Time Out

Devon & Cornwall

timeout.com

Time Out Guides Ltd
Universal House
251 Tottenham Court Road
London W1T 7AB
United Kingdom
Tel: +44 (0)20 7813 3000
Fax: +44 (0)20 7813 6001
Email: guides@timeout.com
www.timeout.com

Published by Time Out Guides Ltd, a wholly owned subsidiary of Time Out Group Ltd.
Time Out and the Time Out logo are trademarks of Time Out Group Ltd.

10 9 8 7 6 5 4 3 2 1

This edition first published in Great Britain in 2010 by Ebury Publishing.
A Random House Group Company
20 Vauxhall Bridge Road, London SW1V 2SA

Random House Australia Pty Ltd 20 Alfred Street, Milsons Point, Sydney, New South Wales 2061, Australia

Random House New Zealand Ltd 18 Poland Road, Glenfield, Auckland 10, New Zealand

Random House South Africa (Pty) Ltd Isle of Houghton, Corner Boundary Road & Carse O'Gowrie,
Houghton 2198, South Africa

Random House UK Limited Reg. No. 954009

Distributed in USA by Publishers Group West
1700 Fourth Street, Berkeley, California 94710

Distributed in Canada by Publishers Group Canada
250A Carlton Street, Toronto, Ontario M5A 2L1

For further distribution details, see www.timeout.com.

ISBN: 9-78184670-184-9

A CIP catalogue record for this book is available from the British Library.

Printed and bound by Firmengruppe APPL, aprinta druck, Wemding, Germany.

The Random House Group Limited supports The Forest Stewardship Council (FSC), the leading international
forest certification organisation. All our titles that are printed on Greenpeace approved FSC certified paper
carry the FSC logo. Our paper procurement policy can be found at http://www.rbooks.co.uk/environment.

Time Out carbon-offsets its flights with Trees for Cities (www.treesforcities.org).

Hall for Cornwall

Take *Time Out* for live entertainment

Truro is home to Cornwall's professional theatre, see live bands, drama, dance and comedy. In the last year HfC (2008) has welcomed Jimmy Carr, Bloc Party, Simon Amstell and ... Des O'Connor to name but a few – check website to see what's on.

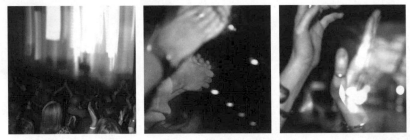

HALL FOR CORNWALL

Published by

Time Out Guides Limited
Universal House
251 Tottenham Court Road
London W1T 7AB
Tel +44 (0)20 7813 3000
Fax +44 (0)20 7813 6001
email guides@timeout.com
www.timeout.com

Editorial

Authors *Devon* Helen Stiles and Deborah Martin with additional writing by Stu Lambert; *Cornwall* Ismay Atkins
Editors Sarah Guy, Elizabeth Winding
Researchers Alex Brown, Gemma Pritchard, William Crow
Proofreader Marion Moisy
Indexer Ismay Atkins

Managing Director Peter Fiennes
Editorial Director Sarah Guy
Series Editor Cath Phillips
Business Manager Daniel Allen
Editorial Manager Holly Pick
Assistant Management Accountant Ija Krasnikova

Design

Art Director Scott Moore
Art Editor Pinelope Kourmouzoglou
Senior Designer Henry Elphick
Graphic Designers Kei Ishimaru, Nicola Wilson
Advertising Designer Jodi Sher

Picture Desk

Picture Editor Jael Marschner
Deputy Picture Editor Lynn Chambers
Picture Researcher Gemma Walters
Picture Desk Assistant Ben Rowe
Picture Librarian Christina Theisen

Advertising

Commercial Director Mark Phillips
Sales Manager Alison Wallen
Advertising Sales Lotte Mahon
Copy Controller Alison Bourke

Marketing

Sales & Marketing Director, North America & Latin America Lisa Levinson
Senior Publishing Brand Manager Luthfa Begum
Art Director Anthony Huggins
Circulation & Distribution Manager Dan Collins
Marketing Intern Alana Benton

Production

Group Production Director Mark Lamond
Production Manager Brendan McKeown
Production Controller Damian Bennett

Time Out Group

Director & Founder Tony Elliott
Chief Executive Officer David King
Group Financial Director Paul Rakkar
Group General Manager/Director Nichola Coulthard
Time Out Communications Ltd MD David Pepper
Time Out International Ltd MD Cathy Runciman
Time Out Magazine Ltd Publisher/MD Mark Elliott
Group IT Director Simon Chappell
Marketing & Circulation Director Catherine Demajo

Thanks to Will Fulford-Jones, Anna Norman, Ros Sales, Aleida Strowger; *Devon* Kevin Brown, Stu Lambert; *Cornwall* Paddy and Ashley Atkins, Helen Gilchrist, Kate Leys, Juliet and Michael Peters, Ben Rowe.

Maps pages 20, 160 Kei Ishimaru.

This product contains mapping from Ordnance Survey with permission of HMSO. © Crown Copyright, all rights reserved. Licence number: 100049681.

Cover photography David Wogan/Photolibrary.

Back cover photography Marc Eade; Andrew Ray; Watergate Tourism.

Photography Bill Bradshaw, except: pages 3, 158-59 ,256, 262, 263, 265, 314 Andrew Ray; page 18-19, 78, 79 Andrew Coulter; pages 21, 50-51, 62, 132, 137, 138 Walter Weber; pages 25, 35, 53, 59, 87, 92 Jonathan Perugia; pages 54 (bottom, left), 203 (top, right), 205 (top) Marc Eade; pages 54 (right), 54 (top, left), 203 (top, right), 204, 205 (middle & bottom), 208 Aleida Stowger; pages 61, 67, 68, 76, 95, 102, 118, 149 www.visitdevon.co.uk; page 64 Sally Dallyn; page 71 Peter Hendrie; pages 75, 190 English Heritage; page 115 First Great Western; pages 120-21 English Riviera; pages 148, 152, 153, 157 Plymouth City Council; pages 161, 216-17, 252, 253, 267, 270 (middle, left), 271, 280, 281, 301, 305 Britta Jaschinski; page 164 www.cornwalls.co.uk; pages 168 (right), 168 (left), 185 Ismay Atkins; pages 176, 188, 248 Michelle Grant; pages 189, 196, 275, 282, 283, 284 Scott Moore; page 211 Sandy Maya Matzen/Shutterstock; page 226 Stephen Aaron Rees/Shutterstock; page 231 Stephen Bardens/Alamy; pages 234, 235 Chris Pierre; pages 264, 255 Ben Rowe; pages 270 (top), 270 (bottom, left) Derek Adams; page 274 Mike Greenslade; page 279 Sam Morgan; page 298 Jeremy Pearson.

The following images were provided by the featured establishment/artists: 12, 13, 15, 31, 43, 44, 56, 109, 130, 136, 143, 156, 168 (top), 170, 171, 187, 218, 222, 240, 243, 258, 259, 261, 203, 218, 224-25, 286, 290, 291, 292, 293, 295, 296, 297, 299.

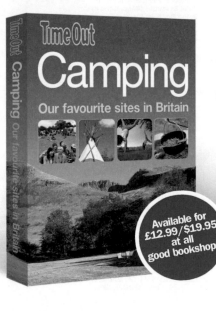

About the guide

Devon & Cornwall is one in a new series of Time Out guides covering Britain. We've used our local knowledge to reveal the best of the region, and while we've included all the big attractions, we've gone beneath the surface to uncover plenty of small or hidden treasures too.

These two counties offer a huge variety of experiences and terrains: landscapes run from wild moorland to luxuriant wooded valleys; several hundred miles of magnificent coastline include hidden coves, pine-backed bays and sandy surfing beaches. Exploring the towns and villages – vibrant Falmouth, independent Totnes, picture-perfect Mousehole – brings rewards too. There's a vibrant arts scene as well as lots of messing about on boats, from million-pound yachts to small sea kayaks. Attractions range from Tate St Ives and the Eden Project to prehistoric sites on Dartmoor. And the region's food and accommodation options are now some of the best in the country, though the delights of Devon cream teas and Cornish pasties are timeless.

TELEPHONE NUMBERS

All phone numbers listed in this guide assume that you are calling from within Britain. If you're calling from elsewhere, dial your international access code, then 44 for the UK; follow that with the phone number, dropping the first zero of the area code.

OPENING TIMES

Part of the charm of the countryside is that it's not like the city. But this means beware opening times; places shut up shop for the winter months, or only open at weekends, and some shops still shut for lunch. If you're eating out, many places still stop serving at 2pm sharp for lunch and at 9pm for dinner. If you're making a journey, always phone to check. This goes for attractions too, especially outside the summer holiday season. While every effort has been made to ensure the accuracy of the information contained in this guide, the publisher cannot accept any responsibility for errors it may contain.

ADVERTISERS

The recommendations in *Devon & Cornwall* are based on the experiences of Time Out's reviewers. No payment or PR invitation has secured inclusion or influenced content. The editors choose which places to include. Advertisers have no influence over content; an advertiser may receive a bad review or no review at all.

FEEDBACK

We hope you enjoy the guide. We always welcome suggestions for places to include in future editions and take note of your criticism of our choices. You can email us at guides@timeout.com.

Contents

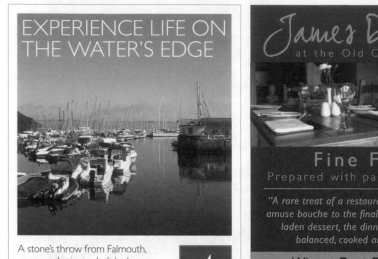

Festivals & Events

Devon

FEBRUARY

Animated Exeter
01392 265198, www.animatedexeter.co.uk. Date mid Feb.
This showcase for world animation includes screenings, free exhibitions and workshops for all ages.

Civil War Battle Anniversary
01805 626140, www.great-torrington.com.
Date mid Feb.
The tramp of feet and the rattle of muskets fill the streets of Great Torrington at this annual battle commemoration, which culminates in a torchlit procession and fireworks.

MARCH

Vibraphonic
www.2020vibraphonic.co.uk. Date early-late Mar.
Musical offerings at this Exeter music festival span a dizzying array of genres, from reggae and blues to urban and experimental music.

APRIL

Crediton Folk Weekend
01363 775695, www.poppyrecords.co.uk.
Date mid Apr.
Celebrating traditional folk music, this tiny, weekend-long festival is held in the Devon village of Cheriton Fitzpaine.

Tuckers Malting Beer Festival
www.tuckersmaltings.co.uk. Date late Apr.
This three-day beer festival showcases over 200 different real ales; for more on Tuckers Malting, see p115.

MAY

North Devon & Exmoor Walking Festival
01271 883131, www.walkingnorthdevon.co.uk.
Date mid May.
Guided walks range from moorland treks to rockpool rambles, and there are opportunities to acquire some bushcraft skills. There's a smaller event in autumn, too.

Plymouth Summer Festival
www.plymouthsummerfestival.com. Date Apr-Sept.
All kinds of events around the city: concerts, dance, theatre and art exhibitions are among the cultural offerings. The Plymouth half marathon is a sporting highlight.

Brixham Pirate & Shanty Festival
01803 850382, www.brixhambuccaneers.co.uk.
Date 1st May bank holiday weekend.
Don your eye patch and join the Brixham Buccaneers for this festival of swashbuckling, family-friendly fun.

Hunting of the Earl of Rone
http://earl-of-rone.org.uk. Date 2nd May bank holiday weekend.
Each year, the villagers of Combe Martin, in North Devon, dress up to enact this ancient ritual over four days, hunting down the earl, before setting him (backwards) on a donkey and throwing him in the sea. Odd, but fun.

International Worm Charming Championships
01803 712149, www.wormcharming.co.uk.
Date early May.
Teams compete to lure the most worms on their respective turf plots. Afterwards, everyone goes to celebrate in Blackawton village hall.

Devon County Show
01392 446000, www.devoncountyshow.co.uk.
Date 3rd weekend in May.
Animals from alpacas to rare-breed pigs are on show at the county showground at Westpoint, near Exeter. Carriage racing, showjumping, a dog show, sheep shearing and craft stalls are among the other draws.

Exmouth Summer Festival
www.exmouthfestival.org.uk. Date late May.
Local art, music and culture take centre stage. Graffitti demos, clowning workshops, shanty singers and classical quartets have featured in previous years.

Brixham Heritage Festival
01803 858362, www.brixhamheritagefestival.co.uk.
Date last week in May.
Brixham celebrates its nautical past with a parade, a sailing trawler race, music and lavish firework displays.

Appledore Visual Arts Festival
07900 021 2747, www.appledorearts.org.
Date last weekend in May.
A showcase for local talent, held in Appledore.

Exmouth Sand Sculpture Competition
www.eastdevon.gov.uk. Date 2nd bank holiday Sun in May.
In past years, sculptures at this competition on Exmouth Beach have included dinosaurs, elephants and mermaids.

JUNE

North Devon Festival
01271 324242, www.northdevonfestival.org.uk.
Date early June.
Art, music and theatre events across the region. The Barnstaple Fringe is a focus for theatre, comedy and music, while Croyde's GoldCoast Oceanfest weekend is all about surfing and music.

Pixie Day
www.pixieday.org. Date mid June.
See p27.

Devon County Show. See p11.

Teignmouth Folk Festival
01803 290427, www.teignmouthfolk.co.uk.
Date mid June.
As well as folk performers, this weekend festival plays host to Morris, Border and Appalachian dancers.

Exeter Summer Festival
01392 265200, www.exeter.gov.uk/festival.
Date late June-early July.
Music, dance, theatre, comedy, street entertainment, crafts and more, culminating in a grand firework finale.

JULY

Ways with Words
01803 867373, www.wayswithwords.co.uk.
Date mid July.
This prestigious ten-day literary festival takes place in the elegant setting of Dartington Hall, with talks by big-name writers and public figures on an eclectic range of subjects.

Teignmouth Summer Carnival
www.teignmouthcarnival.co.uk. Date last Tue-Sat in July.
The carnival incorporates concerts, talent contests and a children's day; on the Friday, the Grand Procession brings a dazzling array of floats. In late July, look out for the town's nine-day regatta (www.teignmouthregatta.co.uk).

Torbay Carnival
www.torbaycarnival.co.uk. Date late July.
Eight exuberant days of carnival bring birds of prey displays, Punch and Judy shows, fireworks, baton-twirling displays and a grand parade to Paignton Green.

Yealmpton Show
www.yealmptonshow.com. Date late July.
Farmers vie for prizes with their finest livestock and produce at this one-day show, while amusements include dog agility shows, pony club games and more.

Sidmouth Folk Week
01395 577952, www.sidmouthfolkweek.co.uk.
Date late July-early Aug.
An impressive line-up of folk artists play at this friendly, phenomenally successful summer festival.

AUGUST
August is regatta month in Devon, and every seaside town worth its salt has its own knees-up. Ask at local tourist information offices for a comprehensive list.

Appledore & Instow Regatta
01271 470500. Date 1st week in Aug.
Different types of craft compete each day at this lovely week-long regatta. Other draws include a sandcastle competition on Instow beach and a greasy pole contest.

Dartmoor Folk Festival

01837 840102, www.dartmoorfolkfestival.co.uk. Date 2nd weekend in Aug.
A cheery festival South Zeal, on Dartmoor's northern edge. The village hall and a marquee host concerts and ceilidhs, with informal music sessions in both village pubs.

British Firework Championship Finals

www.britishfireworks.co.uk. Date mid Aug.
Six top teams compete over two nights to provide the most spectacular firework displays over Plymouth harbour. The Hoe is the prime viewing spot.

Okehampton Show

www.okehamptonshow.co.uk. Date mid Aug.
Entertainments at this agricultural show include tug-of-war, Morris dancing and ferret racing, plus a packed children's programme.

Beautiful Days Festival

www.beautifuldays.org. Date 3rd week in Aug.
This family-friendly roots music festival is set in the glorious rolling parkland of Escot Park, near Ottery St Mary. Bring a tent, or book a yurt or tipi for the weekend.

Dawlish Carnival Airshow

www.dawlishcarnival.co.uk. Date 3rd Thur in Aug.
The airshow is a highlight of Dawlish Carnival week, with thousands of spectators lining the seawall and beach.

Totnes Orange Race

www.totnesinformation.co.uk. Date Tue 3rd week in Aug.
Orange-chasing races down Totnes's steep high street recall Sir Francis Drake's visit in the 1580s, when he presented 'a fair red orange' to a little boy in the street.

SEPTEMBER

Devon Open Studios

www.devonartistnetwork.co.uk. Date early-mid Sept.
Artists' studios across Devon are opened to the public.

Agatha Christie Festival

www.englishriviera.co.uk/agathachristie/festival. Date mid Sept.
This celebration of Torquay's most famous daughter attracts murder mystery fans from around the world. Events include talks, writing workshops, guided walks, screenings, murder mystery dinners and tea dances.

Widecombe Fair

www.widecombefair.com. Date 2nd Tue in Sept.
Subject of the famous folk song of the same name, this immensely popular fair brings sheepdog displays, bale tossing, a gymkhana, sheep shearing and lots of stalls.

South Devon Walking Festival

www.southdevonwalkingfestival.co.uk. Date late Sept-early Oct.
This ten-day festival offers all sorts of guided walks.

Ways with Words

Colyford Goose Fair
www.colyfordvillage.co.uk. Date closest Sat to Michaelmas.
Attractions at this medieval fair run from a ram roast and beer tent to a mummers' play and archery demonstrations.

OCTOBER

Exmoor Food Festival
01643 702624, www.exmoorfoodfestival.co.uk. Date early Oct.
Tastings, farmers' markets, farm visits and special themed suppers feature on the Food Festival's agenda.

Tavistock Goose Fair
www.tavistock.gov.uk. Date 2nd Wed in Oct.
This annual event dates back to 1105, when abbey tenants paid their tithes in geese. The town centre is filled with all manner of stalls and amusements.

Two Moors Festival
01643 831370, www.thetwomoorsfestival.com. Date early-mid Oct
An eclectic programme of classical music is brought to small community venues across Exmoor and Dartmoor.

Exeter Autumn Festival
01392 265200, www.exeter.gov.uk/autumnfestival. Date late Oct-mid Nov.
A two-week festival showcasing the city's vibrant arts scene, with an emphasis on local performers and artists.

NOVEMBER

Tar Barrel Night
01404 813964, www.otterytourism.org.uk. Date 5 Nov.
Dating from 1688, this bizarre event sees locals bearing flaming tar barrels down Ottery St Mary's packed high street.

Teignmouth Jazz Festival
01626 215666, www.teignmouthjazz.org. Date mid-late Nov.
This popular festival attracts international jazz icons such as John Etheridge, as well as West Country talent.

Herring Festival
http://clovelly.co.uk. Date late Nov.
See p67.

Cornwall

MARCH

St Piran's Day
01872 572121, www.perranporthinfo.co.uk. Date 5 Mar.
Cornwall's patron saint is said to have landed on the beach at Perranporth, after being cast out of Ireland. On St Piran's Day, hundreds of people trek across the sands to visit the oratory he built, and to watch the St Piran play.

Walk Scilly & Isles of Scilly Folk Festival
01720 424043, www.walkscilly.co.uk. Date late Mar-early Apr.
Over 30 guided walks take in some of the Isles of Scilly's most stunning landscapes; the event is organised to tie in with the Isles of Scilly Folk Festival, with walks fitting in with the music schedule.

APRIL

Trevithick Day
www.trevithick-day.org.uk. Date late Apr.
Held in Camborne, this free one-day festival celebrates the area's industrial heritage. There are dances through the streets and processions led by miniature steam engines, along with larger displays of steam power.

Porthleven Food Festival
01326 561341, www.porthlevenfoodfestival.co.uk. Date Apr.
A weekend of food-related talks, walks and demonstrations, showcasing the best of the South West, from organic beers to traditionally reared meat.

World Pilot Gig Championships
01720 422670, www.worldgigs.co.uk. Date late Apr-early May.
See these colourfully painted, traditional Cornish rowing boats take to the water around the Isles of Scilly.

MAY

'Obby 'Oss
www.padstow.com. Date 1 May.
On 1 May, dancers and musicians weave through Padstow's narrow streets following the two 'Obby 'Osses, in what is thought to be an ancient celebration of fertility and the arrival of spring.

Flora Day
www.helstonfloraday.org.uk. Date 8 May
On 8 May (unless it falls on a Sunday or Monday), the village of Helston is bedecked with bluebells and gorse,

'Obby 'Oss

Discover the best of Britain's beaches

and a series of dances reenacts St Michael slaying the devil and St George dispatching the dragon. Festivities culminate in the 'Furry Dance', with townsfolk dressing up dancing in and out of the houses.

Daphne Du Maurier Festival of Arts & Literature
01726 879500, www.dumaurierfestival.co.uk. Date mid May.
Held at various locations in and around Fowey, this week-long festival features dance and comedy performances, art exhibitions, walks and film screenings.

Run to the Sun
01637 851851, www.runtothesun.co.uk. Date late May.
A chilled out, Newquay-based festival mixing bands, DJs and comedy with a celebration of the VW Beetle, drawing hundreds of enthusiasts.

Port Isaac Music Festival
www.portisaacmusicfestival.co.uk. Date late May.
Held once every two years (the next is scheduled for 2010), this four-day classical music festival boasts a glorious harbourside setting.

JUNE

Royal Cornwall Show
01208 812183, www.rcaa.org.uk. Date mid June.
The showground at Wadebridge comes alive for the annual county show. Livestock and horses compete in the judging area, while a flower show, steam fair, sheep dog trials, falconry, crafts and games are among the other entertainments.

Polperro Festival
www.polperrofestivalsandlights.co.uk. Date late June.
Music, art, theatre, parades, children's entertainment and morris dancing feature at this fishing village's community-run festival.

JULY

Port Eliot Festival
01503 232783, www.porteliotfestival.com, www.porteliot.co.uk. Date late July.
This hip literary festival has an inspiring setting, in the grounds of the Port Eliot estate, and a playful approach. It attracts leading writers, poets and artists, who are encouraged to offer more than a standard talk.

Lafrowda Festival
www.lafrowda-festival.co.uk. Date early-mid July.
Anything goes at St Just's community arts festival, from Cornish songs and ballroom dancing competitions to samba. Visitors can participate in various arty workshops, making sculptures, lanterns and banners for the festival's closing processions on Lafrowda Day.

St Endellion Summer Festival
www.endellionfestivals.org.uk. Date late July-early Aug.
This long-running festival boasts a stellar programme of choral, chamber, orchestral and operatic works, with performances taking place in the village's lovely 15th-century church. Check the website for details of the Easter Festival.

AUGUST

Relentless Boardmasters
www.relentlessboardmasters.com. Date early Aug.
Five days of surfing, skateboarding, BMXing and partying in Newquay. The world's top professionals show off their skills during the day, and by night some of the biggest acts in the music industry entertain the masses.

Falmouth Week
www.falmouthweek.co.uk. Date mid Aug.
With a week of racing for keelboats, dinghies and traditional craft around the waters of Falmouth Bay, the Carrick Roads and the harbour, this is the largest sailing regatta in the South West. A dazzling firework display rounds off proceedings.

Newlyn Fish Festival
07825 770223, www.newlynfishfestival.org.uk. Date Aug bank holiday Mon.
Tap your feet to a sea shanty or two, before taking in the fish auction, cookery demonstrations, gig racing and RNLI rescue demos. Sustenance runs from seafood paella to good, old-fashioned crab sandwiches.

Fowey Regatta
01726 832133, www.foweyroyalregatta.co.uk. Date mid Aug.
As well as boat races and daredevil overhead manoeuvres from the Red Arrows, Fowey's seven-day regatta features the crowning of the carnival queen, daily storytelling sessions, bands on the quayside, and crab-catching and pasty-eating contests.

Bude Jazz Festival
01288 350300, www.budejazzfestival.co.uk. Date late Aug-early Sept.
This week-long jazz fest brings plenty of international musical talent to town, with events in 14 venues: the Stroller ticket buys you entry to every performance.

SEPTEMBER

Cornwall Food & Drink Festival
www.cornwallfoodanddrinkfestival.com. Date late Sept.
Taking place on the aptly named Lemon Quay in Truro, this three-day feast of foodie events runs the gamut from wine masterclasses and culinary demos to food stalls and special menus in restaurants around town.

World Belly Boarding Championships
www.bellyboarding.co.uk. Date early Sept.
Chapel Porth, St Agnes
See p230.

OCTOBER

Falmouth Oyster Festival
01326 312300, www.falmouthoysterfestival.co.uk. Date mid Oct.
Falmouth's four-day festival marks the beginning of oyster-dredging season. There's Cornish produce, crafts, oyster and shellfish bars, oyster-shucking contests and plenty of family-friendly entertainment (face painting, games, and a shell-painting competition).

Devon

Haytor Rocks. See p88.

Devon

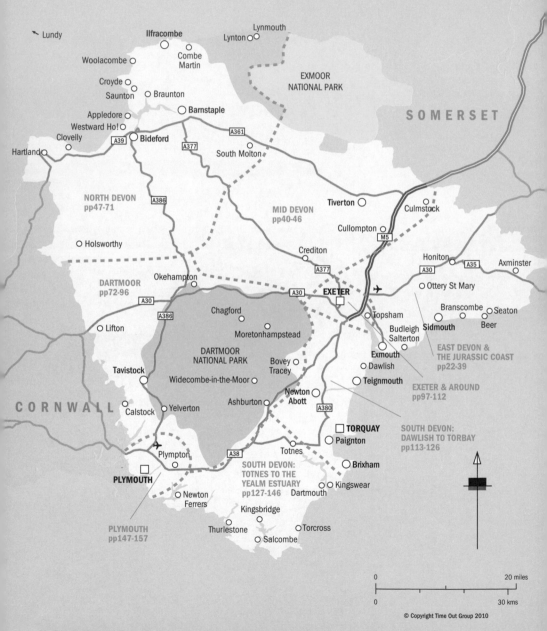

Bristol Channel

Lundy

Ilfracombe
Lynmouth
Lynton
Combe Martin
Woolacombe
Croyde
Saunton
Braunton
EXMOOR NATIONAL PARK
Appledore
Westward Ho!
Barnstaple
SOMERSET
Clovelly
A39
Bideford
A361
Hartland
A377
South Molton

NORTH DEVON pp47-71
A386
MID DEVON pp40-46
Tiverton
Culmstock
Cullompton
Holsworthy
M5
Crediton
Honiton
A377
A35
Axminster
Okehampton
A30
DARTMOOR pp72-96
EXETER
A30
Ottery St Mary
Chagford
Branscombe
Seaton
Lifton
A386
Moretonhampstead
Topsham
Beer
Budleigh Salterton
Sidmouth
DARTMOOR NATIONAL PARK
Bovey Tracey
EAST DEVON & THE JURASSIC COAST pp22-39
Tavistock
Exmouth
Widecombe-in-the-Moor
Dawlish
Calstock
Yelverton
Ashburton
Newton Abott
Teignmouth
EXETER & AROUND pp97-112
CORNWALL
A380
SOUTH DEVON: DAWLISH TO TORBAY pp113-126
TORQUAY
Plympton
Totnes
Paignton
A38
PLYMOUTH
SOUTH DEVON: TOTNES TO THE YEALM ESTUARY pp127-146
Brixham
Newton Ferrers
Dartmouth
Kingswear
Kingsbridge
PLYMOUTH pp147-157
Thurlestone
Torcross
Salcombe

0   20 miles
0   30 kms

© Copyright Time Out Group 2010

Braunton Burrows. See p49.

Devon

East Devon & the Jurassic Coast

The striking red cliffs of Orcombe Rocks, in Exmouth, mark the start of a very special stretch of coastline, known as the Jurassic Coast. Designated a Natural World Heritage Site by UNESCO, putting it in the same league as the Grand Canyon and the Great Barrier Reef, the Jurassic Coast offers a vivid record of 185 million years of geological history. As you head eastwards along the 95-mile stretch of coast, past towering sea stacks and crumbling pebble bed-cliffs, the rocks become progressively younger, making it – in a literal sense – a walk though time.

Along the coast, amid the cliffs, you'll find elegant Regency seaside resorts such as Exmouth, Budleigh Salterton and Sidmouth, along with the pretty fishing villages of Branscombe and Beer. Inland lie heathland, wooded combes and lush river valleys, along with the historic market towns of Honiton and Axminster – it's little wonder that two-thirds of the region has been designated an Area of Outstanding Natural Beauty.

HONITON

Set in the fertile Otter Valley, Honiton has long been a hub for the area. In Roman times it was a stopping-off point on the Fosse Way, which ran from Exeter to Lincoln; in the 18th century, it became a busy coaching stop on the London to Exeter route. The lace trade, introduced by Flemish craftsmen in the Elizabethan era, also shaped the town. The flamboyant fashions of the day demanded extravagant quantities of lace on collars, cuffs and handkerchiefs, resulting in a thriving cottage industry; by the end of the 17th century, over half of Honiton's population were earning a living making lace at home. The town's resulting prosperity funded the construction of its elegant Regency houses; although the arrival of mechanically made lace in the 19th century almost killed off the industry, Queen Victoria's decision to use Honiton lace for her wedding veil saved it from extinction.

Beautiful examples of the intricate designs are displayed in Allhallows Museum (*see p30*), which also holds the remains of Honiton's earliest resident – a venerable hippo, whose bones date back some 100,000 years. Also tucked behind the High Street is the Thelma Hulbert Gallery (Dowell Street, 01404 45006), once the artist's home and studio; her work is displayed alongside temporary exhibitions.

Today, agriculture is Honiton's main industry. The Honiton Show is an annual fixture, and you'll find plenty of produce from local farms on sale along the broad High Street, which also has a market on Tuesday and Saturday. Look out, too, for the bow-fronted window of Pop goes the Weasel (01404 45072), which sells and hires out handmade hats.

In recent years the town has become known for antiques, and dealers and bargain hunters prowl the High Street. At the lower end of the High Street is Yarrow Antiques (01404 44399, www.yarrow155. com), where reclaimed sash windows jostle for space with Buddhist statues and weighty bronzes. The Fountain Antiques Centre (no.132, 01404 42074) holds assorted dealers, while book lovers should beat a path to Graham York Rare Books (no.225, 01404 41727, www.gyork.co.uk). For a childhood nostalgia fix, the cabinets at Honiton Antique Toys (no.38, 01404 41194) are packed with die-cast cars, vintage teddies, lead soldiers and other gems.

Where to eat & drink

Hidden away in a passage just off the High Street, Vine Tea Rooms (Vine Passage, 01404 42889) is pretty as a picture with its window-boxes and hanging baskets. When the sun is shining, take tea in the lovely garden. The small café-chain Boston Tea Party (53 High Street, 01404 548739, www.bostonteaparty.co.uk) has a branch in Honiton.

For special occasion dining, book a table at the restaurant at Combe House (*see p24*), where beautifully presented mains might include john dory with crab croquettes, split pea purée, samphire and sauce vierge or roast tenderloin of pork with sage, potato gratin, black pudding and caramelised apple.

The Holt ★

178 High Street, EX14 1LA (01404 47707, www. theholt-honiton.com). Open 11am-3pm, 5.30-11pm Tue-Sat. Lunch served noon-2pm, dinner served 7-10pm Tue-Sat.

This award-winning gastropub is part of the local Otter Brewery – hence the gleaming taps on the bar, dispensing all five of its superb beers. Tapas dishes are chalked up on blackboards; otherwise, there's Modern British fare such as game terrine with spiced lentils and pickled cauliflower.

Railway
Queen Street, EX14 1LA (01404 47976, www.the railwayhoniton.co.uk). Open/food served noon-3pm, 5.30-11pm Tue-Sat.
Built in the early 19th century as a drinking spot for railway workers building the Exeter to London line, the Railway has been sleekly updated in line with modern tastes: think muted colours, leather sofas and polished-up original features and fireplaces. The menu mixes Italian and gastropub influences, running from brick-fired pizzas to catch of the day. Children are welcome.

Where to stay
There are four well-equipped holiday cottages, sleeping from two to six, at Hembury Court (Broadhembury, 01404 841444, www.hembury-court-barns.co.uk), a 240-acre organic farm on the edge of the Blackdown Hills. Shared facilities include an eight-seater hot tub, a gas barbecue, a croquet lawn for croquet and games and an oak-cruck games barn.

Combe House
Gittisham, EX14 3AD (01404 540400, www.combehousedevon.com). Rates £179-£399 double incl breakfast.
History permeates every panel and flagstone of this Grade I-listed country house, set in rolling parkland where Arabian horses and pheasants roam. The rooms range from light, floral-sprigged rooms in the former servants' quarters to grand suites, sumptuously appointed with rich fabrics and antiques. The Linen Suite apartment occupies the former Victorian laundry, with an airy sitting room and a huge circular copper tub in the bathroom; alternatively, there is a thatched one-bedroom cottage with its own walled garden in the hotel grounds.

Hollies Trout Farm
Slade Lane, Sheldon, EX14 4QS (01404 841428, www.holliestroutfarm.co.uk). Rates £176-£344 per week for 4 people. No credit cards.
If you fancy catching your own supper, a stay at this self-catering log cabin could be just the ticket. Set amid peaceful woodland, in the grounds of a trout farm, the cabin has two bedrooms and an open-plan living area with a wood-burning stove. Guests can book a fly fishing session or lesson on the trout-stocked lakes, or learn the intricacies of fly-tying.

West Colwell Farm
Offwell, EX14 9SL (01404 831130, www.westcolwell.co.uk). Open Feb-Nov. Rates £70-£80 double incl breakfast.
A short drive outside Honiton, this farmhouse B&B feels nicely secluded, with glorious views across the woods and fields. The three guest rooms, named after carthorses, are in the old stone barns on one side of the cobbled yard. Farmer has its own terrace with stunning views of the valley; Captain takes a seafaring theme, with its driftwood furniture; and Blossom is tucked away in the eaves.

AXMINSTER
East from Honiton along the old Roman road (now the A35) is Axminster. The town is best known for its carpets, first produced in the mid-18th century by an enterprising local weaver, Thomas Whitty, who wanted to re-create the Turkish carpets he had seen. The small factory he set up behind the church produced hand-knotted designs for the finest houses in the land; on the completion of each carpet, a peal of bells rang out from the church. After a disastrous fire, however, the business closed in 1835.

Over a century later, carpet manufacturer Harry Dutfield struck up a conversation with a West Country vicar while on a train, who bemoaned the fact that Axminster carpets were no longer made in Axminster. Dutfield decided to resurrect the company – which endures to this day, in a factory on the outskirts of town. Plans are afoot to turn the 18th-century factory at Caster Hill House into a museum; in the meantime, you can admire examples of the celebrated carpet in the church of St Mary the Virgin. To buy your own reduced-price roll, head for the Axminster Factory Outlet (01297 32808, www.axminsterfactoryoutlet.co.uk, closed Sun) on Musbury Road.

Axminster's main streets converge on Trinity Square, which is home to most of the town's shops, along with its Thursday market. Here, too, is the elegant façade of Trinity House (01297 32273, www.trinityhouseaxminster.co.uk, closed Sun) – one of the few remaining independent, family-owned department stores in the country. In nearby Milton's Yard, the White Space Art Gallery (01297 35807, www.whitespacegallery.org.uk, closed Sun) showcases the work of local artists.

Where to eat & drink
In the Old Courthouse building on Church Street, the Arts Café (01297 631455) hosts monthly-changing art exhibitions and serves cakes and light lunches; the courtyard is a lovely hideaway.

Drewe Arms
Broadhembury, EX14 3NF (01404 841267, www.the drewearms.com). Open noon-3pm, 6-11pm Tue-Thur; noon-3pm, 5pm-midnight Fri; noon-midnight Sat; noon-10.30pm Sun. Lunch served noon-2.30pm, dinner served 6.30-9.30pm Tue-Sat. Meals served noon-8.30pm Sun.
Set in an implausibly pretty village of thatch and cob cottages, this flagstone-floored, beamed pub is a paragon of its kind. A log fire roars in the grate on chilly days, and bar staff pull pints of draught cider and real ale from the Otter Brewery. In the bar, drinkers can fill up on chunky doorstep sandwiches, or hearty mains. Sunday lunch, meanwhile, brings roast sirloin of Devon beef.

River Cottage Canteen ★
Trinity Square, EX13 5AN (01297 631862, www.rivercottage.net). Breakfast served 9am-noon Tue-Sat; 10.30am-11.30am Sun. Lunch served noon-3pm Tue-Sun. Dinner served 6.30-9.30pm Thur-Sat.
Locally sourced produce is king at chef/writer Hugh Fearnley-Whittingstall's produce store and café. Take the

DEVON

Branscombe. See p34.

humble – albeit delicious – bacon roll, which uses pork reared at Sydling Brook Farm, just over the border in Dorset, and cured to a River Cottage recipe by a local butchers. The canteen is also open for dinner three nights a week, when the menu shifts up a gear with mains such as slow roast shoulder and seared loin of Sydling Brook lamb with caramelised onion mash, buttered greens and gravy. Baskets and wooden boxes brim with fruit and veg in the shop, which also sells meat, bread, preserves and wine.

Where to stay

Applebarn Cottage

Bewley Down, EX13 7JX (01460 220873, www.apple barn-cottage.co.uk). Rates from £122-£128 double for 2 nights incl breakfast.

Set in a restored cottage garden, this wisteria-covered 17th-century dwelling is very pretty. The Wisteria Suite, inside the main cottage, has views towards Lambert's Castle; wake up to breakfast served in the slate-floored dining room. There is also a detached studio suite with a spacious bedroom, a small kitchen and patio doors on to a terrace.

Kerrington House

Musbury Road, EX13 5JR (01297 35333, www.kerringtonhouse.com). Rates £110 double incl breakfast.

This bijou establishment has five elegant, individually decorated en suite bedrooms, along with a light-filled drawing room overlooking the gardens. The charming decor, friendly hosts and comfortable beds make this a relaxing bolthole; on a summer's evening, unwind with drinks on the terrace before heading into the centre of Axminster for supper.

OTTERY ST MARY

Ottery, as it is affectionately known, is one of the oldest towns in Devon. Its impressive historic pedigree dates back to the 11th century, just before the Norman invasion, when the parish boundaries were first established. Set among the rolling Devon hills, 11 miles from Exeter and six miles from the Jurassic coastline, it makes an ideal base for exploring the eastern side of the county.

Standing proud on a hill overlooking the town, the magnificent St Mary's Church ★ is Ottery's crowning glory. Notable features include the ribbed, vaulted roof of the nave, adorned with bosses and shields and a remarkable 14th-century astronomical clock.

A young Samuel Taylor Coleridge was a regular member of the congregation in the 18th century. The poet was born just opposite the church in the Old School House, adjacent to the Grammar School where his father was headmaster. Both buildings were demolished in the 1880s, although a blue plaque marks the spot. The Heritage Society holds regular exhibitions devoted to the town's history in the Institute (19 Yonder Street) – also the venue for the community market, on the last Saturday morning of the month.

Independent shops include K&M Butchers (01404 812724, closed Sun) in Broad Street, whose sausages run the gamut from Old English pork bangers to tangy fruit and cider concoctions. A sprawling farmers' market is held on the first Friday morning of the month at the Hind Street car park.

The Gallery at Hind Street (01404 815641, closed Sun) displays work by local and international artists, while the Bagpuss Gallery (7 Mill Street, 01404 814272, closed Sun) is a good hunting

River Cottage Canteen. See p24.

ground for gifts, with an eclectic mix of pictures, clothes, decorative glassware and jewellery.

Away from the high street, a stroll down to the unusually named Land of Canaan park, by the mill leat, is particularly pretty in summer, when members of the Ottery in Bloom committee bedeck the riverside and town with flowering plants. The park also hosts various seasonal shindigs, including Pixie Day in June, when the town's children, dressed in elfin attire, spirit the bellringers away from the church and the whole town makes merry at a fête. On Bonfire Night, fireworks are set off here following the infamous Tar Barrel Ceremony.

Where to eat & drink

Season's on Silver Street (no.9, 01404 815751, closed Mon, Sun) is a temple to high tea, and serves mushrooms on toast and welsh rarebit alongside cream teas and a sumptuous spread of cakes.

Golden Lion

Tipton St John, EX10 0AA (01404 812881, www. goldenliontipton.co.uk). Open noon-2.30pm, 6-11pm Mon-Fri; noon-3.30pm, 6-11pm Sat; noon-3.30pm, 7-10.30pm Sun. Lunch served noon-2pm daily. Dinner served 6.30-8.30pm Mon-Sat; 7-8.30pm Sun.
Art deco prints, bejewelled lights and the odd antique bust add a pleasingly eccentric vibe to this beamed country pub, set in one of the picturesque villages around Ottery St Mary. In summer, diners spill out into the pretty beer garden and terrace, bearing ploughman's lunches and Lyme Bay crab sandwiches; in winter, steak and kidney pudding, eaten by the fireside, keeps the cold at bay. The evening menu has a rustic French twist, reflecting the owners' roots, so you might find creamy, cider-infused pork à la Normande on the menu.

Hare & Hounds

Putts Corner, Sidbury, EX10 0QQ (01404 41760, www.hareandhounds-devon.co.uk). Open/food served 10am-11pm Mon-Sat; noon-10.30pm Sun.
Not far from Ottery, this traditional country pub is known for its carvery (with a nut roast option for veggies). Inside are two blazing log fires, oak panelling and squishy sofas; behind the bar you'll find local ales on tap, alongside farm cider. Outside, the garden has valley views, picnic tables and a children's play area. The main menu comprises no-nonsense, filling grub.

Joshua's Harvest ★

Gosford Road, Ottery St Mary, EX11 1NU (01404 815473, www.joshuasharveststore.co.uk). Open Store 9am-6pm Mon-Sat; 10.30am-4.30pm Sun. Café 10am-4.30pm Mon-Sat; 10.30am-4pm Sun.
Set up 20 years ago by organic farmers Mark and Jude Essame, this epicurean emporium is a delight. The deli counter is packed with fresh pasties and pies, pick and mix olives, and cakes, bread, scones and flapjacks produced on site. Try before you buy at the café, which specialises in tasting platters featuring locally sourced meat, fish and cheese, served with an assortment of pickles, crudités, chutney, salads and freshly baked bread.

Where to stay

A mile or so north of Ottery, Gosford Pines (Gosford, 01404 812739, www.gosford-pines.net) offers comfortable, inexpensive B&B accommodation in a grand 18th-century farmhouse. There are five acres of grounds and a tennis court.

An even grander option is Cadhay Manor (*see p30*), where large groups can hire the Elizabethan manor house, waking up in grand four-posters and sweet little attic rooms. Smaller parties can stay in the former stables and coach house.

Hay House

Blacklake Farm, East Hill, Ottery St Mary, EX11 1QA (01404 812122, www.blacklakefarm.com). Rates £425-£975 per week for 6 people.
The old hay house and dairy at this Grade-II listed farm have been sensitively converted into a lovely holiday house, sleeping up to six people. The farmhouse-style kitchen is in the old dairy, while the sitting room has weathered stone walls and a wood-burning stove. Red Ruby cattle and pedigree Dorset Down sheep roam the pastures, while Gloucester Old Spot pigs rootle around the orchard. The farm is organic and Soil Association-certified, and meat is available to buy, along with wool throws and scarves. Holistic massage and aromatherapy are also offered.

Larkbeare Grange

Talaton, EX5 2RY (01404 822069, www.larkbeare.net). Rates £95-£145 double incl breakfast.
A cream-painted Georgian pile, with four en suite bedrooms kitted out with big beds, goose-down duvets, flatscreen TVs and Wi-Fi. Bathrooms are equally plush. At breakfast, guests can slather home-made marmalade on to organic bread still warm from the Aga, while awaiting a full English breakfast, kedgeree or smoked salmon and scrambled eggs. Visiting dogs are welcome to kip in the boot room. Note that the house is closed from 10.30am to 4pm.

Mazzard Farm

East Hill, Ottery St Mary, EX11 1QQ (01404 815492, www.mazzardfarm.com). Rates £350-£650 per week for 2 people-£600-£1,150 per week for 6 people.
The six cottages at this award-winning complex are geared towards luxurious getaways. Flatscreen TVs, DVD players, Wi-Fi and wood-burning stoves (bar Bramley Cottage) are par for the course, and families can borrow toys, games, books, cots and beach towels. Some 17 acres of woodland, fields and orchards provides a glorious backdrop, while on site facilities include barbecue and play areas. Bikes are available for hire, and both reflexology sessions and babysitting can be arranged. An indoor swimming pool and spa are planned.

EXMOUTH

Lying on the eastern side of the mouth of the River Exe, Exmouth sports a two-mile stretch of golden sand. In the early 1800s it was set to become the Bath of the South West, and elegant lodgings were built for the gentry, drawn here by the Regency craze for sea-bathing and salubrious sea air.

Lady Byron and Lady Nelson (the estranged wife of the Admiral) were among the town's fashionable visitors; indeed, the latter spent her final years at

no.6 the Beacon, overlooking the Esplanade.
On Tower Street, another blue plaque marks Pilot
Lights – the former home of Ann 'Nancy' Perriam.
This doughty lady, who lived to the ripe old age of
98, accompanied her husband to sea in the 1790s.
As well as mending the captain's shirts, she served
as a powder monkey in the fleet under Nelson,
loading shells and cartridges with gunpowder at the
battles of L'Orient, Cape St Vincent and the Nile.
On the northern fringes of town, the extraordinary
A La Ronde (see p30) was built at the behest of two
other globe-trotting ladies, at the opposite end of
the social spectrum, to house their souvenirs.

Aside from the town's elegant Georgian terraces
and Victorian villas, its main attraction is the beach.
The broad Esplanade runs from the harbour to the
red rocks of Orcombe Point, where the Jurassic
Coast World Heritage Site starts. The seafront's
sky-blue painted benches, Torbay palms and
colourful municipal gardens are more Deauville
than Devon; take a few moments to sit and soak
up the scene, watching the gigs practising for
their races and the boats coming and going. From
Exmouth Marina, ferries (01626 774770, www.exe
2sea.co.uk, closed Nov-Mar) run across the river to
Starcross, and water taxis (07970 918418, closed
Nov-Mar) nip across to Dawlish Warren. DJ's Café,
just past the Lifeboat Station, hires out kayaks,
while Tiger Charters (07836 792626, www.tiger
charters.co.uk) offers fishing trips.

In summer, Exmouth is a quintessential British
seaside resort, where families can hire a beach hut
(01395 222299), go rockpooling at Maer Rocks,
play a round of crazy golf at Arnold Palmer Putting
Course & Jungle Fun (Queens Drive, 01395
273312) or take a donkey ride along the sands.
On the Esplanade, the Pavilion (01395 222477,
www.exmouthpavilion.co.uk) offers classic seaside
entertainment.

Although Exmouth is renowned for its sailing,
windsurfing and kite-surfing (see p37), its strong
currents are not for novices, who usually start on
the calmer waters of the Duck Pond, by the harbour.
Non-swimming areas are clearly marked on the
beach, and lifeguards are on duty in high season.
At the Orcombe end of the beach, beyond the
volleyball nets, is a nature reserve (www.exmouth-
guide.co.uk/nature.htm). The tidal mudflats and
sands of the estuary are an important habitat for
migrating and wading birds.

The town's main shopping area centres on the
pedestrianised Magnolia Shopping Centre. For
more individual shops, head down the side streets;
the Café Quarter, just off the Strand, has a plethora
of cafés, boutiques and traders. For fresh fish and
deli treats, head to Wet Plaice (see p32).

Where to eat & drink

Beach
*Victoria Road, EX8 1DR (01395 272090, www.thebeach
pub.co.uk). Open 11am-11pm Mon-Thur, Sun; 11am-
midnight Fri, Sat. Lunch served noon-2pm, dinner
served 6.30-9pm daily.*

In a prime position on the Marina, this family-run pub is
decorated with maritime memorabilia and photographs.
The line-up at the bar generally includes at least three real
ales, while a decent menu runs from sandwiches and spuds
to curries, sausage and mash and weekly specials, which
often feature locally caught seafood.

Grove
*The Esplanade, EX8 1BJ (01395 272101, www.grove
exmouth.com). Open 11am-11.30pm daily. Food served
noon-10pm daily.*

You'll find an all-British menu of comfort food and local cask
ales at this family-friendly Young's pub, whose large garden
and balcony overlook the mouth of the River Exe. Venison
and red wine casserole, smoked mackerel fish cakes and 21-
day aged Exmoor beef burgers come in at under a tenner;
there's also a seafood-based specials menu. The barbecue
sizzles into action on sunny weekends.

Les Saveurs at the Seafood Restaurant
*9 Tower Street, EX8 1NT (01395 269459, www.les
saveurs.co.uk). Dinner served 7-9pm Tue-Sat.*

Hidden away in a quiet, pedestrianised street, Les Saveurs
is a quietly accomplished little bistro. The menu includes
plenty of seafood, as you'd expect, ranging from Exmouth
sea bass (served with mash, mussels and fennel and saffron
sauce) to pan-fried local scallops, accompanied by
cauliflower purée and cumin velouté. The French-English
owners have also expanded the menu to include carefully
sourced local meat.

Where to stay
No 33 (33 Waverley Road, 01395 273702,
www.number33.co.uk) has three immaculately kept
rooms, and the owners cheerily accommodate any
special dietary requirements.

Royal Beacon Hotel
*The Beacon, EX8 2AF (01395 264886, www.royal
beaconhotel.co.uk). Rates £105-£120 double incl
breakfast.*

The Royal Beacon stands proud on Exmouth's finest
Regency terrace, with breathtaking sea and estuary views.
There are two restaurants: Fennels, serving brasserie-style
food, and the more informal Donato's – an Italian restaurant
set in the cellars, which does a roaring trade on Friday and
Saturday nights. The hotel also lets out a number of self-
contained apartments.

BUDLEIGH SALTERTON & THE OTTER VALLEY

Budleigh Salterton
A few miles east along the coast from Exmouth,
Budleigh Salterton developed into a genteel seaside
resort in the early 19th century, and has retained
an air of respectability. As you stroll around the
town and along the seafront everything seems
pleasantly staid and English, with few modern
intrusions. There are no chain stores here; shops
are proudly independent, and provide old-fashioned
service. You'll find proper bakers and butchers, a
fishmonger's, a deli, and a sprinkling of gift and

antiques shops. Call in at the Creamery (34 Fore Street, 01395 442064, closed winter) for freshly made ice-cream in a range of flavours.

For a more visual treat, look round the Brook Gallery (01395 443003, www.brookgallery.co.uk, closed Mon) in Fore Street, which hosts exhibitions of prints by Royal Academicians and local artists; there's also some lovely gold and silver jewellery. Just off the High Street, Chapel Street is home to the Isca Gallery (01395 444193, http://iscagallery. co.uk, closed Thur) which displays paintings by contemporary West Country artists. On Fore Street, a thatched house in the 19th-century cottage orné style houses Fairlynch Museum & Arts Centre (no.27, 01395 442666, www.devonmuseums.net/ fairlynch, closed Sat & Nov-Mar), which explores the area's geology and history.

From here, Marine Parade leads to the seafront. To the east, a path follows the sea wall all the way to the mouth of the River Otter. In the other direction, the path gradually climbs to the top of the red sandstone cliffs to reach the high point of West Down. The town's beach is made up of large, rounded pebbles – fall outs from ancient pebble beds in the cliffs. Overlying the pebble beds is rusty-red Otter sandstone, formed some 200 million years ago. Over the centuries, some of the rocks have been eroded away, leaving dramatic, isolated sea stacks (there are some fine examples at Ladram Bay, to the east).

Fishermen's boats are drawn up on the pebbles and brightly painted beach huts dot the seafront, adding to the beach's charm. Attractive as the pebbles may be to look at, getting into the sea is tricky; wear swim shoes to avoid bruised feet.

The Otter Estuary

Budleigh Salterton lies on the western side of the Otter Estuary – which, unlike its neighbour the Exe, is no broad tidal channel. After meandering its way through almost 25 miles of countryside, the river simply trickles into the sea, through the almost enclosing barrier of the shingle ridge. It wasn't always so: in the Middle Ages, ships sailed upriver as far as Otterton, but as the pebble ridge slowly formed, the estuary silted up and put paid to sea-going trade.

The second part of the town's name refers to the salt pans by the river mouth, which once fuelled a profitable salt industry; nowadays, the saltmarsh and mudflats provide a rich habitat for wildlife. Redshank, greenshank, plovers and other migrants can be spotted from hides on the banks, along with native birds including the occasional kingfisher.

There are scenic walks along the South West Coast Path, which loops around the estuary then follows the line of trees along the low cliffs. Other footpaths accompany the river upstream to Ottery St Mary; try the first section from the coast at Budleigh up to to the village of Otterton, just over two miles away. Stop for lunch or tea at Otterton Mill (see p31), before strolling back – or, for a circular ramble, walk through Otterton up to Stantyway Lane and the link to the Coast Path, then head back along the clifftop.

Like many an East Devon village, Otterton is characterised by white-painted cob and thatch cottages. A stream flows in a channel beside the main street, with little bridges leading to the houses. This is an ancient settlement, and Otterton Mill (see p31), which stands beside the river, was recorded in the Domesday Book. Now restored to working order, it is a fascinating place to visit; buy a loaf of wholemeal bread, made from the stoneground flour produced on site. From Otterton, a lane leads to the stunning pebble beach at Ladram Bay, with its splendid sandstone cliffs.

Raleigh Country

In Budleigh Salterton, you may have walked past the Octagon on Fore Street – a white-painted house, where Sir John Millais painted The Boyhood of Raleigh in 1870. (A blue plaque commemorates the fact.) The Elizabethan seafarer was actually born at Hayes Barton Farm (closed to the public), just outside the village of East Budleigh.

About two miles north of Budleigh Salterton, East Budleigh is the heart of the area now dubbed 'Raleigh Country', which encompasses the area between the Exe estuary and Sidmouth. It's an unspoilt village of pretty cob and thatch cottages, with a stream bordering the main street, leading up to the church. The Raleigh family are believed to have settled at Hayes Barton in 1537, and the family pew, which bears their coat of arms, is on the north side of the nave. On the edge of the village are the Bicton Park Botanical Gardens (see p30).

Where to eat & drink

On the seafront below Marine Parade in Budleigh Salterton is the summer-only Longboat Café (01395 445619), where you can sit and watch the waves over lunch; the Premier Café in Chapel Street (no.7, 01395 442962, closed Sun) serves fish and chips.

Over in East Budleigh, the Rolle Arms (Lower Budleigh, 01395 442012, www.therollearms.webs. com) is a sociable boozer, while in the old part of the village, near the church, the 16th-century Sir Walter Raleigh (22 High Street, 01395 442510) is a low, beamed local with an old-world atmosphere.

Further inland in Newton Poppleford, Moores' Restaurant (High Street, 01395 568100, www. mooresrestaurant.co.uk) is an intimate, family-run restaurant which also has three B&B rooms.

A Slice of Lyme

1-2 Rolle Road, Budleigh Salterton, EX9 6JZ (01395 442628). Open/food served 10am-4pm Mon; 10am-3pm, 6-9pm Tue-Fri; 10am-4pm, 6-9pm Sat; noon-4pm Sun.

This licensed café-bistro serves tasty light lunches, speciality coffees and a globally ranging evening menu. In the daytime, a takeaway hatch dispenses local Marshfield Farm ice-cream.

Cosy Teapot

13 Fore Street, Budleigh Salterton, EX9 6NH (01395 444016). Food served 10am-4pm daily. No credit cards.

Places to visit

DEVON

HONITON

Allhallows Museum
High Street, Honiton, EX14 1PG (01404 44966, www.honitonmuseum.co.uk). Open Easter-Sept 9.30am-4.30pm Mon-Fri; 9.30am-1pm Sat. Oct 9.30am-3.30pm Mon-Fri; 9.30am-12.30pm Sat. Admission £2; £1.50 reductions. No credit cards.
Fittingly, the town's museum occupies its oldest building – a 14th-century former chapel. Along with local pottery, a Victorian dolls' house and the weathered, 100,000 year-old bones of the Honiton hippos, the museum houses a fine collection of Honiton lace.

AXMINSTER

Burrow Farm Gardens
Dalwood, EX13 7ET (01404 831285, www.burrow farmgardens.co.uk). Open Apr-Oct 10am-7pm daily. Admission £5; £1 reductions.
This ten-acre garden has been beautifully landscaped over the last 40 years by Mary Benger, and is a true labour of love. Roses entwine the pergola walk, primula and iris dot the woodland garden, and there are great views over the surrounding fields. Light refreshments are available, along with plants from the nursery.

Lyme Bay Winery
Shute, EX13 7PW (01297 551355, www.lymebay winery.co.uk). Open 9am-5pm Mon-Fri; 10am-4pm Sat; 11am-3pm Sun. Closed weekends Jan-Apr.
In addition to its award-winning scrumpy and ciders, this place specialises in reviving old country tipples, made using hedgerow fruits and flowers. The long list of traditional country wines and fruit liqueurs includes cowslip wine and summer fruit liqueur; the sparkling strawberry and elderflower wines are also excellent.

Shute Barton
Shute, EX13 7PT (01752 346585, www.national trust.org.uk/main/w-shutebarton). Open May-Sept 2-5.30pm Wed, Sat. Oct 2-5pm Wed, Sat. Admission £3; £1.50 reductions.
A castellated roof and Tudor gatehouse lend this imposing country house a fairytale quality. Inside, you'll find the largest fireplace in England (over 20 foot wide), along with antique furniture, paintings and photographs belonging to the Pole-Carew family (it's still a family home, though run by the National Trust). The house is said to have its own apparition, the Grey Lady – the ghost of a lady who was ambushed in woods near the house by Parliamentarians, who hanged her from a tree.

OTTERY ST MARY

Ark Pottery
Higher Barnes, Wiggaton, EX11 1PY (01404 812628, www.arkpottery.co.uk). Open Mar-Oct 10am-5pm daily. Admission free.
In a quiet hamlet near Ottery, Ark was established by potters Vaughan and Angela Glanville some 30 years ago. In the studio, once the dairy of their 16th-century Devon longhouse, you can watch pots being hand-thrown. Work on sale includes one-off platters and jugs, tableware and Angela's hand-modelled Ark animals. You can also stay here in one of two B&B rooms.

Cadhay Manor
Ottery St Mary, EX11 1QT (01404 813511, www.cadhay.org.uk). Open May-Sept 2-5.30pm Fri, bank hol weekends. Admission House & gardens £6; £2 reductions. Gardens only £2; £1 reductions.
A splendid Elizabethan manor and gardens. The lush herbaceous borders, walled kitchen garden and medieval fish ponds make for a relaxing afternoon, followed by tea and cakes in the tearoom. The manor house can be hired out as self-catering accommodation, with room for up to 22 people, while the converted stables and coach house sleep up to six apiece.

Escot
Escot Park, Ottery St Mary, EX11 1LU (01404 822188, www.escot-devon.co.uk). Open Easter-Oct 10am-6pm daily. Nov-Easter 10am-5pm daily. Admission £6.95; £5.95 reductions; £24 family.
Wild boar, water vole, red squirrel and a pair of Bavarian beavers are among the wildlife at this historic East Devon estate, whose grounds were originally laid out by Capability Brown. It's a family-friendly place, with woodland walks, a beech maze, letterboxing, an indoor play barn for drizzly days and a fearsomely steep slide, the Forest Leap. Tuck into cream teas in the Coach House, or bring a picnic.

EXMOUTH

A La Ronde ★
Summer Lane, Exmouth, EX8 5BD (01395 265514, www.nationaltrust.org.uk/alaronde). Open Mar-Oct 11am-5pm Mon-Wed, Sat, Sun. Admission £6.40; £3.20 reductions; £16 family.
Two miles north of Exmouth, this delightfully eccentric, 16-sided house has panoramic views over the Exe. It was built in 1795 for cousins Jane and Mary Parminter, to house an impressive collection of mementoes gathered during their Grand Tour. The rooms were laid out so they could follow the sun through the day, finishing with tea in an oval room on the western side of the house. The pair also adorned the interior, created a feather frieze and a shell-encrusted gallery that has to be seen to be believed.

BUDLEIGH SALTERTON & THE OTTER VALLEY

Bicton Park Botanical Gardens ★
East Budleigh, Budleigh Salterton, EX9 7BJ (01395 568465, www.bictongardens.co.uk). Open Summer 10am-6pm daily. Winter 10am-5pm daily. Admission £6.95; £5.95 reductions.
Some 300 years of horticultural history are captured in these magnificent gardens, home to numerous rare plants and an impressive arboretum. Stroll the elegant 18th-century Italian Garden or venture into the marvellous glasshouses, which include a curvaceous 1820s Palm House and a lush Tropical House. The on-site Countryside Museum offers a glimpse of rural life over the last three centuries, while the trim little Woodland Railway, nature trail, maze and play areas keep children happy.

An Elizabethan manor house, with an adjacent medieval hall. The guided tour is led by the owners, who describe its history to visitors; children will perk up at the mention of the ghost. The six-acre gardens were laid out in 1911, and include a long terrace and Edwardian summer-house. There's also a tearoom.

BRANSCOMBE

Old Bakery
Manor Mill & Forge, Branscombe, EX12 3DB (01752 346585, www.thenationaltrust.co.uk). Open Old Bakery Apr-Oct 11am-5pm Wed-Sun. Manor Mill July, Aug 2-5pm Wed, Sun. June, Sept, Oct 2-5pm Sun. Forge 11am-5pm daily. Admission Manor Mill £2.80; £1.40 reductions. No credit cards
The Old Bakery was the last traditional working bakery in Devon, until it closed ust over 20 years ago. Now part of a cluster of buildings run by the National Trust, it is charmingly atmospheric. The old baking equipment remains, as does the water-powered mill, and there's also a tearoom. The thatched forge has also been restored, and sells ironwork forged by the blacksmith. This is the departure point for a number of lovely walks; a leaflet is available.

BEER

Beer Quarry Caves ★
Quarry Lane, EX12 3AT (01297 625830, www.beer quarrycaves.fsnet.co.uk). Open Easter-Sept 10am-4.30pm daily. Oct 11am-4pm daily. Admission £6; £4.25 reductions; £18 family. No credit cards.
Beer stone is prized by stonemasons: perfect for carving fine detail when freshly quarried, it hardens and turns a soft white colour on prolonged exposure to air. This underground quarry provided the stone for 24 great cathedrals, including St Paul's. The caves now house a museum, while an hour-long guided tour explores the vast complex of tunnels (once a hiding place for Catholics taking refuge, and for smugglers' contraband).

Pecorama
Underleys, EX12 3NA (01297 21542, www.peco-uk.com). Open Apr-Oct 10am-5.30pm Mon-Fri; 10am-1pm Sat; occasional Sun, check website for details. Admission £7; £5-£6.50 reductions; £22.50 family.
Run by model train manufacturers Peco, this place will enthrall locomotive-lovers. Model trains layouts include a modern city with underground trains and a tram system; get involved by pushing a button or two. Visitors can also ride the outdoor narrow gauge train, or explore the flower-filled Millennium Gardens.

SEATON

Motoring Memories Museum
Colyford, EX24 6QQ (01297 553815, www.motoring memories.com). Open June-Sept 10.30am-4.30pm Tue-Sat; also by arrangement. Admission £2.50.
Motoring memorabilia and vintage vehicles are proudly displayed at this museum. It's set by the old Colyford Filling Station – built in 1928, but now kitted out with '50s petrol pumps and signs. TE Lawrence was a regular customer here during the 1930s, dropping by to fill up his Brough Superior motorcycle.

Otterton Mill

Otterton Mill
Otterton, EX9 7HG (01395 568521, www.otterton mill.com) Open 10am-5pm daily. Admission free.
This historic watermill is now fully operational once more, and used for its original purpose – using waterpower to produce stoneground flour. An artisan bakery sells bread made from the flour, along with great cakes, and there are regular baking courses with the head baker. On certain days you can watch the milling taking place. The mill complex has also become a centre for arts and crafts, with a gallery space, a shop and two artists' studios; there's also a restaurant, and a lively music programme. The orchard is planted with traditional Devon apple trees, and there's a wildlife meadow and pond.

SIDMOUTH

Donkey Sanctuary ★
Slade House Farm, Sidmouth, EX10 0NU (01395 578222, www.thedonkeysanctuary.org.uk). Open 9am-dusk. Admission free, donations appreciated.
The HQ of the Donkey Sanctuary charity, this place is home to some 160 rescue donkeys. Visitors can wander around the paddocks and yard and meet the donkeys. There are five different walks through the sanctuary and the surrounding countryside, including a challenging footpath to the sea at Weston Mouth; refuel with cake and a cuppa in the Hayloft restaurant.

Norman Lockyer Observatory
Salcombe Hill, Sidmouth, EX10 0NY (01395 579941, www.projects.exeter.ac.uk/nlo). Open phone or check website for details. Admission £5; £2.50 reductions.
Established in 1912, this historic observatory and planetarium has regular opening evenings, many of which tie in with astronomical events such as meteor showers. A visit takes roughly two hours, but can be longer on a clear night if the telescopes are in use; you'll also be shown a planetarium presentation and given a tour of the telescope domes – and possibly a demo of the radio station or weather satellite reception.

Sand House & Gardens
Sidbury, EX10 0QN (01395 597230, www.sand sidbury.co.uk). Open check website for details. Admission House & Gardens £6. Gardens only £3.

Teapots and old books line the walls here, the sugar bowls sport lacy covers, and music from a more leisured age plays discreetly in the background while customers sip tea from bone china cups. Daily specials – local sausages with toasted crumpets – are served alongside cakes and scones.

Otter Inn
Exmouth Road, Colaton Raleigh, EX10 0LE (01395 568434, www.otterinn.co.uk). Open noon-11pm daily. Food served noon-9pm Mon-Sat; noon-8pm Sun.
The interior of the café-style pub is modishly modern, with stripped wood floors, chunky tables, soft cream walls and deep leather sofas. Beers from local breweries include Otter and Branscombe, there's a wide-ranging, family-friendly menu and a childrens' play area in the garden.

Tobias Restaurant
53 High Street, Budleigh Salterton, EX9 6LE (01395 446644, www.tobias-restaurant.com). Lunch served noon-2pm Wed-Sun. Dinner served 6-9pm Tue-Sat.
At lunch, this town-centre restaurant concentrates on bistro fare: salmon and dill fish cakes with sautéed new potatoes, or chorizo and pepper omelette with chips. In the evening, the prices rise and more sophisticated cooking prevails.

Where to stay
A few minutes' walk from the beach in Budleigh Salterton, Appletree Cottage (23 Victoria Place, 01395 445433, www.appletreecottagebudleigh. co.uk) offers simple B&B rooms. Walkers on the South West Coast Path are well catered for, with big breakfasts, drying facilities for wet kit, and luggage transfers arranged on request between Exmouth and Seaton. On the High Street, the Feathers (no.35, 01395 442042, www.feathers-hotel.co.uk, closed dinner Sun) is a traditional pub with an inexpensive bar menu and four nicely appointed B&B rooms.

In East Budleigh, Wynards Farm (Middle Street, 01395 443417) is a working dairy farm with three B&B rooms. Children are welcome. Alternatively, Webbers Park (Castle Lane, Woodbury, 01395 232276, www.webberspark.co.uk, closed Nov-Feb) is a family-run caravan and camping site with well-spaced pitches, good facilities and an animal enclosure with donkeys and goats.

Pebbles
16 Fore Street, Budleigh Salterton, EX9 6NG (01395 442417, www.bedandbreakfastbythebeach.com). Rates £85-£99 double incl breakfast.
You can't get closer to the sea than this beachfront B&B. The three guest rooms have great views – particularly the second-floor Sail Loft, with its sloping ceilings and nautical blue and white decor. The rooms are well equipped (flatscreen TVs, DVD players, Wi-Fi, mini fridges) and the beach lies just beyond the garden gate.

Rosehill Rooms & Cookery
30 West Hill, Budleigh Salterton, EX9 6BU (01395 444031, www.rosehillroomsandcookery.co.uk). Rates £80-£99 double incl breakfast. No credit cards.
Each of the four rooms at this upscale B&B has a different feel – although Wi-Fi, king-size beds, flatscreen TVs and

SEAFOOD SPECIALISTS

Beer Fisheries
Three family-owned boats keep Beer Fisheries (01297 20297, www.beer fish.co.uk) well stocked with brill, bass, mackerel, lobster and more: fish can be speedily filleted or scaled on request. Delicious Lyme Bay crabs are cooked moments after touching dry land and can be bought ready-to-eat, still warm from the broiler.

Millers Farm Shop
Set just off the A35, the superb Millers Farm Shop (Gammons Hill, Kilmington, 01297 35290, www.millersfarmshop. com, closed Sun pm) stocks everything from scrumpy to Colyton Butcher's pies. What's more, fishmonger Simon Bennett (whose foodie fans include Hugh Fearnley-Whittingstall and Mark Hix) runs a fish stall by the main entrance, Tuesday to Sunday; you might find scallops, wild bass, grey mullet and lemon sole.

Sidmouth Trawlers
Located in Fisherman's Yard, at the eastern end of Sidmouth's Esplanade, this family-run fishmongers, (01395 512714, www.sidmouthtrawlers.co.uk, closed Mon) was established in the 1960s by local fisherman Stan Bagwell. Seafood includes brill, dover sole, plaice, lemon sole, mackerel, bass, crabs and lobsters. There's also cooked shellfish (whelks, cockles, mussels, prawns) – and if you fancy a crab sarnie, they'll make one to order.

Wet Plaice
The wet fish counter at Exmouth's award-winning Wet Plaice (16 the Strand, 01395 222717, closed Sun) is a joy to behold, with an impressive array of locally landed specimens. Along with fresh fish of every size and stripe, there's smoked fish, shellfish and deli treats such as squid and octopus salad, fishy pâtés and pies.

bath robes come as standard. The largest room is Sandcastle, with space for a sofa and two easy chairs, along with a vast, sleekly appointed bathroom. Breakfast, consumed around a communal table, is another plus. Cookery courses for adults and kids are also offered.

SIDMOUTH

In the late 1700s, with Napoleon causing an uproar on the continent, the upper classes turned to summer watering holes closer to home. Astute businessman Emmanuel Lousada realised that Sidmouth, a little fishing village at the mouth of the River Sid, flanked by dramatic red cliffs and sheltered by the wooded slopes of the Sid Valley, was ripe for development. He transformed Sidmouth into a fashionable resort, building large houses in an ornate, faux-rustic style known as cottage orné and creating a mile-long esplanade by the broad pebble beach. This was soon lined with elegant, bow-fronted houses with elaborate balconies, many of which are now hotels. With its mild climate and natural beauty, Sidmouth was a hit with high society. In the summer of 1801, Jane Austen came here with her family; and the Duke and Duchess of Kent arrived with their baby, Princess Victoria, in December 1819. They took lodgings at Woolbrook Cottage, now the site of the Royal Glen Hotel, the Duke dying a month later of a feverish cold.

In Sidmouth Museum (Church Street, 01395 516139, www.devonmuseums.net, closed Sun), Hubert Cornish's etching of 1815, the *Long View*, depicts the seafront as it was then, complete with newfangled bathing machines. For those not brave enough to enter the sea, the Marine Baths (now the Kingswood Hotel) warmed up the saltwater. When the railway finally arrived in 1874, the station was built a good mile outside town. Thus Dawlish, further down the coast, was invaded by day-trippers, while genteel Sidmouth preserved its exclusivity.

John Betjeman described Sidmouth as 'a town caught still in a timeless charm.' That's certainly the case by the thatched pavilion at the cricket grounds, where you can hear the satisfying thwack of leather on willow. Fortfield Terrace, with its white façade and canopied balconies, overlooks this quintessentially English scene. Once the home of the Grand Duchess Hélène of Russia, sister-in-law to the tsar, no.8 is marked out by a resplendent double-headed eagle. Further examples of Georgian architecture line York Terrace and Coburg Terrace.

On Church Street, look out for the Old Chancel: the handiwork of 19th-century antiquarian and artist Peter Orlando Hutchinson, it's a medieval-Victorian fusion, created from pieces salvaged from the old parish church.

Among the town's shops are a handful of family-owned establishments that have been going for a century or more. Govier's (55 High Street, 01395 513419, www.goviers.co.uk) has sold fine china, glass and cutlery since 1904, while Fields Department Store (01395 515124, www.fieldsof sidmouth.co.uk) on Market Place first opened its doors some 200 years ago. Trumps (*see p34*) is another atmospheric old-timer.

Newer additions to the shopping scene include Paragon Books (38 High Street, 01395 514516, www.paragon-books.co.uk) and Kaieteur (3 Fore Street, 01395 515561, www.kaieteur.uk.com, closed Sun), which sells renewable energy gadgets and gizmos; on the same street, you'll find covetable homeware at the Secret Garden (01395 577886, www.thesecretgardensidmouth.com). The Dairy Shop (5 Old Church Street, 01395 513018) is a well-established deli and café; for fish landed on the beach and locally grown produce and flowers, head for the town's covered market.

The seafront & beaches

There are candy-striped deckchairs for hire on the Esplanade, by the main beach – although budding marine biologists and sandcastle builders may prefer the beach at Jacob's Ladder, to the west, where low tide reveals an expanse of sand and rock pools. At the back of the beach, the 'ladder' – a steep set of wooden steps – scales the red cliffs, emerging amid the floral displays of Connaught Gardens. The gardens are home to the Clock Tower Tea Rooms; from June to August, Sidmouth Town Band plays a Sunday-evening concert in the bandstand. The musical high point of Sidmouth's calendar, though, is its week-long folk festival, held in August.

For breathtaking views of the Jurassic Coast and Sidmouth, make your way further up Peak Hill; you can also pick up the Coasthopper Bus from here and take a coastal tour of the area.

Where to eat & drink

There are some pleasant country pubs just outside Sidmouth. In the village of Sidford, the thatched Blue Ball Inn (Steven's Cross, 01395 514062, www.blueballinn.net) serves local ales and an extensive menu. Built in 1385, the inn was destroyed by fire in 2006, and has been lovingly rebuilt by the Newton family, who have owned it since 1912. It also offers nine bright en suite rooms.

Dukes

The Esplanade, Market Place, EX10 8AR (01395 513320). Open 10am-11pm Mon-Wed, Sun; 10am-11.30pm Thur-Sat. Food served noon-9pm Mon-Wed, Sun; noon-9.30pm Fri, Sat.
Serving food all day, Dukes is a handy port of call. The sunny patio is a pleasant spot for Lyme Bay crab sandwiches, grilled sardines or a stone-baked pizza. Upstairs are 14 en suite B&B rooms (£42-£52 double incl breakfast), some with sea views.

Old Ship Inn

Old Fore Street, EX10 8LP (01395 512127). Open 11am-11pm Mon-Thur; 11am-midnight Fri, Sat; noon-10.30pm Sun. Lunch served noon-2pm Mon-Sat; noon-2.30pm Sun. Dinner served 6-9pm daily.
A one-time smuggler's haunt, the cob-walled building dates back to 1350; rumour has it there's a secret passage, used to evade the excise men. The beamed interior is decked out with old pictures and seafaring memorabilia, and there's beer from the Branscombe Brewery and Sharp's Brewery.

Trumps of Sidmouth ★

Fore Street, EX10 8AH (01395 512446, www.trumpsof sidmouth.co.uk). Open/food served 9am-5pm Mon-Sat; 11am-4pm Sun. Closed Sun Jan.

Established in 1813, Trumps is one of the oldest grocery stores in the South West. Its long wooden counters, gold and green pillars and beautifully carved shop fittings advertising 'High Class Provisions' are charming, as is the in-store café. Call in for coffee and cake, or welsh rarebit, made with good, sharp cheddar on Otterton Mill bread.

Where to stay

In a regency building on the Esplanade in Sidmouth, the Royal York & Faulkner Hotel (01395 513043, www.royalyorkhotel.co.uk) is a traditional upmarket hotel with spa facilities. Just outside the town, in Bowd Cross, the Barn & Pinn Cottage (01395 513613, www.thebarnandpinncottage.co.uk) is a sweet B&B, set in beautiful gardens. There are six homely en suite rooms, and a residents' dining room and bar in the converted barn.

Groveside

Vicarage Road, Sidmouth, EX10 8UQ (01395 513406, www.thegroveside.co.uk). Rates £74 double incl breakfast. No credit cards.

A relaxed B&B in a detached Edwardian villa around eight minutes' walk from the sea. There are ten en suite bedrooms; all have crisp white linen, tea and coffee making facilities and TVs. Evening meals are available too.

Lower Pinn Farm

Peak Hill, EX10 0NN (01395 513733, www.lower pinnfarm.co.uk). Rates £56-£76 double incl breakfast. No credit cards.

There are three simple en suite bedrooms at this 220-acre working farm. The farm is situated not far from the beach at Ladram Bay. Stroll across the fields and soak up the glorious coastal views.

Royal Glen Hotel

Glen Road, Sidmouth, EX10 8RW (01395 513221, www.royalglenhotel.co.uk). Rates £100-£125 double incl breakfast.

In its time, this distinctive, Grade I-listed building has been a farmhouse, an orphanage, a boarding house, a wartime RAF convalescent home and, finally, a family-run hotel. The rooms retain a gentle, old-fashioned charm, and the hotel has an indoor heated pool and a stately dining room. The location is good: just minutes from the seafront.

Salcombe Close House

Sid Lane, Sidmouth, EX10 9AW (01395 579067, www.salcombeclosehouse.com). Rates £80-£84 double incl breakfast. No credit cards.

Opened in 2009, the house and gardens are a short walk from the river Sid, which you can follow through the Byes (a National Trust owned park) into town. There are two large en suite rooms; both have flatscreen TVs and Wi-Fi.

Salty Monk ★

Church Street, Sidford, EX10 9QP (01395 513174, www.saltymonk.co.uk). Rates £110-£200 double incl breakfast.

This unusual 16th-century building was once a salt works, owned by Benedictine monks. It's now a B&B and restaurant, with six en suite rooms. These vary in style, from simple doubles and twins to plushly appointed suites: the Lavender suite, for example, has a super king-size bed and ultra-modern freestanding bath. The restaurant menu draws extensively on Devonshire produce: tuck into the likes of rilettes of Branscombe rabbit with toasted brioche.

BRANSCOMBE

This delightful village, set along the coast to the east of Sidmouth, was thrust into the limelight in January 2007, when the 62,000 tonne container ship MSC *Napoli* ran aground just offshore. Two days of chaos ensued, as treasure seekers from all over the country descended to pillage its cargo. But Branscombe should really be remembered as one of the loveliest villages in Devon; today, the only memento of the drama is the ship's enormous anchor, displayed on a plinth by the seafront.

Tucked away in a hidden wooded valley, the village enjoys a benign microclimate, and many of its pretty stone and thatch cottages sport colourful fuchsia hedges. Thanks to its meandering, mile-long main street, Branscombe is said to be the longest village in Britain; check out the aerial photographs of the village in the Fountain Head (*see below*).

At the other end of the village, the venerable Masons Arms (*see p35*) has been serving liquid refreshment to locals and the masons, who rode here from Beer Quarry, since 1360. The 12th-century St Winifred's church has fragments of medieval wall paintings and a fine 18th-century triple pulpit. On the outskirts of the village, the forge, watermill and tearooms at the Old Bakery (*see p31*) give a flavour of village life of old.

The village culminates in a long pebble beach – accessible via a wheelchair- and pushchair-friendly gravel footpath; alternatively, you can drive down a steep, narrow lane and park in the car park at the Sea Shanty (*see p35*). Owned by the National Trust, this is one of the most unspoilt beaches in Devon. The cliffs are home to breeding seabirds such as fulmars, the under-cliff linnets and Adonis blue butterflies. Pulled up on the steeply shelving shore are a few fishing boats; the *Branscombe Pearl* (01297 680369, closed Oct-Mar) offers mackerel fishing and scenic coastal excursions.

Where to eat & drink

Fountain Head

Branscombe, EX12 3BG (01297 680359, www.fountain headinn.com). Open 11am-3pm, 6-11pm Mon-Sat; noon-3pm, 6-10.30pm Sun. Lunch served noon-2pm, dinner served 6.30-9pm daily.

This 14th-century pub offers a sterling selection of local brews (including Branoc ale from the Branscombe Vale brewery and Thatchers Cheddar Valley cider), along with dog biscuits and local fudge. A log fire, sloping stone floors and tankards hanging from the beams exude good cheer. Children and dogs are welcome; food runs from crab sarnies to steak pie. In summer, the pub hosts its own beer festival.

Branscombe

Masons Arms

Branscombe, EX12 3DJ (01297 680300, www.masons arms.co.uk). Open 11am-3pm, 6-11pm daily. Lunch served noon-2pm, dinner served 7-9pm daily. Rates £80-£175 double incl breakfast.

The Masons started life in 1360, as a tiny cider house. Over the centuries it has expanded to become an idyllic country inn. With its ship's timbers, slate floors and central log fire, the bar hasn't changed much over the years. There are always five real West Country ales on tap, as well as ciders and scrumpy, and appealing bar food (Branscombe beef and horseradish sausages, for example, or local mussels), with fancier meals served in the restaurant. There are characterful rooms too (*see below*).

Sea Shanty

Branscombe Beach (01297 680577, www.theseashanty. co.uk). Open/food served Easter-Oct 10am-5pm daily.

Just yards from the beach, this thatched restaurant and tearoom has Lyme Bay crab on the menu in season. The snack menu runs from bacon baps to Devon cream teas. Bigger appetites can feast on Thai curry, local bangers and mash or catch of the day. A small shop sells groceries, sandwiches, cakes, ice-cream and a good range of beach goods and swimwear, and is also open winter weekends.

Where to stay

At the Masons Arms (*see above*), you can stay in the main inn or in one of the 12 cottage rooms or two luxury suites. Rooms vary in style from pretty twin rooms with sprigged curtains and garden views to grand bedrooms with four-posters and jacuzzis.

Forge Cottage

Branscombe, EX12 3DB (0844 800 2070, www. nationaltrustcottages.co.uk). Rates £318-£1,042 per week for 4 people.

This thatched two-bedroom cottage stands opposite the working forge across the lane. In summer, make the most of the suntrap garden; in winter, sit by the fire in the snug, pink-painted sitting room. Footpaths lead through the wooded valley down to the pebble beach, and you're within easy reach of the village pub.

Great Seaside Farm

Branscombe, EX12 3DP (01297 680470, www.great seaside.co.uk). Rates £80-£90 double incl breakfast. No credit cards.

This 16th-century thatched farmhouse, surrounded by over 400 acres of National Trust land, is just two minutes' walk from the beach. The guest lounge exudes period charm, with an inglenook fireplace, an original bread oven, flagstone floors and beamed ceilings, while the bedrooms are tucked under the eaves.

Margells

Branscombe, EX12 3DB (01628 825925, www. landmarktrust.org.uk). Rates £794-£2,110 per week for 5 people.

It's thought that this thatched stone cottage, now owned by the Landmark Trust, was once a wing of a much larger house. That would account for its distinctly upmarket interior, with its oak partitions and staircase, and vaulted upstairs rooms – one of which bears the richly hued remains of a late 16th-century wall painting. The cottage is within easy staggering distance of the pub.

BEER

'Down in Devon, down in Devon/There's a village by the sea/It's a little piece of heaven/And the angels call it Beer!'. So runs a local ditty, extolling the virtues of this fishing village – and most visitors would be inclined to agree. Lined with candy-coloured thatched cottages and brimming hanging baskets and windowboxes in summer, Beer's main street is one of the prettiest in the county. A stream runs along an open conduit on Fore Street, down towards the sheltered cove at the bottom of the hill where the fishermen land their catch.

Fore Street is also home to some interesting shops; look out for the lovely tiled exterior of Marine House ★ (01297 625257, www.marinehouseat beer.co.uk, closed Mon mid Nov-Mar). Along with its sister business the Steam Gallery, a few doors away, the gallery is one of Devon's leading centres for fine and applied arts, showcasing work from over 100 artists and craftspeople.

At Woozie's Deli (01297 20707), more down-to-earth temptations include fresh baked pastries and pies, while Rock Villa (01297 21491) sells a huge range of local wines, beers and ciders, including ales brewed in Branscombe. On Lower Fore Street, the funky Jimmy Green (01297 625125, www.jimmy green.co.uk) sells sailing and surf gear.

Follow Fore Street down to the beach, where a dozen or so brightly coloured wooden fishing boats rest on the shingle. On the left-hand side of the beach, Butler Boats (07771 924857) offer self-drive wooden motor boats, with perky names such as *Popeye* and *Boy John*, in which to potter around the bay. An hour's hire costs £18, and staff will lend you a line to catch a mackerel for supper.

Beneath the wooded cliffs, sit at one of the tables on the shingle at the Chapple Café, order a fresh crab sandwich and a pot of tea and soak up the scene. The café also lets the little wooden beach huts at the base of the cliffs. Behind here, steps lead to Jubilee Gardens, which has superb views across the coastline towards Seaton.

At the Fine Foundation Centre (01297 24841, closed Nov-Mar), on the slipway to the beach, you can find out about the history and geology of the area. Local ecologist Patricia Farrell also runs special events throughout the Easter and summer holidays, including wildlife Wednesday and rockpooling safaris (bucket and net provided). The noticeboard details sea-fishing trips with locally based fishermen, while the yard behind the Centre holds the superb Wet Fish Shop (also known as Beer Fisheries; see p32).

In August, Beer Regatta Week fills the bay with all sorts of watercraft, including traditional rigged sailing boats from the Beer Luggers Club. Rattenbury Day, at the end of August, is when the village celebrates one of its most notorious sons. Born in Beer in 1778, smuggler Jack Rattenbury is believed to have been the inspiration for Elzevir Block in the novel *Moonfleet*.

Where to eat & drink

Fore Street's tearooms and numerous pubs all sport impressive seafood specials boards.

Barrel O'Beer

Fore Street, EX12 3EQ (01297 20099, www.barrelo beer.co.uk). Open Summer 11.30am-11pm Mon-Sat; noon-10pm Sun. Winter 11.30am-2.30pm, 6-11pm Mon-Wed; 11.30am-11pm Thur-Sat; noon-10pm Sun.

Lunch served noon-2pm, dinner served 6-9pm Mon-Sat. Meals served noon-10pm Sun.
The Barrel sources its produce as close to home as possible, with Lyme Bay seafood, free-range and organic meat from local farms and game from nearby estates. Classic dishes – roast skate wing with lemon and caper butter and chips – are supplemented by a lighter lunch and snack menu, served in the bar. There's a good range of real ale, cider and wine.

Steamers

New Cut, EX12 3DU (01297 22922, www.steamers restaurant.co.uk). Lunch served noon-2pm, dinner served 7-9pm Tue-Sat.
Housed in the old village bakery, this laid-back bistro is a family-friendly affair, with a children's menu, highchairs, baby-changing facilities, books, toys and puzzles. The menu runs from Med-inspired risottos and bruschetta to hearty English staples, such as sautéed calf's liver with bacon and onion gravy. Local seafood is also much in evidence.

Where to stay

Marine House (*see above*) rents out three two-bedroom apartments above the gallery. For details, call Jean Bartlett Holidays (01297 23221).

Set in 16 acres of farmland on the edge of the village of Salcombe Regis, Salcombe Regis Camping & Caravan Park (01395 514303, www. salcombe-regis.co.uk) is geared towards family fun, with plenty of room for outdoor play, a large field for dogs to exercise in and access to the nearby pebble beach of Salcombe Mouth.

Anchor Inn

Fore Street, EX12 3ET (01297 20386, www.anchorinn-beer.com). Rates £85 double incl breakfast.
The Anchor sits in a prime location, 100 yards from the beach. Six of the eight B&B rooms have sea views, and most are en suite; those who are intrigued by Beer's smuggling past can stay in the Jack Rattenbury-themed room. The restaurant majors in fish; the bar has local real ales and Devon cider, which you can sup by the fire. Come summer it's all about the cliff-top beer garden and barbecues.

Bay View Guest House

Sea Front, Fore Street, EX12 3EE (01297 20489, www.bayviewbeer.com). Rates £60-£70 double incl breakfast.
The South West Coast Path passes right by the front door of this six-room B&B, which overlooks the beach. The en suite rooms are individually styled with nautical colour schemes, and enjoy lovely views. Waffles with maple syrup or smoked haddock with poached egg feature at breakfast.

Coombe View Farm

Branscombe, EX12 3BT (01297 680218, www. branscombe-camping.co.uk). Rates £10-£12 for 2 people.
Set along a hilly lane, this small, friendly farm campsite comprises three grassy camping fields and two or three static mobile homes. Children can play rounders or football in the centre of the first field, collect firewood in the neighbouring thickets (campfires are allowed, in designated areas) or meet the resident ducks, chickens, Berkshire pigs and Exmoor ponies. Other facilities include electric hook-ups and free showers; dogs are allowed, on leads.

Seaton Tramway

AXMINSTER

River Cottage
Park Farm, Musbury, EX13 (01297 630302, www.rivercottage.net).
Hugh Fearnley-Whittingstall's River Cottage HQ, Park Farm, is set in a valley that straddles the East Devon and Dorset border, near Axminster. It's the venue for a wide range of day courses and demonstrations, ranging from cider-making to wild food foraging or butchery. There are also themed evening events, some hosted by HF-W, when you tuck into a seasonal feast in the barn or the garden. Book well ahead.

EXMOUTH

Edge Water Sports
3 Royal Avenue, Exmouth, EX8 1EN (01395 222551, www.edgewatersports.com). Open 9.30am-5.30pm Mon-Sat; 10am-4pm Sun.
Kitesurfing, wakeboarding, powerboating or power-kiting, with expert tuition; equipment can be hired.

Stuart Line Cruises ★
Exmouth Marina, EX8 1DS (Summer 01395 222144, Winter 01395 279693, www.stuartlinecruises.co.uk). Tickets from £5; £3 reductions.
This family-run business offers cruises along the River Exe, the South Devon coastline and the Jurassic Coast between Exmouth and Sidmouth, as well as guided wildlife trips and day excursions to Torquay and Brixham.

World of Country Life
Sandy Bay, Westdown Lane, Exmouth, EX8 5BU (01395 274533, www.worldofcountrylife.co.uk). Open Apr-Oct 10am-5pm daily. Admission £9.85; £7.85 reductions; £32.50-£37.50 family.
Entertainments on offer at this wholesome amusement park include going on a deer safari, taking a pygmy goat for a walk, or petting rabbits and guinea pigs. If that's not your thing, then you can also admiring the gleaming collection of vintage cars, motorbikes and steam engines gathered here. Children can also let off steam in the action-packed adventure playgrounds and covered play area.

SEATON

Seaton Tramway ★
Harbour Road, Seaton, EX12 2TB (01297 20375, www.tram.co.uk). Open Feb-Easter 10am-4pm Sat, Sun. Easter-Oct 10am-4pm daily. Tickets £8.35; £5.85-£7.50 reductions.
This narrow-gauge heritage tramway runs along the route of a former branch line by the Axe Estuary, through the birdlife-rich nature reserves of Seaton Marshes and Colyford Common. The three-mile route takes around half an hour, stopping at Colyford village and terminating at Colyton, where the Tram Stop restaurant serves big breakfasts and simple, reasonably priced meals. Check the website for details of the two-hour birdwatching trips, led by experienced ornithologists.

Beer. See p35.

SEATON, COLYTON & COLYFORD

Seaton

Driving down the hill towards the seaside town of Seaton, a glorious vista of Lyme Bay stretches out before you. With its gently sloping pebble beach and pretty harbour, the town is set by the mouth of the River Axe, with the white cliffs of Beer Head sheltering it to the east and the red sandstone of Haven Cliff to the west.

The arrival of the railway in the late 1860s turned Seaton into a stylish resort, and the remaining Victorian and Edwardian architecture gives the pedestrianised town centre an elegant air. At the Tourist Information Centre next to the tram station

(01297 21660), invest 40p in a leaflet on the town's various heritage trails, ranging from 20-minute strolls to four-hour treks.

The seawall and Esplanade run alongside the mile-long beach, interspersed by the odd beachside kiosk offering crab sandwiches, toasties and ice-cream. Towards the western end of the beach, Seaton Hole is a perfect rock pooling spot at low tide, overlooked by a seasonally-opening café, the Cliffside Cabin (no phone). Get there by walking along the beach (depending on the tide) or via Cliff Field Gardens, whose coastal views make it an ideal picnic spot.

At the eastern end of the Esplanade is the small harbour, where the Axe enters the Bay. There's a café with outdoor tables at the Sea Discovery Centre (01297 24774, closed Nov-Mar); a marine chandlery and tackle shop, it also incorporates an aquarium, where you can peer at conger eels, anemones, baby sharks and other sea critters.

Across the river is the Undercliffs National Nature Reserve (*see below*), which extends to Lyme Regis. The area around Seaton is rich in wildlife and ancient woodlands, carpeted with bluebells in May. Spot wading birds from the open-topped Seaton Tram (*see p37*), which runs alongside the Axe estuary, or explore the Seaton Marshes Nature Reserve on foot. Here, wheelchair- and buggy-friendly paths lead to hides beside the Axe.

Colyton & Colyford

In the 15th century, the small town of Colyton grew rich on agriculture and the wool trade, becoming one of the richest towns in Devon. Located within a conservation area, where the Axe and Coly valleys meet, it is a charming place to explore. The unusual circular street pattern dates back to Saxon times, and the maze of narrow streets is lined with thatched stone cottages and merchant's houses. St Andrew's Church, with its distinctive octagonal lantern tower, dates from the 15th century.

During the Civil War, Colyton was the site of many a bloody skirmish, being caught between the Royalist stronghold at Colcombe Castle, near Axminster, and the Parliamentarians at Stedcombe, close to Lyme Regis. In 1685, it was dubbed the most rebellious town in Devon when over 100 of its men decided to support the Duke of Monmouth's ill-fated campaign to overthrow James II; many were kiled or later hanged. Copies of the town's historic trail are available at Haynes Hardware in the Market Place, and a local historian also runs hour-long guided tours for groups (01297 552828).

In King Street, J & FJ Baker & Co (01297 552282, www.jfjbaker.co.uk, closed Sat, Sun) is the last traditional oak bark tannery in the country. There has been a tannery on this riverside site since Roman times – and although the tannery has been rebuilt several times over the centuries, the methods used to tan the skins are little changed. Over many months the tanning liquor, made from soaking oak bark in river water, results in a rich-coloured leather, used to make bridles and shoes.

Just over a mile away, the pretty village of Colyford is also on the Seaton tramway line. Its main street, dotted with thatched cottages, comes alive in September during the Michaelmas Goose Fayre, which incorporates mummers, medieval music and costume-clad locals in a parade through the village.

Where to eat & drink

Frydays (2 the Burrow, Seaton, 01297 23911, www.frydays.eu) is the locals' choice for a slap-up fish supper.

Terrace Arts Café

6 Marine Crescent, Seaton, EX12 2QN (01297 20225, www.artannapola.com). Open 10am-5pm Tue, Thur; 10am-3pm Wed; 10am-9pm Fri, Sat; 11.30am-3pm Sun.

Overlooking the bay, this licensed gallery café cooks up an inviting array of vegetarian and vegan dishes, such as spicy refried bean tortilla wrap or butternut squash and sweet potato curry. The gallery itself specialises in contemporary artwork, including metalwork, ceramics and paintings.

Wheelwright Inn

Swan Hill Road, Colyford, EX24 6QQ (01297 552585, www.wheelwright-inn.co.uk). Open 9am-11pm daily. Food served 9am-9.30pm daily.

The flower-filled patio outside this thatched inn is perfect for supping a summer pint of Badger ale. Inside, oak floors, cob walls and open fires exude a homely charm. The food – steak and ale pie, liver and bacon – is a cut above pub grub. Children are welcome, as are dogs on leads.

Where to stay

Glebe House

Southleigh, EX24 6SD (01404 871276, www.guests atglebe.com). Rates from £70 double incl breakfast. No credit cards.

Set above the village of Southleigh, some two miles from Colyton, this late Georgian vicarage enjoys superb views over the Coly valley. Its 15-acre grounds include an outdoor heated pool and tennis courts, while the three guest rooms are bright and well-equipped. Breakfast in the conservatory, under a spreading 60 year-old vine, or in the morning room

Mariners

The Esplanade, Seaton, EX12 2NP (01297 20560, www.marinershotelseaton.co.uk). Rates £72-£76 double incl breakfast. Self catering £475-£525 per week for 4 people.

A stone's throw from the beach, this welcoming B&B has nine comfortable en suite rooms, kitted out with flatscreen TVs, DVD players and digital radios (five have sea views). There's also a smart self-catering apartment, with two bedrooms and a sunny private balcony.

Swan Hill House ★

Swan Hill Road, Colyford, EX24 6QQ (01297 553387, www.swanhillhouse.com). Rates £70-£90 double incl breakfast.

A seven-bedroomed B&B decorated with tremendous flair. No.6, for example, sports a playful flamingo print and resplendent white-painted bed. Elemis toiletries, digital TVs and radios, a mini fridge and a refreshment tray complete the picture. Top-notch breakfasts include own-made fruit compotes and Gatcombe Farm apple-smoked bacon.

Across the border

Undercliff National Nature Reserve

East of Seaton, the coast path heads through the marvellous Undercliff National Nature Reserve (0845 600 3078, www.naturalengland.org.uk). Shaped by numerous landslides, it is a romantic wilderness, overgrown with thickets of ash and field maples, brambles and clematis. It's a reasonably strenuous seven-mile walk from the River Axe to Lyme Regis, and the footpath can be precariously muddy; wear proper walking boots and be prepared for a scramble.

Mid Devon

Most of the action in this predominantly rural area is centred on three long-established settlements: Tiverton, Crediton and Cullompton, all former centres of the wool trade and now market towns for their surrounding areas. Between them lie numerous villages, with ancient parish churches, attractive vernacular architecture and traditional, flagstone-floored village inns. There are endless footpaths and bridleways to follow too, across undulating pastures and meandering river valleys, and secret corners waiting to be discovered.

TIVERTON & AROUND

Tiverton

The origins of Mid Devon's largest town go back to Saxon times. The town's name is a corruption of Twyfordton, 'the town of two fords', and refers to Tiverton's position at the junction of two rivers, the Exe and the Lowman.

From medieval times, Tiverton's prosperity was built on the cloth industry, and many of the most impressive buildings that remain are a legacy of the wealthy wool merchants who called the town home. One of the finest is Blundell's School, founded in 1604 by a bequest of Peter Blundell, a manufacturer of Tiverton 'kerseys' (fine woollen cloths). The school was later made famous by RD Blackmore, a former pupil, in his 1869 novel *Lorna Doone*.

Two of the town's historic buildings are worthy of particular attention: St Peter's Church, located on high ground above the River Exe, and impressive when seen from the Exe Bridge; and Tiverton Castle (Park Hill, 01884 253200, www.tivertoncastle.com, closed Mon-Wed, Fri, Sat, closed Nov-Easter). The castle is now privately owned, but open to the public on certain days. You can also stay here, in some unusual holiday apartments (*see p44*).

To learn more about the town's past, visit the Tiverton Museum of Mid Devon Life ★ (Beck's Square, 01884 256295, www.tivertonmuseum. org.uk, closed Sun, closed Jan). The displays are spread across 15 galleries covering agriculture, transport, industry and domestic life, and include the 'Tivvy Bumper', an impressive 75-year-old GWR steam locomotive.

Shopping

Most of the town's shops are concentrated in and around Fore Street and Gold Street. Interesting independents include the Lantic Gallery (38 Gold Street, 01884 259888, www.lanticgallery.co.uk, closed Sun) for art and jewellery; the Painted Door (36 Gold Street, 01884 256694, www.thepainted door.co.uk, closed Mon, Sun) for homewares; and Judith Christie's (42 Gold Street, 01884 258795, closed Mon, Wed, Thur, Sun) for antiques.

The town's pannier market was refurbished a few years ago and is now housed in a covered, glass-walled building. The market hosts antiques dealers and flea-market traders on Mondays; second-hand furniture stalls on Wednesdays and Thursdays; a car boot sale on some Sundays; and a general market every Tuesday, Friday and Saturday, with plenty of local food. Other good food outlets include Reapers Organics (18 Bampton Street, 01884 255310, closed Sun), and the Cake Box (24 Gold Street, 01884 259236, closed Sun).

A couple of farm shops outside town are worth a visit: Exe Valley Farm Shop (01392 861239), just down the Exe Valley at Thorverton, and West Yeo Moor Farm Shop (01884 860313, www.witheridge farmshop.co.uk), further west, on the B3137.

The canal

On the edge of Tiverton, a canal basin marks the end of the Grand Western Canal, part of an ambitious scheme to provide a shipping link between the Bristol Channel and the English Channel. The canal was abandoned when the railways arrived, but following a vigorous revival programme in the 1970s, it now forms an 11-mile, wildlife-filled country park, with a towpath for walkers and cyclists (bike hire from 01884 820728, www. abbotshoodcyclehire.co.uk), horse-drawn barge trips (www.tivertoncanal.co.uk) and boat hire (01884 252178, www.middevonhireboats.co.uk, closed winter). Several of the canalside villages are home to pubs; at the basin, you'll also find a tearoom on Lime Kiln Road (01884 252291, closed Nov-Easter) and Ducks' Ditty Floating Café Bar (01884 253345, closed Mon & Nov-Mar), on Canal Hill.

Exe Valley churches

Several villages near Tiverton, all close to the valley of the River Exe, are worth a visit for their churches. In a quiet wooded valley, St Mary the Virgin at Calverleigh has a 14th-century tower and

Across the border

In Somerset, some 20 minutes' drive from Uffculme, is Cothay Manor (Greenham, 01823 672283, www.cothaymanor.co.uk, closed Mon, Fri, Sat). The moated 15th-century medieval manor is surrounded by 12 acres of glorious gardens, landscaped in the 1920s.

DEVON

Places to visit

TIVERTON & AROUND

Bickleigh Mill
Bickleigh, EX16 8RG (01884 855419, www.bickleigh mill.com). Open Summer 10am-5.30pm Mon-Wed, Sun; 10am-7.30pm Thur-Sat. Winter 10am-5pm Mon-Wed, Sun; 10am-7.30pm Thur-Sat.
Housed in an 18th-century watermill, Bickleigh Mill is primarily a shopping destination, though the huge water wheel and the mill machinery can also be seen in action. The shop sells a wide range of gifts, arts and crafts, and clothing. There's also a pottery, and a bistro.

Devon Railway Centre
Bickleigh, EX16 8RG (01884 855671, www.devon railwaycentre.co.uk). Open times vary, check website for details. Admission £6.40; £5.10-£5.30 reductions; £20.30 family.

Coldharbour Mill Working Wool Museum

The Exe Valley line closed in 1963, but part of the line, along with Bickleigh's old station, has been restored and now houses a large collection of railway memorabilia. Attractions include narrow and miniature-gauge tracks where visitors can enjoy unlimited train rides; a model railway exhibition; an Edwardian model village with exceptional period detail; and, for children, crazy golf, a remote-control car circuit, and indoor and outdoor play areas. Refreshments are served in the restored station.

Holbrook Garden
Sampford Peverell, EX16 7EN (01884 821164, www.holbrookgarden.com). Open Apr-Oct 9am-5pm Tue-Sat. Admission £3; free reductions.
A delightful two-acre garden, at its peak in summer.

Knightshayes Court ★
Bolham, EX16 7RQ (01884 254665, www.national trust.org.uk). Open times vary, check website for details. Admission £7.45; £3.70 reductions; £11.15-£18.60 family. Park & Garden only £5.90; £2.95 reductions.
This National Trust-owned Victorian country house was designed by William Burges for the Heathcoat-Amory family, whose lace-making factory was a major employer in Tiverton. The garden draws as many visitors as the house, especially since the restoration of the walled kitchen garden; much of the produce grown in it supplies a restaurant in Knightshayes' old stables, while the remainder is sold in Tiverton's pannier market (*see p41*).

Yearlstone Vineyard
Bickleigh, EX16 8RL (01884 855700, www.yearlstone.co.uk). Open Apr-Sept times vary, check website for details.
Devon's oldest vineyard has been producing estate-grown wines for years. Self-guided tours of the vineyard include a tasting session. Have lunch in Charlotte's Kitchen – the terrace overlooks the Exe Valley.

CULLOMPTON & THE CULM VALLEY

Coldharbour Mill Working Wool Museum
Uffculme, EX15 3EE (01884 840960, www.coldharbourmill.org.uk). Open Easter-Oct 10.30am-4pm daily. Nov-Easter 10.30am-4pm Mon-Fri. Admission £5; £2.50-£4 reductions; £12.50 family.
A 200-year-old spinning mill that's now a museum. Special events include 'Steam Up' days, when the engines and boilers are brought to life. A shop sells textiles produced at the mill.

CREDITON

Devon Traditional Breeds Centre
Downes, EX17 3PL (01363 772430, www.dtbcentre.co.uk). Open 9.30am-5pm Tue-Sat; 10.30am-4.30pm Sun. Admission free.
This centre dispenses advice and equipment, but even if you don't harbour any smallholding ambitions, it's an appealing place for a wander: Ruby Red cattle and Devon Longwool sheep graze the parkland, and there are pens of chickens, bantams and pigs. There's also a plant centre.

DEVON

Tiverton Canal Company. See p41.

font, but its chief points of interest are the typical Devon wagon roof and, in the churchyard, the pond. North east in Washfield, on a hill overlooking the Exe Valley, the 15th-century church of St Mary the Virgin has a handsome Jacobean screen with fine carvings. A little further out in Loxbeare is the 12th-century church of St Michael and All Angels. The large square Norman tower contains a set of three medieval bells; over the south doorway is a baroque-style royal arms dating from 1725.

Further south of this trio stands the large village of Thorverton, which contains some good vernacular architecture in cob and local stone. The spacious medieval church of St Thomas of Canterbury was restored in the 19th century; of particular interest is the porch ceiling, decorated with carved symbols of the four evangelists and an unusual central boss.

Where to eat & drink

For old world charm in Tiverton, it's hard to beat Four & Twenty Blackbirds (43 Gold Street, 01884 257055, closed Sun), a café within a former wool-worker's house. Just over the Lowman Bridge is Mallards Tea Rooms (Lowman Green, 01884 252258, closed Wed). In Fore Street, Mad Hatters (5 Fore Street, 01884 252635, closed Sun) has a small courtyard at the back. In the evening, try Il Gatto Nero in Bampton Street (no.54, 01884 251166, closed Sun lunch) for Italian food.

Cadeleigh Arms

Cadeleigh, EX16 8HP (01884 855238, www.the cadeleigharms.co.uk). Open noon-2pm, 6-11pm Tue-Sat; noon-3.30pm Sun. Food served 7-9pm Tue-Sat; noon-2.30pm Sun.

The traditions at this country inn extend to open fires, a skittle alley and old-fashioned bar food, but there's also more modern cooking in the dining room: the likes of sautéed lambs' kidneys with mustard sauce and mash. The wine list includes varieties from the nearby Yearlstone Vineyard.

Mason's Arms

Knowstone, EX36 4RY (01398 341231, www.masons armsdevon.co.uk). Open noon-3pm, 6-11pm Tue-Sat; noon-3pm Sun. Lunch served noon-2pm Tue-Sun. Dinner served 7-9.30pm Tue-Sat.

Close to the edge of Exmoor, this thatched village inn dates back to the 13th century. These days, it's known as much for its Michelin-starred food as for its history: since 2005, it's been in the hands of chef-owner Mark Dodson (previously head chef at the Waterside Inn at Bray for more than 12 years). The French-influenced menu takes in dishes such as Devon beef fillet with rich oxtail, parsnip purée and red wine jus.

Quarryman's Rest

Briton Street, Bampton, EX16 9LN (01398 331480, www.thequarrymansrest.co.uk). Open 11.45am-11pm Mon-Thur, Sun; 11.45am-midnight Fri, Sat. Food served noon-2pm, 6-9.30pm Mon-Sat; noon-4pm Sun.

Formerly an old coaching inn, this pub has been renamed in honour of what was once Bampton's main industry. Behind the bar, an airy restaurant offers modern British cooking (caramelised red onion and Somerset goat's cheese tart, for example). There are also three B&B rooms (£60-£80 a night).

Stag Inn ★
Rackenford, EX16 8DT (01884 881369, www.thestag inn.com). Open noon-3pm, 6.30-11pm Mon-Sat; noon-3pm Sun. Lunch served noon-2.30pm daily. Dinner served 6.30-9pm Mon-Sat.
Dating from the late 12th century, the Stag is believed to be Devon's oldest inn, although the beamed bar and dining room are these days complemented by a modern decked patio. Co-owner Sophie Bulley is the daughter of Kate Palmer, who co-runs the nearby organic West Yeo Farm and supplies much of the meat served at the pub. Local fish also features on the varied menu, which takes in local cheeses and Exmoor ales.

Where to stay

Hartnoll Hotel
Bolham, EX16 7RA (01884 252777, www.hartnollhotel. co.uk). Rates £75 double incl breakfast.
The decor at this boutique operation on the edge of Exmoor is elegant and modern. All 16 rooms have their own shower, bath or walk-in wet room; flatscreen TVs and Wi-Fi come as standard. The restaurant is open for lunch and dinner to both guests and non-residents; a range of spa treatments and beauty therapies is also available within the property.

Middlewick Barton
Nomansland, EX16 8NP (01884 861693, www. middlewick-barton-devon.co.uk). Rates £349-£549 per week for 2 people.
This self-catering apartment in a Georgian farmhouse is in the heart of rural Mid Devon. Modern facilities (dishwasher, washing machine) are supplemented by original features such as an inglenook fireplace with a woodburner.

Mill
Lower Washfield, EX16 9PD (01884 255297, www.themill-tiverton.co.uk). Rates from £60 double incl breakfast. No credit cards.
Just north of Tiverton, beside the River Exe, this converted mill is now a friendly B&B. All the rooms have en suite facilities and views over the garden, and in fine weather guests can relax on the terrace overlooking the mill leat. Dinners and picnic lunches can also be provided.

Tiverton Castle
Park Hill, Tiverton, EX16 6RP (01884 253200, www.tivertoncastle.com). Rates £290-£640 per week for 2 people. £350-£840 per week for 4 people. No credit cards.
This castle contains four refurbished apartments: a ground-floor apartment that sleeps two, and three further apartments on the first and second floors (one with a cot) that each sleep four. All of the apartments come with old-world features (exposed beams, Victorian fireplaces, Jacobean staircases) as well as modern conveniences (dishwashers, microwaves).

West Middlewick Farm Campsite
Nomansland, EX16 8NP (01884 861235, www. westmiddlewick.co.uk). Pitches £8-£10 for 2 people. No credit cards.
This family-run camping and caravan site, set on a working dairy farm, is open year round. There are great views towards Exmoor, and access to lovely walks across the farmland and beside the river. B&B is also available in one en suite bedroom, with its own sunroom (£50-£70 double incl breakfast); there are also two self-catering log cabins, each sleeping up to six (£280-£850 per week).

CULLOMPTON & THE CULM VALLEY

The busy market town of Cullompton made an appearance in the Domesday Book, but the settlement dates back even earlier. From the Middle Ages onwards, the town's prosperity was built on the cloth trade, but there was other industry here in the shape of a bell foundry and several corn mills. A path tracks the course of the Mill Leat, a water channel diverted from the River Culm and still flowing today.

Among the historic buildings is St Andrew's Church (off Fore Street), the red sandstone tower

Cadeleigh Arms. See p43.

of which makes for an imposing focal point. The most famous feature is the rather gruesome Golgotha, a massive piece of tree trunk carved with skulls and crossed bones that represents mortality and the path to salvation. It's believed to be the only one in the country. Close by on Fore Street is the Walronds, a Grade I-listed Elizabethan house that's currently being restored by a preservation trust.

Independent shops include Very Nice (15A High Street, 01884 839943, www.theveryniceshop. co.uk, closed Mon), which sells jewellery made on the premises and accessories. Based in the Old Tannery in Exeter Hill, Cullompton Antiques (01884 38476, www.cullomptonantiques.co.uk, closed Sun) specialises in English and French country furniture. There are more antiques in nearby Hele, at Fagins (01392 882062, www.faginsantiques.com, closed Sun), where four floors of an old mill building are stuffed full of furniture, architectural salvage and collectibles. Back in Cullompton, on the second Saturday in the month, the car park on Station Road hosts an excellent farmers' market.

North-east of Cullompton is the upper part of the Culm Valley, scattered with villages, farms and country pubs. If you're visiting Coldharbour Mill Working Wool Museum at Uffculme (*see p42*), have a look at the village church, which has an impressive rood screen dating from 1420. At Hemyock, further up the valley, are the remains of a medieval castle.

South of Cullompton, meanwhile, is the large village of Bradninch, once an important centre for the wool and lace industries. The town's most prominent feature is the Perpendicular-style church, which has an exquisite early-16th-century rood screen, whose 50 original painted panels depict biblical scenes.

Where to eat & drink

Cullompton has a couple of cafés in Fore Street – Pickwick's Tea Room and Ye Olde Tea Shoppe – for daytime eating. The bar and restaurant at the Manor House Hotel (2-4 Fore Street, 01884 32281) are open to non-residents.

At Culmstock, the Culm Valley Inn (01884 840354) supplements its real ales with excellent food. In Clayhidon, the Half Moon Inn (01823 680291, www.halfmoondevon.co.uk, closed Mon) serves a compact, inviting menu and hosts a special pie night on Tuesday evenings. The Wyndham Arms at Kentisbeare (2 High Street, 01884 266327, http://wyndhamarmsdevon. co.uk) is a Grade II-listed coaching inn with ales and hearty pub food. And just outside Uffculme is the Ashill Inn (Ashill, 01884 840506), a traditional village pub.

Five Bells

Clyst Hydon, EX15 2NT (01884 277288, www.fivebells clysthydon.co.uk). Open 6.30-11pm Mon; 11.30am-3pm, 6.30-11pm Tue-Sat; noon-3pm, 7-10.30pm Sun. Lunch served 11.30am-2pm Tue-Sat; noon-2pm Sun. Dinner served 6.30-9pm Mon-Sat; 7-9pm Sun.

Things to do

CULLOMPTON & THE CULM VALLEY

Diggerland

Verbeer Manor, Cullompton, EX15 2PE (0871 227 7007, www.diggerland.com). Open times vary, check website for details. Admission £15; £7.50 reductions.
Attractions include Diggerland dodgems, specially designed courses for dumptrucks and full-size JCBs.

Quad World

Exeter Road, Bradninch, EX5 4LB (01392 881313, www.quadworld.co.uk). Open Mar-Oct 10am-6pm daily. Nov-Feb 10am-4pm daily. Prices vary, phone for details.
The Quad machines for hire are suitable for all sizes at this quad-bike track, with tuition and protective clothing also provided.

Tarka Line

(01752 233094, www.tarkarail.org). Open times vary, check website for details. Tickets £7.40 single; £7.50 return.
This railway line between Exeter and Barnstaple is a great way to see this part of the countryside, not least because you can stop off and explore the region on foot or by bike: the Tarka Line Association has produced a booklet of walks from various stations (phone 01752 233094 for a copy), and there's cycle hire at Barnstaple, Crediton and Exeter. The Rail Ale Trail (01752 233094, www.railaletrail.com) uses the railway as the basis for a pub crawl around a series of country pubs.

CREDITON

Devon Wine School

Redyeates Farm, Cheriton Fitzpaine, EX17 4HG (01363 866742, www.devonwineschool.co.uk). Open times vary, check website for details.
Along with serious – and highly rated – wine tutorials, the Devon Wine School also offers tasting lunches, informal events and midweek suppers. You don't have to sign up for a wine course in order to stay at the school's lovely 17th-century farmhouse (£80-£125 double incl breakfast).

Formerly a farm, this thatched-roof building makes the most of its history, retaining its low beamed ceilings and inglenook fireplace. The array of local ales is supplemented by a sturdy menu: steaks, seafood dishes, pies and a curry of the week are among the choices. There's music too: the second Wednesday of the month sees jazz; the fourth Friday an acoustic duo plays.

Where to stay

The Culm Valley Inn (*see left*) also has rooms.

Lower Ford Farm

Nr Cullompton, EX15 1LX (01884 252354). Rates £62 double incl breakfast. No credit cards.
The family, double and twin rooms in this 15th-century farmhouse B&B all have en suite facilities and pretty views. A traditional breakfast is served in the beamed dining room, with its weighty old oak table and original bread ovens.

Guests are welcome to explore parts of the 350-acre working farm, which includes a peaceful lake and woodland areas.

Upton Farm
Plymtree, EX15 1RA (01884 33097).
Rates phone for details.
Farmhouse-style B&B is available in this 17th-century house, which includes characterful features such as an inglenook fireplace. The setting is quiet and rural and the grounds contain two coarse-fishing lakes. A locally sourced breakfast is served in the elegant oak-panelled dining room.

CREDITON
The recorded history of Crediton begins towards the end of the seventh century with the birth of Winfrith, its most famous son. Later known as St Boniface, Winfrith was one of the founders of the Christian church in Europe, preaching throughout what is now Germany and the Netherlands; indeed, he's now the patron saint of Germany. A statue of St Boniface stands beside Newcombes Meadow.

Like many Devon towns, Crediton was once a centre for the wool trade – woollen cloth was made here from as early as the 12th century up until the 19th. A few weavers' cottages still exist today, but many more were destroyed in a series of fires during the 18th century; most of the buildings in the centre of town date from the Georgian period or later. Among the notable buildings are the handsome Old Town Hall, which sits beside the long main street, and a number of elegant red-brick houses and shops. One of Crediton's most interesting buildings is the substantial red sandstone Church of the Holy Cross, a 12th-century cruciform church that was extensively remodelled in the early 15th century.

Local produce is much in evidence in the town's shops; try Treloars Delicatessen (High Street, 01363 772332, closed Sun). A fine monthly farmers' market takes place in the main square on the first Saturday in the month. Also worth checking out is Crediton Bookshop (100 High Street, 01363 774740, closed Sun).

Crediton's location on the River Creedy means that there are some lovely walks in the low hills overlooking the river valley. Just across the river is the Shobrooke Park estate (www.shobrooke park.com), with public access footpaths through the southern part of the parkland; there's also the opportunity to fish at Creedy Lakes. An amphitheatre was created in the park around the turn of the millennium, and hosts open-air theatre and a music festival during the summer.

Just outside Crediton lies the village of Sandford, which contains a square ringed with attractive cottages and a handsome old church. On the far side of the river stands the tiny hamlet of Upton Hellions, which also contains a fine church; it's a simple 12th-century building with a Norman south doorway. Slightly further away, the larger village of Morchard Bishop is worth a look for its tall-towered 15th-century church, which contains a two-decker pulpit.

Where to eat & drink
Among Crediton's cafés is the Station Tea Rooms (01363 777766), by the rail station. The town's restaurants include the Italian Il Casita (1 St Lawrence Green, 01363 777057, closed Sun); Richie's Bistro (31 East Street, 01363 777779, closed Tue), which offers French-style cooking; and the Three Little Pigs (Parliament Street, 01363 774587), a traditional pub.

The Old Thatch Inn in Cheriton Bishop (01647 24204, www.theoldthatchinn.com) is a village hostelry known for its fish and seafood.

Lamb Inn
The Square, Sandford, EX17 4LW (01363 773676, www.lambinnsandford.co.uk). Open 9am-midnight daily. Lunch served 12.30-2.15pm daily. Dinner served 6.30-9.15pm Mon-Sat.
This charming old village pub may date from the 16th century, but it's no museum piece. The real ales are impeccably kept, the food is excellent (it's heavy on local ingredients), and upstairs there are three modish bedrooms (solar-powered underfloor heating, flatscreen tellies, all for £69 double incl breakfast). The pretty terraced garden is lovely during the summer months, but the pub's most unusual feature is its small cinema, with free screenings most weekends.

New Inn
Coleford, EX17 5BZ (01363 84242, www.thenew inncoleford.co.uk). Open noon-3pm, 6-11pm daily. Lunch served noon-2pm, dinner served 6.30-9.30pm daily.
The New Inn is anything but: originally a 13th-century farmhouse, it comes complete with thatched roof and flagstone floor. The ambience reflects its village inn style, but the food is decidedly current: scallops with lardons and sweet chilli dressing, for example. The wine list includes bottles from Devon vineyards. Coleford is a bit off the beaten track, but you could always stay the night in one of the comfortable rooms, which have king-size beds and flat screen TVs (£85 double incl breakfast). The pub holds various events – from hog roasts to jazz evenings – see the website for details.

Where to stay
The New Inn and the Lamb Inn (for both, *see above*) have B&B rooms. Hele Barton Farm (Black Dog, 01884 860278, www.eclipse.co.uk/helebarton) offers both self-catering and B&B options; while Creedy Manor (Crediton, 01363 772684, www.creedymanor.com) has four well equipped stone-cottage apartments in what was originally the dairy and wood store.

Ashridge Farm
Sandford, EX17 4EN (01363 774292, www.ashridge farm.co.uk). Rates £60-£70 double incl breakfast. No credit cards.
This 200-acre organic farm offers environmentally friendly accommodation, with heating and water provided by a wood-pellet burning system, and insulation by sheep's wool. Wildlife is an integral part of the farm: there are waymarked trails through the fields and woods.

North Devon

It's known for its miles of golden sands and sweeping sea cliffs, but that's only part of North Devon's story. The region's richly varied terrain ranges from the heather-covered moorland of Exmoor to tiny, craggy coves, concealed by jutting headlands; from the wildlife-rich habitats of the Taw-Torridge estuary to the cattle-grazed pastures of inland farming communities.

Reliable rollers have made Croyde a surfing hotspot, while the fine, clean sands of Saunton and Woolacombe draw the bucket-and-spade brigade. A few miles east along the coast, the seaside resort of Ilfracombe is a vision of faded Victorian gentility; for chocolate-box prettiness, though, the cobbled streets and fishermen's cottages of Clovelly win hands down (although the peak season crowds can be maddening).

Once you get to know the area, it's easy to see why so many artists have been inspired by the landscape. The fertile soils also make for a thriving food scene, with an abundance of local produce in the delis, farm shops and restaurants. It's just as well, then, that there are so many opportunities for outdoor activities – including the Tarka Trail, which follows the River Taw through swathes of unspoiled scenery.

BARNSTAPLE

The largest town in North Devon, Barnstaple grew up around the River Taw. Once an important port, sending ships to fight the Spanish Armada, it declined in status after the estuary silted up in the 19th century. Nonetheless, the town remains a focal point for the region.

Close to the 16-arch Long Bridge is the Museum of Barnstaple & North Devon (The Square, 01271 346747, www.devonmuseums.net/barnstaple, closed Sun), whose collections include Barum ware pieces from the town's famous Victorian potteries. There's more on Barnstaple's past at the riverfront Heritage Centre (Queen Anne's Walk, 01271 373003, www.devonmuseums.net, closed Mon, Sun) – an engaging, child-friendly place with hands-on displays, quizzes and brass-rubbing.

At Barnstaple's heart is its historic Pannier Market (01271 379084, www.barnstaplepannier market.co.uk), open six days a week. It was built in 1855 for the traders who brought their goods to town in panniers or baskets, and the lofty, iron-pillared building has changed very little in the intervening years. The market is open year-round: Wednesday is devoted to antiques and collectibles, Monday and Thursday to crafts and general produce, while the general market on Tuesday, Friday and Saturday brings a jumble of produce, clothes, haberdashery and bric-a-brac.

Alongside the market hall is the equally antique Butchers Row. Built in Bath stone, with a canopy to keep off the sun, it originally housed around 30 butchers' shops. Today, food shops and cafés have taken over – among them the excellent West Country Cheese Company (no.10, 01271 379944, www.westcountrycheese.co.uk, closed Sun) and Ballantyne's Delicatessen (no.15, 01271 379742,

closed Sun), where cakes, pasties and pizzas can be sampled in the tiny café. Along Bear Street, the Art Coop at Gallery 39 (no.39, 01271 346415, www.artcoopatg39.co.uk) is an artists' co-operative, selling ceramics, paintings, textiles and jewellery.

On Boutport Street, Queen's Theatre (01271 324242, www.northdevontheatres.org.uk) has an eclectic events programme, including touring productions, drama, music, ballet and comedy; nearby is the Central Cinema (77 Boutport Street, www.scottcinemas.co.uk, 08712 303200).

Where to eat & drink

For inexpensive Italian cooking, try Giovanni's (Boutport Street, 01271 321274, closed Sun lunch) – a longstanding, family-run restaurant. Just up the road is 62 the Bank (01271 324446, www.brend-hotels.co.uk, closed Sun): the food may be standard pub grub, but the ornate ceiling, which dates from 1620, is a show-stopper. On the main square, Lilico's (3-5 Bridge Buildings, 01271 372933, www.lilicos.co.uk, closed Sun) is an airy bistro and bar, with tapas and paella on the menu.

Muddiford Inn, ten minutes' drive from Barnstaple (Muddiford, EX31 4EY, 01271 850243) is a 16th-century coaching inn with plenty of character and a wide-ranging menu.

Boston Tea Party

21-22 Tuly Street, Barnstaple, EX31 1DH (01271 329070, www.bostonteaparty.co.uk). Open/food served 8am-6pm Mon-Sat; 9.30am-5pm Sun.
Part of a small, family-run West Country chain, BTP prides itself on its Fairtrade coffee, loose-leaf teas and use of local produce; over 80% of its suppliers are from the South West. Food is a cut above standard café fare, with Belgian waffles

with warm summer berries and maple syrup at breakfast, then gourmet sarnies, wraps and soups later in the day.

Fremington Quay Café ★
Fremington Quay, Bickington, Barnstaple, EX31 2NH (01271 378783, www.fremingtonquaycafe.co.uk). Open/food served Summer 10.30am-5pm daily (except Mon in school term). Winter 10.30am-4pm Tue-Sun.
Occupying a converted railway station on the Tarka Trail, this café is a welcome sight for walkers. For a quick pick-me-up, try a glass of Luscombe wild elderflower bubbly and an own-made scone with clotted cream and jam. Savoury options range from organic bacon BLTs to fish cakes with chilli mayo, best consumed out on the terrace overlooking the quay.

James Duckett at the Old Customs House
The Strand, Barnstaple, EX31 1EU (01271 370123 www.jamesduckett.co.uk). Open/lunch served noon-2.30pm, dinner served 7-10pm Tue-Sat.
Lunchtime at this polished eaterie sees modestly priced set price menus or 'tapas' versions of the chef's signature dishes, ranging from truffle oil-laced wild mushroom soup to red wine-braised shin of Devon beef with pickled walnuts and spinach. Dinner options include a six-course tasting menu and a compact à la carte, featuring pot-roast pheasant with braised sprout leaves, chestnuts, bacon and thyme, perhaps.

Owl Vegan Café
1 Maiden Street, off Boutport Street, Barnstaple, EX31 1HA (01271 371222, www.owlvegancafe.co.uk). Open/food served 8.30am-5.30pm Mon-Sat; bookings only Sun. No credit cards.
The atmosphere is relaxed at this friendly café: loll on the sofa with the newspapers while you wait for lentil bake, scrambled tofu on toast, or a bowl of spicy bean casserole.

Zena's Restaurant
1 Market Street, Barnstaple, EX31 1BX (01271 378844, www.zenasrestaurant.com). Open 8.30am-11pm Mon-Sat. Breakfast served 9-11.30am, lunch served noon-3pm Mon-Sat. Dinner served 7-9pm Tue-Sat.
This intimate bistro is set in a shady courtyard near the Pannier Market. The menu concentrates on tried-and-tested classics: eggs benedict for breakfast, say, then welsh rarebit or risotto of the day for lunch. In the evening, expect more elaborate food and an eclectic special events programme, celebrating everything from Bastille Day to Burns Night.

Where to stay
Greystones (Church Hill, Fremington, 01271 326341) is a homely, welcoming little B&B in the centre of Fremington, three miles west of Barnstaple.

Beachborough Country House
Kentisbury, EX31 4NH (01271 882487, www. beachboroughcountryhouse.co.uk). Rates B&B £70-£80 double incl breakfast. Apartment from £220 per week for 2/3 people. No credit cards.
Four acres of grounds surround this delightful Grade II-listed Georgian rectory, on the edge of Exmoor National Park. Its window-seats, marble fireplaces, flagstone floors

and old-fashioned sash windows brim with period charm, and its facilities include a tennis court and a games barn. There are three spacious B&B rooms, and the old servant's quarters have been converted into a self-catering apartment.

Bratton Mill
Bratton Fleming, EX31 4RU (01598 710026, http:// brattonmill.co.uk). Rates £75-£95 double incl breakfast. Self-catering £295-£750 per week for 4 people.
Reached via a meandering private lane, this former mill stands in a tranquil valley below the village of Bratton Fleming. The owners offer self-catering and B&B rooms in the 17th-century farmhouse, slate-roofed cottage and romantic folly; outside, a trout stream winds through the 28-acre gardens.

Broomhill Art Hotel
Muddiford Road, Barnstaple, EX31 4EX (01271 850262, www.broomhillart.co.uk). Rates £75 double incl breakfast.
Surprises lurk around every corner at Broomhill, which also incorporates an art gallery and sculpture park (*see p56*). The six-room hotel occupies a Victorian house; there's a swimming pool and tennis court.

Broomhill Farm
Broomhill, nr Muddiford, EX31 4EX (01271 850676, www.broomhillfarmhouse.co.uk). Rates £56-£60 double incl breakfast. No credit cards.
This modern farmhouse is set in a beautiful wooded valley. It has two light and airy en suite rooms upstairs, along with a ground-floor room that's suitable for less mobile guests. A farmhouse breakfast can be served either in the dining room or outside on the patio. The farm also offers B&B for horses, with stabling, grazing and the use of an all-weather manège.

BRAUNTON TO MORTEHOE

Braunton Durrows & Saunton Sands
The small town of Braunton has become the surfing capital of Devon, thanks to its proximity to the seemingly endless sands of Saunton, Croyde and Woolacombe. (There's even a surfing museum planned – see www.museumofbritishsurfing.org.uk.) But there's another reason to visit this northern boundary of the Taw-Torridge estuary – and that's Braunton Burrows.

This vast area of towering sand dunes is a UNESCO-designated Biosphere Reserve, thanks to its rich diversity of flora and fauna. The profusion of wildflowers attracts a host of butterflies, while kestrels and common buzzards hover overhead, in search of unwary rabbits. It's easy to get lost in the huge, otherwordly dunescape, and the best way to see its plantlife is to join a guided walk; for details, contact the Tourist Information Centre (Caen Street, 01271 816400, www.brauntontic.co.uk).

On the seaward side of Braunton Burrows, Saunton Sands is renowned for its three-mile stretch of gleaming white sands. This is a terrific place for surfing, especially for beginners, as well as sand yachting, swimming and kayaking. There's a car park, toilets and café at the beach's northern

DEVON

Braunton Burrows. See p49.

end, while on the cliff stands the white-painted, 1930s Saunton Sands Hotel (*see p53*).

Braunton itself is a busy place, straddling the main Barnstaple to Ilfracombe road and with a multitude of surf shops, pubs, cafés, restaurants and takeaways. For a glimpse of the past, stroll by the traditional cob buildings on Church, East and South Streets, whose walls are made from a mix of mud and straw.

Lying between the village and Braunton Marsh, Braunton's Great Field is another relic of centuries gone by. Almost the only remaining example in England of Saxon strip-system farming, it is still cultivated – although many strips have been amalgamated, and it's hard to visualise the hundreds there once were. There's more on local history at Braunton Museum (01271 816688, closed Sun) on Caen Street.

Croyde

Just around the coast from Saunton is the crescent-shaped Croyde Bay, bounded to the north by the headland of Baggy Point. Croyde beach is another surfing hotspot, attracting devotees year-round. There's a surf school (*see p62*), along with various outfits offering board and wetsuit hire. The beach is also popular with families, and is patrolled by lifeguards in high season.

The seaward part of the village is geared towards the holidaying masses, with all the requisite trappings for a day on the beach. Further inland – and despite an onslaught of cars in summer – Croyde remains a pretty village of thatched cottages and narrow lanes. In the centre of the village, Chapel Farm Gallery (Hobbs Hill, 01271 890429,

www.chapelfarmcroyde.co.uk, closed Nov-Feb) exhibits and sells paintings, pottery, ceramics, glassware and jewellery by local artists.

Equally attractive – and far less busy – is Georgeham, less than two miles away. Here the cottages are grouped around the parish church. In the side chapel is an effigy of a knight, dating from 1294, while *Tarka the Otter* author Henry Williamson is buried in the churchyard. Nearby, his former home, Crowberry Cottage, is identified by a blue plaque.

Woolacombe

Follow the footpath around Baggy Point from Croyde, and you'll be greeted by the spirit-lifting vista of Woolacombe Beach – almost three miles of clean, golden sands. Woolacombe developed as a holiday destination in the late 19th century,

and a sprinkling of seafront Regency villas remain. By and large, though, the town suffers from a surfeit of holiday builds and bungalows, and its main attraction is the beach. Awarded Blue Flag status, it attracts lots of picnic-toting families and is a good surfing beach, with lifeguard protection. Each July there's a popular sandcastle competition, in which teams compete to build the most impressive edifice.

Tucked into the top corner of the beach are some swing-boats and a tiny railway, while the Beachcomber café sits on a terrace just above the sands. To escape the crowds, head to the southern end to the quieter Putsborough Beach, or north to a brace of smaller coves: Barricane Bay (known for its rock pools and exotic seashells), Combesgate and Grunta Bay – though keep an eye on the tides. The coves are backed by untamed, National Trust-owned land, which extends to the headland of Morte Point (*see p52*) and beyond.

Mortehoe & around

The road from Woolacombe eventually leaves the Esplanade behind, and climbs steeply uphill to a different world. In the tiny village of Mortehoe, slate-hung houses cluster around the church. Despite its diminutive size, the village has three pubs, a restaurant and a couple of cafés, as well as the summer-season Mortehoe Shellfish (*see p52*).

Call in at the Heritage Centre (01271 870028, www.devonmuseums.net, closed Fri, Sat) behind the car park to discover more about Mortehoe's swashbuckling history of wrecks and smuggling. For a more vivid understanding of why so many ships came to grief on the razor-edged rocks, though, walk out to Morte Point. Surrounded by treacherous offshore reefs, the jagged, gorse and heather-dotted headland is wonderfully dramatic. Footpaths lead to lovely Rockham Bay, accessible via a long flight of steps, and the lighthouse at Bull Point, built in 1879; for one suggested route, see www.devon.gov.uk/walk17. Colonies of seabirds throng the cliffs, and you may spot a seal or two.

A few miles along the coast is the pretty cove of Lee Bay, backed by a wooded valley. At low tide, its small beach is a great place for rockpooling. Beyond the cove, an indented line of cliffs leads to Ilfracombe (*see p54*). In Lee village, the friendly Grampus Inn (01271 862906, www.thegrampus-inn.co.uk) has a nice beer garden and its own specially brewed Grampus EX34 bitter on tap.

Where to eat & drink

For excellent fish and chips, head for Squires Fish Restaurant (Exeter Road, Braunton, 01271 815533, closed Sun), whose piping-hot takeaways draw quite a crowd. Join the queue, or eat in the restaurant.

In Croyde, the laid-back Thatched Barn Inn (Hobbs Hill, 01271 890349, www.thethatchcroyde.com) is a few minutes' walk from the beach, and abuzz with surfers and holidaymakers; B&B is available.

The seafront Red Barn in Woolacombe (Barton Road, 01271 870264) is another surfers' haunt, with beers from the St Austell Brewery.

Barricane Beach Café ★
The Esplanade, Barricane Beach (no phone). Open Summer 6pm-closing time varies. Closed in bad weather.
On summer evenings, this informal outdoor café on the edge of Barricane Bay serves wonderful Sri Lankan curries. There's no phone, and no advance bookings are taken; you just have to turn up from 6pm onwards and hope to get one of the four tables (if not, you can always sit on the beach). Bring your own beer or wine.

Blue Groove Café
2 Hobbs Hill, Braunton, EX33 1LZ (01271 890111, www.blue-groove.co.uk). Open Late Mar-early Nov 9am-10pm daily. Food served 9am-5pm, 6-10pm daily.
In the heart of Braunton, within walking distance of Croyde Beach, this popular café is adorned with surfing pictures and paraphernalia. On a sunny day, grab a table on the street and watch the world go by; there's also a covered outdoor area at the back. Hungry surfers are appeased with substantial fry-ups, dubbed the Piglet and the Big Pig (the veggie option is the Pig Hugger) and there's a decent children's menu.

Chichester Arms
Mortehoe, EX43 7DU (01271 870411). Open Apr-Oct noon-11pm daily. Nov-Mar noon-3pm, 6-11pm Mon-Fri;
noon-11pm Sat, Sun. Lunch served noon-2pm. Dinner served Apr-Oct 6-9pm daily; Nov-Mar 7-9pm Fri, Sat.
You'll find this 16th-century pub next to the church in Mortehoe. It offers an excellent range of real ales and ciders, including local brews such as Barum Original, Cottage and St Austell, and is a great place to sit outside with a pint on a balmy summer's afternoon. The menu ranges from local seafood specials to hearty steak and ale pies.

Corner Bistro
8 The Square, Braunton, EX33 2JD (01271 813897, www.thecornerbistro.com). Open/breakfast served 9am-noon, lunch served noon-2pm daily. Dinner served 7-9pm Fri, Sat.
The carefully sourced menu at this warm, inviting bistro runs from breakfast (sautéed field mushrooms and poached egg on toast), through lunch (organic burgers, Quickes' cheddar and Devon chutney baguettes), to dinner (West Plaistow lamb with ratatouille). During asparagus season, spears from nearby Broadlands Farm often feature.

The Electric
West Road, Woolacombe, EX34 7BW (01271 871411, www.theelectricrestaurant.co.uk). Open 8am-midnight. Breakfast served 8am-noon, lunch served noon-2.30pm, dinner served 6-11pm daily Apr-Oct, closed Mon, Tue Nov-Mar.
A delightfully relaxed vibe prevails at this bar and restaurant, where cheery staff deliver brilliant breakfasts, daily-changing specials, fresh seafood (herb-crusted fillet of hake, perhaps) and stellar puddings.

Mortehoe Shellfish ★
5 Kinevar Close, Mortehoe, EX34 7EE (01271 870633, www.mortehoeshellfish.co.uk). Open Easter-Sept Lunch served noon-3pm, dinner served from 6pm daily.
Fish caught on the family boat is the mainstay at this low-key seafood shack. The lunch menu is a treat, running from simple crab sarnies to lobster and prawn gratin. In the evening (phone to book dinner), diners can feast on piled-high seafood platters, or roll up their sleeves to tackle a

---

Across the border
Porlock & Porlock Weir

Set in a hollow amid the hills, Porlock retains a sweetly old-fashioned feel. The high street has a good array of antique shops, hotels and pubs, including the cosy Ship Inn (01643 862507, www.shipinnporlock.co.uk). Porlock is also known for its fearsomely steep hill, with its one-in-four gradient and hairpin bends; those with shaky brakes or nerves should take the toll road instead.

The working harbour at Porlock Weir, around a mile and a half to the west, is low-key but lovely, with its bobbing yachts, craft workshops, pub and restaurant with rooms, Andrew's on the Weir (01643 863300, www.andrewsontheweir.co.uk, closed Mon, Tue). A couple of miles – mainly uphill – along the wooded South West Coast Path stands the lonely, medieval Culbone Church; the 'leper squint' window in the north wall enabled sufferers from the local leper colony to follow the services.

Watermouth Cove. See p55.

whole lobster. Meals are served in the family's front room, or on the patio; while you're there, peek inside the garden Shell Shack.

Wild Thyme Juice Café
5 Caen Shopping Centre, Caen Street, Braunton, EX33 1EG (01271 815191, www.wildthymecafe. co.uk). Open/food served 9am-4pm Mon-Fri, Sun; 9am-5pm Sat.
Though the café is licensed, juices and smoothies are the point here. Examples include the Instant Energiser (carrot, orange, apple and ginger) and the Immune Booster (blueberries, apple, banana and raspberries). Food is simple and tasty – burgers, chilli con carne, Devon blue cheese and pear salad – with children's portions available.

Where to stay
Chapel Farm in Croyde (*see p50*) also has five sweetly old-fashioned B&B rooms.

In addition to the campsites listed below, Lobb Fields Caravan & Camping Park (Saunton Road, Braunton, 01271 812090, www.lobbfields.com, closed Nov-Feb) is a spacious, well-equipped site, about a mile out of Braunton, with views over Braunton Burrows to the estuary.

Rather more staid and formal is the Watersmeet Hotel (Mortehoe, 01271 870333, www.watersmeet hotel.co.uk) – but it does have breathtaking views over Woolacombe Bay, an outdoor pool, plus an indoor swimming pool and steam room.

Cherry Tree Farm Campsite
Croyde, EX33 1NH (01271 890495, www.cherry treecroyde.co.uk). Open May, July, Aug; phone for dates. Rates £9-£12 per person, min 3 nights.
Set on a hillside just outside Croyde, with views to the coast and footpaths to Putsborough Beach and Baggy Point, this quiet, eight-field campsite is for tents and campervans only. Boards and wetsuits are available for hire.

Grey Cottage
Lee, EX34 8LN (01271 864360, www.greycottage. co.uk). Rates £70 double incl breakfast. No credit cards.
Honeysuckle and wisteria entwine this Georgian house, set in two-and-a-half acre grounds on the outskirts of Lee. Its three B&B rooms are traditional without being cloying, with crisp floral linen and dark wood antiques. Owner Julia Waghorn used to run an organic bakery and is passionate about food; breakfast might include vanilla poached prunes, blueberry and sour cream muffins and French toast with cinnamon and banana. Dinners can be pre-booked too.

North Morte Farm Campsite
Mortehoe, EX34 7EG (01271 870381, www.northmorte farm.co.uk). Open Mar-Oct. Rates £6.50-£9 per person.
Spectacular views across the Bristol Channel to Lundy Island are the crowning glory at North Morte – a large but friendly site, with immaculately clean showers, a playground and well-maintained (if sloping) camping fields. Those in the know camp in the shelter of the gorse hedges, as the site is relatively exposed. A stony path leads down to the beach, and it's a five-minute amble into Mortehoe. There's no advance booking, so you have to take a chance in high season.

Saunton Sands Hotel
Saunton Road, Braunton, EX33 1LQ (01271 890212, www.brend-hotels.co.uk). Rates £150-£300 double incl breakfast.
It's all about the location at this boxy, bright white 1930s hotel, perched above Saunton's three-mile stretch of sand, so it's worth paying extra for a sea view. Rooms are understated but comfortable, and facilities include indoor and outdoor pools, a sauna, tennis and squash courts; there's also an Ofsted-registered playroom for under-eights.

Southcliffe Hall ★
Lee, EX34 8LW (01271 867068, www.southcliffehall. co.uk). Rates £100 double incl breakfast. No credit cards.
This grand Edwardian mansion has superb grounds and sea views. The three spacious, antique-furnished guest rooms have lavish flourishes such as Chinese rugs, hand-printed William Morris wallpaper and mahogany sleigh beds, while the bathrooms are appealingly idiosyncratic. With no traffic noise to drown out the birdsong, no TVs in the rooms and no children (it's grown-ups only), tranquillity reigns.

Victoria House
Chapel Hill, Mortehoe, EX34 7DZ (01271 871302, www.victoriahousebandb.co.uk). Rates £90-£120 double incl breakfast. No credit cards.
Perched high above the coast, this comfortable B&B promises sea views from every room. As well as two doubles (one of the rooms has a freestanding bath, from which you

Cherry Tree Farm Campsite. See p53.

can watch the waves), there is the Beach House room, with a private terrace overlooking the beach. Breakfast times are flexible, allowing guests a restorative lie-in.

ILFRACOMBE & COMBE MARTIN

Ilfracombe

It was the Victorians who 'discovered' Ilfracombe – a centuries-old fishing port, built around a natural harbour in the midst of spectacular cliffs. The new railway line brought carriage-loads of daytrippers, and the town expanded into a popular resort. Today, the town's Victorian and Regency terraces and villas have a slightly down-at-heel air – although it's not immune to the steady march of gentrification, as 11 the Quay (*see p55*) demonstrates.

The High Street exudes faded grandeur, with wrought iron balconies above the shopfronts. At no.6 you can watch chocolates being made and visit the small chocolate museum at Walkers Chocolate Emporium (01271 867193, www. chocolate-emporium.co.uk, closed Sun), before sampling one of 12 different types of hot chocolate in the café.

One not-to-be-missed feature from the town's 19th-century heyday are the extraordinary Tunnels Beaches (Bath Place, 01271 879123, www. tunnelsbeaches.co.uk, closed Nov-Easter). In 1823, Welsh miners were brought in to carve tunnels through the rock, allowing access to the previously inaccessible beaches. Tidal swimming

pools were built for ladies and gentlemen (separate, of course), one of which still exists, and the sheltered beach remains popular for bathing and rockpooling. A charge is levied to visit the beach, which also has a café-bar, and deckchairs and kayaks for hire.

To the east of the Tunnels, along the coast towards the harbour, Wildersmouth Beach is a mix of sand and rocks, in the shadow of Capstone Hill. A path climbs to the top of the hill, affording a glimpse of the Welsh coast across the Bristol Channel.

Lantern Hill & the harbour

Continuing east, Cheyne Beach stands beside Lantern Hill; for centuries a lantern burned here at night, to indicate the harbour entrance. At its summit stands St Nicholas' Chapel, said to be the oldest lighthouse in the country, built in 1320.

Below Lantern Hill is the small, east-facing harbour, nestling between the mainland and a narrow protective promontory to the north. Here, you can board the MS *Oldenburg* for a trip to Lundy (*see p68*), or take a wildlife-spotting cruise aboard the *Ilfracombe Princess* (bookings at the pier kiosk, 01271 879727, www.ilfracombeprincess.co.uk, closed Nov-Easter); there's a good chance of seeing seals on the latter, as well as some breathtaking coastal scenery. Tucked away in a corner of the quay, the old lifeboat house is now home to Ilfracombe Aquarium (The Pier, 01271 864533, www.ilfracombeaquarium.co.uk, closed Dec, Jan).

Here, too, is Damian Hirst's restaurant, 11 the Quay (see below), which showcases some of his work; next door, there's more affordable art on display at the Driftwood Gallery (no.10, 01271 862590, www.driftwoodgallery.co.uk). Nearby, Roly's Fudge Pantry (01271 867373, www.rolys fudge.co.uk, closed winter) sells creamy, crumbly fudge, made on the premises. Turning left into Broad Street you'll reach the uphill-climbing Fore Street, which links the harbour with the High Street. As the town's oldest street, it is home to the 14th-century George and Dragon inn, and the old police station – now enjoying a new lease of life as La Gendarmerie (see right).

Back on the Promenade, the Landmark Theatre (Wilder Road, 01271 324242, www. northdevontheatres.org.uk) is easy to spot, thanks to its eye-catching design – two cones, built out of white brick; the café-bar has a terrace overlooking the sea. Alongside, through the pretty Jubilee Gardens, is Ilfracombe Museum (Wilder Road, 01271 863541, www.ilfracom.org.uk/ museum, closed Mon, Sat, Sun Nov-Mar), full of curiosities.

Along the coast
East of Ilfracombe the main road follows the coast, past Hele Bay and Watermouth to tho famously long, spindly village of Combe Martin. Set on the edge of Exmoor, it stretches for some two miles along a narrow valley and culminates in a rocky cove, with a decent expanse of sand and some alluring rock pools to poke about in at low tide. For South West Coast Path walkers, this is the last pit-stop for some time before a long clifftop stretch: there are cafés, pubs and shops, along with a museum (Cross Street, 01271 889031, closed Nov-Easter) that has lots of activities for kids.

Each spring bank holiday, the villagers re-enact the bizarre ritual of the Hunting of the Earl of Rone, which has to be seen to be believed.

Where to eat & drink
In Ilfracombe, fast-food outlets straggle along the promenade. For smarter dining, try the quayside or wander down Fore Street, which has a cluster of decent restaurants. At no.54, Basil's (01271 862823, closed lunchtimes & all day Wed) has crisp white cloths on the tables and plenty of local seafood on the menu. For a more Mediterranean feel – and alfresco dining, weather permitting – try the evenings-only Terrace Tapas & Wine Bar (01271 863482, www.terracetapasbar.co.uk). The intimate restaurant at the Elmfield Hotel (see right) showcases local produce, and puddings are deliciously indulgent.

11 The Quay & White Hart Bar ★
11 The Quay, Ilfracombe, EX34 9EQ (01271 868090, www.11thequay.co.uk). Restaurant Lunch served noon-2.30pm, dinner served 6-9pm Mon-Sat. Meals served noon-3pm Sun. Bar Apr-Sept 10am-midnight daily. Oct-Mar 10am-3pm, 6pm-midnight Wed-Sat; 10am-3pm Sun.

Artist Damian Hirst masterminded the reinvention of this century-old harbourside inn, now a modish restaurant and bar. On the first floor, the Harbourside Room is home to some of Hirst's Modern Medicine artworks, and has floor to ceiling windows overlooking the harbour. There are similarly lovely views from the Atlantic Room, whose ceiling is shaped like an upturned boat. Alongside local seafood, the menu includes meat and game from nearby Exmoor. Downstairs in the White Hart Bar, you can watch the fishing boats go by over tapas and a glass of wine.

La Gendarmerie
63 Fore Street, Ilfracombe, EX34 9ED (01271 865984). Meals served Summer 6.30-9.30pm Tue-Sun. Winter 7-9.30pm Thur-Sat.
This spacious, modern brasserie occupies the town's old police station – hence the name. It's an appealing space, with exposed stone walls, candles glinting on little wooden tables and an open kitchen. The compact menu might include grilled venison loin with creamed cauliflower; Gressington duck with spring onion mash, or twice-cooked pork belly with Asian spices (a speciality).

No.6 St James Restaurant & Bar
6 St James Place, Ilfracombe, EX34 9BH (01271 866602, www.no6stjames.co.uk). Open/food served phone for details.
No.6 St James serves seasonal grub, mostly sourced from within six miles of the restaurant. Caramelised pear and organic Cropwell blue salad is a typical lunchtime dish; in the evening, you might find slow-roasted mutton with rosemary mash. The premises are light and airy, and there's a terrace.

Where to stay
A short but steep walk from the town centre and harbour, the Montpelier (20 Montpelier Terrace, 01271 879646, www.montpelierbandb.com) offers elegant, inviting B&B accommodation and magnificent breakfasts.

Elmfield Hotel
Torrs Park, Ilfracombe, EX34 8AZ (01271 863377, www.theelmfield.com). Rates £95 double incl breakfast.
Hidden away at the top of town, the Elmfield is worth seeking out. Its ten rooms have plenty of character: there's a four poster, and a nicely laid-out family suite. Children are warmly welcomed, and there's an indoor pool, a games room and Wii games on the cine-screen in the lounge. Child-free guests may prefer to wander the lovely gardens or retreat to the bar. The restaurant is another draw; booking is essential.

Little Meadow Campsite ★
Watermouth, EX34 9SJ (01271 866862, www.little meadow.co.uk). Open Easter-Sept. Rates £8-£16 2 people. No credit cards.
Perched on a hillside overlooking the coast, just to the east of Ilfracombe, the site is arranged in tiered, flower-bordered terraces; this means the pitches are level, and there are unobstructed vistas across the Bristol Channel. The facilities are simple but well-maintained – and this being an organic farm, the site is run on eco-friendly lines. A private path leads to Watermouth Harbour.

DEVON

Broomhill Sculpture Garden

BARNSTAPLE

Arlington Court

Arlington, nr Barnstaple, EX31 4LP (01271 850296, www.nationaltrust.org.uk/main/w-arlingtoncourt). Open Mar-Nov 11am-5pm daily. Feb noon-4pm daily. Admission £7.45; £3.70 reductions; £18.60 family. Gardens & Carriage Museum £5.35; £2.65 reductions.
This neoclassical house features a glorious clutter of Regency and Victorian furniture, along with intriguing *objets* collected by its globe-trotting former owner, Miss Rosalie Chichester. A colony of lesser horseshoe bats inhabit the roof, and can be spied on via 'bat-cam'. The Carriage Collection comprises 50 splendid horse-drawn vehicles; in summer, visitors can trot around the grounds.

Broomhill Sculpture Garden

Muddiford, nr Barnstaple, EX31 4EX (01271 850262, www.broomhillart.co.uk). Open 11am-4pm daily. Admission Sculpture Garden £4.50; £1.50-£3.50 reductions; £10 family. Gallery free.
Set on a hillside, Broomhill's ten-acre gardens provide a leafy backdrop to the 300-strong collection of sculpture. Artworks range from stately African stone sculptures to playful,
large-scale abstract pieces. There is also an exhibition gallery, a restaurant and a hotel (*see p49*).

Exmoor Zoo

South Stowford, EX31 4SG (01598 763352, www.exmoorzoo.co.uk). Open May-Sept 10am-6pm daily. Apr, Oct 10am-5pm daily. Nov-Mar 10am-4pm daily. Admission £7.25-£8.25; £5-£7.25 reductions; £23-£26.50 family.
This family-friendly zoo specialises in smaller animals and exotic birds – although recent additions include cheetahs and wolves.

Marwood Hill Garden

Marwood, Barnstaple, EX31 4EB (01271 342528, www.marwoodhillgarden.co.uk). Open Gardens 10am-5.30pm daily. Tearoom and plant shop Mar-Oct 10am-4.30pm daily. Admission £5.50; children under 12 free.
Centered on three lakes and a large bog garden, with a good range of plants for sale, and a tearoom.

BRAUNTON TO MORTEHOE

Borough Farm

Nr Woolacombe (01271 870056, www.borough farm.co.uk). Check the website for details.

On Wednesday evenings (6pm) in July and August, farmer David Kennard and his sheepdogs demonstrate the art of sheep-herding. David is joined by falconer Jonathan Marshall, who puts on striking displays with his birds of prey.

ILFRACOMBE & COMBE MARTIN

Chambercombe Manor

Chambercombe Lane, Ilfracombe, EX34 9RJ (01271 862624, www.chambercombemanor. org.uk). Open July, Aug 10am-5.30pm Mon-Fri; noon-5.30pm Sat, Sun. Easter-June, Sept, Oct 10am-5.30pm Mon-Fri; noon-5.30pm Sun. Admission phone for details.

The Manor was mentioned in the Domesday Book and features include a Tudor frieze and a secret chamber, where a skeleton was discovered in 1865. Gardens, an arboretum and a tearoom complete the picture.

Hele Corn Mill

Hele Bay, EX34 9QY (01271 863185, www.hele cornmill.com). Open July, Aug 11am-5pm Mon-Fri, Sun. Apr, June, Sept, Oct 11am-5pm Fri, Sat; 1-5pm Sun. Admission £3; £1.50-£2.50 reductions. No credit cards.

This restored 16th-century mill, which has a working waterwheel, still produces and sells stone-ground flour. There's also a tearoom and a pottery.

EXMOOR

Castle Hill Gardens

Filleigh, EX32 0RH (01598 760336, www.castlehill devon.co.uk). Open Apr-Sept 11am-5pm Mon-Thur, Sun. Oct 11am-4pm Sun. Admission £4; £3.50 reductions.

Landscaped gardens, and parkland containing some unusual follies. A more recent addition is the box- and lavender-edged Millennium Garden. The house is not open to the public.

BIDEFORD & THE TORRIDGE ESTUARY

Tapeley Park Gardens

Nr Instow, EX39 4NT (01271 860897, http:// tapeley-park.co.uk). Open Apr-Oct 10am-5pm Mon-Fri, Sun. Admission £4; £2.50-£3.50 reductions.

Sustainability looms large on the agenda at this beautiful estate: displays document the estate's progress towards self-sufficiency, there's a straw bale building to demonstrate eco-living in action, and organic vegetables flourish in the walled garden and permaculture garden. There's also a tearoom, a picnic area, and a plant shop.

THE HARTLAND 'PENINSULA'

Docton Mill Gardens ★

Lymebridge, EX39 6EA (01237 441369, www.doctonmill.co.uk). Open Mar-Oct 10am-5pm daily. Admission £4.50.

Created around the waterways of an old mill and set in a sheltered valley, this nine-acre garden is a delight. In spring, the narcissi are glorious. The tearoom serves Brixham crab sandwiches and cream teas.

Hartland Abbey

Hartland, Bideford, EX39 6DT (01237 441234, www.hartlandabbey.com). Open House Mid May-Oct 2-5pm Mon-Thur, Sun. Apr-mid May 2-5pm Wed, Thur, Sun. Gardens & grounds Apr-Oct noon-5pm Mon-Fri, Sun. Admission £9.50; £5 gardens & grounds only; £1.50-£3.50 reductions; £11-£22 family.

The abbey's setting is sublime: a tranquil river valley, which stretches to the sea. Following the dissolution of the monasteries, the abbey became – and has remained – a family home. Although the house contains some fine paintings, porcelain and furniture, its gardens (part-designed by Gertrude Jekyll) are the main draw.

GREAT TORRINGTON

Dartington Crystal

Great Torrington, EX38 7AN (01805 626242, www.dartington.co.uk). Open 9.30am-3.15pm Mon-Fri. Admission £6; free-£5 reductions.

This famous crystal glassware factory has been going strong since the 1960s. Visitors can watch the craftsmen at work or have a go at glass-blowing (book ahead). There's an exhibition space and a well-stocked shop.

RHS Rosemoor ★

Great Torrington, EX38 8PH (01805 624067, www.rhs.org.uk/gardens/rosemoor). Open Mar-Oct 10am-6pm daily. Nov-Feb 10am-5pm daily. Admission £7; £2.50 reductions.

Set in the lush Torridge valley, RHS Rosemoor encompasses 65 acres of horticultural delights, and a mix of formal and informal planting: allow the best part of a day to see it all. Plants are on sale in the visitors' centre, which also houses a restaurant and gift shop.

RUBY COUNTRY

Bradworthy Transport Museum

Bradworthy, nr Holsworthy, EX22 7RW (01409 241597, www.bradworthy-transport-museum.co.uk). Open 10am-5pm Mon-Thur, Sun. Admission £5.50; free-£4.50 reductions; £16 family.

A collection of more than 100 historic vehicles, plus associated memorabilia.

Gnome Reserve & Wild Flower Garden ★

West Putford, nr Bradworthy, EX22 7XE (01409 241435, www.gnomereserve.co.uk). Open Mar-Oct 10am-6pm daily. Admission £2.95; free-£2.75 reductions.

Over 1,000 gnomes and pixies populate this four-acre 'reserve', making for a kitsch day out. Cream teas, sandwiches and ice-cream are served in the Gnome Kitchen, and can be consumed in the grassy picnic area.

Winsford Walled Garden

Winsford Lane, Halwill Junction, nr Hatherleigh, EX21 5XT (01409 221477, www.winsfordwalled garden.com). Open Apr-Oct 9am-5pm daily. Admission £5.

A restored Victorian garden, notable for its vibrant colours and wonderful greenhouses, with their Burmese teak frames and exotic, richly hued plants.

DEVON

Old Rectory Hotel

Martinhoe, EX31 4QT (01598 763368, www.old rectoryhotel.co.uk). Rates Hotel from £140 double incl breakfast. Hollowbrook Cottages from £400 per week for 2-4 people. Closed Nov-Easter.

The South West Coast Path lies at the end of the garden at this delightful Georgian rectory, which is flanked by National Trust-owned land. Its eight rooms have glorious views over the sea or the garden, and are furnished with rich fabrics and antiques. Flatscreen TVs, Wi-Fi and White Company toiletries add to the air of understated luxury. Candlelit four-course dinners are also available, while the former stables have been converted into self-catering cottages, combining period features with modern comforts to great effect.

Westwood

Torrs Park, Ilfracombe, EX34 8AZ (01271 867443, www.west-wood.co.uk). Rates £80-£110 double incl breakfast.

The three double rooms at Westwood are decorated in bold, boutique hotel fashion. All have widescreen TVs, L'Occitane toiletries, bathrobes, DVD players and Wi-Fi access.

EXMOOR

Heather-covered moorland, beautiful river valleys, ancient oak woodland and a spectacular coastline combine to create the unique landscape of Exmoor. A National Park (01398 323665, 01398 323841, www.exmoor-nationalpark.gov.uk) since 1954, it straddles the Devon-Somerset border, with the westernmost third lying in Devon. Its history has also been shaped by thousands of years of human habitation, and the landscape is punctuated by Bronze Age burial mounds and hut circles, Iron Age hillforts, deserted medieval villages and more recent relics of agricultural and mining activity.

Red deer have lived on Exmoor since prehistoric times, and one of the joys of walking on the moor is unexpectedly coming upon a grazing herd. Far easier to spot than the wary deer are the sturdy, sure-footed Exmoor ponies, which have also roamed the moor for thousands of years. Moorland and woodland birds thrive here too, as do bats, butterflies and an extraordinary array of insects.

Hundreds of miles of footpaths and bridleways criss-cross the park, and the South West Coast Path runs the length of Exmoor's coastline, from Minehead, in Somerset, to Combe Martin. Meanwhile, the Two Moors Way links the park with Dartmoor, starting on the coast at Lynmouth.

Heddon Valley to Woody Bay

East of Combe Martin (*see p55*) rise the dramatic hills of Little and Great Hangman, the latter being

North Morte Farm Campsite. See p53.

the highest point on the South West Coast Path. The scenery is superb, and it's worth stopping in one of the parking areas on Trentishoe Down and strolling along the meandering grassy paths.

The high-level panorama is abruptly interrupted by Heddon's Mouth Cleave, a strikingly narrow, steep-sided valley. Paths follow the stream down to the sea and Heddon's Mouth, where there's a restored Victorian lime-kiln. Back up the valley, towards Parracombe, the Hunters Inn (see p60) is a good place to stop for refreshments. There's also a National Trust shop, information centre and car park.

For sublime sea views, walk eastwards along the cliffs to Woody Bay. It's easy to make it into a circular route (about five miles in total) by taking the two parallel paths, one near the top of the cliffs and one (the coast path) midway down; both are signposted to Heddon Valley and Woody Bay. Park in the Heddon Valley National Trust car park, or on the minor road just beyond Martinhoe. Woody Bay has a stony beach, set among rocky cliffs; it's also home to Woody Bay Station and the steam trains of the Lynton & Barnstaple Railway (see p62).

Narrow country lanes wind their way inland to the village of Parracombe. There is a rich sense of history here: the common is dotted with Bronze Age barrows, and the remains of a Norman motte-and-bailey castle stand on high ground near the village. The old church of St Petrock, on the edge of the moor, was threatened with demolition in the 1870s, but survived thanks to a spirited campaign, championed by writer and art critic John Ruskin. Its Georgian interior is beautifully preserved, from the wooden hat-pegs to the pulpit.

Lynton & Lynmouth

Despite being neighbours, these twin towns are separated by a 500-foot cliff. Lynton stands at the top of the gorge, Lynmouth at the bottom, by the sea. During the Napoleonic wars, when foreign travel was curtailed, the area's craggy scenery brought an influx of sightseers, artists and poets; later, the Victorians would dub it 'Little Switzerland'.

The towns are linked by the vertiginous Cliff Railway (01598 753486, open mid Feb-mid Nov), built in 1890 as a means of transporting both goods and tourists. Setting off from the Esplanade, it is an ingenious piece of water-powered engineering, based on a counter-balance system; as one car goes down, the other is pulled up. A zigzag path climbs alongside, for those who prefer to stay on terra firma.

Lynton is largely the functional half of the duo, with a farmers' market in the Town Hall on the first Saturday of the month. The excellent Lyn Valley Art & Crafts occupies a former chapel on Lee Road (01598 753611, closed Jan). Catch a film in the tiny auditorium of Lynton Cinema (Lee Road, 01598 753397, www.lyntoncinema.co.uk); screenings are twice daily in summer and evenings only in winter.

The cliff walk out of Lynton to the Valley of Rocks, a mile or so to the west, is not to be missed. The level, well-surfaced path winds its way along cliffs topped by extraordinary rock formations, and

populated by a herd of wild goats. There is also road access to the Valley, with a car park at the end, but it's infinitely more impressive approached on foot.

Lynmouth, which also lies at one end of the Two Moors Way (see p58), is more geared towards tourism. The line of pretty, whitewashed thatched cottages curving above the quay is a much-photographed scene, and gift shops, cafés and takeaways cluster along the roads leading to the harbour. It's all a far cry from the devastation wreaked by the disastrous flood of August 1952, when the East and West Lyn turned into raging torrents, sweeping people and houses into the sea. The tragedy is commemorated in a display inside the Flood Memorial Hall, by the harbour.

Doone Country

The area around the East Lyn river valley and its tributary, Badgworthy Water, is indelibly associated with RD Blackmore's romantic account of Exmoor's fictional brigands, Lorna Doone. The villages of Malmsmead, Oare and Brendon are at the centre of this untamed region, with its plunging, wooded combes, limpid rivers and remote heather moorland.

The tiny Norman church of St Mary's, in the sleepy hamlet of Oare, is where Lorna was shot at the altar on her wedding day; on the road to Porlock Hill, the small, stone-built Robbers' Bridge also featured in the book. West of Oare, Malmsmead is a photogenic spot, with an old stone packhorse bridge alongside the ford, some attractive cottages and a tearoom.

The village is at the foot of Badgworthy Water, and footpaths follow the stream up into the heart of Doone country, past a memorial stone to RD Blackmore and into the rustling Badgeworthy Wood. (Bring an OS map.) A footbridge crosses the stream flowing from Lank Combe – the site of the waterslide where John Ridd and Lorna first met; above here is heather-clad moorland, and the remains of a medieval village at Hoccombe Combe. From here, loop back to Malmsmead, or retrace your steps along this most magical of valleys.

Further west is Brendon, alongside the East Lyn River. It's an unspoilt village of thatched cottages and narrow lanes, with a cosy pub, the Stag Hunters Inn (see p60). Footpaths accompany the tumbling, gurgling river on its rocky course down to Watersmeet, about two and a half miles away, at times crossing wooden footbridges.

At Watersmeet, the East Lyn is joined by the Hoar Oak Water, which drops in small cascades. Watersmeet House, an Edwardian fishing lodge, is now a National Trust tearoom and shop (01598 753348, www.nationaltrust.org.uk/watersmeet, closed Nov-mid Mar), with tables dotting the lawn.

South Molton

The small, attractive market town of South Molton lies just to the south of Exmoor, and is a focal point for the rural community around the moor's southern fringes. A signposted trail takes in the town's medieval remains and Elizabethan and Georgian

DEVON

buildings, with an accompanying booklet on sale at the Tourist Information Centre (1 East Street, 01769 574122). On Broad Street, the town hall now houses the South Molton Museum (01769 572951, www.southmoltonmuseum.org, closed Sun, closed Nov-Mar), whose exhibits include a horse-drawn fire engine, a penny farthing and an enormous 18th-century cider press.

On Thursdays and Saturdays the covered Pannier Market swings into action, selling local produce and all sorts of collectibles, and the town buzzes with activity. South Molton is also known for its smart independent shops. Look out for sumptuous fabrics and trimmings at Partridge & Pear Tree (East Street, 01769 574865, www.partridgeandpeartree.com, closed Sun) and contemporary jewellery and leather bags at Vanilla (2 East Street, 01769 579557, closed Sun). Griffin's Yard and Griffin's Gallery (North Road, 01769 574284, www.craftsgallery griffinsyard.co.uk, closed Sun) is an organic food shop, café and craft gallery; one of the exhibitors is Jenny Wilkinson, who weaves gorgeous rugs.

The George Hotel (1 Broad Street, 01769 572514, www.georgehotelsouthmolton.co.uk) runs a wide-ranging entertainment programme, including film screenings, comedy and musical performances.

Where to eat & drink

In Parracombe, the Fox & Goose (01598 763239, www.foxandgoose-parracombe.co.uk) serves ales from the Cotleigh and Exmoor breweries, sturdy food and tempting own-made puddings.

Stumbles in South Molton (131-134 East Street, 01769 574145, www.stumbles.co.uk) is a restaurant with rooms (£55-£60 incl breakfast), offering courtyard dining when the weather allows.

Corn Dolly Tea Shop

15a East Street, South Molton, EX36 3DB (01769 574249). Open 9.30am-5pm Mon-Wed, Fri, Sat; 8.30am-5pm Thur; 11am-5pm Sun.
Serving proper loose-leaf teas, this quaint tea shop has won a clutch of awards from the Tea Guild. The menu offers light lunches and superb cakes and scones, and the owner knows a thing or two about the right way to toast a teacake.

Hunters Inn

Heddon Valley, EX31 4PY (01598 763230, www.thehuntersinn.net). Open 10am-11pm daily. Lunch served noon-3pm, dinner served 6-9pm daily.
Set in the wooded Heddon Valley, the Hunters is a haven for walkers. A no-nonsense menu of baguettes, jacket potatoes and more substantial mains (lamb shank, beer-battered fish and chips) provides sustenance, along with a fine line-up of ales. In the evening, there's a choice between eating by the fire in the bar or in the candlelit restaurant.

Rising Sun

Harbourside, Lynmouth, EX35 6EG (01598 753223, www.risingsunlynmouth.co.uk). Lunch served noon-2.30pm, dinner served 6.30-9pm daily.
This picturesque, thatched 14th-century inn, overlooking Lynmouth harbour, has appeared on countless postcards. Inside, it lives up to its image with low ceilings, oak panelling and a candlelit dining room. The menu features Exmoor game, salmon from the River Lyn and local seafood; you can't go far wrong with half a Lynmouth Bay lobster with new potatoes and salad. The inn also has 16 rooms (£120-£150 double incl breakfast), furnished in keeping with its character; there is a private suite in Shelley's Cottage (£160 incl breakfast), where it is said the poet spent his honeymoon.

Rockford Inn

Brendon, EX35 6PT (01598 741214, www.therockford inn.co.uk). Open noon-11pm Tue-Sun. Lunch served noon-3pm, dinner served 6-8.30pm Tue-Sun.
Just down the road from Brendon in the hamlet of Rockford, this beamed, 17th-century village inn overlooks the wooded banks of the East Lyn River. Known for its ciders and cask ales, such as Cotleigh Barn Owl, it also serves good-value grub. Puddings are comfortingly old-school (rhubarb crumble and custard, syrup sponge).

Stag Hunters Inn

Brendon, EX35 6PS (01598 741222, www.stag hunters.com). Open noon-11pm daily. Lunch served noon-2.30pm, dinner served 6-9pm daily.
This village inn has an idyllic setting on the banks of the East Lyn River. Order a pint of malty Exmoor Gold at the bar, then head out to the garden. As well as the bar menu, there's smarter dining in the restaurant: Exmoor venison features, as you'd expect, along with locally caught fish. Clean, basic B&B rooms (£60 double incl breakfast) are also available.

Where to stay

For a delightfully rural retreat, the Rockford Inn has five snug, spotlessly clean B&B rooms. Another B&B option in Brendon is the Stag Hunters Inn (*see above*); the Rising Sun and Stumbles (*see left*) also offer rooms.

Alternatively, camp at Channel View Camping & Caravan Park (Manor Farm, Lynton, 01598 753349, www.channel-view.co.uk, £6 per person). The hillside site overlooks Lynton and Lynmouth, although the sea-view pitches soon get snapped up. There's a shop and café on site, a children's play area and a pub almost next door.

Hunters Inn (*see left*) offers B&B (and dinner), staying in one of its quaintly old-fashioned rooms – several of which have four-posters.

Cloud Farm

Oare, near Brendon, EX35 6NU (01598 741234, www.doonevalleyholidays.co.uk). Open all year. Rates £5.50-£7; £4.50-£5.50 children.
Occupying an idyllic site in the Doone valley, the riverside fields at Cloud Farm are a beautiful place to pitch camp – although the site can get crowded in high season, and you can't book ahead. Campfires are allowed, and there's a well-equipped shop, along with a tearoom and horse riding stables.

Sea View Villa ★

6 Summerhouse Path, Lynmouth, EX35 6ES (01598 753460, www.seaviewvilla.co.uk). Rates £110-£130 double incl breakfast.

Exmoor. See p58.

A Grade II-listed Georgian villa that's now a luxurious B&B, overlooking the harbour. Decor throughout is warm and elegant, with the odd theatrical flourish. Breakfast options include smoked kippers or omelette Arnold Bennett. Dinners (not served Wed & Sun) and picnics can be provided.

BIDEFORD & THE TORRIDGE ESTUARY

Bideford

Bideford is the only remaining commercial port on the north coast of Devon, with a quay along the tidal waters of the River Torridge. The ancient 24-arch Long Bridge is magnificent, but has been supplanted by the Torridge Bridge, which spans the river downstream. As a port and market town, Bideford has a long history, and a stroll around its narrow, sloping streets is always rewarding. In Kingsley Road, Burton Art Gallery & Museum (01237 471455, www.burtonartgallery.co.uk) has a varied exhibition programme, along with a craft gallery, a café and a museum documenting the town's history.

The quay is a fascinating place to while away an hour or so – especially at high tide, when commercial and pleasure craft come and go. Lundy's supply ship and passenger ferry, the MS *Oldenburg*, is often moored here. Just across the road is the former Custom House, built in 1695; it's now Quigley's, a popular local. Further along is the equally ancient Kings Arms, and there's no shortage of cafés from which you can watch the world go by. Across the river, look out for the graceful outline of the *Kathleen & May*, built in 1900 and the only wooden triple-masted sailing schooner still in existence.

The high street runs at right angles to the Quay; just off it, the narrower Mill Street is lined with a higgledy-piggledy mix of cafés, food shops, craft and antique shops. Further up the high street is Grenville Street, which leads to the Pannier Market. Admire the artful window display of Deco World (2-3 Grenville Street, 01237 422355, www.deco-world.com), filled with 1930s finds. A little further on, Old Bridge Antiques (no.19, 01237 420909, closed Sun) is packed with curios. The 19th-century Pannier Market is one of Bideford's treasures, hosting market days on Tuesday and Saturday year round. Running through the centre of the building is Butchers' Row; these days, the butchers have been replaced by shops selling crafts, clothes, toys and vinyl records.

Appledore & Instow

Downstream from Bideford, just before the Torridge merges into the Taw, the villages of Appledore and Instow face each other across the water. The estuarine expanse of water and sky, combined with the pastel-painted cottages, are wonderfully scenic, so it's no surprise to find a thriving artistic community here. Devon Duck Tours' (01271 861077, www.devonducktours.co.uk, closed Nov-Easter) amphibious craft has a regular summer service of round trips between the two villages and Crow Point. The most scenic way to arrive in Instow, though, is to cycle along the Tarka Trail (*see p63*) from East-the-Water.

Marine Parade overlooks the village's sandy beach, safe for bathing and with views westward to Bideford Bay. On a corner of the Parade, the Waterside Gallery (01271 860786, www.waterside art.co.uk) is good for a mooch, while you'll find picnic provisions at Johns' store (01271 860310).

Things to do

Torrs Walk

BRAUNTON TO MORTEHOE

North Devon Surf School
01237 474663, www.northdevonsurfschool.co.uk.
Prices from £28 half day.
Lessons take place at the Northam Burrows end of the beach at Westward Ho!, where wipe out-prone novices are safely out of the way of more experienced surfers. All equipment is provided.

Sea Kayaking Southwest
01271 813129, www.seakayakingsouthwest.co.uk.
Prices from £150 2 days.
Taking to the waves in a sea kayak is a brilliant way to see hidden inlets and coves along the coast, and get close to wildlife. This friendly outfit offers trips and courses at various locations along the coast.

Surf South West
01271 890400, www.surfsouthwest.com.
Prices from £25-£28 half day.
Awarded level 4 status by the British Surfing Association, Surf South West operates out of Croyde and Saunton Sands. A surfboard and wetsuit are provided, and tuition ranges from beginners' lessons to advanced coaching.

Surfing Croyde Bay
01271 891200, www.surfingcroydebay.co.uk.
Prices from £35 half day taster session.
Surfing Croyde Bay promises no more than five students to every instructor in its group sessions, and offers all manner of courses and equipment hire.

Woolacombe Riding Stables
Eastacott Farm, Woolacombe, EX34 7AE
(01271 870260). Open 9am-5.30pm daily.
Admission 30mins £12; 1hr £20; 90mins
£30; 90mins sand £35; 105mins beach £50.
No credit cards.
Whether you want a gentle amble along the coast or a serious hack through the sand dunes, you'll find a variety of rides on offer at this farm-based stables.

ILFRACOMBE & COMBE MARTIN

Lynton & Barnstaple Railway
Woody Bay Station, Martinhoe Cross, Parracombe, EX31 4RA (01598 763487, www.lynton-rail.co.uk). Open June-Sept daily, check website for timetable. Reduced service Mar-May, Oct-Dec. Tickets £6 return; £3-£4 reductions.
Closed in 1935, this narrow-gauge railway is now enjoying a new lease of life. A doughty little steam loco, Axe, powers along the mile-long stretch of track between Woody Bay and Killington Lane. The station café is open whenever trains are running. Check the website for special events aimed at children.

Torrs Walk
Ilfracombe (www.nationaltrust.org.uk/main/w-morte).
To the west of Ilfracombe is the National Trust-owned area of the Torrs. The Torrs Walk, a cliff-top footpath, offers stunning views over the coast and can be followed all the way to Lee Bay; alternatively, take one of the paths back through Torrs Park.

EXMOOR

Doone Valley Trekking
Cloud Farm, Oare, Lynton, EX35 6NU (01598 741234, www.doonevalleytrekking.co.uk). Prices from £25/hr.
Escorted rides for all abilities are offered in and around the beautiful Doone Valley, ranging from one- or two-hour jaunts to whole day excursions.

Exmoor Coast Boat Trips
Lynmouth Harbour, EX35 6ER (01598 753207, www. theglenlyngorge.co.uk). Trips Mar-Sept 11am, noon daily (weather/tides permitting). Rates £10 per hr.
Take an hour-long trip to Woody Bay, past looming cliffs circled by seabirds, lonely bays and deep river valleys. Drift fishing for mackerel is also offered.

Exmoor Coastal Link ★
08453 45955, www.somerset.gov.uk. Tickets £4.90 return.
Linking Lynmouth with Porlock and Minehead, service 300 is one of the best bus journeys in the country. It follows the high-level main road close to the coast, and the views are stupendous. In summer, look out for the Exmoor Explorer, a vintage double-decker (£6 return).

Outovercott Riding Stables
Lynton, EX35 6JR (01598 763341, www.outovercott.co.uk). Prices from £20/hr.

Bike hire

Bideford Cycle Hire
Torrington Street, East-the-Water, Bideford, EX39 4DR (01237 424123, www.bideford bicyclehire.co.uk). Bike hire from £10.50 day.

Biketrail
Fremington Quay, nr Barnstaple, EX31 2NH (01271 372586, www.biketrail.co.uk). Bike hire from £10 day.

Otter Cycle Hire
Station Road, Braunton, EX33 2AQ (01271 813339). Bike hire from £12 day.

Tarka Trail Cycle Hire
Railway Station, Station Road, Sticklepath, Barnstaple, EX31 2AU (01271 324202/01271 879617, www.tarkabikes.co.uk). Bike hire from £10.50 day.

Torrington Cycle Hire
Station Yard, Station Hill, Torrington, EX38 8JD (01805 622633, www.torringtoncyclehire.co.uk). Bike hire from £10.50 day.

This is splendid riding terrain, whether you opt to trot through the Lyn valley, across the moor or along the coast. All abilities are catered for, and tuition is available.

BIDEFORD & THE TORRIDGE ESTUARY

The Big Sheep
Abbotsham, Bideford, EX39 5AP (01237 472366, www.thebigsheep.co.uk). Open Apr-Oct 10am-6pm daily. Nov-Mar 10am-5pm Sat, Sun. Admission £5-£9.95.
Activities at this unexpectedly engaging sheep-themed attraction range from feeding the lambs and watching sheep-shearing displays to tackling the adrenaline-charged high ropes course. The site also has an indoor play barn, its own brewery and a restaurant.

THE HARTLAND 'PENINSULA'

Clovelly Charters
01237 431405, www.clovelly-charters.ukf.net. Trips from £35 return. Open Apr-Oct.
Take a boat trip from Clovelly to Lundy (*see p68*), aboard the shipshape *Jessica Hettie*, keeping your eyes peeled for seals en route. The owner also runs seal-spotting trips where you can swim with friendly pinnipeds. Some wetsuits and goggles can be provided, but bring your own if possible.

Tarka Trail

Across the water in Appledore, the view is of Instow's white buildings, set against gently rising green hills. Appledore's long history of fishing and shipbuilding stretches back centuries; shipbuilding still continues at Bidna Yard, and catch of the day appears in pride of place on most menus. The original quayside houses were along Market Street, with jetties at the end of their gardens; only in 1845 was a proper quay constructed.

At its seaward end, the Quay curves to the left as the estuary broadens. Just below the slipway beside the car park is Marcus Vergette's *Time and Tide Bell*. Installed in 2009, this unique bronze bell is activated by the rising tide, the pitch varying with the water level. Further on is Irsha Street, where pretty terraced fisherman's cottages huddle together; from the small promenade, you can look over to Crow Point on the northern shore, with Braunton Burrows behind. The road ends at the Lifeboat Station, while the Coast Path continues to Northam Burrows.

Narrow streets lead off from the quay into Appledore's heart: a tangle of streets, where some of the buildings date from Elizabethan times. Bude Street holds various galleries and studios; after a browse, head to Schooners Tea Shop & Delicatessen (01237 474168) at no.25 for a coffee and a slab of cake. Running off Market Street is the pretty One End Street, which is too narrow for cars.

Myrtle Street leads down to the Quay; it's also home to Walter's Emporium (no phone) – a garage bursting with second-hand books and bric-a-brac,

with proceeds going to the village library. While you're on the junk shop trail, check out Uncle Wainwright's Charity Shop (no phone) on the Quay for an enticing jumble of clothes, china, records, jigsaw puzzles and more. It's open on Wednesdays and Saturdays year round, plus Fridays in August.

The North Devon Maritime Museum (Odun Road, 01237 422064, www.devonmuseums.net, closed Oct-Apr) is an essential port of call for anyone with an interest in seafaring. Set in imposing Georgian premises, it explores the area's maritime past, from salmon boats to shipwrecks.

In and around Appledore, look out for the wonderfully retro Hockings' ice-cream vans. This local company has been making ice-cream to its own unique recipe since 1936; cones are only available in vanilla, so don't ask for anything too exotic.

Northam Burrows

Stretching along the southern entrance to the Taw-Torridge estuary, not far from Appledore, is Northam Burrows. Flanked by a pebble ridge, its salt marsh, grassland and sand dunes are a designated Site of Special Scientific Interest, with an important range of maritime plant life. The Burrows is also used by walkers, horseriders and birdwatchers, and is home to the oldest golf links in the country. The sandy beach beyond the pebble ridge stretches south for almost two miles to Westward Ho!, and is a popular spot for sand-yachting, kite-flying and surfing – although there's better surf to be found at other

Hunters Inn. See p60.

beaches further north. Still, the mellow waves are ideal for beginners, and the North Devon Surf School (*see p62*) has its base here.

Vehicular access to Northam Burrows is by toll road (the gates close at 10pm), and a visitor centre near the dunes provides information on the park. The northern end, beside the estuary, is a good place to see birdlife, as waders and seabirds feast on the rich mudflats.

Westward Ho!

Those who tend to shun the more brash, kiss-me-quick sort of seaside attractions could be forgiven for thinking that Westward Ho!'s most notable feature is its exclamation mark. (Named after Charles Kingsley's novel, it is the only place name in Britain to have one.)

Nevertheless, the resort bends over backwards to cater for families, and has beguiled many a toddler. For a start, the sandy beach is perfect for building sandcastles and kite-flying (it also has designated swimming and surfing areas). Where the sand gives way to rocks, there are rock pools to explore, along with a man-made swimming pool that is exposed at low tide. The seafront promenade is a gaudy galaxy of cafés, takeaways, amusement arcades and souvenir shops, while plenty more shops and eateries can be found in the main streets.

If a surfeit of chips and candy floss leaves you craving more wholesome food, head for Marshford Organic Foods Farm Shop (Churchill Way, 01237 477160, www.marshford.co.uk, closed Mon, Sun). There's a huge range of organic produce, including vegetables grown in the farm's own nursery.

Where to eat & drink

Bideford is well-supplied with uncomplicated eateries. Refuel with Fairtrade coffee and Dunstaple Farm ice-cream at Cleverdon's Café (18 Mill Street, 01237 472179, closed Sun), or a pasty from the Happy Pasty shop (no.13, 01237 470340, closed Sun) in nearby Allhalland Street. On Mill Street, Cafecino Plus (01237 473007, www.cafecinoplus.com, closed Sun) is an all-day affair, with a courtyard for alfresco drinks.

In Westward Ho!, Tea on the Green (Golf Links Road, no phone, closed winter) has a sophisticated beach hut meets Doris Day vibe, and serves dreamy afternoon teas as well as light lunches.

Beaver Inn

Irsha Street, Appledore, EX39 1RY (01237 474822, www.beaverinn.co.uk). Lunch served noon-2pm, dinner served 7-9pm daily.
The inn's location should soon blow any cobwebs away: looking out over the estuary, it has picnic tables on a patio by the water. Local ales on tap include Otter and Doom Bar, and the menu includes a good selection of fresh fish.

Boathouse ★

Marine Parade, Instow, EX39 4JJ (01271 861292, http://www.instow.net/boathouse/boathouse.htm). Lunch served noon-2pm daily. Dinner served 6-9.30pm Mon-Sat; 7-9pm Sun.

Renowned for its seafood and set opposite the beach, this popular establishment is a great place to watch the sunset while you dine. The kitchen sources as much locally sourced produce as possible: baked Lundy crab and prawns with a cheesy crust or sautéed fillet of local beef with madeira sauce might feature. Book in advance for an estuary view.

9 the Quay

9 The Quay, Appledore, EX39 1QS (01237 473355, www.9thequay.co.uk). Breakfast & lunch served 10am-3.30pm, dinner served 7-9pm Tue-Sun.
Paintings by local artists adorn the walls at this welcoming coffee shop, which serves Fairtrade coffee and organic juices, along with breakfast and lunch. The upstairs restaurant offers a nicely balanced menu of smart, bistro-style food (grilled sardines with rocket salad and tomato compote, say).

Phansit's Kitchen

9 Grenville Street, Bideford, EX39 2EA (01237 429942, www.phansitskitchen.com). Open 6-10pm Thur-Sat.
The Thai owner of Phansit's Kitchen cooks up a storm in its open plan kitchen, serving up old favourites (green curry, pad thai noodles, prawn tempura) and inspired specials, such as jungle curry made with pheasant breast. The quality of the cooking has garnered this place a loyal following.

Potwallopers Bistro

Golf Links Road, Westward Ho!, EX39 1LH (01237 474494, www.potwallopers.co.uk). Meals served Winter 6.30-9.30pm Mon-Sat; 10am-2.30pm, 6.30-9.30pm Sun. Easter-June 10am-2.30pm, 6.30-9.30pm Wed-Sun. July, Aug 10am-2.30pm, 6.30-9.30pm Tue-Sun.
A relaxed place, overlooking the seafront at Westward Ho!, Potwallopers' has an appealing international menu, which runs from burgers to bouillabaisse.

Wayfarer Inn

Lane End, Instow, EX39 4LB (01271 860342, http://thewayfarerinstow.co.uk). Open 11am-11pm daily. Lunch served noon-2pm, dinner served 6.30-9pm daily. Room rates £80 double incl breakfast; 6 rooms available.
Just 20 yards from the beach, this busy local pub serves a great range of real ales. Locally caught fish and game feature on the menu, and there is a sunny, enclosed beer garden for clement afternoons; children and dogs are welcome.

Westleigh Inn

Westleigh, EX39 4NL (01271 860867, www.westleigh inn.co.uk). Open 11.30am-11pm Mon-Sat; 11.30am-10.30pm Sun. Lunch served noon-2.30pm, dinner served 6-9pm Mon-Sat. Meals served noon-3pm Sun.
This cosy old hostelry has views over the estuary from its garden, where children swing from the climbing frame and grown-ups sup Hartland Blonde. The kitchen delivers classic pub grub, such as breaded Brixham whitebait with salad, crusty bread, own-made coleslaw and lemon mayo.

Where to stay

Instow's Wayfarer Inn (*see above*) has six en suite B&B rooms, some with sea views.

On Appledore's quay, the Seagate Hotel (01237 472589, www.seagatehotel.co.uk) is a sturdy, white-painted 17th-century inn with

DEVON

old-fashioned rooms and a restaurant; in summer, you can dine on the patio overlooking the estuary.

Commodore Hotel
Marine Parade, Instow, EX39 4JN (01271 860347, www.commodore-instow.co.uk). Rates £110 double incl breakfast.
Owned and managed by the Woolaway family for over 30 years, the Commodore has a breathtaking waterside location, with views across the estuary from its manicured, palm-fringed lawns. Rooms are plush and traditional rather than cutting edge chic. Mid-afternoon, indulge in a cream tea overlooking the lawns and the water; more substantial meals are served in the bar or the Marine Restaurant.

The Mount
Northdown Road, Bideford, EX39 3LP (01237 473748, www.themountbideford.co.uk). £60-£70 double incl breakfast.
This handsome Georgian house, set within its own tranquil, partially walled garden, is five minutes' walk from the centre of Bideford. Inside, an impressive winding staircase leads up from the chequerboard-tiled hallway; the lounge is equally stately, with its open fire, grand piano and well-stocked library. Eight en suite bedrooms are tastefully furnished.

Old Shippon & The Sparrows
Beara Farmhouse, Buckland Brewer, EX39 5EH (01237 451666, www.bearafarmhouse.co.uk). Rates Old Shippon £300-£550 per week for 4 people. The Sparrows £350-£650 per week for 6 people. No credit cards.
Two delightful self-catering properties: the Old Shippon is a converted cowshed, attached to the farmhouse but with its own entrance, a wood-burning stove and glorious country views. The detached, slate-roofed Sparrows also offers a lovely vista across the fields from its first-floor living area. A cream tea welcomes new arrivals.

Polly-Dora's Guest House
13 Market Street, Appledore, EX39 1PW (01237 421059). Rates £65 double incl breakfast. No credit cards.
Owned by a globe-trotting artist, this cob-walled 18th-century house is full of character, and set in the heart of the village. The bedrooms are en suite and there is a guests' lounge, while homebaked bread and organic produce feature on the breakfast menu, served in a light-filled garden room.

Rufus Stone Houseboat
Clarence Wharf, Bideford, EX39 4AE (07790 989595, www.rufusstone.com). Rates £650 per week for 6 people. No credit cards.
Built in 1963, this steel-hulled oil bunkering barge has now been converted into a static houseboat. Moored on the River Torridge, the boat has a spacious main saloon (equipped with a large-screen TV, Sky, DVD player and PlayStation 2), a smaller aft saloon, a kitchen and dining area, two shower rooms and sleeping quarters for up to eight people. There's also a small swimming pool, heated by two solar panels. The decor throughout is quietly chic, with dark wood floors, leather sofas and vanilla cushions, and the setting is lovely.

West Farm
Irsha Street, Appledore, EX39 1RY (01237 425269, www.wolseylodges.com). Rates £98 double incl breakfast.
Set in a Grade II-listed house, this three-bedroom B&B is a delightfully relaxed establishment. The bedrooms are old-fashioned and spotlessly clean; for direct access to the lovely gardens, book into the twin-bed garden suite.

THE HARTLAND 'PENINSULA'
This corner of north-west Devon forms a little region on its own, with a wild, wave-lashed coastline that juts into the Atlantic at Hartland Point. The high cliffs are punctuated at intervals by deep combes and dramatic coastal waterfalls, tumbling on to the pebbly foreshore. The undulating terrain means that the coastline remains unspoilt by seaside developments; inland, the rural landscape is scattered with villages and patches of ancient woodland. Other than Clovelly, it's all a bit off the beaten track – but that's part of the appeal.

Hartland
A few miles inland from Hartland Point lies the small town of Hartland. In the square stands the stone-built market hall, with its 400-year-old clock; these days, there is a thriving community of artists and craftspeople in the area, and the hall regularly hosts arts and crafts fairs. In his workshop on the corner of the square, James Morley (01237 441890, closed Sun) makes contemporary-style furniture using traditional skills. Nearby is Two Harton Manor (*see p69*), where Merlyn Chesterman's woodcuts are displayed. Just off West Street, you'll find earthenware pots and tiles at Springfield Pottery (01237 441506, www.springfield-pottery. com, closed Sun), and in Fore Street, Millthorne Chairs (01237 441590, closed Sat, Sun) sells hand-made chairs. Antiques can be found at Darville Gallery in West Street (01237 441984, closed Mon-Thur, Sun). Hartland Farm Shop (Fore Street, 01237 441332, www.hartlandfarm shop.co.uk, closed Sun) is good for provisions, and has a quality tea shop.

To the west of the town, in a damply romantic wooded valley, is Hartland Abbey (*see p57*). The road past the abbey leads to Stoke, home to Hartland's 14th-century parish church, dedicated to St Nectan. Its soaring tower once provided a useful landmark for sailors; inside is a fine 15th-century carved oak rood screen. From Stoke, it's not far to the shingle beach and small museum at Hartland Quay (*see p67*), by road or footpath; another path descends to the River Abbey and on to the coast at Blackpool Mill Cove.

Alternatively, Cheristow Lavender (01237 440101, www.cheristow.co.uk, closed Nov-Feb) is a five-minute drive away; after a stroll around the fragrant lavender nursery and rose gardens, head for the tearoom for lavender and chocolate brownies.

Clovelly
The tourist honeypot of Clovelly needs little or no introduction. Privately owned by the same family since 1738, it is a bewitchingly pretty place, with its car-free, stepped and cobbled streets and tiers of white-painted cottages.

Crow Point. See p61.

Herring fishing was the village's main source of income until the early 19th century, when the fickle shoals of so-called silver darlings headed elsewhere. These days herring are somewhat scarce, although a few fishermen remain; you can also taste the traditional delicacy at the Herring Festival in November.

There is limited roadside parking above the village, but most visitors have to park and enter through the visitor centre, and pay an admission charge to the village. (Walkers have free access from the Coast Path.) As you stroll down the cobbled main street you'll probably see some of the resident donkeys, whose forebears used to bring goods in and out; today, deliveries are transported on sledges. About halfway down the street is Kingsley House (01237 431781), where a small museum tells of Clovelly's seafaring past and its connection with the novelist Charles Kingsley; beyond it is a fisherman's cottage, furnished as it would have been in the 1930s.

Further down, the street twists around to reach the harbour, and the quayside Red Lion Hotel (see p68). Walk out along the harbour wall and look back up at the village to appreciate its extraordinary location, set among near-vertical wooded cliffs. If you can't face the walk back up, a Land Rover service (Easter-Oct) follows a back road to the top. Just beyond the car park is Clovelly Court, the manor house for the Clovelly Estate; the house is closed to the public, but the walled gardens are open year-round.

East of Clovelly is the Hobby Drive – a three-mile walk from the top of the village to the viewpoint and back. Built as a scenic carriage drive in the early 19th century, it's reasonably level; through the trees, you catch glimpses of the sea and harbour.

West of Clovelly

To the west of Clovelly, the South West Coast Path takes an even more scenic route as it strikes out towards Hartland Point. The path drops steeply to sea level at Mouth Mill Cove, where the arched Blackchurch Rock rises from the beach. Beyond this is another deep valley; once you're back at the top, the path stays at clifftop level all the way to Hartland Point.

It's a ten-mile walk from Clovelly to Hartland Quay; if you'd prefer to tackle a shorter stretch, car parks at Brownsham, Exmansworthy and East Titchberry have footpaths connecting with the South West Coast Path. There's also a paying car park close to the headland of Hartland Point, where the coastline turns abruptly south. On a rock plateau below stands a lighthouse, built in 1874; at the bottom of the cliff, the Atlantic rollers pound the rocks relentlessly. From here down to the Devon-Cornwall border at Marsland Mouth, the coastline is nothing short of spectacular – and the best way to enjoy it is on foot.

It's a challenging, three-mile walk from Hartland Point to the once-bustling harbour at Hartland Quay ★, which fell into disuse in the 1890s. The old quay buildings now house the Hartland Quay Hotel (see p69); opposite is the small Shipwreck Museum. A slipway leads to the shingle beach, where a stretch of sand is exposed at low tide. From here, it's less than a mile south along the Coast Path to the impressive waterfall at Speke's Mill Mouth, and the curved crescent of beach below; inland of here are the lovely Docton Mill Gardens (see p57).

More towering cliffs lead on to Embury Beacon, where an Iron Age hillfort once stood. Far below at Welcombe Mouth, there's a small car park at the end of a very rutted track, and a waterfall that tumbles on to the shingly beach; at low tide, a generous expanse of sand is revealed, attracting intrepid bodyboarders.

A short, steep scramble over the cliff leads to Marsland Mouth and the border with Cornwall, marked by signs at the footbridge. Access to the rock and shingle beach is via a small path by the stream; inland, the wooded Marsland Valley is a flourishing nature reserve (01392 279244, www.devonwildlifetrust.org), home to otters, roe deer, green woodpeckers and rare butterflies.

Further inland is the tiny village of Welcombe. Sermons at the ancient St Nectan's church are delivered from a carved Tudor pulpit, and there's a wonderful 14th-century screen; across from the church is a holy well, in its own little stone building. Half a mile away is the other half of the village, Darracott, where you'll find the Welcombe Pottery Studio (01288 331361, www.welcombepottery. co.uk, closed Nov-Easter). Almost next door, the Old Smithy (01288 331305, http://theold smithyinn.co.uk) is a thatched country pub with good food.

DEVON

Lundy Island

Twelve miles north of Hartland Point, the 400-foot high granite outcrop of Lundy Island rises from the sea. Some three miles long and half a mile wide, it offers visitors blissful respite from the pressures of 21st-century life.

Much of its charm lies in its sense of remoteness. Without the intrusions of modern life (there is no internet access, and no mobile phone signal), the pace of life is less hurried; in place of noisy traffic, there are a handful of tractors and vehicles needed for essential tasks.

The island's colourful history adds to its appeal. There have been numerous shipwrecks around its craggy shores, and in the 12th century it belonged to a family of pirates, who terrorised the neighbouring coast. In the 18th century it was used for smuggling, before embracing the more respectable trade of granite-quarrying in the 19th century, when it was purchased by William Hudson Heaven. Its buildings reflect this rich history, from the medieval castle and the remains of the battery on the west coast to the three lighthouses. (The original lighthouse, on the island's highest point, was frequently obscured by fog, and had to be replaced; today, you can climb the spiral staircase to the redundant lamp chamber for a bird's-eye view of the island.)

Sold to the National Trust in the 1960s, Lundy is now managed by the Landmark Trust. As a result, the island's unique atmosphere and exceptional array of wildlife have survived. The huge variety of resident and migratory seabirds includes kittiwakes, razorbill, oystercatchers and, most famously, puffins (the name Lundy comes from the Old Norse for 'puffin island'). The Lundy cabbage, with its bright yellow flowers, blooms on the south-eastern cliffs; offshore, seals and basking sharks are frequently spotted, and the sea around the island is a Marine Nature Reserve, thanks to its wealth of underwater life. It's a great place for diving and snorkelling, as well as climbing on the near-vertical sea cliffs.

Most people come here as day visitors on Lundy's own vessel, the MS *Oldenburg* (01271 863636, www.lundyisland.co.uk), which sails several times a week from Bideford and Ilfracombe, from March to October. In winter, a helicopter service operates.

It is also possible to stay in one of the quirky self-catering properties on the island, let out by the Landmark Trust (01628 825925, www.landmark trust.org.uk); there is also a small campsite. Properties include the castle keep, a converted piggery, the former lighthouse keeper's quarters and the remote Admiralty signal station.

The jetty is at the south-east corner of the island – the only possible landing place amid these formidable cliffs. From here, it's a steep climb up to the village – a cluster of houses with a church, a shop selling provisions, gifts and special Lundy postage stamps, and the Marisco Tavern. The hub of island life, the latter is open all day and serves breakfast, lunch and dinner.

The road soon turns into a track, which runs along the spine of the island to the northern tip. The best way to explore, however, is to take one of the footpaths around the perimeter. The west side has dramatic cliffs, lashed by Atlantic storms, while the east coast is softer, with wild flowers in spring followed by a purple carpet of (unfortunately invasive) rhododendrons. Here, there's a good chance of spotting some of Lundy's Sika deer herd. Inland, follow the footpaths that criss-cross the island to see peacefully grazing Soay sheep, along with wild goats and Lundy ponies. Guided walks led by the warden run for most of the year, and are a good way to find out more about the island's wildlife.

Where to eat & drink

In Clovelly, the New Inn Hotel (*see p69*) has a restaurant and bar open to non-residents.

Anchor Inn

Fore Street, Hartland, EX39 6BD (01237 441414, www.theanchorinnhartland.co.uk). Lunch served noon-2pm Mon, Thur-Sat; noon-3pm Sun. Dinner served 6-9pm Mon, Wed-Sun. Rates £60 double incl breakfast.
This 16th-century inn is known for its well-kept real ales, which include a brew or two from the local Forge Brewery. A down-to-earth menu ranges from sausage, egg and chips to Devon sirloin steak; or order a giant Yorkshire pudding filled with roast beef, pork, own-made curry or chilli.

Hart Inn

The Square, Hartland, EX39 6BL (01237 441474, www.thehartinn.com). Open noon-3pm, 6-11pm
Mon-Sat; noon-3pm Sun. Lunch served noon-3pm Tue-Sun. Dinner served 6-9pm Tue-Sat.
Parts of this old coaching inn, in the centre of Hartland, date back to the 14th century. It's still going strong, thanks to its characterful interior, welcoming atmosphere and supremely fresh, good-quality grub – ingredients might include Lundy Lamb, locally caught game and fish from Bidna Yard in Appledore.

Red Lion Hotel

The Quay, Clovelly, EX39 5TF (01237 431237, www.clovelly.co.uk). Lunch served noon-2.30pm, dinner served 6.30-8.30pm daily.
Clovelly lobster with garlic butter is typical of the local food served in the hotel restaurant. Less fancy fare is offered in the back bar, below ancient beams and old photographs. Rooms are also available (£124 double incl breakfast), with sea or harbour views.

DEVON

Where to stay

A few miles outside Hartland, and minutes from the South West Coast Path, the 32-room Elmscott Youth Hostel (01237 441276, www.elmscott. org.uk) occupies a Victorian schoolhouse. Another rugged, rural option, half a mile from Hartland Point, is West Titchberry Farm (01237 441287), a Devon longhouse with three bedrooms. Even closer to the action is Hartland Quay Hotel (01237 441218, www.hartlandquayhotel.com). Popular with walkers, it has 17 plain, clean bedrooms, most of which have en suite bathrooms and views across the Atlantic.

In Clovelly, the quayside Red Lion Hotel (*see p68*) is an alternative to the New Inn Hotel.

Donkey Shoe Cottage

21 High Street, Covelly, EX39 5TB (01237 431601, www.donkeyshoecottage.co.uk). Rates £54 double incl breakfast. No credit cards.
This pretty B&B on the cobbled high street oozes old-world charm. There are three bedrooms, including a family room, and a full English breakfast is served in the dining room.

East Dyke Farmhouse

Higher Clovelly, EX39 5RU (01237 431216, www.bedbreakfastclovelly.co.uk). Rates £60 double incl breakfast. No credit cards.
A 350-acre working farm, close to the remains of an Iron Age hill fort. The 19th-century farmhouse has open fires, exposed beams and polished flagstone floors; upstairs are three generously proportioned rooms. Breakfast, cooked on the Aga, is a veritable feast.

Now Inn Hotel

High Street, Clovelly, EX39 5TQ (01237 431303, www.clovelly.co.uk). Rates £102 double incl breakfast.
For the full Clovelly experience, book into the 17th-century New Inn, set in the heart of the village. Refurbished in the style of William Morris, it has eight light, elegantly appointed en suite bedrooms.

Stoke Barton Farm Campsite

Stoke, Hartland, EX39 6DU (01237 441238, www.westcountry-camping.co.uk). Rates £5.50; £3.50 reductions per night for 1 person.
A few fields back from the South West Coast Path, this is a site for lovers of low-key camping. There are spirit-lifting views over the Atlantic and Lundy (though beware the tent-lifting winds), flat pitches and a café, serving hearty breakfasts and, at weekends, clotted cream and jam-laden cream teas. It's all refreshingly free and easy: campfires are allowed, you can pitch where you like on the 12-acre site, and dogs and children are welcome.

Two Harton Manor

The Square, Hartland, EX39 6BL (01237 441670, www.twohartonmanor.co.uk). Rates £70 double incl breakfast. No credit cards.
This 400-year-old house is full of character – and bang in the centre of Hartland. The beautifully decorated double room has a four-poster, and there's also a twin and a sweet little single room; all have Wi-Fi access. Children and pets are welcome, and the owner also offers woodcut printing courses.

Yapham Coastal Cottages

Yapham, Hartland, EX39 6AN (01237 441916, www.yaphamcottages.co.uk). Rates £320-£820 per week for 2-4 people. No credit cards.
Seven acres of grounds surround the three small cottages at Yapham, with wide open views across the fields, towards the sea. Although the cottages are self-catering, meals can be delivered to the door.

GREAT TORRINGTON

Follow the main road south from Bideford towards Okehampton, alongside the River Torridge, and you'll reach Great Torrington. The town is perched on an inland cliff high above the river, and it's easy to see why the Normans built a castle here. Although the castle was destroyed, the town itself prospered, first from the wool trade then from glove-making – which, by the 19th century, was its biggest industry.

Great Torrington is best known, though, for the part it played in the Civil War. A Royalist stronghold, it was attacked by the Roundheads in 1646; their victory marked the end of Royalist resistance in the South West. It was a black day for the king's followers: some 200 of the captured soldiers were imprisoned in the church, where the Royalists had their gunpowder store. The inevitable explosion killed them all, and the cobbled mound outside the church is believed to be a mass grave. The anniversary of the battle is marked by a torchlight procession and firework display each February; see a recreation of events at Torrington 1646 (Castle Hill, 01805 626146, www.torrington-1646.co.uk, closed winter).

The 19th-century Market House on the main square marks the entrance to the glass-roofed Pannier Market ★. There's a parade of small shops (closed Sun) selling everything from old-fashioned sweets to antiques, along with a general market on Thursdays and Saturdays and bric-a-brac stalls on Fridays. South Street, leading off the square, is also good for a browse: second hand bookshop River Reads (no. 21, 01805 625888, www.river reads.co.uk, closed Sun) specialises in angling books and fishing tackle.

The ★ Plough Arts Centre (9-11 Fore Street, 01805 624624, www.plough-arts.org, Box office closed Mon, Sun) is the hub of the region's cultural scene. Film, theatre, dance, music, art and workshops all feature on the agenda.

If you're here for the August bank holiday, don't miss the spectacular conflagrations laid on by the Torrington Cavaliers, a local fundraising group. Themes change from year to year, but past efforts have included building a full-size replica of HMS *Victory*, which was then set aflame.

Just outside town are Dartington Crystal and the lovely RHS Rosemoor Garden (for both, *see p57*).

Where to eat & drink

In the centre of town, the Black Horse Inn (High Street, 01805 622121, www.blackhorse devon.co.uk) is a 16th-century hostelry with traditional food and three B&B rooms. The Green Lantern Café (no.6 High Street, 01805 622178, closed Sun) is another spot where time has stood still: a green-painted, no-frills establishment that's perfect for a pot of tea.

In the nearby hamlet of Frithelstock, the Clinton Arms (01805 623279, closed) is a classic country pub. Overlooking the village green and church, it's a pleasant place for a pint on a summer's afternoon.

Yarde Orchard ★

East Yarde, EX38 8QA (01805 601778, www.yarde-orchard.co.uk). Open/food served June-Sept 10.30am-5pm daily. Oct-May 10.30am-5pm Sat, Sun. No credit cards.

This eco-friendly café is right beside the Tarka Trail in the hamlet of East Yarde. Tables dot the orchard and terrace; on chilly days, retreat indoors to the warmth of the woodburner. Next door is a timber bunkhouse (£12 per person, £40 family room). Local beer and cider feature on the menu, and spirited special events include gigs and curry nights.

Where to stay

The bunkhouse at Yarde Orchard (*see above*) is impressively eco-friendly, with solar water heating and reedbed water treatment.

Huntshaw Barton

Huntshaw, EX38 7HH (01805 625736, www.huntshawbarton.com). Rates B&B £65-£90 double incl breakfast. Cottage £250-£595 per week for 4 people. No credit cards.

This Grade II-listed farmhouse is full of period features, including a 13th-century inglenook fireplace in the dining room. There are two en suite bedrooms, and a two-bedroom converted barn in the grounds; it's self-catering, but you'll find a cream tea awaiting on your arrival.

Rosemoor House Apartments

Great Torrington, EX38 8PH (01805 626810, www.rhs.org.uk/Gardens/Rosemoor). Rates £264-£770 per week for 2 people; £297-£975 per week for 4 people.

Guests at Rosemoor's three self-catering apartments, set in the wisteria-entwined main house, are afforded the rare privilege of exploring its glorious gardens (*see p57*) after the crowds have gone home. The apartments are elegantly decorated and comfortable.

RUBY COUNTRY

The rural inland area of north-west Devon has become known as Ruby Country, named after its Red Ruby Devon cattle. Hit hard by the foot-and-mouth crisis of 2001, it's an unspoiled landscape of open meadows, woodland and farmland, scattered with small villages and bisected by quiet, green lanes. The main centres are the two market towns of Hatherleigh and Holsworthy – but even here, life proceeds at an unhurried pace.

Hatherleigh

Dotted with cob and thatch cottages, the small market town of Hatherleigh dates back to Saxon times. The market still takes centre stage on Tuesday mornings, when the town is abuzz with activity from early morning till lunchtime. A colourful assortment of stalls sells a huge range of produce, crafts, clothes and bric-a-brac. In the covered area, an auctioneer rattles through various lots of furniture and household effects; there are also regular sheep and cattle auctions.

To escape the throng, stroll up Market Street and into the flower-filled, cobbled courtyard that houses Hatherleigh Pottery (01837 810624, www.hatherleighpottery.co.uk, closed Jan-Easter, Sun Easter-Dec). Further down the hill, in Bridge Street, is the Salar Gallery (01837 810940, closed Mon, Wed, Sun). Regular exhibitions showcase individual painters, sculptors and photographers, while the shop stocks a good range of crafts, prints and cards.

Around Hatherleigh

The area surrounding Hatherleigh is dotted with picturesque villages, largely overlooked by visitors. At Sampford Courtenay, five medieval stone crosses mark the five roads into the village, with its cob and thatch houses, 16th-century pub and elegant granite church. It was here, on the Whit Monday of 1549, that outraged villagers rose up in protest at the introduction of the Book of Common Prayer, which replaced the Latin prayer books, sparking the ill-fated Prayer Book Rebellion. A mile north is the tiny church of St Mary at Honeychurch, the core of which is almost unchanged since the 12th century.

Further north is the large hilltop village of Winkleigh, whose broad main street contains an ornate conduit, built in 1832. In the centre of the square is the venerable King's Arms

Woolacombe Beach. See p50.

(01837 83384, www.thekingsarmswinkleigh.co.uk); nearby, All Saints' Church has a remarkable wagon roof, supported by 70 carved angels.

Holsworthy

Close to the border with Cornwall, the small town of Holsworthy has a long history, and even merited a mention in the Domesday Book. Today, it is chiefly known as a market town. A good range of independent shops caters for everyday needs, while Wednesday's market fills the square with stalls.

Held each July, the week-long St Peter's Fair is a cherished tradition. Look out too for the vintage vehicle and engine rally in June. For more on the village, pop into Holsworthy Museum (Manor Offices, 01409 259337, www.devonmuseums. net/holsworthy, closed Sat, Sun).

Just to the north, on the road to Bideford, Lizzy's Larder (Blackberry Farm, Milton Damerel, 01409 261440, www.lizzyslarder.freeuk.com, closed Mon) is a fine farm shop and tearoom.

Where to eat & drink

Hatherleigh's Bridge Inn (Bridge Street, 01837 810085, www.thebridgeinnhatherleigh.co.uk) is a convivial local with a riverside patio. Another option is Hatherleigh Tea Rooms (Bridge Street, 01837 810693, closed Wed, closed Thur Nov-mid Feb).

Duke of York ★

Iddesleigh, EX19 8BG (01837 810253). Open 11am-11pm daily. Food served 11am-9pm daily.
An unspoilt village inn completely lacking in modern intrusions, once a favourite haunt of the poet Ted Hughes. The focus is on real ale, real cider and good food. The pub also offers B&B (£70 double incl breakfast).

Half Moon Inn

Sheepwash, EX21 5NE (01409 231376, www.half moonsheepwash.co.uk). Open 11am-2.30pm, 6-11pm Mon-Sat; noon-2.30pm, 7-11pm Sun. Lunch served noon-2pm daily. Dinner served 6.30-9pm Mon-Sat; 7-9pm Sun.
Not far from the River Torridge, the Half Moon Inn is one of Devon's original fishing inns. It has its own fishing rights, on a ten-mile stretch of the river, and can issue licences. A huge fireplace, polished horse brasses, wooden beamed ceilings and well-worn settles give the bar an authentic atmosphere; game features prominently on the menu. The inn has 13 bedrooms (£90 double incl breakfast) in the main building and annexe.

Where to stay

The Duke of York and the Half Moon Inn (for both, *see above*) also offer rooms.

Raymont House ★

49 Market Street, Hatherleigh, EX20 3JP (01837 810850, www.raymonthouse.co.uk). Rates £65 double incl breakfast. No credit cards.
The rooms at this dapper, Grade II-listed house are more boutique hotel than B&B. The biggest is the French Room, with its ornately carved bed, antique dressing table and pretty glass chandelier.

Thomas Roberts House

2 Higher Street, Hatherleigh, EX20 3JD (01837 811278, www.thomasrobertshouse.com). Rates £70 double incl breakfast. No credit cards.
Originally built as a school, this gracious Georgian building is now a superior B&B run by Charles and Anna Chalcraft. The three en suite rooms are prettily old-fashioned, without being fussy or twee.

DEVON

Dartmoor

Dartmoor's 368 square miles encompass the last remaining area of true wilderness in southern England. Much of the heather- and gorse-covered moorland is set on an immense granite plateau, and the rocky tors that characterise the landscape are the result of the weathering of the underlying granite over millions of years. The layer of peat that covers the higher parts of the moor gives rise to treacherous bogs and mires, memorably evoked in Conan Doyle's *The Hound of the Baskervilles*. But don't be deterred by Watson's fearful account of the 'green scummed pits and foul quagmire', or thoughts of the phantom hound: steer clear of the shooting ranges and the mires, and Dartmoor offers some of the best opportunities for walking you'll find anywhere in the country.

It's also a paradise for anyone interested in the past, with the largest concentration of prehistoric sites in Britain, from weathered hut circles to enigmatic stone rows. Centuries of mining and peat-cutting have also left their mark on the moors: you might come across the tumbledown walls of a medieval tinner's hut, or the ruins of an 19th-century mine, now clothed in heather and blending unobtrusively into the landscape. Stone crosses are another man-made feature, marking the ancient trackways that crossed the uplands, between the powerful abbeys.

Yet Dartmoor also has its gentler side. River valleys radiate from all sides of the moor; some sheltered and wooded, others open and heathery, with grassy banks overlooking fast-flowing streams. Idyllic picnic spots are not hard to find, and quaint tearooms and stone-built farmhouses offer classic cream teas. The quietly dignified, old-fashioned market towns and pretty hamlets, approached via winding country lanes, are also a far cry from the lonely, wind-scoured moors.

OKEHAMPTON & AROUND

Okehampton

Set at the foot of the high moor, Okehampton was established by the Normans soon after the Conquest; the motte and bailey castle that they built above the River Okement was extended over the centuries to become one of the largest castles in the South West. Today, only the ruins remain (01837 52844, www.english-heritage.org.uk, closed Oct-Mar), about a mile south-west of the town centre. Next to the castle, part of the medieval deer park is now a nature reserve: steep footpaths weave through the mossy oak trees, amid violets, bluebells and wood anemone, and you might still glimpse the odd deer.

In medieval times, the wool trade brought the town prosperity, and funded a clutch of fine buildings – you can't miss the 15th-century granite tower of St James' Chapel, which dominates the town centre. On the third Saturday of the month, the chapel square hosts a lively farmers' market. The town was also a staging post on the Exeter to Cornwall route, and a handful of dignified-looking coaching inns remain.

Just off the main shopping drag of Fore Street is the glass-roofed Victorian arcade – a sweetly old-fashioned affair, with an interesting mix of independent shops. Red Lion Yard also has some gems, including an organic bakery and a greengrocer's that sells locally made preserves and apple juice. Arts and crafts can be found at no.7, the Arts Gallery (01837 658820, www. theartsgallery.co.uk, closed Sun).

The best way to explore Okehampton is by following the Town Trail: pick up a leaflet at the Tourist Information Centre in the pretty cobbled courtyard behind the White Hart Hotel. Here, too, is the Museum of Dartmoor Life (01837 52295, closed mid Dec-Easter), housed in a former granary with a working waterwheel.

Although the mainline railway no longer runs, a scenic stretch of track has been reopened as the Dartmoor Railway (01837 55164, www.dartmoor-railway.co.uk), with trains heading west to the spectacular Meldon Viaduct and east to Sampford Courtenay. Another stretch of railway has become the Granite Way (*see p76*) cycle path; bikes can be hired from Okehampton Youth Hostel (*see p75*) next to the station, Okehampton Cycles (North Road, 01837 53248), Moor Cycles (6 the Arcade, Fore Street, 01837 659677, www.moorcycles.com) or Devon Cycle Hire (01837 861141, www.devon cyclehire.co.uk), in the village of Sourton Down.

Okehampton is at the foot of High Willhays and Yes Tor, the moor's highest points, so there is also

DEVON

some good – if strenuous – walking to be had. Bring OS Explorer Map OL28, and proper walking boots. The 36-mile West Devon Way also starts at Okehampton, tracing the western edge of Dartmoor all the way to Plymouth and passing through Lydford en route.

A few miles from Okehampton, Meldon Reservoir occupies a steep-sided Dartmoor valley and is popular with walkers; there's a car park near the dam, and a two-mile path all the way round. If you continue beyond the head of the reservoir up the West Okement Valley, after about a mile you'll reach Black Tor Copse, one of the three remaining ancient oak woodlands on Dartmoor.

The Beacon villages

Belstone, Sticklepath, South Zeal and South Tawton (collectively known as the Beacon Villages) lie just to the east of Okehampton, on the edge of the moor.

Belstone is a particularly good starting point for walks, with a parking area on the way into the village. It's an attractive, mellow-looking place, where the old stone stocks stand idle amid the daisies on the village green. To the west of the village, out on the moor, a jagged stone circle known as the Nine Maidens surrounds a Bronze Age burial cairn.

From Belstone, a glorious mile-and-a-half walk follows the valley of Belstone Cleave and the River Taw down to the village of Sticklepath; the footbridges en route are carved with quotations from *Tarka the Otter*. At Sticklepath, Finch Foundry (01837 840046, www.nationaltrust.org.uk, closed Tue & end Oct-late Mar) is the last working water-powered forge in England. Its enormous trip hammers can be seen in action (call to check demonstration times), and there's a small tearoom in the summerhouse; beyond it lies an old Quaker burial ground. The village is also home to the Taw River Inn (01837 840377, www.tawriver.co.uk), which has real ales on tap and a grassy beer garden.

South Zeal lies at the foot of the looming Cosdon Beacon – an excellent viewpoint for those steeled for a serious walk. Known for its copper mining heritage, the village centres on a medieval market cross, and the diminutive chapel of St Mary. The main visitor attraction in the small village of South Tawton is the Grade I-listed St Andrew's Church, and neighbouring Church House. Dating from the 1490s, the latter is a sturdy, thatched granite building where villagers once gathered for 'Church Ales' – beer-fuelled gatherings, used to raise money for the church's upkeep and to feed the poor. Now meticulously restored, the building is used for local events and exhibitions, and on occasion is open to the public in summer (01837 840418, www.thechurchhouse.org.uk).

Lydford

Just off the Okehampton to Tavistock road, the attractive village of Lydford now comprises one long street. Once an important town, its far-reaching parish boundaries still encompass most of the high moor, while its ruined castle is a grim reminder that this was once the site of the stannary courts and prison, for those who transgressed the tinners' laws. The iniquities of 'Lydford Law' became notorious: in his poem of the same name, William Browne wryly described 'How in the morn they hang and draw/And sit in judgment after'. The castle is flanked by the congenial Castle Inn (01822 820241, www.castleinnlydford.co.uk) and St Petrock's church, where a witty epitaph adorns the tombstone (now displayed inside the church) of a local watchmaker, who died in 1801.

Just down the road, Lydford Gorge (01822 820320, www.nationaltrust.org.uk, closed Nov-mid Feb) boasts a spectacular three-mile circular walk that follows the ravine alongside the river to reach the White Lady waterfall; it's slippery terrain, so wear walking boots. There are tearooms at both entrances, and a picnic area in the orchard.

Where to eat & drink

In Okehampton the choice includes the dolls' house-sized parlour at the Victorian Pantry Tearoom (The Courtyard, West Street, 01837 53988, closed Sun) for cream teas, heavenly cheese scones and no-nonsense hot lunches; and Vines Pizzeria (01837 52730, closed Mon, Tue, Sun) at the White Hart Hotel (*see below*). The pick of the eating options around Red Lion Yard is the Dovecote Café (01837 54662).

South of Okehampton, on the A386, the Bearslake Inn (01837 861334, www.bears lakeinn.com) was originally a Devon longhouse, accommodating its human and animal residents under one roof. Converted into a pub in 1959, it serves straightforward, local food.

In Belstone, the Tors (01837 840689, www. thetors.co.uk), serves a hearty pub grub menu. In South Zeal the imposing, 12th-century Oxenham Arms (01837 840244, www.theoxenhamarms. co.uk) oozes rural chic, with its log fire, polished flagstones and smart seasonal menu. The King's Arms just outside South Zeal(01837 840300) serves real ales. The ivy-draped Seven Stars Inn (01837 840292, closed Mon) in South Tawton, meanwhile, does a fine line in Devonshire real ales and ciders, along with filling mains.

Pickled Walnut

Fore Street, Okehampton, EX20 1DL (01837 54242, www.pickledwalnut.net). Lunch served 11am-3pm Tue-Sat. Dinner served 7-10pm Thur-Sat.
This cellar restaurant kicks off with own-made muesli, pancakes with maple syrup and a fried breakfast. Simple lunches are followed by evening meals such as ricotta ravioli with sage butter. An eclectic events programme ranges from art exhibitions to classical guitar performances.

Where to stay

The Tors offers B&B, as does the Bearslake Inn (for both, *see above*) – the latter's Hayloft room, with its kingsize bed and views over the garden and the moors, is particularly charming.

Okehampton Castle. See p73.

In Okehampton, the 18th-century White Hart Hotel (Fore Street, 01837 52730, www.thewhitehart-hotel.com) is a central, serviceable place to stay, with a bar, a restaurant and a pizzeria.

South Zeal's Oxenham Arms (*see left*) has seven plushly decorated rooms that combine modern comforts with antique flourishes – several rooms have fine four-posters – and there's a treatment room too. For an even more upmarket option, try Lewtrenchard Manor (Lewdown, 01566 783222, www.lewtrenchard.co.uk) a Jacobean mansion set in a tranquil wooded valley.

Dartmoor Inn

Lydford, EX20 4AY (01822 820221, www.dartmoor inn.com). Rates £120 double incl breakfast.

Think *Country Living* does Dartmoor with a touch of New England and a whiff of Scandinavia. This delightful hostelry has three double bedrooms, painted in calm pastel hues and artfully decorated with antiques and fresh, pretty fabrics. Note that there are no TVs; instead, you get a Roberts radio. Downstairs, sample local ales and classy comfort food in the bar, warmed by a roaring log fire, or cosy up in one of the small, stylish dining areas. One room is given over to a little shop; handmade quilts, Swedish glassware and jewellery, all sourced by the hotel's interiors-savvy owner.

Fox & Hounds Hotel

Lydford, EX20 4HF (01822 820206, www.foxand houndshotel.com). Rates Tent £6.50 for 2 people; camping barn £8 per person; hotel £70-£75 double.

Something of a jack of all trades, the Fox & Hounds Hotel offers nine simple rooms (three of which are in the adjacent cottage), a no-frills camping barn (extra charges apply for linen and breakfast) and a large campsite, with direct access to the moor. There's unpretentious bar food and a seasonal restaurant menu featuring a selection of local fish and meat.

Knole Farm

Bridestowe, EX20 4HA (01837 861241, www.knole farm-dartmoor-holidays.co.uk). Rates £60 double incl breakfast.

A curving avenue of beeches provides a glorious approach to this Victorian farmhouse, perched on the edge of Dartmoor. The B&B is an old-school affair, with comfortably chintzy decor, a log fire in the lounge and evening meals by advance request (bring your own wine, as it's not licensed).

Okehampton Youth Hostel

Klondyke Road, Okehampton, EX20 1EW (0845 371 9651, www.yha.org.uk). Rates from £13.95 per person, £37.90 double.

Things to do

OKEHAMPTON & AROUND

Adventure Okehampton
Klondyke Road, EX20 1EW (01837 53916, www.adventureokehampton.com). Open 24hrs daily. Activities varies, check website for details.
Adventure Okehampton – based at Okehampton Youth Hostel – runs two outdoor activity centres, with a focus on groups and families. Kayaking, gorge scrambling and bushcraft weekends feature on the action-packed agenda.

Granite Way
www.devon.gov.uk.
Between Okehampton and Lydford, a disused stretch of railway line has become the Granite Way, forming part of the Devon Coast to Coast route. The 11-mile path is mainly off-road, with lovely views of the moor, and crosses two huge viaducts at Meldon and Lake.

Skaigh Stables
Belstone, EX20 1RD (01837 840917, www.skaighstables.co.uk). Open Easter-Oct 10am-4.30pm daily. Closed Nov-Easter. Cost £60 6hrs; £36 morning/afternoon ride; £18 per hr. No credit cards.
Riding across the moors is gloriously exhilarating, whatever your level of ability. Skaigh Stables offers rides of various lengths, for both experienced and novice horse riders.

TAVISTOCK & AROUND

Cholwell Riding Stables
Mary Tavy, PL19 9QG (01822 810526). Open 10am-3.15pm daily. Cost £29 2hrs; £23 90mins; £16 1hr. No credit cards.
The stables at Cholwell Farm offer moorland rides, as well as tuition; book well ahead in peak season.

Drake's Trail
www.drakestrail.co.uk
Opened in 2009, this network of off-road cycling and walking routes includes a cycle path between Tavistock and Plymouth. It forms part of the longer National Cycle Network Route 27, which crosses Devon from coast to coast. Podcasts describing places of interest along the route can be downloaded at www.drakestrail.co.uk.

Wharf Arts Centre
Canal Road, Tavistock, PL19 8AT (01822 611166, www.tavistockwharf.com). Open Box office 11.15am-2.15pm; 11.15am-2.15pm, 6-8pm Tue-Sat. Coffee shop 10am-4.30pm Mon-Fri; 10am-4pm Sat. Gallery 10am-4.30pm, 6-8pm Mon-Sat. Bar open 1hr before film or live event.
Set between the river and the canal, the Wharf Arts Centre incorporates a theatre, concert hall, cinema and art gallery. There's also a bar and a coffee shop, with a tranquil waterside terrace.

CHAGFORD, MORETONHAMPSTEAD & AROUND

Chagford Pool
Rushford, Chagford, TQ13 8BB (01647 432929, www.chagfordpool.co.uk). Open May-Sept 8-9am

Mon; 2-6pm Tue; 2-6pm Wed, Thur, Sat, Sun; 1-2pm, 2-6pm Fri. Admission £3.20; £1-£1.80 reductions.
Chagford's open-air swimming pool, on the edge of the town near Rushford Mill, is unusual in that it is fed by river water. Originally created from a duck pond beside the river, it has been in use for three-quarters of a century; there can be few more scenic spots to cool off after a moorland walk.

Fernworthy Reservoir ★
Fernworthy, nr Chagford (01647 277587, www.sw lakestrust.org.uk). Open 24hrs daily. Fishing season Mar-Oct. Admission free. Fishing £12; £3-£10 reductions. No credit cards.
Around ten minutes' drive from Chagford, Fernworthy Reservoir is home to a rich array of birdlife. A three-mile walk loops around the lake, and there's a car park with toilets and a picnic area beside the water. The area below the dam is particularly attractive when the rhododendrons are in flower in late May. Inexpensive fly-fishing permits are available from the kiosk, for those keen to get their hands on the resident brown trout.

BOVEY TRACEY & AROUND

Becky Falls
Manaton, Newton Abbot, TQ13 9UG (01647 221259, www.beckyfalls.com). Open mid Feb-Nov call to check opening hours. Admission £6.50-£6.95; £5.50-£5.95 reductions; £20-£22 family.
Famed for its eponymous waterfalls, this woodland park is run as a family attraction, with an entrance fee and assorted entertainments, ranging from a letterboxing challenge to animal feeding sessions involving the resident rabbits, miniature Shetland ponies and, in season, lambs.

ASHBURTON, BUCKFASTLEIGH & WIDECOMBE-IN-THE-MOOR

Dartmoor Llama Walks
Newton Abbot, TQ13 7PJ (01364 631481, www.dartmoorllamawalks.co.uk). Open by prior arrangement only. Rates £30 2hrs. No credit cards.
For a walk with a difference, try one of these guided treks with your own llama companion – who will also obligingly carry your rucksack. The walks explore moorland areas around Widecombe, and include a picnic or cream tea.

DEVON

Dartmoor Riding Centre
Widecombe-in-the-Moor, TQ13 7TF (01364 621281, www.dartmoorstables.com). Rides Summer 10am. Winter 9.30am. Cost £50 2hrs; £35 1hr.
This British Horse Society-approved centre offers treks on Dartmoor for novice and experienced riders, as well as riding lessons.

River Dart Country Park
Ashburton, TQ13 7NP (01364 652511, www.river dart.co.uk). Open Summer 10am-dusk daily. Winter 8am-5pm Sat, Sun. Admission Summer £6.75; free-£3 reductions. Winter £5 per car. Activity prices vary.
This 90-acre park provides a scenic backdrop for a heady array of outdoor activities, from rock-climbing and canoeing to water-zorbing; check the website for details. There's also riverside walks, zip wires and adventure playgrounds, along with a campsite.

South Devon Railway
The Station, Dart Bridge Road, Buckfastleigh, TQ11 0DZ (0845 345 1466, www.southdevonrailway. co.uk). Timetable/tickets call or check website.
The South Devon Railway's steam trains chug along a scenic seven-mile route, through the River Dart valley to Totnes. There's a museum at Buckfastleigh with historic locomotives and rolling stock, a picnic area and a café. On selected days, a shiny vintage double-decker bus runs between the station, the town and Buckfast Abbey, and is free to train ticket-holders.

PRINCETOWN, POSTBRIDGE & CENTRAL DARTMOOR

Burrator Reservoir
Nr Yelverton (01822 855700, www.swlakestrust. org.uk). Open 24hrs daily. Admission free.
Just off the B3212 south of Princetown, towards Yelverton, a minor road leads to the wooded shores of Burrator Reservoir. Footpaths follow the lakeside, or you can walk up to Sheeps Tor on the south side for great views. There's parking near the dam and also at Norsworthy Bridge, at the top end of the reservoir. In summer you'll find ice-cream vans at both places.

WEST OF DARTMOOR

Roadford Lake
Between Okehampton & Launceston, EX20 4QS (Café 01566 784859, Angling & Watersports Centre 01409 211507, www.swlakestrust.org.uk). Open Café 11am-5pm daily. Angling & Watersports Centre Summer 10am-5pm daily. Winter 10am-5pm Sat, Sun.
Just off the A30, heading towards Launceston, this large reservoir is a magnet for watersports enthusiasts, with sailing, rowing, canoeing and windsurfing on offer. Tuition is available, and boats and equipment can be hired. The lake is stocked with brown trout, and anglers can buy day permits at the Angling and Watersports Centre. On the other side of the lake is a visitors' centre and café, both open daily. A network of footpaths and a four-mile cycle track, which can be linked to country lanes to make a longer route, wind through the woodland and along the shore of the lake.

Attractively housed in a Victorian railway goods shed, the Okehampton outpost of the YHA has good facilities (pool and table tennis in the lounge, a decent self-catering kitchen) and a brilliant activity centre (*see left*), offering everything from gorge-scrambling to archery.

TAVISTOCK & AROUND

Tavistock
Its celebrated Pannier Market and attractive town centre, along with its location on the western edge of Dartmoor, make Tavistock a popular place with visitors. The town grew up around its powerful Benedictine abbey, founded in the tenth century; after the dissolution of the monasteries, the abbey's greenish Hurdwick stone was commandeered for many of Tavistock's secular buildings.

Mining has long played a part in the town's fortunes, thanks to the copper, lead, silver, zinc and tin lodes found around Dartmoor and the Tamar Valley. In the Middle Ages, Tavistock was one of four stannary towns where Dartmoor tin was weighed and valued; today, it is part of the Tamar Valley World Heritage Site.

In the mid-19th century, the seventh Duke of Bedford remodelled the town, building cottages for the mine workers and creating the covered Pannier Market and spacious Bedford Square, with its handsome Victorian town hall. On the corner of the square, next to St Eustachius' Church, stand the graceful ruins of the abbey cloisters. The church itself is a 15th-century construction, enlarged and altered over the centuries and containing some beautiful carvings. Opposite, next to the Bedford Hotel, stands a striking, though crumbling, structure known as Betsy Grimbal's Tower – named, some say, for an unfortunate young woman who was thrown from its walls by a jealous monk. The square is also home to Tavistock Museum (01822 612546, closed end Oct-Easter), which houses displays on local history, the mining industry and the town's most illustrious son, Sir Francis Drake, whose statue loftily surveys the traffic at the bottom of Plymouth Road.

A riverside path along the Tavy affords lovely views of the town's historic buildings, and, in particular, the abbey bridge and weir. Alternatively, take a stroll by the Tavistock Canal, which once linked Tavistock with Morwellham Quay on the River Tamar.

The famous Pannier Market (01822 611003, www.tavistockpanniermarket.co.uk) dates back to 1105, when a royal charter was granted. Occupying the grand, 19th-century market hall, it is open from Tuesday to Saturday, with different goods sold on specific days. Tuesdays is antiques and bric-a-brac, while Friday is produce; look out for the WI's home-made cakes. Permanent traders include BagsAnd (www.bagsand.com), whose Fairtrade wares include some sumptuously strokable velvet bags, and Sponzi's (01822 614247, closed Mon) – a delightful Italian deli, run by the affable Giovanni

DEVON

Haytor Rocks. See p88.

DEVON

Places to visit

TAVISTOCK & AROUND

Buckland Abbey
Yelverton, PL20 6EY (01822 853607,
www.nationaltrust.org.uk/buckland). Open mid Feb-Jan
days/times vary; check website for details. Admission
£8.20; £4.10 reductions.
Originally a Cistercian abbey, and later home to
Tavistock-born Sir Francis Drake, Buckland Abbey is
now owned by the National Trust. It houses interactive
displays on Devon's seafaring history, along with
Drake's Drum – said to sound when England is in grave
peril. There's also a magnificent tithe barn, and an
Elizabethan garden.

Garden House ★
Buckland Monachorum, PL20 7LQ (01822 854769,
www.thegardenhouse.org.uk). Open Feb 11am-4pm
Sat, Sun. Mar-Oct 10.30am-5pm daily. Admission
£6; £2.50 reductions.
Run by a charitable trust, this eight-acre garden is a
magical place, brimming with colour and life. Highlights
include the walled garden, with its 16th-century tower,
the wild profusion of the cottage garden, dotted with
foxgloves, poppies and forget-me-nots, and the richly
hued Acer Glade (at its best in autumn). Tearooms
can be found in the 18th-century vicarage.

Yelverton Paperweight Centre
Leg O'Mutton, Yelverton, PL20 6AD (01822
854250, www.paperweightcentre.co.uk). Open
Apr-Oct 10.30am-5pm daily. Admission free.
Fans of quirky museums will relish Yelverton
Paperweight Centre, which has an astonishing
collection of antique and modern paperweights
for viewing and for sale.

CHAGFORD, MORETONHAMPSTEAD & AROUND

Castle Drogo ★
Drewsteignton, EX6 6PB (01647 433306,
www.nationaltrust.org.uk/castledrogo). Open times
vary, check website for details. Admission Castle &
Garden £7.80; £3.90 reductions; £11.70-£19.60
family. Garden only £5; £2.75 reductions.
The last castle to be built in England (it dates from the
1930s), this austere, mock-medieval granite edifice
perches high above the Teign Gorge. Designed by Sir
Edwin Lutyens at the behest of a self-made millionaire,
it is surrounded by formal gardens and woodland walks.
The café is open throughout the day.

Miniature Pony Centre
Wormhill Farm, North Bovey, TQ13 8RG (01647
432400, www.miniatureponycentre.com). Open late
Mar-Nov 10.30am-4.30pm daily (closes 5pm July,
Aug). Admission £6.95; £5.50-£5.95 reductions;
£24 family.
The centre's miniature donkeys and Shetland ponies
exert a powerful appeal for small visitors, as does the
whirl of wholesome activities (pony-grooming, pond
dipping, duck-feeding and more). There's also a pets'
paddock, with rabbits, chipmunks, mice and guinea
pigs, various play areas, trampolines and a cafeteria.
Look out, too, for the daily birds of prey display.

Stone Lane Gardens
Stone Farm, Chagford, TQ13 8JU (01647 231311,
www.mythicgarden.eclipse.co.uk). Open 2-6pm daily.
Exhibition Apr-Oct 2-6pm daily. Admission Garden &
Exhibition £4.50; £2.50 reductions. Garden only £3;
£2 reductions. No credit cards.
Every summer, this five-acre arboretum becomes
a backdrop for the work of West Country sculptors,
blending art and nature to great – and often surprising
– effect. As you wander between the birches and
alders, you might find anything from a leggy metal
flamingo to a group of abstract, undulating stone
torsos, looming amid the trees.

BOVEY TRACEY & AROUND

Canonteign Falls
Christow, EX6 7NT (01647 252434, www.canonteign
falls.co.uk). Open end Mar-Nov 10am-4.30pm daily
(last entry 3pm). Admission £5.75; £4.50-£5
reductions.
Three scenic walks wend their way around the lakes,
meadows, woodland and wetlands of this lovely estate.
The most exciting path leads through the shady secret
garden and fern dell to the 220-foot falls; involving
a winding set of 90 steps, constructed in Victorian
times, it's only for the stout of shoe and firm of
purpose. If the children still have energy to burn,
there's a play area with trampolines and an assault
course. Bring a picnic.

Devon Guild of Craftsmen
Riverside Mill, Bovey Tracey, TQ13 9AF (01626
832223, www.crafts.org.uk). Open 10.30am-
5pm daily.
Contemporary crafts, art and design are showcased
in the Craftsmen's headquarters, set in a restored mill
by the river. There's a lively programme of exhibitions,
and plenty of pieces to buy in the shop, which sells
everything from prints, handmade jewellery and textiles
to furniture and sculpture. The Terrace Café has a
rooftop terrace with lovely views.

House of Marbles
The Old Pottery, Pottery Road, Bovey Tracey,
TQ13 9DS (01626 835285, www.houseofmarbles.
com). Open 9am-5pm Mon-Sat; 10am-5pm Sun.
Admission free.
Housed in an 18th-century pottery, the glass and
games factory incorporates a splendid Marble
Museum. Along with what is reputedly the largest
collection of marbles in the world, visitors can gawp
at some mesmerising marble runs. The main shop
is a wonderland of marbles, games, toys and puzzles,
and in the glass-blowing factory you can watch the
craftsmen at work from a viewing platform.

Parke Estate
Bovey Tracey, TQ13 9JQ (01626 834748,
www.nationaltrust.org.uk/parkeestate).
Open 24hrs daily. Admission free.
The Parke Estate belongs to the National Trust,
and most of it is open to the public on a free-access
basis. The circular riverside walk is beautiful, especially
in spring, when the bluebells and wood anemone
are in bloom.

Stover Country Park
Stover, TQ12 6QG (01626 835236).
Open 24hrs daily. Admission free.
Encompassing over 100 acres of woodland, heath and marshland, with Stover Lake at its centre, the park is home to a wealth of wildlife. Squirrels dart through the branches and lizards bask on the heathland; sharp-eyed visitors might also glimpse a graceful roe deer, framed by the trees. For a bird's-eye view of the flora and fauna, walk through the lower tree canopy on the sturdy aerial walkway. For more on the flora and fauna, visit the interpretation centre.

ASHBURTON, BUCKFASTLEIGH & WIDECOMBE-IN-THE-MOOR

Buckfast Abbey
Buckfastleigh, TQ11 0EE (01364 645500, www. buckfast.org.uk). Open Church (outside service times) 9am-6pm Mon-Thur; 10am-6pm Fri; noon-6pm Sun. Admission free.
The original abbey was founded in the 11th century, but fell into ruin after the dissolution of the monasteries. At the turn of the 20th century, a community of Benedictine monks began to painstakingly rebuild it; in 1932, the church was finally consecrated. Now a living monastery once again, it is also a visitor attraction, with an exhibition on the abbey's history, three shops and a restaurant. The gardens are based on medieval plans, and include an aromatic lavender garden and a medicinal herb garden.

Hill House Gardens & Nursery
Landscove, TQ13 7LY (01803 762273, www.hill housenursery.co.uk). Open 11am-5pm daily, closed 2wks Christmas. Admission free.
This old vicarage garden is at its peak in late summer, when it is a tapestry of colour. The attached nursery includes glasshouses specialising in unusual and exotic plants, and there's a licensed tearoom which serves delicious scones.

Pennywell Farm & Wildlife Centre
Buckfastleigh, TQ11 0LT (01364 642023, www.pennywellfarm.co.uk). Open mid Feb-Oct 10am-5pm daily. Admission £9.95; £6.95 reductions.
It's all action at Pennywell, which keeps its young visitors occupied with half-hourly activities, a miniature railway, giant trampolines, a willow maze and covered and outdoor play areas. Then there are the animals – including the scene-stealing miniature pigs, which the children will want to smuggle home. Refreshments are of the fast food variety, so bring a picnic.

PRINCETOWN, POSTBRIDGE & CENTRAL DARTMOOR

Dartmoor Prison Museum
Princetown, PL20 6RR (01822 322130, www. dartmoor-prison.co.uk). Open 9.30am-4.30pm Mon-Thur, Sat; 9.30am-4pm Fri, Sat. Admission £2.50; £1.50 reductions.
Next door to the prison, this intriguing museum gives an insight into the history of the building, and its varied inmates over the years. The Black Museum is a highlight for the macabre-minded, with its collection of crudely made confiscated weapons, home-made bongs and escape gear (including the time-honoured classic of knotted bedsheets).

Powdermills Pottery
Nr Postbridge, PL20 6SP (01822 880263, www.powdermillspottery.com). Open Easter-mid Oct 10am-5pm daily. Late Oct-Easter 10am-5pm Sat, Sun.
This pottery studio and craft shop is housed in part of a 19th-century gunpowder works. The shop has some lovely products – not only pottery, but a range of crafts. In summer, cream teas are served in the courtyard.

IVYBRIDGE & SOUTH BRENT

Delamore Gallery
Cornwood, Ivybridge, PL21 9QT (01752 837711, www.delamore-art.co.uk). Exhibition May 10.30am-4.30pm daily. Admission £5; free reductions.
Each May, this country house estate hosts an exhibition of painting and sculpture in the house and its lovely gardens, in aid of a chosen charity.

Lukesland Gardens ★
Harford, Ivybridge, PL21 0JF (01752 691749, www.lukesland.co.uk). Open Apr-June 2-6pm Wed, Sun. Mid Oct-mid Nov 11am-4pm Wed, Sun. Admission £4.50; free under-16s. No credit cards.
This 24-acre woodland garden occupies a beautiful, sheltered little valley, with a stream cascading through ponds and over waterfalls towards the River Erme. It has some impressive magnolias flowering in spring, and gorgeous autumn colours, reflected in the water. There's a treasure trail for children in the garden, and teas and light refreshments are served in the Old Dilliard Room, or out on the patio.

Two Moors Way
www.devon.gov.uk/walking/two_moors_way.html.
Ivybridge is at the southern end of the Two Moors Way, a 103-mile route across Exmoor and Dartmoor. (From here, it links with the Erme-Plym Trail to create a coast-to-coast route.) For a short circular walk on the Two Moors Way, follow the signs from the town centre up to the moor gate, then head due east to the rocks on Western Beacon; from here, the view extends right across South Devon to the coast. Now follow the ridge northwards over Butterdon Hill, then down to join a clearly defined track (the former Redlake tramway); turn left and follow the track back to the moor gate.

WEST OF DARTMOOR

Dingles Fairground Heritage Centre
Milford, PL16 0AT (01566 783425, www.fairground-heritage.org.uk). Open mid Mar-Nov 10.30am-4.30pm Mon, Thur-Sun (daily during school hols). Nov-mid Dec 10.30am-4.30pm Sat, Sun. Admission £7; free-£5 reductions.
Gorgeously painted carousels, showman's wagons and rides are on display at this unique museum, devoted to the history of funfairs. A highlight is the Rodeo Switchback with its wooden cowboy figures, dating from the 1880s, which has been restored to working order. You may be able to try some of the vintage rides and there are also steam engines and historical machinery on display.

DEVON

Cleave Inn. See p88.

Sponziello. Just outside the market, Country Cheeses (Market Road, 01822 615035, www. countrycheeses.co.uk) is a fragrant emporium of West Country cheeses, ranging from nettle-covered Cornish yarg to creamy, crumbly Beenleigh blue.

Tucked away down Church Lane, you'll find ash-glazed ceramic bowls, recycled glass jewellery and hand-crafted leather bags at South West Crafts (01822 612689, www.southwestcrafts.co.uk). In Duke Street, the ArtFrame Gallery (no.17, 01822 611091, www.artframegallery.co.uk) sells fine art, ceramics and bronze sculptures as well as limited edition prints – easy on the eye, if not the pocket. Just off Brook Street, quaint Paddons Row is lined with delightful small-scale shops.

Roborough Down, to the south of Tavistock and west of the A386, is perfect for a gentle stroll, affording superb views of south-west Dartmoor without any challenging gradients. There are car parks at Bedford Bridge and Grenofen Bridge, and various parking areas on the minor roads across the down. For a scenic drive, the B3357 across Dartmoor to Two Bridges and on to Ashburton on the eastern side is hard to beat, and includes the Merrivale stone rows (*see p91*).

Between Roborough Down and the River Tavy is the village of Buckland Monachorum, best known for its abbey (*see p80*) and the verdant Garden House (*see p80*). Sporting a fine pinnacled tower, the church of St Andrew dates from the 15th century. Inside, a pew bears a carving of the *Golden Hind*; Sir Francis Drake bought Buckland

Abbey in 1581. Next to the church, the 12th-century Drake Manor Inn (*see p83*) is a good spot to toast the great man's memory.

The Tavy Valley

North-east of Tavistock are the villages of Mary Tavy and Peter Tavy (named for their respective churches, both of which are worth a visit, and the river). Just to the north of Mary Tavy, beside the A386, is the striking ruined engine house of Wheal Betsy, once a lead, silver and zinc mine. It's an easy walk along the bridleway from St Mary's church to Peter Tavy, where you can stop for lunch and a half or two of West Country ale in the cosy, beamed Peter Tavy Inn (01822 810348, www. petertavyinn.com).

Further up the valley, the River Tavy flows through the spectacular Tavy Cleave; park at Lane End and walk north to reach the leat (water channel) then turn right and follow the leat into the Cleave. There are large rock slabs to scramble over and pools to paddle in, but don't attempt this when the river is in spate.

Brent Tor

Perched on the volcanic outcrop of Brent Tor, five miles north of Tavistock, the Church of St Michael de Rupe (Saint Michael of the Rock) is a landmark for miles around. Some say it was built by a seafaring merchant, in gratitude at being spared from shipwreck; another legend has it that the Devil tried to thwart the church's construction,

moving the stones to a seemingly impossible site to build on. What is certain is that there has been a church here since the 12th century, and it's still in regular use today. A footpath winds its way up to the church from the nearby car park; the views over Dartmoor and west into Cornwall are outstanding.

Where to eat & drink

Tavistock has plenty of restaurants and cafés, and endless opportunities to sample a cream tea: indeed, 11th-century manuscripts suggest that they originated at Tavistock Abbey, where monks fed travellers with bread, clotted cream and preserves.

Hidden away at the end of Paddons Row, Donella's (no.5, 01822 612888, closed Sun) is a friendly spot for afternoon tea or a light lunch, with a handful of tables on the wooden decking out front. The riverside terrace at the East Gate Café & Brasserie (3 Market Road, 01822 615665) is another appealing hideaway, while Duke's Coffee House (8-11 Pannier Market, 01822 613718, closed Sun) is a popular locals' meeting place. On West Street, at the Cornish Arms (01822 612145), Monterey Jack's is famed for its enjoyable – if slightly incongruous – Mexican specials, and is a hit with families.

Drake Manor Inn ★
Buckland Monachorum, PL20 7NA (01822 853892, www.drakemanorinn.co.uk). Open 11.30am-2.30pm
Mon-Thur; 11.30am-2.30pm, 6.30-11.30pm Fri; 11.30am-3pm, 6.30-11.30pm Sat; noon-11pm Sun. Lunch served noon-2pm daily. Dinner served 7-10pm Mon-Sat; 7-9.30pm Sun.
In the centre of Buckland Monachorum, this unspoilt, centuries-old pub serves local real ales, malt whiskies and an extensive bar menu. The pretty little garden is ideal for enjoying a sundowner or a summer lunch; if you can't tear yourself away, there's an unexpectedly modish little oak-beamed suite upstairs, available for B&B (£80) or self-catering stays (from £150 for 2 nights).

Horn of Plenty
Gulworthy, PL19 8JD (01822 832528, www.the hornofplenty.co.uk). Lunch served noon-2pm, dinner served 7-9.30pm daily. Rates £120-£200 double incl breakfast.
People travel for miles to dine at this elegant Georgian country house hotel, thanks to chef and co-owner Peter Gorton's assured, high-end cuisine. Assembled with a scrupulous commitment to local suppliers, this is light, elegant fare: steamed red mullet on a sautéed crab cake to start, perhaps, followed by roast loin of Devonshire lamb with wild mushroom salsa and basil mash. Monday's 'pot luck' night offers three courses for £28.

Robertson's Café & Pizzeria
4-8 Pepper Street, Tavistock, PL19 0BD (01822 612117, www.robertsonsorganic.co.uk). Open 9am-4pm Mon-Wed; 9am-9pm Thur-Sat.
This superior café impresses by dint of its attention to detail. The sandwiches are made from bread baked that morning,

FIVE DEVON FOLLIES

Belvedere Tower

Standing proud on Hatherleigh Common, just outside Hatherleigh (see p70) in north Devon, this crenellated brick and stone structure was built in 1879 to celebrate George Pearse, a celebrated marksman and winner of the Queen's Prize for rifle shooting. Later used as a wartime lookout, it is certainly a good viewpoint: it's said that 12 church spires can be seen from here.

Haldon Belvedere

Also known as Lawrence Castle, this curious Grade II-listed white triangular tower with castellated turrets dates from 1788. It was built as a memorial to Major-General Stringer Lawrence, founder of the Indian army. Perched on Great Haldon Hill, some six miles south of Exeter (see p96), it offers a panoramic view over the Exe Valley and can be seen for miles around. These days it is a popular venue for weddings, while the top floor has been converted into a lavishly appointed little holiday apartment (01392 833668, www.haldonbelvedere.co.uk), with access to the roof terrace. The rest of the building is open to the public on Sunday and bank holiday afternoons (Feb-Oct).

The Pimple

Walkers exploring Whitchurch Down, just outside Tavistock (see p77), may encounter the Pimple: a small, triangular stone structure with a pointed roof, built in 1914. Despite its unflattering name, it is thought to be the work of Sir Edwin Lutyens, and marks the entrance to an underground reservoir (the interior is closed to the public). It also acts as a kind of gazebo, with seats around the edge from which you can admire the view.

The Pleasure House

Silhouetted against the sky, on the cliffs near Hartland Quay (see p67) in north Devon, is the ruin of a small square stone building with a broad arch in one wall. Built in the late 16th century on the Hartland Abbey estate, its purpose is a mystery: it might have been a lookout, a summer house, a chapel or a warrener's house.

The Toot & the Labyrinth

There are several buildings that might be called follies on the Tapeley Park estate (see p57), near Bideford in north Devon. One is a small pavilion with brick pillars, a herringbone floor and a silver ball atop the roof; sweetly dubbed the Toot, it dates from the estate's early days. In contrast is a modern folly, the Labyrinth: a maze-like pattern on the ground constructed in stone from the ruins of a former obelisk.

while soup and salad ingredients hail from named local suppliers, or the owners' organic garden. The pizzas are a treat, and there's a good children's menu.

Where to stay

The Horn of Plenty (see p83) is a delightful place to stay. The interiors are luxurious but unfussy; glorious views over the countryside are another draw. Drake Manor Inn (see p83) in Buckland Monachorum is another option.

At Kingfisher Cottage (Mount Tavy Road, Tavistock, 01822 613801), a cosy B&B, guests can breakfast in a conservatory overlooking the river. Another riverside option is Harford Bridge Holiday Park (Peter Tavy, 01822 810349, www.harfordbridge.co.uk), which accepts tents, motor homes and touring caravans, and has static vans for hire.

In Horrabridge, the Old School Guest House (Whitchurch Road, 01822 852437, www.theold schoolguesthouse.co.uk) is set in a lovely Victorian schoolhouse. The decor may be slightly dated, but the en suite bedrooms are equipped with all manner of mod cons (free Wi-Fi, digital radios and DVD players); downstairs, there are big sofas in the guest lounge, and a log fire in winter. Burnville Farm (Brentor, 01822 820443, www.burnville.co.uk) has two B&B rooms and four self-catering cottages in elegant surroundings with a tennis court and outdoor heated swimming pool.

Browns Hotel

80 West Street, Tavistock, PL19 8AQ (01822 618686, www.brownsdevon.co.uk). Rates £79-£249 double incl breakfast.
This 17th-century coaching inn is a dependable – and popular – bet for a comfortable stay and a good dinner. The decor is elegantly traditional, and rooms are well equipped, with Molton Brown toiletries, DVD players, Wi-Fi and Egyptian cotton bedding. There's smart dining in the restaurant, and a cheaper, less formal brasserie menu, served in the bar and Orangery.

Mount Tavy Cottage

Tavistock, PL19 9JL (01822 614253, www.mounttavy.co.uk). Rates £70 double incl breakfast. Self-catering £180-£250 per week, for 2 people.
Rural retreats don't come much lovelier than this 250-year-old former gardener's cottage. For a start, it's set in ten acres of land, with its own lake, organic walled garden, beehives and cider orchard. A mix of B&B rooms and self-catering accommodation is divided between the main cottage, the Garden Studios, the two-bedroom Wood Shed and the teeny-tiny Pump House, overlooking the lake.

Sampford Manor

Sampford Spiney, PL20 6LH (01822 853442). Rates £48-£70 double. No credit cards.
An ancient manor house now run as a B&B and smallholding, incorporating a growing herd of alpacas. The slate floors, beamed ceilings and mullioned windows ooze history, while the three en suite rooms have lovely views over the moors, which stretch beyond the garden gate. Dogs are welcome, as are horses.

CHAGFORD, MORETONHAMPSTEAD & AROUND

Chagford

It would be hard to find a more idyllic location than that of Chagford. Lying at the foot of Meldon Hill, with the River Teign just a stone's throw away, its views extend across the river to the uplands of north Dartmoor. Chagford grew in importance in medieval times, thanks to the wool trade and tin mining, and was one of Devon's four stannary towns, where Dartmoor tin was weighed and valued.

It's an appealing place, with handsome granite buildings and a central square – home to the octagonal Market House, better known as the Pepperpot. Just off the square stands St Michael's Church; it was here, in 1641, that Mary Whiddon was shot dead on her wedding day by a spurned suitor, an event that inspired the famous scene in *Lorna Doone*. Opposite the church, a cluster of ancient, thatched stone buildings includes the Three Crowns Hotel (High Street, 01647 433444, www.threecrowns-chagford.co.uk).

Back on the square, opposite the Market House, the century-old emporiums of James Bowden & Son (01647 433271) and Webber & Sons (01647 432213) are still going strong. Each comprises a labyrinth of rooms and stairways, packed with household goods, gardening tools, outdoor clothing, china, books and much more. Bowden's also has a small museum with exhibits from the shop's early days. At the Big Red Sofa (no.11, 01647 433883, www.thebigredsofa.co.uk) bookshop, customers are encouraged to curl up with a coffee on the eponymous sofa while looking through the books. Tucked away in a corner is the redoubtable Black's Delicatessen (no.28, 01647 433545, www.blacks-deli.co.uk); at no.42 the Moorland Dairy (01647 432479) sells delectable cream and ice-cream, courtesy of the owners' herd of pedigree Guernseys.

Soon after passing Chagford, the River Teign enters a wooded, steep-sided gorge, where you can set off on some beautiful riverside walks. There's parking near the old stone packhorse bridge at Fingle Bridge, and a pub, the Fingle Bridge Inn (01647 281287). An enjoyable four-mile circular walk runs along the river then up Hunters' Path, which climbs steeply uphill then levels out to give wonderful views over the gorge and of Castle Drogo (*see p80*); you can find full details of the route at www.devon.gov.uk/walk35.

Moretonhampstead

Moreton, as it's known locally, lies on a crossroads – which can give it a slightly hectic air, particularly in summertime. It's very much a 'lived-in' place, with shops catering for everyday needs, but also makes a good base for visiting Dartmoor. The best place to begin is the Tourist Information Centre (01647 440043, www.discoverdartmoor.co.uk) in the square, where you can pick up leaflets on three town trails. On a wall overlooking the square is the sparrowhawk sculpture that is the town's symbol; when King John granted Moretonhampstead its market charter in 1207, the rent was one sparrowhawk a year.

The town's best-known landmark is the Cross Tree (or Dancing Tree), near the 15th-century almshouses in Cross Street. Although the massive elm tree below which couples once danced is long gone (replaced by a copper beech, planted in 1912), its history is recounted in the Red Trail leaflet.

Several craftspeople have studios in town. At the Studio (44 Court Street, 01647 440708, closed Sun), Penny Simpson makes and sells hand-thrown, glazed earthenware pots. Other crafts can be found at the LongHouse Originals (01647 440935, closed Sun) gift shop, on the square. There's also a bookshop specialising in antiquarian books, an antiques and curios shop and a butcher's and delicatessen, which does a fine line in pies.

Where to eat & drink

In Chagford, the Old Forge Tea Room (6 the Square, 01647 433226, closed Tue) is renowned for its cakes; soups and light lunches complete the menu. The Courtyard Café (76 The Square, 01647 432571, closed Sun) specialises in organic and vegetarian grub. In the evening, try 22 Mill Street (01647 432244, www.22millst.com, closed Mon, Sun). It's a small but stylish place, serving a modern European menu (seared foie gras, wild Exmoor venison); there's also a simpler lunch menu.

Of the town's pubs, visit the Globe Inn (9 High Street, 01647 433485, www.theglobeinnchagford.co.uk) for real ales and speciality fish dishes, and the Bullers Arms (7 Mill Street, 01647 432348) for trad pub food plus a Sunday carvery.

In the nearby village of Drewsteignton, the thatched Drewe Arms ★ (The Square, 01647 281224, www.thedrewearms.co.uk) is worth sampling for the ambience alone. The tap room, where ales are served straight from the cask, has hardly changed in decades. Dining, however, is right up to date.

Moretonhampstead's oldest hostelry, the Union Inn (Ford Street, 01647 440199), is a traditional local, while the White Hart Hotel (The Square, 01647 441340, www.whitehartdartmoor.co.uk) has a smart but cosy brasserie, open all day.

Dartmoor Tearooms

3 Cross Street, Moretonhampstead, TQ13 8NL (01647 441116, www.dartmoortearooms.co.uk). Food served Mar-Oct 10.30am-5pm Wed-Sat; 11am-5pm Sun.
All is just as it should be: cheery geraniums in the window, a superb range of loose-leaf teas, and a menu of cream teas and the likes of Devon rarebit with real ale chutney.

Sandy Park Inn

Sandy Park, TQ13 8JW (01647 433267, www.sandyparkinn.co.uk). Open noon-11pm Mon-Sat; noon-10.30pm Sun. Lunch served noon-2.30pm, dinner served 6-9pm daily.
A classic country pub, Sandy Park has a whitewashed, thatched exterior and a beamed bar, with inviting settles,

snugs and log fires. A range of hand-pumped beers, maps for walkers and dog biscuits behind the bar are further pluses. The blackboard menu draws on produce from the moor and beyond, and there are five smart B&B rooms (£85) upstairs.

Where to stay

In Chagford, 22 Mill Street (*see p85*) has two well-equipped guest rooms, with stripped oak floors, DVD players and en suite bathrooms. The Sandy Park Inn (*see 85*) has five cosy rooms, with Wi-Fi and flatscreen TVs, while the Globe Inn (*see p85*) also has seven comfortable rooms.

Sparrowhawk Backpackers' Hostel (Ford Street, Moretonhampstead, 01647 440318, www.sparrow hawkbackpackers.co.uk) is a small eco-hostel in lthe centre of Moretonhampstead, with solar-heated showers and recycling facilies. The 14-bed dorm is in the old hayloft, and there's also a modestly priced double and family room.

Drewsteignton's Drewe Arms (*see p85* has three B&B rooms, along with budget-rate bunks (bedding and towels provided) in the converted stables.

Gate House

North Bovey, TQ13 8RB (01647 440479, www.gate houseondartmoor.co.uk). Rates £74-£78 double incl breakfast & afternoon tea.
The thatched medieval longhouse dates from the 1400s; these days it's a B&B, with three double rooms available. There are hearty breakfasts, delicious teas and supper trays on request. In winter, toast yourself in front of a roaring log fire; in summer, sit by the pool and soak up the gorgeous view.

Gidleigh Park Hotel

Chagford, TQ13 8HH (01647 432367, www.gidleigh. com). Rates £310-£450 double incl breakfast.
Set in its own 107-acre estate, with the wild moors to the rear and the River Teign running by its front door, this half-timbered Tudor-style country hotel is famed for its culinary credentials. At the helm is chef Michael Caines, who has won two Michelin stars for his efforts. The prices, like the quality, are high – although the lunchtime menu won't break the bank. The 24 individually decorated bedrooms are equipped with enormous beds, marble bathrooms and appealing little luxuries (L'Occitane smellies, a decanter of Madeira).

Higher Westcott Farm

Westcott, TQ13 8SU (01647 441205, www.higher westcottfarm.com). Rates £80-£115 double incl breakfast.
Its design-conscious owners have done a sterling job in converting this 300-year old Devon longhouse into a charming, chintz-free retreat. The four guest rooms, all with beautiful views and deep window seats, are elegantly furnished with king-size beds, duck-down bedding and flatscreen DVD players (there's a well-stocked DVD library). Downstairs, the lounge bar features leather sofas, a crackling log fire and a well-stocked honesty bar. Breakfast features home-made bread, Devon yoghurts and eggs courtesy of Jean-from-next-door's chickens. Families are made welcome.

Mill End Hotel

Chagford, TQ13 8JN (01647 432282, www.millend hotel.com). Rates £90-£160 double incl breakfast.
The sound of the waterwheel at this former corn mill, just outside Chagford, proves wonderfully relaxing – aided by its calm decor and cosy vibe. There are 14 rooms, most of which have garden views, and a restaurant serving nicely honed comfort food, such as slow-roasted beef with truffle potato.

Parford Well B&B

Sandy Park, TQ13 8JW (01647 433353, www. parfordwell.co.uk). Rates £70-£85 double incl breakfast.
With its pretty walled garden, stately interiors and friendly owner, this little B&B is a delight. There are three well-appointed bedrooms, generous cooked breakfasts, and a spacious residents lounge.

Ring of Bells

North Bovey, TQ13 8RB (01647 440375, www.ring ofbells.net). Rates £80 double incl breakfast.
Overlooking the village green in the sleepy village of North Bovey, this thatched, beamed 15th-century inn is a vision of rural bliss. The landlord dispenses pints of Otter and St Austell Tribute, and there's a cracking little food menu and wine list. The five rooms are appealingly understated; several have four-posters and window seats.

BOVEY TRACEY & AROUND

Bovey Tracey

Close to the eastern edge of Dartmoor, and with easy access to the main A38, Bovey (short 'o' as in 'dove') is one the main gateway towns to the moor.

The town's Heritage Centre (St John's Lane, 01626 834331, closed Sun & Nov-Easter), set in its 19th-century railway station, has displays on its history – including the Battle of Bovey Heath, where the Royalists were roundly defeated. From the mid-18th century onwards, the local clay deposits formed the basis of a flourishing pottery industry (though Josiah Wedgwood, visiting in 1775, was unimpressed, loftily declaring it to be 'a poor trifling concern, and conducted in a wretched slovenly manner'). The remaining kilns are now listed buildings, and the old potteries are home to the House of Marbles (*see p80*).

Most of the town's shops are found along the long main street, leading up to an impressive parish church (notable for its delicately carved 15th-century rood screen). Don't miss Mann & Son (43 Fore Street, 01626 832253, www.the cheeseshed.com), whose deli treats include a lavish spread of West Country cheeses. A dazzling array of yarns (some from Dartmoor sheep) fills the shelves at Spin a Yarn (26 Fore Street, 01626 836203, www.spinayarndevon.co.uk). If you need outdoor gear for moorland walking, make tracks to Moor & Tor (55 Fore Street, 01626 835522).

There are also some splendid cafés and coffee shops – not least Pinks Place (*see p88*), at the upper end of Fore Street.

Runnage Farm. See p94.

Bovey Valley

Upstream of town, the River Bovey flows through steep-sided Lustleigh Cleave. This is a local beauty spot, where a network of footpaths meander alongside the river or climb through the woods to reach the open moorland higher up. River crossings include the picturesque packhorse bridge in Hisley Wood, a wooden footbridge and, further upstream, the massive boulders known as Horsham Steps (a certain amount of agility is needed to negotiate the latter). On the east side of the Cleave, the highest path will take you along the ridge to the hill fort at Hunter's Tor. From this vantage point, there is a spectacular vista over the wooded valley, and the moorland tors beyond.

Footpaths also connect the villages of Manaton and Lustleigh, which lie on either side of the Cleave. Manaton has an attractive green beside the church, with a footpath leading to the Manaton Rocks. Its local pub, the Kestor Inn (01647 221204, closed Mon), is further down the road in the tiny hamlet of Water. It's a friendly place, serving homely food. Nearby, the Becka Brook cascades among vast, mossy boulders at Becky Falls (see p76), which can be reached either from the B3344 or on foot from the Cleave.

To the east, between Bovey Tracey and Moretonhampstead, is Lustleigh. Set on the Wray Brook, a tributary of the Bovey, the village centre is a chocolate-box scene of thatched cottages grouped around the church. One of those dwellings houses Primrose Cottage Tea Rooms (01647 277365, closed Winter Mon-Fri), which serves a classic cream tea; for something stronger, drop by the Cleave Inn (see below). Inside the 13th-century church is the ancient burial monument of Datuidoc's Stone, thought to date from around AD 600.

Lustleigh is also home to a community-owned orchard; amid the apple trees, look out for the rock carved with the names of the village's May Queens.

Teign Valley villages

To the north-east of Bovey Tracey stretches the central swathe of the Teign Valley. For aficionados of church architecture, this is happy hunting ground. From the B3193, ascending the valley on the eastern side, first comes the village of Higher Ashton, whose church has a beautiful and elaborately decorated late medieval rood screen. A little further on, the church at Doddiscombsleigh has five 15th-century stained glass windows, in jewel-like hues. Just over the hill towards Exeter is the small red sandstone church at Dunchideock, which also has an ancient rood screen and carvings.

Returning down the valley, high up on the west side, Bridford's Church of St Thomas Becket has an exceptional painted screen dating from the early 1500s. Another hillside village on this side is Hennock, whose screen features early 16th-century paintings of apostles. Closer to the valley floor, Christow's fine granite-towered church contains some fragments of old stained glass.

The Teign Valley also has some superb village pubs, namely the Artichoke Inn at Christow (see below), the Manor Inn at Lower Ashton (01647 252304) and the Cridford Inn (see below), a former longhouse at Trusham.

Haytor Rocks

Around ten minutes' drive from Bovey Tracey, just outside the village of Haytor Vale, Haytor Rocks is one of the most popular tors on Dartmoor, thanks to its proximity to the road. It is a striking granite outcrop – or two outcrops, to be precise, both of which have roughly hewn steps to enable non-climbers to reach the top. There's a car park next to the National Park Information Centre (01364 661520), and another further along the road. It's an easy, though uphill, stroll to the tor from either car park. But be warned: if you don't like crowds, this is not the place to be on a summer's weekend.

On your way, don't miss the award-winning Ullacombe Farm Shop & Barn Café (Haytor Road, 01364 661341, closed Mon), just off the road between Bovey Tracey and Haytor.

Where to eat & drink

In Bovey Tracey, the tearoom at Pinks Place (76 Fore Street, 01626 835363, www.courtenay house.co.uk, closed Wed) has pale pink walls, lacy tablecloths and a three-course Sunday lunch, while the Old Cottage Tea Shop (20 Fore Street, 01626 833430, closed Sun, no credit cards) lives up to its name with its beams and old-world atmosphere. Just below the bridge, Brookside Tea Rooms (Station Road, 01626 832254) is modern, light and airy, and a popular place for lunch.

The thatched 12th-century Artichoke Inn in Christow (Village Road, 01647 252387, www. theartichokeinn.co.uk) has a snug bar, hung with pewter tankards, a wood-panelled dining room and a large terrace.

Cleave Inn
Lustleigh, TQ13 9TJ (01647 277223, www.thecleave inn.co.uk). Open 6-10pm Mon, Tue; noon-3pm, 6-11pm Wed-Sat; noon-9pm Sun. Meals served Summer noon-3pm, 6-9pm Mon-Sat; noon-4pm Sun. Winter noon-3pm, 6-10pm Wed-Sat; noon-4pm Sun.
Although food is taken seriously at this pretty village pub, it remains an unstuffy sort of place. Weary walkers can consume a restorative pint of Otter Ale and an own-made scotch egg, while weighing up the merits of a ploughman's or pie of the day. There's a polished evening menu: Brixham scallops with chervil and pea purée and home-cured bacon is typical.

Cridford Inn
Trusham, TQ13 0NR (01626 853694). Open 11am-3pm, 6-11pm Mon-Fri; 11am-11pm Sat; noon-10pm Sun. Lunch served noon-2.30pm Mon-Sat, noon-2pm Sun. Dinner served 7-9.30pm Mon-Sat; 7-9pm Sun.
A thatched Devon longhouse: note the rare medieval stained glass window in the bar, and the marks made by the masons who built the house on the beams. The splendid bar menu runs from inexpensive mezze to gamekeeper's cobbler – slow-braised venison, rabbit and pheasant in a red wine and thyme gravy, served with spuds, veg and

herby scones. For fancier food, book a table in the Vanilla Pod restaurant. There are also four comfortable en suite rooms (£80 incl breakfast).

No Body Inn
Doddiscombsleigh, EX6 7PS (01647 252394, www.nobodyinn.co.uk). Open 11am-11pm Mon-Sat; noon-10.30pm Sun. Lunch served noon-2pm Mon-Sat; noon-3pm Sun. Dinner served 6.30-9pm Mon-Thur; 6.30-9.30pm Fri, Sat; 7-9pm Sun. Rates £90 double incl breakfast.
Dating back to the 1600s, the inn is now known for its cheeses, wines, and 240-strong collection of whiskies, while its menu includes hearty British stalwarts such as game pies, venison stew and traditional puddings. Upstairs are five en suite boutique hotel-style rooms; downstairs, the walls and beamed ceiling have the sort of honeyed patina interior designers adore.

Rock Inn
Haytor Vale, TQ13 9XP (01364 661305, www.rock-inn.co.uk). Open 11am-11pm daily. Lunch served noon-2.15pm Mon-Sat; noon-2.30pm Sun. Dinner served 7-8.30pm Mon-Wed; 7-9.15pm Thur-Sun.
Tourists have flocked to the Haytor Rocks for centuries – and stopped off at this nearby coaching inn, founded in the mid 18th century, to nurse a drink by the fire. Walkers drop by for a pint of local Jail Ale and a hearty pub lunch. The inn has nine individually designed en suite rooms (£78-£117 double incl breakfast): Sheila's Cottage features a resplendent carved four-poster; Master Robert has a private balcony.

Where to stay
The No Body Inn and Rock Inn (for both, *see above*) also offer upscale B&B accommodation.
   In the moorland village of Manaton, the inexpensive B&B at Wingstone Farm (01647 221215, www.wingstonefarm.co.uk) is delightfully off the beaten track; stabling is available. Rather larger in size is Ilsington Country House Hotel (Ilsington, 01364 661452, www.ilsington.co.uk) where the facilities include an indoor pool, a sauna and a gym.

Easdon Cottage & Barn
Long Lane, Manaton, TQ13 9XB (01647 221389, www.easdoncottage.co.uk). Rates from £65 double incl breakfast. Barn £225-£355 2-3 people per week.
There's a spacious, en suite double or twin B&B room in the main cottage, while the stone barn provides a romantic self-catering hideaway. There's an oil-fired Rayburn, a king-size double bed and glorious views of the moors, along with an extra sleeping space downstairs. If you're staying at the B&B, the imaginative, organic vegetarian and vegan breakfasts are a treat. Suppers and packed lunches can be provided too.

Moorstone Guest House
Bridford, EX6 7HS (01647 252071, www.moorstone.net). Rates £60-£70 double incl breakfast.
A chic refurbishment has transformed this 18th-century house, set in the peaceful Teign Valley. There are three guest rooms, all different in style. Breakfasts are excellent,

as are the optional dinners – expect wholesome English food with a French twist. (It's unlicensed, so bring a bottle.)

Vogwell Cottage
Manaton, TQ13 9XD (01647 221302, www.vogwell cottage.co.uk). Rates £60 double incl breakfast. No credit cards.
Set in the woods, down a quiet country lane, this former gamekeeper's cottage is wonderfully secluded (there's no TV, as there's no signal here). There is one large double room and one single, with an extra pull-out bed. Breakfast is served in the conservatory, overlooking the garden; the owner is a dab hand in the kitchen, and it's worth staying in for the two-course evening meal. Decor is traditional, without being twee.

Yurtcamp
Gorse Blossom Farm, Staplehill Road, Liverton, TQ12 6JD (01626 824666, www.yurtcamp.co.uk). Rates £395-£625 per week small yurt (sleeps 2), £495-£745 large yurt (sleeps 5).
Set amid 40 acres of oak woodland on the eastern edge of Dartmoor, this is camping at its most glamorous. Instead of a saggy tent, you sleep in a spacious, modern yurt, with proper beds and duvets, a crackling wood-burning stove and paraffin lamps. Each yurt also comes equipped with a two-ring camping stove and a coolbox, and you can also fry bacon and eggs over the outdoor firepits (there's a licensed café, if campfire cooking isn't your forte). Red deer roam the surrounding woodland, and buzzards fly overhead; bring wellies, as the site can get muddy. Children love exploring the woods, playing on the see-saw, swings and woodland assault course and meeting the pygmy goats.

ASHBURTON, BUCKFASTLEIGH & WIDECOMBE-IN-THE-MOOR

Ashburton
Narrow streets and tall buildings give Ashburton its distinctive character – both elegant and intimate. Several buildings feature fine, slate-hung frontages; above Somerfield, the slates are carved with playing-card suits, indicating the building's original use as a gaming house. The parish church, with its lofty 15th-century tower, and the nearby Methodist Chapel are both imposing buildings, and it's worth taking a detour down St Lawrence Lane to seek out St Lawrence's Chapel – it now houses a heritage centre (www.stlawrencechapel.org.uk, closed Oct-Apr). More history can be found in Ashburton Museum (1 West Street, 01364 652698, closed Mon, Wed, Sun, closed Oct-Apr).
   Ashburton's fortunes were founded on the cloth trade and tin mining, and it was one of the four stannary towns where the tinners took their metal to be valued. Certain old traditions die hard: this is one of the few places still to elect a portreeve – a role that dates back to AD 820. Bread-weighers and ale-tasters are also appointed, and carry out their duties in a special annual ceremony in July.
   Today, the town is known for its antiques shops, most of which are on North Street. Selling an eclectic mix of fireplaces, furniture, garden statuary

DEVON

Walking on Dartmoor

How to get started

There is free access to most of Dartmoor's open moorland, and a network of footpaths and bridleways around the fringes of the moor. In places there are well-trodden footpaths, while in others the terrain is pathless. Many of the granite tors are surrounded by clitter (broken chunks of granite formed by weathering). It is important to be well equipped for walking on the high moor. Boots and waterproof clothing are essential; so too are a map and compass. The Ordnance Survey OL28 map is recommended.

Guided walks

Dartmoor National Park Authority organises a programme of guided walks and talks throughout the year, which give a good introduction to the moor. Details are published in the free Dartmoor Guide and also online at www.dartmoor-npa.gov.uk. A charge is made for these events.

ACCESS POINTS FOR WALKS

For those who prefer to do their own thing, the choice of walks is endless. Below are some suggestions for starting points, with car parking and access directly on to the moor (OS grid references in brackets). Further access points are mentioned in the main text.

● Belstone, car park on edge of village at Brenamoor Common (SX621938): a good access point for the northern moor, with tracks leading to Yes Tor and High Willhays, plus Belstone Tor south of the village and Cosdon Beacon across the river.

● Car park on B3212 between Moretonhampstead and Postbridge (SX698834): walk south over Shapley Common to Grimspound and on over Hameldown ridge, or cross the road below Grimspound to reach Challacombe Down.

● Postbridge car park (SX646788): paths lead upstream on both sides of the East Dart to reach a waterfall (about 2 miles) where it's usually possible to cross the river; southwards, tracks through Bellever Forest take you to Bellever Tor, a good viewpoint.

● Two Bridges, small car park by cottage opposite hotel (SX609751): a path goes up the West Dart valley to Wistman's Wood – one of Dartmoor's wonders, where ancient, stunted oak trees grow among granite boulders; several tors stand on the ridge above, including the conical pile of Longaford Tor, another good viewpoint.

● Bel Tor Corner on B3357 between Ashburton and Dartmeet (SX695732): from here there's a more or less level walk along the grassy track known as Dr Blackall's Drive, overlooking the wooded Dart Valley.

● Venford Reservoir, two car parks, one either side of the dam (SX685713 and 689709): for a view of the Dart Valley from the other side, walk north from the eastern end of the dam to Bench Tor, where you can hear the river far below. To the south is the open expanse of Holne moor, and to the west the valley of the O Brook with the remains of Hooten Wheals tin mine; there's also a footpath around the reservoir.

● Car park on B3357, east of Merrivale Bridge (SX561749): this is called 'Four Winds' and the walled area was once a school for quarry workers' children.

---

and ornate chandeliers, and based in the former United Reformed Chapel, Adrian Ager (01364 653189, www.adrianager.co.uk, closed Sun) is always good for a browse. Both North Street and East Street are dotted with interesting independents, such as Lamplite Glass Studio (22 East Street, 01364 653431) among many others. On a more down-to-earth note, Trailventure (7 North Street, 01364 652522) has a comprehensive range of outdoor gear and maps, and knowledgeable staff.

Gourmands will want to head for the town's two delis. In North Street, Ashburton Delicatessen (no.16, 01364 652277, closed Sun) is a traditional establishment, whose stock includes pâtés, cheeses and wine – and bread, if you get there early. Round the corner in East Street, the Fish Deli (no.7, 01364 654833, www.thefishdeli.co.uk, closed Sun) sells superior olives, oils and tapas, alongside locally caught fish. For organic veg, chutneys, lamb and other local produce, there's a covered all-day market in Tuckers Yard (Chuley Road, at the bottom of St Lawrence Lane), Tuesday to Saturday.

Buckfastleigh

A working town that grew up around the woollen mills, Buckfastleigh has few airs and graces. The wool industry survived until well into the 20th century – joined, in the 19th century, by corn and paper mills. The town's industrial heritage is reflected in its narrow streets, which are lined with mill workers' cottages; note, too, the iron bollards in the shape of wool bobbins along the curving main street, with its colourfully painted façades.

There's not a great deal for tourists to tarry over in the town centre, save the intriguing Valiant Soldier (Fore Street, 01364 644522, www.valiantsoldier.org.uk, closed Mon, Tue, Sun; Nov-Mar). The pub was left in a timewarp after the landlady shut up shop in the 1960s, leaving everything exactly as it was – even down to the change in the till, and a jar of pickled eggs on the bar. A trust took over this perfectly preserved slice of '60s Britain some 40 years later, and it's now open to visitors. The prime tourist draw (Buckfast Abbey, see p81) lies a mile north of town.

From the lower end of the town, 196 stone steps lead up to the ruined Holy Trinity Church. The church burned down in the 1990s, leaving only the spire intact, and its empty arches and roofless shell are eerily atmospheric. Beneath the ruins lies an ancient cave system, where the fossilised remains of sabre-toothed tigers have been found; the caves are home to a colony of horseshoe bats, however, and are closed to the public.

Widecombe-in-the-Moor

Devon's most famous village lies in the lovely East Webburn Valley, bounded on all sides by moorland. The village itself is small, but the extent of the

The remains of Swelltor and Foggintor quarries are to the south, beside the former Princetown railway; nearby, to the south-west, are the Merrivale stone rows and circle. Across the road to the north is Great Mis Tor and beyond is a vast expanse of moorland, with plenty of scope for high moor walks.

● Car park on B3212 between Princetown and Yelverton (SX561709): cross the road and walk up to Sharpitor for a view over Burrator Reservoir and, close by, the craggy outcrop of Leather Tor; dropping down to the forest beyond you'll reach the Devonport Leat (built in 1797 to supply water to Plymouth and Devonport) – follow it upstream to the aqueduct to see it cascading down the hill opposite.

FIRING RANGES

When walking on Dartmoor, be aware that there are three military firing ranges, covering a large area of the northern moor. A leaflet showing the location of the ranges is available from National Park information centres. When firing is taking place, red flags are flown at points on the range boundaries and access is prohibited; on non-firing days there is free access. The firing programme can be checked in advance on www.dartmoor-ranges.co.uk or 0800 458 4868.

There is no firing on any of the ranges during August and on public holidays. Weekends are also clear on Okehampton and Merrivale ranges, but on Willsworthy range, firing may take place on the second weekend in the month. It is worth emphasising that there are far fewer firing days than clear ones.

parish is reflected in the scale of its church, known as the Cathedral of the Moor and topped by a soaring, pinnacled stone tower. Inside the church, verses recount the history of the Great Thunderstorm of 1638, when the building was struck by lightning and four people were killed. Next door is the granite-pillared, 16th-century Church House (01364 621321, www.national trust.org.uk) and the Sexton's Cottage. On the last Saturday of the month, Church House hosts the village market, where local produce is sold and refreshments raise money for charity.

Outside the church, facing the large village green, a plaque commemorates the song that is the reason for Widecombe's enormous popularity, *Widdecombe Fair*. (The fair itself is held in a nearby field on the second Tuesday in September each year.) Around the green are a couple of souvenir shops, a café and an ice-cream kiosk.

Widecombe's two pubs both live up to its quaint, olde-worlde image. Near the green, the Old Inn (01364 621207) has a beamed bar and a large restaurant. Around a quarter of a mile from the village is the rustic Rugglestone Inn ★ (01364 621327, www.rugglestoneinn. co.uk), with its low-ceilinged bar, wood-burning stove and home-cooked food. It also has a sheltered beer garden, across a pretty stream, where you might find chickens pecking about on the grass.

Where to eat & drink

Ashburton has a good choice of daytime eateries. The Studio Teashop (4 Kingsbridge Lane, 01364 653258, closed Mon, Sun) dispenses tempting cakes and simple lunches, while Café Green Ginger (26 East Street, 01364 653939, www.cafegreen ginger.com) occupies an elegant townhouse; on sunny afternoons, nab a table in the walled garden and order a glass of Pimms. Moorish (11 West Street, 01364 654011, closed Mon, Sun) serves tapas at lunch and more substantial dishes in the evening. For traditional bar food, the Royal Oak (5 East Street, 01364 652444) is a good local.

Between Buckfast and Buckfastleigh, the Abbey Inn (30 Buckfast Road, 01364 642343) is right beside the River Dart and has a waterside terrace – a pleasant place for a pint of Tribute and a bite to eat.

In Widecombe, the Wayside Café (01364 621313, www.waysidecafe.co.uk, closed Fri, Sat, closed mid Dec-Feb) has indoor and outdoor seating, and a pleasing menu that includes cream teas.

Agaric

30 North Street, Ashburton, TQ13 7QD (01364 654478, www.agaricrestaurant.co.uk). Coffee served 10am-noon, lunch served noon-2pm Wed-Fri. Dinner served 7-9pm Wed-Sat.

Chef Nick Coiley, formerly of the Carved Angel in Dartmouth, is the culinary talent behind this acclaimed restaurant with rooms. Everything is made in house, from bread and ice-creams to fruit vinegars and salamis. Most ingredients come from within a 20-mile radius of the restaurant. It's open for coffee and cakes in the morning, too. The five beautifully-decorated rooms are two doors away at no.36, in a former merchant's townhouse (£110 double, incl breakfast).

Where to stay

In the pretty village of Holne, four and a half miles from Ashburton, Church House Inn (01364 631208, www.churchhouseinn-holne.co.uk) is an atmospheric old hostelry, next to the church. There are four en suite rooms, and dogs are welcome.

Hockmoor Garden Cottage

Buckfast, TQ11 0HN (01364 644174). Rates £300-£500 per week for 2 people.

This stone-built cottage makes for a sweet hideaway, with its wooden-floored kitchen and living area and airy, cream-painted bedroom, heated by a wood-burning stove. The cottage adjoins the owners' house, in a 14-acre smallholding in Hembury Woods. Guests can roam the extensive gardens and private woodland. Dogs can stay for £5 per night.

Kilbury Manor

Colston Road, Buckfastleigh, TQ11 0LN (01364 644079, www.kilburymanor.co.uk). Rates £65-£75 double incl breakfast.

Draped with wisteria, this 17th-century longhouse is set in four acres of grounds, which include a riverside meadow.

DEVON

Yurtcamp. See p89.

There are four B&B rooms (two in the main house, two in the converted barn). For self-catering stays, there's the one-bedroom Apple Loft Cottage.

Old Rectory
Widecombe-in-the-Moor, TQ13 7TB (01364 621231). Rates £50-£70 double incl breakfast. No credit cards.
Beautiful gardens surround this Georgian country house. The owners are keen artists, and the interior is dotted with sculptures and exotic finds from their travels. The place is run on green lines, and breakfast features organic produce. Book ahead – there are only three bedrooms.

PRINCETOWN, POSTBRIDGE & CENTRAL DARTMOOR

Princetown
With its dour grey buildings, Princetown is an unprepossessing sort of place – yet it draws visitors from all over the world, who come here to gaze on the famous Dartmoor Prison. Built in 1809 to house prisoners from the Napoleonic wars, its austere granite walls loom large as you approach Princetown from Two Bridges. The museum (*see p81*) recounts the stories

of former inmates and displays various items, from Victorian convicts' attire to lethal-looking home-made weapons found in the cells.

The prison aside, the best reason to visit Princetown is to drop into the National Park's High Moorland Visitor Centre (Tavistock Road, Princetown, 01822 890414, www.dartmoor-npa.gov.uk). The *Dartmoor Guide* lists current events, while an exhibition explores the moor's wildlife and history. Staff are well informed, and the shop sells maps, gifts and outdoor gear. Close by, the recently opened Duchy Square Centre for Creativity (Tavistock Road, 01822 890828, www.duchysquare.org) runs craft workshops and exhibitions.

A railway line once ran from Plymouth to Princetown – an ambitious scheme dreamed up by the town's founder, Thomas Tyrwhitt, who also built the prison. Opened in 1823, the railway transported lime and other goods up to Princetown, and carried locally quarried granite on the return leg. Having closed in 1956, it makes for a wonderful off-road cycle route (it can be walked too; ask for a map of cycle routes at the Visitor Centre. Access to the railway line is beyond the car park and past Dartmoor Brewery's premises, where the well-known Jail Ale is brewed.

East of Princetown on the B3357 towards Ashburton, the road descends sharply to cross Dartmeet – the point where the East Dart and West Dart river tributaries converge. Alongside the road bridge are the remains of an ancient granite clapper bridge, while footpaths lead upstream and downstream to riverside picnic spots. Badger's Holt Tea Rooms (01364 631213, closed Jan-Mar) are at the top of the car park; for a touch of old-world charm, there's Brimpts Farm Tea Rooms (01364 631450, www.brimptsfarm.co.uk, closed Mon-Fri term-time) at the top of the hill, where you can eat clotted cream slathered scones in a cottage garden

Postbridge

Right in the centre of Dartmoor, this small village is also home to a magnificently preserved medieval clapper bridge. Spanning the East Dart River, alongside the 18th-century road bridge, its sturdy piers are topped with massive slabs of rough granite, clearly built to withstand raging floods.

Postbridge is a good starting place for walks, with paths both north and south, easy access to the open moorland and a large car park. The Transmoor Link bus (no.82, run by First; 0871 200 2233) also has a regular service along the B3212, stopping at the village, making linear walks a possibility.

The small shop-cum-post office in the village serves takeaway cream teas. Alternatively, pop into the East Dart Hotel (01822 880213, www. eastdart.co.uk), beside the bridge. At one stage in its history, this was a temperance house; these days you can enjoy a pint there too.

Where to eat & drink

For solid grub and ales, head to the Plume of Feathers (Princetown, 01822 890240). Housed in Princetown's oldest building, its wooden beams, log fires and oil lamps lend it a cosy feel.

Fox Tor Café

Two Bridges Road, Princetown, PL20 6QS (01822 890238, www.foxtorcafe.co.uk). Open/food served 9am-5pm Mon-Fri; 7.30am-6pm Sat; 7.30am-5pm Sun.
No-nonsense fry-ups are the main attraction at this friendly café – perfect fuel for hikers. There's seating in the garden out back; in inclement weather, stay close to the cosy log burner and open fire. This place is also a general store, and can kit you out with anything from a bottle of rum or a torch battery to painkillers and chocolate. Attached is a backpackers' hostel (sleeping 12 people in three four-person rooms; £9.50 per person, with bedding and towels extra).

Prince of Wales

Tavistock Road, Princetown, PL20 6QF (01822 890219). Open 11.30am-11pm Mon-Thur; 11am-midnight Fri, Sat. Lunch served noon-2.30pm, dinner served 5-8.30pm Mon-Sat. Food served noon-8.30pm Sun.
Master Brewer Simon Loveless started the Dartmoor Brewery here in 1994, in a converted garage behind the pub. His subsequent success with its award-winning Jail Ale and Dartmoor IPA meant that in 2005, the brewery moved to a purpose-built site at the old Princetown Railway. The pub, which is between the prison and the visitor's centre, remains a popular local.

Tavistock Inn ★

Poundsgate, TQ13 7NY (01364 631251). Open/food served 11am-11pm Mon-Fri, Sun; 11am-midnight Sat. (Closed Winter 3-6pm Mon-Fri.)
This friendly moorland pub has been welcoming walkers and their four-legged friends for decades. In summer, sup a pint in the flower-filled garden; in winter toast in front of a blazing log fire and admire the granite spiral staircase and flagstone floor. Game pie and pasties are among the menu staples.

Warren House Inn ★

Postbridge, PL20 6TA (01822 880208, www.warren houseinn.co.uk). Open 11am-11pm Mon-Sat; 11am-10.30pm Sun. Meals served Summer noon-9pm Mon-Sat; noon-8.30pm Sun. Winter noon-4.20pm Mon, Tue; noon-9pm Wed-Sat; noon-8.30pm Sun.
High on the moors stands one of Dartmoor's most famous pubs. It's an isolated place, running on its own generators; it once provided a social hub for the tin miners who lived and worked here during the week. The inn's most famous feature is its fire – said (with perhaps a pinch of artistic licence) to have been burning continuously since 1845. Its warmth was essential when the inn was snowed in; in 1963 it was cut off from the outside world for almost 12 weeks. In more clement weather, there are picnic tables across the road with a panoramic view. The inn's name refers to the artificial rabbit warren constructed at a local farm to feed the miners; Warrener's Pie is still on the menu.

Where to stay

Along with its summer-only tearoom, Brimpts Farm in Dartmeet (*see above*) offers inexpensive B&B accommodation in its converted granite barns.

Corndonford Farm
Poundsgate, TQ13 7PP (01364 631595). Rates from £60 double incl breakfast. No credit cards.
Situated just a hop, skip and a jump from the Two Moors Way, this stone-built Devon longhouse is a working horse farm, with shire horses and Dartmoor ponies. B&B visitors are made to feel like guests in a private home, and there are freshly laid eggs for breakfast. A stone staircase leads up to two bedrooms, with a shared bathroom and garden views.

Forest Inn
Hexworthy, PL20 6SD (01364 631211, www.theforestinn.co.uk). Rates £65-£75 double.
This country inn, which started life in the 1850s as an anglers' ale house, proclaims 'muddy boots and dogs welcome'. The rooms are simple but comfortable; specify if you'd like an en suite bathroom. In the bar, the emphasis is on Devon beers and cider. Stables and grazing are available for those who arrive on horseback.

Prince Hall Hotel
Two Bridges, PL20 6SA (01822 890403, www.princehall.co.uk). Rates £140-£160 double.
After a long and varied history, including a short stint as Lord and Lady Astor's summer residence, this 18th-century house has become an eight-room hotel. Big beds, crisp white cotton linen and home-made biscuits await in the spacious guest rooms; downstairs, log fires and squashy sofas welcome tired walkers. Salmon and trout fishing can be arranged on the nearby West Dart, as can as fly-fishing tuition. It is an emphatically dog-friendly establishment.

Runnage Farm
Postbridge, PL20 6TN (01822 880222, www.runnagecampingbarns.co.uk). Rates £7.50 per person. No credit cards.
Just outside the village, this centuries-old moorland farm sprawls over some 220 acres. A working farm, it has two spacious camping meadows, one of which is set aside for families and small groups; paths lead from the site up into the pine woods and out on to the open moor.

YHA Bellever
Postbridge, PL20 6TU, (0845 371 9622, www.yha.org.uk). Rates £11.95 per person.
This 38-bed hostel, once a part of a Duchy farm, occupies a prime spot in the heart of the National Park, close to the East Dart River and Bellever Forest and a host of walking and cycle tracks. It's a relaxed sort of place, with discounted rates for guests who arrive by bus, bike or foot. A hearty meal is on offer every evening. Rooms vary in size from four to eight beds, with some family rooms; facilities include a games room, lounge, library, shop, cycle store and drying room.

IVYBRIDGE & SOUTH BRENT

Ivybridge
Its 13th-century ivy-clad bridge was once the subject of a painting by Turner, but today Ivybridge is more workaday than picturesque. Nonetheless, its position on the southern edge of Dartmoor and proximity to the A38 make it a useful base. Another plus is its mainline railway station. The town is set beside the River Erme, which crashes boisterously

along its rocky bed. The fast-flowing water drove the mills that formed the basis of the town's prosperity from the 16th century onwards; today, just one paper mill remains. The old turbine known as the Snail, which sits on a plinth near the packhorse ivy bridge, is a reminder of the past.

Another striking piece of engineering is the massive granite and brick viaduct that carries the railway across the deep river valley. It was constructed in 1893, replacing an earlier viaduct built by Brunel in 1848. The latter's tall piers still stand alongside it, and if you take the riverside path going north from the town you'll get a neck-craning view of these imposing structures. For a longer walk, continue along the path, through woods and then fields; at the minor road turn left to Hall Cross, then left on a track to cross Hanger Down and Henlake Down back to Ivybridge.

The town's rather prosaic array of shops is mainly along Fore Street and in Glanville's Mill precinct. The Leisure Centre on Leonards Road (01752 896999) has an indoor and a summer-only outdoor pool. The Watermark (Leonards Road, 01752 892220, www.ivybridgewatermark.co.uk, closed Sun), nearby, houses a cinema, theatre space and café.

South Brent
Quite different from its neighbour, South Brent is a large and tranquil village. In Church Street, the old tollhouse displays a list of charges levied on market days, dated 1889. Further on, the street turns a corner into the attractive Wellington Square, lined with quaint, pastel-painted houses. Just beyond here is the massive Norman tower of St Petroc's Church. A sanctuary ring is attached to the door (in the Middle Ages, fugitives who touched the ring were immune from arrest). In the village centre, on Station Road, Artworks (01364 649424) showcases the work of local craftspeople. A few doors away, the Pantry (01364 73308) has a good deli counter. For refreshments, call in at Crumbs & Cuppa (01364 73004, closed Sat afternoon, Sun).

Where to eat & drink
The restaurant at Plantation House (*see p96*) is also open to non-residents.

Julie's Café
16 Glanvilles Mill, Ivybridge, PL21 9PS (01752 698576). Open served 8.45am-5pm Mon-Sat; 11am-4pm Sun. No credit cards.
This locals' café is open every day for coffee, lunch and tea. In fine weather you can sit on the terrace overlooking the River Erme – the place has a slightly dog-eared air, but the river is mesmerising and the cakes are scrumptious.

Packhorse Inn
Plymouth Road, South Brent, TQ10 9BH (01364 72283, www.thepackhorse.co.uk). Open 4pm-midnight Mon-Thur; noon-midnight Fri-Sun. Dinner served 6-9pm Tue-Sat. (Tearoom open 9am-3pm Mon-Thur.) Rates £55 double incl breakfast.
Dating from medieval times, this is believed to be the oldest inn in South Brent. Once a resting place for the packhorse

St Michael de Rupe, Brent Tor. See p82.

Postbridge clapper bridge. See p93.

trains, it is now known for its traditional folk music (every Wednesday, and on alternate Tuesdays) and traditional pub games. The bar serves unpretentious pub grub and pizza, and teas are served in the grassy beer garden in summer. Three comfortable B&B rooms are available.

Royal Oak
Station Road, South Brent, TQ10 9BE (01364 721333, www.oakonline.net). Open 10am-11pm daily. Lunch served noon-2pm, dinner served 6-9pm daily. Rates £65-£85 double incl breakfast.
Two-times South Devon CAMRA Pub of the Year, this family-owned pub has a sterling line-up of real ales on the pumps. Keep the wolf from the door with a toasted teacake, or fill up on devilled kidneys on toast. Upstairs is fine dining restaurant Charlie's, whose Modern European menu employs locally sourced ingredients to good effect. There are also five en suite bedrooms.

Where to stay
Glazebrook House Hotel (01364 73322, www.glazebrookhouse.com) is a country house hotel in the traditional vein but on a small scale, with ten bedrooms in all.

Plantation House
Totnes Road, Ermington, PL21 9NS (01548 831100, www.plantationhousehotel.co.uk). Rates £95-£140 double incl breakfast.
Set in a former Georgian rectory, this boutique hotel and restaurant stands in delightful gardens overlooking the river Erme. The nine en suite bedrooms are beautifully decorated, with appealing attention to detail (fresh flowers, cafetière coffee, fluffy bathrobes). Breakfasts, best consumed on the leafy terrace, are a feast. The restaurant menu might include grilled turbot with lemon chive hollandaise, followed by luscious dark chocolate truffle terrine.

WEST OF DARTMOOR
Extending from Dartmoor to the Tamar Valley and the border with Cornwall is a pastoral landscape of small villages and quiet roads. With no towns to draw tourists in, this area tends to escape the notice of most visitors. Its attractions include the vast resevoir at Roadford Lake (*see p77*), with its angling and watersports centre, and the more colourful charms of Dingles Fairground Heritage Centre (*see p81*).

While you're in the vicinity, pop into Lifton Farm Shop (01566 784605, www.liftonstrawberry fields.co.uk). As well as the shop there's a restaurant and you can pick your own strawberries.

Where to eat & drink

Harris Arms
Portgate, EX20 4PZ (01566 783331, www.theharris arms.co.uk). Open/food served noon-2pm, 6.30-9pm Tue-Sat; noon-2pm Sun.
The Harris Arms promises 'honest' food – braised pork cheek with potato and apple hash, own-made fish cakes with chips – made from locally caught fish and meat from the

excellent Phillip Warren & Son in Launceston. There's a thoughtfully chosen wine list, art adorning the walls and a terrace with a view over the western edge of Dartmoor.

Percy's Country Hotel & Restaurant
Coombeshead Estate, Virginstow, EX21 5EA (01409 211236, www.percys.co.uk). Dinner served 7-9pm daily. Rates £125-175 incl breakfast & dinner.
Tina and Tony Bricknell-Webb have created a haven for food-lovers keen to keep their food miles low and experience real Devonshire food. The lucky 'ingredients' have the run of the 130-acre organic estate, where pigs roam free, Jacob sheep graze, and free-range geese, ducks and chickens wander at will. There's also a huge kitchen garden. Cookery workshops are available. Deluxe rooms have king-size beds and flatscreen TVs; bring or borrow a pair of wellies and explore the beautiful grounds

Where to stay
Percy's Country Hotel & Restaurant (*see above*) accommodates guests in its converted granary.

There are three B&B rooms at Higher Woodley dairy farm (Lamerton, 01822 832374, www. woodleybandb.co.uk), where breakfast features prize-winning sausages. Another working farm, Beera Farm in the Tamar Valley (Milton Abbot, 01822 870216, www.beera-farm.co.uk) also has three rooms, one of which has a four-poster; the warm welcome includes a cream tea on arrival.

Arundell Arms
Lifton, PL16 0AA (01566 784666, www.arundell arms.com). Rates £170-£195 double incl breakfast.
This flyfishers' paradise on the bank of the river Tamar is one of the country's top sporting hotels. Hundreds of guests have learned to fly-fish on its 20 miles of privately owned waters, or shoot in the nearby fields and woods. There are 21 elegant en suite rooms; downstairs guests can cosy up around a roaring fire in the bar with a toasted steak sandwich or a spiced venison burger. In the dining room, a more elaborate menu is served in polished surrounds.

Barbaryball Barns
Barbaryball House, Lifton, PL16 0AU (01566 780457, www.devoncountrybarns.co.uk). Rates £450-£1125 per week for 2-6 people.
Twelve acres of lush pasture on the Devon and Cornwall border, with beautiful views of the River Thrushell, surround these luxurious barn conversions. Each of the three properties is finished to a high standard, and has its own character. Dogs can stay in the purpose-built kennels adjacent to the barns.

Tor Cottage
Chillaton, PL16 0JE (01822 860248, www.torcottage. co.uk). Rates £140-£150 double incl breakfast.
A romantic retreat hidden away in its own private valley, amid 28 acres of land. Converted from an ancient carthouse, the Garden Room has a vaulted, beamed ceiling and its own private terrace and garden, while the Craftsman's Garden and Craftman's Deco occupy an old craftsman's workshop by the stream. For more seclusion, Laughing Waters is a woodland hideaway with hammocks and a gypsy caravan outside. There's a heated outdoor pool too.

DEVON

Exeter & Around

If you fell from the sky into one of Exeter's gleaming new glass and steel developments, you might think you'd arrived in a totally modern city. Turn a corner, though, and you could find yourself staring up at the lofty Norman towers of the cathedral. Such juxtapositions typify the city's character, with history overlaid by a thriving modern town. Exeter remains at the centre of life in the South West: not as large as Plymouth, but Devon's capital nonetheless.

The city's history goes back to Roman times, when the settlement of Isca was founded in about AD 50 on a ridge above the river. Later, the Normans arrived, building the cathedral and Rougemont Castle. Other buildings represent later periods in the city's history: the medieval Guildhall; the Tudor and Stuart houses in the High Street; and, elsewhere, some fine Georgian terraces. Large parts of the city centre were destroyed during World War II, and much of the rebuilding that followed has itself recently been replaced by more aesthetic developments.

There's more to explore just outside the city. The historic town of Topsham is an interesting place, and the Exe Estuary is a wildlife refuge of some renown.

EXETER

Exeter's city centre can conveniently be divided into 'quarters' for exploration: the Cathedral Quarter, the Castle Quarter, the West Quarter and the Quayside, plus the main artery of the High Street. A good way to discover Exeter's historical roots is to follow the three self-guided trails (see p104).

The Cathedral Quarter

Dominated by the cathedral and ringed by a medley of period buildings, Cathedral Close is at the heart of Exeter. A large area around the cathedral is occupied by the Green; to the north is a cobbled way bounded by a sequence of medieval red-stone buildings, including the Chapter House. Continue east along New Cut towards Southernhay and you'll pass under a charming iron footbridge, built in 1814.

The west side of Cathedral Close, called Cathedral Yard, is home to the imposing frontage of the Royal Clarence Hotel, dating from 1769 but reworked in 1827. On the other corner is the tiny church of St Martin, first consecrated in 1065. Next to it is the prominent black-and-white Mol's Coffee House, four storeys high and bearing the date 1596; the upper Dutch-style gable was added in the 1880s.

Two narrow alleys lead off from this corner. On the right is Catherine Street; where this opens out into a square, you'll find some ruins in red stone that were once 15th-century almshouses. The other, narrower, alleyway is St Martin's Lane. Along here is the Ship Inn, where Drake and Hawkins are reputed to have plotted their campaign against the Spanish Armada.

Back in Cathedral Close, past the Royal Clarence's outdoor tables, is the Well House Tavern, which has a grandstand view of the cathedral's West Front. Other 17th- and 18th-century timber-framed buildings, and a more grandiose 19th-century structure, house a variety of shops.

Curving around the south side is the Palace Gate, one of the seven former gateways surrounding Cathedral Close. Here stands the medieval Bishop's Palace, largely remodelled in the 18th century but currently closed for building work; the medieval chapel behind it remains intact. All of these features can be explored in the Red Coat Guides' 'Close and Cloisters' tour (see p105).

Exeter Cathedral

Work on Exeter's best-known building (01392 255573, www.exeter-cathedral.org.uk, closed Sun, admission £5) began in the early 12th century on the site of an earlier Saxon minster. The two huge towers are the main survivors from these Norman origins; the major part of the structure dates from a rebuilding programme that began in the 1270s and continued for over a century.

The cathedral is famous for its exquisitely carved West Front, decorated with tiers of intricately worked figures representing apostles, kings and angels. Other treasures include 13th-century misericords depicting a range of subjects (including an elephant), the ornate bishop's throne and an astronomical clock. Look out, too, for the catflap in the door near the clock: at one time, the cathedral's cat was paid a penny a week to catch intruding mice. The library (open 2-5pm Mon-Fri) contains the famous Exeter Book of Anglo-Saxon poetry and the Exon Domesday. There's also a shop and a café.

The Castle Quarter

Just to the west of High Street lie the remains of Rougemont Castle, accessible via the broad, pedestrianised opening of Castle Street midway up the High Street. As you walk up Castle Street (the left-hand fork), ahead is a stone archway built in about 1770 that leads to the original inner bailey,

which now houses the county's law courts (closed to the public). But before reaching the archway, turn left into Rougemont Gardens. Here, to the right, is the gatehouse of the Norman castle, built in 1068 following the siege of Exeter and now the best-preserved early Norman gatehouse in the country.

Located on a small hill, Rougemont Castle was a key element in the city's defences, surrounded by a large bank and ditch within the Roman wall. In the 12th and 13th centuries, a series of towers were added around the perimeter to consolidate its defences; some of the foundations are still visible. The paths in Rougemont Gardens give a good view of the dips and mounds of the Norman earthworks.

From here, paths lead through the city wall into Northernhay Gardens, where you can see a good stretch of the Roman wall. Located on high ground, the gardens were laid out in the 17th century and remodelled in the 19th. Today, they afford good views over the city, and are a fine place for a picnic.

Along the southern edge of the Castle Quarter is the narrow, cobbled and traffic-free Gandy Street ★. Most of the buildings here date from the early 19th century and the street has a Dickensian charm, especially around Christmas. There are plenty of niche shops here, among them Kintamani (jewellery and ornaments), Silver Lion Jewellers and Martian (records, CDs and DVDs), while the Paragon Gallery is a showcase for local artists. There are more interesting shops in New Buildings, a narrower alley just off Gandy Street.

The High Street

Along with the streets radiating off it and the precinct developments of the Guildhall Centre, Harlequins and Princesshay, the High Street (open only to buses and pedestrians) is the commercial centre of Exeter, home to branches of major chains such as Marks & Spencer, Boots and Gap. At its north-eastern end is Sidwell Street, where you'll find smaller chains such as Lush, independent shops and a daily market.

Heading south-west along the High Street, off on the left is Princesshay, which opened in 2007. This distinctive development represents a new stage in Exeter's architectural history, creating a spacious pedestrian zone that speaks of its own time while also paying homage to the past; notice the way the building lines converge on a spectacular view of the Cathedral. Chain retailers such as Fat Face are joined by independent shops, such as the Chandos Deli in Roman Walk, and some eateries (see p105).

Continuing down the High Street, on the other side is the top of Queen Street, which has many 19th-century buildings. A short way down on the right is a grand Victorian edifice that houses the Royal Albert Memorial Museum (closed until 2011; see p110). Further down, on Paul Street, is the entrance to the Harlequins shopping mall. Also on Queen Street is the Cavern (nos.83-84, 01392 495370, www. cavernclub.co.uk), a well established platform for post-punk, indie and roots music.

Moving back towards the top of Queen Street, you may notice the long, neo-classical frontage with fluted columns that graces the entrance to the Guildhall shopping centre. This imposing 19th-century façade is all that remains from this period; behind it is a functional 1970s shopping precinct, home to a supermarket, some other chains and independent stores such as Exeter Rare Books. Incongruously set in a paved square at the centre

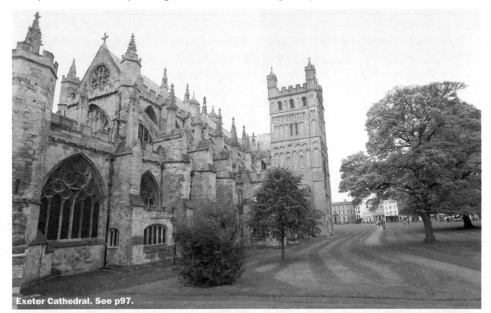

Exeter Cathedral. See p97.

Exeter Cathedral

Come and visit one of England's most beautiful Decorated Gothic cathedrals. Discover the world's longest continuous medieval vault.

Visitor opening times: Monday - Saturday 09.00 - 16.45
Admission charges apply.
Daily guided tours available. Roof tours by arrangement.

Cathedral Café

Set in the historic cloisters serving locally sourced freshly prepared food.
Outdoor seating available.
Open: Monday - Saturday 10.00 - 16.45

Cathedral Shop

Located within the Cathedral supplies a wide variety of books, CDs, postcards, greeting cards and gifts.
Open: Monday - Saturday 09.30 - 16.30

Photo Credit: Angelo Hornak

01392 285983   www.exeter-cathedral.org.uk

is the tiny medieval church of St Pancras, restored in the 19th century; note, in particular, the late-medieval wagon roof.

Leaving the Guildhall shopping centre on its east side, you'll emerge on to the High Street and the magnificent Guildhall itself. For more than 800 years, it's been the chamber of Exeter's mayor and council. The present building dates from 1330, though it was remodelled in 1468-69; the grand portico that extends over the pavement is Elizabethan. When it's not in use, the Guildhall is open to the public on selected weekdays (call 01392 665500 to check) and, in summer, on Saturday mornings.

Beyond the Guildhall, you'll arrive at a crossroads with North and South Streets. Turning right into North Street will take you to the Iron Bridge, built in 1835 and once the main entrance to the city from the north. It's an ornate structure with several arches and Gothic cast-iron balustrades. Heading left along South Street, meanwhile, affords the opportunity to visit the White Hart, a 14th-century alehouse with a later Georgian frontage, and the Nonconformist George's Meeting, built in 1760 and now in the hands of a large pub chain.

The West Quarter

At its south-western end, the High Street eventually becomes Fore Street, which lies at the heart of the West Quarter. The shops in this part of town are predominantly independent, selling everything from surfing gear to toys. Within McCoy's Arcade, the Real McCoy offers a huge selection of vintage clothing and a café (01392 410481, closed Sun), while Mansons Guitar Shop has a huge range of instruments. Down at the foot of the hill, Otto Retro stocks what it describes as 'jolly junk', from old furniture to Victoriana and tin soldiers. The paved area at the top of Fore Street, meanwhile, is the venue for the weekly Exeter Farmers' Market, held on Thursdays from 9am to 2pm.

Notable buildings on Fore Street include the late medieval church of St Olave and Tuckers' Hall, built in 1471 as a chapel for Exeter's woollen cloth workers. Just around the corner, in the Mint, is St Nicholas' Priory, founded in the 11th century (see p110). Nearby, on Mary Arches Street, sits another of the city's medieval parish churches, St Mary Arches – damaged in the war, it has been restored, and contains several interesting old monuments.

Running parallel with Fore Street is Smythen Street, which at its lower end becomes the delightful, cobbled Stepcote Hill. At the bottom is a little cluster of ancient buildings, and on the right is the 15th-century church of St Mary Steps. Its chief attraction is the 17th-century clock on the outside of the tower, which represents a miller named Matthew and his two sons: apparently, Matthew, who worked at a nearby mill, was so punctual that people could tell the time by him, and when he died a clock was made to take over the job. On the hour, Matthew nods his head, while his sons strike the bells at their feet.

To the left is a three-storey timbered medieval building. More or less opposite is a property known locally as 'the House That Moved'. When nearby Western Way was constructed in 1964, this timber-framed Tudor merchant's house was lifted on to rollers and rolled 75 yards along the road.

Walk up West Street and then turn left into New Bridge Street to look down on the ruins of the medieval Exe Bridge. Built in 1200 to allow packhorses and carts to reach the city from west of the river, its series of arches can be seen, with the remnants of a church that stood at the end. The bridge was in use until the 18th century.

Back along Bartholomew Street West, the Exeter Picturehouse (no.51, 0871 704 2057, www.picture houses.co.uk) shows a judicious mix of mainstream releases and arthouse flicks, and has a nice café.

The Quayside ★

The Romans were the first to construct a quay in Exeter. In the Middle Ages, it became a major port, until the city's trade was thwarted by the building of weirs across the river near Topsham. Things improved again with the building of the Exeter Ship Canal (see below), which opened in 1566; from then on, the cloth trade flourished, with wool mills powered by leats diverted from the river. The buildings that remain from this era – five-storey warehouses and bonded cellars that are now home to small shops selling artisan-made goods – tell the story of a flourishing trading centre.

The most impressive building is the red-brick Custom House, built in 1680 and remarkably well preserved. Nearby is the gabled Wharfinger's House, built in 1778 for the wharfinger (or harbourmaster) who collected the wharfage fees. Next to it is the Quay House Visitor Centre, a former warehouse and transit shed that also dates from 1680; it now houses an exhibition on the history of the quay, an information service and a shop selling local guidebooks (01392 271611, closed Mon-Fri Nov-Mar). Close at hand is the former Fishmarket, now part-occupied by an antiques centre and a café.

To reach the canal basin, cross the river either on Butts Ferry (a kind of floating bridge) or walk over the Cricklepit footbridge. The new development around here, known as Piazza Terracina, affords a panoramic view of the quay, backed by the graceful Georgian buildings of Colleton Crescent.

Just along from the quay, in Commercial Road, is Cricklepit Mill, parts of which date from the 17th century. Now restored, the mill is occupied by the Devon Wildlife Trust, which has turned part of it into a wildlife interpretation centre (01392 279244, open 9am-5pm Mon-Fri). The trust organises various events, talks and film shows; you can also learn about the Trust's Exeter Wild City project, aimed at creating more wildlife habitats within the city.

Exeter Ship Canal

Work on the venerable Exeter Ship Canal began in 1564, making it one of the oldest man-made waterways in Britain. The canal opened two years later, originally rejoining the river just below Countess Weir less than two miles away; in the 1670s, it was extended to reach the river opposite

Exeter

Princesshay. See p99.

DEVON

Cathedral Close. See p97.

Topsham. In the early 19th century, the canal was widened, deepened and extended a further mile and a half, as far as the Turf Lock – although with the coming of the railways, canal traffic slowly but irrevocably dried up.

Like so many obsolete waterways, the canal is now enjoying a new lease of life. In summer, the Kingsley (07984 368442, www.exetercruises.com), a 1920s passenger boat, takes tourists from Exeter Quay to the Double Locks; her sister vessel, the White Heather, connects the Double Locks to Turf Lock. Visitors can also travel between Topsham and Turf Lock on the Sea Dream II (07778 370582, www.topshamtoturfferry.co.uk) – or explore under their own steam, hiring kayaks or canoes from Saddles & Paddles at Exeter Quay (No.4 Kings Wharf, 01392 424241, www.sadpad.com), which also offers bike hire.

Open to walkers and cyclists, the five-mile Exeter Canal Towpath Trail runs alongside the canal, from its basin by the quay to its outflow into the Exe Estuary at Turf Lock. Safe and easy to follow, the trail affords some great waterside panoramas, from the canal itself over to the upper part of the estuary. The trail is part of the longer Exe Estuary Trail (www.exetrail.co.uk), an as-yet incomplete 26-mile cycle route that will extend along both sides of the estuary from Exeter's quay, linking Exeter, Exmouth and Dawlish.

The canal basin lies just across the footbridge from the quay in Exeter (*see p101*). A bridge at the lower end of the basin gives access to paths on either side of the canal, as well as a further route through the Riverside Valley Park between the canal and the river. The main cycle route starts on the eastern side of the canal; look back towards the city for a panorama of buildings along the rising ground above the river, with the cathedral's towers crowning the view.

The surroundings soon become more rural, with fields lining the route. A swing bridge carries a minor road leading to the Double Locks pub (01392 256947, www.doublelocks.com); built as a lock-keeper's cottage, it now offers fine real ales and a pub-grub menu. The large lock was built to accommodate two vessels at a time, hence the pub's name. At Double Locks, the trail crosses to the west side of the canal.

The trail crosses the main road at Countess Wear Bridge and soon after passes under the M5 viaduct. A former lock-keeper's cottage still stands beside the derelict Topsham Lock and a swing bridge over the canal; there are good views of Topsham's waterfront. If you want to visit the town, you can catch the little foot ferry (07801 203338) across the river; you'll probably have to wave, though, as it's normally moored on the far side. The ferry runs every day except Tuesday from April to September, and on weekends in winter, and bikes are allowed on board.

Back on the west side of the canal, it's a mile and a half down to the Turf Lock. At the time of the lock's construction in the 1820s, the Turf Hotel was built to provide accommodation for the lock-keeper and hospitality for the crews of visiting

Things to do

EXETER

Barnfield Theatre
Barnfield Road, EX1 1SN (01392 270891, www.barnfieldtheatre.org.uk). Box office 10am-4pm Mon-Fri; 10am-1hr before performance Sat. Tickets £8-£12.
The resident Exeter Little Theatre Company are joined by other amateur theatre groups in this central theatre, which also hosts concerts and other events. The café is open daily, even when there's no performance.

Crealy Adventure Park
Sidmouth Road, EX5 1DR (01395 233200, www.crealy.co.uk). Open Apr-Sept 10am-6pm Mon, Thur-Sun. Oct-Mar 10am-5pm Thur-Sun. Admission £13.50-£14.50; free-£10.50 reductions.
This large family attraction has activities for children of all ages, with lots of indoor things to do on rainy days. It's divided into six realms: animals, adventure, action, farming, nature and magic. There are small animals to cuddle, ponies to groom, nature trails to follow and a train to ride around the park. And, of course, there are the rides, guaranteed to cause much shrieking and laughter. It's open daily during the school holidays.

Exeter Corn Exchange
Market Street, EX1 1BU (01392 665866). Tickets prices vary, check website for details.
This city-centre auditorium, under the auspices of the city council, is a major venue for concerts, comedy nights and other performances, as well as events such as CD and book fairs.

Exeter Heritage Trails
Dix's Field, EX1 1GF (01392 665700, www.exeter.gov.uk). Open Summer 9am-5pm Mon-Sat; 10am-4pm Sun. Winter 9am-5pm Mon-Sat.
Exeter's Tourist Information Centre offers three leaflets that plot simple, self-guided walks around the city. The City Wall Trail guides visitors around the wall built by the Romans nearly 2,000 years ago, much of which can still be seen; the Exeter Woollen Trail explores key sites associated with the woollen cloth trade, including the mills and warehouses by the river; and the Medieval Trail gives an insight into life in the Middle Ages.

Exeter Northcott
Stocker Road, EX4 4QB (01392 493493, www.exeternorthcott.co.uk). Box office 10am-8pm Mon, Tue, Thur-Sat; 11am-8pm Wed; 10am-1hr before performance Sun. Tickets £8-£15.
Exeter's professional repertory company presents a year-round programme of serious drama, plus children's shows and pantomime. The highlight is the annual Shakespeare in the Gardens production, performed in Rougemont Gardens during the Exeter Summer Festival. The Northcott also hosts visiting opera, ballet and touring productions, plus student theatre.

Exeter Phoenix
Bradninch Place, Gandy Street, EX4 3LS (01392 667080, www.exeterphoenix.org.uk). Tickets prices vary, check website for details.
The Phoenix arts centre hosts theatre, music, dance and comedy performances, along with screenings organised by the Exeter Film Society (open to all) and four exhibition spaces. Upstairs is the Voodoo Lounge, a more intimate setting for acoustic sessions.

Exeter University Streatham Campus
Northcote House, EX4 4QJ (01392 661000, www.exeter.ac.uk/fineart).
Located north of the city centre, Exeter University's Streatham Campus is a beautiful spot, with extensive views across the city. The attractive gardens were originally laid out in the 1860s, when the estate was privately owned; they've been developed and extended over the years, and are now a delightful mix of formal and informal areas and a rich wildlife habitat. Recent years have seen the development of a sculpture walk, which includes a Barbara Hepworth. (Note that access to indoor sculptures is restricted to weekdays and Saturday mornings only). Pick up a leaflet from the Tourist Information Centre or on campus.

Go Ape!
Haldon Forest Park, Bullers Hill, Kennford, EX6 7XR (0845 643 2056, www.goape.co.uk). Open phone for details. Admission from £30; £20 reductions.
Discover your inner Tarzan by shinning up rope ladders and zooming along zip wires at this treetop adventure trail in Haldon Forest Park, just off the A38 south of Exeter. Safety harnesses and instructors provide reassurance. Booking is essential.

Haldon Forest Park
Haldon Forest Park, Bullers Hill, Kennford, EX6 7XR (01392 834251, www.forestry.gov.uk/haldonforestpark).
In handsome Haldon Forest Park, bikes can be hired at the Forestry Centre, where there are also toilets, a shower and a café. The forest itself contains footpaths and wildlife trails, along with play trails suitable for families with buggies. The gallery at the Centre for Contemporary Art & the Natural World (01392 832277, www.ccanw.co.uk) displays sculptures fashioned from wood and natural materials.

Mama Stone's
1 Mary Arches Street, EX4 3BA (01392 848485, www.mamastones.com). Open 5pm-midnight Tue; 5pm-2am Thur-Sat; 5pm-1am Sun. Admission varies, check website for details.
Run by Joss's mum, Mama Stone's offers a mix of singer-songwriters and bands. The bar dispenses mojitos and long island ice teas, while the menu oozes an easygoing, Southern-influenced vibe: fried chicken wings, Cajun pork patties, cheese-topped fries and other guilty pleasures. Singing lessons and workshops are also available, for those keen to hone their own vocals.

New Theatre
Friars Gate, EX2 4AZ (01392 277189, www.cygnetnewtheatre.com). Tickets vary, check website for details.
Home to the Cygnet Theatre Company, which trains young actors, this intimate venue runs a programme of drama performed both by the Cygnet troupe and by touring companies.

DEVON

Red Coat Guided Tours
01392 265203, www.exeter.gov.uk/guidedtours.
See website for details.
Exeter's Red Coat Guides run a programme of 18 free walking tours, generally illuminating some aspect of the city's history and occasionally allowing access to places that are otherwise off-limits (the medieval refectory of St Nicholas Priory, for instance). Themes include Cathedral to Quay, Medieval Treasures, Exeter's City Wall and Ghosts & Legends. Most of the tours last about 90 minutes and start from Cathedral Yard; there's no need to book. For a schedule, check online or pick up a leaflet from the Tourist Information Centre.

Rock Centre
Chudleigh, TQ13 OEE (01626 852717, www.rockcentre.co.uk). Open by appointment only. Admission varies, check website for details.
Another venue for would-be apes lies just over the hill in Chudleigh, where there are more treetop adventures along with indoor and outdoor rock climbing and abseiling. There's also a chance to see some of the caves in this limestone outcrop.

TOPSHAM & AROUND
RSPB Avocet Cruises
01392 432691, www.rspb.org.uk.
See website for details.
The RSPB operates birdwatching cruises of varying lengths during the winter months. All have with expert commentary, and run from from Topsham, Exmouth and Starcross.

Stuart Line Cruises
Exmouth Marina, EX8 1DS (01395 222144, www.stuartlinecruises.co.uk). Cruises Easter-Oct (times dependent on tides). Tickets from £5; £3 reductions.
Between Topsham and Exmouth, Stuart Line Cruises operates a 'Round Robin' boat and train cruise: travel one way by boat on the River Exe, explore your destination, then come back by train. In addition, there are a couple of ferry services between Topsham and Turf Lock; see p103.

Topsham Outdoor Swimming Pool
Fore Street, EX3 0HF (01392 874477, www.topshampool.com). Open Mid May-mid Sept times vary, check website for details. Admission £3; £2 reductions.
Numerous children have learnt to swim at Topsham's open-air pool, set next to the bowling green behind Matthews Hall and opened in 1979. The water is heated by solar panels, and awash with giant inflatables during the twice weekly 'serpent attack!' childrens' sessions.

Topsham Society Walks
01392 873457, www.topshamsociety.co.uk. Open May-Sept 2pm Mon, Sat. Admission free.
The Topsham Society runs free walking tours of the town at 2pm on Wednesdays and Saturdays, from May to September. Meet at the Holman Way car park; there's no need to book.

boats. It remains open for business (Exminster, 01392 833128, www.turfpub.net) as one of the few pubs in the country that can't be reached by car. In summer, the menu extends to barbecues in the huge beer garden.

You can continue from here along the narrow path on the embankment beside the estuary to reach the minor road at Powderham Church; the road can then be followed to Starcross.

Leaflets on the canal and estuary are available from Exeter's Tourist Information Centre (Dix's Field, 01392 665700, closed Sun Winter), and there are displays on the history of the waterways at the Quay House Visitor Centre (*see p101*).

Where to eat & drink
There are plenty of cafés in the city centre, including several in Cathedral Close that have outdoor tables. The menu at Tea on the Green (01392 276913) includes a selection of set teas; there's also a Sunday lunch menu. At the far end, the small Plant Deli (01392 428144) offers wholesome, vegetarian fare. And No.21 (01392 210303) serves light lunches and afternoon teas. For lunch on the go, try a sandwich or a salad from Michael Caines' nearby MC Boutique (01392 256200, www.michaelcaines.com), opposite the Ship Inn in Martins Lane.

Many national chains have outlets in the city centre. Among them are casual, family-friendly Giraffe on Princesshay (01392 494222, www.giraffe.net) and, near where Princesshay meets Bedford Street, upscale Italian café Carluccio's (01392 410492, www.carluccios.com), the Strada pizzeria group (01392 432727, www.strada.co.uk) and the Spanish-inspired La Tasca chain (01392 434488, www.latasca.co.uk). Unique to Exeter are colourful Exeshed (01392 420070, www.shedrestaurants.co.uk) and, on Queen Street, Juice Moose (01392 427900, closed Sun), majoring in juices and smoothies.

Cat in the Hat
29 Magdalen Road, EX2 4TA (01392 211700, www.cathat.co.uk). Lunch served noon-2.30pm, dinner served 6-9.30pm Tue-Sat.
The Cat in the Hat offers reliable modern British cooking over in the St Leonard's area, a little way from the city centre. The dinner menu might take in the likes of marinated wood pigeon with a roast shallot, beetroot and hazelnut salad; black bream fillet with olive mash; and roast lamb rump with dauphinois potatoes. At lunchtime there's a shorter menu. The room is small, and booking is advisable.

Herbies
15 North Street, EX4 3QS (01392 258473). Lunch served 11am-2.30pm Mon-Fri; 10.30am-4pm Sat. Dinner served 6-9.30pm Tue-Sat.
Informal, friendly Herbies has been feeding local vegetarians for more than 20 years with an array of simple, wholesome dishes. The menu includes spicy beanburgers, dahls, salads and a Mediterranean platter (olives, houmous and so on); there's a soup special every lunchtime, when the restaurant is particularly popular. There's also a children's menu.

LOCAL WILDLIFE

Bowling Green Marsh RSPB Reserve
01392 824614, www.rspb.org.uk
An excellent viewing point with a bird hide and a platform on the edge of Topsham Park in Topsham.

Dawlish Warren Nature Reserve
www.dawlishwarren.co.uk
A range of habitats make up this large nature reserve. There's detailed information at the on-site visitors' centre, along with details of the regular guided walks. The car park is signed off the A379 Exeter to Dawlish road.

Exe Reed Beds
Devon Wildlife Trust Reserve
01395 279244,
www.devonwildlifetrust.org
This area of reed bed and saltmarsh at the upper end of the estuary is a breeding site for warblers and is visited by winter migrants. It can be viewed from the canal towpath. Park inside the South West Water treatment works entrance, beside the Countess Wear bridge.

Exminster Marshes RSPB Reserve
01392 824614, www.rspb.org.uk
At this large area of marshland and wet pasture on the west side of the upper estuary, birds can be seen roosting at high tide. It's also a spring breeding area for waders and wildfowl. To reach it, follow the footpaths from Exminster village or the car park by the railway bridge on Station Road, past the Swan's Nest Inn.

Exmouth Local Nature Reserve
01395 222299, www.eastdevon.gov.uk/ exmouth_local_nature_reserve
This reserve covers a large area of mudflats known as Cockle Sand, which can be explored at low tide or viewed from the riverside path between Exmouth and Lympstone (parts of which are accessible to wheelchairs). It's a good place to see waders and wildfowl, especially either side of high tide. Park in Exmouth.

Powderham
The sea wall between Powderham and the Turf Lock gives good views over the middle part of the estuary. There's a small parking area beside the railway line near Powderham church.

Jack in the Green Inn ★
Rockbeare, EX5 2EE (01404 822240, www.jackinthe green.uk.com). Open 11am-2.30pm, 5.30-11pm Mon-Thur; 11am-3pm, 5.30-11pm Fri; 11am-3pm, 6-11pm Sat; noon-10.30pm Sun. Lunch served 11.30am-2pm Mon-Thur; 11.30am-2.30pm Fri, Sat. Dinner served 6-9.30pm Mon; 6-10pm Tue-Sat. Food served noon-9.30pm Sun.
Head chef Matthew Mason leans heavily on local produce for his menus at this traditional-looking pub, about five miles outside Exeter. Served in a stylish, understated dining room, the regular menu takes in the likes of smoked fish from Dartmouth and pork belly from Kenniford Farm in Clyst St Mary, while the list of daily specials reflects what's just been caught, foraged or harvested: hand-dived scallops from Lyme Bay, for instance. The bar has a good range of local brews on tap, and a simpler food menu that includes the likes of posh prawn cocktail and a hearty beef and stilton cobbler.

Lily's
153 Fore Street, EX4 3AT (01392 278641, www.lilys restaurantexeter.co.uk). Lunch served 11.30am-2.30pm, dinner served 6-11pm Tue-Sat.
One of several restaurants to have opened in recent years in Exeter's West Quarter, Lily's is a handsome, modern room with an informal ground-floor bar and a smart mezzanine dining room. The food could be described as global comfort cooking: you might find the likes of roasted chicken wings with barbecue sauce, potato skins with cheese and jalapeño peppers, fajitas, steaks and calamares on the menu.

Michael Caines at ABode Exeter
Cathedral Yard, EX1 1HD (01392 223638, www.michaelcaines.com). Lunch served noon-2.30pm, dinner served 6-10pm Mon-Sat.
Having taken over the former Royal Clarence Hotel by the cathedral, local-boy-made-good Caines has developed this fine-dining restaurant within it. The use of locally sourced ingredients is central to the menu, which might include confit of duck liver with rhubarb compote and shitake mushrooms; River Exe salmon; and roasted saddle of Devon lamb. A café-bar and grill offers more informal dining; upstairs, there are 53 contemporary-style bedrooms (£79-£165 double incl breakfast).

Where to stay
Michael Caines' ABode hotel by the cathedral offers some of Exeter's smartest and best accommodation; see above.

Exeter Globe Backpackers
71 Holloway Street, EX2 4JD (01392 215521, www.exeterbackpackers.co.uk). Rates from £16.50 per night.
An independent hostel in an 18th-century townhouse close to the city centre, this place has three private rooms (for two to four people) and five dormitories, plus a self-catering kitchen and free showers. Facilities include Wi-Fi.

Exeter YHA Hostel
Mount Wear House, 47 Countess Wear Road, EX2 6LR (0845 371 9516, www.yha.org.uk). Rates £15.95 per night; £11.95 under-18s.

Jack in the Green Inn

This 66-bed hostel occupies a 17th-century house on the city outskirts, close to the river. It has a full range of facilities, with breakfast and evening meals available.

Old Mill Guest House

Oil Mill Lane, Clyst St Mary, EX5 1AG (01392 259977, www.oldmillbedandbreakfast.co.uk). Rates from £68 double incl breakfast.

On the outskirts of the city, this historic converted mill building is set in its own grounds, and contains four B&B bedrooms along with a guests' lounge. There's a regular bus service to the city centre.

Park View Hotel

8 Howell Road, EX4 4LG (01392 271772, www.park viewexeter.co.uk). Rates £58-£65 double incl breakfast.

This Grade II-listed Georgian house overlooks Bury Meadow, a small park between the city centre and the university. There are ten double or twin rooms, one single and two family rooms, most with en suite facilities. The dining room opens on to a handsome patio.

Raffles

11 Blackall Road, EX4 4HD (01392 270200, www. raffles-exeter.co.uk). Rates £72 double incl breakfast.

This sympathetically restored, antiques-packed Victorian townhouse is a well-appointed, comfortable place. The owners use organic produce wherever possible, and most of the items on the breakfast menu are of local origin.

St Olaves Hotel

Mary Arches Street, EX4 3AZ (01392 217736, www. olaves.co.uk). Rates £115-£155 double incl breakfast.

This elegant, 200-year-old building is set in its own walled garden near the city centre. There are 14 bedrooms in the hotel, all with en suite facilities, plus a one-bed apartment and a three-bed house in a medieval building. The hotel's Treasury restaurant, open to non-residents, is named in honour of the nearby Mint. A more informal 'garden menu' can be enjoyed in the lounge and conservatory overlooking the garden.

Townhouse

55 St David's Hill, EX4 4DT (01392 494994, www.townhouseexeter.co.uk). Rates £70-£75 double incl breakfast.

The Townhouse offers modern B&B accommodation in a spacious Edwardian house, within walking distance of the city centre and the main station. The nine rooms are named after fictional characters, from Arthur Dent to Bathsheba Everdene; facilities include Wi-Fi and a peaceful garden.

Wood Barton

Farringdon, EX52HY (01395 233407). Rates £60-£65 double incl breakfast. No credit cards.

The rooms at this farmhouse, a few miles east of Exeter, are traditional and comfortable. Breakfast is based on farm fare, and is cooked the old-fashioned way on an Aga. Farringdon is surrounded by countryside, but is handy for the M5.

DEVON

TOPSHAM & AROUND

Throughout its history, Topsham's position near the head of the Exe Estuary has been its defining feature. Four miles from the city of Exeter and bypassed by the main traffic routes, this former port could easily have faded into obscurity. Instead, it remains firmly on the map, thanks to its nautical heritage, varied architecture and flourishing shopping and foodie scenes.

The Roman port here was active for almost 400 years, serving Exeter. However, the town's fortunes really took off in the 13th century, when Countess Isabella de Fortibus effectively cut off Exeter's link with the sea by having a weir built across the river above Topsham. Her successors, the de Courtenays, built on her initiative, and the port of Topsham flourished: the quay was extended, shipbuilding yards were established and foreign trade grew. Although Exeter regained its link with the sea when the Exeter Ship Canal was opened in 1566, Topsham remained the more important port, and prospered up until the 19th century.

Today, Topsham's estuary is used for leisure. A little ferry boat plies to and fro across the river (daily except Tuesdays in summer, weekends in winter), giving access to the canalside path that runs from Exeter quay to the Turf Lock. On the east bank, Topsham is connected to Exeter by a short railway line that ends at Exmouth.

Major honeypot sights are absent from Topsham, but there are plenty of notable buildings throughout the town. Many are private residences that date from the town's heyday. Among them are the Dutch-style houses in the Strand, built around 1700 with bricks brought back from Holland as ballast by ships whose outward cargo was Devon cloth; the imposing red-brick Broadway House on the High Street, built in 1776 and now a tearoom and B&B; and, on Fore Street, the Salutation Inn, here since 1720, and two small, timber-framed medieval houses (at nos.61 and 62). Running parallel with Fore Street along the river, Ferry Road has several houses that were once sail lofts (Wixels and Furlong among them) and some old warehouses. Dating from 1721, the Passage Inn has a fine pedimented doorcase.

Ferry Road and Fore Street converge at the quay; the oldest part of it, where the Lighter Inn now occupies the old Custom House, is said to date from the early 14th century. The quay's present form took shape in 1861, when it was extended to house a spur of the Great Western Railway. As you stroll around the quay, note the sailing trawler *Ros-Ailither*, moored alongside. The boat was built in 1954 and used for commercial fishing for 46 years before being bought by its present owners, who now live on it. Since their five-year restoration of the boat, they've sailed it across the Atlantic and back.

It's well worth walking to the end of the Strand, past the aforementioned 'Dutch' houses and the Topsham Museum (*see p110*), to the point at which a slipway drops to the water and the whole estuary opens out like a watercolour painting, with Exmouth on the horizon. A raised path known as the Goat Walk continues alongside the sea wall; take in the estuary views or continue to the lane, which curves past Bowling Green Marsh beside the River Clyst and returns beside the railway to Topsham.

Bowling Green Marsh itself is a low-lying area beside the River Clyst, close to its outflow into the Exe. Part of the Exe Estuary Site of Special Scientific Interest, it's a prime spot from which to watch the abundant birdlife; a hide overlooks the marsh. There's also a raised viewing platform, from which you can look across the mud as the tide goes out and watch a range of feeding birds. Information boards give details of what species are likely to be seen. For more on the estuary's wildlife, *see below*.

Away from the historic architecture and abundant birdlife, the town is dotted with small shops, many specialising in bijou homewares. Notable exceptions on Fore Street include Country Cheeses, which offers plenty of mouth-watering English artisan cheeses, and Joel Segal Books, which specialises in rare and antiquarian volumes. Galleries on Fore Street include the Art Room (above the Café, closed Mon-Fri) and Tony Isham's nauticalia-packed Gallery @ 58 (closed Sun). And down on the quay, an old red-brick warehouse is now packed to the gunnels with antiques; it's open 10am-5pm daily.

The Exe Estuary

Once a focus of maritime trade, today the estuary of the River Exe is a prime site for wildlife, and a site of great importance thanks to the numbers of resident and migratory birds it attracts. At almost one and a half miles wide at its seaward end and more than six miles long, it's Devon's largest estuary. This rich environment, with many areas of sandbanks and mudflats, is home to millions of tiny creatures, creating a food chain that supports large numbers of fish and birds.

On the west side of the estuary's mouth, the sand dunes of Dawlish Warren provide a habitat and a high-tide roost for birds. More than 600 species of plant have been recorded here, including orchids, evening primrose and the Warren crocus, which flowers in April and is found at only one other location in Britian. Invertebrates such as moths, dragonflies and damselflies thrive here, and sand lizards can be seen from late spring onwards.

Spring and autumn bring thousands of migratory birds, but winter is the peak time for birds in the estuary. One eye-catching winter visitor is the avocet, which can be seen on the mudflats of the upper estuary and at Bowling Green Marsh. Wildfowl are also here in significant numbers during the colder months, when wigeon, teal, pintail, mallard, eiders, red-breasted mergansers, Brent geese and mute swans are all likely to make an appearance. Also regularly found on the mudflats are redshank, curlew, lapwing, black-tailed godwit, greenshank and little egret; further downstream, you may find sanderling, turnstone, oystercatcher, dunlin and plovers, among others.

Where to eat & drink

For lunch and daytime snacks, the Avocet Café on Fore Street (01392 877887, www.avocetcafe. co.uk, closed Sun) offers own-made soups, scones,

DEVON

Darts Farm

Just under a mile outside Topsham on the road towards Exmouth, Darts Farm (01392 878200, www.dartsfarm. co.uk) has picked up the concept of the farm shop and run with it. The standard farm-shop ethos – home-grown produce, sold at fair prices – is at the heart of the enterprise, but this is virtually a complete shopping village under one roof.

Central to the business is the farm shop, which sells produce from this working farm (meat, vegetables, salad crops and fruit), augmented by seasonal produce from other local growers. There's also a food hall, where you'll find a huge range of artisan products from the West Country and beyond, plus a bakery, a deli, a florist and a butcher (Gerald David). The Fish Shed is a combination fishmonger–fish 'n' chip shop with a twist: customers can choose their fish from the wet fish counter and have it cooked for them on the spot (grilled or battered). Beers and ciders are offered in the Cider Works and Ale House, and upmarket homewares are sold at a couple of outlets.

Given Darts Farm's proximity to the Exe Estuary, it's appropriate that the RSPB has a shop on site, at which you can buy bird food and feeders as well as binoculars and gifts for birdy friends. If you need weatherproof gear, Cotswold Outdoor should be able to help. Naturally enough, there's also a restaurant here, at which you can enjoy dishes based on products from the shops.

To reach Darts Farm from Topsham, leave the town along Bridge Hill (past the Bridge Inn); the farm is on the right, about a mile from Fore Street.

juices and a range of things on toast. Topsham's most famous café, though, is the very traditional Georgian Tearoom in Broadway House on the High Street (01392 873465, http://broadway house.com, closed Mon, Sun), which serves Devon cream teas alongside a range of more substantial dishes.

Topsham holds a certain level of notoriety in some quarters due to the tradition of the 'Topsham Ten' pub crawl, a freeform stagger around the village's hostelries. Among them are the historic, CAMRA-friendly Bridge Inn (Bridge Hill, 01392 873862, www.cheffers.co.uk), run by the same family since 1897 and famous as the only pub in the country ever visited by the Queen; the Globe (Fore Street,

01392 873471, www.globehotel.com), an old coaching inn with 19 en-suite rooms; and the Lighter Inn (Fore Street, 01392 875439), located on the quay. Full details of the ten can be found at www.topsham.org.

Galley

41 Fore Street, Topsham, EX3 0HU (01392 876078, www.galleyrestaurant.co.uk). Lunch served noon-2pm, dinner served 6.30-9.30pm Tue-Sat.

Paul Da-Costa-Greaves's restaurant is housed in a Grade II-listed building close to the quay. Appropriate, then, that fish is a speciality, sourced daily from Brixham down the coast and from other local fishermen. The menu might include a mixed grill of fish with a Cajun edge; fillets of turbot on a

Places to visit

EXETER

Killerton
Broadclyst, EX5 3LE (01392 881345, www.national trust.org.uk/killerton). Open House Mar-Nov 11am-5pm daily. Dec 2-4pm daily. Feb 2-4pm Sat, Sun. Gardens 10.30am-7pm daily. Admission £8.40; £4.20 reductions; £20.70 family.
This 18th-century house was built for one of Devon's oldest families, the Aclands, who also oversaw the creation of its stunning hillside gardens and wooded parkland. The magnolias and rhododendrons are glorious in springtime, while summer brings outdoor concerts. Inside the main house, changing displays showcase pieces from the vast historical clothing collection. The estate extends to Marker's Cottage in nearby Broadclyst, a lovely little medieval cob-and-thatch cottage, and the Old Post Office in Budlake, preserved 1950s style with a pigsty, a henhouse and a cottage garden (both closed Nov-Mar).

Royal Albert Memorial Museum
3 Queen Street, EX4 3RX (01392 665858, www.exeter.gov.uk/ramm). Closed until 2011.
The city's main museum is undergoing a major refurbishment. When it reopens in 2011, it will centre on a double-height courtyard space for public events, surrounded by a series of galleries. Until then, look for the Out & About programme of events outside the Queen Street building.

St Nicholas Priory
The Mint, off Fore Street, EX4 3BL (01392 665858, www.exeter.gov.uk/priory). Open 10am-5pm Mon-Sat school hols; 10am-5pm Sat term time. Admission £2.50; £1-£2 reductions.
This ancient building was originally part of a medieval priory, and later became the home of a wealthy Tudor merchant family. It's furnished in the style of an Elizabethan townhouse. There's a small garden too, planted with Tudor herbs.

Spacex
45 Preston Street, EX1 1DF (01392 431786, www.spacex.co.uk). Open 10am-5pm Tue-Sat. Admission free.
Housed in a 19th-century warehouse in the West Quarter, this contemporary arts space exhibits both established and new artists. It also has a programme of talks, children's activities and other events.

Tobys Reclamation ★
Station Road, Exminster, EX6 8DZ (01392 833499, www.tobysreclamation.com). Open 8.30am-5pm Mon-Fri; 9.30am-5pm Sat; 10.30am-4pm Sun.
If you're restoring a period house, or simply enjoy poking through architectural salvage and old furniture, head to this reclamation shop. Its varied wares include everything from Victorian candelabra to ornate fountains, heavy church pews and old red telephone boxes.

Tuckers' Hall
140 Fore Street, EX4 3AT (01392 412348, www.tuckershall.org.uk). Open June-Sept 10.30am-12.30pm Tue, Thur, Fri. Oct-May 10.30am-12.30pm Thur. Admission varies, check website for details.
Belonging to the Guild of Weavers, Fullers & Shearmen, this Grade II-listed building was constructed in 1471 as a chapel for cloth workers. It was converted into a guildhall at the Reformation, and is worth seeing for its beautifully panelled rooms.

Underground Passages
2 Paris Street, EX1 1GA (01392 665887, www.exeter. gov.uk/passages). Open June-Sept 9.30am-5.30pm Mon-Sat; 10.30am-4pm Sun. Oct-May 11.30am-5.30pm Tue-Fri; 9.30am-5.30pm Sat; 11.30am-4pm Sun. Admission £5; £3.50-£4 reductions; £15 family.
Built in the 14th and 15th centuries to carry fresh water from springs outside the city, Exeter's intriguing network of vaulted underground passages can now be explored on foot, giving a fascinating glimpse into this subterranean world. There's an exhibition and interpretation centre with interactive displays, and visits begin with a short film. Claustrophobics beware.

TOPSHAM & AROUND

Kenton Vineyard
Helwell Barton, Kenton, EX6 8NW (01626 891091, www.kentonvineyard.co.uk). Open May-Sept 3pm Sun. Admission Wine tasting free. Vine Trail £2. Vineyard Tour £7.
The Kenton Vineyard was planted in 2003 on south-facing slopes not far from the Exe Estuary. It's now producing wines made on the premises, which can be sampled in the shop. Tours take visitors through the vineyard and winery.

Powderham Castle
Powderham Park, Powderham, EX6 8JQ (01626 890243, www.powderham.co.uk). Open July, Aug 11am-5.30pm Mon-Fri, Sun. Apr-June, Sept, Oct 11am-4pm Mon-Fri, Sun. Admission £9.50; free-£8.50 reductions; £26.50 family.
Idyllically located in its own deer park beside the estuary, this stately pile, belonging to the Earl of Devon, is one of the oldest family houses in England. It started life as a medieval fortified manor house, but was extensively remodelled and extended in the 1840s. Tours take you from the medieval core to the grand mid 18th-century staircase, neo-classical music room (which dates from 1796) and the Victorian kitchen. Outside, there are acres of deer park to explore. Other attractions include regular birds of prey demonstrations, an adventure play castle, and, if you climb to the foot of the curious triangular belvedere, views over the estuary. Also on site are a tearoom, a gift shop and the Powderham Country Store, selling a wide range of West Country foods.

Topsham Museum
25 Strand, Topsham, EX3 0AX (01392 873244, www.devonmuseums.net/topsham). Open Apr-Oct 2-5pm Mon, Wed, Sat, Sun. Admission free.
Housed in one of the 17th-century buildings on the Strand, with a garden overlooking the river, this museum explores Topsham's maritime history through a fine display of historic rivercraft. Other rooms contain period furnishings; one is devoted to a display of memorabilia connected with the film star Vivien Leigh. Round off the day with a cream tea in the tearoom.

DEVON

Tobys Reclamation

FIVE DEVON BEERS

Albert Ale, Totnes
The sign of the Albert pub, Bridgetown Brewery's base in Totnes, shows not the usual Prince Consort but shock-haired genius Albert Einstein. Its Albert Ale is a 3.8% pale session beer which, in January 2009, was a guest ale at the Houses of Parliament. A rapid result for a beer that was first brewed less than a year earlier.
Tasting notes Light and floral.

Break Water, Bishopsteignton
You'll find Red Rock bottled beers behind the bar at many of the coolest drinking places in the South Hams. The beers are brewed using spring water and crushed barley from the company's farm, malt from nearby Tuckers Maltings, whole hops and fresh yeast. Red Rock makes eight beers, from Back Beach (3.8%) to Christmas Cheer (5.2%); the 4.8% Break Water is made with three kinds of hops and three kinds of malt, and won a bronze award in the Taste of the West Awards 2009.
Tasting notes A mouth-filling flavour of roasted malt, balanced with a heavy hop finish.

Druid's Fluid, Ilfracombe
Drinkers describe tastes of toffee and caramel in this red-brown 5% beer from the Wizard Brewery, which started out in Warwickshire but is now firmly established in Ilfracombe.
Tasting notes Full bodied and rich, with a bitter aftertaste.

Jail Ale, Dartmoor
The name of this amber 4.8% premium bitter refers to the nearby Dartmoor prison. Princetown-based Dartmoor Brewery is the highest brewery in England, at 1,400 feet above sea level. Its Jail Ale is widely available south of Exeter, and also comes in bottles.
Tasting notes Full bodied and well rounded, with a sweet finish.

Otter Amber, Honiton
Otter Brewery's new Amber 4% beer, with a citrus and pine aroma, is available in over 20 pubs and gained a silver award in the Taste of the West Awards 2009. To cut its energy consumption, the brewery has built an eco-cellar with a grass roof to store 5,000 barrels.
Tasting notes Soft tropical fruit and spices, traditional bitter aftertaste.

seaweed mash; and even posh fish 'n' chips with 'Yorkshire caviar'. Vegetarian and vegan dishes are also available. Children aged 12 and over are welcome, but this is not what might be termed a family restaurant. Booking is essential.

Oliva Restaurant
6-7 Fore Street, Topsham, EX3 0HF (01392 877878, www.olivarestaurant.co.uk). Lunch served noon-2pm Wed-Sat. Dinner served 6-9.30pm Mon-Sat.
The style of cooking at Tim Golder's Oliva is predominantly Mediterranean, focusing especially on seafood and paella; there's a choice of five different paellas, including a seafood variety with River Teign mussels. Other dishes might include oven-roasted rack of Devon lamb, and wild mushroom risotto topped with mozzarella; tapas is available every lunchtime and on Thursday evenings. On days when the weather is in tune with the menu, you can dine outside on the terrace.

La Petite Maison
35 Fore Street, Topsham, EX3 0HR (01392 873660, www.lapetitemaison.co.uk). Lunch served by appointment, dinner served 7-10pm Tue-Sat.
This attractive little house curves around the corner where Fore Street descends to the quay. The food is modern British, made with local produce; menus might include such dishes as fillet of sea bass and monkfish with chive potato cakes and beurre blanc, Somerset pork in a herb crust with black pudding on creamy leeks and dauphinois potatoes. Warm almond and apricot tart with amaretto mascarpone cream is a typical dessert.

Where to stay

Ebford Cottage
Lower Lane, Ebford, EX3 0QT (01392 877914, www.ebfordcottage.co.uk). Rates from £55 double incl breakfast. No credit cards.
Just outside Topsham, this 17th-century thatched cottage has one comfortable double room available for B&B, with evening meals offered by arrangement. Next door is the Studio, where hot stone massage, reflexology, reiki and other therapies are available; guests are offered a 15% discount.

Highfield Farm Campsite
Clyst Road, nr Topsham, EX3 0BY (01392 876388, www.highfieldfarm.org). Open Mar-Oct. Rates £5-£6 per night for 2 people.
This small, simple caravan park and campsite is on a mixed organic farm just outside the town, close to the River Clyst. Facilities are basic – there's no hot water or showers – but everything is eco-friendly, and there's a farm trail that runs through traditional grazing meadows.

Steam Packet Apartments
Route 2 Café Bar, 1 Monmouth Hill, Topsham, EX3 0JJ (01392 873471, www.route2topsham.co.uk/ accommodation). Rates £100 double.
Three fully serviced apartments are located above the Route 2 Café Bar in what was formerly the Steam Packet, one of Topsham's oldest inns. Now run as an annexe to the Globe Hotel's accommodation, they've been refurbished in a modern style and offer en suite bath or shower rooms and sitting rooms with Wi-Fi connections.

South Devon: Dawlish to Torbay

Stretching from the River Teign to the mouth of the Exe is the area known as Teignbridge. To the north is the sedate seaside town of Dawlish and the sandy dunes of Dawlish Warren – part tranquil nature reserve, part caravan park and stomping ground for the bucket-and-spade brigade. The mouth of the Teign Estuary is flanked by Teignmouth, another classic Victorian resort, and the pretty village of Shaldon; upriver, Newton Abbot remains a thriving market town.

South along the coast is Torbay – the collective name given to the three very different holiday towns set around the sheltered, sandy arc of Tor Bay. First and foremost comes Torquay – the jewel in the English Riviera's crown, with its yachts, palm tree-lined boulevards and continental dash. With its broad sands and Victorian pier, Paignton is geared towards classic seaside fun, while Brixham is a colourful fishing port, where pastel-painted fishermen's cottages cling to the hill above the harbour.

FROM THE EXE TO THE TEIGN

Dawlish

A few miles south of the Exe Estuary is the seaside town of Dawlish. Turning its attentions from fishing to tourism in the early 19th century, with the coming of the railways, it soon became a watering hole for the literary greats of the day: Jane Austen stayed here (and dispatched Lucy Steele here for her honeymoon in *Sense and Sensibility*), as did Charles Dickens, who designated it his eponymous hero's birthplace in *Nicholas Nickleby*.

Like its larger neighbour Teignmouth, Dawlish's architecture is a mix of Georgian and Victorian. Running through the heart of town is the Lawn; once an area of swampy marshland, it was reclaimed in 1808 and transformed into an ornamental park, with trim and tidy flower beds, meandering paths and Torbay palms.

In the evening, necklaces of coloured lights strung along the paths make this a magical place for a stroll, and the Lawn becomes a hub of activity during August's carnival week. In 2009, a new piazza was created at the eastern side of the Lawn, where a once-monthly Friday farmers' market is held.

To discover the older parts of Dawlish, stroll away from the seafront and up to Manor House gardens, crossing one of the footbridges over the brook and wandering past Manor House, a classic example of grand Regency architecture. On Old Town Street you'll find the thatched cottages of the old village, untouched by the glitzy goings-on at the seafront; the 700-year-old parish church of St Gregory's, with its ancient yew tree; and the tiny, cobbled Albert Street.

To reach the main town beach, which stretches all the way to Dawlish Warren, walk under the railway viaduct at the end of the Lawn. The indomitable Isambard Kingdom Brunel built the station and train line on the sea wall – a remarkable piece of Victorian engineering, making for dazzlingly scenic journeys. If you're after a less crowded beach, try Boat Cove, at the foot of Lea Mount, or Coryton Cove at the end of the seawall, sheltered by steep red cliffs. The rumble of passing trains is a given at all three.

North east from Dawlish, the broad footpath along the sea wall runs past the Red Rock café and on to Dawlish Warren, a sandy spit on the mouth of the Exe. Its sand dunes and the surrounding land form an internationally important 55-acre nature reserve, whose flora and fauna includes the tiny, very rare sand crocus. At the same time, though, the Warren is home to a funfair, crazy golf, go-karts, cafés, holiday chalets and a golf course, and its sandy blue-flag beach, patrolled by lifeguards during high season, is popular with families.

Teignmouth

South-west from Dawlish, at the mouth of the Teign Estuary, Teignmouth combines a busy working port with classic seaside attractions and a wealth of fine Georgian and Victorian architecture.

In 1690, the town was pretty much razed to the ground by a band of marauding French troops, in what was to be the last foreign invasion on English soil. As its fisheries declined in the early 19th century, Teignmouth began to attract the fashionable crowd – hence its splendid Regency houses. With the arrival of Brunel's railway line

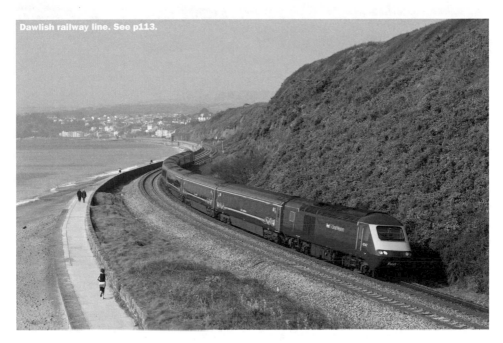

from Exeter in 1846, crowds of Victorian pleasure-seekers came to stroll the seafront and take steamer trips from the pier.

At the harbour entrance stands a diminutive lighthouse, completed in 1845; beyond here, the sandy swath of the main town beach stretches from the mouth of the Teign towards Dawlish. The Victorian pier offers old-fashioned amusements such as penny slot machines and a palm reading ball; once you've squandered your small change, take in the glorious views along the coast or stop for cake and tea at the Beachcomber Café (01626 778909) on Den Promenade.

In summer, the main beach can get busy – but there is a second beach, on the estuary mouth. Known as the river beach or back beach, this is a much quieter spot where you can watch fishing boats going into the harbour to land their catch. The candy-coloured beach huts lined up along the Spit and the boats pulled up on the shore imbue the scene with a dreamy, time-warp feel, and there are plenty of pubs and eateries facing the estuary.

Back on the main seafront, sandwiched between Upper Den Road and Den Crescent, the Den is a landscaped expanse of lawns and flowerbeds with a play area, an adventure golf course, football pitches and a food kiosk. In summer it becomes a hive of activity, playing host to Teignmouth's summer carnival and other family-friendly events. At the end of Den Promenade, at Eastcliff Walk, Teignmouth Lido (01626 215637, www.teignbridge.gov.uk, closed Oct-May) is an open-air heated seafront pool.

Behind the sweep of the seafront, with its colourful flower displays and Torbay palms, is the town centre. The oldest part, which backs on to the river, is a

maze of narrow alleys. Set back from Teign Street, behind a courtyard, Thomas Luny House is a classic Georgian gentleman's residence.

The Triangle is Teignmouth's pedestrianised town square and the centre of its café society; make a detour to Luders Patisserie (01626 773060, closed Sun) in Waterloo Street for delectable French and Swiss pastries and handmade chocolates. The Triangle is also home to the local produce market, on the third Saturday of each month. Further retail therapy can be found in Wellington Street and Bank Street, where high street names rub shoulders with quirkier independent outlets.

On balmy evenings, make your way to the Ship Inn (01626 772674) on Queen Street, where you can sit outside with a pint and watch gig teams practising out on the water. Other notable pubs include Ye Olde Jolly Sailor (46 Northumberland Place, 01626 772864), a rare 12th-century survivor of the French raid in 1690, and the beachside New Quay Inn (01626 774145) – a former smugglers' haunt which has replaced duty-dodgers with bands.

Teignmouth Folk Club hold gigs at the Devon Arms Hotel (Northumberland Place, 01626 774400) on the last Thursday of each month, and there are bluegrass sessions on the first Thursday of the month. The town also hosts an annual jazz festival and folk festival.

Shaldon

With its thatched cottages and village green, this pretty riverside village is the antithesis of the rather grand seaside resort across the water. Drive over the bridge, or check if the little passenger ferry

Shaldon

from Teignmouth (suspended at the time of writing) has resumed service; see www.teignferry.com for the latest update.

The Strand runs alongside Shaldon beach, where wooden gigs and seine boats are pulled up on the shingle. Across the road are a handful of pubs and bistros; with its chalkboard of daily specials from the sea, estuary views and riverside gardens, the Ferry Boat Inn (01626 872340) is a classic spot at which to soak up the scene.

Continue along the Strand and Marine Parade towards the red sandstone headland known as the Ness. Here, you'll find Ness House (01626 873480), a Georgian hotel and pub set in extensive grounds. The views across the estuary are superb, extending beyond Teignmouth towards the red cliffs of Dawlish and the distant beaches of Budleigh and Beer. You can access the little beach at Ness Cove, on the other side of the headland, via an old smugglers' tunnel behind the pub.

Further up the hill, Shaldon Wildlife Trust and Homeyards Botanical Gardens (for both, *see p118*) also afford glorious views over the estuary.

Newton Abbot

At the head of the Teign Estuary is Newton Abbot – transformed, like so many of the towns in this area, by the arrival of the railway in the mid 19th century. The simple market town became a major industrial base, as Great Western Railways established its locomotive and carriage repair works here. Discover more about GWR and its impact on the town at the Newton Abbot Museum (2A St Paul's Road, 01626 201121, www.museum-newtonabbot.co.uk, closed Nov-Feb), by the Town Hall.

The town still proudly retains its market heritage. The main markets are held in the historic Butter Market Hall on Market Walk, where the pannier market (closed Sun) sells everything from flowers and pet food to kitchen utensils. The outdoor market is held in the adjacent square on Wednesdays

and Saturdays; on Fridays, magpie-eyed collectors come here for the Trash and Treasure Market.

Newton Abbot farmers' market is held on Tuesday morning in pedestrianised Courtenay Street, offering everything from pasties and rare breed pork to olives, cheese and chutney. The livestock market, an institution since 1221, takes place on Wednesday morning at the Cattle Market.

Newton Abbot is also home to the only working malthouse in Britain that is open to the public. Tuckers Maltings (Teign Road, 01626 334734, www.tuckersonline.co.uk, closed Sat, Sun) produces malt for over 30 breweries. The shop stocks a superb selection of West Country beers, and there's a three-day beer festival in April.

On the outskirts of town, on Newton Road, Newton Abbot Racecourse (01626 353235, www.newtonabbotracing.com) is the UK's leading summer jumping course; if you fancy a flutter, there are regular meetings from March to September.

Decoy Country Park, on the south-east edge of town, is a former clay pit that is now a haven for wildlife and humans. Its facilities include a large play area, a BMX race track and dirt jumps and a lake for fishing, sailing and canoeing. Another green escape is the 114-acre Stover Country Park (01626 835236) on the A382 Newton Abbot/Bovey Tracey road. Encompassing woodland, heathland, lake and marsh, it has a bird hide and an aerial walkway through the trees. Stover is also home to the Ted Hughes Poetry Trail, dotted with 'poetry posts' featuring the great man's nature poems.

To the east of town, the Council Recycling Centre (Brunel Road, 0845 155 1010, www.devon. gov.uk) is an unexpected treasure trove. Kayaks and surfboards are lined up in rows outside, and trestle tables brim with bargains, from wooden wine boxes to old zinc baths. Inside the warehouse are furniture and books.

Where to eat & drink

In Newton Abbot, Ye Olde Cider Bar (01626 354221) on East Street is one of the few cider bars left in the country. It's pretty spartan inside, though you may not notice after a glass of parsnip wine or a pint of scrumpy.

Coombe Cellars

Combeinteignhead, TQ12 4RT (01626 872423, www.thecoombecellars.co.uk). Open 11.30am-11pm daily. Food served noon-9pm Mon-Thur; noon-10pm Fri, Sat; noon-8pm Sun.
On the southern banks of the Teign Estuary, between Newton Abbot and Teignmouth, this rambling village pub is big, bright and airy. Stripped wooden floors, table lamps made from driftwood and estuary views add a seaside feel, and there are plenty of tables outdoors. Food ranges from seasonal specials (seared scallops on black pudding mash with a creamy mustard sauce) to pub classics.

Elizabethan Inn ★

Fore Street, Luton, TQ13 0BL (01626 775425, www.elizabethaninn.co.uk). Open noon-3pm, 6-11pm Mon-Sat; noon-11pm Sun. Food served noon-3pm, 6-9.30pm Mon-Sat; noon-9.30pm Sun.
Set in the hamlet of Luton, this tiny, 16th-century inn sources all its produce within a five-mile radius. The owners are passionate about preparing good, honest food, doing all the butchery in house, dry curing bacon from locally reared pigs and smoking haddock, mackerel, duck and chicken with cherry wood. Bar food ranges from fish cakes to risotto; in the restaurant, the blackboard offers dishes such as ragoût of local venison with woodland mushrooms.

Ode

21 Fore Street, Shaldon, TQ14 0DE (01626 873977, www.odetruefood.co.uk). Lunch served noon-1.30pm Thur, Fri. Dinner served 7-9.30pm Wed-Sat.
Set in a three-storey Georgian townhouse, Ode has won a clutch of awards for its food. Under head chef Tim Bouget the menu is a confident affair. Lyme Bay mackerel, glazed with chilli and teamed with pickled carrots and coriander, is typical of the kitchen's quietly inventive twists. A genuine commitment to organic produce and wild-caught fish is a key part of the ethos, while the interior's reclaimed wood and recycled glass continues the eco theme. Book ahead.

Old Mill Tea Room

23 Brunswick Place, Dawlish, EX7 9PD (07852 314708, www.oldmilltearoom.co.uk). Food served 10.30am-5pm daily. No credit cards.
A lovely place for a cream tea, this tearoom is set in the Strand Mill. The huge waterwheel has now been restored; inside, you can see all the internal working of the mill and the mill stones as you tuck into scones, freshly ground coffee, light lunches and own-made cakes.

Owl & the Pussycat

3 Teign Street, Teignmouth, TQ14 8EA (01626 775321, www.theowlandpussycat.co.uk). Lunch served 10am-2.30pm Mon-Sat; noon-3pm Sun. Dinner served 6-9.30pm Mon-Fri, Sun; 6-10pm Sat.
Local meat and fish plays a starring role on the compact menu at the Owl & the Pussycat, with dishes like assiette of seafood in lemon and herb broth, and pan-roasted rump of South Devon lamb with boulangère potatoes and onion purée. Housed in a Grade II-listed Georgian house with a lovely bow-fronted window, the restaurant is open for brunch, lunch and dinner, and has a loyal local following.

Shaldon Coffee Rush

27 Fore Street, Shaldon, TQ14 0DE (01626 873922). Open 8am-5pm Mon-Sat; 9am-5pm Sun.
With its sky blue-painted exterior and huge picture windows, this place exudes an easygoing charm. The menu runs from coffee and Aga-baked cakes through to jacket potatoes and pies. It's licensed, so Devon cider also features.

Take 2

Old Cinema, Den Crescent, Teignmouth, TQ14 8BQ (01626 879614, www.take2teignmouth.co.uk). Lunch served 11am-3pm, dinner served 5.30-11pm Mon-Fri. Food served 11am-11pm Sat; 11am-5pm Sun.
When Teignmouth's seafront Assembly Rooms opened in 1826, complete with a ballroom, they became the social hub of the town. Later converted into a cinema, the building is now home to a stylish bistro, bar and café. The menu changes seasonally; in winter, steaks and grills often feature, while summer brings a lighter menu. The decor is quietly chic, and the sweeping views from the terrace are a treat.

Where to stay

Just outside Newton Abbot, in Preston, Sampsons Farm (01626 354913, www.sampsonsfarm.com) has 15 rooms and suites in the farmhouse and its converted barns; there's a smart restaurant too. The owner, a professional artist, also runs art courses.

Bay Hotel

15 Powderham Terrace, Teignmouth, TQ14 8BL (01626 774123, www.bayhotelteignmouth.co.uk). Rates £76 double incl breakfast.
Built for the Earl of Devon in 1869, this hotel is one of the historic buildings that make up the elegant face of Teignmouth's seafront. The hotel has fabulous views of the bay, and is an easy walk to the beach. There are 17 en suite bedrooms, including a four-poster suite and three family rooms, prettily decorated in muted pastels. The bistro offers a locally sourced menu, and the bar has an outdoor terrace.

Passage House Hotel

Hackney Lane, Kingsteignton, TQ12 3QH (01626 355515, www.passagehousehotel.co.uk). Rates £95 double incl breakfast.
Set on the Teign Estuary, this hotel is situated at the site of what was once a tidal ford across the River Teign, with gorgeous riverside walks and the Hackney Marshes Nature Reserve close at hand. The hotel offers 90 modern en suite rooms, many with estuary views; next door is the 17th-century Passage House Inn.

TORQUAY

Driving along the coast road into Torquay, you may – on a sunny day, at least – see a fleeting resemblance to St Tropez. White villas are scattered among seven pine-covered hills, which plunge down to an azure bay, while tufted Torbay palms (introduced from New Zealand in the 1820s) line the coast road.

Places to visit

FROM THE EXE TO THE TEIGN

Homeyards Botanical Gardens
Nr Horse Lane, Shaldon, TQ14 0BA (www.shaldon botanicals.wordpress.com). Open 24hrs daily. Admission free.
A romantic Italianate garden on a hillside, created in the late 1920s and early '30s, with rockeries, a terraced arboretum and a ruined summer house, built in the style of a castle. It's a peaceful place for a wander, with views of the estuary and coastline.

Old Walls Vineyard
Old Walls Road, Bishopsteignton, TQ14 9PQ (01626 770877, www.oldwallsvineyard.co.uk). Open Summer 11am-4pm Tue-Sun. Winter 11am-3.30pm Thur-Sat; 11am-4pm Sun. Tours £5.
The steep south-facing slopes of this vineyard were once tended by the Romans. Now the Dawe family have returned it to its ancient use. Tours of the vineyard are followed by tastings, and there's a tearoom and shop.

Shaldon Wildlife Trust
Ness Drive, Shaldon, TQ14 0HP (01626 872234, www.shaldonwildlifetrust.co.uk). Open Summer 10am-6pm daily. Winter 10am-4pm daily. Admission £5.75; £3.25-£4.50 reductions; £14.75 family.
Set in an acre of lush natural woodland gardens, planted with semi-tropical species, this small zoo aims to nurture and preserve some of the world's most endangered smaller animals. Rare residents include the Madagascan giant jumping rat, golden lion tamarin, red-footed tortoise and golden poison dart frog.

TORQUAY

Babbacombe Model Village
Hampton Avenue, Babbacombe, TQ1 3LA (01803 315315, www.babbacombemodelvillage.co.uk). Open times vary, phone for details. Admission £8.50; £6.25-£7.75 reductions.
This world in miniature, with thousands of scaled-down buildings, people and vehicles, opened in 1963. Models include an intricately made castle and a fully animated circus; there are also two model railways. The village is set in lovely gardens and – for wet days – there's a 4D cinema and café. The whole place is lit up after dark.

Brunel Manor Gardens
Teignmouth Road, Watcombe, TQ1 4SF (01803 329333, www.brunelmanor.com). Open Summer 2.30-5.30pm Tue-Thur, Sun. Winter 2.30-4.30pm Tue-Thur, Sun. Admission by donation.
Brunel Manor and its grounds were designed by Isambard Kingdom Brunel, who worked on the project up until his death in 1859. The real draw are the grounds. A garden trail, equipped with interpretation panels takes you through the great man's designs.

Bygones
9 Fore Street, St Marychurch, TQ1 4PR (01803 316874, www.bygones.co.uk). Open Apr-Oct 10am-6pm daily. Feb, Mar 10am-5pm daily. Jan, Nov, Dec 10am-4pm daily. Admission £6.50; £4.50-£5.50 reductions; £20 family.
Go time-travelling at this distinctive attraction, whose exhibits include a full-size recreation of a Victorian

Living Coasts

street, a World War I trench, and a row of 1940s and '50s shops. The Station Café serves own-made scones and traditional cakes, and the souvenir shop is a mine of memorabilia.

Kents Cavern ★
Cavern House, 89-91 Ilsham Road, TQ1 2JF (01803 215136, www.kents-cavern.co.uk). Open 9.30am-4.30pm daily. Admission £8.50; £7 reductions; £29 family.
Experience the life of our prehistoric ancestors in the cave system they once called home. Kids can paint a woolly mammoth, while budding archaeologists will love excavating at the Dig. Access to the cave is by guided tour only, and there's a sound and light show to take you back in time some 400 million years, when the cavern formed at the bottom of a warm tropical sea.

Living Coasts
Torquay Harbourside, Beacon Quay, TQ1 2BG (01803 202474, www.livingcoasts.org.uk). Open 10am-3.30pm daily. Admission £8.35; £6.25-£6.50 reductions; £26.25 family.
Get up close to local bird- and wildlife at the carefully reconstructed beaches, cliff faces and estuary that make up Living Coasts, Torquay's zoo and conservation centre. South American fur seals bask and swim at Fur Seal Cove, penguins roam the sand at Penguin Beach and kittiwakes, puffins and guillemots perch and dive at Auk Cliff.

Torquay Museum
529 Babbacombe Road, TQ1 1HG (01803 293975, www.torquaymuseum.org). Open July-Sept 10am-5pm Mon-Sat; 1.30-5pm Sun. Jan-June, Oct-Dec 10am-5pm Mon-Sat. Admission £4.50; £2.85-£3.40 reductions; £14 family.
Artefacts here run the gamut from a 40,000-year-old Neanderthal jaw bone to Agatha Christie's fur coat. The Time Ark takes children back to Torquay's Jurassic past and allows them to handle fossils, lion skins and elephant tusks.

Torre Abbey & Gardens ★
The King's Drive, TQ2 5JE (01803 293593, www.torre-abbey.org.uk). Open Mar-Oct 11am-6pm daily. Feb, Nov, Dec 10am-5pm Tue-Sun. Admission Abbey & Garden £5.90; £2.50-£4.90 reductions; £14.50 family. Garden only 75p; 35p-50p reductions.
Torre Abbey was once one of England's wealthiest religious houses. Then came the Dissolution of the

Monasteries – and in 1539, the White Canons were forced to surrender it. In 1662, it was sold to the Cary family, who lived there for almost 300 years. The art collection includes works by William Holman Hunt and Edward Burne-Jones, while the magnificent gardens include a palm house. There's a café too.

PAIGNTON

Occombe Farm ★
Preston Down Road, TQ3 1RN (01803 520022, www.occombe.org.uk). Open 9am-5.30pm. Admission free.
Children love getting stuck into life at this organic farm. Children's events include hands-on cookery sessions and bugs and beasts expeditions; most popular of all is Meet the Farmer, when kids help the farmer feed his livestock and find the eggs laid by the Sussex hens. The farm also has a collection of vintage tractors just begging to be climbed on, a farm shop (*see p124*) and a café serving organic grub.

Paignton & Dartmouth Steam Railway
Queens Park Station, Torbay Road, TQ4 6AF (01803 553760, www.pdsr.co.uk). Open 10.30am-5.30pm. Tickets £10 return; £7.50-£9 reductions; £30 family. With Ferry £12; £8.50-£11 reductions; £35 family.
Puff along the English Riviera on the Paignton to Kingswear line, enjoying coastal and river views.

Paignton Zoo & Environmental Park ★
Totnes Road, TQ4 7EU (01803 697500, www. paigntonzoo.org.uk). Open 10am-4pm daily. Admission £12.50; £8.80-£10.30 reductions; £39.50 family.
Visit the desert, cross the savannah and trek through the tropics at this zoo, where 1,200 animals live in 75 acres of landscaped gardens. Crocodile Swamp, with its sinister snappers, and Monkey Heights are among the highlights. A small train trundles around the park every half hour. There's also a playground and café, plus refreshment huts and picnic areas.

Seashore Centre
Tanners Road, TQ4 6LS (01803 528841). Open Apr-Oct times and prices vary, phone for details.
Discover the hidden world of local marine life at this hands-on centre, next to Goodrington Sands. Seawater tanks replicate the underwater environment of Torbay, with inhabitants including seahorses and jewel anemones. There are also interactive displays and a video microscope for examining finds.

BRIXHAM

Berry Head National Nature Reserve ★
Gillard Road, TQ5 9AP (01803 882619, www.berry head.org.uk). Open 24hrs daily. Admission free.
One of the area's most important plant and wildlife reserves. Its caves are home to greater horseshoe bats, and during spring and summer the cliffs house one of the largest breeding colonies of guillemots on the south coast: watch their antics on CCTV in the Visitor Centre. The centre provides information on all the reserve's rare residents. A café now occupies one of the headland's two Napoleonic War-era forts; views from the outdoor tables are superb.

Torquay started life as a little fishing village with a sideline in lime-quarrying, and gradually grew. Word of Torquay's mild climate and fresh sea air (just the thing for convalescents and consumptives) spread, and the arrival of the railway in the late 1840s sealed its popularity. By the 1850s, Torquay was frequented by the crème de la crème of Victorian society, who built grand Italianate villas in exclusive areas such as the Warberries and Wellswood; one of the smartest addresses in town remains Ilsham Marine Drive (aka Millionaires' Row), which affords splendid sea views across the bay to Brixham. Charles Kingsley, author of *The Water Babies*, was among the famous visitors of the day, while Isambard Kingdom Brunel fell under Torquay's spell while working on the railway in 1847, buying a plot of land at Watcombe (*see p120*).

Born in Barton Road in 1890, Agatha Christie spent much of her life in Torquay, roller-skating along Princess Pier and honeymooning at the Grand Hotel. Both locations feature on the Agatha Christie Mile, a gentle walking route around some of the places associated with her life and work. It starts at the harbourside Tourism Information Centre (5 Vaughan Parade, 01803 211211, closed Sun winter), where you can pick up a leaflet. Torquay Museum (*see p118*) has a gallery dedicated to the author and her life in Torquay, and the town pays homage to its most famous daughter with an annual festival.

One place Christie would have known very well is the seafront Pavilion – an extraordinary, white-tiled concoction, adorned with cherubs, pineapple-topped urns and flowery scrolls. Dubbed the 'Palace of Pleasure' when it opened in 1912, this was the place to go for concerts and dances. The building now houses a collection of independent shops, selling china and collectibles, homeware, handmade candles and the like. A ground floor café revives shoppers with cappuccino and cake, while the Terrace Restaurant & Bar (01803 211801) has harbour vistas.

Nearby, the Princess Theatre (Torbay Road, 01803 290288, www.princesstheatre.org.uk) has a varied programme, running from American wrestling to touring ballets. Next to the theatre is Princess Pier; it curves around the marina, which has berths for over 400 yachts. Torquay has always had a strong connection with yachting, and hosted the yachting events for the 1948 Summer Olympics. The quayside is lined with cafés, gift shops and kiosks offering bay cruises and mackerel-fishing trips.

The dramatic, steel-finned Harbour Bridge connects the Marina to the new Beacon Quay development. Artist Bob Budd's *Quay Ring*, which consists of a painted 23-foot steel ring, encircles the new quayside walkway, while LED lights run along the ground. The lights spell out 'vanishing point' in morse code, in memory of the troops that set off from here to the D-Day battles and were never to return. Alongside the quay are galleries, shops, pubs and cafés, while Living Coasts (*see p118*), with its seals, seahorses and penguins, is a hit with families. Just beyond here is Beacon Cove, a small pebbly cove.

Overlooking the Marina, the busy Strand is the heart of Torquay. The street has more than a whiff of the French Riviera on a summer's evening, thanks to the yacht masts and palms. There are a huge range of restaurants and cafés, while the town's main shopping area leads up from here on to Fleet Walk, Fleet Street, Union Street and Union Square.

Torquay has an impressive array of parks and gardens, including the seafront Abbey Park, with its avenue of cherry trees and Italian garden. Get a bird's eye view of the scene by taking a ride on the Hi-Flyer (01803 298550, www.thehiflyer.com), a tethered balloon that ascends 400 feet in the air. Next to Abbey Park are the gardens of Torre Abbey Meadow (*see p119*) – perfect for a picnic. By the marina, Princess Gardens opened in 1894, and are home to a magnificent cast-iron fountain, where cherubs sit astride leaping dolphins.

Torquay's beaches

You're never far from a beach in Torquay. Torre Abbey Sands, in the heart of Torquay, is good for swimming and sandcastle building; in neighbouring Abbey Park, there's pitch and putt and crazy golf. Just along the coast, Corbyn Head Sands is a lovely little sand and shingle beach with a café, deckchair hire and a beach shower. Easily accessed from the promenade, near the Osbourne Hotel, pebbled Meadfoot Beach is backed by spectacular cliffs; hire a deckchair or commandeer a pedalo. South of town, Hollicombe Beach is a sheltered, sandy spot, and one of the area's quieter beaches.

Between Torquay and Babbacombe is the rock and shingle covered Anstey's Cove, which has a seasonal café and beach shop; look for signs off the main coast road, just past the Palace Hotel. North of here, steep tree-clad cliffs shelter the shallow sandy strands of Babbacombe and Oddicombe. In summer, the glorious, 1920s cliff railway makes the steep ascent to the beaches from grassy Babbacombe Down.

Beyond here, towards Shaldon, sandy Watcombe Beach tends to be quieter than other local beaches, as the steep climb makes access difficult. It's good for swimming, and facilities include a beach café and shop. A little further along the coast, Maidencombe Beach (also sand and shingle) offers safe and sheltered swimming, and limpid rock pools at low tide.

Torquay

Where to eat & drink

On the harbourside at Beacon Quay, Quay Reflections (01803 214715, www.quayreflections. co.uk) is a gallery and café, with big leather sofas, Italian coffees and views over the bay.

Drum Inn

Cockington, TQ2 6XA (01803 690264, www.vintage inn.co.uk/thedruminncockington). Open noon-11pm Mon-Sat; noon-10.30pm Sun. Food served noon-10pm Mon-Sat; noon-9.30pm Sun.

DEVON

This thatched pub was designed and built by architect Sir Edwin Lutyens in 1936. The pub offers a good range of real ales and an all-day menu of country pub classics, such as steak and ale pie. The village itself is picturesque, with chocolate-box cottages, a forge and a millpond.

Elephant Restaurant & Brasserie
3-4 Beacon Terrace, TQ1 2BH (01803 200044, www.elephantrestaurant.co.uk). Food served Brasserie noon-2pm, 6.30-9pm Tue-Sat. Restaurant 6.30-9pm Tue-Sat.
The ground floor brasserie in this elegant Georgian property is smart yet relaxed, with a polished main menu (pea and truffle risotto with Cornish yarg and wild mushroom foam) and a simpler – and cheaper – set menu. Upstairs, Michelin-starred head chef Simon Hulstone presides over an intimate fine dining restaurant and a six-course tasting menu (£47.50).

Nourish Café & Deli
Fore Street, St Marychurch, TQ1 4PR (01803 311314, www.nourish-cafe-deli.co.uk). Open/food served 8.30am-5pm Mon-Sat.
This delightful, family-run café and deli is known for its hearty breakfasts, seasonally inspired specials and traditional Sunday roasts. The deli offers own-made pies (from venison and sweet red onion to spinach, feta and mushroom), along with ready meals, chutneys, fresh bread, baguettes, paninis and pretty cupcakes.

Number 7 Fish Bistro
7 Beacon Terrace, TQ1 2BH (01803 295055, www.no7-fish.com). Lunch served Summer 12.15-1.45pm daily. Winter 12.15-1.45pm Wed-Sat. Dinner served Summer 6-9.30pm daily. Winter 6-9.30pm Tue-Sat.
The menu at this family-run bistro is supplemented by chalked-up daily specials, which soon sell out. Lemon sole, turbot, sea bass, red mullet and John Dory are expertly roasted or grilled to perfection. Smaller portions (and a non-fishy menu) are available for children. Service is friendly, and homely nautical knick-knacks adorn the walls.

Orange Tree Restaurant
14-16 Parkhill Road, TQ1 2AL (01803 213936, www.orangetreerestaurant.co.uk). Dinner served 7-9pm Mon-Sat.
Set on a quiet, and mainly residential road, this simply decorated little restaurant is pleasantly removed from the bustle of the town centre. The menu is seasonally inspired: expect the likes of Brixham crab bisque with pan-seared scallops to start, followed by pork medallions with black pudding and shallots.

Where to stay
Accommodation is plentiful in Torquay, ranging from stately seafront hotels to old-fashioned B&Bs. There are also increasing numbers of swanky new clifftop and harbourside holiday lets, which afford amazing views of the bay.

Barcelo Torquay Imperial Hotel
Park Hill Road, TQ1 2DG (01803 294301, www.barcelo-hotels.co.uk). Rates £71-£230 double incl breakfast.

Built in 1866 on a headland overlooking the bay, the Imperial is a comfortable, reliable option. In its heyday, guests included Edward VII and Benjamin Disraeli; it also features in Agatha Christie's *Peril at End House*, under the guise of the Majestic, and its terrace is the setting for the final scene of *Sleeping Murder*. The hotel has 152 en suite rooms, 77 of which are sea-facing. There are also indoor and outdoor pools, a health club and a spa.

Cary Arms ★
Beach Road, Babbacombe, TQ1 3LX (01803 327110, www.caryarms.co.uk). Rates B&B £200-£250 double incl breakfast. Self-catering £750-£2,500 per week for 2-8 people.
The Cary Arms has been transformed from a humble beachside inn into a glamorous boutique hotel, with eight en suite rooms and three well-equipped self-catering cottages. The crisp linens, white-painted furniture and red striped ticking cushions are the embodiment of coastal chic, and the views are heavenly. The South West Coast Path is yards from the front door. The beamed bar offers classic comfort food (a half pint of prawns, potted Brixham crab, chicken and tarragon pie); in summer, the outdoor pizza oven and barbecue spring into action.

Osborne Hotel
2 Hesketh Crescent, TQ1 2LL (01803 213311, www.osborne-torquay.co.uk). Rates £119-£230 double incl breakfast.
Standing on an elegant Regency crescent, Osborne Hotel overlooks six acres of landscaped grounds, stretching down to Meadfoot beach. There are 32 en suite bedrooms, many with sea views; mod cons include free Wi-Fi and, in pricier rooms and suites, extras such as iPod docks and binoculars. The hotel also has indoor and outdoor heated swimming pools, a health and leisure suite and two restaurants.

PAIGNTON
Sandwiched between Torquay and Brixham, Paignton is a traditional bucket-and-spade resort with all the trimmings, from broad sandy beaches to tuppenny falls on the pier. Children also adore the 75-acre zoo (*see p119*).

Paignton started life as a fishing village, before the construction of its harbour in the 1840s, and the arrival of the railway a decade later attracted the holidaymaking hordes. In the late 19th century, American sewing machine tycoon Isaac Singer built the 100-room Oldway Mansion on Torquay Road – later extravagantly remodelled by his son Paris, who took his inspiration from the Palace of Versailles. It is currently the rather grand offices of Torbay Borough Council, and the landscaped grounds are open to the public.

The Victorian pier dominates the seafront, awash with gaudy amusements and candy floss-toting kids. A stroll along its boardwalk offers wonderful views of the bay; on rainy days, retreat to the nearby Apollo Cinema, once a seafront theatre.

The beaches
The town beach, Paignton Sands, is a gently sloping stretch of fine red sand, backed by the promenade. Behind it, Paignton Green is often busy with funfairs

in summer, and comes alive for July's carnival. On Wednesday nights from June to September it also plays host to Bike Night (www.bmad.co.uk), when leather-wearing bikers gather to show off their gleaming motorbikes and raise money for charity.

The beach itself offers old-fashioned seaside fun. Its shallow waters are perfect for paddling and pedalos, and boats can be hired in summer. Beyond the Redcliffe Hotel (see p125), the beach turns into Preston Sands; when the tide is out, you can walk from one to the other. Painted beach huts survey the red sands, and the long promenade is dotted with refreshment kiosks. At low tide, rock pools are revealed at the beach's northern end.

A stroll around the sandstone cliffs of Roundham Head takes to broad, sandy Goodrington Sands. In summer, the Paignton to Dartmouth steam train puffs by the South Sands area of the beach. There are beach huts, deckchairs and pedalos for hire, and several shops and cafés en route from the car park. The slides and rapids of Quaywest Water Park (see p125) are close at hand for watery thrills, as is the more educational Seashore Centre (see p119). Nearby Goodrington and Youngs Park is a good picnic spot, complete with bumper boats, wonderfully retro swan pedalos and crazy golf.

Further south, towards Brixham, Blue Flag Broadsands Beach lives up to its name with a vast expanse of red sand, between two rocky headlands. Popular with families, it offers sheltered swimming and plenty of scope for sandcastle building. From here, follow the footpath over the golf course for around half a mile to reach Elberry Cove. Wooded slopes back the pebbly, crescent-shaped cove, and to one end of the beach are the ruins of Lord Churston's bathhouse. The waters are crystal clear: water-ski boats shatter the tranquillity, although buoys limit how close they can come to the shore.

Where to eat & drink

While you're in Paignton, look out for beers from the local Bays Brewery, established in 2007. You'll find Bays Best, Bays Gold and Bays Breaker on tap in local pubs; alternatively, drop by the brewery in Aspen Way (01803 555004, closed Sat, Sun) for a tasting, and to pick up some beers from the shop.

In a lovely location on the water's edge, Harbour Light (North Quay, The Harbour, 01803 666500, www.theharbourlight.co.uk, closed Dec-Apr) occupies an ancient whitewashed building with sky-blue shutters. Inside, the decor is quietly old-fashioned and the menu is of a retro bent: think garlic mushrooms and duck in morello cherry sauce. For something more up-to-date, try Cilantro (75 Torquay Road, 01803 664626, www.cilantro online.co.uk) for modern Indian food.

Church House Inn ★
Village Road, Marldon, TQ3 1SL (01803 558279, www.churchhousemarldon.com). Open 11.30am-3pm, 5-11pm Mon-Thur, Sun; 11.30am-3pm, 5-11.30pm Fri, Sat. Lunch served noon-2pm, dinner served 6.30-9.30pm daily.

THINGS TO DO AFTER DARK

● Join a Megaliths by Moonlight guided walk on Dartmoor, organised by the Dartmoor National Park Authority during the summer months. See p90.
● Sleep with the sharks at Plymouth's National Marine Aquarium (see p152) – if you dare.
● Watch beavers at Escot Park (see p30); call to book a place on one of the special evening visits, to see these nocturnal creatures.
● Book a place on Badger Watch at Paignton Zoo (see p119). Peek out from the hide to see the badgers foraging for food, illuminated by artificial moonlight.
● Take a moonlit paddle down the Dart. Try Canoe Adventures (01803 865301, www.canoeadventures.co.uk) or Wildwise (01803 868269, www.wildwise.co.uk).
● Join the sky-gazing crowds on Plymouth Hoe for the annual British Fireworks Championship in August.
● Scour Exmoor in search of deers, with Exmoor National Park Rangers. Contact the National Park Centre in Dulverton (01398 323841, www.exmoor-national park.gov.uk). No dogs allowed.
● Look at the night sky at the Norman Lockyer Observatory (see p31) in Sidmouth. Regular opening evenings are held, many of which tie in with astronomical events such as meteor showers.
● Go on a bat walk on the Great Western Canal. They're popular events, so book a place with the Canal Ranger Service (01884 254072). No children under seven and no dogs are allowed; participants should bring their own torches.

DEVON

Things to do

Babbacombe Cliff Railway

FROM THE EXE TO THE TEIGN

Riviera Cruises
*8 Ivy Lane, Teignmouth, TQ14 8BT (01626 774868).
Times and prices vary, phone for details.*
Riviera Cruises offers excursions around Teignmouth
Bay and along the Teign, as well as mackerel fishing
trips. All cruises depart from the ferry beach.

Seasports South West
*Vinnicombe Stores, New Quay Street, Teignmouth,
TQ14 8DA (01626 772555, www.seasports-
sw.com). Open Summer 9am-6pm daily. Winter
10am-4.30pm daily.*
Based at the back beach, this RYA-accredited centre
has experienced instructors in a variety of watersports.

Courses range from learning to sail a dinghy or drive
a powerboat to jet skiing, windsurfing and kayaking.

TORQUAY

Babbacombe Cliff Railway
*Babbacombe Downs (01803 328750). Open Easter-
Sept 9.30am-5pm daily. Tickets £1.80 return; £1.20
reductions.*
Save your legs by taking this dapper little funicular
railway, which has been in operation since 1926.

Jibset Marine
*Beacon Quay, The Harbour, TQ1 2BG (01803 295414,
www.jibsetmarine.co.uk). Open 9am-5pm daily. Price
£20 for 2hrs; £60 for family of 4.*

A few miles inland from Paignton is Marldon. At its heart,
the 14th-century Church House Inn was built to house the
artisans working on the church next door. An 18th-century
makeover added lovely Georgian windows – which have
miraculously escaped stray cricket balls from the village
green. Food is taken seriously here, with a menu that might
include roast butternut squash soup with cinnamon cream,
or slow cooked shoulder of lamb with Moroccan spiced sauce;
on Sundays, there are superior roasts.

Occombe Farm Shop & Café ★
*Preston Down Road, TQ3 1RN (01803 520022,
www.occombe.org.uk). Open 9am-5pm Mon-Sat;
9.30am-4.30pm Sun.*
This brilliant farm shop offers a cornucopia of West Country
produce. Wicker baskets brim with fruit and veg (some still
muddy from the fields), and the excellent butcher's counter
sells organic meat reared at Occombe and other local farms.
There's a deli counter and a bakery. All produce is sourced
as locally as possible and labelled as such, and there is an
organic and fair trade buying policy. Upstairs in the
excellent café, tuck into splendid breakfasts, snacks (cheese
scones with local chutney, say) and lunches.

Old Singer Tea Shop
*41 Torquay Road, TQ3 3DT (01803 666635,
www.theoldsingerteashop.co.uk). Open Easter-Dec
9am-4.30pm Mon-Sat; 10am-2.30pm Sun.*
This quaint teashop is filled with Singer sewing machine
memorabilia and Victorian bric-a-brac. It's a sweetly old-
fashioned place, with embroidered tablecloths, and tea
served in a teapot with fine bone china cups and saucers. In
addition to cakes and cream teas, the menu includes all-day
breakfasts, roast dinners, omelettes, jacket potatoes and
hearty soups.

Where to stay

Compton Pool Farm ★
*Compton, TQ3 1TA (01803 872241, www.compton
pool.co.uk). Rates vary, check website for details.*
Set in 14 acres of land, this cluster of ten stylishly
renovated self-catering cottages are perfect for tranquil
getaways. Boutique touches include plasma screen TVs
and Bose sound systems in the cottages, and there's an all-
weather tennis court and an indoor heated pool. Children,

As well as selling specialist clothing and equipment, this watersports centre hires out kayaks (with wet suits and buoyancy aids) from May to September during set session times, when there is also a safety boat on the water.

Waves Leisure Pool
Riviera Conference Centre, Chestnut Avenue, TQ2 5LZ (01803 299992, www.rivieracentre.co.uk). Open 7.30am-7pm Mon-Wed; 7.30am-9pm Thur; 7.30am-8pm Fri; 9am-4pm Sat, Sun. Admission £3.90; £3.10-£3.60 reductions; £12.90 family.
This large, family-friendly heated indoor pool is equipped with a wave machine and giant water flume, and is a good standby for a rainy day.

PAIGNTON

Quaywest
Goodrington Sands, TQ6 6LN (01803 550034, www.quaywest.co.uk).Open June-Sept 10am-6pm daily. Admission £11; £5 reductions; £42 family.
Quaywest is child heaven. Thrill-seekers can plummet 65 feet in the Devil's Drop, take an enclosed speed slide in the Screamer, or ride the Raging Rapids in a tube, while little ones paddle, splash and slide in the Toon Town pool.

BRIXHAM

Brixham Ghost Walks
Tours leave from the William of Orange Statue, Harbour Front (01803 857761, http://myweb.tiscali. co.uk/devondawdlers). Tours June, Sept Tue, Thur. July Tue, Thur, Sun. Aug Tue-Thur, Sun. 31 Oct. Tours £5; £3-£4 reductions. No credit cards.
Join Deadly Dave and his harem of lost souls to explore Brixham's darker side, and hear about its ghostly tales and unquiet souls. The 90-minute walk sets off from the harbourfront at 7.30pm, and is suitable for all ages.

Greenway Ferry
0845 489 0418, www.greenwayferry.co.uk. Times and prices vary, phone for details.
Options include ferries to Dartmouth and to Greenway House, fishing expeditions and themed cruises, ranging from Agatha Christie specials to trips to watch Dartmouth Royal Regatta from the waves.

Ocean Adventures
07900 953658, www.ocean-adventures.net. Times and prices vary, phone for details.
Ocean Adventures offers power boat cruises from Brixham Marina for up to 12 people. You'll reach speeds of 50mph on the Bay Blast; or take the quieter Wildlife Cruise around Berry Head to see grey seals, kittiwakes, guillemots and oyster catchers.

Pirate Thursdays ★
Quayside (01803 850382, www.brixhambuccaneers. co.uk). Events July, Aug; check website for details.
Every Thursday during the summer holidays, Brixham is overrun by pirates great and small, under the command of Cap'n Blood 'n' Guts of the Brixham Buccaneers. Proceedings kick off with the quayside Pirate Parade at 10am, followed by all manner of piratical games, including pirate language lessons, storytelling, crafts workshops, face painting and treasure hunts.

Shoalstone Pool ★
Berry Head Road, TQ5 9AH (01803 207975, www.shoalstoneseawaterpool.co.uk). Open May-Sept 9am-5pm daily. Admission free.
This open-air seawater swimming pool was built in the 1890s on the site of a natural rock pool that was already used for swimming by locals. There's plenty of space around its 25-metre length to bask in the sun (deckchairs can be hired). The Waterside Café serves light snacks and drinks, and Shoalstone Beach is close.

though, will be more excited by the trampolines, slides and resident Vietnamese pot-bellied pigs, goats and chickens; bring your wellies.

Redcliffe Hotel
Marine Drive, TQ3 2NL (01803 526397, www.redcliffe hotel.co.uk). Rates £116-£130 double incl breakfast.
A landmark on the seafront, this superbly located hotel was built in 1856 at the behest of Colonel Robert Smith, who served with the Royal Bengal Engineers and designed his seaside home with an unmistakably Indian theme. Converted into a hotel in 1904, it retains an old-fashioned elegance. There are 68 rooms, many of them with sea views and balconies; families are well catered for, with interconnecting rooms, a small play area and early suppers for younger children. There are outdoor and indoor swimming pools too.

BRIXHAM

Brixham is the rough diamond of Torbay. A jolly and colourful fishing port, its fishing history stretches back some 900 years. On New Road, Brixham

Heritage Museum (01803 856267, www.brixham heritage.org.uk, closed Mon, Sun) is packed to the gunwhales with relics of the town's maritime past.

These days, Brixham mixes its fishing heritage with tourism. The *Vigilance* – a beautifully restored 78-foot ketch, built in 1926 – offers trips around the bay (07764 845353, www.vigilanceof brixham.co.uk, closed Nov-Feb). But Brixham is actually the real thing – a working fishing village. Below the steep hillside, scattered with colourful rows of fishermen's cottages, the harbour is busy with day boats and trawlers unloading their catch. Fishermen in yellow bibs banter over ice-filled boxes of squid, turbot, plaice and monkfish, and lobster pots are loaded on to the crabbing boats. Over 100 fishing boats land and sell their catch at the fish market on the quayside – currently undergoing a multi-million-pound redevelopment.

Moored in the inner harbour is a full-size replica of Sir Francis Drake's *Golden Hind*. The on-board museum (01803 856223, www.goldenhind.co.uk) offers a glimpse into the world of the 16th-century sailor. Brixham has embraced the salty seadog theme with gusto, and on Pirate Thursdays (*see p125*) the harbourside is awash with buccaneers and pirate-themed entertainments. Looking on with lofty distain is a statue of William of Orange, who landed in Brixham in 1688, and successfully overthrew King James II.

The Quay, the Strand and King Street border the inner harbour. Gift shops, cafés and seafood restaurants rub shoulders along the Quay and the Strand, while King Street is home to a bizarre, 17th-century coffin-shaped house, and the tiny, aptly-named Hole in the Wall pub. Further shops, including the Brixham Deli (*see right*), can be found along Fore Street. Stefan's Fishmongers (01803 853957), in nearby Middle Street, sells fish fresh off the boats.

A waterside walkway leads from the inner harbour to the new marina, where dinghies and yachts bob gently on the water, their rigging clinking in the breeze. The walkway ends at the pebble-scattered Breakwater Beach, sheltered by the man-made breakwater. Nearby, the Breakwater Café (*see below*) offers takeaways as well as sit-down meals. To the east, Shoalstone Beach is a small, shingly beach, set by Shoalstone Pool (*see p125*).

North-west of here, a steep footpath leads down from the coastal path and through the woods to the diminutive pebble beach at Churston Cove. Sheltered by the cliffs and wooded hillside, it is something of a sun trap, and a good spot for snorkelling and fishing – although the resident seal may offer some competition. There are no facilities, so pack a picnic. It's a short but enjoyable walk from Brixham, though it feels a world away.

Slightly easier to access is the adjacent Fishcombe Cove – this is another small, pebbly beach at the foot of the cliffs, equipped with toilets and a basic café offering tea, coffee and ice-creams. The nearby holiday park means the cove can get busy.

Brixham's sole sandy beach is St Mary's Bay, on the other side of town and around the limestone promontory of Berry Head. Steps lead down to the sandy cove, which is backed by steep cliffs; the reward is a secluded spot in which to bathe and bask. The coastal path has amazing views across the bay.

Where to eat & drink

Breakwater Bistro & Café ★
Berry Head Road, TQ5 9AF (01803 856738, www.thebreakwater.co.uk). Food served Summer 9am-9.30pm daily. Winter 10am-4pm Mon-Thur, Sun; 10am-9pm Fri, Sat.
Conveniently close to the main town beach and marina, the Breakwater is a cheery all-day affair. In the daytime, you can sit out on the balcony and order up a full English, a fresh crab sandwich or a bowl of seafood chowder – or admire the view over a hot chocolate and toasted teacake. In the evening it becomes a bistro, where you can watch the sun go down over the bay and choose from the seafood-packed specials board.

Brixham Deli ★
68a Fore Street, TQ5 8EF (01803 859585, www.the brixhamdeli.co.uk). Food served Summer 9am-5.30pm Mon-Sat. Winter 9am-4pm Mon-Sat.
Treats at this friendly deli run from roasted artichoke hearts to local ciders and fantastic breads. There is also a great café, which does a mean coffee and croissant and top-notch light lunches. For picnics, you won't better the sandwich bar's offerings (stilton, blackcurrant jam and red onion, say, or kiln-roasted salmon with lime mayonnaise and watercress).

Where to stay

Overlooking the waves from its perch on Berry Head, the grand Berry Head Hotel (Berry Head Road, 01803 853225, www.berryheadhotel.com) was once home to the vicar of All Saints' Church, Reverend Francis Lyte, who composed the hymn *Abide With Me* while watching dusk fall over Torbay. Staid, rather dated decor may deter some, but plus points include superb views, an indoor pool and a croquet lawn.

Campers and caravaners can stay at Upton Manor Farm (St Mary's Road, 01803 882384, www.uptonmanorfarm.co.uk), a sheltered site with good, clean facilities. It's ten minutes' walk from St Mary's Bay beach, and a regular bus service runs from outside the site into Brixham.

Churston Court
Church Road, Churston Ferrers, TQ5 0JE (01803 842186, www.churstoncourt.co.uk). Rates £95-£110 double incl breakfast.
This Grade I-listed manor house is full of period charm. Its 20 en suite rooms are decorated in rich, warm colours, and several have magnificent four-posters. Candlelit dinners in the restaurant bring smart, traditional fare: think Brixham crab thermidor followed by braised lamb shank with creamed potatoes and confit garlic. The bar offers no-nonsense grub and local ales; in summer, enjoy the sun in the walled garden.

Sampford Guest House & Cottage
57-59 King Street, TQ5 9TH (01803 857761, www.sampfordhouse.com). Rates £54-£66 double incl breakfast. Self-catering £420-£504 per week for 4 people.
This B&B occupies an 18th-century fisherman's house, overlooking the inner harbour. Rooms are prettily and comfortably appointed, and decorated in calming pastel hues; for those seeking more independence, the self-contained Fisherman's Cottage has a lounge, kitchenette and double bedroom, with a four-poster bed.

White House
35 North View Road, TQ5 9TF (0844 561 2001, www.bluechipvacations.com). Rates £329-£789 per week for 4 people.
This appealing, end-of-terrace Victorian cottage has views over Brixham harbour, and its hotchpotch backdrop of brightly painted cottages. Original fireplaces aside, the decor is resolutely contemporary, with white-painted wooden floors, vibrant red rugs and cushions and chunky sand-coloured sofas. There is one double and one single bedroom.

South Devon: Totnes to the Yealm Estuary

The South Hams is real Famous Five country. The hills roll, the brooks babble, and the green lanes lead to secluded bays where you can have a smashing time and, if you remember to bring it, lashings of ginger beer. 'Ham' essentially means 'sheltered or enclosed place', and the hidden villages, unspoilt beaches and secret coves help the area live up to both its name and its status as part of the South Devon Area of Outstanding Natural Beauty.

The area stretches from the borders of Torbay in the east to the edge of Plymouth in the west, taking in part of Dartmoor National Park to the north. Along the 60-odd miles of coastline, around half of which is overseen by the National Trust, you'll find sandy beaches, craggy coves and wooded river valleys to explore by foot or boat. There are five estuaries along the coast – the Dart, the Salcombe-Kingsbridge, the Avon, the Erme and the Yealm – and plenty of worthwhile towns and villages, from the upscale likes of Dartmouth and Salcombe to smaller, less heralded settlements such as Beesands.

TOTNES & AROUND

Totnes

In Elizabethan times, Totnes was a flourishing market town, spread over a steep promontory overlooking the River Dart. Some 500 years later, it continues to flourish, and not only as a historic relic. Totnes was the first place in England to sign up to the Transition Town initiative, an ethos built around reducing reliance on the world's diminishing supplies of oil. Its residents have taken the 'shop local' concept to heart, and a wealth of independent retailers line the streets.

Start your exploration by the river, then walk up higgledy-piggledy Fore Street, which then turns into the High Street. Note the handsome 16th-century houses of pilchard baron Nicholas Ball (16 High Street) and cloth merchant Walter Kelland (70 Fore Street); the latter is now Totnes Museum (01803 863821, closed Nov-mid Mar). Other buildings are given over to shops and galleries; squeezed between them, pretty alleyways lead to hidden courtyards. Ticklemore Street holds a number of fine food shops, including Country Cheeses ★; Annie's greengrocer; and Ticklemore Fish.

Close to the East Gate arch on Fore Street, look out for the Brutus Stone, set into the pavement. According to 12th-century historian Geoffrey of Monmouth, this granite boulder was the first stone stepped upon by Brutus of Troy, the mythical founder of Britain, when he reached these shores. You'll also see signs for the castle ramparts and the town's 14th-century Guildhall. A little further up on the right is the 15th-century church of St Mary, with its distinctive red sandstone tower.

Continue up the hill along the High Street, passing the excellent, independent Totnes Bookshop (01803 863273), to reach the Civic Square, home to a market on Fridays and Saturday. On Tuesday mornings from May to September there's also an Elizabethan Market, with crafts and costumes galore. Opposite the square runs the pretty Butterwalk, home to a number of shops and the Devonshire Collection of Period Costume (01803 862857, open Tue-Fri June-Sept).

A right turn up Castle Street will take you to Totnes Castle (see p134). Alternatively, follow the High Street around to the left and into the historic Narrows, a skinny street lined with specialist retailers. From here, cut down Leechwell Street, by the 17th-century Kingsbridge Inn (01803 863324). Follow the alley behind the pub down to the Leech Wells; fed by three springs flowing into three granite troughs, and believed by some to have healing powers, it was once a place of pilgrimage.

Just to the south of Totnes, there's a lovely riverside walk at Longmarsh. Benches are scattered along the broad gravel path, and members of the Dart Totnes Amateur Rowing Club can often be seen practising on the water. Another option is to walk or cycle the sometimes hilly route that links Totnes with the village of Ashprington. Part of the National Cycle Network, it's four and a half miles long; join the trail at the back of the Steam Packet pub. Sharpham Vineyard (see p140) is en route.

Dartington Hall Estate

Set on a 1,200-acre estate outside Totnes, the Dartington Estate ★ (01803 847000, www.dartington.org) was established in the 1920s as

a centre for progressive education. The boarding school that was founded here in 1926 has long since closed; more controversially, Dartington College, a specialist arts college, recently merged with University College Falmouth. Still, education remains a going concern thanks to the International Summer School, which offers music tuition in a variety of disciplines, and the year-round Schumacher College, which deals in holistic education. And even if you've no interest in signing up to any of the courses, Dartington merits a visit. Visitors can walk or cycle to Dartington along a signposted river path, which can be picked up at the back of Totnes station and shows off the estate at its best.

The first attraction is the complex of buildings itself, set in spectacular grounds that sweep down to the Dart. The Great Hall dates from 1388, but the estate also has some fine buildings from the more recent past: look out, in particular for High Cross House, an eye-catching white, 1930s Modernist structure (closed Mon, Sat, Sun & all Nov-Apr), built by Swiss-American architect William Lescaze for the school's first headmaster. The house remains in mint condition, both inside and out, and is now a showcase for Dartington's fine collection of paintings and ceramics; there's a £5 admission charge. The beautiful gardens (open to all) by the Great Hall include a number of sculptures – including a serene reclining figure by Henry Moore.

The public events programme includes regular concerts, with a particular focus on classical and folk music; theatre, film screenings and family-friendly events are among the other cultural riches. A charming café is supplemented by the White Hart (01803 847111), a lovely, pubby bar and restaurant. There is also some keenly priced hotel accommodation.

Where to eat & drink

For casual eats, try Effings (50 Fore Street, 01803 863435, www.effings.co.uk, closed Sun), a fine deli/café; Rumour (no.30, 01803 864682) on the High Street, popular for its pizzas and daily specials; or the Fat Lemons Café (01803 866888, closed Mon, Sun) on Ticklemore Court, open during the day for simple vegetarian fare. Just across the river in Bridgetown, the Albert Inn (32 Bridgetown, 01803 863214) is a fine local that brews its own ales.

Maltsters Arms ★
Tuckenhay, TQ9 7EH (01803 732350, www.tuckenhay. com). Open 11am-11pm daily. Lunch served noon-3pm, dinner served 7-9.30pm daily.
A few miles outside Totnes, the Maltsters Arms was once owned by the late Keith Floyd. Overlooking the creek, the restaurant offers gastropub-style food; in the bar, you'll find several ales and 15 wines by the glass. The four bedrooms (£75-£125 double incl breakfast), all delightfully and eccentrically furnished, offer lovely views of the water.

Old Church House Inn
Torbryan, TQ12 5UR (01803 812372, www.oldchurch houseinn.co.uk). Open 11am-11pm daily. Lunch served noon-2.30pm, dinner served 7-9pm daily.

Tucked away off the Totnes to Newton Abbot road, this venerable building was erected in 1340 by stonemasons working on the church across the lane. Food is served in one of five dining rooms, candlelit in the evening; the menu draws on ingredients from nearby farms, with dishes such as rack of West Country lamb. The inn has 16 rooms (£69-£79 double incl breakfast) many with historic features.

Riverford Field Kitchen ★
Wash Barn, Buckfastleigh, TQ11 0JU (01803 762074, www.riverford.co.uk). Lunch served 12.30pm daily. Dinner served 7.30pm Mon-Sat.
The Riverford Field Kitchen gives diners the full field-to-plate culinary experience: if you want to eat here, you have to tour the farm, whether on a full guided tour or a quick DIY potter around. Jane Baxter and her team dish up a set menu of five vegetable dishes and one meat dish (a vegetarian alternative to the meat dish can be arranged; ask when booking) in a canteen-style setting, with organic ciders among the drinks. Booking is essential. For more, *see p140*.

Sea Trout Inn
Staverton, TQ9 6PA (01803 762274, www.seatrout inn.co.uk). Open 11am-11pm Mon-Thur, Sat; 11am-11.30pm Fri; 11am-10.30pm Sun. Lunch served noon-2pm Mon-Fri, Sun; noon-2.30pm Sat. Dinner served 6-9pm Mon-Thur, Sun; 6-9.30pm Fri, Sat.
This lovely Devon inn dates back to the 15th century. Food and drinks are served in a variety of different areas, none of them very formal and most of them quite pubby; apt, then, that real ales are a strong point. Dishes might include a leek and three cheese tart with tomato chutney, or roasted pork belly with bubble and squeak; the bar menu offers hearty pub grub such as venison casserole with dumplings. There are also ten very pleasant rooms (£79-£85 double incl breakfast). Staff are helpful and welcoming.

Sharpham Café ★
Sharpham Estate, Totnes, TQ9 7UT (01803 732178, www.thevineyardcafe.co.uk). Open times vary, phone for details.
Run by local girl Rosie Weston, this little organic café on the Sharpham Estate isn't exactly posh: the kitchen is in a trailer, while the tables occupy an outdoor deck area and marquee. However, the views over the Dart are lovely, and so is the food: the likes of pork, pistachio and prune pâté; smoked fish platters; dressed Dartmouth crab; and Sharpham cheeses. The restaurant's closed in winter, and even in summer the hours are weather-dependent; call ahead to check.

Tangerine Tree Café
50 High Street, Totnes, TQ9 5SQ (01803 840853, www.tangerinetree.co.uk). Open 9am-5pm Tue-Sat. Breakfast served 9-11.30am, lunch served noon-3.30pm Tue-Sat.
Spread over two floors, with plump sofas and chunky wooden chairs, the Tangerine Tree is part-gallery and part-brasserie. It's a friendly place, with a daily specials board detailing dishes such as Brixham crab salad with mango dressing, and pork belly and butterbean stew.

Watermans Arms
Bow Bridge, Ashprington, TQ9 7EG (01803 732214, www.thewatermansarms.net). Open 11am-11pm daily.

Dartington Hall Estate. See p127.

Lunch served noon-2.30pm Mon-Fri; noon-3pm Sat, Sun. Dinner served 6-8.30pm Mon-Thur; 6-9pm Fri-Sun.
Built in the 17th century, the Watermans Arms has served as a smithy, a brewhouse, a prison and a haunt for the feared press gangs. Today, it's a lovely waterside pub. Kids can play in the shallow creek while adults relax with a pint on the terrace. The menu has a strong local theme, and there are 15 en suite bedrooms (£60-£90 double incl breakfast).

Waterside Bistro
10 Symons Passage, The Plains, Totnes, TQ9 5YS (01803 864069, www.watersidebistro.com). Open 9.30am-midnight daily. Food served Summer noon-3pm, 6-10pm daily. Winter noon-2.30pm, 6-9.30pm daily.
Locally caught seafood plays a major role at the Waterside Bistro, with dishes such as fish pie, Bigbury Bay oysters, and pan-fried sea bass with Thai green coconut curry.

Where to stay

Great Grubb
Fallowfields, Plymouth Road, Totnes, TQ9 5LX (01803 849071, www.thegreatgrubb.co.uk). Rates £55-£70 double incl breakfast.
This contemporary-styled B&B displays work by local artists in the guests' lounge, the dining room and the bedrooms (all of which have en suite bathrooms, Wi-Fi and DVD players). Breakfast features a wealth of Devon produce.

Old Forge
Seymour Place, Totnes, TQ9 5AY (01803 862174, www.oldforgetotnes.com). Rates £66-£99 double incl breakfast.
A few minutes' walk from the centre of town, this friendly B&B is housed in a 15th-century building with a very pretty garden. As well as the cosy rooms, there's accommodation for up to four people in Wheelwright's Cottage.

Royal Seven Stars Hotel
The Plains, Totnes, TQ9 5DD (01803 862125, www.royalsevenstars.co.uk). Rates £119-£149 double incl breakfast.
Believed to have been built in the 1660s, this operation is a stone's throw from the river. As well as 18 cheery, attractive bedrooms, some of which come with jacuzzi bathtubs, there are two bars and a restaurant on site.

Steam Packet Inn
St Peter's Quay, Totnes, TQ9 5EW (01803 863880, www.steampacketinn.co.uk). Rates £79.50 double incl breakfast.
This pub and restaurant, which offers a decent food menu alongside its real ales, has four pleasant rooms overlooking the river. You can pick up the River Rat water taxi from here (Tim Burke, 07814 954869); it heads upstream to the South Devon Steam Railway.

DARTMOUTH & AROUND

Dartmouth
In the 1720s, Daniel Defoe described Dartmouth as a harbour 'able to receive 500 sail of ships of any size'. Three centuries later, boats still bob on the water, but the naval warships and merchant vessels have been replaced by yachts. This is now one of the area's most prosperous towns. Dartmouth's maritime history has shaped its buildings, which are clustered around the half-moon of the quay and up the steep hillside. Many are decorated with intricate and sometimes ribald carvings. Look out, too, for the mosaic tiling in shop entrances; much of it is the work of Italian craftsmen who later gave up building in favour of making ice-cream.

Perhaps the town's most notable building is St Saviour's Church. Consecrated in 1372, its features include a 15th-century carved-oak screen of vine leaves, grapes and wheat, and a carving of the pagan 'Green Man' symbol. Some of Dartmouth's most interesting shops sit on nearby Smith Street (glassware at Blown Studio Glass, food and flowers at the Smith Street Deli) and Foss Street (canvas goods at the Canvas Factory, punning gifts at the Simon Drew Gallery).

The oldest parts of Dartmouth are on its steeper slopes, lined with 13 stepped alleyways that weave between the houses. The prettiest is Brown's Hill, a former packhorse route; in summer, it's a riot of colourful window boxes, terracotta pots and hanging baskets. Similar floral displays can be found at the Cherub Inn (*see p132*) on Higher Street; built in around 1380, it's the oldest medieval house in town.

A stroll along Lower Street, reached via one of the alleyways, will lead you to the ancient, cobbled quay of Bayards Cove, lined with 18th-century houses and home to the Bayard's Cove Hotel & Coffee House (*see p133*), once the home of a Tudor merchant. In 1620 this was one of the last ports of call for the Pilgrim Fathers as they set sail aboard the *Mayflower*. At the end of the quay sit the remains of a single-storey fort, built in 1510 to protect the quay from Spanish and French ships. The real guardian of the Dart, though, is Dartmouth Castle (*see p134*), a mile south of town. From the car park by the castle, steps lead down to the pebbly Castle Cove. Locals have been taking to the water here for years, and it's a fine rock-pooling spot at low tide.

Between April and September, parking is tricky. It's best to use the Park & Ride facility, signposted off the A3122 by the Dartmouth Leisure Centre; buses run every ten minutes from 8am (9.30am Sun) until 2pm, then every 20 minutes until 6.40pm. Alternatively, you can avoid the problem entirely and arrive by boat, via the River Link from Totnes.

The pretty riverside village of Dittisham (pronounced 'Ditsum') lies a few miles upriver from Dartmouth. The village was once famous for its orchards, where the celebrated Dittisham plum was harvested over ten days near the end of July. A few orchards remain, but these days the village is more famous as a hideaway for those who can afford the house prices. A ferry (0845 489 0418) runs across the river to Greenway (*see p135*), Agatha Christie's secluded Devon hideaway, and the village is also on the Dart Valley Trail.

Across the estuary

Across the river from Dartmouth lies Kingswear, an attractive town with more than a touch of Balamory about it. Keen-eyed film buffs may recognise the town from *The French Lieutenant's Woman*; even without cinematic familiarity, the town's pastel-coloured cottages are a scenic sight. Also on this side of the river is Coleton Fishacre house and gardens (*see p134*).

Two car ferries cross the Dart between Dartmouth and Kingswear. The Higher Ferry leaves Dartmouth from near the marina on the edge of town and will put you across just outside Kingswear, while the Lower Ferry departs from Bayards Cove and deposits you in the heart of Kingswear, by the steam railway station. Once you're in Kingswear, it's easy to reach towns and villages on this side of the Dart, such as Brixham; otherwise, the nearest river crossing is back in Totnes.

Where to eat & drink

For casual dining in Dartmouth, you can't go far wrong with Café Alf Resco ★ on Lower Street (01803 835880, www.cafealfresco. co.uk). Commonly known as 'Alf's', the café offers substantial breakfasts in the morning and comfort cooking in the evening; there are also two B&B rooms and a one-bed flat for hire upstairs.

The folks behind the new Dart Marina development (www.dartmarina.com) are responsible for three restaurants: the River Restaurant, a smart operation within the Dart Marina Hotel & Spa; the Wildfire Bistro, a contemporary grill; and the Floating Bridge, a traditional pub by the Higher Ferry serving the likes of beer-battered fish and chips.

Anzac Street Bistro & Guesthouse

Anzac Street, Dartmouth, TQ6 9DL (01803 835515, www.anzacstreetbistro.co.uk). Dinner served 6.30-9.30pm Tue-Sat.

Much of the produce on the menu at this good-looking restaurant, located in an elegant Georgian house, is raised or grown on a family farm at nearby Blackawton. The cooking at the Anzac Street Bistro has a continental theme – cheese and mustard soufflé with creamed spinach, classic steak-frites – but the kitchen also does a cracking Sunday roast. Upstairs are two beautifully furnished double bedrooms (£75-£85 double incl breakfast).

Cherub Inn

Higher Street, Dartmouth, TQ6 9RB (01803 832571, http://the-cherub.co.uk). Open 11am-11pm daily. Lunch served noon-2.30pm, dinner served 6.30-9pm daily.

This gorgeous 14th-century inn is packed with character, thanks to its old ship's beams, leaded light windows and huge stone fireplaces. Behind the bar, you'll find Sharp's Doom Bar supplemented by guest ales and more than a dozen wines by the glass, along with a good bar menu. The menu upstairs is fancier (Dartmouth smokehouse salmon, say).

Totnes Castle. See p134.

Jan & Freddies Brasserie ★

10 Fairfax Place, Dartmouth, TQ6 9AD (01803 832491, www.janandfreddiesbrasserie.co.uk). Lunch served 11.45am-2pm Tue-Sat. Dinner served 6.30-10pm Mon-Sat.

The rather chirpy name of this operation belies a serious restaurant. Chef Richard Hilson trained at Gidleigh Park under Michael Caines; his influence is visible in brasserie-style dishes such as bisque of spider crab finished with saffron oil, River Teign mussels in white wine broth, and chargrilled sirloin of Devon beef. Popular with locals, and with good reason.

New Angel

2 South Embankment, Dartmouth, TQ6 9BH (01803 839425, www.thenewangel.co.uk). Food served Summer 9-11am, noon-2.30pm, 6.30-9.30pm Tue-Sat; 9-11am, noon-2.30pm Sun. Winter 9-11am, noon-2.30pm, 6.30-9.30pm Tue-Sat.

John Burton Race is in charge of the kitchens here, delivering a menu rich in local produce and served at elevated prices. The enterprise also includes six B&B rooms (£75-£105 double incl breakfast), housed in a nearby building,

Seahorse ★

5 South Embankment, Dartmouth, TQ6 9BH (01803 835147, www.seahorserestaurant.co.uk). Lunch served noon-3pm Wed-Sat. Dinner served 6-10pm Tue-Sat.

Fishworks founder Mitch Tonks showcases seafood landed at Brixham in this excellent eaterie. The menu changes daily to reflect what's been caught that morning, but might take in the likes of red gurnard fillets, roasted with sage and lemon, or silver mullet with North African spices. There's also meat, though, with Cornish lamb chops and beef rib on the agenda. The restaurant has a courtesy boat that can take you across the Dart after your meal.

Where to stay

This is Agatha Christie territory. Stay at Greenway (*see p135*) in a luxurious holiday apartment, or in the one-bedroom Lodge by the entrance. Or at the Royal Castle Hotel (Dartmouth, 01803 833033, www.royalcastle.co.uk) which features in her thriller *Ordeal by Innocence* as the Royal George.

Bayards Cove Hotel

Bayards Cove, Dartmouth, TQ6 9AN (01803 839278, www.bayardscovehotel.co.uk). Rates £75 £105 double incl breakfast.

This former Tudor merchant's house, in one of the oldest parts of Dartmouth, has seven bedrooms, with a beguiling mix of historic features (wooden beams, leaded light windows) and mod cons (Wi-Fi, for instance). Nelson's Penthouse is a luxurious two-bedroom suite with room for up to six people.

Dart Marina Hotel & Spa

Sandquay Road, Dartmouth, TQ6 9PH (01803 837120, www.dartmarina.com). Rates £150-£195 double incl breakfast.

The better rooms at this stylish hotel and spa come with private balconies or patios, while suites have their own sitting rooms. The Devon Health Spa adds further appeal; facilities include a steam room, a jacuzzi, a small pool and a full programme of treatments. The hotel also runs three restaurants and several self-catering riverside apartments.

Fingals

Dittisham, TQ6 0JA (01803 722398, www.fingals. co.uk). Rates B&B £100-£190 double incl breakfast. Self-catering £600-£900 per week for 4 people.

Although there's a tennis court on site, this ten-room family-friendly hotel, set in a secluded valley about a mile from Dittisham, really places the emphasis on relaxation. Attractions include gorgeous gardens, a heated pool and a hot tub jacuzzi and sauna. Served on one long table, dinner includes plenty of local produce. There's also a self-catering option in a newly built green oak barn.

Fir Mount House

Higher Contour Road, Kingswear, TQ6 0DE (01803 752943, www.mannafromdevon.com). Rates £90 double incl breakfast.

As well as running the Manna from Devon Cookery School, Holly and David Jones offer two B&B rooms in their beautiful Victorian villa, on the banks of the Dart. (There is also an additional attic room, which can be booked to form a suite with the Blue Room.) There are dreamy harbour views from the outdoor decking area; breakfast, served in the large family kitchen, brings masses of local produce.

Kingswear Castle ★

Kingswear, TQ6 0DX (01628 825925, www.landmark trust.org.uk). Rates £931-£2,842 per week for 6 people.

The Landmark Trust rescued this medieval castle from decay, restoring the gun deck and converting the floors above it into comfortable, appealing accommodation. The windows afford panoramic views of the Dart; at night, climb up on to the battlements for star-gazing. The Trust even supplies a Union Flag for you to raise at dawn and lower at dusk.

Nonsuch House

Church Hill, Kingswear, TQ6 0BX (01803 752829, www.nonsuch-house.co.uk). Rates £100-£150 double incl breakfast.

The four large and sunny rooms at this luxurious B&B all have fabulous views across the water. Stellar breakfasts are served in the conservatory; the owners also offer a three- or four-course dinner made with local seasonal produce on selected evenings, and will happily provide picnic lunches on request.

River Dart. See p127.

DEVON

Places to visit

TOTNES & AROUND

Berry Pomeroy Castle
nr Totnes, TQ9 6LJ (01803 866618, www.english-heritage.org.uk/berrypomeroycastle). Open Apr-June, Sept 10am-5pm daily. July, Aug 10am-6pm daily. Oct, Nov 10am-4pm daily. Admission £4.50; £2.30-£3.80 reductions.
Said to be one of the most haunted castles in Britain, this magnificent ruin sits on a precipitous cliff overlooking Gatcombe Valley. There are some lovely woodland walks, and refreshments are available in a café by the castle.

Dartington Cider Press Centre
Shinners Bridge, Totnes, TQ9 6TQ (01803 847500, www.dartington.org/cider-press-centre). Open 9.30am-5.30pm Mon-Sat; 10am-5pm Sun.
Formerly an apple-pressing mill and small-scale cider factory, this corner of the Dartington empire is now home to a number of interesting arts and crafts shops. There are also two cafés, one with a kids' play area.

Totnes Castle
Totnes, TQ9 5NU (01803 864406, www.english-heritage.org.uk/totnescastle). Open Apr-June, Sept 10am-5pm daily. July, Aug 10am-6pm daily; Oct, Nov 10am-4pm daily. Admission £3.20; £1.60-£2.70 reductions.
Built by Judhael, a knight from Brittany who was given Totnes as a gift by William the Conqueror, this motte-and-bailey structure affords commanding views across the town rooftops and the River Dart.

Totnes Rare Breeds Centre
Totnes, TQ9 5JR (01803 840387, www.totnes rarebreeds.co.uk). Open Apr-Oct 10am-5pm daily. Admission £4.75; £3.80-£4.25 reductions; £15 family. No credit cards.

Youngsters can feed a red squirrel, make friends with a pygmy goat, meet Wizard the eagle owl and cuddle a guinea pig at this family attraction. You can arrive by steam train from Buckfastleigh or Staverton: ask at the station for a joint ticket to get a discount for the farm and train. There's also a café.

DARTMOUTH & AROUND

Coleton Fishacre
Brownstone Road, Kingswear, TQ6 0EQ (01803 752466, www.nationaltrust.org.uk/coletonfishacre). Open Mar-Nov 10.30am-5pm Wed-Sun. Admission £7; £3.50 reductions; £10.50-£17.50 family.
A lovely, Arts and Crafts-style house, once owned by the family that founded the D'Oyly Carte Opera Company. There's an excellent tearoom and subtropical gardens. Free, hour-long guided walks take place at 2.15pm on Fridays, and this is also the starting point for some bracing coastal walks.

Dartmouth Castle
Dartmouth, TQ6 0JN (01803 833588, www.english-heritage.org.uk/dartmouthcastle). Open Jan-Mar, Nov, Dec 10am-4pm Sat, Sun. Apr-June, Sept 10am-5pm daily. July, Aug 10am-6pm daily. Oct 10am-4pm daily. Admission £4.50; £2.30-£3.80 reductions.
Built in the 14th century, this fine castle enjoys panoramic views of the river and the sea. Within the castle is the 12th-century church of St Petrox, originally a monks' cell and later a chapel for the castle garrison. Above the castle are the remains of a Civil War fort.

Dartmouth Museum
The Butterwalk, Dartmouth, TQ6 9PZ (01803 832923, www.devonmuseums.net/dartmouth). Open Summer 10am-4pm Mon-Sat. Winter noon-3pm Mon-Sat. Admission £1.50; 50p-£1 reductions. No credit cards.
An impressively decorated merchant's house, now a museum about the area and its maritime history.

Old Brewhouse
Manor Street, Dittisham, TQ6 0EX (01628 783118, www.theoldbrewhousedittisham.co.uk). Rates £310-£785 per week for 4 people. No credit cards.
This Grade II-listed two-bed cottage lies a stone's throw from the water in Dittisham. It retains many original features, but has been kitted out in a bright and contemporary style, with a Bose iPod docking station and a handcrafted oak kitchen. There's a small courtyard with a barbecue and a shower.

River Dart YHA
Maypool, Galmpton, TQ5 0ET (0845 371 9531, www.yha.org.uk). Rates from £13.95 per person.
This Victorian mansion overlooks the Dart estuary and backs on to the Greenway estate (*see p135*). There are 70 beds, along with a café and a bar; in summer, look out for barbecue nights. The hostel features in Agatha Christie's 1956 thriller *Dead Man's Folly* as Hoodown Youth Hostel.

TOWARDS PRAWLE POINT
From the Dart estuary, Start Bay's sweeping arc of high cliffs and picturesque shingle beaches

stretches some miles, all the way to the jagged arm of Start Point (*see p136*). South-west of Start Point lies the dramatic headland of Prawle Point (*see p136*), used as a lookout point for centuries.

Blackpool Sands & Strete
Set in a sheltered bay ringed by steep, pine-clad slopes, defined on sunny days by its sweep of golden shingle and clear turquoise waters, this privately owned Blue Flag beach ★ is a beautiful place. Facilities include showers, toilets, deckchairs and, in summer, lifeguards; you can also hire surf-skis, kayaks, boogie boards and wetsuits. The Venus Beach Café (01803 712648, www.venus company.co.uk) offers a menu of local produce; needless to say, the views are lovely. If you're feeling adventurous, Lushwind (07849 758987, www.lushwind.co.uk) operates windsurfing, kayaking and paddle boarding courses.
From Blackpool Sands, hairpin bends lead to the clifftop village of Strete. Once inhabited by smugglers, it has spectacular views of Start Bay and, on a more mundane level, a fine village shop and post office.

Greenway ★

Greenway Road, Galmpton, TQ5 0ES (01803 842382, www.nationaltrust.org.uk/greenway). Open Mar-June, Sept, Oct 10.30am-5pm Wed-Sun. July, Aug 10.30am-5pm Tue-Sun. Admission £7.45; £3.75 reductions; £11.20-£18.65 family.

Agatha Christie purchased Greenway in 1938, and spent her summers and Christmases here. In 2000, Christie's family gave the property to the National Trust, and it opened to the public in spring 2009. Access to the 18th-century house is limited, with timed tickets allocated on arrival; in Christie's bedroom, you can see the clothes she would have worn, while the library contains editions of every book she wrote. The house is surrounded by beautiful woodland gardens, and footpaths criss-cross the estate. Visitors are encouraged to arrive by public transport, taking the ferry from Dartmouth, Brixham, Dittisham or Torquay (Greenway Ferry, 0845 489 0418), or the bus (Riverlink 01803 834488); alternatively, walk here via the Greenway Walk, the Dart Valley Trail or the John Musgrave Trail. If you do drive, you'll need to pre-book a parking space, and admission costs more.

Newcomen Engine

The Engine House, Mayors Avenue, Dartmouth, TQ6 9YY (01803 824224, www.discoverdartmouth.com). Open Easter-Oct 9.30am-5pm Mon-Sat. Nov-Easter 9.30am-4.30pm Mon-Sat. Admission free.

The world's first successful steam engine, invented by local ironmonger Thomas Newcomen in 1710 to help pump water out of Dartmoor's tin mines.

TOWARDS PRAWLE POINT

Start Point Lighthouse

Start Point (01803 771802, www.trinityhouse.co.uk). Open July, Aug 11am-5pm daily. Other times vary, phone for details. Admission £3; £1.60 reductions; £8 family. No credit cards.

The walk to Start Point Lighthouse offers commanding views of Start Bay. The distinctive and still-working lighthouse, built in 1836 to warn ships off the Skerries, is open for guided tours on selected summer days.

KINGSBRIDGE & AROUND

South Devon Chilli Farm

Wigford Cross, Loddiswell, TQ7 4DX (01548 550782, www.southdevonchillifarm.co.uk). Open Jan-Easter 10am-4pm Mon-Fri. Easter-Dec 10am-4pm daily.

The 110-foot polytunnel here is home to more than 200 chilli plants, from the comparatively mild Hungarian wax to the positively scalding naga jolokia. The chillies are at their peak in the late summer, transforming the tunnel into a riot of colour as they ripen. The shop has a wealth of fiery wares, from chilli seeds to chilli-spiked chocolate.

SALCOMBE TO SHARPITOR

Overbeck's

Sharpitor, TQ8 8LW (01548 842893, www.national trust.org.uk/overbecks). Open Garden only Jan, early Feb, Nov, Dec 11am-5pm Mon-Fri. Mid Feb-mid Mar 11am-5pm daily. House & Garden Mid Mar-June, Sept, Oct 11am-5pm Mon-Wed, Sat, Sun. July, Aug 11am-5pm daily. Admission Summer £6.40; £3.20 reductions; £9.60-£16 family. Winter £3.50; £1.75 reductions.

This splendid Edwardian house, on the cliffs above Salcombe Bar, is named in honour of eccentric inventor Otto Overbeck, who lived here between 1928 and 1937. Learn about Overbeck's Rejuvenator, a deeply strange electric-shock beauty treatment, in the museum, which also showcases a fine toy collection. There are also subtropical gardens, a café and a youth hostel.

Slapton Sands & around

On the other side of Strete, Slapton Sands stretches some three miles along the coast. It's a pretty, if inappropriately named, place: the beach is not made of sand but of small shingle. However, its fame comes not from its natural beauty but from its history. In April 1944, this was the site of the ill-fated Exercise Tiger: a convoy of Allied ships, gathering to rehearse for the D-Day landings, were attacked by German E-boats, and some 700 US servicemen lost their lives. A plaque commemorates the event, and the car park at nearby Torcross contains a Sherman tank, recovered from Start Bay in 1984.

At the northern end of the shingle stretch lies Pilchards Cove, a well established and lovely naturist beach. This end of the beach, with its sheltering wooded slope, is something of a sun trap; you may spot a naked body basking in the sun while, at the other end of the beach, fleece-clad hikers stride grimly into the wind. West from Pilchards Cove, Strete Gate is a pleasant picnic spot, with access to a woodland walk and a pay-and-display car park.

Behind the beach and the A379 is the freshwater lagoon of Slapton Ley, a National Nature Reserve and a Site of Special Scientific Interest. With its sheltered reed beds and woodlands, the ley has become a haven for all sorts of birdlife. The Slapton Ley Field Centre (01548 580466, www.field-studies-council.org) on Sands Road, in Slapton village, has regular updates on sightings.

The circular Slapton Ley Nature Trail (01548 580685, www.slnnr.org.uk) crosses the reed marshes on a boardwalk and continues around the ley to Slapton Bridge and Slapton Sands. The site is under constant threat from coastal erosion.

Just inland from the ley is the pretty village of Slapton. Notable buildings include the 14th-century church of St James and the Grade I-listed Tower Inn (01548 580216, www.thetowerinn.com, closed Mon Oct-Mar), originally part of the Collegiate Chantry of St Mary. The remains of the chantry tower provide a dramatic backdrop to the beer garden at the inn, which was built in about 1347 to house the men working on the monastery buildings.

At the southern end of the lagoon, huddled on the shingle shore and protected by a large sea wall, is

Torcross. Located at the more sheltered end of Slapton Sands, the village has plenty of B&Bs, holiday apartments and cottages, many of which are right on the beach. Inland of here, there are more options at Stokenham – also home to the well stocked Stokeley Farm Shop (01548 581010, www.stokeley.co.uk).

Beesands, Start Point & Prawle Point

A few miles south around the coast is the fishing village of Beesands. As you follow the steep, high-sided green lane down to the village, you'll get tantalising glimpses of Start Bay and the Start Point lighthouse. A sturdy sea wall and thousands of tonnes of huge boulders protect the beachside cottages, St Andrew's Church, the wonderful Britannia Shellfish shop ★ (and café in summer) and the Cricket Inn (see p137) from winter storms.

The former fishing village of Hallsands, just south of here, could have done with such protection on 26 January 1917, when a combination of easterly gales and high tides breached the villages' defences, and washed away most of its buildings. You can see what remains from a viewing platform in South Hallsands.

Until the 16th century, Start Bay was notorious as a hangout for pirates. Even after they left, danger remained in the form of treacherous fog, which proved the undoing of many a ship. With the construction of the still-operational Start Point lighthouse (see p135) in 1836, the bay became a considerably safer place. The headland's grassy, rocky ridge offers commanding views of Start Bay and beyond Slapton to the Dart estuary.

Around the point, a walk through a field followed by a scramble down the cliff path will bring you to Great Mattiscombe Sands, a small, sheltered cove without a café or a deckchair in sight. Basking seals sometimes sunbathe on the rocks, however; ask the car park attendant where best to spot them.

The Coast Path then curves around Lannacombe Bay, with its tiny sliver of sandy beach, and on to Prawle Point, Devon's most southerly headland. This was another shipwreck hotspot – hence the lookout station perched at the top. The headland can also be reached via a single-track lane from the serene village of East Prawle; after parking in the National Trust car park, continue on foot.

With no end of superb coastal walks, plenty of birdwatching and a lovely local pub, the Pig's Nose Inn (see p137), East Prawle is popular among Devonians keen for a spot of simple seaside camping. On the green, the Piglet Stores & Café (01548 511486, www.piglets atprawle.com/index.htm) covers pretty much all eventualities, selling everything from magnums of Moët to fresh bread and fishing tackle.

Driving west will bring you to the Salcombe-Kingsbridge Estuary and East Portlemouth, the most notable village on the estuary's eastern bank. Much quieter than Salcombe (see p142), its glitzy neighbour across the water, East Portlemouth is home to a couple of beautiful sandy beaches. A ferry runs from here to Salcombe in summer (see p142). The village itself is up on the hill; highlights include the 12th-century church of St Winwaloe.

Fingals. See p133.

Start Bay

Where to eat & drink

In addition to the venues below, it's worth checking out Stokenham's two fine village pubs: the Church House Inn (01548 580253, www.churchhouseinn-stokenham.co.uk), which has three low-beamed rooms and a large garden, and the Tradesmans Arms (01548 580996, www.thetradesmans arms.com), a thatched pub overlooking the village green, where sheep graze. Both pubs offer simple, hearty food; the Tradesmans Arms also has B&B accommodation (£65-£75 double incl breakfast).

In the village of Chillington, which is about a mile west of Stokenham, whitehouse (see p140) is a laid back but luxurious place for a meal. Non-residents are welcome, but it's best to book ahead.

Cricket Inn

Beesands, TQ7 2EN (01548 580215, www.thecricket inn.com). Open Summer 11am-11pm daily. Winter 11am-3pm, 6-11pm Mon-Fri; 11am-11pm Sat, Sun. Lunch served noon-2.30pm, dinner served 6-9pm daily.
This small, friendly pub, right on the beach at Beesands, first opened its doors in 1867, and has been popular with locals, fishermen and walkers ever since. The inn was recently refurbished but retains its charm, with plenty of black and white photographs of village life on its whitewashed walls. The extensive menu is renowned for its seafood, landed yards from the front door. Upstairs are four beautiful B&B rooms (£60-£100 double incl breakfast); another four were being added at the time of writing.

Kings Arms

Dartmouth Road, Strete, TQ6 0RW (01803 770377, www.kingsarms-dartmouth.co.uk). Open 11.30am-3pm, 6-10.30pm Tue-Sat; noon-3pm, 7-10pm Sun.
Lunch served noon-2pm Tue-Sat; noon-3pm Sun. Dinner served 6.30-9pm Tue-Sat; 7-9pm Sun.
Located in a former Edwardian hotel in the heart of Strete, the Kings Arms employs local fish and seafood to great effect in dishes such as fillet of sea bass with ginger, spring onion and Thai shellfish broth. Drinks include local ales and a number of unusual wines. Booking is essential for dinner and Sunday lunch.

Millbrook Inn ★

South Pool, TQ7 2RW (01548 531581, www.millbrook innsouthpool.co.uk). Open noon-11pm daily. Lunch served noon-2pm, dinner served 7-9pm daily.
This 16th-century village inn comes with a posse of ducks; they entertain customers with their antics in the brook behind the pub. The lovely location is complemented by well kept ales and seasonally inspired cooking, which extends from simple crab sandwiches to more elaborate dishes (bouillabaisse, assiette of lamb). In warmer months, the barbecue is fired up. Some diners choose to arrive under sail; by road, it's roughly three miles away from both Beeson and East Portlemouth.

Pig's Nose Inn ★

East Prawle, TQ7 2BY (01548 511209, www.pigsnose. co.uk). Open noon-3pm, 6-11pm daily. Lunch served noon-2.30pm, dinner served 6-9pm daily.
This country pub in East Prawle (another establishment that dates back to the 16th century) is decorated with all sorts of mismatched rustic paraphernalia, from hunting crops to ships in bottles. It's now in the hands of former band manager Peter Webber, which explains the occasional gigs from the likes of the Boomtown Rats and Chris Farlowe. The ales are local and the food uncomplicated: curries, chillies and the like.

DEVON

Slapton Sands. See p135.

DEVON

Rocket House Tearooms

Torcross, TQ7 2TQ (01548 581096). Open Summer noon-4pm daily (weather dependent).
Tuck into fluffy pancakes with crisp bacon or an own-made pecan and maple Danish at this family-run tearoom, set in the former lifeboat house by the beach. Inside, the decor is all Cath Kidston and knitted cupcakes; outside there is a pretty garden.

Start Bay Inn ★

Torcross, TQ7 2TQ (01548 580553, www.startbayinn. co.uk). Open 11.30am-11pm daily. Lunch served noon-2.15pm, dinner served 6-9.30pm daily.
This 14th-century inn was once crammed to the gills with fishermen, who worked their boats from the beach on the other side of the sea wall. Today, it's hugely popular with locals and visitors, who pitch up (there's no advance booking) in the hope of getting a chance to tuck into the renowned fish and chips. The specials board lists what's been caught in Start Bay that day. Drink pints of Otter Ale, or choose from the very decent wine list.

Where to stay

In summer, you may be able to camp in East Prawle, in a field near the Pig's Nose Inn (*see p137*); facilities are basic. Ask at the pub for information. At the opposite end of the spectrum, there are some jaw-droppingly opulent self-catering properties in these parts. In East Portlemouth, Harbour Watch (01548 853089, www.toadhall cottages.co.uk) is a superbly swanky waterside residence. Prices start from over £2,000 per week, but it does sleep 12. Downsteps (01637 881942, www.uniquehomestays.co.uk), in Torcross, is another superbly located pad. Oozing low key luxe, the 200-year-old whitewashed fisherman's cottage is set in its own secluded cove, with a terrace overlooking the waves; with two doubles and one bunk room, it sleeps six.

Somewhere in the middle, Higher Beeson House, near Beesands (01548 580623, www.higherbeeson.co.uk) is a plush B&B on a family-run organic farm, which also offers craft workshops. Down Farm (01548 511234, www.downfarm.co.uk), a working farm a short stroll from the sands of Lannacombe Bay, offers both B&B and self-catering.

Beacon Cottage & Landward Cottage

(01386 701177, www.ruralretreats.co.uk). Rates Beacon Cottage £801-£1,646 per week for 6 people. Landward Cottage £747-£1,201 per week for 5 people.
Next to the Start Point lighthouse, just off the South West Coast Path, sit two well equipped stone cottages, both with three bedrooms and superlative sea views. Landward Cottage adjoins the lighthouse; Beacon Cottage is a detached property opposite Landward, with an alfresco dining area that offers lovely views of the bay. The lighthouse's fog signal operates automatically when needed; ear plugs are provided.

Buckland Court Holiday Cottages

nr Slapton, TQ7 2RE (07970 617513, www.buckland court.com). Rates vary, check website for details.
A mile and a half from Slapton, Buckland Court is an elegant, 250-year-old Georgian farmhouse. A number of the former farm buildings have been converted into self-catering holiday cottages, set around two large courtyards. There are nine cottages in total, sleeping between four and 12 apiece; facilities include a badminton and cricket area, and a barbecue.

Frogwell B&B

Strete, TQ6 0RH (01803 770273, www.frogwell.net). Rates £75-385 double incl breakfast. No credit cards.
This pretty cottage dates back to the 17th century, and has three beautifully decorated en suite B&B rooms. It's within walking distance of Blackpool Sands.

Kittiwake Cottage

East Prawle, TQ7 2BY (01548 511471, www.kittiwake cottage.com). Rates £330-£725 per week for 4 people. No credit cards.
This semi-detached, 19th-century fisherman's cottage has been sympathetically restored. Decor draws on seaside colours, with soft blues and creams, and there is a double bedroom with a balcony and a sweet attic room. Outside, the garden has glorious views across the valley to the sea, and a gate that opens on to the village green.

Sea Breeze

Torcross, TQ7 2TQ (01548 580697, www.seabreeze breaks.com). Rates £85-£125 double incl breakfast.
The decor inside this pretty, thatched cottage, with sky-blue shutters and a seafront location, is simple and stylish, with window-seats from which you can watch the sun or moon rise over the sea. There are three en suite B&B rooms (two doubles and a family suite). Downstairs is a delightful café where, if the sun's out, you can sit by the sea wall and tuck into a hearty breakfast or a bacon sarnie.

Seacombe

East Portlemouth, TQ8 8PN (01647 24474, www.seacombe-devon.co.uk). Rates £750-£2,700 per week for 7 people.
Cedar-clad Seacombe enjoys a magnificently secluded location, overlooking the coast between East Prawle and East Portlemouth. The house is beautiful, with nice bedrooms (there's space for seven), a state-of-the-art kitchen, geothermal heating and its own cinema. The modern design, with floor-to-ceiling window walls and glazed balconies, brings the outside in, and the beach is a short scramble down the hill.

Tilly's Tuckaway

Stokenham (01548 853089, www.toadhallcottages. co.uk). Rates £248-£777 per week for 4 people.
Roughly 300 yards from the Stokeley Farm Shop (*see p136*), this two-bed, self-catering barn conversion overlooks the ley. Upstairs are a double bedroom and a twin with a shared bathroom. Outside, there are flower-filled gardens.

2 Prospect House

South Hallsands, TQ7 2EY (07525 758363, www.2 prospecthouse.net). Rates £500-£1,280 per week for 4 people. No credit cards.
In the 1920s, the Trout sisters used the compensation they received for the destruction of their cottage at Hallsands in the 1917 gale to build the Trout Hotel, on the cliff above the

deserted village. The hotel has now been converted into luxury holiday apartments; this two-bed apartment has fabulous views over Start Bay and access to an outdoor heated pool. The beach is a two-minute stroll away.

whitehouse ★
Chillington, TQ7 2JX (01548 580505, www.white housedevon.com). Lunch served noon-4pm, dinner served 6.30-9.30pm daily. Rates £180-£240 double incl breakfast.
The decor inside the beautifully proportioned rooms of this Georgian house is effortlessly chic. Upstairs are six slickly appointed boutique-style rooms (think gigantic plasma screen televisions, baths big enough for two, Frette linens and Nespresso coffee machines). But you don't have to be staying here to eat in the attractive, airy dining room. Lunchtime is all about inviting, low-key fare (lemon, artichoke, green olive and parsley linguine), while the evening brings a good haul of local seafood.

KINGSBRIDGE & AROUND
At the head of the Kingsbridge-Salcombe estuary is the market town and local transport hub of Kingsbridge. Over the years, the area around the quay here has changed beyond recognition: the mudflats have been covered with tarmac and riverside housing, while the cargo ships have long since been replaced by bobbing yachts and dinghies. The market, established in 1219 to allow monks from Buckfast Abbey to sell their wares, still takes place on the first and third Saturday of the month, in the square by the quay – although the monks have been usurped by farmers and artisanal producers.

Nearby Fore Street offers further food-shopping opportunities. Lidstone's sells locally reared organic meat; there's seafood at Catch of the Day; and, on adjoining Duke Street, the Red Earth Deli & Café has cheese, charcuterie and other tempting edibles, plus a nice café. Other notable shops include the Harbour Bookshop, just off Fore Street on Mill Street.

Towards the top of Fore Street sit some fine old 18th- and 19th-century merchant's houses. The former town hall is home to Wednesday's Country Market, with stalls selling food and other goodies, and the independent, family-run

Things to do

TOTNES & AROUND

Canoe Adventures ★
Tuckenhay, TQ9 7EH (01803 865301, www.canoe adventures.co.uk). Open by arrangement only. Trips from £19 per person.
Canoe Adventures offer visitors the opportunity to explore the Dart by getting out on the water, on guided four- to five-hour trips in a 12-seater canoe. No experience is necessary, and all equipment is provided.

Dart Round Robin
Steamer Quay, Totnes, TQ9 5AL (01803 834488, www.riverlink.co.uk). Open Apr-Oct; phone for timetable details. Admission £19.50; £12.50-£17.50 reductions; £58 family.
The Dart Round Robin includes a boat trip (with audio commentary) from Totnes down the Dart to Dartmouth, passing Sharpham, Dittisham and Greenway; the ferry across to Kingswear; a ride on a steam train from Kingswear to Paignton; then an open-top bus ride through the Devon countryside back to Totnes. You can linger as long as you like at each destination, but be aware that the boat sailing times depend on the tides. Or simply take the boat to Dartmouth and back (75 minutes each way).

Riverford Farm Pick & Cook Days
Wash Barn, Buckfastleigh, TQ11 0JU (01803 762074, www.riverford.co.uk). Open times vary, check website for details. Admission varies.
Encourage kids to love their vegetables by getting them to harvest their own lunch from the fields at Riverford Farm. Their rich pickings will then be taken back to the Field Kitchen, where the children cook it (under supervision) and eat it. Check the website for details of seasonal events, along with regular farm tours.

Sharpham Estate & Vineyard
nr Totnes, TQ9 7UT (01803 732203, www.sharpham. com). Open Mar-May, Oct-Dec 10am-5pm Mon-Sat. June-Sept 10am-5pm daily. Tours from £5.
This 500-acre estate has been farmed for a thousand years, and now produces wine from its riverside vineyards and unpasteurised cheeses from its organic Jersey herd. There are a variety of tasting tours, ranging from a quick walk around the vineyard followed by wine and cheese tastings (£5) to the day-long Sharpham Wine Experience (£49.50; booking essential). Or just pop in to browse the shop, or eat in the excellent café (*see p129*).

Totnes Ghost Walk
(01803 847930). Tours Easter-Oct 8pm Tue. Admission £5; free reductions. No credit cards.
A guided walk on which you'll hear spine-chilling tales about Totnes's darker side, before calming your shredded nerves with a drink in a supposedly haunted pub. Historical or literary walks are also available.

DARTMOUTH & AROUND

Britannia Royal Naval College Tours
College Way, Dartmouth, TQ6 0HJ (01803 834224, www.discoverdartmouth.com). Tours Easter-Oct 2pm Wed, Sun; booking essential. Admission £15.95; £6.50-£15.30 reductions.
The Royal Naval College was built to replace the Royal Navy's original floating training base in Dartmouth. Located on a hill overlooking Dartmouth, the building was completed in 1905. Book a tour through the Tourist Board, who can supply details of dates and regulations. You'll need to bring photo ID.

Picnic Boat
Double Steps, Dartmouth (01404 42449, www.the picnicboat.co.uk). Open Mid Mar-Oct by arrangement only. Trips from £30-£70 per person.

Reel Cinema (01548 856636, www.thereelcinema.
co.uk). Next to the town hall is the Shambles, a
granite-pillared Elizabethan arcade. Up the hill
from here, the old, 17th-century grammar school is
now home to the Kingsbridge Cookworthy Museum
(01548 853235, www.kingsbridgemuseum.org.uk,
closed Nov-Easter).

Where to eat & drink

Fortescue Arms ★
*Green Lane, East Allington, TQ9 7RA (01548 521215,
www.fortescue-arms.co.uk). Open 6-11pm Mon; noon-
2.30pm, 6-11pm Tue-Sat; noon-2.30pm, 6-10.30pm
Sun. Lunch served noon-2pm Tue-Sun. Dinner served
7-9.30pm daily.*
Some ten minutes' drive from Kingsbridge, this old pub has
been spruced up a little for modern times, but has retained
a certain cosiness in the bar and dining areas. Dishes from
Austrian chef/proprietor Werner Rott might include
pheasant wrapped in Black Forest ham and apple strudel.
There's B&B accommodation available upstairs (£60
double incl breakfast).

Old Bakery Café & Restaurant
*The Promenade, Kingsbridge, TQ7 1JD (01548
855777, www.theoldbakerykingsbridge.co.uk). Food
served Summer 10am-3pm, 6.30-9.30pm Mon-Sat;
10am-3pm Sun. Winter 10am-3pm Mon; 10am-3pm,
6.30-9.30pm Tue-Sat.*
The Old Bakery's premises used to be occupied by a tapas
bar, and the new owners have continued the tradition,
supplementing small tapas plates with paella (24 hours'
notice required) and other main dishes that rely on local
produce. Coffees and cakes are available all day.

Where to stay
Upmarket lodgings can be had at Buckland Tout-
Saints (Goveton, 01548 853055, www.tout-
saints.co.uk) an elegant William-and-Mary manor
house, set in four acres of landscaped gardens.

Chantry
*Loddiswell, TQ7 4EH (01548 559372, www.chantry
devon.co.uk). Bed & breakfast £70-£120 double incl
breakfast. Self-catering £305-£705 per week for
2-4 people.*

With room for up to 12 people, the Picnic Boat offers
trips from Dartmouth Castle upstream to Dittisham
and back. Staff can provide picnics of locally sourced
goodies, taking in everything from fresh seafood to
champagne. Kids may enjoy the themed Pirate Picnic.

Woodlands Leisure Park
*Blackawton, TQ9 7DQ (01803 712598, www.
woodlandspark.com). Open Mar-Oct 9.30am-5pm
daily. Admission phone for details.*
Set in 90 acres of countryside, this theme park's
adrenaline-fuelled attractions include a commando
course, bumper boats and three water-coasters.
It's also home to a huge indoor play centre, with
slides, climbing nets, rides and play areas for
smaller children. Other attractions include a
falconry centre and the Big Fun Farm.

KINGSBRIDGE & AROUND

Mountain Water Experience
*Courtlands, Kingsbridge, TQ7 4BM (01548 550675,
www.mountainwaterexperience.co.uk). Courses vary,
check website for times and prices.*
On-site attractions at this outdoor activity centre include
an assault course, an orienteering course and an
archery range; away from the centre, staff can organise
body-boarding, kayaking, caving and rock-climbing.

Rivermaid boat tours
*Boatyard Quay, Kingsbridge (01548 853607). Open
May-Sept; phone for timetable details and ticket prices.*
These 90-minute trips on the *Rivermaid* allow close-up
views of the estuary's extensive birdlife.

SALCOMBE TO SHARPITOR

Sailing in Salcombe
There are plenty of opportunities for novices to take
to the water in Salcombe. Based on a permanently

moored old ferry, the Island Cruising Club (01548
531176) is a one-stop shop for would-be sailors,
offering reasonably priced sailing courses for all
comers (it's very child-friendly). Salcombe Dinghy
Sailing (01548 843927, www.salcombedinghy
sailing.co.uk), with headquarters at Whitestrand
Quay, rents boats to competent sailors; it also
offers taster sessions and lessons with qualified
instructors, as does South Sands Sailing (01548
843451, www.southsandssailing.co.uk).

SOAR MILL COVE TO
BURGH ISLAND

Discovery Surf School
*Bigbury Beach, Bigbury-on-Sea, TQ7 4AZ (07813
639622, www.discoverysurf.com). Open by
arrangement only. Lessons from £38 2hrs.*
The two-hour beginners' lesson is suitable for
ages six and up, but there's also tuition for more
experienced wave-catchers. And if you want to try
something new, there's always the more sedate
stand-up paddle-surfing (SUP). Equipment is
available for hire even if you haven't signed up
for tuition. (Discovery Surf School also offers
lessons at Tregonhawke Beach and Tregantle
Beach in south east Cornwall.)

ERME MOUTH TO BOVISAND

Discovery Divers
*Fort Bovisand, PL9 0AB (01752 492722,
www.discoverydivers.org). Open by arrangement
only. Dives from £15.*
Discovery Divers offers a variety of diving courses,
along with guided dives. There are some excellent
dive sites near Plymouth, from deep wrecks to
shallow scenic dives; in the latter category is the
HMS Scylla, a former warship that's ideal for
novices. Check the website for full details.

DEVON

Two imaginative barn conversions – one perfect for couples, and the other geared towards families. Both properties are available for short-term holiday lets or for B&B stays. Kingsbridge is around three miles away.

Hazelwood House
Loddiswell, TQ7 4EB (01548 821232, www.hazelwood house.com). Rates £72-£145 double incl breakfast.
This grand Victorian country house was once the home of the Peek family, whose fortune was made in the biscuit trade. It's long since been converted into a hotel, with 14 bedrooms (seven of which have en suite facilities). Some are simple and elegant; others are altogether grander and retain more of their original character.

SALCOMBE TO SHARPITOR
There's an easy, casual confidence about Salcombe – which stems, in part, from the affluent second home-owners who gravitate towards it in summer. The population of 1,500 increases tenfold in August, as the pretty bay fills with visiting boats, and the town becomes Chelsea-by-the-Sea.

For all Salcombe's latterday affluence, the town's origins are more humble. Built on the steep western side of the estuary, it used to be a centre for boat-building and sail-making; it was also once a bustling port. Learn more about Salcombe's past at the Maritime Museum in Market Street (closed Nov-Easter), behind the Tourist Information Centre (01548 843927). The town's nautical heritage is upheld around Island Street, where you'll find boat yards, chandleries, and clinker-boat makers and restorers, including the Salcombe Boat Store (01548 843708, www.salcombeboatstore.co.uk). The ground floor has a chandlery; upstairs, there's clothing and a splicing service. During the week-long Salcombe Town Regatta at the start of August, watercraft of all shapes and sizes descend on the town. But even outside festival-time, the estuary is never short of boats.

Further along the waterfront is Victoria Quay, which, at summer high tides, is thronged with youngsters crabbing. There are several galleries around here, among them the Loft Studio, Through the Quay Hole and, in Island Square, Bangwallop.

Fore Street, the town's main street, runs parallel to the water's edge, with little alleyways leading up the hill or down to the quay. The street is lined with clothes shops, from upmarket chains to local boutiques such as Amelia's Attic, and places to eat. You can pick up bits and pieces for a picnic at the Salcombe Delicatessen on Fore Street, or Casse-Croûte Deli on nearby Clifton Place.

Continuing south along the waterside, past the ornamental gardens of Cliff House, you'll come to North Sands, one of the town's two beaches. Nicely sheltered between two headlands, the beach has parking, toilets and disabled access. Time your visit with care, though, as the beach disappears at high tide. Further south is South Sands, accessible via the coastal path, by car (parking is limited) or by ferry from Whitestrand Quay in Salcombe (01548 561035, closed Nov-Easter).

Salcombe is a small place, and traffic can be problematic in summer. A park-and-ride scheme operates every weekend in June and daily during July and August. Boat parking is available in the Creek Boat Park, via Gould Road (book on 01548 843791) and the South Sands dinghy park. And you could always arrive by ferry from Kingsbridge (01548 853607, closed Oct-Apr) or East Portlemouth (01548 842053).

Along the coast from Salcombe, in the village of Sharpitor, is the cliff-top Overbeck's Museum & Gardens (*see p135*) – home to some bizarre inventions, and with amazing views towards Salcombe from its terraced, six-acre gardens. From Sharpitor, the coast path winds south to the rocky promontory of Bolt Head, guarding the estuary mouth.

Where to eat & drink
It's not cheap to eat in Salcombe, so try to make sure you get a view thrown in with your meal. For casual meals, the Wardroom (19 Fore Street, 01548 843333), serves light lunches and cream teas at tables by the quay wall. Also on Fore Street is the Ferry Boat Inn (01548 844000): it isn't the prettiest pub, but it does serve a fair crab sandwich and offers river views from the garden. Nearby, the smarter Dick & Wills (01548 843408, www.dickandwills.co.uk, closed Jan-Mar) bar and brasserie has stunning views across the estuary.

Winking Prawn ★
North Sands, Salcombe, TQ8 8LD (01548 842326, www.winkingprawn.co.uk). Open 10.30am-4pm Mon-Thur; 8.45am-8.30pm Fri, Sat; 8.45am-4pm Sun. Breakfast served 8.45-10.45am Fri-Sun. Lunch served 11am-4pm daily. Dinner served 6-8.30pm Fri, Sat.
Over the last decade or so, this casual, family-friendly eatery has become a Salcombe institution. After breakfast, drinks and snacks are served all day. For dinner, pick something from the barbecue (weather permitting), or choose from the lengthier menu, which includes platters of fruits de mer.

Where to stay
Salcombe's South Sands Hotel (01548 859000, www.southsandshotel.co.uk) is scheduled to open in spring 2010, with 22 rooms and five self-catering apartments, all with a contemporary feel.

Bar Lodge
Salcombe, TQ8 8LW (07795 064012, www.bar lodgesalcombe.co.uk). Rates £695-£1,500 per week for 8 people.
The detached, Edwardian-era Bar Lodge is located on a wooded slope, with panoramic views across Salcombe Bar. The property sleeps up to eight people in four double bedrooms (three with balconies). South Sands beach is five minutes' walk away.

Sharpitor YHA
Salcombe, TQ8 8LW (0845 371 9341, www.yha.org.uk). From £15.95 per person.

Accommodation at these prices doesn't often come with such sublime views: this beautiful Edwardian property sits above the estuary. At the bottom of the drive is a sandy beach, and at the top the South West Coast Path. Sleeping arrangements range from two-bed rooms to eight-bed dorms.

Tides Reach Hotel

South Sands, Salcombe, TQ8 8LJ (01548 843466, www. tidesreach.com). Rates £120-£284 double incl breakfast.
The Tides Reach has 35 bedrooms, from singles to expansive family rooms (no under-eights); most have sea views, and some also have balconies. There's an indoor pool, a sauna and a spa, and a restaurant.

Yeoman's Cottage

Salcombe (01548 853089, www.theyeomanscottage. co.uk). Rates £285-£739 per week for 3 people.
Attached to a 17th-century thatched longhouse, this pretty south-facing cottage was once a granary, and then housed a cider press – outside, you can stroll amid the orchard's apple trees. There's a double bedroom, a single and a small balcony with views across the valley.

SOAR MILL COVE TO BURGH ISLAND

Soar Mill Cove to Hope Cove

Some five miles west of craggy Bolt Head, across the National Trust-managed coastal grassland of Bolberry Down, lies the lovely Soar Mill Cove. The remote, sandy beach is accessible via a steep little footpath, lined with wildflowers in summer. The beach itself is surrounded by great chunks of rock, while the water is shallow and safe for swimming.

West along the coast at Hope Cove, the fishing villages of Inner Hope and Outer Hope are connected by the cliff path. In 1588, one of the Spanish Armada's ships came to a nasty end on the Shippen Rock between the villages, and timbers from the wreck were built into the Village Inn (01548 563525) at nearby Thurlestone. Today the area is popular with divers, who explore its numerous wrecks.

With cottages clustered around a cobbled square, Inner Hope has a quaint charm. The hub of village life, though, is in Outer Hope, which has a pub, the Hope & Anchor (01548 561294), and a village shop. Both villages have sandy beaches and local boats still land lobster and crab.

From Hope Cove, you can pick up the coastal path and walk along the clifftop west towards Thurlestone. On a clear day, you can see the Cornish coast, some 30 miles in the distance.

Thurlestone Sands to Bantham

Thurlestone Sands is essentially one long shingle and sand beach, split into two very distinct parts. The westerly end, Thurlestone, tends to be the quieter section, as there are no facilities. By contrast, the National Trust-managed, sand dune-

whitehouse. See p140.

Noss Mayo. See p146.

backed South Milton Sands, at the eastern end, has a car park, toilets, lifeguards (in summer) and a café. Beyond the car pack is the small wetland area of South Milton Ley, a birdwatching hotspot.

North of Thurlestone, the large, sandy surfing beach at Bantham sits at the mouth of the Avon Estuary. Boards and wetsuits can be hired at Tri Ocean Surf, down the road in Churchstow (01548 854676, www.trioceansurf.co.uk). For non-surfers, there's a flag-marked swimming area, monitored by a lifeguard from May to September. The main seaward stretch of the beach can get busy, but the estuary side tends to be quieter. Like Thurlestone and South Milton, this is an exposed beach, and can be breezy.

The beach is also the starting point for the Avon Estuary Walk, a lovely, eight-mile stroll that connects Bantham, Bigbury and Aveton Gifford; see www.southdevonaonb.org.uk for details. Back in Bantham, warm up with a pint and a bite to eat at the 14th-century Sloop Inn (01548 560489).

Bigbury Beach, Burgh Island & around

On the other side of the estuary sits long, sandy Bigbury Beach. You'll find plenty of safe paddling and rock pools here, along with excellent surfing; the Discovery Surf School (see p141) can help with equipment and tuition. There are lifeguards on duty is summer, and refreshments courtesy of the Venus Café (01548 810141, www.venus company.co.uk). Be wary of wading across the estuary to or from Bantham, as rip currents make

it more dangerous than it appears. Better to use the summer-only pedestrian ferry, or drive via the bridge at Aveton Gifford.

A mere 200 metres across the water from Bigbury Beach is bijou Burgh Island, accessible on foot across a sandy causeway or, when the tide's in, by sea tractor. Quaff a half at the Pilchard Inn (see p145) then walk up to the Huer's Hut; until the late 1800s, a lookout was posted up here during the pilchard season, shouting out to the fishermen below when he saw the shoals arriving; the views are stunning. However, the island's main attraction is the Burgh Island Hotel (see p145).

West of Bigbury, sandy, secluded Ayrmer Cove is a gem. Footpaths run from the village of Ringmer to the cove; alternatively, park at the National Trust car park just south of the village and pick up a path from there. The cove itself is in a dramatic setting, backed by sheer cliffs; keep an eye on the tide.

Where to eat & drink

Oyster Shack ★

Milburn Orchard Farm, Stakes Hill, Bigbury, TQ7 4BE (01548 810876, www.oystershack.co.uk). Food served Summer 9-10.30am, noon-2pm, 7-9pm Mon-Sat; noon-2pm Sun. Winter 9-10.30am, noon-2pm, 7-9pm Wed-Sat; noon-2pm Sun.

You don't have to like oysters to eat here, but it certainly helps: a large section of the menu is dedicated to molluscs, raised in the Avon. Hidden away down a track, this is a refreshingly casual place. Non-oyster main courses might include skate wing or crab; sides are excellent chunky chips and a rocket salad. If the tide's out, reach the shack via the tidal road off the Timbers roundabout as you enter Aveton Gifford; if it's in, take the B3392 to St Ann's Chapel, then head left by the post office.

Pilchard Inn
Burgh Island, TQ7 4BG (01548 810514, www.burgh island.com/pilchard.html). Open 11am-11pm daily. Lunch served noon-3pm daily. Dinner served 7-9.30pm Fri, Sat.
Squatting next to the slipway in Burgh Island, this fine old 14th-century smugglers' pub makes the most of its history and its location. There are ales and ciders aplenty at the bar, while food includes basic bar snacks and a Friday-night curry club.

Where to stay
For rustic green camping, try Higher Aunemouth Farm (01548 560339, www.aunemouth camping.co.uk), a 15-minute stroll from the beach in Bantham.

Burgh Island Hotel ★
Burgh Island, TQ7 4BG (01548 810514, www.burgh island.com). Rates £360-£385 double incl breakfast & dinner.
In the 1930s, the Burgh Island Hotel was described as 'the smartest hotel west of the Ritz', as aristocrats, celebrities and royals beat a path to its door. Following a post-war decline,

the hotel was rescued in the 1980s and restored to its former glory. The 25 suites are beautifully furnished, with plenty of period detail. Outside, there's a croquet lawn, a tennis court and a 1930s seawater rock pool. Non-residents can book for black-tie dinner or Sunday lunch.

Old Colonial House
Hope Cove, TQ7 3HH (01564 732309, www.hopecove. co.uk). Rates £350-£1,500 per week for 5 people.
Built in the 1920s, the Old Colonial House is split into three two-bed self-catering apartments: Port, Starboard, and the larger Midships. The house retains much of its original character, with the living rooms and bedrooms at the front of the building, maximising the glorious views.

Soar Mill Cove Hotel
Malborough, TQ7 3DS (01548 561566, www.soarmill cove.co.uk). Rates £140-£240 double incl breakfast.
The hotel is home to a number of spacious, good-looking rooms, with private patios and a variety of mod cons. There's also a smart restaurant and a spa.

Thurlestone Hotel
Thurlestone, TQ7 3NN (01548 560382, www. thurlestone.co.uk). Rates £180-£360 double incl breakfast.
This upmarket hotel is set in 19 acres of subtropical gardens, close to the sea. Alongside the 64 en suite rooms, which range from simple doubles to sea view suites, facilities include a golf course, two pools (indoor and outdoor), a restaurant and bar, a sauna and tennis courts.

Ship Inn. See p146.

ERME MOUTH TO BOVISAND

The Erme Estuary

Where the river Erme reaches the sea, the estuary is flanked by the sandy beaches of Wonwell and Mothecombe. Much of the land around the estuary is owned by the Flete Estate, which lets out a number of holiday properties (*see below*), and the countryside has remained gloriously unspoiled.

On the eastern side of the estuary, Wonwell is accessible via a single-track lane from the village of Kingston (note that there's very little parking down here), or via the coastal path. There are rocks to climb on, shallow, sheltered bathing and a sweeping expanse of fine sand at low tide. On the other side of the estuary is Mothecombe (also known as Meadowsfoot Beach), which is open to the public on Wednesdays and at weekends. Again, access is via a single-track lane; unlike Wonwell, there is a car park and toilets, along with a summer-season teashop. There are fine walks along this part of the coast, west to the Yealm Estuary and the creekside village of Noss Mayo.

The Yealm Estuary & around

The River Yealm reaches the sea just below Newton Ferrers and Noss Mayo. Unlike at the Avon or Dart, there's no trail around the estuary. However, during the summer, a ferry service connects Newton Ferrers, Noss Mayo and Warren Point.

Just west of the estuary is the village of Wembury. Its main draw is the Wembury Marine Centre (Church Road, 01752 862538 www.wembury marinecentre.org), which has displays on the region and its wildlife, and organises a variety of hands-on activities in season. Wembury's small and secluded rocky beach is surrounded by low cliffs. When the tide's out, plenty of sand is exposed; when it's in, there are good snorkelling opportunities. Half a mile from here is a tiny rocky island known as the Great Mew Stone. It's now a nature reserve, and a popular fishing spot for cormorants and shags.

If you're staying in Wembury, the Moostone Meats Farm Shop at New Barton Farm (01752 863420, www.moostonemeats.co.uk, closed Mon, Tue, Sun) is a great source of provisions. There's another excellent farm shop north of here at Yealmpton: Riverford's outpost at Kitley (01752 880925, www.riverfordfarmshop.co.uk), where additional attractions include a café and pick-your-own.

If you're staying over in Noss Mayo, there's a water taxi service from Wembury in high season (10am-4pm, weather permitting). But Wembury itself is a good starting point for a walk west along the coastal path towards Bovisand – a large beach in Down Thomas, on the edge of Plymouth. Rocky outcrops split it into four main areas, of which three are child-friendly, sandy beaches with rock pools between. Access to all the beaches is via the coast path or from the clifftop car park (where you'll also find toilets, a café and shop with a grassy play area for children). When the tide is out, the vast expanse of sand is a popular spot for ball games and castle building. Nearby Fort

Bovisand, built to defend the entrance of Plymouth Sound, is now home to Discovery Divers (*see p141*).

Where to eat & drink

Dolphin Inn

Kingston, TQ7 4QE (01548 810314, www.dolphin-inn.co.uk). Open Summer noon-3pm, 6-11pm daily. Winter noon-2.30pm, 6-11pm Mon-Sat; noon-3pm, 7-10.30pm Sun. Food served Summer noon-2pm, 6-9pm Mon-Fri; noon-2.30pm, 6-9pm Sat, Sun. Winter noon-2pm, 6-9pm Mon-Fri; noon-2.30pm, 6-9pm Sat; noon-2.30pm, 7-9pm Sun.

Tradition is the watchword at this 16th-century inn, a mile or so's walk from the beach at Wonwell. Ales and local ciders can be accompanied by straightforward food (sandwiches, soups, ploughman's lunches and heartier dishes such as steak and ale pie); in summer, retreat to the beer garden. Accommodation ranges from three B&B rooms (£68 double incl breakfast) to two sweet self-catering cottages (£295-£840 per week for 4 people).

Ship Inn

Noss Mayo, PL8 1EW (01752 872387, www.noss mayo.com). Open 11am-11pm Mon-Sat; 11am-10.30pm Sun. Food served noon-9.30pm Mon-Sat; noon-9pm Sun.

Walkers love this popular creekside pub in the pretty village of Noss Mayo, as do sailors, who can tie their boats up outside and pop in for a pint. The interior includes pictures of the local area, bookshelves and assorted nauticalia; you can also sit outside, overlooking the estuary. Some of the beers are local; food runs from burgers and pies to risotto.

Where to stay

Stay in a grand old Elizabethan house at Kitley House Hotel & Restaurant (Yealmpton, 01752 881555, www.kitleyhousehotel.com) or in one of the deluxe self-catering properties at the beautiful, 5,000-acre Flete Estate (Holbeton, 01752 830234, www.flete.co.uk). Less fancy, but with an unbeatable location almost on Wembury Beach, is Mill Cottage (0844 800 2070, www.nationaltrustcottages.co.uk).

Bugle Rocks

Battisborough, PL8 1JX (01752 830422, www.bugle rocks.co.uk). Rates B&B £70 double incl breakfast. Self-catering £294-£858 per week for 4 people.

Occupying a former coachhouse, once part of Lord Mildmay's country residence, this B&B offers three en suite rooms, all with doors leading out to a courtyard garden. There's a two-bed self-catering cottage. The sands of Mothecombe Beach are five minutes away.

Churchwood Valley Holiday Cabins

Wembury Bay, PL9 0DZ (01752 862382, www. churchwoodvalley.com). Rates £255-£875 per week for 4 people.

Set in a wooded valley, running down to the sea, these two-bedroom timber cabins afford lovely vistas across the valley or towards the sea. On-site facilities include a shop and a launderette, and Wembury Beach is just a ten-minute stroll away.

DEVON

Plymouth

For visitors arriving at Devon's most populous city by road, the first evocative sight of the City of Discovery may well be a supermarket. The Sainsbury's superstore at Marsh Mills, just off the A38, is a local landmark that has striking, tensioned fabric 'sails' along its roof – a modern homage to the centuries-old connection between the city and the sea. The sea and waterfront are central to the experience of Plymouth old and new, whether you are treading in the footsteps of Sir Francis Drake at the Hoe, sleeping with sharks at the National Marine Aquarium, watching the vast ferries and warships in Plymouth Sound, or admiring the adventurous architecture of the sleek apartment blocks – a product of the recent, and continuing, regeneration of the city.

The views of Plymouth Sound have an inexpressible wow factor. Running from the Plym Estuary in the east to the Tamar Estuary in the west, this natural harbour offers a diverse, ever-changing scene. Water traffic large and small goes to and fro, while the light falls across the forest of masts in the marina, the offshore Drake's Island and, to the west, Mount Edgcumbe Park and the Rame Peninsula – a first glimpse of Cornwall. Even a Devonian accustomed to cover-star beaches and stupendous views from the South West Coast Path can be stopped in his or her tracks by a new perspective from a café or terrace between Mount Batten and Devonport.

The importance of the waterfront is reinforced by the curious absence of a 'heart' to the city. Plymouth's Victorian city centre was almost totally destroyed by heavy bombing during World War II, and although the centre was rebuilt in the 1950s, it is more functional than attractive. In many ways, Plymouth feels like a scattering of areas that hardly connect to one another, so creating a harmonious link between the city centre and the sea is one of the council's ongoing projects.

Another recent project has been the £3.5m facelift of the West End's 'Independent Quarter', around Frankfort Gate, the indoor Pannier Market and Market Avenue. Small boutiques, delis, cafés and stalls cluster here, offering a quirky alternative to the usual bland, big chain shopping experience.

BARBICAN & SUTTON HARBOUR

Sutton Pool (now Sutton Harbour) was the dominant port and naval base in Elizabethan times. It is bordered by the cobbled streets, narrow alleyways and slanting buildings of the historic Barbican district, which escaped the worst of the bombing during the war. It's an interesting place to wander; for a flavour of how people lived in the time of the Virgin Queen, head for the timber-framed Elizabethan House (see p152), now a small museum.

Boat trips and ferries to Mount Batten set off from the harbour, including the Cawsand Ferry (07971 208381, www.cawsandferry.com, closed Nov-Easter) – a scenic half-hour jaunt across the Sound, past the Breakwater, to the little Cornish village of Cawsand. On West Pier, a small, crumbling arch marks the Mayflower Steps, where the Pilgrim Fathers departed for America in 1620 to escape religious persecution and found Provincetown. (Sticklers for accuracy should note that the actual causeway they set off from, demolished centuries ago, was closer to the present-day site of the Admiral MacBride pub.)

In the middle of the cobbled walkway is the 'Barbican Prawn' – a curious sculpture of an impaled green metal crustacean, atop a pole. Around the seats at its base, a series of small plaques celebrate the colonisation of the world by Plymouth's famous sailors (see p151), including Sir Humphrey Gilbert, who settled Newfoundland in 1583, and his better-known half-brother, Sir Walter Raleigh. Looking at the landmark sailings commemorated here, it's obvious why there are over 40 places named after Plymouth scattered across the globe.

With its views over the water, Sutton Harbour is the café and restaurant quarter. Menus tend to concentrate on fish dishes, tapas and light bites, and there's plenty of outdoor seating in summer. For a more down-to-earth fast food hit, Cap'n Jaspers (see p251) is a favourite haunt of bikers and boaters, and a Plymouth institution.

Barbican Area

A swing footbridge just past the Mayflower Steps leads across to the National Marine Aquarium (*see p152*) on the Coxside bank. With over 50 live exhibits, including sleek sharks and majestic rays, the Aquarium is a must-do. Backtracking a little more takes you to the Cattewater, an estuary of the River Plym. This is where Drake departed on his circumnavigation of the world, and where the English fleet was prepared for the Armada. There is a striking modern shrine to St Christopher at the junction of Cattedown Road and Breakwater Hill, wrought in stainless steel.

Back in the Barbican, you'll find some interesting shops and bars. Housed in a beautiful old building opposite the Custom House, Art 2 Frame on the Parade (01752 204069, www.art2frame.com, closed Mon, Sun) sells huge glass bowls and wall pieces, and has prints displayed in the beamed gallery upstairs. Also on the Parade, the Book Cupboard (01752 226311) is a bibliophile's dream, with narrow aisles cutting between racks piled high with second-hand books of every description.

The next street back, Southside Street, is home to the Black Friars Distillery (*see p152*), where Plymouth Gin, the favoured tipple of the Royal Navy's officers, can be sampled in medieval surroundings. Opposite, naked Plymothians adorn the House That Jack Built craft market (*see p152*).

The Royal Citadel

From the Barbican, the waterfront takes you past more personal plaques of remembrance, mostly to those lost at sea or with connections to the sea, and the wall shrine to Stella Maris, 'The Star of the Sea, the Virgin, the Patron Saint of all Mariners', represented by a small, seaworn Madonna, rescued from a cargo of marble. On nearby Lambhay Street is the St James Scallop, marking Plymouth as one of two places licensed for the embarkation of pilgrims to Santiago de Compostela in medieval times.

On up Madeira Road, you walk under the looming bulk of the Royal Citadel, though the encounter can be postponed by a visit to the superbly placed Dutton's Café (01752 255245), whose terrace affords magnificent sea views. Nearby Fisher's Nose is a military blockhouse, incorporated into the Citadel but much older, dating from the early 1500s.

The 70-foot high limestone walls of the Citadel loom over Plymouth Sound – although its austerity is broken by a rather frivolous, baroque-style entrance gate. The Citadel was built by Charles II in 1666, on the site of an earlier fort, to defend the city from seaward attacks. An unusual feature is that some of the gun emplacements point at the city – possibly with the intention of keeping its unruly citizens in check, after they took Parliament's side during the English Civil War. Although it is still an active military base, guided tours run between May and September; ask at the Tourist Office (3-5 the Barbican, 01752 306330, www.visitplymouth. co.uk, closed Sun Nov-Mar) for details. The views from the battlements are exceptional, taking in the sea and the old flying boat base at Mount Batten, along with Dartmoor to the north.

PLYMOUTH HOE & AROUND

The Citadel stands at the eastern end of Plymouth Hoe – a broad, grassy esplanade, with superb views over Plymouth Sound, Drake's Island and the breakwater beyond. The Hoe is a great spot from which to watch the world famous British Firework Championships in August; stake out your spot early on, and send runners for refreshments.

Along the Hoe, you'll find a liberal sprinkling of monuments, honouring the armed services. The Royal Marine Memorial is a dramatic bronze of St George, dagger in hand, grappling with a sea monster and flanked by two military statues. Meanwhile, the Naval Memorial obelisk towers above the Armada Memorial, the RAF Memorial and – a little further along – Sir Francis Drake's statue. Drake is said to have been playing bowls on Plymouth Hoe when the Spanish Armada was sighted in August 1588; legend has it, the great man coolly finished his game before sailing to meet them. (Others pooh-pooh the story, saying the delay was more a matter of wind and tide conditions than bravado.)

In front of the statue is the red and white striped Smeaton's Tower, where a stiff climb (there are 93 steps) is rewarded by breathtaking views. The tower (closed Mon, Sun) was once part of Eddystone Lighthouse, built in 1759. Sited on

Smeaton's Tower

Eddystone Rocks, some 14 miles out to sea, the lighthouse marked the treacherous Eddystone Reef, whose jagged rocks lurk just below the waves. When, in 1882, the lighthouse was replaced, it was dismantled stone by stone and erected on the Hoe.

A little further along Hoe Road is Tinside Lido (see p157), an elegant seawater pool that has been restored to its Jazz Age glory. Beyond are more sea pools hewn into the rocks, and high diving boards into the deeper water beyond; at low tide, a network of paths and jetties are revealed. A group of hardy local ladies swim in the waters off the Hoe year round, sporting floral bathing caps and equipped with flasks of hot coffee for afterwards.

The Belvedere, a three-tiered bandstand known locally as the wedding cake, is a genteel spot at which to soak up views to Drake's Island ahead, and the Tamar Estuary to the right. A nearby memorial garden marks the site of the Bull Ring, where bull-baiting with dogs took place until 1815.

It was at West Hoe pier that Francis Chichester returned in 1966 from his record-breaking solo circumnavigation of the world, aboard his yacht Gypsy Moth IV, to flag-waving crowds and amid an armada of small craft. He was later knighted with the sword of the first circumnavigator, Drake. Further along West Hoe Road, there are portholes set into the seaward wall, allowing children to peep at the wonderful view.

At the end of Millbay Road lies Durnford Street, where Arthur Conan Doyle practised as a doctor in the 1880s. He left Plymouth years before publishing A Study in Scarlet, Holmes' debut; nonetheless, quotes from the books are set into the pavement. Following the road round to the right, a pathway takes you to the Artillery Tower, a 15th-century fortification that is now one of Plymouth's foremost restaurants (see p151). Nearby is the Devil's Point blockhouse, where you can gaze out across the Sound.

Admiralty Road curves around the coast to the impressive buildings of Royal William Yard, jutting out on to the water on an 18-acre peninsula. Built in the early 19th century, this former Royal Navy victualling yard supplied ships with the three Bs on which they survived: beef, biscuit and beer. It was a huge operation, slaughtering up to 100 cattle and grinding 120 tons of flour a day. It remained under military control and out of bounds to the public until 1990, although it had not been working to capacity for decades. After standing disused for nine years, it found a new lease of life as a marine-side village. The Grade 1-listed buildings have been sensitively converted into glossy commercial ventures and apartments; occupying an old warehouse, Urban Brew (01752 227598) has stylish decor, exposed brick walls and classic café fare. The adjoining Martin Bush Gallery (07703 231150, closed Mon, Tue) displays the artist's vibrantly hued abstract paintings.

A short walk will bring you to the Cremyll Ferry (01752 822105, www.tamarcruising.com) at Admiral's Hard, which crosses the River Tamar to Cornwall's Mount Edgcumbe – a route in operation since the 11th century. Elvira's Café (7 Admirals

Hard, 01752 661015) is close at hand, cooking up all-day breakfasts and daily specials; on the frontage, under the main sign, a knitted breakfast proclaims its devotion to the humble fry-up.

STONEHOUSE TO DEVONPORT

From here, you are entering the Stonehouse district of Plymouth, long the home of dockyard workers and Naval types. The entrance to the Millbay Docks is to the left; from the mid-1800s, when the Great Western Dock was built, this became a popular arrival and departure point for America.

During the heyday of the great ocean liners in the first half of the 20th century, this was where the big stars from the USA first set foot on British soil. The Wall of Stars gives a full roll call of the great and the glamorous who stepped off the boat here, from Bing Crosby and Duke Ellington to Boris Karloff and Charlie Chaplin. Although the transatlantic liners no longer anchor here, you can see Brittany ferries glide out on their way to Roscoff and Santander.

West of here, set on the Hamoaze (the local name for the Tamar Estuary), is Devonport. The Royal Naval Dockyard was built here at the very end of the 17th century, as Sutton Pool had become too small for the Navy's operations. Her Majesty's Naval Base (HMNB) Devonport, also known as HMS Drake, remains one of three UK operating bases for the Royal Navy, along with Clyde and Portsmouth. The largest naval base in Western Europe, it is home to the Navy's biggest ship, HMS *Ocean*, and its only repair and refuelling station for nuclear submarines. There are two tours a day, Monday to Thursday, which must be booked well in advance (01752 552326, www.royalnavy.mod.uk). This is a working military base, so various restrictions apply. Alternatively, you can get a good view of the dockyards from a Tamar river cruise (*see p156*).

Trains run from Devonport station to the main Plymouth station. Check the timetable, as there is often a gap of almost two hours between services.

Where to eat & drink

The outdoor heated terrace at the Watering Hole pub (6 Quay Road, 01752 667604) overlooks the harbour, while the menu offers pub grub with style, at reasonable prices. Hotel Mount Batten (Lawrence Road, Mount Batten, 01752 484660, www.hotelmountbatten.co.uk) has a low-key menu of baguettes and scampi but lovely views across the water to the Hoe from the outside terrace and the conservatory. More upmarket dining is to be had at Italian restaurant Positano's (36 Mayflower Street, 01752 661290, closed Sun) in the city centre.

Rocco y Lola (*see p154*) is one of five Sutton Harbour eateries owned by local restaurateur Edmond Davari. Asia Chic has an open kitchen, and an 'Asian Fusion' menu that hops from sushi to red curry, while diners at the Fish Market eat below a billowing sailcloth ceiling, choosing from a menu based on the day's catch. By contrast, Souk is decorated with elaborate tiling and Middle Eastern lamps, while tagines and mezze dominate

Sir Francis Drake

the menu. Zucca is more restrained, majoring on pasta, pizza and brasserie fare, and with full-length windows overlooking the marina. All five restaurants offer bargain lunchtime deals. For full details, visit www.eatsuttonharbour.co.uk.

Artillery Tower ★

Firestone Bay, PL1 3QR (01752 257610, www.artillery tower.co.uk). Open noon-3.30pm, 7pm-midnight Tue-Sat. Lunch served noon-1.45pm Tue-Fri. Dinner served 7-9pm Tue-Sat.

Set at the water's edge, this early 16th-century battlemented tower protected the passage between Drake's Island and the town. In style as well as age, the Artillery Tower vies with Tanners for the top spot in Plymouth's dining league table. Owners Peter and Debbie Constable emphasise 'honest' cooking that complements the ingredients, which come from named, mostly local, suppliers. Smoked Tamar eel with beetroot and horseradish or sea bass with crushed potatoes are typical dishes. It's worth securing a table at a window to make the most of the experience.

Barbican Kitchen

Black Friars Distillery, 60 Southside Street, PL1 2LQ (01752 604448, www.barbicankitchen.com). Lunch served noon-3pm daily. Dinner served 5-10pm Mon-Sat; 6-10pm Sun.

The metropolitan feel of the Tanner brothers' brasserie comes as something of a surprise, as the Barbican Kitchen is set within the centuries-old Black Friars Distillery (*see p152*). While the whitewashed stone walls and wooden ceiling evoke the past, the lime-green vinyl chairs and angular tables are defiantly modern. For the most part, the menu tends towards classic brasserie grub: kick off with chicken liver parfait and chutney, prawn cocktail or fish cake with tomato salsa, before moving on to surf 'n' turf, steak, calf's liver with horseradish mash and bacon, or butternut squash risotto. It's much simpler than Tanners (*see p154*) – and considerably cheaper. It's been said that the Kitchen needs to decide what it is: a casual, open-shirt brasserie, or a slower-paced fine dining establishment with more formal service. The quality of the food is undisputed, though, and the surroundings are a delight.

Cap'n Jaspers ★

Whitehouse Pier, PL1 2LS (01752 262444, www.capn-jaspers.co.uk). Open/food served 7.30am-midnight Mon-Sat; 8am-midnight Sun. No credit cards.

This legendary fast-food joint started life as a wooden hut (the size of a garden shed) at the old fishmarket. It moved to new premises on Whitehouse Pier in the 1990s, but has stayed true to its roots with a menu of cheap, filling food. The truly hungry can tackle 'half a yard of hot dog', or try to get their teeth round the Jasperizer – a quarter pounder bacon burger perched on a quarter pounder cheese burger, topped with fried onions. Otherwise, there's a range of baguettes, torpedoes, breakfast baps and hot rolls.

Chocaccino Chocolate Café & Shop

58 Southside Street, PL1 2LA (01752 256655). Open Mar-Oct 10am-5pm Tue-Sat; 11am-4.30pm Sun. Nov-Feb 10.30am-4.30pm Tue-Sat; 11am-4pm Sun.

Behind a cherry red-painted window, this little chocolate shop offers around 25 varieties of loose chocolates, made to its own recipes. Traditionalists can stick to dark chocolate

DEVON'S GREAT SEAFARERS

During the Elizabethan era Devon produced an impressive clutch of intrepid seafarers, who expanded England's horizons by discovering new lands and founding British colonies overseas.

Sir Francis Drake (c1540-1596)

Drake was born at Crowndale Farm, just outside Tavistock, and was apprenticed to a sea captain at an early age. Famed for his skirmishes with the Spanish, and circumnavigation of the world in the *Golden Hind*, he is best known for his legendary – and probably apocryphal – game of bowls on Plymouth Hoe before the defeat of the Armada. In 1581 he bought Buckland Abbey (*see p80*) from Sir Richard Grenville, and lived there whenever he was not at sea.

Sir Richard Grenville (c1541-1591)

Brought up at Buckland Abbey, near Tavistock, adventurer Richard Grenville commanded the expedition that founded the colony of Virginia in the USA. He is best known for his heroic death off the Azores when his ship, the *Revenge*, was massively outnumbered and eventually defeated by Spanish warships. Indeed, his final stand was the subject of a poem by Tennyson, which recounts how 'The little Revenge ran on, sheer into the heart of the foe/With her hundred fighters on deck, and her ninety sick below'.

Sir John Hawkins (1532-1595)

Born in Plymouth into a wealthy shipbuilding family, Hawkins made numerous voyages to West Africa and the West Indies. Like many of his fellow seafarers, he was a privateer as well as an adventurer, and has the unhappy distinction of being the first Englishman to be involved in the slave trade. Treasurer to the Navy 1573-89, he was knighted for his role in helping to defeat the Spanish Armada.

Sir Walter Raleigh (1552-1618)

Courtier, soldier and explorer Walter Raleigh was born at Hayes Barton in East Devon, in 1552. Before he was 20 he had joined his half-brother Humphrey Gilbert in attacking Spanish treasure ships returning from the Americas. He helped to put down the Irish rebellion in 1580, and swiftly became a favourite of Queen Elizabeth – although he incurred royal wrath when he secretly married one of her ladies-in-waiting. After Queen Elizabeth's death he was imprisoned by James I, and later executed after a failed expedition to South America.

DEVON

Places to visit

Black Friars Distillery
60 Southside Street, Barbican, PL1 2LQ (01752 665292, www.plymouthgin.com). Open 10am-5.30pm Mon-Sat; 11am-4.30pm Sun. Admission £6.
Brewed with Dartmoor's soft water, Plymouth Gin has been produced at this distillery since 1793. The tipple of choice of Winston Churchill and Ian Fleming, it's a smooth, aromatic blend. See for yourself on one of the guided tours and tastings, on which you can also sample the company's tart, delicious Sloe Gin and its Navy Strength Gin – a powerful 57% abv blend.that was supplied to every Navy ship that left from Plymouth. Post-tour snifters can be consumed in the gorgeous Refectory Bar, where the Pilgrim Fathers are said to have spent their final night on English soil – not knocking back shots, mind: in those days, the building was a Dominican monastery.

Elizabethan House
32 New Street, Barbican, PL1 2NA (01752 304774, www.plymouth.gov.uk). Open Mar-Oct 10am-5pm Tue-Sat. Admission £2; free-£1 reductions; £4.80 family. No credit cards.
This 16th-century merchant's house is a rare – and mainly intact – survivor of Elizabethan Plymouth. Original features include hefty oak beams, probably salvaged from a ship, and a central newel post that was once a ship's mast, and the lime-washed rooms are kitted out with period furniture. It doesn't take long to explore, but it's an atmospheric glimpse into Plymouth's past nonetheless.

House That Jack Built
11-12 Southside Street, Barbican, PL1 2LA (01752 266149, www.housejackbuilt.co.uk). Open times vary, check website for details.

Just across the road from Black Friar's Distillery is one of the city's most striking sights, and a bizarre retail experience. *The Last Judgement*, a mural by celebrated local artist Robert Lenkiewicz, covers the façade of the three-storey building. Painted in 1985, it caused a stir at the time as most of the subjects (including some local people) were painted nude. Inside the craft market, Jack Nash, another Barbican-based artist and friend of Lenkiewicz, provided the paintings: along the narrow corridors, colonies of gnomes nestle against forest backdrops, along with a tipsy-looking dragon and an 'enchanted waterfall'. The market itself comprises ten boutiques, whose treasures run the gamut from militaria and coins to handknits and voodoo dolls; there is also a Chinese restaurant.

Merchant's House
33 St Andrew Street, Plymouth, PL1 2AH (01752 304774, www.plymouth.gov.uk). Open Mar-Oct 10am-5pm Tue-Sat. Admission £2; free-£1 reductions; £4.80 family. No credit cards.
A historic gem that survived the blitz unscathed, the 16th-century Merchant's House stands on one of the city's oldest streets. Inside it is packed with old curiosities, such as a ducking stool and an enormous Victorian doll's house. On the top floor you'll find a perfectly preserved Victorian pharmacy, which was painstakingly transported and reassembled here in the 1980s.

National Marine Aquarium ★
Rope Walk, Coxside, PL4 0LF (01752 600301, www.national-aquarium.co.uk). Open Apr-Sept 10am-6pm daily. Oct-Mar 10am-5pm daily. Admission £11; free-£9 reductions; £30 family.

Black Friars Distillery and Gin Bar

Marine beasties large and small can be gawped at at this enormous aquarium, whose reconstructed habitats range from craggy Devon shoreline, where crab and lobster scuttle, to coral seas, populated by shoals of vividly coloured fish. The Mediterranean zone has the deepest tank in Europe, which you can view from different levels for spectacular sightings of the sand sharks. Along with ten species of shark, the aquarium has a dazzling array of seahorses and tropical fish, while star residents include Snorkel, a loggerhead turtle that was rescued in Cornwall in 1990, and Mad Jack, a 100-year-old-lobster. The aquarium has a daily programme of talks and activities, including drop-in kids' sessions in the Discovery Zone. The 'Sleeping with Sharks' sleepover events (£40) for children and families include a twilight tour to see what the fish get up to after hours, games and crafts, a movie in front of the Atlantic reef tank, a midnight feast and breakfast.

Peninsula Arts
University of Plymouth, Roland Levinsky Building, Drake Circus, Plymouth, PL4 8AA (01752 585050, www.plymouth.ac.uk).
The public arts programme organised by the University of Plymouth's Faculty of Arts is wonderfully varied, taking in everything from special cinema seasons to art exhibitions, piano recitals and lectures. Events are held in the impressive, copper-clad Roland Levinsky building; check the website for details of the latest events.

Plymouth Arts Centre
38 Looe Street, Plymouth, PL4 0EB (01752 206114, www.plymouthartscentre.org). Open Box office 10am-8.30pm Tue-Sat, 4-8.30pm Sun. Café 11am-8.30pm Tue-Sat. Tickets vary, check website for details.
Established in 1948, this is one of the oldest art centres in the country. Over the years, it has staged exhibitions by artists of international repute, such as Andy Goldsworthy and Sir Terry Frost; in 1975, Beryl Cook held her first exhibition here. There's also an independent cinema showing arthouse releases and foreign films, and a relaxed café-bar.

Plymouth City Museum & Art Gallery
Drake Circus, PL4 8AJ (01752 304774, www.plymouthmuseum.gov.uk). Open 10am-5.30pm Tue-Fri; 10am-5pm Sat. Admission Free.
Along with displays devoted to Plymouth and its port, the city museum's collections include Egyptian amulets and jewellery, archaeological finds, and jars of pickled sea creatures. On the artistic side of things, there are ceramics, an exhibition on the artists of St Ives and the south west, and a Beryl Cook tribute wall (Cook lived and worked in the city for many years). Touring exhibitions, talks and events for adults and children, classical concerts and holiday workshops in the school holidays and half terms are also on the agenda.

Saltram ★
Plympton, PL7 1UH (01752 333500, www.national trust.org.uk/main/w-saltram). Open House late Feb-mid Mar noon-4.30pm Sat, Sun. Mid Mar-Oct noon-4.30pm Mon-Thur, Sat, Sun. Gardens & gallery Feb-mid Mar 11am-4pm Sat, Sun. Mid Mar-Oct 11am-4.30pm Mon-Thur, Sat, Sun. Nov-end Jan 11am-4pm

Elizabethan House

Mon-Thur, Sat, Sun. Admission £8.70; £4.30 reductions; £21.70 family. Garden & gallery only £4.50; £2.30 reductions.
As Austen acolytes may know, this gorgeous Georgian pile stood in for the Dashwood family's lost estate in Ang Lee's 1995 version of *Sense and Sensibility*. The mansion, which was the seat of the earls of Morley, boasts a magnificent Robert Adam interior, with original Chippendale furniture, Wedgwood china and portraits by Sir Joshua Reynolds (a Plympton boy and family friend) and his protégée, Angelica Kauffmann. A network of paths criss-cross the lovely gardens and parkland, overlooking the Plym estuary and dotted with secluded bowers and follies. If you simply want to wander around the grounds, park in the car park just inside the entrance gate. There is a café in the old stable block, while the estate's 19th-century chapel is now a shop and art gallery, with regular exhibitions in summer.

truffles, while more tongue-tingling combinations include strawberry and black pepper. The café serves a mean hot chocolate, along with brownies, slices of rich white chocolate cheesecake, and many more chocolate-infused goodies.

Chloe's
Gill Akaster House, Princess Street, PL1 2EX (01752 201523, www.chloesrestaurant.co.uk). Lunch served noon-2pm, dinner served 5.30-10pm Tue-Sat.
Ambitious French cuisine is on the menu at Chloe's, where the à la carte kicks off with a three-part starter of foie gras, frogs' legs and snails. Mains follow equally classic lines: traditional cassoulet, perhaps, or confit duck leg with sauté potatoes. There is a piano player in the evenings – for some, adding a touch of romance, for others reinforcing the impression of a very formal dining experience. For lower prices – and no musical accompaniment – try the less elaborate lunchtime and pre-theatre set menu.

Langdon Court Hotel ★
Adams Lane, Down Thomas, PL9 0DY (01752 862358, www.langdoncourt.com). Open Bar/Bistro 11am-11pm daily. Lunch served noon-2.30pm, dinner served 7-11pm daily. Restaurant dinner served 6.30-9.30pm daily.
Thanks to its beautiful façade and gardens, this Grade-II listed Tudor manor house is much in demand as a wedding venue. Consequently, it can be almost impossible to stay here during the summer season (from £109 double incl breakfast). Nonetheless, you can still enjoy the sumptuous restaurant and a stroll through its glorious ten-acre grounds. Head chef Carl Smith works with fish from Plymouth or Brixham, local meat and game and seasonal vegetables from the hotel's own garden. Expect intricate dishes with luxurious flourishes in the restaurant (beef carpaccio with a rocket salad and parmesan tuille, oven roasted tournedos of salmon and foie gras with cocotte potatoes), and considerably less formal eating in the bistro. It's a 15-minute drive from the centre of Plymouth.

Rocco y Lola
Eau 2 East Quay House, Sutton Harbour, PL4 0HX (01752 224711, www.eatsuttonharbour.co.uk). Open noon-3pm, 6-11pm daily. Lunch served noon-2.30pm, dinner served 6-10pm daily.
This new waterside restaurant is tucked away next to the China House pub on Sutton Harbour. Once found, it proclaims itself boldly with a jagged neon sign that stretches the width of the building, and hot-red upholstery and lampshades. The menu features tapas mainstays such as salt cod fritters and manchego with membrillo, alongside more unusual combinations: crab cakes with coriander paste, say, or lamb and cinnamon-stuffed risotto balls. Mains include tuna carpaccio with orange, fennel and mint, braised monkfish with chocolate sauce or chicken with caramelised apples.

Tanners ★
Prysten House, Firewell Street, PL1 2AE (01752 252001, www.tannersrestaurant.com). Lunch served noon-2pm Tue-Sat. Dinner served 7-9pm Tue-Thur; 7-9.15pm Fri, Sat.
Opened in 1999 by brothers Chris and James Tanner, this is one of Plymouth's most polished eateries. It's set in the oldest surviving dwelling in the city, dating from 1498, and the stone-walled, beamed dining rooms and covered

DEVON CHEESES

Blissful Buffalo
Devon's only mozzarella is produced with milk from Mike Greenaway's herd of 150 or so water buffalo, at Belland Farm in Tetcott. Greenaway also makes a semi-soft blue cheese called Blissful Blue Buffalo – a smooth, light cheese with a rich and creamy texture and soft blue tang.

Curworthy Cheese
The milk for Rachel Stephens' superb cheeses (www.curworthycheese.co.uk) comes from her herd of Friesians at Stockbeare Farm, near Okehampton. A full-fat semi-hard cheese, Curworthy has a light buttery taste when young and a fuller flavour when aged. It comes in several forms: traditional, Devon oke (mature), Meldon (with mustard), Vergin (with stem ginger), Chipple (with spring onion) and Belstone (made with vegetable rennet).

Norsworthy Goat's Cheese
Available at a number of farmers' markets and West Country delis (http://norsworthydairygoats.blogspot.com), this medium soft, full-fat unpasteurised cheese has a mild flavour, and is made to a Dutch recipe with milk from Dave and Marilyn Johnson's 200-strong herd of goats. Based near Crediton, the Johnsons also produce two semi-hard goat's cheeses (Gunstone and the paprika-laced Posbury), two soft cheeses (Tillerton and Chelworth Ash) and a blue goat's cheese, Nanny Bloo.

Quickes Traditional
Mary Quicke's traditional truckle cheddar cheeses (www.quickes.co.uk) are real show-stoppers. Her vintage cheddar, matured for 24 months, won gold at the World Cheese Awards, and has a lovely rich flavour. Other goodies produced at the dairy at Home Farm, set to the north-west of Exeter, include a traditional red leicester and double gloucester.

courtyard are suitably atmospheric. Fresh local ingredients are put to inventive use in dishes such as John Dory with linguine, chorizo and crab cream sauce at dinner or Cullompton cauliflower soup with Devon blue cheese beignet at lunch. The kitchen is happy to adapt dishes on the menu for special diets and intolerances, and there's a vegan menu with three choices per course.

Veggie Perrin's

95 Mayflower Street, PL1 1SD (01752 252888, www.veggieperrin.co.uk). Open/food served noon-2pm, 6-10pm Mon-Sat.
Veggie Perrin's Gujarati Indian restaurant – motto: 'I didn't get where I am today by eating meat' – is a shining example of its kind. Family-run and ethically principled, it has a wondrously cheap, daily-changing lunch menu (a buffet plate plus a popadom, chapati and chutney will set you back under £3). The evening menu offers a varied array of dals, paneers and vegetable curries, while dessert options include pistachio or mango kulfi.

Where to stay

Bowling Green Hotel

9-10 Osborne Place, Lockyer Street, PL1 2PU (01752 209090, www.thebowlinggreenplymouth.com). Rates £70 double incl breakfast.
This welcoming, 12-room B&B occupies a Georgian building with views over the bowling green, the Hoe and Smeaton's Tower. The spotlessly clean rooms feature flatscreen TVs, while breakfasts go the extra mile, with four strengths of coffee and plenty of options, from greek yoghurt with honey and walnuts to no-nonsense fry-ups.

Crownhill Fort

Crownhill Fort Road, PL6 5BX (01628 825925, www.landmarktrust.org). Rates £622-£1,458 per week for 8 people.
Set high above the city and sheltered by earth ramparts, Crownhill Fort dates from the 1860s, when it was built to defend the Royal Dockyard at Devonport. Now run by the Landmark Trust, it's open to visitors; book into the Officers' Quarters, which sleep eight, and you can stay the night here and have the full run of the fort and its grounds.

Drake's Wharf ★

Royal William Yard, PL1 3PA (01803 782461, www.plymouthapartment.com). Rates £295-£765 per week for 2-6 people.
Set in Royal William Yard (*see p149*), these three luxury apartments feature exposed stone walls, oak and walnut floors and sleek, contemporary kitchens and bathrooms. Most importantly, the smell and slap of the water is yards from your door, and the views are stupendous.

New Continental Hotel

Millbay Road, PL1 3LD (01752 276798, www.new continental.co.uk). Rates £108-£120 double incl breakfast.
This impressive Grade-II listed Victorian building is yards from the Pavilion, and very convenient for the city centre, Theatre Royal and Barbican. It's a large-scale establishment, with 99 recently refurbished en suite rooms, a well equipped gym and a reasonably large indoor pool.

Sharpham Cheeses

These cheeses, made by Debbie Mumford, use organic Jersey milk from the Sharpham Estate's own herd, which grazes the banks of the River Dart. You can watch the cheese being made in daily tours as part of the Sharpham Vineyard experience (www.sharpham.com). Cheeses include Elmhirst, a mould-ripened cheese made with double Jersey cream and full-fat milk, resulting in a soft, white rinded cheese; Sharpham Brie, an unpasteurised mould-ripened cheese with a lovely nutty flavour and creamy texture; and Sharpham Rustic (plain or with herbs), a semi-hard unpasteurised cheese with a rich creamy texture and gentle flavour.

Ticklemore Cheese

Robin Congdon was one of the first British cheesemakers to start milking sheep in the 1970s, initially for yoghurt and later for making Beenleigh Blue – a vegetarian, pasteurised ewe's milk cheese with a rich creamy flavour and medium blue tang. From its headquarters near Totnes, Ticklemore Cheese (www.ticklemorecheese.co.uk) now produces a range of blue cheeses, including Harbourne Blue (a blue pasteurised goat's cheese with a crumbly texture and medium blue tang) and the smooth, buttery Devon Blue, made from cow's milk.

Vulscombe

At Higher Vulscombe Farm, near Tiverton, Josephine and Graham Townsend make goat's cheeses using a traditional, rennet-free process. Vulscombe is a pasteurised, soft, fresh cheese with a rich, creamy finish and mild flavour. There are four flavours: plain, black pepper, herb and sun-blush tomato.

Things to do

Barbican Theatre
*Castle Street, Plymouth, PL1 2NJ (01752 267131,
http://barbicantheatre.co.uk). Open Box office
10am-6pm Tue-Fri; noon-8pm Sat. Tickets Free-£10.*
Expect an adventurous programme of contemporary
drama and dance at this small, lively theatre, including
performances by the resident youth theatre group.

Hippo
*9 Bath Street, Plymouth, PL1 3LT (01752 223737,
www.hippolive.co.uk). Open 8pm-late Thur-Sat.
Admission £3-£15. No credit cards.*
Formerly known as the Hub, but now spruced up and
relaunched as the Hippo, this dedicated music venue
hosts gigs by local and national rock and dance talent,
three evenings a week. The main bar is quite narrow
and can be hectic, but the cellar bar under the
backstage area is usually quieter.

Mount Batten Centre
*70 Lawrence Road, Mount Batten, PL9 9SJ
(01752 404567, www.mount-batten-centre.com).
Open Apr-Oct 8am-11pm daily. Nov-Mar 8am-6pm
daily.*
There are plenty of activities to burn off excess energy
at this outdoor activities centre, including sailing,
canoeing, windsurfing, climbing, caving, gorge walking
and coasteering. On site accommodation (from £41)
means you can get out of bed and be at the water's
edge in half an hour. Those in less of a hurry to get
wet can tarry at the Isobar café, whose floor-to-ceiling
windows and outside deck offer panoramic views over
Cattewater towards Sutton Harbour.

Mount Batten Ferry
*01752 408590, http://mountbattenferry.com/
info.html. Tickets £1.50; free-£1 reductions.
Open daily year-round; check website for timetable.
No credit cards.*
From the Mayflower Steps, a bright yellow water taxi
ferries pedestrians – and bikes and dogs – to the jetty
at Mount Batten, cutting out a rather dull walk. Set on
a peninsula jutting into the Sound, Mount Batten is
home to a 17th-century artillery tower (generally closed
to the public), and a now-defunct RAF base, where TE
Lawrence (alias Lawrence of Arabia) served under the
name of Aircraftsman Shaw from 1929 to 1933. During
World War II, the huge hangars housed Sunderland
flying boats, and a propeller from one of the boats is
mounted on a tall plinth by the shoreline. Mount Batten
remained an active RAF base until the 1980s. The
ferry company also offers various cruises, including
one that takes in Plymouth's National Firework
Championships in August.

Plymouth Ghost Walks
*07747 739605, www.hauntedplymouth.com.
Tours 7.30pm, days vary, check website for details.
Tickets £5; free-£3 reductions.*
Interested in the city's ghostly goings-on? Take a
guided tour of Plymouth's haunted inns, houses and
sites of spectral interest, with chilling tales related by
paranormal investigator Kevin Hynes. The walk lasts
over an hour; wear suitable shoes, and enough clothing
for an evening by the sea. Walks set off from outside
the Tourist Information Centre (3-5 the Barbican).

TR2 (Theatre Royal)

Plymouth Hoe Cruises
*Pebbleside Steps, Hoe Road, PL1 2IA (07971
208381, www.plymouthhoecruises.co.uk). Open
times vary, phone for details. Tickets £6.50; £3.50-
£5.50 reductions; £18 family.*
Plymouth Hoe Cruises offers a one-hour harbour cruise,
as well as a wildlife trip, on which you might spot
sunfish, minke whales, dolphins, basking sharks and
leatherback turtles. Its sister company, Fish'n'Trips,
runs mackerel fishing trips and four-hour deep sea
fishing forays; call the affable owner for details.

Plymouth Pavilions
*Millbay Road, Plymouth, PL1 3LF (08451 461460,
www.plymouthpavilions.com). Open 10am-6pm Mon-
Sat. Admission varies, check website for details.*
The arena hosts everything from basketball games
and touring ballet companies to visiting rock and pop
bands. The complex also has an ice rink, and a child-
friendly pool with flumes and a wave machine.

Plym Valley Railway
*Marsh Mills Station, Coypool Road, Plympton, PL7
4NW (www.plymrail.co.uk). Open Sun from 11am;
check website for timetable. Tickets prices vary,
check website for details.*
Volunteers have restored over half a mile of track of the
old Plym Valley Railway, which closed in the 1960s.
Thanks to their efforts, passenger trains are chugging
along the track once more, on the short stretch from
Marsh Mills, on the outskirts of Plymouth, to Lee Moor
Crossing. Albert, a steam locomotive, runs one or two
days a month, and there's a buffet and shop.

Sound Cruising
*01752 408590, www.soundcruising.com.
Open Apr-Oct. Tickets from £6 return.*
Those of a military bent can opt for the Dockyards and
Warships cruise, which takes in RAF Mount Batten and
Devonport Naval Dockyard; alternatives include cruises
along the coast, or along the River Tamar to the village
of Calstock, across the border in Cornwall. Another
day-long trip ventures beyond Calstock and upriver to

DEVON

Morwhellham Quay, with its Victorian copper mine and 16th-century inn. The company also runs a ferry service to Saltash, in Cornwall.

Theatre Royal

Royal Parade, Plymouth, PL1 2TR (01752 267222, www.theatreroyal.com). Open Box office 10am-8pm Mon-Sat. Tours 11am Wed, Sat. Tickets £10-£50. Tours £3.50; £2 reductions.

This large, impressive theatre showcases touring West End productions, operas and ballet companies. Next door, the smaller Drum Theatre has built a national reputation for cutting-edge work in new writing and physical theatre, often collaborating with companies such as London's Royal Court and the Lyric Hammersmith. Well-informed, enthusiastic guides lead backstage tours of the theatre twice a week, and there's a café. TR2 (12 Neptune Park, 01752 230575), the new production and creative learning wing, is 1.5 miles away.

Tinside Lido ★

Hoe Road, Plymouth, PL1 3DE (01752 261915, www.plymouth.gov.uk). Open late May-late July noon-6pm Mon-Fri; 10am-6pm Sat, Sun. Late July-Sept 10am-6pm Mon, Tue, Thur-Sun; 10am-7.30pm Wed. Admission £6.40 day ticket; free-£4.25 reductions; £17.05 family.

This magnificent art deco sea pool opened in 1935, closing in 1992 – a victim, like many British lidos, of decades of neglect, and the boom in foreign holidays. It triumphantly reopened in 2005, after a £3.4m restoration project, and gained Grade II listed status to boot. Set below Plymouth Hoe, the semicircular pool is filled with filtered seawater, and has a spectacular central fountain. There are three other, unregulated, tidal pools built into the adjoining coastline.

Waterfront Walkway ★

www.plymouth.gov.uk/tourismwaterfront.

By the end of the 20th century, Plymouth's once noisy, dirty waterfront had undergone a sea change. Its industrial areas, docks and workshops were defunct, but what remained was a rich history – and, in comparison to the city's somewhat clinically rebuilt heart, districts with plenty of character. In 2002 the council created the ten-mile Waterfront Walkway, which runs from the ferry slip at Admirals Hard to Jennycliff, and forms part of the South West Coast Path (www.southwestcoastpath.com). It's a great way to soak up Plymouth's seagoing and military past, and the views across the bay are spectacular; there is a also an entertaining podcast to download, narrated by the late Edward Woodward.

It's easy walking for the most part, though the stretch between Laira Bridge and Mount Batten is relatively steep, and involves some steps. The sections from Barbican to the western end of the Hoe, and around Mount Batten, are wheelchair and pushchair friendly. In Mount Batten, look out for the curious 'Codeword Steps'. To condense telegraph messages, codes were devised where single words substituted for sentences. Words engraved on the steps, taken from Captain DH Bernard's *Nautical Telegraph Code Book*, include Ringbolt, which stands for 'My health has improved wonderfully down here' and the useful Sheave – 'Send me results of today's race'. A full listing of all the codes can be found at www.houwie.net/ntele01.html.

Tinside Lido

Cornwall

Helford River. See p259.

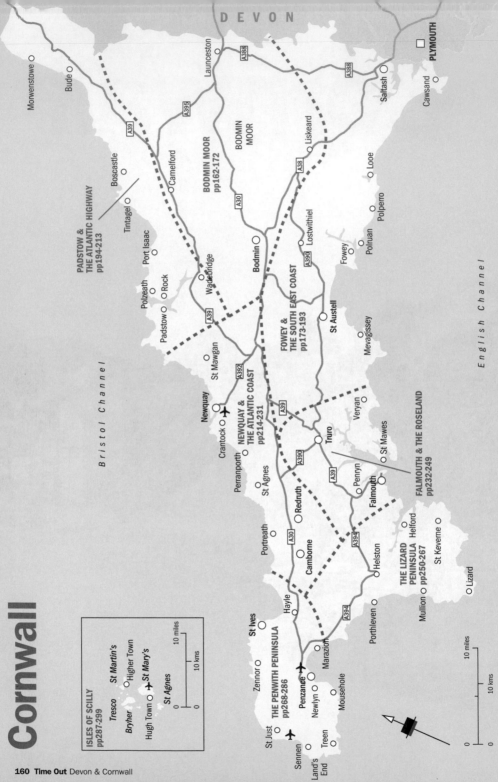

Cornwall

DEVON

Morwenstowe

Bude

Boscastle

Tintagel

Camelford

A39

A395

A388

Launceston

PLYMOUTH

Saltash

Cawsand

A388

BODMIN MOOR

pp162-172

BODMIN MOOR

A30

A38

Liskeard

Looe

Polperro

**PADSTOW &
THE ATLANTIC HIGHWAY**
pp194-213

Port Isaac

Polzeath

Rock

Wadebridge

Padstow

A39

Bodmin

Lostwithiel

A390

Fowey

Polruan

**FOWEY &
THE SOUTH EAST COAST**
pp173-193

St Austell

Mevagissey

St Mawgan

A392

Newquay

Crantock

A39

Veryan

Truro

St Mawes

**NEWQUAY &
THE ATLANTIC COAST**
pp214-231

Perranporth

St Agnes

A390

A39

Penryn

Falmouth

FALMOUTH & THE ROSELAND
pp232-249

Redruth

A30

Camborne

A394

Helston

Helford

St Keverne

Portreath

**THE LIZARD
PENINSULA** pp250-267

Lizard

Hayle

Mullion

A394

Porthleven

St Ives

Marazion

THE PENWITH PENINSULA
pp268-286

Zennor

Penzance

St Just

Newlyn

Mousehole

Land's
End

Treen

Sennen

Bristol Channel

English Channel

ISLES OF SCILLY
pp287-299

Tresco   *St Martin's*

Bryher   Higher Town

Hugh Town   *St Mary's*

St Agnes

10 miles

10 kms

0

0

10 miles

10 kms

0

0

© Copyright Time Out Group 2010

Sennen Cove. See p285.

Cornwall

Bodmin Moor

Bodmin Moor might be smaller in scale than Dartmoor further east, but there is enough drama and unprocessed beauty within its 80 square miles to stir even the most jaded of travellers: surreal, weather-warped granite tors towering over wild expanses of moorland and vast, treeless downs. Remote as the moor may feel, high on the granite spine of Cornwall, it is actually deceptively well connected, thanks to the A30 main road that slices through its centre, from Launceston in the east to Bodmin in the west. The north and south coasts are both an easy drive away, as are the Eden Project, the gastronomic delights of Padstow and the windswept ruins of Tintagel Castle.

Bodmin & the western moor

The sober, no-frills town of Bodmin is the largest of the settlements around the moor. An important religious centre in the Dark Ages, thanks to the foundation of a priory at St Petroc in the sixth century, the town has an impressive 15th-century granite church dedicated to the saint.

Bodmin was also once the county town of Cornwall before administrative and judicial powers moved to Truro, as evinced by some important-looking public buildings in the centre. Beyond the old-fashioned high street, there is a handful of visitor attractions, including the foreboding Bodmin Jail (*see p166*) on the outskirts, the Courtroom Experience (*see p170*) and the quaint Bodmin & Wenford Railway (*see p170*).

One of the most attractive villages on the moor is Blisland, on its western edge. It centres on a pretty green surrounded by granite cottages, a Norman church and the superb Blisland Inn (*see p169*). Three miles north-east of Blisland is Hawk's Tor; home to a circle of neolithic standing stones known as the Stripple Stones, it's a wild and primitive spot.

By car, the narrow and at times very steep country lanes to the west of the moor take in some gorgeous countryside, covered in ancient deciduous woodland. Traditional villages such as St Mabyn and St Tudy are also worth a look.

The southern moor

South of the A30, Bodmin Moor is characterised by wide open expanses of heath, softened by tracts of thick woodland, deep river valleys and gorges. Viciously prickly, vivid yellow gorse bushes proliferate, competing by midsummer with the subtler purple of moorland heather.

Prehistoric stone circles and burial sites are concentrated on the south-eastern edge of the moor, and are the source of a host of local legends involving piskies and spriggans. More recently, these mythical creatures have been joined by the Beast of Bodmin Moor, a puma, panther or wild cat that is blamed for the unexplained slaughter of ponies and sheep on the moor – though little scientific evidence has been forthcoming.

From Jamaica Inn (*see p166*) of du Maurier fame, the geographical heart of Bodmin Moor, it's a mile or so's stroll south to Dozmary Pool, which on sunny days is visible for miles around as a bright blue diamond. Some say this spot is the watery lair of the Lady of the Lake and the final resting place of King Arthur's sword, Excalibur, although there are other contenders.

Close to Dozmary are two much larger recreational lakes, offering plenty of scope for birdwatching, fishing and walks year round. Colliford Lake attracts over-wintering wildfowl and is a top spot for natural brown trout fishing, while Siblyback Lake has sandy beaches and a watersports centre (01579 346522). South of here, Dranesbridge is the starting point of a riverside ramble to Golitha Falls – a wooded valley where the rapid waters of the river Fowey hurtle along a deep gorge, and over a series of cascades.

Further west, the villages of Warleggan, Cardinham and St Neot are good starting points for exploring the lush, wooded fringes of the moor. St Neot is a delightful place, and worth visiting for its church alone, which boasts a beautiful 15th-century interior with stunning stained glass. Warleggan is the subject of the film *A Congregation of Ghosts*, released in 2009, which tells the true story of the Reverend Frederick Densham, who, influenced by Gandhi and his travels in India, returned to live in the village in the 1930s to preach to a remote and deeply traditional community.

The south-eastern corner of the moor, meanwhile, has some desolate scenery around the peaks of Kilmar Tor, Hawk's Tor and Trewortha Tor, as well as a concentration of Bronze Age remains clustered around Minions, the highest village in Cornwall. The most impressive of all the prehistoric sites is the Hurlers, just outside the village, which consists of three circles of massive standing stones. Although their original purpose is unknown, local lore recounts that they are men turned to stone for playing the Cornish game of hurling on a Sunday.

South of Minions, near the village of Darite, is a huge Stone Age burial chamber known as Trevethy Quoit. To the north, meanwhile, the Cheesewring is

Cheesewring

Bodmin Moor

a quite extraordinary top-heavy pillar of granite slabs that has been eroded by the moorland winds. It's hard to believe that it was formed entirely naturally – or that it isn't about to topple over.

Just beyond the moor's southern fringes is the ancient stannary and market town of Liskeard, on the mainline railway. Not in the slightest bit touristy, it is a working town with a traditional centre.

Launceston

Launceston (pronounced 'Lanson' locally), the ancient 'capital' of Cornwall, is a charming, richly historic market town. It acts as the traditional gateway between Dartmoor and Bodmin Moor, and is one of the area's most interesting inland towns for a wander. Although not much of the 12th-century town wall remains, evidence of Launceston's medieval fortifications endures in the shape of Southgate Arch (originally one of three entries to the town) and the 11th-century castle (*see p166*), the seat of the first Earl of Cornwall. In the town centre, the 16th-century St Mary Magdalene Church, famous for its ornate carved exterior, is a striking sight.

The town centre also supports a healthy crop of smart, independent shops on the lanes radiating out from the main square. Names to look for include long-established free-range butcher Philip Warren (1 Westgate Street, 01566 772089, www.philipwarrenbutchers.co.uk, closed Sun), the Bray Farm Shop (7 Church Street, 01566 775677, closed Sun) and the recently opened Deli (6-8 Church Street, 01566 779494, closed Sun), which sells pastel-coloured cupcakes alongside local and imported cheeses, and Italian specialities.

Places to visit

There are several interesting churches around Bodmin Moor, including the 16th-century St Mary Magdalene Church in Launceston, with its elaborately carved granite exterior; the Church of St Neot, on the south-western edge of the moor, known for its medieval stained glass; and the high-towered Church of St Nonna at Altarnun, known as the 'Cathedral of the Moor'.

Bodmin Jail
Berrycoombe Road, Bodmin, PL31 2NR (01208 76292, www.bodminjail.org). Open 10am-dusk daily. Admission free. Jail Walk tour £5.50; £3.25-£3.75 reductions.

Until 1862, public executions took place at this infamous jail, with crowds flocking from all over the county to witness the grisly events. The glowering, 18th-century granite building is still a disquieting place to visit, with a grim display of dungeons, cells, pillories, execution blocks and the original hanging pit. Perfect sightseeing, then, for a cold, steely grey day before a walk on the moor. Ghost walks are held here in the evenings, along with occasional paranormal nights; check the website for details.

Jamaica Inn
Bolventor, Launceston, PL15 7TS (01566 86250, www.jamaicainn.co.uk). Open Museum Summer 10am-5pm daily. Winter 11am-4pm daily. Admission £3.95; £3.45 reductions.

At the heart of Bodmin Moor, this inn was an important staging post on the turnpike road for several centuries, and a hotbed of smuggling. It only came to prominence as a tourist attraction, though, when Daphne du Maurier set her bestselling novel here, after frequent visits to the inn in the 1930s. The inn now feels like little more than a tourist trap – all the more so thanks to its location on the A30, which makes it a convenient stop for coaches. Nonetheless, there is some interest to be found here at the Smugglers Museum, containing a quirky collection of smuggling devices from times gone by, and the small du Maurier exhibition (including her desk). There is a dated hotel attached, a pub and a shop (which does, at least, sell the du Maurier classics alongside less useful fridge magnets and trinkets).

Lanhydrock House ★
Bodmin, PL30 5AD (01208 265950, www.national trust.org.uk/lanhydrock). Open House Mar-Sept 11am-5.30pm Tue-Sun. Oct 11am-5pm Tue-Sun. Garden 10am-6pm daily. Admission £9.90; £4.90 reductions; £24.80 family. Garden only £5.80; £2.90 reductiions.

Two and a half miles south-east of Bodmin is one of Cornwall's grandest houses, situated above the Fowey valley. Lanhydrock House was first constructed in the 17th century but was rebuilt after a fire in the late 1800s, resulting in a profusion of high Victoriana. The house is now owned by the National Trust, with 50 or so rooms open to the public; allow plenty of time for your visit. One of the few remaining 17th-century interiors is the long gallery, which has a stunning barrel-vaulted ceiling depicting scenes from the Old Testament. Another highlight is the restored Victorian kitchen and servants' quarters. In spring, the bloom of camelias, azaleas, magnolias, rhodedendrons and bluebells is breathtaking; footpaths lead from the gardens into the 1,000-acre area of park and woodland beyond.

Launceston Castle
Launceston, PL15 7DR (01566 772365, www.english-heritage.org.uk). Open Apr-June, Sept 10am-5pm daily. July, Aug 10am-6pm daily. Oct 10am-4pm daily. Admission £3.20; £1.60-£2.70 reductions.

Strategically placed high above town on a grassy mound surveying the Cornish border, this Norman castle must have been a fearsome sight for enemy forces. Much of the original construction has disappeared over the centuries, but enough remains to make the steep trip up to the keep worthwhile. On a clear day the views in every direction are spectacular, taking in deeply undulating valleys and, on the horizons to the east and west, the dramatic profiles of Dartmoor and Bodmin Moor.

One of the loveliest of the villages around Launceston is Altarnun, where founder of Methodism John Wesley often stayed on his frequent preaching trips to Cornwall. (Wesley Cottage is open to the public, some half a mile from Altarnun in the hamlet of Trewint; www.wesleycottage.org.uk). In the village, a picturesque 15th-century packhorse bridge straddles the river Inney, overlooked by the stunning church of St Nonna.

Camelford & the northern moor
In the moor's north-eastern corner, Camelford is a compact town on the river Camel, often clogged with slow-moving traffic thanks to its position on the tourist-heavy A39. Although its name actually derives from a conflation of 'cam' (meaning crooked) and 'hayle' (estuary), Camelford has become associated over the years with Camelot, legendary court of King Arthur. The myth has been perpetuated by the presence of a carved sixth-century stone at nearby Slaughterbridge, which supposedly marks the site of the king's final battle at Camlann. What's certain is that a battle did take place here in the ninth century between the Saxons and the Celts, but Arthurian enthusiasts insist the stone is evidence of Arthur's fatal wound at the hand of Mordred. The myths and countermyths are explored in full at Slaughterbridge's Arthurian Centre (01840 213947, www.arthur-online.co.uk, closed Nov-Mar).

Camelford also provides easy access to the moor and its highest peaks: Rough Tor (1,311 feet), pronounced 'rowter', and Brown Willy (1,375 feet). The latter's name is enough to raise a smile in all but the most strait-laced of visitors, but is in fact a corruption of 'bronewhella' or 'highest hill'. Both peaks can be seen for miles around, and offer gobsmacking views over Cornwall from their summits, with the gorse and granite of the moorland giving way to green fields and the sea. Rough Tor, three miles south-east of Camelford,

Blisland Inn. See p169.

South Penquite Farm. See p172.

is the more accessible of the two, with a small car park close to its base. There are ruins of a medieval chapel on the summit, and the southern slopes are dotted with Bronze Age hut circles.

Both peaks can be tackled in a day's hiking, starting and finishing at the car park at the foot of Rough Tor (follow signs to from Camelford). You can descend Rough Tor on its southern slopes to continue on to Brown Willy. No technical expertise is required for the walk, but bring waterproofs (beware the 'Brown Willy effect', a meteorological phenomenon resulting in heavy rain showers), food and drink, and an OS Map – and avoid walking when visibility is poor.

Where to eat & drink

Self-evidently, Bodmin Moor isn't a wining and dining destination – cosy pints of Cornish ale and hearty cooking are more the order of the day. Almost every village on the moor has its own intimate, fire-warmed inn, one of the nicest of which is the Blisland Inn (*see below*). Other options include the characterful Old Inn at St Breward (01208 850711, www.theoldinnand restaurant.co.uk), the highest in Cornwall and also one of the oldest; the London Inn at St Neot (01579 320263, www.londoninn.info); and the cosy Crow's Nest (01579 345930) at Darite, near St Cleer.

For more sophisticated eating and drinking options, look to Rock (*see p207*) to the north, or Lostwithiel (*see p175*) to the south, both of which are easily accessible by car. The excellent gastropub at St Kew (*see p199*) is also not far from the western edge of the moor.

Blisland Inn

Blisland, PL30 4JF (01208 850739). Open 11.30am-11.30pm Mon-Sat; noon-10.30pm Sun. Food served noon-2pm, 6.30-9pm Mon-Sat; noon-2pm, 6.30-8.30pm Sun.
This pretty, old-time pub attracts beer buffs from miles around with its choice of draught real ales (between seven and nine). A gentler proposition than the moor's more desolate-feeling inns, the Blisland is bedecked with hanging flowers and faces the tranquil village green, with lots of bench seating outside. Pub food is served, with mains such as steak in a bap and the 'beast' burger all keeping close to the £5 mark.

Where to stay

In Bodmin itself, organically oriented Bedknobs (Polygwyn, 01208 77553, www.bedknobs.co.uk) is an attractive B&B with three good-sized guest rooms and a named-source breakfast. A short drive south of the moor, near Lostwithiel, the unspoilt farmstead of Botelet (*see p186*) offers B&B in season and self-catering year-round.

Artisan Farmhouse

Grogly Farm, Withial (01637 881942, www.unique homestays.com). Rates £650-£1,800 per week for up to 7 people.

FIVE ARTISAN CHEESES

Cornish Blue
This is a soft, mild, young cow's milk cheese, more akin to gorgonzola than traditional British blue cheeses, with a sweet, mellow flavour. It is produced by the Cornish Cheese Co (01579 363660, www.cornishcheese.co.uk), based near Liskeard.

Cornish Yarg
Lynher Dairies Cheese Company (01872 870789, www.lynherdairies. co.uk), near Truro, makes this moist, caerphilly-esque pasteurised cow's milk cheese. Its unique, delicate taste derives from the rind, which is made from nettle leaves; a delicious wild garlic version is also available.

Gevrik
Meaning 'little goat' in Cornish, Gevrik is a full-fat goat's milk cheese with a clean, nutty flavour and a creamy texture. It hails from the Cornish Country Larder (01460 281688, www.ccl-ltd.co.uk) in Trevarrion, on the north coast.

Menallack Farmhouse
Matured for two months, this hard, full-fat, unpasteurised cow's milk cheese is based on Cheshire. It is produced at Menallack Farm near Penryn, and is available in classic, baby or vintage versions. Buy it online from the Cheese Shed (07703 965595, www.the cheeseshed.com).

Trelawny
A traditional farmhouse mould-ripened cheese, made with pasteurised cow's milk, Trelawny has a clean, lemony flavour with a creamy aftertaste. The texture is deliciously moist and slightly crumbly. Buy a block from Lobbs Farm Shop (01726 844411, www.lobbsfarmshop.com) near the Lost Gardens of Heligan.

Things to do

Camel Valley Vineyard

Bodmin & Wenford Railway ★
General Station, Bodmin, PL31 1AQ (01208 73666, www.bodminandwenfordrailway.co.uk). Open June-Sept daily. Feb-May, Oct-Dec times vary. Check website for details. Tickets £11.50; £6-£10.50 reductions; £30 family.
Cornwall's only full-size steam railway connects with the mainline at Bodmin Parkway, and can be accessed via the Camel Trail at Boscarne Junction, or the beautifully preserved heritage station of Bodmin General (where the classic GWR brown and cream benches and signage invites sighs about the way rail travel used to be) in the centre of Bodmin. The railway makes a 13-mile round trip through the freshly unfurling countryside – and kids go loco for the Thomas and Santa specials in the school holidays. Adults, however, may be more interested in alighting at Boscarne Junction for the idyllic Camel Valley Vineyard (*see below*), a 25-minute walk away. Full details and timetables can be found on the website.

Camel Trail cycling
Since the extension of the Camel Trail (*see p183*) a few years back, you can now cycle off-road from Bodmin Moor all the way to Padstow. You can pick up the trail near the village of St Breward; bikes can be hired at nearby East Rose (01208 850674, www.eastrose.co.uk).

Camel Valley Vineyard ★
Little Denby, Nanstallon, PL30 5LG (01208 77959, www.camelvalley.com). Open Apr-Oct 10am-5pm Mon-Sat. Nov-Mar times vary, phone for details. Guided tour Apr-Sept 2.30pm Mon-Fri. Grand tour & tasting Apr-Oct 5pm Wed (& 5pm Thur in Aug). Tours £6-£10.
Credited with putting Cornish wine on the map, Camel Valley is one of the UK's leading vineyards. Making the most of the valley's mild climate and fertile slopes, the Lindo family produce a small range of superlative wines. Their most famous offerings are the Cornwall

Brut, a multi-award-winning sparkler with delicate fruity notes and fine bubbles, and the Bacchus white, which won gold at the International Wine Challenge in 2009. Tours of the vineyard, usually conducted by one of the winemakers, are fascinating and friendly – and include a taste of the finished product. The vineyard is easily accessible from the Camel Trail (three miles from Bodmin), and is a 25-minute walk from Boscarne Junction station, which you can reach by steam train on the Bodmin & Wenford Railway.

Carnglaze Slate Caverns
St Neot, PL14 6HQ (01579 320251, www.carnglaze. com). Open 10am-5pm Mon-Sat (10am-8pm in Aug). Admission £6; £4 reductions; £17.50 family.
Guided tours take visitors underground through three vast caverns, created by slate mining, to reach a huge, blue-green lake. Bring a jumper, as it's chilly even on the hottest of days.

Courtroom Experience
Shire Hall, Mount Folly, Bodmin, PL31 2DQ (01208 76616, www.cata.co.uk/attractions/the-courtroom-experience.html). Open Easter-Oct 10am-5pm Mon-Sat. Nov-Mar 10am-5pm Mon-Fri. Sessions hourly 11am-4pm. Admission £3.75; £2.25-£2.75 reductions; £10 family.

A new addition to the Unique Homestays portfolio, Artisan Farmhouse is located deep in the Ruthern Valley countryside, a short drive from Bodmin and Wadebridge. Style-wise it's the last word in farmhouse chic, with a smart navy blue Aga in the kitchen, a cream woodburner in the hearth, artfully scattered vases of wild flowers, and even a resident peacock. The farmhouse is mainly let on a self-catering basis, but the owner, trompe l'oeil artist Janet Shearer, also runs art courses with B&B accommodation.

Belle Tents
Owls Gate, Camelford, PL32 9XY (01840 261556, www.belletentscamping.co.uk). Open mid May-mid Sept. Rates £75 per night for 2 people (min 2 night stay).
Located on the northern edge of the moor, Belle Tents offers a handful of generously furnished, candy-striped bell tents for hire. The set-up is perfect for small groups of campers, as the site is portioned up into three terraces, each with a fully equipped kitchen tent. Tents have proper beds (duvets are provided), raised flooring, carpets and kitchens. The footpath to Rough Tor is close by, and the north coast just six miles away.

Cornish Yurt Holidays
Greyhayes, St Breward, PL30 4LP (01208 850670, www.yurtworks.co.uk). Rates £335-£650 per week for 2-5 people. No credit cards.
Each of the three comfortable yurts here has rugs and carpets, lanterns and OS maps, books and games, and a barbecue outside (as well as towels and bedding for an extra charge). A compost toilet is tucked into a yurtlet behind each yurt, and there's a lovely shared bathroom yurt, with woodfire water heating, a full-sized bath and a star-spangled view overhead. The yurts are situated on the edge of Bodwin Moor; to get here, you must leave your car and stroll the final (short) stretch on foot.

Higher Lank Farm
St Breward, PL30 4NB (01208 850716, www. higherlankfarm.co.uk). Open Mar-Oct. Rates B&B £790-£1,025 per week. Self-catering £700-£1,650 per week, for up to 4 adults & 5 children.
Lucy Finnemore, her husband 'Farmer Andrew' and their four children run 'toddler dream holidays' from their farm near Bodmin Moor. As the idea is to cater specifically for the needs of families with babies and young children, the holidays are reserved for families who have at least one child under six. The en suite rooms and self-catering Nursery Rhyme Barns come with all the equipment you could ever need: cots, high chairs, toys and even feeder cups (Higher Lank's green policy also means that washable nappies are lent free of charge, and there's a laundering service). The farm has its own woodland and river walks, as well as farm-themed play areas. But the best fun of all for the young guests is joining in with poultry feeding and egg collecting, giving bottles to spring lambs, grooming and riding the pony and putting the livestock to bed. Lucy provides a nursery tea for tinies (£7) and suppers for grown-ups (£20), while substantial, Cornish-sourced breakfasts are included in the room prices. Babysitting is also available (and free on Tuesday); Higher Lank Farm may be all about providing dream holidays for the urban toddler, but parental fantasies of peaceful evenings in Cornish country pubs are also indulged.

In a wood-panelled room of the old County Court building in Bodmin (judicial power moved to Truro in the late '80s), moving and talking models re-enact the trial of Matthew Weekes, who was controversially hanged for the murder of his lover Charlotte Dymmond in 1844. Visitors get to decide for themselves if he is guilty or not. The most haunting part of the experience, though, is the basement, where you can see the original holding cells for the accused (in use until 1922); a dank dungeon smell is piped in, and spooky voices help to recreate the sinister scene.

Launceston Steam Railway
St Thomas Road, Launceston, PL15 8DA (01566 775665, www.launcestonsr.co.uk). Open times vary, check website for details. Tickets £8.50; £5.50 reductions. No credit cards.
Locomotives from the late 19th century chug along several miles of narrow-gauge tracks from a small transport museum at St Thomas Road in Launceston to Newmills. The five-mile round trip follows the route of the old Waterloo to Padstow line through the Kensey valley; tickets are valid for the day, so you can stop for a picnic. Opening hours are strictly seasonal, with extra services laid on in high summer and the half term holidays.

CORNWALL

FIVE CAMPER VAN COMPANIES

Campers for Hire
01872 575275,
www.campersforhire.co.uk.
With just three smart, early 1970s VW campers on offer – named Sennen, Gwithian and Lizard – Campers for Hire, based in Perranporth, is a small but slick operation. All vans are right-hand drives, and cost between £405 and £660 per week. As with all of the camper van hire companies listed here, bedding, where required, is extra.

Campers in Cornwall
01209 890218,
www.campersincornwall.co.uk.
Campers in Cornwall offers four right-hand drive VW camper vans. Vintage models George, Sherbie, Skippy and Molly hail from Australia and New Zealand, and date from the 1960s and '70s; green- and cream-painted Sherbie is the oldest. The vans cost from £400 to £660 per week. The company's headquarters are in Menagissey, in northern Cornwall.

Classic Campervan Hire
0800 970 9147,
www.classiccampervanhire.co.uk.
Although based in Tavistock, Devon, this company will happily supply its fully restored VW campers for touring holidays in Cornwall too. Ten (and counting) colourful, classic vans are available, dating from the late 1960s to the late '70s. The campers can be provided with bike racks, and prices for a week's hire range from around £490 to £665.

Cornwall Campers
01872 571988,
www.cornwallcampers.co.uk.
Based in Goonhavern, near Truro, Cornwall Campers has six iconic VW camper vans for hire – Ella, Miss Molly, Eric, Ringo, Lucy and Jimi – some of which are left-hand drives. Costing between £395 and £670 per week (with cheaper deals for weekend and mid-week breaks), all are fully equipped, with two-ring cookers and a small grill, plus freestanding awnings.

North Coast Campers
01840 230232,
www.northcoastcampers.co.uk.
North Coast Campers has a definite surfing focus – as befits its location, in Bude. As well as supplying English VW camper vans for exploring the off-the-beaten-track surfing spots of Cornwall and Devon, it also hires out surf equipment (and mountain bikes), and can help guests book surfing lessons. Prices range from £375 to £485 per week, and vans come fully equipped (including a fridge and a colour TV).

Pip & Pip's Cabin
Rezare, Launceston, PL15 9NX (01579 370219, www.quirky-holidays-cornwall.co.uk). Rates £195-£234 for three nights for 2 people.
Pip is a diminutive 1930s steamroller wagon, now converted into a snug little bedroom with a double bed. The rest of the living quarters (a spacious bathroom, lounge and kitchen) are in the timber-clad Pip's Cabin, just across the clearing. On chilly evenings, light up the woodburner or build a campfire in the fire pit – sometimes the simple things in life really are the best. Check the website for the details of the other options on site, which include a 1940s railway wagon and a converted barn.

South Penquite Farm ★
Blisland, PL30 4LH (01208 850491, www.south penquite.co.uk). Open May-Oct. Rates £12 per night for 2 people. Yurts from £220 per week.
Two grassy fields of this Soil Association-certified organic farm, surrounded by open moorland, have been set aside for camping. The solar-powered shower block is both eco- and user-friendly, with enormous, thoughtfully appointed shower cubicles, while the equally smart loos feature gleaming white circular sinks and pine-clad walls. Campfires are allowed, and children can play table football in the lounge or real football out on the playing field, which also has two swings. Visitors hankering for a few extra home comforts can hire one of the four Mongolian yurts in the bottom field, equipped with woodburners, futons, lamps and gas stoves. Book ahead – it's a very popular site.

South Tregleath
Washaway, PL30 3AA (01208 72692, www.south-tregleath.co.uk). Rates £65-£80 double incl breakfast. No credit cards.
There are three contemporary en suite rooms at this farmstay B&B, overlooking the Camel Valley. With 500 acres of farmland and a 250-strong dairy herd, it's the ideal place to get your feet dirty and reconnect with the land. Visitors can watch milking sessions at 7.30am or 4pm, made all the more engrossing by the knowledge that the milk from South Tregleath is used to make such widely bought cheeses as Davidstow Cheddar, Cathedral City and M&S's Cornish Cruncher. Breakfast is a highlight, made with predominantly own-produced ingredients (including butter, eggs, cream, marmalade, jam and, of course, milk in plentiful supply). The Camel Valley Vineyard (*see p170*) is just a mile away.

Trevenna
St Neot, PL14 6NR (07872 647730, www.trevenna. co.uk). Rates £120-£150 per night for 2 people, £150-£240 for 4, £285-£480 for 8 (min 2 night stay).
Stylish digs are few and far between in the wild environs of Bodmin Moor – but the self-catering barns at Trevenna provide a haven for design acolytes. A series of upmarket, eco-friendly barn conversions on the southern edge of the moor, they offer up-to-date kitchens, underfloor heating, iPod docks and hotel-style bathrooms (deluge showers, oversized sinks, fluffy towels). Heating is fuelled by wood chips (sustainably grown in the grounds), plumbing is water-efficient and the kitchen garden project is reaching fruition. The Farmhouse Eatery opens daily for dinner, and, at the time of writing, was gearing up to offer room service in the barns.

Fowey & the South East Coast

From Mevagissey up to the Tamar River, this portion of the Cornish Riviera has been a favourite family holiday destination for generations – not least for the endless opportunities it offers for messing about on the water. Every little coastal town has its regatta week, when bunting is put up, fireworks organised and flotillas of colourful sails take to the water.

For those who are prepared to explore, there is a beach for every taste: small, sheltered coves, miraculously empty on account of the lack of car access and toilets; wild and windy expanses; surf breaks; craggy bays, teeming with rock pools at low tide; and good old-fashioned sandcastles-and-cornets beaches.

Beyond the busy tourist strongholds of Fowey, Looe and Mevagissey, the area is replete with hidden treasures: sleepy creeks and tiny beaches, jungly gardens and stately homes, and windswept heights that reward your scramble with fabulous views over clear-watered bays. And whatever you do, don't forget Cornwall's 'forgotten corner': the stunningly scenic and vividly historic Rame Peninsula, right on the border with Devon.

THE RIVER FOWEY

Fowey

You can swiftly identify a newcomer to the south Cornish coast by his stated intention to visit 'Fowee Hall'. It is pronounced 'Foy', and the place is as intriguing as its name. With its steep winding streets and busy little port, located at the mouth of the river of the same name, this natural harbour is always busy with visiting yachts and boats. Regatta week in Fowey, usually the third full week of August, is considered to be one of the best local regattas in the country; the spectacular Red Arrows display over the harbour is a highlight.

With its classy boutiques, galleries, delis and cafés, and smartly painted houses, Fowey makes a well-heeled base for trips upriver and out to the nearby beaches. Taking to the water is a must. It is thought that Kenneth Grahame drew inspiration for *The Wind in the Willows* from the creeks and quiet waters of the Fowey estuary, and most of Fowey would agree with Ratty's sage advice to Mole: 'There is nothing – absolutely nothing – half so much worth doing as simply messing about in boats.'

Fowey was also the home of Daphne du Maurier, whose legacy is celebrated every May with an arts and literature festival. There is also a small Literary Centre in the centre of Fowey, next to the church, which has a modest exhibition on Du Maurier, and sells her complete, in-print works; the Tourist Information Office (5 South Street, 01726 833616, www.fowey.co.uk) is on the same site. Good holiday reading for romantics would be Du Maurier's *The House on The Strand*, *Frenchman's Creek*, *Rebecca* or *Jamaica Inn*, all of which are set in and around Cornwall.

Around the estuary

The Fowey estuary offers some of the county's most bewitching waterside scenery, its quiet creeks backed by dense woodland and sprinkled with quaint hamlets. From Fowey, there are foot ferries upriver to pretty Bodinnick, the home of the Du Maurier family, and across the river to the old fishing village of Polruan, which has perfect views of the pastel-shaded houses of Fowey across the water. The beautiful 'Hall Walk' takes you along the serene banks of Pont Pill creek from Polruan all the way around the river to Bodinnick, where you can catch a ferry back to Fowey.

Stowed away at the head of a tidal creek is the peaceful village of Lerryn, which has fantastic woodland walks nearby, picnic tables by the river and the friendly Ship Inn (Fore Street, 01208 872372, www.theshipinnlerryn.co.uk). A regular car ferry crosses from Fowey to Bodinnick, giving access to the eastern side of the river, and Looe beyond.

Fowey is within easy reach of several sandy beaches. The cliff-sheltered Ready Money Cove is the closest option – an idyllic spot that can be easily accessed on foot from Fowey (head out along the Esplanade). Polkerris Cove – great for watersports – is a quick drive away, or a more rewarding walk around the coastal footpath, which takes you past the promontory of Gribbin Head and its 84-foot high red-and-white stripey daymark tower.

Fowey. See p173.

The more intrepid should seek out the clear waters and white sands of Lantic Bay ★, a short drive away via the Bodinnick ferry (or a few miles' walk along the cliffs from Polruan). The steep path down to the beach is not suitable for pushchairs and there are no toilets or facilities, but this refusal to pander to modern sensibilities, combined with the scenery, makes this one of the best beaches in Cornwall. To the west of Fowey is the big sandy beach at Par Sands, a popular family beach with facilities.

In season, a ferry chugs west along the coast from Fowey to the village of Mevagissey (see p184).

Lostwithiel

The attractive town of Lostwithiel, at the head of the Fowey estuary, was a major port for the export of tin back in Norman times. Today it has a more tranquil, genteel feel, with a pretty church and a five-arched bridge spanning the River Fowey – although the stunning remains of the Norman fortress of Restormel (see p188), just outside town, are a potent reminder of the town's past strategic importance. Much quieter than its more touristy neighbour Fowey, downriver, Lostwithiel nonetheless supports a number of interesting independent enterprises in its two quaint main streets.

The unofficial antiques capital of Cornwall, the town has a cluster of shops selling objets and artefacts, as well as more modish establishments, such as Nanadobbie (8 Fore Street, 01208 873063, www.nanadobbie.com, closed Sun), featuring choice retro pieces from the 1950s up to the 1980s, and characterful organic emporium

Tamar Bridge. See p191.

Watts Trading (12 Fore Street, 01208 872304, www.wattstrading.co.uk, closed Sun), selling everything from bamboo towels and candles to eco-friendly toilet cleaner.

The zesty new Bella Mama deli ★ (24 Fore Street, no phone) sells Cornish cheese and light lunches, as well as superb cakes and artisanal bread. A farmers' market takes place in the community centre (01840 250586) every other Friday from 10am until 2pm and, as of 2009, Lostwithiel even has its own food festival in October, testament to a flourishing interest in local produce.

Where to eat & drink

The departure of Michelin-starred Nathan Outlaw from Fowey in late 2009 – when the rising young chef moved his fine dining restaurant to Rock on the north coast (*see p207*) – was something of a blow to the upwardly mobile Fowey dining scene. But plenty else warrants your attention in and around the Fowey estuary, from seaside-chic cafés to smart seafood restaurants and historic waterside pubs.

If you're planning a picnic, stock up at Kittow Bros butcher and deli (South Street, 01726 832639, www.kittowsbutchers.co.uk, closed Sun winter), packed to the rafters with cheeses, cold meats and own-made cheese and pork pies.

Conveniently placed on the road back from Ready Money Beach, with tables and customers spilling out on to the quiet lane in summer, the Red Herring (34 the Esplanade, 01726 834941, closed Mon-Fri winter) is a casually cool spot for post-beach tapas and wine, or a handmade thin-crust pizza.

Enthusiasts of the great British pub will be amply diverted by the pubs in the area, many of which have soul-soothing locations on the river. In addition to the Rashleigh at Polkerris (*see p179*) and the Crown (*see p180*), in the peaceful inland village of Lanlivery, it's worth taking a pint stop at the following: the terrace at the Old Ferry Inn (01726 870237, www.oldferryinn.co.uk) next to the ferry at Bodinnick for superb river views; the friendly Russell Inn (01726 870292, www.russell inn.co.uk) in Polruan, which makes up for its lack of views with a friendly atmosphere, affordable pub food (including curry by the Little Cornish Curry Company) and free Wi-Fi; and the idyllically located Ship Inn (01208 872374, www.theshipinn lerryn.co.uk) at Lerryn, with a large beer garden.

Dwelling House ★

6 Fore Street, Fowey, PL23 1AQ (01726 833662, www.thedwellinghouse.co.uk). Open Summer 10am-6.30pm daily. Winter 10am-5.30pm Mon, Wed-Sun. No credit cards.

This delectable little period tearoom is a must for cake aficionados, particularly girls who swoon at the sight of three tiers of pastel-hued cupcakes. (Think dainty lavender sprigs on light purple icing, a sprinkling of mini marshmallows on a vanilla cream topping, or an artful swirl of chocolate.) Said cupcakes are served on their very own vintage cake stand, and are ideally accompanied by

Carlyon Beach, St Austell Bay. See p183.

CORNWALL

Gorran Haven, Mevagissey. See p184.

a pot of loose leaf tea (25 varieties available). Less cute offerings include a superb walnut and coffee cake, sticky toffee pudding and light lunches (cold platters, soup, sandwiches). Forget about nervously clattering teacups and pretension: the staff are charming, the prices reasonable and the menu rather sweetly concedes that, while fine leaf tea is a wonderful thing, they understand that sometimes only a strong teabag will do. There's a small walled garden out the back.

Muffins
32 Fore Street, Lostwithiel, PL22 0BN (01208 872278, www.muffinsdeli.co.uk). Open 10am-5pm Tue-Sat.
In summer, the walled cottage garden at Muffins is just the place for afternoon tea. If the weather is inclement, sit in the spacious tea shop, with rustic pine furniture. Friendly staff serve a variety of tasty, affordable meals inspired by local produce, such as smoked salmon open sandwiches, Cornish yarg ploughmans, and the popular Muffins Tasting Plate, featuring local cheeses and cold meats with own-made bread and chutney on the side. The Cornish cream tea, with Trewithen clotted cream and local Boddingtons Berries strawberry jam, is just the job for appetites sharpened by fresh air. Note that the Cornish traditionally put the cream on top of the jam. Own-made muffins are, of course, another speciality – and the tea served here is approved by the UK Tea Council, no less.

Pinky Murphy's Café
19 North Street, Fowey, PL23 1DB (01726 832512, www.pinkymurphys.com). Open 9am-5pm Mon-Sat; 9.30am-4pm Sun. No credit cards.
Polka dots, candy stripes and florals come together in chaotic harmony at Fowey's most colourful café. Eclectic

Things to do

THE RIVER FOWEY

Fowey Marine Adventures
35 Fore Street, Fowey, PL23 1PQ (01726 832300, www.fowey-marine-adventures.co.uk). Open & rates phone for details.
Trying out your sea legs is essential on a visit to Fowey. Marine Adventures offers hour-long boat trips up the river estuary and along the coast to spot gannets, cormorants and seals; if you're lucky, dolphins, whales and basking sharks might make an appearance too. Waterproof clothes, life jackets and underwater viewers are all provided. Charters and family outings are also available, as well as cruises out to Looe Island. The boats leave from Town Quay, and advance booking are required.

Polkerris Beach Company
The Pilchard Store, Polkerris, PL24 2TL (01726 813306, www.polkerrisbeach.com). Closed winter.
The RYA-recognised watersports centre, right on the beach at Polkerris, provides training for all levels in windsurfing, sailing and stand-up paddlesurf. It also hires out one- or two-person sit-on kayaks.

ST AUSTELL BAY & AROUND

China Clay Country Park
Wheal Martyn, Carthew, PL26 8XG (01726 850362, www.chinaclaycountry.co.uk). Open Jan 10am-4pm Tue-Thur, Sat, Sun. Feb-Easter, Sept-Dec 10am-4pm daily. Easter-June 10am-5pm daily. July, Aug 10am-6pm daily. Admission £7.50; free-£6 reductions.
The series of white peaks that characterise the landscape around St Austell look, at first sight, like the peaks of some unmapped mountain range. They are, in fact, the piles of waste deposited by the local china clay industry. This extensive visitor attraction takes you on a journey through the history of china clay, with a modern exhibition and a walking trail around the 19th-century clay works, past old locomotives, wagons and a 35-foot waterwheel, all the way out to a viewing platform at the rim of a working china clay pit. To see everything on this 26-acre site you would need the best part of an afternoon. Another such crater was filled by the Eden Project (*see p188*), which is accessible on foot or by bike as part of the Clay Trails project (*see p183*).

Pentewan Valley Cycle Hire
1 Westend, Pentewan, St Austell, PL26 6BX (01726 844242, www.pentewanvalleycyclehire.co.uk). Open Easter-Sept. Bike hire from £12 per day.
This cycle hire shop is usefully placed at the start of the Pentewan Valley Trail, a manageable route that takes you through a river valley for around three miles towards St Austell. Alternatively, pedal along the trail to Mevagissey. Bikes are rented by the half- or whole day.

St Austell Brewery Visitor Centre
63 Trevarthian Road, St Austell, PL25 4BY (01726 66022, www.staustellbrewery.co.uk). Open varies, phone for details. Admission £8; £5-£6 reductions.
Revered for its real ales – such as Tribute, Tinner's and Proper Job – the St Austell Brewery is one of Cornwall's most famous independent breweries. Visitors are taken on a tour of the Victorian-built brew-house, and shown the different stages of the brewing process. There's a small interactive museum at the entrance, and the ticket includes tastings and a pint in the bar.

LOOE BAY & AROUND

St Mellion International Resort
St Mellion, Saltash, PL12 6SD (01579 351351, www.st-mellion.co.uk). Open Summer 7am-dusk. Winter 8.30am-dusk. Green fees £40-£90. Club hire £50.
One of the two 18-hole golf courses at St Mellion was designed by the world-renowned Jack Nicklaus, and is considered a most demanding course. Due to host the England Open in 2011, the resort has recently pumped £20 million into a makeover, adding a new luxury hotel.

Wild Futures' Monkey Sanctuary
Murrayton House, St Martins, PL13 1NZ (01503 262532, www.monkeysanctuary.org). Open Easter-Sept 11am-4.30pm Mon-Thur, Sun. Admission £7.50; £3.50-£5 reductions; £20 family.
You'll find failsafe animal magic at the headquarters of primate protection charity Wild Futures, set in woodland just off the coastal footpath. It was the first place in the world to breed the Amazonian woolly monkey outside its native habitat, and also rehabilitates monkeys formerly kept as pets. Lesser horseshoe bats, visible via live video link, are also resident in the cellar, and there's a play area, Victorian garden and veggie café.

furniture creates a carefree, beach-hut vibe – your seat could be anything from a sarong-draped director's chair or a vintage armchair with a crochet blanket to a (cushioned) plastic crate on the tiny outside terrace, shaded by a shocking-green faux-rush parasol. The fun-packed menu takes in big breakfasts (including the Breakie Bocker Glory – fruit, yoghurt and muesli), filled ciabattas, veggie platters with fresh dips, excellent own-made cakes, and Pinky's Cream Tease. There's free Wi-Fi too.

Rashleigh Inn
Polkerris, PL24 2TL (01726 813991, www.rashleigh innpolkerris.co.uk). Open Summer 11am-11pm daily. Winter 11am-11pm Mon-Sat; noon-10pm Sun. Food served noon-9pm daily.

Ruling the roost in the tiny cove of Polkerris, this thriving pub is housed in the centuries-old lifeboat station on the beach, making it an ideal fuel stop on the coastal footpath. The huge beach-side terrace makes the most of its sea-facing position, while the interior is well-kept and traditional – and we can vouch for the very good, reasonably priced crab sandwiches. If you're based in Fowey, consider a circular walk out along the coastal path and back on the inland footpath, making the Rashleigh your halfway point.

Sam's
20 Fore Street, Fowey, PL23 1AQ (01726 832273, www.samsfowey.co.uk). Open/food served Bistro noon-9.30pm daily. Bar Summer 5-11.30pm Mon-Thur, Sun; 5pm-1am Fri, Sat. Winter 5pm-1am Fri, Sat.

The retro diner decor, zippy service and unfussy food have made this bistro a Fowey institution – something that will become immediately apparent when trying to procure a table in peak season. No bookings are taken, but the addition of a cool new upstairs bar and the uplifting, rock-inflected soundtrack do at least take the pain out of the wait. There is plenty of fresh, simply cooked fish on the menu, along with chunky chargrilled burgers and children's portions of grown up meals. Pan-fried scallops in garlic butter with salad and bread is a time-honoured classic, as is the Scooby Burger, piled high with pineapple, egg and bacon and held together with a skewer. Sam's on the Beach (The Old Lifeboat House, 01726 812255), up the road at Polkerris, serves pizzas, salads and seafood – and takes bookings. Reserve an upstairs table with a harbour view, or people-watch in the café downstairs.

Trewithen
3 Fore Street, Lostwithiel, PL22 0BT (01208 872373, www.trewithenrestaurant.com). Open/lunch served 11am-2pm, dinner served 6.30-9pm Tue-Sat.

There is something reassuringly simple about Trewithen restaurant – two small, candlelit rooms on Lostwithiel's pretty main street with white Lloyd Loom chairs, fresh white tablecloths, a short, assured menu and attentive service. A key player on Lostwithiel's newfound food scene, the tiny place is run with flair by experienced chef Paul Murray and his wife Claire, who oversee a seasonally led menu of Modern European classics, with the occasional Asian and Cornish twist: a warm duck confit salad with hoisin sauce, say, a salmon and halibut Thai curry, or local Bocadden Farm veal (aka 'the Real Veal Company') caponata.

Old Quay House. See p181.

Where to stay

Crown Inn

Lanlivery, PL30 5BT (01208 872707, www.wagtailinns.com). Rates £49.95-£89.95 double incl breakfast.

Those wanting to stay in a 'proper' old country pub in a pretty Cornish village must customarily endure the low-grade furnishings and scratchy linens that seem to go with the territory. But the Crown is a notable, and very good-value, exception: a handsomely preserved 12th-century pub with nine tastefully rustic rooms attached (some in the old outhouses). It also serves good, fresh food, with plenty of mains under a tenner, three real ales at any one time and ten wines by the glass. Guest rooms have solid pine chests of drawers, white cotton sheets, flatscreen tellies and up-to-date (but shower-only) bathrooms. It's a simple package but it's no less appealing for it, especially when you factor in the period drama romance of the village setting, opposite a striking granite church. It's also handily located for visiting the Eden Project, Fowey and the south coast.

Fowey Hall Hotel

Hanson Drive, Fowey, PL23 1ET (01726 833866, www.foweyhallhotel.co.uk). Rates £150-£305 double incl breakfast.

Lost Gardens of Heligan. See p189.

This luxury family hotel is perfectly situated above Fowey, with views up the river in one direction and the open sea in the other. A Queen Anne chateau-style mansion (reputedly the inspiration for Toad Hall in *The Wind in the Willows*), Fowey Hall is the sort of extravagant setting that would usually have parents hovering uncomfortably over their children. Here, however, familes are welcomed wholeheartedly. Under-12s sharing their parents' room are accommodated for free, and the hotel caters for all ages, with the Ofsted-registered Four Bears Den nursery for under-sevens, a baby-listening service, a games room, a PlayStation room, badminton, croquet and much more. The interior decor is chateau chic (chandeliers, grand fireplaces and the reassuring whiff of expensive leather), but with contemporary art on the walls, Roberts digital radios in the rooms and a pleasing lack of florals. The new Aquae Sulis Retreat spa has a hot tub overlooking the estuary, treatment rooms and a glass-walled swimming pool, making sure that guests are never without those views. High-end Hanson's restaurant is a traditional dining experience, with starched napkins, oak-panelled surrounds and formal service.

Golant Youth Hostel

Penquite House, Golant, Fowey, PL23 1LA (0845 371 9019, www.yha.org.uk). Rates vary; phone for details.

Children can run free in three acres of grounds and 14 acres of woodland beyond them at this family-friendly Georgian country pile. The hostel looks out over the Fowey estuary and is well off the beaten track, down a long lane off the B3269 Fowey Road. There are plenty of family rooms, including four four-bedders, and seven six-bedders, so Golant tends to attract large, outdoorsy families who make good use of the space. Breakfast, picnic lunches and evening meals are served (the dining room is licensed), and there's a self-catering kitchen.

Old Quay House

28 Fore Street, Fowey, PL23 1AQ (01726 833302; www.theoldquayhouse.com). Rates £170-£230 double incl breakfast.

One of Cornwall's finest boutique hotels, the Old Quay House has just ten luxurious rooms – so book early. The cliché-free cream and black colour scheme shows style and sophistication, and makes a refreshing change from the usual seaside colours of Cornish hotel rooms. Lovely touches abound: contemporary art in the corridors (for sale); involved service from a small team; and a plethora of little extras, such as a small hot water bottle in your bedroom in winter, a computer for guest use on each level and a mini-fridge in the corridor containing fresh milk for tea. The

hotel's unique selling point, though, is its smart riverside terrace, jutting out into the Fowey River, which ripples gently at the sides. Guests can sip a glass of wine on the terrace or dine at the highly competent Q restaurant, serving bistro classics and seafood. As per most characterful old Cornish fishing villages, parking is problematic. The hotel has no dedicated space for cars, but the trade-off is more than fair: who needs wheels when you're this close to the water? No under-12s.

Pencalenick House
(www.pencalenickhouse.com). Rates see website for details.
As holiday lets go, it doesn't get much more private – or dream-like – than Pencalenick House. A stunning modernist property built into the contours of the banks of the Pont Pill creek, it is shrouded in thick woodland, and further camouflaged by a green roof planted with local grasses and a curving, cedar-clad front. Designed by Seth Stein architects, and shortlisted for the Wood Awards in sustainable architecture, the house, available for hire by a maximum of 16 guests, is breathtakingly creative. Inside, you'll find Starck fittings, Cornish slate detailing, and glass walls looking on to the calming waters of the creek. And did we mention the private beach, with its own boat? Naturally, Pencalenick is an expensive – make that very expensive – proposition, but what it offers is genuinely one of a kind.

ST AUSTELL BAY & AROUND

St Austell
Unlike the more nostalgically attractive towns of Fowey and Lostwithiel, St Austell has a mainly industrial heritage, and a slightly grittier feel. Ever since the discovery of huge deposits of china clay in the mid 18th century, the town has been at the heart of the area's enormous china clay operation – an industry that, though in decline, is still trading. The landscape around St Austell has been shaped by centuries of intense mining, leaving a collection of surreal-looking white conical mountains and chasmic pits (one of which was famously converted into the world's largest greenhouse by Tim Smit; see the Eden Project, *p188*).

With its down-at-heel atmosphere and tired high-street, St Austell has largely been bypassed by tourists. But its fortunes could be changing, as a number of regeneration projects zone in on the area: the £75 million White River Place complex opened in 2009, with the county's first new cinema in over 70 years and a rather predictable shopping centre, while the government is moving forward with a plan to build 5,000 homes as part of a new carbon-neutral eco town in former china clay mines.

Charlestown & the coast
An unusually straight road, designed to take horse-drawn clay wagons three abreast, runs down the hill from St Austell to the sea at Charlestown. Built at the end of the 18th century, the port was planned and laid out by Charles Rashleigh, after whom it is named. Its little dock was designed to load china clay and copper ore from the nearby pits and mines on to ships for export. The dock is now home to a collection of old sailing ships, used in film projects

CORNISH CYCLE TRAILS

Camel Trail
Setting off from Padstow, on the North Cornish coast, the 17-mile Camel Trail (www.sustrans.org.uk) follows a disused railway line along the Camel Estuary to Wadebridge, then on to Bodmin and Poley's Bridge. The first stretch, to Wadebridge, affords wide open views across the mud flats (bring your binoculars and look out for wading birds) and water; the second cuts through wooded river valleys, en route to the western fringes of the moor. There are bike hire outfits in Padstow, Wadebridge and Bodmin, if you haven't brought your own set of wheels (*see p206*).

Clay Trails
The Clay Trails, or China Trails, weave across the still-operational clay-mining districts surrounding St Austell (*see left*). It's a tranquil landscape of woodland and open terrain, punctuated with crumbling brick chimneys, clay pits and mines; the trails are also a nice way to reach the Eden Project. The trails consist of three main routes: the five-mile Wheal Martyn Trail, past the China Clay Country Park; the relatively easy four-mile Bugle to Eden Trail; and the three-mile St Blazey to Par Beach Trail. Recent additions to the network include the Green Corridor, linking the Wheal Martyn trail with St Austell. For further information, see www.claytrails.co.uk or www.sustrans.org.uk.

Mineral Tramways
This ambitious project has opened up almost 40 miles of trails, following the tramways and railway lines that once served the region's thriving tin and copper mines. The best known trail is the 11-mile Coast to Coast Trail between Devoran on the south coast and Portreath on the north coast. Tracing the route of the horse-worked Portreath tramroad and the Redruth and Chasewater Railway, which opened in 1825, it passes through picturesque heathland, woodland and historic mining sites. It also links in with other Mineral Tramway routes, such as the Tolgus Trail and Wheal Busy Loop. There are bike hire shops and refreshment stops along the route; for a map, see www.cornwall.gov.uk/mineral-tramways.

all over the world – and the elegant houses of the Georgian new town are also a favourite with film and television location scouts.

To the south-west, Porthpean is regarded as St Austell's town beach, and is a local favourite.

Mevagissey

Mevagissey is an ancient port and fishing village that dates back to the 14th century. In the 19th century, pilchards were the main catch here, and the fish were salted and stored in cellars in the town and exported. The painted cob and slate houses cling to the hillside overlooking the two harbours, and the old fish cellars have been converted into tourist-oriented shops and eateries. These days, the fishermen supplement their income by taking visitors out on fishing trips; there is shark fishing for the adventurous, and mackerel trips for families who want to catch their own supper.

Polstreath beach, a lovely stretch of sand and shingle, lies below the cliffs on the north edge of town, reached by 200 steps. More accessible is the beach at Pentewan to the north, which marks the start of a cycle trail that winds through a wooded river valley towards St Austell (*see p183*). Nearby Portmellon Cove, a 20-minute walk south along the coastal footpath from Mevagissey, has a pretty, sandy stretch – and further south, Gorran Haven is another fishing village with two safe, sandy village beaches, good for swimming and snorkelling.

The Lost Gardens of Heligan (*see p189*) are a short drive (or bus ride) from Mevagissey proper, where there is also the excellent, family-run Lobbs Farm Shop (01726 844411, www.lobbsfarmshop.com).

Where to eat & drink

St Austell and its surrounding towns on the coast don't go in for destination dining as a rule, with restaurants generally geared towards fleeting tourist trade. For the top tables, you're better off heading just up the coast to Fowey or along to Lostwithiel.

In Mevagissey, try Portuguese-themed Alvorada (17 Church Street, 01726 842055) for tapas, or Salamander (4-6 Tregoney Hill, 01726 842254, www.salamander-restaurant.co.uk, closed Mon, Sun later) for a more formal setting.

Fountain Inn

3 Cliff Street, Mevagissey, PL26 6QH (01726 842320). Open noon-midnight daily. Lunch served noon-2pm, dinner served 6-9pm daily.
There's nothing flashy about the Fountain, but therein lies its charm. A smugglers' haunt of old, the plant-covered inn dates back to the 15th century, making it the oldest pub in Mevagissey. The tidy, well-kept bar displays well-preserved original features: low oak beams, a fine open fireplace and smooth, old slate floors. Simple pub food is served: go for the fish and chips, then smuggle yourself away for a few hours in the corner with a pint of Tinners.

Where to stay

Despite its proximity to one of the UK's most widely visited attractions – the unstoppable Eden Project

(*see p188*) – St Austell town offers next to nothing in the way of good accommodation. This seems bound to change but, for now, better pickings can be found towards the coast.

Lower Barn ★

Bosue, St Ewe, PL26 6ET (01726 844881, www.bosue. co.uk). Rates £100-£130 double incl breakfast.
The location might be profoundly rural (though if you have a car, it is very convenient for the Lost Gardens of Heligan and the Eden Project), but there's nothing rustic about the styling at this boutique B&B. The four big guestrooms are decorated in bold, vibrant colours, and guests are lavished with soft white dressing gowns, high-end linens, Sanctuary toiletries, chocolates on the pillow and a flatscreen TV, with a selection of DVDs – there's even a hot tub bubbling away in the garden. Inevitably, Lower Barn isn't the cheapest B&B on the market, but you'd struggle to find a hotel offering these sorts of extras in this price range. Dinner (pre-book and BYO) is served in the Shack, a fairy light-lit hideout in the garden. The Hideaway and the Garden Suite are the most private of the rooms; the former is particularly popular with honeymooners, being tucked away down the garden with a super-king-size bed and a freestanding bath.

Pier House Hotel Charlestown

Harbour Front, Charlestown, PL25 3NJ (01726 67955, www.pierhousehotel.com). Rates £96-£132 double incl breakfast.
This small hotel, right on the harbourside in the enchanting port of Charlestown, can be spotted in numerous film and television productions (most recently, Walt Disney Pictures' The Three Musketeers). It is warm and friendly, and the renovated rooms (as a rule, the ones with sea views) are great value, with muted tones and new bathrooms. The restaurant – not yet updated, at the time of going to press – extends to a large patio, where you can watch the world sail by.

Trevalsa Court

School-Hill, Mevagissey, PL26 6TH (01726 842468, www.trevalsa-hotel.co.uk). Rates £105-£230 double incl breakfast.
Mevagissey's most attractive hotel stands high on the cliffs above the village (and directly on the coastal footpath), with all but two of the 13 rooms offering open sea views. Once a seaside home, Trevalsa was built in the late 1930s but has the feel of an older, more extravagant country manor, on account of its mullioned windows and oak panelling, which were incorporated from a historic mansion in Leeds. The owners, who took over the reins in 2007, have freshened up the rooms and public areas, adding turquoise and pink accents, Designers' Guild rugs and curtains, and modern new bathrooms. The two-and-a-half acre subtropical gardens are a delight in summer, and it's a short walk down some steep steps to the lovely beach below.

LOOE BAY & AROUND

Looe

In contrast to upscale Fowey, with its multi-million-pound riverside properties and chichi interiors boutiques, a feel of pre-gentrification British seaside prevails at Looe, with buckets and spades, fudge and bags of chips unashamedly courting the summer trade. What it may lack in sophistication, however, it does make up for with a fantastic town beach and a memorable setting – not to mention the bonus of landing some of the freshest fish around, thanks to its day boats.

The bustling port occupies both sides of the valley at the mouth of the river, with narrow streets of old fishermen's cottages twisting and turning steeply up on either side. Once distinct settlements, East and West Looe are connected by a seven-arched 19th-century bridge; from here, Fore Street runs on the eastern side of the estuary as far as Buller Quay and the busy harbour. Tourists began arriving in Looe in the early 19th century to bathe on the surrounding beaches, but the town didn't really begin to draw the crowds until the building of the railway in 1879. The delightful Looe Valley Line (*see p245*) still runs from the mainline station at Liskeard, its one carriage following the river to the sea.

South West Coast Path ★

At some 630 miles (1,014 kilometres), the South West Coast Path is the longest national walking trail in Britain, running from Minehead in Somerset right round the coastline of Devon and Cornwall to finish at Poole harbour in Dorset. It encompasses some of the most spectacular coastal scenery in the country – and despite its length, there is hardly a dull mile on the whole route. The path passes through Areas of Outstanding Natural Beauty, Heritage Coasts, Exmoor National Park, a UNESCO Geopark and a Biosphere reserve, not to mention industrial heritage sites, fine seaside towns and picturesque harbours.

The Cornwall part is by far the most extensive section of the trail, encompassing some 300 miles of terrain, from Marsland Mouth on the north coast to Cremyll on the south-east coast. It also provides some of the most challenging walking conditions and most varied scenery – starting with the high cliffs and rugged landscape around Sandy Mouth and the surfing hubs of Bude and Widemouth Bay, and on to Tintagel Castle; moving on to the Camel Estuary near Padstow (served by a series of small ferries). After that, the terrain becomes a little easier, passing by the sand dunes known as 'the towans' between Newquay and Hayle, where you may have to walk on the beach at certain points, before winding round the Penwith peninsula – full of steep ascents and rocky terrain just beyond St Ives and Penzance. Then comes the greener scenery of the south coast, where forests, rivers and valley estuaries (Helford, Fal, Fowey, Looe and Tamar) make up the views, and there are plenty of rest opportunites at pretty fishing villages and beaches.

In Devon, the path traces the outline of both north and south coasts, climbing to the Great Hangman on Exmoor's edge, the highest point on the whole route. The broad Taw-Torridge estuary involves a lengthy riverside detour, while on the south coast several estuaries have to be crossed; some of these are served by ferries, while one (the Erme) can be waded at low tide. The route passes lighthouses and coastal lookouts, and broad sandy beaches provide contrast to clifftop panoramas. The cliffs are at their most colourful in early summer when wild flowers such as sea thrift are at their peak; later, the intense yellow of gorse fills the scene. In autumn and winter wave-lashed rocks stand out against an often intensely blue sea.

To walk the whole trail requires at least six weeks, but most people opt to do sections at a time or simply include parts of the coast path in circular day walks. There's no shortage of permutations on using the trail, including catching a bus in order to explore linear stretches of coast path. All the Tourist Information Centres have leaflets about local coastal walks, and there are a number of guidebooks to the whole trail. For more information visit www.southwestcoastpath.com and www.swcp.org.uk.

A busy fish market is still held on the east side of the harbour – but if you're keen to make your own catch, check out the blackboards along the quay for fishing trips. Looe is the centre for shark-fishing in the UK, but mackerel fishing and pleasure boating are also widely available. For exclusively Cornish produce, don't miss the Purely Cornish Deli (Buller Street, 01503 262680, www.purelycornish.co.uk), and its farm shop just outside town at St Martins.

One of the most popular boat excursions is to Looe Island (otherwise known as St George's), lying a mile offshore and measuring a mile in circumference. Once the site of a Celtic monastery, the island was bought in the 1970s by two sisters, who lived alone there for over 20 years. Now uninhabited and owned by the Cornwall Wildlife Trust, it has become a fascinating nature reserve.

Beyond the harbour, the protective arm of the Banjo Pier extends out into the bay, marking the western end of popular East Looe Beach. Further east and accessible via the coast path is Millendreath, not to mention endless little coves and rock pools. The coast path continues east from here to the sandy beach at Seaton and to the linear clifftop villages of Downderry and Portwrinkle on the edge of Whitsand Bay. West of Looe, meanwhile, there's Hannafore Beach – good for rockpooling and snorkelling.

Polperro

During the 19th century, the harbour village of Polperro – four miles from Looe – was a prosperous smuggling port, with many fishermen stashing contraband among the hauls of pilchards. Although the village is still a quaint sight, in midsummer it is suffocatingly touristy, as its tiny streets are jammed with daytrippers surveying the endless fudge displays and ye olde tea shoppes. Whatever you do, leave your car at the top – from there, you can take the bizarre, if useful, 'horse bus' service into the village (summer only).

The village still supports some fishing vessels, which unload their catch on to the quay, and out of season Polperro is a pleasant place for a wander, particularly for a pint at the shipshape Blue Peter Inn (see right).

For walkers, however, the major attraction is the jagged stretch of coastline between Polruan and Polperro, owned almost entirely by the National Trust and thus blissfully unexploited. Nearby is the sleepy village of Porthallow – the halfway point in the 630-mile South West Coast Path, marked by a new sculpture in 2009 – and the pink-grey rocks at Talland Bay.

Where to eat & drink

For snacking in Looe, you can rely on the quality of Sarah's Pasties on Buller Street, and the artisanal ice-cream sold at Treleavens (Fore Street, 01503 220969, www.treleavens.co.uk, closed Jan, Dec). One kitchen to watch for finer fare is Blue Plate (Main Road, 01503 250308, www.blueplate cornwall.com, closed Mon, Sun), just east of town at Downderry. It launched as we went to press, with

the area's most renowned chef, Nick Barclay, at the helm. As well as more formal dinners, you can stop by from 5pm for a selection of tapas-style dishes to share – a bowl of Fowey mussels, say, or four mini burgers with a scattering of mini fries.

Other respected restaurants in the area include Trawlers on the Quay (01503 263593, www.trawlersrestaurant.co.uk, closed Mon, Sun) in Looe, which matches its supremely watery location with a predominantly fishy theme; the dining room at Barclay House (see below); and Couch's Great House Restaurant (Saxon Bridge, 01503 272554, www.couchspolperro.com) in Polperro, run by Ramsey- and Blanc-trained chef Richard McGeown.

Blue Peter
Quay Road, Polperro, PL13 2QZ (01503 272743, http://bluepeterinn.awardspace.com). Open 11am-11.30pm daily. Lunch served noon-2.30pm, dinner served 6-9.30pm daily.
A genuine find in over-touristed Polperro, the Blue Peter is an old, whitewashed fisherman's pub lodged into the cliff. The topsy turvy angles, tiny blue windows and low ceilings create a jolly, ship-like vibe – you can even buy a 'I've been wrecked at the Blue Peter' T-shirt before you disembark. There's a tiny amphitheatre of a terrace overlooking the quay, which should be bagged if at all possible.

Talland Bay Beach Café
Talland, PL13 2JA (01503 272088, www.tallandbaybeachcafe.co.uk).
There's nothing else at secluded Talland Bay beach, bar this beach café, but it has all the provisions you're likely to need: crab sandwiches, cream teas, 11 flavours of Roskillys ice-cream and beach-going essentials such as buckets and spades, sun cream, windbreaks and puzzle books. It even rents sit-on kayaks by the hour, in the right weather.

Where to stay

On the whole, Looe and Polperro's accommodation is in desperate need of an update, with floral-filled B&Bs and guesthouses making up the majority of the rooms. But it's worth keeping an eye on the Talland Bay Hotel (Porthallow, 01503 272667, www.tallandbayhotel.co.uk), which changed hands in late 2009 and is promising a lighter, more contemporary new look.

Barclay House
St Martins Road, East Looe, PL13 1LP (01503 262929, www.barclayhouse.co.uk). Rates £100-£175 double incl breakfast.
Looe's smartest rooms can be found at Barclay House, a spotless white guesthouse with views over the river and woodland below. The rooms (some of which have fantastic river views) are refined and light in tone, with traditional but not fuddy-duddy decor. The staff are exceptionally warm and accommodating, the restaurant is accomplished and among the six acres of lush gardens is a heated swimming pool.

Botelet ★
Herodsfoot, PL14 4RD (01503 220225, www.botelet. com). Rates B&B £80 double incl breakfast. Self-catering

Port Eliot Festival. See p190.

£290-£1,200 per week for 5 people. Yurts £300 per week for 2 people. Camping £5 per night for 1 person. No credit cards.

There is a uniquely unspoilt feel to Botelet – a 300-acre farm sequestered down a long, muddy lane a few miles from Lostwithiel. Arriving at the farmhouse is like stepping into another century: reclaimed granite standing stones mark the driveway, and everything from the traditional Cornish hedging to the slate roofs, ancient trees and wooden gates is wonderfully time-weathered and covered in a layer of moss. The Tamblyn family have been working this land for the best part of two centuries and place great value on its heritage, restoring the buildings with a gentle touch and farming the land sustainably. Self-caterers can choose between the Grade II-listed Manor House, dating back to the the 17th century and with masses of intriguing original features (a mahogany spiral staircase, a floodlit well in the kitchen, flagstone floors, a huge granite fireplace and a private walled garden,

composed of remains that appeared in the Domesday Book), or the 19th-century Cowslip Cottage, a whitewashed hideaway with a big farmhouse kitchen table and open fireplaces. In summer you can rent an antique-strewn yurt in the meadow, pitch a tent, or stay at the farmhouse B&B, where breakfast with own-toasted granola, fresh berries from the farm and home-baked bread is served (no cooked breakfasts). The setting could hardly be more rural, with no sound or light pollution, and the lack of mobile phone signals seals the deal for a holiday away from it all.

Higher Town Campsite

Lansallos, PL13 2PX (01208 265211, www.national trust.org.uk). Rates £4-£5 per night for 1 person.

Set in the blink-and-you'll-miss-it hamlet of Lansallos, half a mile from the Cornish coast, Higher Town offers stripped-down camping: one lush field, by an old granite church, with room for 16 tents. Owned by the National Trust, it's an eco-conscious place, with solar-heated water in the showers and

Places to visit

Charlestown Shipwreck & Heritage Centre

THE RIVER FOWEY

Restormel ★

*Lostwithiel, PL22 OEE (01566 774911, www.
english-heritage.org.uk/restormel). Open July-Aug
10am-6pm daily. Apr-June, Sept 10am-5pm daily.
Oct 10am-4pm daily. Admission £3.20; £1.60-
£2.70 reductions.*

The highly evocative relics of this Norman circular
keep and moat are probably the best preserved
remains of their kind in the country. Located just
upriver of Lostwithiel, with commanding views over
the River Fowey, its lawns are a lovely spot for a
picnic. The shop sells kids' swords and chainmail
vests for would-be valiant knights.

ST AUSTELL BAY & AROUND

Caerhays Castle

*Caerhays, Gorran, PL26 6LY (01872 501310,
www.caerhays.co.uk). Open Gardens Feb-May 10am-
5pm daily. House Tours March-May noon, 1.30pm
& 3pm Mon-Fri. Admission Garden & House Tour
£9.50; £3.50 reductions. Garden only £5.50;
£2.50-£5 reductions.*

In the spring, members of the public may take a tour
of the romantic grounds of Caerhays Castle, designed
by John Nash in the early 19th century – and one
of few remaining Nash castles in the country. It's a

spectacular sight, as the vast collection of magnolias,
rhododendrons, camellias and azaleas explode into
colour. As if the scene weren't impressive enough,
Caerhays overlooks the secluded beach at Porthluney
Cove. If you are visiting at a time when the estate is
closed to the public, you can still get a good view of
the castle, framed by age-old woodland, from the road.

Charlestown Shipwreck & Heritage Centre

*Quay Road, Charlestown, PL25 3NJ (01726 69897,
www.shipwreckcharlestown.com). Open Mar-Oct phone
for details. Admission £5.95; £2.95-£3.95 reductions.*

The Shipwreck & Heritage Centre is housed in old china
clay loading premises on the waterfront, and visitors can
walk through the tunnels that the clay wagons trundled
along before their contents were tipped into the holds
of the waiting ships. The Centre has a fascinating mix of
objects rescued from shipwrecks, along with exhibitions
relating to local life, and an intriguing collection of old
diving equipment. Younger visitors can play with remote-
controlled boats in a miniature port and dock.

Eden Project ★

*Bodelva, PL24 2SG (01726 811911, www.eden
project.com). Open July, Aug 10am-6pm daily. Feb
10am-6pm daily. Jan 10am-4pm Mon-Thur; 10am-9pm
Fri; 9.30am-9pm Sat; 9.30am-6pm Sun. Mar-June,
Sept-Dec 10am-4.30pm daily. Admission £16;
£5-£11 reductions; £38 family.*

Believe the hype: this place is amazing. All ages love the Eden Project, and it's well worth braving the queues and crowds to explore the largest greenhouses on earth. The vast 'bubble-wrap' domes of the Rainforest and Mediterranean biomes house a world of natural wonders – lush jungle greenery, coffee plants, cocoa beans and rubber plants, as well as herbs, vines, clementines and olive trees – while the Core is home to Eden's inspirational Educational Centre. The brainchild of Dutch-born entrepreneur Tim Smit – whose first Cornish project was the Lost Gardens of Heligan (*see right*) – Eden rose from the barren depths of a disused china clay pit into a project of extraordinary vision.

The message at Eden is green, but the tone tends to be more factual than moralising: a razed section of Amazonian rainforest, a fraction of what is destroyed every ten seconds, brings home the reality of soya production, while olive oil is bigged up as a sustainable superfood. You can also travel to the Eden Project in an environmentally friendly way. Green buses run from many local resort towns, offering a discounted journey and entrance ticket. Even better, cycle: arrive at the biomes feeling healthy and virtuous – and claim a £4 discount for your trouble. The Eden Project is on three different cycle trails; see p183.

There need never be a dull moment for kids, with an array of home-grown play structures and hideaways, stepping stones and rope swings, sandpits and tunnels – not to mention sing-songs, workshops and trails. In winter there is ice-skating in the arena, which in summer hosts a series of big-name gigs at the Eden Sessions.

Lost Gardens of Heligan ★
Pentewan, PL26 6EN (01726 845100, www.heligan. com). Open Summer 10am-6pm daily. Winter 10am-5pm daily. Admission £8.50; £5-£7.50 reductions; £23.50 family.

The romantically named Lost Gardens of Heligan were once part of a historic estate owned by the Tremayne family. The gardens fell into decline when 16 of the 22 gardeners were killed during World War I, and lay neglected for the best part of a century. They were rescued from oblivion in the mid 1990s, when Tim Smit (later the brains behind the Eden Project, *see left*) and John Nelson set about restoring them. The project not only gives a sense of the dedication of the 18th- and 19th-century plant-hunters, but also conveys a wider message of ecological sustainability. There are jungle boardwalks, tranquil woodland hikes and, at the heart of the project, the garden itself – not just a showpiece but a productive enterprise. On-site facilities include a farm shop, a tearoom and a picnic area.

Mevagissey Model Railway
Meadow Street, Mevagissey, PL26 6UL (01726 842457, www.model-railway.co.uk). Open Apr-Oct 10am-5pm daily. Admission £3.95; £1.95-£3.60 reductions.

Trainspotters of all ages unite in this dinky Mevagissey attraction. Around 30 visitor-operated model trains roll through all sorts of landscapes, including an Alpine snowscape, gritty urban scenes, seaside settings and a Cornish tin mine. Kids adore the interactive Thomas the Tank Engine section, and the great shop.

Eden Project

Places to visit

Restormel

RAME PENINSULA

Cotehele
St Dominick, PL12 6TA (01579 351346, www.nationaltrust.org.uk/cotehele). Open House Mar-Oct 11am-4.30pm Mon-Thur, Sat, Sun. Garden 10am-dusk daily. Admission House & Garden £8.30; £4.15 reductions; £20.75 family. Garden only £5; £2.50 reductions; £12.50 family.
This granite-built Tudor manor is set in a particularly beautiful portion of the Tamar river valley. Acquired by the Edgcumbe family in 1353, the house was largely rebuilt in the early 1500s and has altered very little since. Arranged around three courtyards, the buildings contain an impressive array of tapestries, richly carved furniture and Tudor armour. Stroll through the parkland to reach an 18th-century folly tower, where you can climb the dingy stone staircase for fantastic views of the Tamar valley. Strolling through the grounds, you will eventually reach the restored quay, with a new exhibition centre at the bottom, and the *Shamrock*, a beautiful sailing barge built at the turn of the 20th century.

Mount Edgcumbe House
Cremyll, PL10 1HX (01752 822236, www.mount edgcumbe.gov.uk). Open House & Earls Garden Apr-Sept 11am-4.30pm Mon-Thur, Sun. Gardens 24hrs daily. Admission House & Earls Garden £6; £3.50-£5 reductions; £12.50 family.
Council-owned since the early 1970s, this vast country park and stately home on the banks of the Tamar was once the seat of the Edgcumbe family,
who laid out its formal gardens, deer park and orangery. The house, built in the 16th century and restored after it was gutted during the Blitz, is open for visits, and the wider parkland is open to all free of charge, year-round; the views across to Plymouth across the sound are superb. Also on the site are the National Camellia Collection and the Orangery Restaurant.

Port Eliot
St Germans, PL12 5ND (01503 230211, www.port eliot.co.uk, www.porteliotfestival.com). Open Mar-June 2-6pm Mon-Thur, Sat, Sun. Admission House & Grounds £7; £3.50 reductions. Grounds only £4; £2 reductions.
The Port Eliot estate, Grade I-listed both inside and out, has a richly layered history that spans more than 1,000 years. Still the home of Lord and Lady St Germans, Port Eliot now opens to the public for 100 days a year, thanks to a deal struck with the government in 2008 in lieu of inheritance tax (masterpieces by Sir Joshua Reynolds, on display, were also donated). The medieval priory was significantly redeveloped by Sir John Soane in the 18th century, while the gardens and parklands were the work of the great landscape designer Humphrey Repton. During the open days, visitors can take in the faded grandeur of the house – still endearingly unmodernised – and roam freely in the grounds, which border the Lynher estuary. The 6,000 acres of parkland were once the venue for the Elephant Fayre arts festival in the 1980s, but now host the Port Eliot literary festival.

washing-up tap (bring a stash of 20p coins), recycling facilities and two compost loos (there are conventional toilets too). The sand and shingle Lansallos Cove is a 15-minute walk through the woods, although the nearest shops, pubs and restaurants are several miles away, so bring supplies.

Well House Hotel & Restaurant

St Keyne, nr Looe, PL14 4RN (01579 342001, www.wellhouse.co.uk). Rates £130-£215 double incl breakfast.

Escape artists have long known about the Well House. Hidden away down a country lane, partway between Liskeard and Looe – and not one Mrs Sat-Nav is particularly familiar with – this intimate country house hotel thrives on the traditional values of kind service, total peace and quiet, and great food. Once you've shifted down a gear, you'll be thankful you don't have to leave for dinner; there is an excellent Modern European restaurant on site (it's worth considering a dinner, bed and breakfast deal). Other amenities include a tennis court, a heated outdoor pool, a croquet lawn and acres of gardens.

RAME PENINSULA

Cornwall's 'forgotten corner' – as the Rame Peninsula is often dubbed – is also one of the county's most beautiful areas. Bafflingly overlooked by tourists and travel guides, the south-eastern tip of Cornwall, on the Devon border, is the stuff of daydreams: romantic creeks, historic country mansions and snug waterside villages that give way to wild, unspoilt cliffs. It is perhaps the out-of-the-way location, and the proximity of Plymouth across the water, that has saved this small peninsula from development – most people dart straight over the Tamar Bridge rather than detour into the meandering country lanes, which culminate in a breathtaking dead end when they reach the sea.

For the ultimate in slow travel, take the ferry over from the Barbican in Plymouth right on to the beach at Cawsand (5 sailings daily, Easter to Oct, 07971 208381, www.cawsandferry.com). Apart from being a valuable service, it is also a scenic trip – and dolphins sometimes swim with the boat in summer.

Among the sweetest places in all of Cornwall are the twin villages of Kingsand and Cawsand, which were once divided down the middle by the old border between Devon and Cornwall. Despite their peaceful atmosphere and seclusion (access is via rambling country lanes), the villages have a quietly sophisticated air, with a couple of smart deli-cafés and a plethora of well-preserved pubs.

Inland, the village of St Germans, with its 16th-century almshouses and 12th-century church, is the idyllic setting for the Port Eliot estate, now open to the public for several months of the year (*see left*) – as well as for the Port Eliot literary festival. A walk along the River Tiddy from St Germans quay affords lovely glimpses upstream, through the splendid arches of the railway viaduct.

From here, it is a fantastic walk south around the coast to the timeless drama of Rame Head, where there's a candlelit 11th-century church on top of the promontory, and stunning views over the sheer cliffs and white waters of Whitsand Bay. This enormous cliff-backed beach stretches for three miles at low tide; note that swimming can be dangerous due to hidden rip currents (there are lifeguards at Freathy, Tregonhawke, Sharrow and Tregantle). Tregantle Beach is often closed for use as a firing range by the MoD, which occupies a fort up on the cliff.

North from the peninsula stretches the long and winding Tamar Valley, the official division between Devon and Cornwall. It has been designated an Area of Outstanding Natural Beauty on account of its woodlands, quiet waters and rich wildlife, but also for its fascinating industrial heritage; in the late 19th century, mining activity made the river and its quays a hive of activity. The best place to take in the scenery and the history is Cotehele House (*see p190*) and, on the river below, the National Trust-preserved Cotehele Quay (free entrance), which is home to the *Shamrock*, a 57-foot ketch-rigged vessel constructed in 1899. The nearby village of Calstock can be easily spotted on account of its spectacular 120-foot-high viaduct, bridging the valley.

Where to eat & drink

The villages of Cawsand and Kingsand are disproportionately well equipped with good pubs. Among them are the cosy Devonport Inn (The Cleave, Kingsand, 01752 822869), right on the water; locals' choice, the Rising Sun (The Green, Kingsand, 01752 822840, closed Mon); and the aptly named Halfway House (Fore Street, 01752 822279), which stands on the old border between Devon and Cornwall. The village's smart deli and café, Moran's (Garrett Street, 01752 829257, closed Tue winter), is worth a stop for cakes, bread, pastries and – on weekend evenings – bistro food.

Finnygook Inn

Crafthole, PL11 3BQ (01503 230338, www.finnygook.co.uk). Open 11am-11pm Tue-Sat; noon-10.30pm Sun. Food served noon-9.30pm Tue-Sun. Rates £55-£65 double incl breakfast.

The reopening of this newly spruced-up 15th-century coaching inn, in the coastal village of Crafthole, has added a smart gastropub to the area's growing foodie portfolio. Smartened up with oak tables, shelves of books and chic bathrooms, the Finnygook nonetheless retains a homely, traditional atmosphere, with log fires, sofas, and stacks of newspapers. The bar serves ten wines by the glass and a frequently tweaked menu of classy pub food, such as gourmet fish and chips (local haddock deep-fried in Tamar real ale batter), steak burger with gruyère, and steak and Guinness pie – all served with stacks of local veg. The guest bedrooms upstairs are due for a similar overhaul in 2010; check the website for details. The quirky pub name can be traced back to the 18th century, when Silas Finny made himself unpopular by informing on local smugglers to the authorities. When the aforementioned crooks were released from prison, they sniffed Finny out and killed him – his 'gook' is rumoured to haunt the neighbourhood.

Old Boat Store

The Cleave, Kingsand, PL10 1NF (01752 829011, www.theoldboatstore.co.uk). Open/food served Summer 10am-4pm daily. Winter 10am-4pm Fri-Sun.

WRITERS ASSOCIATED WITH CORNWALL

Sir John Betjeman (1906-1984)

The former Poet Laureate's immense fondness for Cornwall stemmed from childhood holidays. The county he eventually chose to call home is vividly evoked in his poems, including 'Greenaway' and the lovely 'Cornish Cliffs' ('And in the shadowless, unclouded glare/Deep blue above us fades to whiteness where/A misty sea-line meets the wash of air'). Another poem, 'Trebetherick', remembers the town in which he lived and died. He is buried in the churchyard at St Enodoc's church.

WJ Burley (1914-2002)

William Burley was a prolific writer, penning some 800 books, but was best known for his crime fiction set in Cornwall, featuring the detective Charles Wycliffe. The books were made into a popular TV series, *Wycliffe*, filmed in the county and broadcast in the mid 1990s. Born in Falmouth, Burley spent most of his life in the village of Holywell, near Newquay.

Susan Cooper (born 1935)

Two of the books in Susan Cooper's *Dark is Rising* series – *Over Sea, Under Stone* (1965) and *Greenwitch* (1974) – are set in Cornwall, and make heavy use of Arthurian legend and local folklore. The highly acclaimed books for teenagers follow the Drew children's adventures as they are drawn into the struggle between the Light and Dark, during their holidays in the village of Trewissick – a made-up town closely based on Mevagissey, on the south coast, where Cooper used to holiday as a child.

Daphne du Maurier (1907-1989)

Born in London, du Maurier lived in Cornwall from the age of 20, and the county's landscapes were a huge influence on her work. The family holiday home was in Bodinnick, near Fowey. An annual literary festival is held in Fowey in the writer's honour. Du Maurier later moved to the then-derelict estate of nearby Menabilly; the secluded house was, most famously, the inspiration for Manderley, in *Rebecca*, and also featured in *My Cousin Rachel* and *The King's General*.

It's impossible to walk by this nostagically styled, bright yellow café on the front at Kingsand and not dive in for a cupcake, a traditional Cornish hevva (heavy) cake, a handmade pasty or merely a very good Italian coffee. Consult the specials board for tasty, mainly vegetarian lunches such as stone-baked pizza, stuffed focaccia, paninis and wraps. A more unusual feature is the 'Museum of Celebrity Leftovers' – a wooden shelf containing bottled crumbs from star visitors to the café, such as Prince Charles' leftover bread pudding and crumbs from Pete Doherty's toastie. Coffee geeks might be interested to know that this is also the only outlet in the UK of David Lynch's signature coffee.

Rod & Line

Tideford Church Road, Tideford, PL12 5HW (01752 851323). Open noon-midnight daily. Food served noon-10.30pm daily.

A fine antidote to homogeneous pubs throughout the land, the Rod is a quirky hideaway – it's small, dark and friendly, and the low, beamed ceiling provides minimal head clearance. Pull up a church pew for a pint of Tribute ale and some of landlord Mike's legendary chilli crab claws from Looe, pheasant or game pie. Off-season, there's a popular late Sunday lunch at 5pm.

The View ★

Treninnow Cliff Road, Millbrook, PL10 1JY (01752 822345, www.theview-restaurant.co.uk). Open Apr-Oct 11.30am-2pm, 7-9pm Wed-Sun.

If surfer-chef Matt Corner were in the business of chasing stars, rosettes and accolades, we get the impression he has more than enough talent to catch them. As it is though, he's more interested in serving superb local fish and seafood simply, and without extraneous frills. You might find such clean-cut delights as line-caught sea bass with crab risotto and lime, or watercress risotto with green-rinded Cornish goat's cheese, or panna cotta with roasted pear. The interior decor is correspondingly clean-cut and starkly chic – smart pine chairs, white tablecloths and white walls hung with local contemporary art. And then, of course, there's the view: a soul-stirring panorama from high on the cliffs out into Whitsand Bay, across to Rame Head and out west as far as the Lizard on a clear day. Widescreen windows maximise the vista, and service is flawless. One of Cornwall's rising stars.

Where to stay

The Rame Peninsula is delightfully undeveloped, which means accommodation tends to be small-scale and individual in style. But nowhere, perhaps, is quite so quirky as a stay in a dinky old train carriage, which is what's on offer at the Old Luggage Van at sleepy St Germans station (Nut Tree Hill, 01503 230783, www.railholiday. co.uk). The Finnygook Inn (*see p191*) in Crafthole was in the process of renovating its rooms as this guide went to press and, if the new pub interior is anything to go by, they should be traditional-chic in style.

In the village of Cawsand, ask at the Old Boat Store (*see p191*) for details of the owners' Cath Kidston-accented, pastel-toned holiday apartment, which has direct sea views; it can also be rented through Cornish Cottage Holidays (01326 573808, www.cornishcottageholidays.co.uk).

Buttervilla
Buttervilla Farm, Polbathic, PL11 3EY (07788 155048, www.buttervilla.com). Rates phone for details.

Buttervilla – a boutique B&B located on the romantic Port Eliot estate – takes local, organic sourcing to the next level, with almost everything it serves produced on the farm itself. The bread and granola is home-made, the preserves contain Buttervilla fruit, the eggs are from the hens scrabbling about outside, and the fruit and vegetables are own-grown. This place is sure to appeal to the sort of person who mourns the disappearance of 'real' tomatoes – in season, you can sample Buttervilla's heirloom tomatoes, served at Fifteen Cornwall and Michelin-starred Gidleigh Park in Devon. There are three spacious, well-equipped double rooms with peaceful views.

Rame Barton
Rame, PL10 1LG (01752 822789, www.ramebarton. co.uk). Rates B&B £75-£85 double incl breakfast. Self-catering £325-£770 per week for 6 people.

Interior designer Karen Cardew and ceramicist husband Paul have spent two years rejuvenating this magnificent 18th-century listed farmhouse on the Rame Peninsula, just shy of Rame Head itself. The two self-catering apartments (within the house) are immaculately clean and comfortable, but it's the two B&B rooms that really catch the eye. Spacious, stylish and with glamorous touches (mirrored bedside tables, elegant heavy curtains and even a silver toilet lid), they are the ultimate style-conscious country retreat. Breakfast is served in the deep-red dining room, with a chandelier overhead and pop art on the walls. Budding potters can try their hand in Paul's studio next door, or just take a tour of his collection of eccentric teapots – as well as the Natwest pigs, which he designed some 25 years ago.

Westcroft ★
Market Street, Kingsand, PL10 1NE (01752 823216, www.westcroftguesthouse.co.uk). Rates £100-£140 double incl breakfast.

With the word 'boutique' now in such free currency, its impact has been lost in a sea of fancy fonts and scented candles. But at the Westcroft, an unpretentiously hip B&B housed in a waterfront Georgian coaching inn, the concept is passionately embraced. Warm, effortlessly hospitable hosts Sarah and Dylan McLees-Taylor seem to have an innate sense of what their guests might want and when: if you're travelling with a small child, a cot, blankets and a pile of toys appear as if by magic. Nor are there any time limits on breakfast; they will even leave a pot of tea and fresh croissants on the step as a first course before you surface. Of the three rooms, the top-floor Clocktower Suite is the most romantic, with a claw-foot bath for two, views of the stars from the French antique bed and the sound of the waves hitting the shore. But it is the treats sprinkled liberally throughout that really set Westcroft apart: fishing nets for children, bathrooms strewn with high-end toiletries, pillowcases sprinkled with lavender water, home-made cake and a stack of glossy magazines. What's more, one of Britain's most exquisite peninsulas lies just outside the door. The snag? After a stay at Westcroft, prepare to measure every B&B you ever stay in by these exceptional standards.

Patrick Gale (born 1962)
Probably the most acclaimed present-day writer associated with Cornwall, Gale has lived near Land's End since 1987. Cornish landscapes feature in his first novel – *The Aerodynamics of Pork* – and have made a progressively stronger presence in his works with time, featuring in *Rough Music*, *A Sweet Obscurity* and, in particular, his 2007 novel *Notes from an Exhibition*.

Winston Graham (1908-2003)
Graham is best known for his 'Poldark' saga – 12 novels set in 18th-century Cornwall, which he wrote over half a century, between 1945 and 2002. In the 1970s, *Poldark* became an extremely popular BBC TV series, with scenes filmed across the county and locals often hired as extras for the crowd scenes. The author himself was born in Manchester, but moved to Perranporth (*see p229*), on Cornwall's north coast, at the age of 17, and lived there for more than 30 years.

Rosamunde Pilcher (born 1924)
Born in the village of Lelant, not far from St Ives, Pilcher is known for her romance novels, and started her career writing for Mills & Boon under the pen name Jane Fraser. Her most famous book – *The Shell Seekers* – was written later in her life (published in 1987) and depicts the relationship between the protagonist, Penelope Keeling, and her grown-up children, over several decades; it's set in both London and Cornwall, and has been adapted for the stage and television.

Arthur Quiller-Couch (1863-1944)
Quiller-Couch was born in Bodmin. His first novels – including *Dead Man's Rock*, a romance set in Cornwall – were published under the pen name 'Q' while the writer was studying at Oxford University. He later moved back to Cornwall, setting up home in Fowey. He edited the *Oxford Book of English Verse, 1250-1900*, and he also completed Robert Louis Stevenson's novel, *St Ives*. Quiller-Couch's final work – *Castle Dor* – was unfinished upon his death, but later completed by Daphne du Maurier.

Padstow & the Atlantic Highway

Such has been its rise to fame as restaurant capital of the region, Padstow scarcely needs an introduction. True to its reputation, the culinary repertoire of this pretty fishing village is nothing if not impressive, with Rick Stein's original Seafood Restaurant now joined by an array of boutique bistros, wine bars and dining rooms more in keeping with the offerings of a prosperous city than a West Country fishing village. Suffice to say, if you like food, you can't go wrong in Padstow and Rock, where you'll find a handful of master-chefs, scrupulously sourced local produce, and more top-notch eateries than you can poke your knife and fork at.

Moving up the Atlantic Highway, more prosaically known as the A39, the shifting yellow sands and blazing blue of the Camel Estuary give way to decidedly more daunting scenery: jagged, black cliffs plunging deep into gale-ravaged seas, wind-pummelled moorland and steeply cut valley villages. Crowds and tourist tat notwithstanding, there is no better place from which to survey the rugged landscape than the ruined castle of Tintagel, cast out on a lonely island and perpetually bludgeoned by Atlantic storms. Even if some aspects of Tintagel seem ridiculous, the wild, rock-girt fortress itself can't fail to impress.

Following Thomas Hardy's 'wandering western sea' towards the Devon border, the Atlantic Highway threads all the way to Cornwall's north-eastern corner and the breezy seaside resort of Bude.

PADSTOW & AROUND

An unparalleled destination for gastronomy, estuary views and coastal charm, Padstow is the epitome of fishing-village-turned-chic. A warren of smart cobbled streets lead to the hubbub of the harbour, an animated mix of crabbers, netters, working boats, yachts and pleasure cruisers, with slate-hung, red brick and grey stone cottages trimming the edges, accommodating pasty shops, boutiques, chippies, pubs and increasing numbers of classy restaurants. The Tourist Information Centre by the quay (North Quay, 01841 533449, www.padstowlive.com, closed Sun) is a good starting point for exploration.

Evidence suggests that Padstow has been used as a port since the 16th century, though the decline of shipping here is down to the Doom Bar – shallow sandbanks at the mouth of the estuary on which many ships have foundered. But the fishing industry survives in Padstow, not least thanks to a leap in interest in premium local produce in recent years, so you'll find plenty of activity in and around the busy working port.

While the Stein 'theme park' can become slightly infuriating (you have to look hard to avoid his stamp on everything from your T-shirt to your beer bottle), to his credit he was the first chef to showcase the calibre of Cornish produce to the foodie world. This in turn has given rise to a whole host of noteworthy restaurants, and Padstow is now considered to be the best place to eat out in Cornwall.

At the expense of more practical retail outlets for local residents, upmarket tourism has also brought an influx of boutiques and galleries. For contemporary pieces, have a browse in the Padstow Contemporary Art Gallery (Parnell Court, 01841 532242, www.padstowgallery.com) and Beyond the Sea (22 Middle Street, 01841 533588, www.beyondthesea.co.uk). Inevitably, there's no shortage of sailing and surf labels (Musto, White Stuff, Fat Face et al), but there are also more original finds to be had among the decor, craft and jewellery outlets. In the unlikely event that you will be cooking for yourself in Padstow, try the Padstow Farm Shop (Trethillick Farm, 01841 533570, www.padstowfarmshop.co.uk) on the outskirts of the village. One of the county's best farm outlets, it supplies many of the town's top restaurants.

One of the UK's most vibrant May Day festivals is Padstow's 'Obby 'Oss, which celebrates the rite of spring. Two 'Oss'es – monstrous effigies made out of hoop-work, tarpaulin and sprays of horsehair – are paraded through the streets to the accompaniment of song, accordions and drums. The pulsing rhythms go on until midnight, marking

Padstow

the continuation of a tradition going back around 900 years, and the resilience of the community.

Although Padstow's narrow, winding streets create a picture-postcard setting, they are ill-equipped to deal with peak-season traffic – so ditch the car and explore on foot or by bike (or boat). There are wonderful walks along the estuary and out to Stepper Point, or you can walk or cycle inland along the famous Camel Trail (see p206), a flat, traffic-free path leading inland to Wadebridge and on to Bodmin.

There is a regular foot ferry across the water to Rock (see p207) during daylight hours, and a water taxi (South Slip, 01208 862815, www.rock-watertaxi.co.uk, see website for timetable) for those staying out late. And while Rock and Padstow out-smug each other across the Camel Estuary, the stolid market town of Wadebridge looks on to see fair play from the inland tip.

The Seven Bays

Padstow and the Camel Estuary have no shortage of scenic riches, but the real drama is to be found nearby on the Atlantic coast and its 'Seven Bays' – a string of impressive sandy beaches that lace the cliffs together all the way from Porthcothan to the entrance to the Camel Estuary. Just north of Bedruthan Steps (see p219), Porthcothan offers a eye-popping sequel to its neighbour, with cliffs, caves and blowholes. Other highlights include the skeletal remnants of a German war ship buried into the sands at Booby's Bay, the pristine white sands of Mother Ivey's Bay, and the breakers bulldozing into Constantine and Treyarnon – two more surfers' favourites that join at low tide to create a vast sandy expanse (swimming is not always safe on account of rip tides). A walk on to Trevose Head, edging out into the ocean, makes for spectacular views all around.

Where to eat & drink

From its beginnings at the flagship Seafood Restaurant, 'Padstein' now sees the celebrity chef's signature on three restaurants, a fish and chip shop, a deli (South Quay, 01841 533466 ext 432, www.rickstein.com), pâtisserie (Lanadwell Street, 01841 533901), gift shop (8 Middle Street, 01841 532221), accommodation (see p202) and a seafood school (see p206).

Although Stein turned heads towards the area's perfect marriage of top-quality produce and stunning scenery, he is by no means the only name in town with a strictly 'source local' manifesto and a smart dining room to boot. The best of a very good bunch are reviewed below, but you might also consider a hot steak pasty from Chough's by the quayside (The Strand, 01841 532835, www.thechough bakery.co.uk, closed Sun).

In Wadebridge, coffee geeks should stop at Relish (Foundry Court, 01208 814214, www.relish wadebridge.co.uk, closed Sun), whose barista Jack Hudspith won a top ten place in the UK Barista Championships; there is an excellent deli next door stocking a wide range of Cornish goodies.

Cornish Arms ★

Churchtown, St Merryn, PL28 8ND (01841 520288, www.rickstein.com). Open 11.30am-11pm daily. Lunch served noon-3pm, dinner served 6-9pm daily.

When news broke that Stein had acquired the fine old village pub in St Merryn, it was hard not to envisage, with inescapable cynicism, a chic makeover, a gastrofied menu and prices pitched at global voyagers, not villagers. To his credit, Stein hasn't taken that route. The menu is made up of simple British pub fare (steak and Tribute ale pie, ploughmans, pea and ham soup, apple pie) prepared with care, the prices are mainly under a tenner, and the decor is traditional and rustic, with old black-and-white photos on the wall, and bottles of ketchup and malt vinegar sitting prosaically on each wooden table. Note that reservations are not taken.

Custard

1A The Strand, Padstow, PL28 8AJ (01841 532565, www.custarddiner.com). Open Summer 9am-5pm, 6.30-10.30pm daily. Winter 9am-3pm, 7-9.30pm Tue-Sat; 9am-3pm Sun.

With just enough gentle irony to counterbalance the weighty gastro-temple image of modern-day Padstow, these retro-styled 'British dining rooms' are a refreshing new addition to the town's eateries. An upmarket and thoroughly updated British refectory, Custard is decorated with button-dimpled, buttery leather banquettes, chocolate-coloured wood and choice retro accents (such as an impeccably restored jukebox by the entrance, Cath Kidston floral flourishes and a vintage TV mounted like art on the wall). Despite the light-hearted atmosphere, the food, care of ex-Seafood Restaurant chef Dan Gedge, is perfectly serious. The menu subtly updates old-fashioned British classics of the ilk of ham and piccalilli sandwiches, prawn cocktail, ploughmans and Welsh rarebit, and the Custard Sunday roast is garnering quite a following.

London Inn

Lanadwell Street, Padstow, PL28 8AN (01841 532554). Open 11am-11.30pm daily. Food served Summer noon-2.30pm, 6.30-9.30pm daily. Winter noon 2.30pm Mon-Thur, Sun; noon-2.30pm, 6.30-9pm Fri, Sat.

Originally three fishermen's cottages cuddled into the inner streets behind the quay, this is a proper local boozer. It's a fine place to nurse a traditional Cornish ale – just don't expect a trendy wine list or plump sofas to sit on. What you will find, however, is plenty of local character, as well as lots of local characters.

Margot's Bistro

11 Duke Street, Padstow, PL28 8AB (01841 533441, www.margotspadstow.blogspot.com). Lunch served noon-1.30pm, dinner served 7-9.30pm Tue-Sat.

Margot's may not have the celebrity status of a Rick Stein's, but it's almost as difficult to get a table. Even out of season it is often fully booked. Happily, there's only one sitting per night, which, when you do get a table, makes it a very relaxed affair. Small and quirky, it has a blue and sand-coloured interior, an intimate atmosphere and chatty staff. Food comes in sizeable portions and is sourced daily from local suppliers: mackerel fillets with truffle oil, say, plump and juicy scallops, succulent Cornish lamb cutlets with rosemary jus, or wild sea bass on herby mash.

Places to visit

Tintagel

PADSTOW & AROUND

National Lobster Hatchery

South Quay, Padstow, PL28 8BL (01841 533877, www.nationallobsterhatchery.co.uk). Open Summer 10am-8pm daily. Winter 10am-4pm daily. Admission £3; £1.50-£2 reductions; £7 family.

This hatchery, a charitable enterprise, nurtures giant crabs and lobsters for release into the Cornish seas as a means to conserve stocks. You get to see baby lobsters up close, and learn about the crustaceans that end up in the Stein kitchens. Those so inclined can even adopt a baby lobster for £1.50, and watch on the website for news of when (and where) it was released into the wild.

BUDE & AROUND

Bude Castle Heritage Centre

The Castle, Bude, EX23 8LG (01288 357300, www.bude-stratton.gov.uk). Open Easter-Oct 10am-5pm daily. Nov-Easter 10am-4pm daily. Admission £3.50; £2.50-£3 reductions; £10 family.

Victorian inventor Sir Goldsworthy Gurney had this neo-Gothic castellated home built into the dunes in 1830. Now a state-owned heritage centre, Bude Castle houses a short but interesting exhibition on the history of Bude and its canal, as well as an art gallery showing temporary exhibitions and a new restaurant (*see p211*). Exhibits include the grand railway clock that stood in Bude station before it was closed in 1966 (and

subsequently destroyed), and a male figurehead salvaged from an Italian ship that foundered along this stretch of coast in 1900. Famous as the first man to make the long journey from London to Bath in a steam carriage, Gurney also revolutionised lighthouses by combining oxygen with revolving mirrors to intensify illumination and create a flashing beam. His genius is honoured by a stark illuminated spike, known as the Bude Light, in the grounds of his former home, which uses fibre optics to create a nightly zodiacal pageant.

TINTAGEL & BOSCASTLE

Museum of Witchcraft

The Harbour, Boscastle, PL35 0HD (01840 250111, www.museumofwitchcraft.com). Open Easter-Oct 10.30am-5.30pm Mon-Sat; 11.30am-5.30pm Sun. Admission £3; £2 reductions.

This spooktastic collection of witchy history has been giving children (and easily perturbed adults) the heebie-geebies for 50 years, with its weird and wonderful collection of spells, tableaux, pickled foetuses, charms, curses, paintings, woodcuts and satanism and shapeshifting paraphernalia. Assorted witches' equipment such as cauldrons and herbs and nasty devices used to persecute witches complete the collection.

Old Post Office

Fore Street, Tintagel, PL34 0DB (01840 770024, www.nationaltrust.org.uk/tintageloldpostoffice).

Open Mar-Sept 11am-5.30pm daily. Oct 11am-4pm daily. Admission £3; £1.50 reductions; £7.50 family. The National Trust looks after the Old Post Office, a restored Victorian post room set in a charming 600-year-old slate Cornish longhouse, surrounded by pretty cottage gardens.

Tintagel ★

Tintagel, PL34 0HE (www.english-heritage.org.uk/tintagel). Open Apr-Sept 10am-6pm daily. Oct 10am-4pm daily. Nov-Mar 11am-3.30pm daily.
Like many of Cornwall's most beautiful places, the blackened remains of this ancient castle reward visitors who come out of season – a blustery day in December is the perfect time to experience its full power. The fact that it's a bit of a challenge to reach (there are 100 steps, a lot of uneven ground and a vertiginous bridge over the rocky valley to Tintagel Head to contend with) makes it all the more exciting. What's left of the 13th-century castle – steep stone steps, stout walls and a lofty space where the Great Hall once stood – contributes to the sense of drama. Tintagel was thought to have been a trading settlement in the fifth century (pottery has been unearthed by archaeologists to back this up). Less empirically, the site is rumoured to be where the legend of King Arthur was born, resurrected by Victorian poet Alfred Lord Tennyson in his *Idylls of the King*. The potential for fantastic stories and family games of noble knights and holy grails are endless, and the views unfailingly stirring.

No.6 ★

Middle Street, Padstow, PL28 8AP (01841 532093, www.number6inpadstow.co.uk). Food served June-Sept noon-2.30pm, 6-10pm Tue-Sat; noon-3pm Sun. Oct-May noon-2.30pm, 6-10pm Tue-Sat.
Keeping Stein's Seafood Restaurant well and truly on its toes, No.6 was launched in a good-looking Georgian townhouse by a team headed up by one of Gordon Ramsay's protégés, Paul Ainsworth. Bedecked in a glamorous, contemporary style (nautical trimmings blessedly absent) with black and white checked floors, cool crockery and suited waiters, the restaurant is as well dressed as the food. Sweet chilli and spiced avocado accompany perfectly seared carpaccio of tuna, and Launceston lamb is made daringly complex courtesy of sweetbreads, liver and kidneys. Every dish is beautifully presented and bursting with innovative flavour. A sorbet palate cleanser, for example, comes with popping candy, and a dessert of caramelised banana is served with peanut butter ice-cream. Well worth a detour.

Pescadou

Old Custom House, South Quay, Padstow, PL28 8BL (01841 532359, www.oldcustomhousepadstow.co.uk). Lunch served noon-2pm, dinner served 7-9pm daily.
As the name suggests, this is a place for fish-lovers. Mixing classic and contemporary influences in both design and cuisine, Pescadou tailors its menu around the best of what is caught on its doorstep (it has a prime harbourside position). And even if it's not plucked from the ocean outside, pickings such as the succulent Fowey river mussels won't be sourced from too far away. While the menu attempts to range beyond seafood, options such as steak-frites or risotto are never going to sound as exciting as a whole Padstow lobster or half-shell scallops with lemongrass and lime, fresh from the day boat.

Rick Stein's Café

10 Middle Street, Padstow, PL28 8AP (01841 532700, www.rickstein.com). Breakfast served 8-10.30am, coffee & cake served 10am-noon, lunch served noon-2.30pm, dinner served 6.30-9pm daily.
One of the more relaxed and affordable venues under the Stein banner, this is the sort of place you can be just as happy slurping coffee behind a newspaper as dressed up for Sunday lunch. The fresh, nautical decor befits its location, with stripy cushions and watery paintings adorning wood-panelled walls, and there's a small courtyard for sunny afternoons. The seafood, even in its simplest form, is fantastic, with globally inspired favourites such as Thai fish cakes, grilled cod with spicy noodles or skewers of squid with cumin, coriander and lime. Breakfasts of own-made granola compote with berries, Stein pastries and trademark huevos rancheros see this tiny space heaving in high season.

St Kew Inn ★

St Kew, PL30 3HB (01208 841259, www.stkewinn.co.uk). Open 11am-11pm Mon-Sat; noon-10pm Sun. Lunch served noon-2pm daily. Dinner served summer 6.30-9pm daily, winter 6.30-9pm Mon-Sat.
It's not often you get to sample the work of an acclaimed chef, particularly one who has notched up a Michelin star, somewhere as relaxed as a fine old Cornish pub. The St Kew Inn – taken over by Paul Ripley, previously of Ripley's in St Merryn – is one such happy exception. The idyllic setting, in a village some four and a half miles from Wadebridge

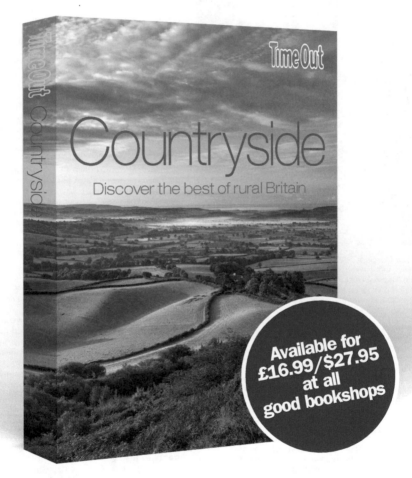

(think handsome church, soothing river, age-old cottages) conjures up scenes from a period drama, and the pub's beamed interior offers the sort of simple, trend-resistant comfort that makes you want to linger all night. Since taking over the pub in late 2008, Ripley has attracted an impressive following – even on a Monday evening in the dead of winter, we found the place warm and buzzing with locals, part-time locals and tourists settling in for an evening of St Austell brewery ales served straight from the barrel and food by the talented Mr Ripley. The simple menu changes daily, but sublime locally sourced steak, served with delicate young local greens (from the St Kew farm shop) and chips, is a constant. Other traditional British dishes include a fine Welsh rarebit and watercress salad, roast leg of Cornish lamb and rosemary gravy and sticky toffee pudding.

St Petroc's Bistro
4 New Street, Padstow, PL28 8EA (01841 532700, www.rickstein.com). Lunch served noon-2.30pm daily. Dinner served 6.30-9.30pm Mon-Thur, Sun; 6.30-10pm Fri, Sat.
Set in the fifth-oldest building in Padstow, St Petroc's has blended its traditional rustic character with a contemporary Stein twist. A simple bistro menu bears all the hallmarks of the man himself, but his signature seafood theme is supplemented by a meat-heavy grill section and various vegetarian dishes. The menu changes daily according to what's in, what's left and what's been caught, and although it makes light reading it caters for all tastes – and comes with an affordable price tag. The ribeye steak with bearnaise sauce is cooked to perfection, and the sea bass with roasted veg says everything about the superb quality of local fish that Rick Stein has been raving about for years.

Seafood Restaurant
Riverside, Padstow, PL28 8BY (01841 532700, www.rickstein.com). Llunch served noon-2.30pm daily. Dinner served 7-10pm Mon-Thur, Sun; 6.30-10pm Fri, Sat.
The jewel in the crown of the Stein empire, the flagship establishment is the place to book if you're out to impress and there's no limit to your budget. The seafood is beyond reproach, from simple Padstow lobster and oysters sourced from the Duchy Oyster Farm on the Helford River to innovative combinations such as sea bass with tomato, butter and vanilla vinaigrette, mackerel stuffed with ginger and chilli masala or salmon marinaded with passionfruit, lime and coriander. With a sleek reception desk, a stylish seafood bar in the centre of the room and opinion-dividing modern art on the walls, the Seafood Restaurant looks and feels like a destination restaurant – Cornwall's first, back in 1975, and still one of the best. Flaws are few, but will inevitably be judged heavily at these prices: whichever way you look at it, £8.50 is a lot to pay for a dessert.

Stein's Fish & Chips ★
South Quay, Padstow, PL28 8BL (01841 532700, www.rickstein.com). Restaurant & Take-away Lunch served noon-2.30pm, dinner served 5-8pm daily.
The impressive choice of fish varieties on offer here blows your average fish and chip shop out of the water. The pebbled counters, shell-framed mirrors and clean interior create a comfortable beachy atmosphere – although it's all too easily packed out by the hordes of families clamouring to sample the Stein reputation. Ultimately, it's the food that matters, and the quality of the fish is impeccable. Expect

Cornish Arms. See p197.

St Moritz. See p210.

generous portions of plump, juicy fillets encased in a perfect golden batter (or grilled if you prefer), served with steaming hot, crisp-shelled chips and a slice of fresh lemon – to eat in (in boxes) or take away. It's worth the wait.

Where to stay
There's no shortage of accommodation in Padstow, but as peak season sees the whole area bursting at the seams, book in advance.

Cornish Tipi Holidays ★
Tregeare, nr Pendoggett, PL30 3LW (01208 880781, www.cornishtipiholidays.co.uk). Rates £375-£495 per week for 2 people. £435-£555 per week for 5 people. £625-£745 per week for 8 people.
Amid the ferns, bluebells and gently nodding foxgloves of this wooded 16-acre site stand 40 canvas tipis, arranged in convivial clusters (the 'village fields') or in leafy clearings, for those seeking romantic seclusion. At the centre of the site is a long, crystal-clear lake, where campers can swim, fish, or go boating. Campfires are allowed, and tipis are equipped with camp stoves, coolboxes, rugs, lanterns and kitchenware – though you'll need to bring your own camp beds, bedding, towels and torches. The coast is a few minutes' drive; Wadebridge, some ten miles away, is the nearest town.

Old Custom House
South Quay, Padstow, PL28 8BL (01841 532359, www.oldcustomhousepadstow.co.uk). Rates £100-£135 double incl breakfast.
Standing right on the quayside, the Old Custom House is a listed building that has been refurbished to create an intimate contemporary hotel. Most of the rooms boast harbour views, so you can wake up to the early morning light flooding the estuary. The superior rooms are elegant and spacious, emphasising the seaside location with sand-coloured furniture and framed drawings of shells. The only downside to being smack-bang in the middle of town is being perched right above the pub.

Prospect House
4 New Street, Padstow, PL28 8EA (01841 532700, www.rickstein.com). Rates £210-£270 double incl breakfast.
The latest four guestrooms in the Stein empire are also the most private – hidden away behind St Petroc's Hotel & Bistro, but accessed via an independent entrance (guests are given their own key). The style is slick and contemporary, with subdued, natural shades, black and white seascapes on the walls and, in the best rooms, deluge showers, glass-encased gas fires and huge baths. A superb breakfast is served a few metres up the road at St Petroc's.

St Edmund's House ★
St Edmunds Lane, Padstow, PL28 8BY (01841 532700, www.rickstein.com). Rates £270 double incl breakfast.
There are some stylish rooms above the Seafood Restaurant and at St Petroc's, but the best accommodation in the Stein stable is at St Edmund's House. Think a Hamptons-style beach house, with six minimalist yet luxurious rooms overlooking private gardens and the Camel estuary. Each room bears the name of a local bay, etched into its driftwood

Cornish Tipi Holidays

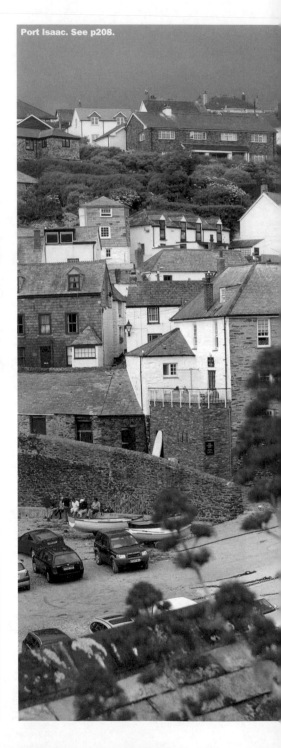
Port Isaac. See p208.

TEN CORNISH ARTISTS

Works by many of the artists mentioned
below are owned by Tate St Ives
(*see p282*).

Elizabeth Forbes (1859-1912)

Canada-born Forbes (née Armstrong)
came to London in the 1870s, moving
to Cornwall in the 1880s, where she met
her husband, fellow painter Stanhope
Forbes. Their Newlyn School of Painting,
set up at the turn of the century,
was a joint enterprise, and Forbes, known
for her paintings of local children and
landscapes, became one of the most
established female artists of the time.

Stanhope Forbes (1857-1947)

Forbes was born in Dublin, but moved
to Cornwall at the age of 27, where
he lived until his death in 1947. Along
with his wife Elizabeth Forbes, he was
a key member of the Newlyn School,
which focused on Impressionist-style
landscapes (particularly scenes
depicting fishermen), natural light
and figurative painting.

Terry Frost (1915-2003)

One of Britain's most prominent abstract
artists, known for his distinctive use of
circles, lines and colour in his painting.
Frost made the decision to become a
painter at the end of World War II,
attending Camberwell School of art and
subsequently St Ives School of Art. After
working briefly as an assistant to Barbara
Hepworth, he moved to Newlyn, his
home for the remainder of his life; the
Cornish landscape and the sea were
an inspiration for much of his work.

Barbara Hepworth (1903-1975)

One of Britain's most prominent
sculptors, Hepworth was also a key
member of the St Ives School and the
breakaway Crypt Group. Hepworth
purchased the Trewyn Studio in St Ives
in 1949, where she worked and lived –
it's now the Barbara Hepworth Museum
& Sculpture Garden (*see p282*).
Hepworth was married to fellow artist
Ben Nicholson (*see p205*) between
1938 and 1951; she died in a fire in
her studio in 1975.

Patrick Heron (1920-1999)

Another St Ives-based artist, Heron
moved to west Cornwall with his family
in 1925. After training at London's
Slade, he returned to Cornwall to draw,
and subsequently became an assistant
at the Bernard Leach Pottery in St Ives,
where he met Ben Nicholson, Barbara
Hepworth and other key members of
the St Ives School; he started to develop
his own abstract style during this time,
painting from his home overlooking
the cliffs at Zennor.

CORNWALL

Roger Hilton (1911-1975)
One of the pioneers of British abstract art, and a prominent member of the St Ives School, Hilton was born in London and studied at the Slade. He started to spend long periods in west Cornwall during the 1950s, moving there permanently in 1964. His work, unusually, became less abstract in his later years.

Peter Lanyon (1918-1964)
Born in St Ives, Lanyon was a painter, printmaker and sculptor known for his abstract paintings that clearly referenced Cornish landscapes, and for his constructions. He was a central member of the Crypt Group (a breakaway group of St Ives School artists), alongside Ben Nicholson and Barbara Hepworth, and subsequent founding member of the Penwith Society of Arts in the late 1940s. St Ives remained his home for much of his life.

Bernard Leach (1887-1979)
Known as the father of British studio pottery, Leach was born and brought up in Asia, and was greatly influenced by Far Eastern – particularly Japanese – approaches to pottery. In 1920, he set up the Leach Pottery School (still open today, partly as a museum; see p282) in St Ives, with Japanese potter Shoji Hamada. Together they promoted pottery from a standpoint that emphasised the fusion of Western and Eastern techniques and philosophies.

Ben Nicholson (1894-1982)
A pioneer of the Constructivist movement during the 1930s, and a key figure in British abstract art in the 1940s and '50s, Nicholson's paintings and prints are easily recognisable thanks to his distinctive geometric style. Many of his most famous works are lino cuts (often of domestic crockery), carvings and painted reliefs. He was greatly inspired by the direct style of the paintings of Cornish fisherman Alfred Wallis.

Alfred Wallis (1855-1942)
One of Cornwall's most famous artists, known for his direct, 'naïve' style that was much celebrated by the St Ives group; Wallis, based first in Penzance and later in St Ives, was a fisherman for much of his life, taking up painting in his late 60s. Having limited funds (he lived and died in poverty), he used industrial paint and cardboard as a canvas.

Things to do

PADSTOW & AROUND

Camel Trail ★
(01872 327310, www.sustrans.org.uk)
Cornwall's best-known cycle trail follows a disused railway line between Padstow, Wadebridge, Bodmin and Poley's Bridge, which was once used to transport slate and sand. The entire trail is flat and manageable – and therefore ideal for families – but the most popular and scenic portion hugs the estuary between Padstow and Wadebridge for five miles. You can hire bikes from Bridge Bike Hire in Wadebridge (01208 813050, www.bridgebikehire.co.uk), whose range includes child and adult trailer bikes, tandems and bikes for special needs, or at Padstow Cycle Hire (South Quay, 01841 533533, www.padstowcyclehire.com). In 2006, two extensions to the Camel Trail were completed, one up into Bodmin and the other towards Bodmin Moor.

Cornwall's Crealy Great Adventure Park
Trelow Farm, Tredinnick, PL27 7RA (01841 541286, www.crealy.co.uk). Open Mar-Oct School Holidays 10am-6pm daily. Term-Time 10am-6pm Mon, Thur-Sun. Sept-Feb 10am-6pm Sat, Sun. Admission £13.95; £9.95 reductions.
Theme park-lovers will do well at Crealy; once you've invested in a family ticket, you can come back as often as you like for the next week. Children like it very much, and adults are rather beguiled by the animal attractions, which include noble shire-horses, sucky-mouthed koi carp that feed from your hand, bunnies, calves, piglets, lambs, guinea pigs, ferrets and bumptious goats. The rides are especially good for tinies, and there's a big sandpit, helter skelter and adventure playground, as well as mini diggers to ride and two indoor playzones. A little safari train takes you though the 100 acre-slice of woodland and meadows in which Crealy sprawls. Check out the glorious sunflower maze in the summer months. We advise taking your own picnic rather than shelling out for the café offerings.

Harlyn Surf School
23 Grenville Road, Padstow, PL28 8EX (01841 533076, www.harlynsurf.co.uk). Open Apr-Oct; times vary, phone for details. Lessons from £38.
Small student to instructor ratios are promised at Harlyn Surf School, whose dizzying array of courses ranges from intensive learn to surf weekends to summer surf camps for kids and teenagers. Instruction in the art of stand-up paddleboarding – easier to master than surfing, and involving a reassuringly wide board – is also offered.

Padstow Boat Trips
www.padstowboattrips.com
Zoom off on a high-speed boat trip (Oct-Easter), or experience the gentler thrill of a fishing trip or cruise from Padstow harbour. Prices vary: see the website for details of the various operators, or visit Padstow's Tourist Information Centre (01841 533449).

Padstow Seafood School
Riverside, Padstow, PL28 8BY (01841 532700, www.rickstein.com). Dates vary, check website for details. Lessons from £185 per day.
Stein's esteemed Seafood School offers one- and two-day courses in a wide range of international cuisines (including Japanese sashimi and sushi, Thai fish and French fish). Students get to work with some of the freshest seafood around, in a combination of hands-on sessions, chef demonstrations and, most importantly, tasting sessions. All in all, something of a dream sequence for foodies.

ROCK, POLZEATH & PORT ISAAC

Animal Surf School
Polzeath Beach (0870 242 2856, www.animalsurf academy.co.uk). Open 8am-dusk daily. Courses from £25.
Girls-only lessons, private lessons for individuals, groups and families, and workshops with pro surfers are among the options at Animal.

Camel Keelboats
Kirland, Chapel Anvle, PL27 6EP (01208 841246, 07811 875321). Open by arrangement only. Courses & Charters from £25 per hour. No credit cards.
Tuition onboard skippered charters. Fishing charters (equipment included), tours both on the river and further out (weather dependant), sailing lessons. Boats (two) take up to six people.

Camel School of Seamanship
The Pontoon, Rock, PL27 6LD (01208 862881, www.camelsailing.co.uk). Open Summer 10am-5pm daily. Winter by arrangement only. Courses from £37 per hour.
This family business offers sailing taster sessions and longer courses on the Camel Estuary, along with power boat instruction. More experienced sailors can also hire Wayfarer dinghies.

Camel Ski School
The Pontoon, Rock, PL27 6LQ (01208 862727, www.camelskischool.com). Open Easter-Oct 9am-dusk daily. Courses from £24 per person.
For a bit more welly on the water, the Camel Ski School offers waterskiing and wakeboarding tuition.

Era Adventures
Valley Caravan Park, Polzeath, PL27 6SS (01208 862963, www.era-adventures.co.uk). Open times vary, check website for details. Activities prices vary; check website for details.
Daredevil activities offered by this Polzeath-based adventure company include surfing (including surf safaris), mountain biking, kite surfing, sea kayaking, rock climbing and power-boating.

St Enodoc Golf Club
Rock, PL27 6LD (01208 863216, www.st-enodoc.co.uk). Open Summer 8am-dusk daily. Winter 8am-1pm daily. Green fees £20-£65. Club hire £25.
St Enodoc Golf Club in Rock incorporates two beautifully sited courses on the edge of the estuary, one of which allows unrestricted access for visiting players. Also, enjoying a spectacular position over Constantine Bay is Trevose Golf Club (01841 520208, www.trevose-gc.co.uk), which has extensive country club facilities.

Surf's Up!

21 Trenant Close, Polzeath, PL27 6SW (01208 862003, www.surfsupsurfschool.com). Open Jan, Mar-Dec 10am-dusk daily. Lessons from £26.
This friendly surf school offers lessons and coaching for all levels, from nervous novices to accomplished surfers looking to polish their technique.

BUDE & AROUND

Big Blue Surf School

Summerleaze Beach, Bude, EX23 8HN (01288 331764, www.bigbluesurfschool.co.uk). Open phone for details. Lessons from £25.
Taking full advantage of Bude's varied beaches, this well-established surf school operates at Middle Beach and Crooklets, as well as Summerleaze. Half-day introductions are good value at £25 – and the more sessions you book in for, the lower prices drop.

Bude Sea Pool

Summerleaze Beach (01208 262822, www.cornwall. gov.uk). Open May-Sept 10am-6pm daily.
Not as elaborate as the art deco Jubilee Pool in Penzance, Bude's sea pool was built into the rocks on Summerleaze Beach during the lido boom of the 1930s – and is filled and emptied twice a day by the tides. There's a lifeguard in high season. Terraces for sunbathing and a sloping bottom make for a comfortable bathing experience, but the occasional encounter with a crop of slimy seaweed – not to mention the all-natural temperature – lend it the invigorating feel of a wild swim.

Bude Surf Centre

Bude (www.thebudesurfcentre.co.uk). See website for details.
The Surf Centre offers both equipment hire and lessons. Small groups can book the Surfari package (£75 per person), which involves heading off in a Landrover to chase the best waves in the area; a surf coach and packed lunches are included.

Bude Surfing Experience

Adventure International, Belle Vue, EX23 8IP (07779 117746, www.budesurfingexperience.co.uk). Lessons Easter-Sept 10am & 2pm daily. Oct-Easter by arrangement. Lessons from £25. No credit cards.
Expert tuition for beginners, groups and experienced surfers, with hot showers and indoor changing rooms.

Tamar Lakes

Near Bude, EX23 9SB (01288 321712, www.sw lakestrust.org.uk). Open 24hrs daily. Watersports Centre & Café Apr-Oct times vary, phone for details. Admission free.
Straddling the border with Devon are the reservoirs and campsite at Tamar Lakes. The lower lake is a nature reserve, with a small car park and pedestrian access along the dam, connecting with the towpath beside the former Bude Canal. The larger upper lake has a car park and visitor centre with a café and offers watersports facilities (Apr-Oct), with the chance to try sailing, windsurfing and kayaking. Walkers can follow a path right round the lake, and coarse fishing permits are sold at the visitors' centre.

door sign, plus four-poster beds, en suite marble bathrooms, oak flooring and an air of seaside luxury; ground-floor rooms also have a private deck. Once you've sunk into the bath with the twinkling estuary in view or reclined by the bay windows, you won't want to leave the comfort of your self-contained retreat – but you're forced out for breakfast, which is served in the Seafood Restaurant (*see p201*).

Treann House ★

24 Dennis Road, Padstow, PL28 8DE (01841 553855, www.treannhousepadstow.co.uk). Rates £80-£110 double incl breakfast. No credit cards.
In terms of design nous, this Padstow newcomer is one of the most polished B&Bs we've seen in Cornwall. The rooms have been flawlessly styled by owner Emma Caddis to create a look that combines new, old and rejuvenated vintage pieces, against a background of fresh whites and creams. All three rooms are way above average (even in chic Padstow), but our money would go on the ethereal Estuary room, with white deco armchairs, a superking-size white cast-iron bed and breathtaking estuary views. All rooms come with a glossy black digital radio, iPod dock, locally blended toiletries, robes, and a mini fridge stocked with complimentary wine, nibbles and water as standard.

Tregea Hotel

16-18 High Street, Padstow, PL28 8BB (0871 871 2686, www.tregea.co.uk). Rates £120 double incl breakfast.
Behind the door of an ivy-fronted cottage at the top of the town, the Tregea (which literally translates as 'the house on the hill') is set back from the bustle of Padstow's harbourfront. Having retained much of its 17th-century charm and character, and the intimate room size of the period, it has been refurbished with a lick of contemporary coastal chic. Relax in the sumptuous sofas by the fireside, take the weight off over a tipple at the licensed bar, and retire to one of eight individual rooms (all en-suite). Local artwork, a sprinkling of shells, whitewashed and wicker furniture, and hues of blues and beiges enhance the beachy feel of the interior. There's also parking, which is rare in Padstow.

Treverbyn House

Station Road, Padstow, PL28 8DA (01841 532855, www.treverbynhouse.com). Rates £80-£115 double incl breakfast. No credit cards.
Occupying a grand Edwardian house, Treverbyn is an elegant B&B with coveted views over the estuary. For a romantic weekend, hide out in the stylish decadence of the Turret Room, or choose a room with a cosy open fire for a winter retreat. Traditional furnishings complement period features, but the rooms are bright, airy and comfortable. A delicious breakfast with organic own-made preserves is served in your room, so you can relax happily in your night attire and gaze out at the water.

ROCK, POLZEATH & PORT ISAAC

Rock to Polzeath

Facing Padstow across the river, and easily accessed by ferry, is the tiny village of Rock. It's actually very sandy, but takes its name from the quarry that used to provide the rocky ballast for sailing ships emptied of cargo across the river. Increasingly popular with

Port Gaverne

CORNWALL

wealthy folk from the city since it became associated with royalty (William and Harry came here for watersports, and now hundreds of public school pupils follow suit), Rock is reputed to be the home of more millionaires than anywhere else in Cornwall, and has to endure the label 'Kensington-on-Sea' – which irritates the locals no end.

It is lovely, however – especially out of season, when the beach that stretches along the side of the Camel all the way around to Daymer Bay ★ at low tide is empty of all but dog walkers, hardy windsurfers and lots of pre-schoolers, unrestricted by term dates and enchanted by the rock pools. You can get to Rock's beaches via a scenic coastal walk or across the 18-hole golf course at St Enodoc, named after the diminutive church with a crooked steeple nestling prettily in the valley. St Enodoc Church is probably best known through its association with poet John Betjeman, who is buried in the graveyard alongside sailors and fishermen who lost their lives on the infamous Doom Bar at the entrance to the Camel Estuary.

The estuary is superb for watersports, and Rock has a smart sailing club (*see p206*). The nearby holiday village of Polzeath, overlooking Padstow Bay, is a good place for novice surfers and bodyboarders, as the waves are gentle and the sand is fine. A beautiful, two-mile walk around the edge of the bay from Rock, Polzeath offers an attractive – and considerably more down-to-earth – cluster of cafés, surf shops and restaurants, and a large sandy beach. There's a sprinkling of surf schools (*see p206*); for equipment hire, head to Anne's Cottage Surf Shop (Polzeath Beach, 01208 863317, www.annscottagesurf.co.uk). From Polzeath, it's a fantastic walk to the remnants of an Iron Age castle at Rumps Point.

Port Isaac

Port Isaac may not attract the same hordes of beach-bound holidaymakers as Rock and Polzeath, but it does suffer from an infestation of second-homers. In this pint-sized fishing village, where white slate-hung cottages cling to a steep incline above a 700-year-old harbour, it seems every other home belongs to someone distinctly un-Cornish. Explore the little alleyways between the cottages (look for the one called Squeeze-ee-belly Alley), have a pint overlooking the harbour at the snug Golden Lion pub (*see p209*), and banish all thoughts of estate agents.

There's a sprinkling of one-off shops and galleries, including Dennis Knight Fish Merchant in Port Isaac (1 Fore Street, 01208 880498, closed Sun), with an excellent range of fresh fish, and mini design emporium Hooper & Shaw ★ (01208 880845, www.hooperandshaw.co.uk), which sells limited-edition screen-printed posters featuring playful one-liners, ceramics and stationery, as well as Cornish ice-cream.

Being part of a working harbour, albeit a very quaint one, the beach at Port Isaac isn't your best bet for a traditional day out at the beach. Adjacent Port Gaverne has a sheltered pebbly beach that's better for swimming, but for sand and space, head for Polzeath.

Where to eat & drink

An affluent tourist trade in these parts supports a variety of excellent restaurants – most notably the new Nathan Outlaw fine dining restaurant, which was preparing to open at the St Enodoc Hotel (*see p209*) as we went to press. Relocating from Fowey, Outlaw looks set to build on his reputation as the rising star of Cornwall's restaurant scene in his new premises, where he will continue to concentrate on British food of the highest order, with an emphasis on seafood.

In addition to the restaurants, pubs and cafés below, the following pubs and cafés make for low-key stops with views: the Rock Inn (Rock Road,

Rock, 01208 863498, www.rockaccommodation.co.uk), a modern pub and café with huge windows and balcony tables overlooking the estuary; the neat Blue Tomato café & takeaway (01208 863841) a few doors down, with a small veranda affording views of the estuary; and the Waterfront (Beach Road, 01208 869655, www.thewaterfrontcornwall.co.uk, closed winter) at Polzeath, with a large deck overlooking the beach.

L'Estuaire
Pavilion Building, Rock Road, Rock, PL27 6JS (01208 862622, www.lestuairerestaurant.com). Lunch served noon-2pm, dinner served 7-9pm Wed-Sun.
On the site of the much-lauded Black Pig, L'Estuaire serves fine French cuisine crafted from local produce, care of French chef Olivier Davoust-Zangari. Hues of beige hint at understated sophistication and, with a chef who has worked with the likes of Raymond Blanc, the food pulls off the continental style and Cornish sourcing with aplomb. Terrine of duck confit is served with crunchy vegetables, while Porthilly oysters are gently doused in shallot cider vinegar. Mains include beef fillet tournedos with foie gras sauce and new potatoes roasted in own-grown rosemary, and Cornish lobster with black truffle risotto. Cheese platters take in the best of Cornish, with some French classics for good measure.

Golden Lion
Fore Street, Port Isaac, PL29 3RB (01208 880336). Open 11.30am-11.30pm Mon-Thur; 11.30am-midnight Fri, Sat; 11.30am-11pm Sun. Lunch served noon-2.30pm, dinner served 6-9pm daily.
This delightful old village pub overlooks the harbour – and played a starring role in the ITV series *Doc Martin*. It feels comfortably aged and rickety, with a sloping floor and pictures of ancient mariners and RNLI heroes on the walls. Many of the dishes on the pub food menu feature Port Isaac seafood, and the fish and chips are excellent – an enormous piece of freshly battered haddock, fried to perfection. Crab sandwich and pint of St Austell HSD in hand, make your way to the sweet spot: the small balcony directly overlooking the harbour and beach.

Mariners Rock
Slipway, Rock, PL27 6LD (01208 863679, www.marinersrock.com). Open/food served Summer 10am-midnight daily. Winter 11am-3pm, 5.30-11.30pm Mon-Fri; 11am-midnight Sat; 11am-11.30pm Sun.
If you want to mix with the sailing crowd, there's nowhere better to catch them than in this smart bar and restaurant overlooking the yacht club, while supping on super-fresh seafood accompanied by a flute of something expensive and cold. If you're not there to talk boating – or tune into the Kensington-on-Sea scene – you can focus on the stunning views over the water to Padstow, or cosy up by the fire in the bar on a winter's evening. There's laid-back bar food downstairs (mussels, crab sandwiches, pizzas) and a smarter restaurant upstairs, with white tablecloths and a more weighty menu.

Nathan Outlaw Seafood & Grill ★
St Enodoc Hotel, Rock, PL27 6LA (01208 863394, www.nathan-outlaw.co.uk). Lunch served 12.30-2.30pm, dinner served 6-9.30pm daily.

Those wanting to size up Cornwall's hottest chef without paying fine dining prices at his new venture next door should secure a table at Outlaw's more affordable outpost (for which don't read 'cheap' – mains stop just short of £20), also at the St Enodoc Hotel. As the name implies, surf and turf are given joint billing, served in uncomplicated ways but nonetheless with exceptional results. Chargrilled Cornish ribeye with pickled mushrooms was superbly succulent, served with chunky, hand-cut chips. Local Porthilly mussels and oysters also feature, and dishes such as black pig with nectarines and earl grey panna cotta with blackberries hint at the culinary creativity going on behind the scenes. Decor is bistro-chic and unpretentious; fishy photography, smart wooden chairs and safe navy blues.

Trevathan Farm
St Endellion, PL29 3TT (01208 880164, www.trevathanfarm.com). Open phone for details.
A working farm with 11 holiday cottages to let, Trevathan also has a shop with locally produced food and wine, a pick-your-own soft fruit business, plus this jolly tearoom and restaurant. Perched on the hillside outside St Endellion village, the tearoom and conservatory have splendid views over the valley to St Austell. On Sundays it's worth booking in for the roast Trevathan-reared lamb or beef with home-grown vegetables, but during the week you're safe enough just turning up for the daily specials menu of salads, lasagne, fish pie or filled paninis. These may well star the legendary Cornish yarg cheese (also sold in the shop), with its nettle covering. Breakfasts, own-made cakes and cream teas are also on the agenda. The biggest attraction for children is the play area with zip slide, mini diggers and tractors to play on, and a pets corner with rabbits, angora goats, wallabies, guinea pigs, poultry and, in spring, lambs.

Where to stay
In Port Isaac, the Slipway Hotel (The Harbour Front, 01208 880264, www.portisaachotel.com), above the bar-restaurant of the same name, has an unbeatable location next to the beach, its ten rooms are chintz-free and comfortable.

St Enodoc
Rock, PL27 6LA (01208 863394, www.enodoc-hotel.co.uk). Rates £130-£235 double incl breakfast.
This family-friendly hotel is a bastion of taste and decorum, without being frosty. From the airy reception and adjoining lounge with slate floors and original art, you climb up stairs and landings carpeted in candy stripes to equally bright rooms. The grounds are pleasantly landscaped and the sheltered outdoor pool, heated from May to September and with wooden steamer chairs dotted around it, is a delight. Baths are big, showers torrent forth, handbasins are double-sized and fluffy bathrobes and decent toiletries are provided. Adding to the already extensive list of assets, Nathan Outlaw Seafood & Grill (*see left*) appeared on the scene in 2009 (with his fine dining operation open in 2010 and gunning for Michelin stars), so St Enodoc looks set to be one of Cornwall's hottest addresses for destination dining. Outside, the terrace looks over the gardens and pool to the Camel Estuary and a little gate in the garden sets you on the footpath for the golf course, the beach, dunes and St Enodoc church, evading the ghastly road down to the beach – it's crammed with 4X4s and has little or no pavement.

FIVE CORNISH ALES

Betty Stogs

Truro-based Skinner's makes this bestselling 4% pale amber bitter, which won Champion Best Bitter at the Great British Beer Festival 2008. To celebrate the accolade, the brewery redesigned the label to feature busty Betty with the Union Jack.

Tasting notes Mid-strength golden bitter, with fruity notes and hoppy overtones.

Chalky's Bite

Rick Stein challenged Sharp's Brewery in Rock to make a beer with individuality to 'stand alongside the Belgian greats'. The result – named after Stein's late canine companion – is a 6.8% beer of immense character, with a refreshing hint of wild Cornish fennel and higher than average levels of (natural) carbonation, making it a great accompaniment to seafood and fish. It is served in Stein's numerous enterprises in Padstow, among other outlets.

Tasting notes A distinctive, triple-fermented golden beer, perfect as an aperitif or with seafood.

Doom Bar

Sharps' legendary bitter is named after the notoriously dangerous sandbank of the Camel Estuary. It's an award-winning 4.3% ale, widely drunk in Cornwall for its warm, distinctive flavours and smooth consistency.

Tasting notes Delicious hints of spice and all things nice, but easy-going enough to be a session beer.

Spingo

Crafted on a small scale by the Blue Anchor (see p252) in Helston, thought to be the UK's oldest brew-pub, Spingo is a strong, dark ale. It comes in four incarnations: IPA, Middle, Bragget and, the strongest, Special (6.5%) – we recommend the copper-coloured Middle. Other than at the Blue Anchor, it is served at the Falmouth Townhouse (see p238) and the Dock Inn (01736 362833) in Penzance. Bottles can be bought in Helston's Oliver's. Worth the pilgrimage.

Tasting notes: sweet and strong with unusual, memorable flavours.

Tribute

St Austell Brewery first brewed this premium 4.2% pale amber beer for the solar eclipse in 1999, and it is now its hugely popular flagship beer, drunk throughout the West Country.

Tasting notes Bronze-coloured, refreshing light citrusy notes.

St Moritz

Trebetherick, PL27 6SD (01208 862242, www.stmoritz hotel.co.uk). Rates £99-£220 double incl breakfast.
When it arrived on the scene in 2007, St Moritz was the first new purpose-built luxury hotel to be built in Cornwall in over 30 years – a gleaming white, art deco-accented complex, bringing with it up-to-speed decor and facilities. A palpably ambitious affair, St Moritz matches its chic looks and ocean-facing views with plenty of substance: exceedingly comfortable beds, switched-on staff, and a superb leisure area equipped with pool, jacuzzi, hammam, steam and a Cowshed spa. Families take note: St Moritz is proactively child-friendly, with a kids' play room (Wii and Xbox present and correct), a baby pool and basics such as cots and high chairs at the ready. St Moritz mightn't be the place to live out any nostalgic dreams of simple fishermen's cottages and log fires, but there's plenty of characterful old Cornwall within easy striking distance, not to mention Rock and Padstow close by.

BUDE & AROUND

Less standoffish than Padstow, and considerably more innocent than Newquay, Bude is a gusty, open-planned resort town high up in the north-east of the county. While developing its prospects as a lively seaside resort with a jazz festival (01288 356360, www.budejazzfestival.co.uk), a long-standing surf scene and a good family beach, this is a town that still values its industrial past, having recently ploughed over £5.5 million into a major regeneration of the Bude Canal.

An early 19th-century construction built to carry the calcium-rich sand of the coast to the infertile uplands of Exmoor, the canal was part of a grand plan to link with the upper Tamar, thus joining the Bristol and English Channels. But the railway arrived long before that ambition could be realised, and the canal rapidly declined (as, eventually, did the railway, with the Bude branch line closed by the 1960s). The canal is now an attractive asset, with rich birdlife and wildlife, towpaths for walking and cycling, and pedalos and rowing boats for hire; the new Tourist Information Centre (The Crescent, 01288 354240, www.visitbude.info) has more details and an exhibition on the canal's history.

Most of all, though, visitors come for the expansive beaches in the vicinity, where Atlantic breaks create a splendid swathe of surf. The most central of Bude's beaches is the wide, sandy Summerleaze, with its own seawater swimming pool (see p207) and a saddlebacked breakwater. Just to the north, Crooklets is the site of numerous surfing and lifesaving competitions, while Sandy Mouth beyond lives up to its name with a sweep of sand and rock pools. Offshore reefs create some good surf at the narrow sandy cove of Duckpool, a little further on. To the south is the mightily impressive span of Widemouth Bay, whose golden sands and reliable waves attract hordes of beachbums.

Morwenstow

Ducking out of the bullying Atlantic gales, between Bude and Hartland Point to the north, Morwenstow fits tidily into a small wooded combe close to the

Bude Canal and Beach

featuring large portions of old favourites such as spag bol, nachos, fajitas, bacon sarnies and an array of sundaes.

Bay View Inn
Widemouth Bay, Bude, EX23 0AW (01288 361273, www.bayviewinn.co.uk). Open 9am-11.30pm daily. Breakfast served 9am-10pm daily. Lunch served noon-2.30pm, dinner served 6-9pm Mon-Sat. Food served noon-9pm Sun.
A pub with light-hearted, surfy aesthetics, the Bay View Inn is set on the coastal road, a few miles from Bude. It's worth a stop for good, crowd-pleasing food (lasagne, sticky toffee pudding, Cornish fillet steak and chips, fish pie) and exhilarating views across the panorama of Widemouth Bay. Sit on the wide decking for maximum, cobweb-clearing effect. There are several rooms for B&B (£90-£100 double incl breakfast) upstairs.

Castle ★
The Wharf, Bude, EX23 8LG (01288 350543, www.thecastlerestaurantbude.co.uk). Lunch served noon-2.30pm daily. Dinner served 6-9.30pm Mon-Sat.
Old-school Bude could do with more places like the Castle, an informally chic café-restaurant located within the historic surrounds of Bude Castle, open for coffees, express lunches and smart dinners. With attractively kooky art on the walls (hand-sewn birds perched on a real branch on our latest visit) and views out over the breakwater from the terrace and window seats, the Castle has a short but engrossing menu, which goes beyond the usual suspects with dishes like black pudding with curried apple purée and herb oil, deep-fried leek and potato terrine with truffled poached egg, or red wine and Cornish blue cheese risotto. This is also one of few places in the area serving good cocktails – try the espresso martini.

Life's a Beach
Summerleaze Beach, Bude, EX23 8HN (01288 355222, www.lifesabeach.info). Open/food served Summer 11am-4pm, 7-11pm Mon-Sat; 11am-4pm Sun. Winter 7-11pm Thur, Fri; 11am-4pm, 7-11pm Sat, Sun.
Every crowd-pleasing Cornish beach worth its salt has a cool café-restaurant – and Bude's town beach, Summerleaze, is no exception. Overlooking the crests rolling in off the Atlantic from its clifftop seat, Life's a Beach is a multi-purpose chill-out zone for hungry families, surfers and the salty-haired of all ages by day, serving ice-creams, lattes and laid-back lunches (burgers, baguettes, bruschettas). Come the evening, the prices, cuisine and atmosphere are all more bistro than beach café – and local seafood dominates proceedings.

Rectory Tea Rooms
Rectory Farm, Crosstown, Morwenstow, EX23 9SR (01288 331251, www.rectory-tearooms.co.uk). Open phone for details.
Opposite Morwenstow Church, the Rectory Tea Rooms has been serving up cream teas for some 60 years – during which time the art of afternoon tea has been lovingly perfected. The house blend of loose leaf tea is Smugglers' Choice, and the plump scones and jams are own-made. There is a lovely garden area, and the interior is steeped in history – the house dates back to the 13th century, and the beams, flagstone floors and fireplaces are original. There is also a window serving ice-creams and soft drinks in season.

Devon border. The tiny hamlet is most famous for its connection to the eccentric, opium-smoking Victorian vicar Reverend Stephen Hawker, who served at the parish chuch and is credited with the introduction of the Harvest Festival in English churches. Hawker's presence looms in the stepped mock-Tudor gables and Gothic windows of the Morwenstow Vicarage, where each chimneypot mimics the spire of a church. The Grade I listed church itself, set against the ocean backdrop, is a memorable sight.

Where to eat & drink
As you move up the coast away from the gastro epicentre of Padstow, the number of notable restaurants thins out, giving way to centuries-old inns and cosy tearooms, ideal for breaks from the scouring Atlantic winds.

Among the most attractive pubs in the area is the Bush Inn (01288 331242, www.bushinn-morwenstow.co.uk) in Morwenstow, a rugged 13th-century pub just back from the coastal footpath. Once the smugglers' boozer of choice, the inn is thought to have provided the inspiration for Daphne du Maurier's Jamaica Inn – and the snug, pared-down old bar is instantly evocative of past times. The Bush also has three comfortable country-styled bedrooms, with views, for B&B.

Atlantic Diner
5-7 Belle Vue, Bude, EX23 8JL (01288 354167). Open/food served Summer 10am-9pm Tue-Sun. Winter 11am-6pm Tue-Thur; 11am-9pm Fri, Sat; 11am-4pm Sun. No credit cards.
With ice-cream-coloured chairs, a neon palm tree and an old jukebox, the Atlantic has the surf shack look down to a T. The menu is perfectly pitched at après surf appetites,

Where to stay

Beyond the Camel Estuary, classy hotels become more scarce, with self-catering cottages and B&Bs dominating. In addition to the accommodation reviewed below, try Dylan's Guesthouse (12 Downs View, 01288 354705, www.dylansguesthousein bude.co.uk) in Bude, whose clean, contemporary rooms are good value for money. Bangors Organic (Bangors House, Poundstock, Bude, 01288 361297, www.bangorsorganic.co.uk), one of only a handful of B&Bs certified organic by the Soil Association, has a number of spacious, tastefully rustic rooms, and serves its own organic produce at breakfast and in the restaurant.

Beach Hut

Nr Widemouth Bay (01637 881942, www.unique homestays.com). Rates £1,575 per week for 2 people.
Beach huts don't get much more desirable than this one, managed by the eminently luxurious Unique Homestays brand. The wooden Beach Hut in question sits in splendid isolation on the fringes of a remote north coast beach. The look, both inside and out, is stripped-down seaside chic, with white wood-panel walls, natural wood floors and cream-painted furniture. However, the real excitement is right outside your door – the sea, stars, cliffs and solitary silence. Sleeps two.

Beach Modern

Various locations around Bude (01288 275006, www.beachmodern.com). Rates see website for details.
A total of five luxury self-catering properties come under the slick Beach Modern umbrella, all within easy reach of Bude's beaches. The biggest (no.28) sleeps up to 20 people, and all are stylishly minimalist, with lashings of white.

Elements Hotel & Bistro

Marine Drive, Bude, EX23 0LZ (01288 352386, www. elements-life.co.uk). Rates £105 double incl breakfast.
Bude's only boutique hotel sits high on the cliffs between Bude and Widemouth Bay. Despite clean, contemporary styling in the 11 rooms, there is an easygoing, surfy feel to the place, with epic views of the jagged coastline from the decking area, a heated drying room for beachware and wetsuits, and even storage space for surfboards. You can book yourself a surf package or borrow the hotel's foam boards. The bistro is a bright, competent affair, with the daily-changing menu taking inspiration from the day boats.

TINTAGEL & BOSCASTLE

It's best to visit Tintagel on a turbulent day. Not only will you see vast blooms of spray coming off the beach, but the straggling village blends in with its bleak setting. Surrounded by moorland and crashing seas, its dark slate cottages look both menacing and mystical. But most visitors to Tintagel come to see its spectacular ruined castle (*see p199*), the mythical birthplace of the King Arthur. Despite the boisterous commercialism that has attached itself to Arthurian legend, the remnants of Tintagel castle – set against the vivid green-turquoise of the surrounding sea (so coloured due to the copper content in the sand) – are by any measure an extraordinary sight.

The surrounding coast is just as wild and menacing – renowned for ferocious storms, heavy seas and shipwrecks. South of Tintagel, the waves at Trebarwith test the skills of surfers, with the hump of Gull Rock looming offshore; the beach, a long stretch of sand backed by cliffs and caves, all but disappears at high tide.

The village of Boscastle, three miles north of Tintagel, is an altogether more quaint sight. A tiny natural harbour at the end of a deep, narrow valley (or combe), where the River Jordan reaches the sea, Boscastle has endured worse onslaughts than a tide of holidaying humanity; in 2004, it was practically washed away by flash floods, when some 440 million gallons of water poured through the village in one day. Miraculously, no one was seriously hurt, but some ancient cottages were irreparably damaged.

The scenically placed village has tearooms, pubs and knick-knack shops, as well a new visitors' centre (01840 250010, www.visit boscastleandtintagel.com) on the harbour, which contains a well-executed exhibition on the history and geography of Boscastle, as well as some interesting exhibits relating to Thomas Hardy and his connection with the area. Hardy first visited Cornwall in 1870, when contracted to work as an architect on nearby St Juliot's Church, where he would meet and court Emma Gifford, later to be his wife (make your holiday reading Hardy's *A Pair of Blue Eyes*, inspired by

St Enodoc. See p209.

CORNWALL

the area around Boscastle). A scenic footpath leads out of Boscastle several miles through the Valency valley to the church in question.

Off the road between Tintagel and Boscastle (the B3263) you'll see signs for Rocky Valley. A parking place leads you to this beauty spot and towards St Nectan's Kieve, where a 60-foot waterfall plunges into a deep rock basin – considered a sacred place since pre-Christian times, and reputed to be one of Cornwall's most haunted locales.

Where to eat & drink

Tintagel is largely given over to lacklustre pubs and tearooms, unsubtly themed to appeal to the thousands of tourists traipsing through in search of traces of King Arthur. For more accomplished dining or just a quiet pint of local ale, try the 18th-century Mill House Inn below.

Mill House Inn

Trebarwith, PL34 OHD (01840 770200, www.themillhouseinn.co.uk). Open 11am-11.30pm daily. Lunch served noon-2.30pm, dinner served 7-8.30pm daily.

This 18th-century corn mill is set in pretty woodland, halfway up the valley from the surfing beach at Trebarwith Strand – and completely removed from the throng of Tintagel proper, a mile or so down the road. The old pub itself is an informal place with slate floors and a wood-burning stove for chilly days, while the newer restaurant behind is a more refined (but still family-friendly) affair, with light wood floors and white tablecloths. Dishes throughout are made from locally sourced meat, fish and vegetables, with the bar menu featuring the comforting likes of Cornish bangers and mash, snakebite-battered haddock and chips, and courgette and Cornish brie lasagne (all of which cost under a tenner). The restaurant menu is more cosmopolitan and elaborate, showing imaginative use of ingredients: own-cured veal and saffron-smoked mozzarella, leek-roasted organic sea trout with rosemary and Cornish potato soufflé, and lavender panna cotta, for example. Sharp's ales (as well as beers from the local Tintagel brewery) are served throughout, and bands play in the pub. There are also eight guestrooms (£90-£120 double including breakfast).

Where to stay

The Mill House Inn (*see above*) has eight attractive rooms, with rustic wooden furniture and white linens. For superior self-catering accommodation, check out the luxuriously converted barns at Fentafriddle Farm (Trebarwith Strand, Tintagel, 01637 881942, www.fentafriddle.com), all of which are within walking distance of the surf at Trebarwith Strand.

Avid readers of Thomas Hardy's novels might be interested in staying a night or two at the Old Rectory (01840 250225, www.stjuliot.com) at St Juliot, near Boscastle. Rooms are traditional but light and airy, and it's all set in three acres of lush grounds. This is where Hardy stayed while working on the local church in 1870, and where he courted his wife-to-be.

Boscastle Harbour Youth Hostel

Palace Stables, Boscastle, PL35 OHD (0845 371 9006, www.yha.org.uk). Open Apr-Nov. Rates from £13.95 per night for 1 person.

Located next to the water in Boscastle's lovely harbour, this comfortable little hostel is housed in a former stables, once occupied by the horses that pulled the boats ashore. The full force of the 2004 floods devastated the hostel's interior, but it has been completely refurbished and looks reborn. Modernisations include a number of great three- and four-bed family rooms, sparkling new bathrooms and a self-catering kitchen.

Boscastle House ★

Tintagel Road, Boscastle, PL35 OAS (01840 250654, www.boscastlehouse.com). Rates £120 double incl breakfast.

The young, charming owners of this boutique guesthouse, overlooking the steep combe of Boscastle, have injected some much-needed style into the mainly weary-looking hotel options in this corner of Cornwall. Boutique accents abound – outsized floral wallpaper, statement colour accents, rich fabrics – and each of the rooms sports a different colour scheme, ranging from fresh greens and creamy tones to Beaujolais-red. Rooms are unusually spacious, with features that normally command a more substantial price tag: roll-top baths, wrought-iron beds, walk-in showers, chandeliers and a beauty treatment menu. There is no restaurant, so technically this isn't a hotel – but nor is it a suffocatingly intimate B&B, since the rooms feel appealingly independent. Other bonuses include complimentary tea and cakes on arrival, a croquet lawn at the front and a stylish guest lounge. Eco policies include partial solar powering, locally sourced food and a £5 discount if you arrive by public transport.

Orchard Lodge

Gunpool Lane, Boscastle, PL35 OAT (01840 250418, www.orchardlodgeboscastle.co.uk). Rates £84 double incl breakfast.

Orchard Lodge is a bright newcomer in Boscastle, offering five scrupulously well-kept and contemporary B&B rooms – think fresh cream carpets, sparkling white bathrooms and thick, hotel-style towels. A member of CoaST (Cornwall Sustainable Tourism Project), the Orchard Lodge shows remarkable committment to local sourcing at breakfast: the milk is from nearby Delabole, the apple juice from Liskeard, the smoked fish from Widemouth Bay and, most impressively, the sausages are made from their own pigs, kept on an organic farm down the road. Note that discounts are offered to those arriving on foot, by bike or by public transport.

Tintagel Youth Hostel

Dunderhole Point, Tintagel, PL34 ODW (0845 371 9145, www.yha.org.uk). Open Apr-Nov. Rates from £13.95 per night for 1 person.

This place is wonderfully remote, and people who've stayed here say it feels as if it's on the edge of the world. The views out to sea are incredible, so you can understand why competition for the two four-bed and two six-bed rooms is so fierce during school holidays. Tintagel Hostel has a little shop where you can buy the wherewithal for a cook-up in the kitchen (no meals are served). It's staffed mainly by volunteers, who are friendly and helpful.

CORNWALL

Newquay & the Atlantic Coast

The north coast is what one might call 'classic Cornwall': great sashes of bright sand, melodramatic cliffs and crags, and an endless supply of Atlantic breakers. We'd probably even go so far as to say that this stretch of coast has the greatest concentration of fine beaches in the country.

But while scenic beauty explains how the north coast came to be the engine house of Cornwall's booming tourist trade, historically the area was defined by the twin industries of fishing and mining. Ivy-choked mine stacks punctuate the landscape around Camborne, Redruth and St Agnes, while Newquay was built on the once-lucrative pilchard trade. Now much of the area earns its crust, directly or indirectly, from leisure and tourism. Property developers throng, keen to cash in on the stunning views and the SUV-loads of families, surfers and partygoers who wend their way down the Atlantic highway to luxury hotels, B&Bs, holiday cottages, campsites, surf shacks and – less happily for the Cornish – second homes.

The largest resort on the north coast (and in all of Cornwall) is Newquay, the self-proclaimed surf capital of Britain and, less attractively, party central for binge-drinking school leavers and single-sex groups on the lash. But for all those who pile in for a potent mix of sticky shots, late-night drinking and cheesy clubs, there are plenty of others who come despite it – more interested in watersports, walking and, increasingly, chic retreats and restaurants.

NEWQUAY & AROUND

Newquay

When, in separate incidents just weeks apart, two teenagers fell to their deaths from the cliffs after an evening of underage drinking in 2009, it stoked the smouldering debate over Newquay – its unbridled property development and rampant construction, but, most of all, the rivers of underage, post-exam drinkers that flow through every summer to behave badly in someone else's backyard.

While the discussion rages on – the police calling for a clean-up, others enjoying the funfair – Newquay's natural assets retain an indelible appeal. For an idea of the raw materials that first made Newquay a resort, make your way to the western side of the harbour; from here, you can take in the entire sweep of cliff-vaulted beaches across the bay.

Newquay was known as Towan Blystra (sandy hill) until adventurous Elizabethans built the Newe Keye for their sailing vessels in the 15th century. With the development of mass tourism and the thriving surf scene, the basis of the town's original claim to fame, the humble pilchard, tends to get forgotten. Yet until the early 20th century, it was plentiful shoals of small herring that provided Newquay's income.

Above the western side of the bay perches the Huer's Hut, which provided shelter for the pilchard watcher. His job was to cry 'Heva!' through a long horn when he saw the silvery fish, then direct the sailors as they manoeuvred their boats around the entire shoal. Millions of plump fish were netted from the boats, and the whole town would turn out to offload the hauls.

Newquay's insignia is still two pilchards, even though the town lost its pilchards when they took it into their fishy heads to change their migration pattern. This, combined with the coming of the railways in the 19th century, put paid to maritime trade and sent the area into a steep financial decline, until the arrival of mass tourism buoyed it up once again.

Although you wouldn't believe it from the downmarket town centre, eminently stylish new additions to Newquay's eastern beaches – Jamie Oliver's Fifteen Cornwall (*see p221*) at the chic Watergate Bay resort, the striking new Scarlet hotel (*see p226*) in Mawgan Porth – herald a shift upmarket. Even more irrefutable evidence of Newquay's gentrification has arrived in the shape of Prince Charles's plan to develop his second ideal village project here, dubbed 'Surfbury' and based on the original Duchy of Cornwall venture in Poundbury, Dorset.

Bedruthan Steps. See p219.

Green and glamorous

How the Scarlet reinvented eco-chic.

One minute, Mawgan Porth was muddling along in a distinctly untrendy way – a few holiday lets, a low-key pub and a shop – the next, one of the country's hottest new hotels landed on the edge of the cliff, drawing the attention of travel editors nationwide – not to mention legions of eco worriers, architects and foodies. Although it has been some years since ecology and style were mutually exclusive, it is still rare to come across such hefty eco credentials (the realm of biomass heaters, not just botanical toiletries) so close to the cutting edge, particularly in the seemingly paradoxical field of eco luxury.

You'd need hours, if not days, to read the specifics of the Scarlet's environmental policies and its from-scratch architecture, but a few key points warrant highlighting. All power comes from renewable sources; carbon emissions are over 70% less than the average for a building of its size; grey water and rain water are both harvested; the ventilation heat exchange system removes the need for air-con; heating comes care of a wood-chip, carbon-neutral biomass boiler; and so the list goes on...

By any measure, the architecture is dazzlingly creative, achieving that much sought-after but rarely realised blending of building and landscape. An infinity pond at the entrance leads the eye seamlessly into the seascape behind; the natural outdoor swimming pool is strewn with granite boulders and cleaned by the reedbeds; reclaimed wood from Plymouth harbour creates the divisions between private terraces; and, best of all, two deep-red hot tubs stand outside on the cliff, silhouetted against the sea. Each of the 37 rooms has ocean views; splash out on one of the upper categories and you might get your own private garden, and a spiral staircase leading up to a little roof terrace. The styling is low-key luxe: think rich, tactile fabrics, statement light fittings and gorgeously sleek bathrooms.

At the helm in the restaurant is local chef Ben Tunnicliffe, who turned heads – including those of the Michelin Guide's inspectors – during his time at the Abbey in Penzance (*see p285*). While we wouldn't go quite so far as to call the food avant-garde, you should come expecting a sprinkling of surprises: peppered satsumas, say, or a strawberry tart with an olive base. This being an eco hotel, local ingredients take centre stage in dishes such as roast sea bass with nettle gnocchi and purple sprouting brocolli, or rabbit and damson stew with suet dumplings.

In a departure from standard high-dining attire, the staff wear Thai-style fisherman trousers and Clarks shoes, and there is a compellingly creative feel to the place. Like the rest of the hotel, the restaurant's decor would be stylish even for Soho – so for a distinctly unhip coastal community near Newquay, it's clean off the trendometer. Scarlet coloured textile lampshades and metal chairs patterned like tree branches set the tone, and there are glorious sunset views across the sea.

The lovely, lantern-lit Ayurvedic spa offers a naturally inspired menu of treatments, with refreshingly realistic aims (wellbeing, not wrinkle reduction) and hanging canvas pods for post-treatment cocooning. Throughout, there's an intelligent, conceptual feel to the place – the *Rough Guide to Happiness* takes the place of the Bible, engaging art hangs in public spaces, and the welcome book requests guests don't bark down their mobiles in communal areas. But there are a few unusual decisions that seem bound to frustrate: there is no reception area, just a grouping of fashionable sofas and a lot of confusion, and there's no Wi-Fi, in a didactic bid to induce you to relax (cables are available from reception). Overall, though, this is a deeply desirable hotel, and for many the very embodiment of 'new Cornwall': creative, sustainable and drenched in coastal cool.

Great surf accounts for a huge chunk of Newquay's visitors and also for some of the biggest summer events in the South-West, including the English National Surfing Championships and Relentless Boardmasters. The attraction here is not just the consistent swell, but also the sheer number and variety of surf beaches – making it possible to choose a beach to make best use of prevailing conditions. *See p228.*

The beaches

Tourist blurb often makes mention of Newquay's chain of 11 golden beaches. While the numbers depend a little on your definition of 'Newquay' and 'beach', there seems little point in splitting hairs: by anyone's measure, this short stretch of coast has an embarrassment of beaches.

In the town centre, Towan Beach, next to the harbour, is the busiest stretch of sand in high season, backed by watersports-hire outfits and beachside tat markets. Beyond the harbour, the road continues past the Huer's Hut to the Towan Head clifftop, where the views are terrific. On the west side of the headland is Little Fistral Beach, followed by Fistral Beach proper – a west facing strand that bears the full brunt of the Atlantic, where a 'surf's up' vibe prevails.

At the far end of the beach, East Pentire Head overlooks the Gannel Estuary as it noses out to sea. On the south side of the estuary – reached by ferry from the Pentire hamlet (10am-6pm daily, summer only) – the village of Crantock is a secluded suburb with a large, north-west facing beach, bordered by grassy dunes; close by, sandy Porth Joke is small and idyllic. Beyond the protrusion of the Kelsey Head, Holywell Bay is another popular stretch with parking, toilets and cafés, backed by the gentle peaks of a vast dune system.

Travelling north from Newquay harbour, Towan Beach makes way for Great Western, Tolcarne and Lusty Glaze (the latter being by far the best name for a beach we've ever heard), all of which join into one mile-long stretch at low tide. Tolcarne has been in and out of the news since 2003, when a proposal to build an artificial surf reef here was aired. That plan appears to have been blown out of the water by Newquay's bigger cheeses, much to the disappointment of the many wetsuited entrepreneurs who ply their trade here. In a new twist, as we went to press, Bournemouth was in the final stages of completing its own artificial reef, designed to turn out perfect waves – amid concerns in Cornish quarters that the Newquay surf scene would suffer as a result.

Porth Beach, with Porth Island at its northern side, was the site of an Iron Age settlement, and is linked to the mainland by a footbridge. It's quiet compared to Watergate Bay round the corner, but it does have ice-cream shops, toilets and cafés. Beyond Trevelgue Head, before reaching Watergate, is hidden Whipsiderry Beach, a quiet, rugged beach with access via steps in the cliff.

Newquay's most fashionable beach has to be Watergate Bay, a watersports resort and chic dining destination. Here, you can ride the waves and master the arts of kitesurfing, wave-skiing or paddle-surfing at the Extreme Academy (*see p221*), or simply watch the beach action through the wraparound windows at Jamie Oliver's Fifteen Cornwall (*see p221*) or the chilled-out Beach Hut (*see p221*), before crashing out at the hip hotel (*see p226*).

Bedruthan Steps & Mawgan Porth

Cornwall may be famous for its rocky coast, but Bedruthan Steps takes cragginess to new extremes. Here, the beach plays second fiddle to the towering rock stacks – some chiselled and pyramid-like, others resembling barnacle-encrusted turrets. According to legend, they were the stepping stones of a giant.

Surveyed from the top of the cliff, this is an intimidating spot; you can watch the scenery being carved before your eyes. As the ocean pummels the cliffs, new rocky outcrops are slowly formed by the constant crumbling. (In 1980, for instance, the distinctive crown of the Queen Bess rock stack was lost to the waves.) And so it follows that visitors are advised to steer clear of the cliff edges – both above and below – which are gradually collapsing. Closed from November to February, Cornwall's stormiest season, Bedruthan Steps is not for the faint-hearted, even in clement weather. The steep path down to the beach may induce vertigo, and the return journey will give your lungs a workout. Refreshment is on hand in a small National Trust café by the car park.

As you get swept away by the romance of it all, don't get swept away by the incoming waves – at high tide, much of the beach disappears. And don't even think about swimming or surfing here. Though a few hardened locals do bring their boards, they take their life in their hands: Bedruthan is very much a case of beauty with cruelty. The currents are treacherous and the rocks can be deadly.

If the stone staircase is too perilous, take in the scene from the coastal footpath above. Gentle on the legs yet with plenty of drama, the cliff-top walk between Carnewas Point and Park Head is superb, and the remains of Redcliff Castle – an Iron Age fort – are near the path.

Bedruthan Steps has but one hidden neighbour: Mawgan Porth, a sheltered, sandy beach resort tucked into the next valley, and a better bet for a proper day at the beach. It is also now home to the county's hottest new hotel, the eco-luxe Scarlet (*see left & p226*).

Where to eat & drink

Despite all the fuss surrounding the town's improbable gastrification after Jamie Oliver set up shop at Watergate Bay (well out of the circus of the town centre, we might add), Newquay town centre is decidedly unrewarding when it comes to food – burger bars, boozy curryhouses and Mexicans, fudge and ice-cream vans dominate.

An oasis of wholesomeness comes in the shape of the Fore Street Deli (40 Fore Street, 01637 851465, www.forestreetdeli.co.uk), near the

harbour. It's a lively delicatessen and wholefood shop, selling local cheeses, meat, pies and quiches, as well as takeaway tea and coffees (there are just two tiny tables outside).

Inland, in Summercourt, is Viners Bar & Restaurant (Carvynick, 01872 510544, www. vinersrestaurant.co.uk, closed Mon, lunch Tue-Sat). It's run by Kevin Viner, who was Cornwall's first chef to earn a Michelin star, some years back (at Pennypots in Falmouth). We'd recommend it more heartily if it weren't for the uninspiring setting, in the midst of a mobile home holiday park; the food, on the other hand, is very good, and the location is handy for the A30.

Keep an eye out for the new incarnation of the Lusty Glaze restaurant (Lusty Glaze Beach, 01637 879709, www.lustyglaze.co.uk/restaurant), due to reopen for the 2010 season as a laid-back beach bar with a modern British menu.

Beach Hut
Watergate Bay, TR8 4AA (01637 860877, www. watergatebay.co.uk). Food served 10am-4pm Mon-Thur, Sun; 10am-9pm Fri, Sat.
Downstairs from Fifteen, the family-friendly Beach Hut, once a bucket and spade shop, retains a lighthearted, beachside vibe. Being part of the über-slick Watergate Bay brand, it's a fashionable spot, with smart rattan chairs, stripped wooden floors and mood lighting. Nonetheless, staff won't bat an eyelid at the sight of sandy flip-flops or boardshorts. Fresh fish, Fowey river mussels, burgers, steak, salads and mugs of hot chocolate for après-surf comfort troughing are the order of the day, but a sprinkling of Asian dishes hit the spot too – our chicken and prawn laksa didn't shy away from serious spice. A wholesome children's menu runs from grilled free-range chicken with chips and peas to fish with new potatoes and peas, and there is a takeaway window – often with a snaking queue in high season – for those who want to picnic on the beach.

Fifteen Cornwall ★
Watergate Bay, TR8 4AA (01637 861000, www. fifteencornwall.co.uk). Breakfast served 8.30-10.30am, lunch served noon 4.30pm (last sitting 2.30pm), dinner served 6.15pm-midnight (last sitting 9.15pm) daily.
Despite mutterings from some quarters relating to hype and high prices, Fifteen Cornwall has proved a resounding success. Part of the Fifteen Foundation charity, and spearheaded by the indomitable Jamie Oliver, it employs 21 local people as student chefs, trained at Cornwall College. Even more impressive is the fact that 80% of the ingredients the chefs work with are sourced locally. Being devised by Mr Oliver, the menu has an Italianate feel, with original touches – courgette and goat's cheese risotto was pepped up by the citrus flavours of some locally foraged wild sorrel. Starters might include the likes of bruschetta of Cornish sardines and chargrilled squid with Amalfi lemon, with fisherman's stew or slow-cooked veal with polenta to follow.

Even those harbouring residual resentment about the stringent booking procedure (advance reservations are crucial) seem to find themselves caught up in the excitement. The young, friendly staff exude positive energy, and the peppy soundtrack and playful decor diffuse the tension associated with expensive dining. Add superb food and charitable foundations, and you can't help but leave smiling.

Things to do

NEWQUAY & AROUND
For more on the surf scene in Cornwall, including surf schools, *see p228*.

Adventure Centre
Lusty Glaze Beach, Lusty Glaze Road, Newquay, TR7 3AE (01637 872444, www.adventure-centre.org).
Turning Lusty Glaze beach into a giant adventure playground, this centre offers abseiling, rock climbing, surfing, coasteering and a spectacular zip wire across the beach. The Cliffhanger is Lusty Glaze's newest adrenaline-pumping activity, taking you on a high-rope traverse over crashing waves, caves and cliffs.

Cornwall Karting
St Eval, Pl27 7UN (01637 860160, www.cornwall karting.com). Open Mar-Oct 10am-6pm Mon-Sat. Nov-Feb hours vary; check the website for details. Admission from £22; £4 reductions.
The largest circuit in the south-west offers four circuits and five types of kart (catering for all ages, from three and up). Speed freaks will want to check out the pro karts, which max out at 70mph.

Extreme Academy
Watergate Bay, TR8 4AA (01637 860543, www.watergatebay.co.uk).
Watergate's adventure sport centre has wind- and wave-driven pursuits covered, with traction-kiting, kitebuggying, waveskiing and paddlesurfing, as well as good old-fashioned surfing. Alternatively, book an 'Extreme Day' to pack them in (£75 per person).

Lappa Valley Railways
St Newlyn East, Newquay, TR8 5LX (01872 510317, www.lappavalley.co.uk). Open Apr-Nov. Tickets £7- £9.50; £5.20-£7.80 reductions; £22-£30 family.
The stars of this family attraction, set in a wooded valley, are the miniature steam trains. Varying in size from the 15in-gauge Zebedee to the tiny, seven-inch-gauge petrol-powered Mardyke Miniature APT, they chuff around merrily, taking families from the café and pedal car track to the boating lake and crazy golf, then round to the play castle and brick path maze. The railway used to carry wagonloads of ore from the East Wheal Rose mine, which now houses an exhibition.

ST AGNES, PERRANPORTH & THE COAST
For more about cycling or walking the network of Mineral Tramways in the area, *see p183*.

Bike Barn
Elm Farm Cycle Centre, Cambrose, TR16 5UF (01209 891498, www.cornwallcycletrails.com). Open 10.30am-5.30pm daily. Cycle hire from £12.
This bike hire centre near Portreath, right on the Coast to Coast cycle trail, offers mountain bikes (some with suspension), tandems, child trailers and free parking.

Perranporth Golf Club
The Clubhouse, Budnic Hill, Perranporth, TR6 0AB (01872 572454, www.perranporthgolfclub.com). Open dawn-dusk daily. Rates from £34.
A scenic links course, on the cliffs above Perranporth.

Beach Hut. See p221.

Fistral Blu

Fistral Beach, Headland Road, Newquay, TR7 1HY
(01637 879444, www.fistral-blu.co.uk). Open/food served
Restaurant 9.30am-4.30pm Mon, Tue, Sun; 9.30am-late
Wed-Sat. Café 11am-6pm daily.

Fistral Beach is an exceedingly popular place, so it can be tricky snagging an early evening sunset and sea-view table at this laid-back restaurant and bar, located in the new Fistral Blu International Surf Centre. The café and fish and chip shop downstairs is accommodating at all times, however, serving breakfast, lunch, afternoon teas, Ben & Jerry's ice-creams and snacks to stoke beachgoers. The upstairs restaurant offers slightly fancier brasserie fare (surf 'n' turf, risottos, fish cakes), but this is a low-key, crowd pleasing spot throughout.

Lewinnick Lodge

Pentire Headland, Newquay, TR7 1NX (01637 878117,
www.lewinnick-lodge.info). Open 9am-11pm daily.
Breakfast served 9am-11.30am, lunch served noon-5pm,
dinner served 5-10pm.

There is hardly a shortage of restaurants in Cornwall with sea views, but there aren't many, if any, that allow you to wine and dine literally on the top of a cliff (practically overhanging the Atlantic, if you venture out on to the decking area). Although the exterior isn't particularly prepossessing, once inside this large bar-restaurant is a smart perch for dinner or drinks, with contemporary decor, a sunny soundtrack, cut-above Med-influenced brasserie fare and huge cliff-top views from the Pentire Headland. Prices are accessible, and the wind-in-the-hair feeling makes it worthy of a stop. It's also accessible via the footpath from Fistral Beach.

Scarlet

Tredragon Road, Mawgan Porth, TR8 4DQ (01637
861800, www.scarlethotel.co.uk). Lunch served noon-
2pm, dinner served 7-9.30pm daily.

You'll find accomplished cooking and top-notch local ingredients at this hotel/restaurant, Cornwall's newest eco-conscious epicentre of cool (*see p218*).

Where to stay

With the exception of the Headland Hotel and the Bay (for both, *see right*), central Newquay has a distinct dearth of classy accommodation. Instead, it's mainly given over to grotty guesthouses and budget surf lodges (crashpads involving bunk beds, cramped conditions and low prices).

Probably the most upmarket of the lodges is the Reef Surf Lodge (10-12 Berry Road, 01637 879058, www.reefsurflodge.info), with flatscreen tellies beaming out surf videos, and a bar area;

meanwhile, Base Surf Lodge (20 Tower Road, 01637 874852, www.basesurflodge.com) overlooks Fistral Beach. A guesthouse alternative to the rowdy surf lodge scene is an en suite room at Trewinda Lodge (17 Eliot Gardens, 01637 877533, www.trewindalodge.co.uk), whose owners also run the Dolphin Surf School (01637 873707, www.surfschool.co.uk) next door.

The Bay
Esplanade Road, Pentire, Newquay, TR7 1PT (01637 852221, www.newquay-hotels.co.uk). Rates £60-£130 double incl breakfast.
Recently revamped at great expense, and incorporating the Fistral Spa, the Bay is now Newquay's smoothest mid-range choice. In an elevated position on the Pentire Headland, nicely removed from the scrum of Newquay proper, the Bay has 90 rooms. The best rooms feature oversized bathtubs looking out over the sweep of Fistral Beach; bring binoculars to get a close-up of the surfers cruising in or wiping out. The grey exterior doesn't inspire, but inside the decor is contemporary, and the staff attentive and on the ball. The 'check in and chill out' spa packages clearly appeal to couples, who kick off their stay with an Espa body massage and a snooze in the low-lit relaxation area. A few doors down, the Esplanade Hotel (01637 873333) is the Bay's family-oriented sister establishment, and home to the Quiksilver Surf School.

Beach Retreats
01637 861005, www.beachretreats.co.uk.
Rates from £202 for 3 nights.
If the lace curtains and earthenware jugs of mainstream Cornish holiday homes don't do it for you, browse the 60 polished properties on the books at this north coast self-catering specialist. Some of its houses and apartments feature such luxuries as a pool, jacuzzi, barbecue area or domed ceilings – but even on a lower budget you can count on clean, stylish decor. Locations include Watergate Bay, Porth, Fistral, Mawgan Porth and the Camel Estuary.

Bedruthan Steps Hotel
Mawgan Porth, TR8 4BU (01637 860555, www. bedruthan.com). Rates £158-£262 double incl breakfast & dinner.
In the age of rampant greenwashing, it's getting harder to separate eco-chat ('We try to use locally sourced ingredients where possible.') from eco-commitment ('We guarantee that 70% of the produce used in our restaurant is locally sourced.'). The Bedruthan Steps Hotel, occupying an enviable cliff-top perch between Newquay and Padstow, falls into the latter category, putting its money – three million pounds, to be precise – where its mouth is to become the first independent hotel in the country to bag the toughest green accreditation of all: the serious-sounding ISO 14001. What makes this feat all the more impressive is that the team aren't running a dinky boutique B&B, but a four-star resort hotel with 101 bedrooms, a 280-seat restaurant, a bar, a spa (with steam rooms, treatments, a sauna and pool), tennis courts and conference facilities.

Bedruthan's child-friendly credentials are almost as momentous. Widely considered to be one of the UK's most family-friendly hotels, it has a variety of indoor and outdoor play areas and no less than five Ofsted-inspected children's clubs (for which extra charges apply). Children and babies can take tea separately from the aged Ps, and there is also a family dining area.

Harbour Hotel
North Quay Hill, Newquay, TR7 1HF (01637 873040, www.harbourhotel.co.uk). Rates £120-£140 double incl breakfast.
Five en suite rooms with balconies make the most of the Harbour's enviable location, looking out into Newquay Bay. The decor goes in for traditional aesthetics, with a scattering of antiques and iron bedsteads, but whatever it looked like you'd be spending most of your time surveying the view. A welcome oasis of calm, directed at the chardonnay rather than alcopop crowd.

Headland Hotel
Fistral Beach, Newquay, TR7 1EW (01637 872211, www.headlandhotel.co.uk). Rates £99-£209 double incl breakfast.
Looming over Little Fistral Cove from its own promontory, this imposing hotel may look familiar, thanks to its role in the unsettling film adaptation of Roald Dahl's *The Witches*. But despite its size, Victorian grandeur and purported ghosts, there's nothing sinister about Carolyn and John Armstrong's hotel. Service is friendly, the guestrooms are classically elegant and the views inspirational. The Headland has ten acres of grounds, as well as two heated pools, a sauna, a small gym, snooker, croquet and a nine-hole golf approach course and putting green. Alongside

Watergate Bay. See p219.

the hotel is a 'village' of 40 nicely appointed holiday cottages (think contemporary but cosy interiors) overlooking Newquay Bay and Little Fistral beach. The cottages can be rented for a minimum of three nights and enjoy access to the hotel's facilities.

Sands Resort Hotel
Watergate Road, Porth, TR7 3LZ (01637 872864, www.sandsresort.co.uk). Rates £100-£156 double incl breakfast.

With the sandy pleasures of Porth Beach to the fore, rolling green farmland aft and vast tracts of play area in the middle, Sands is well positioned and equipped to keep holidaying families happy. This gives it the air of a holiday village rather than a top banana hotel, but the children won't be complaining as they work their way through the treats and diversions laid on for them. Sands is a big, bright block of a hotel, with a playground, mini golf, a large outdoor pool, a maze and tennis courts out back. Inside are games rooms, playrooms, an indoor pool, various lounge areas, an entertainments hall called the Atlantic Suite and a large, canteen-like restaurant. During school holidays, guests can arrange for their kids to be whisked away and organised into Ofsted-inspected clubs, divided by age. While their progeny are thus diverted, grown-ups can let their hair down at the Ocean Breeze Spa, where treatments run from quick manicures to unhurried massages.

Scarlet ★
Tredragon Road, Mawgan Porth, TR8 4DQ (01637 861800, www.scarlethotel.co.uk). Rates £180-£395 double incl breakfast.

Newquay's hippest hotel is the place to sample luxurious eco-living (*see p218*).

Watergate Bay Hotel ★
Watergate Bay, TR8 4AA (01637 860543, www.watergatebay.co.uk). Rates £103-£180 double incl breakfast.

The grand old Victorian exterior of the hotel at Watergate Bay now conceals a series of super-chic rooms and suites, decorated in hip beach-house style with solid oak floors and juicy pink pinstripes, as well as luxurious extras such as Wi-Fi, plasma screen tellies, DVD players, MP3 player docks, L'Occitane freebies and thick towelling robes. The Coach House has decidedly smaller, less la-di-da suites with no views, as a budget option.

One of the original players in the child-friendly hotel game, Watergate provides all sorts of school holiday activities (animal encounters, discos, arts and crafts), as well as heated pools, tennis and squash, and indoor games rooms. Younger children can have an early supper and bedtime, while parents dine later while tuning into the baby listening service. On site, there's the Living Space bar-café, with its huge, sea-facing terrace and laid-back food, or the smarter Brasserie. A few paces away are the Beach Hut or, for a blowout, Fifteen Cornwall – both of which fall under the Watergate Bay brand. The Extreme Academy surf school and surf equipment hire (for all, *see p221*) are also part of the resort. With so many bases covered, you may struggle to find reasons to leave the bay.

REDRUTH & CAMBORNE
The advent of cool Cornwall has, for better or for worse, completely bypassed Redruth and Camborne. Those chasing chic retreats or celebrity chefs will find nothing to detain them in these parts, but as the capital of the once-mighty Cornish mining

Wheal Coates Tin Mine. See p230.

Places to visit

NEWQUAY & AROUND

Blue Reef Aquarium
Towan Promenade, Newquay, TR7 1DU (01637 878134, www.bluereefaquarium.co.uk). Open Mar-Oct 10am-5pm daily. Nov-Feb 10am-4pm daily. Admission £8.95; £6.95-£7.95 reductions; £30 family.
These days, every seaside resort worth its salt has an aquarium for rainy days and, to its credit, Newquay's is a modern, child-friendly affair. Highlights of the 'undersea safari' include the jellyfish nursery; the displays of captive-bred species, such as clownfish and seahorses; Turtle Creek and Turtle Rescue; and, most excitingly, the Underwater Tunnel. Local marine life is also bigged up, with mock-ups of rocky Cornish habitats created for lobsters, spider crabs, gurnards, pipefish and conger eels.

Dairyland Farm World
Near Newquay (A3058), TR8 5AA (01872 510246, www.dairylandfarmworld.com). Open Apr-Oct 10am-5pm daily. Admission £8.35; free-£6.60 reductions; £34.50 family.
Dairyland was born in 1975, when the Davy family, owners of Tresilian Barton Farm, decided to upgrade their milk production using a form of milking parlour pioneered in America, called the Rotary. A source of fascination for the public, the milking parlour attracted increasing numbers of visitors and became the UK's first farm-themed tourist attraction. Today, there's an indoor fun centre as well as playgrounds, climbing nets, pat-a-pet, pony riding, animal feeding and pet parades – not to mention the farm museum, nature trail and gift shop. For all this, the attraction still centres on the working dairy farm, and the milking demonstration educates supermarket-nourished children.

Newquay Zoo
Trenance Gardens, Newquay, TR7 2LZ (01637 873342, www.newquayzoo.org.uk). Open 10am-5pm daily. Admission £10.95; £8.25 reductions.
Opened in 1969 as a pets' corner in the ornamental gardens, Newquay Zoo was a small and undistinguished affair until about a decade ago, when new ownership and redevelopment upped the ante. It's now a much-loved small zoo, with a strong conservation and captive breeding programme for red pandas, pied tamarins, Humboldt penguins and lynx, among others. The tropical house contains a slice of jungle that can be viewed both from ground- and first-floor level; every so often, a man-made rainstorm deluges it to keep it steamy. New for 2009 was the Philippines species area, where spotted deer and curious-looking warty pigs, both endangered species, make themselves at home, and the three-acre African Savannah exhibit, where zebra, wildebeest and nyala antelopes roam.

Trerice
Kestle Mill, nr Newquay, TR8 4PG (01637 875404, www.nationaltrust.org.uk/trerice). Open Mar-Oct 11am-5pm Mon-Thur, Sat, Sun. Admission £7.40; £3.70 reductions; £18.20 family.
Down a winding country lane, a few miles inland from Newquay, the Elizabethan country manor house of Trerice and its sleepy, sheltered grounds is an idyllic scene. Beyond the Dutch-gabled, limestone façade are a series of handsome rooms filled with portraits and tapestries, including the Great Hall, with a musicians' gallery where players could be heard but not seen. The Great Barn café at the back is an attractive space.

REDRUTH & CAMBORNE

Cornish Mines & Engines
Pool, TR15 3NP (01209 315027, www.nationaltrust.org.uk/main/w-cornishminesandengines). Open Mar-Nov 11am-5pm Mon, Wed-Fri, Sun (open Sat July, Aug). Admission £6.40; £3.20 reductions; £16 family.
Despite the uninspiring approach through a Morrisons car park, the hulking engine-houses at this historically significant visitor attraction stand in the heartland of Cornish mining. Inside, you can get up close to the Cornish steam-powered beam engine, invented by local boy Richard Trevithick; at over 52 tonnes, it's an arresting piece of equipment. Across the road you can watch one in motion (visible for free from the road), now powered by electricity. Narrated with a tone of Cornish pride, the short film on hard-rock mining shown in the low-key Heritage Centre acts as a reminder that this run-down area, now the butt of many a local joke, was once one of the most innovative and prosperous industrial areas in the world. Richard Trevithick's cottage is in nearby Penponds (open Wed 2-5pm).

King Edward Mine
Troon, Camborne, TR14 9HW (01209 614681, www.kingedwardmine.co.uk). Open May-Sept 10am-5pm, days vary. Admission £5; £1 reductions. No credit cards.
Up until a few years ago, this site was used by the Camborne School of Mines as a training mine and, as a result, it is one of the oldest intact mining complexes in Cornwall. There is an old-fashioned but absorbing museum, a guided tour of the machinery in action in the mill – some of the last such examples in the world – and a small shop. The site is also home to the Mineral Tramways Heritage Project, a network of cycling trails, and the starting point for the circular, seven-and-a-half-mile Great Flat Lode Trail.

ST AGNES, PERRANPORTH & THE COAST

Outside St Agnes, the Blue Hills Tin Stream (Wheal Kitty, 01872 553341, www.bluehillstin.com, closed Sun, closed Nov-Easter) visitor centre recreates early methods of tin smelting and casting.

Healey's Cornish Cyder Farm
Penhallow, Truro, TR4 9LW (01872 573356, www.thecornishcyderfarm.co.uk). Open Apr-Dec daily. Jan-Mar Mon-Fri. Times vary; check website for details. Admission free. Tours £6.50; £4.50 reductions.
As well as being the place to stock up on Cornish Rattler (Cornwall's most popular cider), apple brandy, fruit wines and scrumpy of varying strengths, all made on site, the Cyder Farm is a cheery visitor attraction. You'll have to pay for the full distillery tour and museum, and the tractor ride around the orchards, but the pretty courtyard, farmyard, shire horse stables, jam room and Mowhay café-restaurant are open to all. Just down the road, Callestick Farm (01872 573126, www.callestickfarm.co.uk, free), of ice-cream fame, is open to visitors in summer.

industry, a hotbed of industrial innovation, and for a taste of the 'real' Cornwall, the area merits further investigation.

During the 1850s this was a hugely important mining area, at one point producing some two-thirds of the world's copper. However, the discovery of cheaper deposits of ore overseas at the end of the 19th century heralded the start of the decline of Cornish mining, and a steep drop in the area's fortunes. Evidence of the region's mining heritage is everywhere; following the once-profitable underground mineral lodes, the landscape is dotted with granite stacks, engine houses and old industrial buildings. Most are derelict, but some have been turned into fascinating heritage centres (*see p227*).

Self-evident, too, are the signs that the conurbation of Camborne, Redruth and Pool now has some of the lowest incomes in the country. One particularly poignant reminder of the area's struggling economy is the graffiti scrawled on the walls outside the closed South Crofty mine, the words taken from Robert Bryant's folk song: 'Well Cornish lads are fishermen/And Cornish lads are miners too/But when the fish and tin are gone/What are the Cornish boys to do?'. South Crofty (not open to the public) was the last Cornish mine to close in the late 1990s, leaving hundreds jobless. Plans to reopen the mine have been aired over the past few years, although debate rumbles on. In the meantime, the £29 million Heartlands project has been awarded to the area, with the aim of creating a vast cultural park and rebooting the local economy.

Aside from some dignified civic architecture and a handsome old Cornish thoroughfare in the shape of Redruth's Fore Street, the streets of Redruth and Camborne – lined with lacklustre low-cost chains and charity shops – provide few reasons to dawdle. More cultural interest can be found in the historical sites out-of-town: the National Trust-owned Cornish Mines & Engines and the King Edward Mine (for both, *see p227*). Then there's the Mineral Tramways project – a network of old industrial tram and rail routes that are perfect for traffic-free biking or walking (*see p183*).

Beyond the towns, the moorland is bracing, with wrecked engine houses and swathes of bracken creating a desolate scene. Dominating the whole region is the ragged, boulder-strewn summit of Carn Brea, 738 feet above sea level. One of Cornwall's most stirring yet seldom-visited vantage points, it is crowned by a towering Celtic cross, visible from miles around, and a slightly surreal folly castle (home to a Middle Eastern restaurant in the evenings).

The life of local inventor Richard Trevithick (1771-1833), is celebrated on Trevithick Day, on the last Saturday in April. Trevithick was the creator of the first beam engine, allowing the mining of much deeper shafts.

Where to eat & drink
Redruth and Camborne offer few, if any, restaurants of note. For a supremely bohemian café-bar in Redruth, call by the Melting Pot (West Park, 07915

TEN TOP SURF SPOTS

Fistral Beach
Fistral Beach in Newquay is a long, straight beach, whose consistent waves have made it a popular spot for surfers. It's home to the British Surfing Association, the Newquay Surf Life Saving Club and the Newquay Boardrider Club, and is also known for its international competitions and surf museum. Fistral Surf School (01792 360370, www.fistral surfschool.co.uk) caters for all levels.

Gwithian
The surf breaks very slowly at this gently sloping beach, located at the northernmost point of St Ives Bay. With rideable surf year-round and relatively warm waters, it's a good spot for novices. Contact Gwithian Academy of Surfing (01736 755493, 01736 757579, www.surfacademy.co.uk) for lessons.

Harlyn Bay
This large, crescent-shaped beach near Padstow, backed by dunes, has a good expanse of sand at low tide and is a safe place to learn the ropes, with tuition from Harlyn Surf School (01841 533076, www.harlynsurfschool.co.uk, closed Nov-Mar). In summer, the lack of swell might deter the more advanced.

Holywell Bay
This tranquil, clean, family-orientated spot – the National Trust's flagship beach – has some of the best surf in Cornwall, without the crowds of nearby Newquay. Hone your technique at the Holywell Bay School of Surf (01872 510233, www.holywellbayschoolofsurf.com, closed Nov-mid May).

Perranporth
Ten miles south of Newquay's beaches, and much less crowded, Perranporth has long stretches of sand and a good variety of waves. The Perranporth Surf School (07974 550823, www.perranporthsurf school.co.uk) can provide instruction, and lifeguards man the beach between May and September.

252757, www.themeltingpotonline.co.uk, closed Sat, Sun). Part of local arts and studio space Krowji (www.krowji.co.uk), it's decorated in an appealingly eclectic manner, with old red-velvet cinema seats. Good, traditional pasties don't come much better than at Berrymans (www.cornish-pasty.co.uk), a third-generation-owned bakery with outposts in Redruth, Camborne and Perranporth.

Where to stay
Redruth and Camborne come up very short on good hotels. Your best bet in Redruth town centre is probably the comfortable but stiflingly old-fashioned Penventon Park Hotel (West End, 01209 203000, www.penventon.co.uk); otherwise, head out to the coast for better picks.

ST AGNES, PERRANPORTH & THE COAST
The coast north of Redruth and Camborne is dotted with popular surfing beaches, notably Porthtowan, a small community with an excellent, wide beach that's also home to the invariably buzzing Blue bar (see p230). Nearby, the old mining harbour village of Portreath – which once shipped out thousands of tonnes of copper ore to Wales for smelting – is now an unassuming place, in possession of a sandy beach and a scattering of surf shops and cafés; most tourists, however, know it as the start or finish of the Coast to Coast cycle trail, part of the Mineral Tramways project (see p182).

St Agnes & Chapel Porth
The largest settlement on this stretch of coast is a few miles east at St Agnes, a fishing village that grew in significance in the late 18th century, when the harbour at Trevaunance Cove began exporting copper and tin, and importing coal for the local mines. A model of the harbour is among the historical exhibits on display at the one-room St Agnes Museum (Penwinnick Road, 01872 553228, closed Nov-Easter).

Today's straggling town, half a mile inland, centres around the Victorian parish church and a chummy squeeze of galleries, shops (butcher, baker, post office, groceries) and cottages. A little further down is Stippy Stappy hill, beloved of photographers for its steep row of wisteria-clad stone cottages.

At St Agnes's small but dramatic Trevaunance Cove, there is a tangible sense of the force of nature. The stony remains of a harbour embedded in the cliff – the last of five harbours built here, all eventually obliterated by winter storms – can be seen to the left, and crumbling granite cliffs loom high overhead. It's a popular surfing spot, with a couple of cafés down on the shore and the lively Driftwood Spars pub (see p230).

To gain some perspective on the impressive landscape, climb up to the heathery summit of the St Agnes Beacon (629 feet) for one of Cornwall's best views. Beyond the steep cliffs of Porthtowan

Porthleven
Located north of Kynance Cove, between Land's End and Lizard Point, Porthleven is one for experts and hardcore locals, and is known for having the best reef break in the country. It can be a dangerous place for novices, however.

Praa Sands
One of West Cornwall's most popular beaches, Praa Sands has an appealingly unpretentious vibe – and is the proud host of the World Crap Surfing Championships, usually held in December. Surfers are catered for by Stones Reef Surf Shop (01736 762991) on the beach, and by a lively après-surf scene.

Sennen Cove
A stone's throw from Land's End, Sennen Cove is a stronghold of free surfing – the belief that grace and fun define a surfer, rather than competitive success – and is good for both beginners and serious surfers. Lessons and board hire are available from Sennen Surfing Centre (01736 871227, www.sennensurfing centre.com, closed Nov-Mar) and the Smart Surf School (01736 871817, www.smartsurf.co.uk).

Whitsand Bay
In south-east Cornwall, Whitsand Bay has sheer, lofty cliffs, dramatic scenery and extensive stretches of sandy beaches, suited to beginners and intermediates. Discovery Surf School (07813 639622, www.discoverysurf. com) runs classes here in summer (mainly July and August).

Widemouth Bay
In North Cornwall, three miles south of Bude, Widemouth Bay offers varied conditions and is frequented by beginners and intermediates, who aren't quite ready to tackle the largest waves. Raven Surf School (01288 353693, www.raven surf.co.uk), set up by former surfing champion Mike Raven, offers instruction here, and at nearby Summerleaze Beach in Bude. RNLI lifeguards patrol its sands in high season.

and Portreath – drizzly days excepted – you can make out the dark lump of Godrevy Head and even St Ives, a staggering 22 miles west. From here, you also get a good view of the remains of the Wheal Coates tin mine, embedded in the cliffs and with its engine house silhouetted against the sea. Probably the most scenically placed of all the mine stacks on Cornwall's coast, or at least the most photographed, this old tin mine can also be seen up close from the coastal path just east of Chapel Porth, against a vivid purple heather backdrop.

The nearby beach at Chapel Porth is something of a secluded gem, completely undeveloped save for a tiny National Trust café, serving, among other simple fare, a famed hedgehog ice-cream cone – a fantastically calorific affair involving a thick layer of clotted cream and a coating of chopped roasted hazelnuts. Low tide opens up huge stretches of sand to the east and west, but take care not to get cut off as the tide rises. Each year in September, Chapel Porth hosts the World Bellyboard Championships. A niche event in which retro wooden boards are ridden with no wetsuit, no leash and no fins, it's free to enter and open to all.

Perranporth

Architecturally, the holiday town of Perranporth is a less than alluring sight; a sprawling mass of chalets, bungalows, new-builds and older terraces, joined by chippies, kebab shops and brassy pubs. But it's worth pushing past first impressions and on to the vast expanse of smooth golden sands beyond – which, at low tide, stretches several miles around Perran Bay to the west. Surf is good here, with the bay receiving steady swell – in particular at Penhale Sands, at the north end of the bay.

Where to eat & drink

Fistral beach

Blue

Eastcliff, Beach Road, Porthtowan, TR4 8AD (01209 890329, www.blue-bar.co.uk). Open 10am-11pm Mon-Fri, Sun; 10am-midnight Sat. Food served noon-9pm Mon-Fri; 10am-9pm Sat, Sun. (Closed dinner Mon, Tue in winter.)

Burrowed into the dunes at Porthtowan, Blue has the rare pedigree of being a locals' hangout that is popular year round. Serving post-surf comfort food par excellence, in the shape of burgers, stone-baked pizzas, beer-battered pollock and chunky chips, it also draws crowds for its weekend gig nights. The alcoves built into the front give views on to the beach and out to sea, and there's also a beachside terrace. The feel is youthful and laid-back, but it attracts the surfer-haired of all ages.

Driftwood Spars

Trevaunance Cove, St Agnes, TR5 0RT (01872 552428, www.driftwoodspars.com). Lunch served Apr-Oct noon-2.30pm, dinner served 6.30-9.30pm daily. (Closed dinner Mon, Tue, Sun Nov-Mar.)

An honourable classic, the Driftwood – down by the beach at St Agnes – is a sprawling and perennially lively old inn dating back to the 17th century. Its array of rooms and

nooks mean you can, to a degree, choose your vibe: cosy pints in the dark-beamed old bar downstairs, games of pool next door or lunch with sea views in the hotel's bright, pine-filled upstairs restaurant. The same menu of solid pub classics and fish dishes is served throughout. Several of the pub's own microbrews are on tap at any given time; bottles are also sold at the Into the Brew shop opposite. The Driftwood hosts a beer festival every year – check online for details.

Schooners Bistro

Trevaunance Cove, St Agnes, TR5 0RY (01872 553149). Open/food served phone for details.

The straight line of brown leather bucket chairs by the bar, all facing seawards, seems like a logical design reponse to this sort of view – Schooners is bang on the beach at Trevaunance Cove, looking directly out to sea and the surf action. The nautically themed upstairs restaurant is smarter, venturing into more upmarket territory, but downstairs and on the terrace there's an ambience of post-surf informality, with worn wooden floors, order-at-the-bar service and warming hot chocolate with marshmallows. A simple daytime menu (ham, egg and chips, crab sandwiches, tapas) keeps everything under a tenner.

Watering Hole

Perranporth Beach, Perranporth, TR6 0JL (01872 572888, www.the-wateringhole.co.uk). Open 9am-11pm Fri Sun.

Perranporth's venerable beachside venue stands in the middle of the Perran's wide sands. There is a menu of standard-issue bar food – burgers, steaks, Mexican beach fillers – but this is more of a beer-at-sunset spot. The views are fantastic, and this is just about as close to the sand as you can get.

Where to stay

In St Agnes, the Driftwood Spars (*see left*) has decent-value rooms with not-so-subtle nautical theming, and the St Agnes Hotel (Churchtown, 01872 552307, www.st-agnes-hotel.co.uk) has six neutral-toned en suite guestrooms at budget prices in the heart of the village.

More upmarket is the Rose-in-Vale (Mithian, 01872 552202, www.rose-in-vale-hotel.co.uk), an idyllic Georgian country manor hotel with formal, flowery furnishings and a candlelit restaurant, set in 11 acres of wooded grounds.

Aramay

Aramay House, Quay Road, St Agnes, TR5 0RP (01872 553546, www.thearamay.com). Rates £90-£105 double incl breakfast.

This spritely new addition sets itself apart from St Agnes's more traditional (read chintzy) B&B options. The Aramay feels more like a small hotel in atmosphere and price, thanks to a reception desk, a chic breakfast room and high-spec bedrooms (32-inch TVs, quality linens, bathrobe and slippers). Its location places you midway between the beach and the village.

Beacon Cottage Farm

Beacon Drive, St Agnes, TR5 0NU (01872 552347, www.beaconcottagefarmholidays.co.uk). Open Apr-Sept. Rates £15-£21 per night for 2 people.

On the lower slopes of the St Agnes Beacon, not far from the cliffs, this campsite has uninterrupted vistas across miles of dramatic Cornish coastline – so the potential for a pitch with a view is high. The facilities are excellent and the crowd generally quiet and respectful, leaving just the sound of the wind racing across the moor to sing you to sleep, and the birds to wake you up. Chapel Porth, some 15 minutes on foot via the coastal path, is the nearest beach.

Falmouth & the Roseland

The surf lessons, blustery cliffs and stag-do image of holidays in Cornwall may dominate the headlines, but the creeks, inlets and coves in and around the Carrick Roads estuary are another world – quietly beautiful, romantic and largely untouched. The merging of rivers, protected from the Atlantic swell by the protrusion of the Lizard Peninsula, has created endless watery escapes: silent wooded creeks, soft-sanded beaches hidden from view and rolling green hills that dip gently into the sea. With the villages of the Roseland also painting an idyllic picture, thanks to their well-kept white cottages, miniature harbours and traditional pubs, it all amounts to a powerful tranquilliser for stressed souls.

The wide waterway dividing Falmouth and the Roseland Peninsula is the world's third largest natural harbour (after Rio de Janeiro and Sydney), and countless ships and sails dot the horizon. Overseeing the entrance is the lively town of Falmouth, currently enjoying its new-found status as Cornwall's most happening town.

FALMOUTH

The town

Seat of the county's first and only university, hotly tipped as Cornwall's boom town and home to the new-this-millennium National Maritime Museum (*see p240*), Falmouth has the feel of a town that's on its way up.

Where other Cornish seaside towns tend towards old-fashioned bucket-and-spade charm or cutesy chic (St Ives, Padstow, Fowey), Falmouth has a more youthful, cosmopolitan air, thanks in large part to the creation of University College Falmouth, which specialises in arts, design and media. There's now a plethora of hip bars and cafés, and a full calendar of festivals and events; as this guide went to press, Rick Stein was set to launch his first West Cornwall restaurant (a fish and chip restaurant, with oyster bar) in Discovery Quay.

Until the 17th century, however, Falmouth was little more than a fishing village. Penryn, two miles to the north-west, was the main town, with Pendennis Castle protecting the mouth of the river. Established as the chief base for the Packet Ships in 1689, which took the first international mail to the Continent and the colonies, Falmouth developed quickly, and its huge natural harbour – the first or last stop before heading out or back across the Atlantic, and a safe haven in bad weather – sealed the town's fortunes.

From the modern, piazza-like Discovery Quay and Events Square, home to the National Maritime Museum, the road narrows into charming Arwenack Street, with its pretty Georgian façades, via the attractive granite Church of King Charles the Martyr (whose palm-framed square tower, overlooking the harbour, features on many a postcard), before becoming Church Street.

At the far end of town, after the usual chain stores, mobile phone shops and estate agents, is the charismatic old High Street. Here you can browse galleries, antique shops and second-hand stores. Buy beautiful bread at Stones Bakery (07791 003183, www.stonesbakery.co.uk, closed Mon, Sun); drink coffee and flick through the records at Jam (*see p235*); or head for the cobbled enclave of Old Brewery Yard, home to Cinnamon Girl (*see p235*) and the Tap Room (*see p235*).

On the Moor, a large, continental-style square that serves as both marketplace and bus terminal, is another testament to the town's strong artistic identity: the award-winning Falmouth Art Gallery (01326 313863, www.falmouthartgallery.com, closed Sun). It houses original works by major 19th- and 20th-century artists – including Alfred Munnings, HS Tuke, JM Waterhouse and Henry Moore – and also features contemporary art exhibitions. It's very family-friendly, with automata, a papier mâché show and children's workshops.

Opposite are the 111 steps of Jacob's Ladder, which ascend the large hill above the town. The steps have no real biblical association – they were installed by Jacob Hamblen, a builder and property owner, to facilitate access between his business (at the bottom) and some of his property (at the top). Once you get your breath back, follow the road to the left around the brow of the hill for a fabulous panorama over the town and across the bay. You can take it all in over a quiet pint at the Seaview Inn (Wodehouse Terrace, 01326 311359, www.seaviewfalmouth.co.uk).

Out on the promontory stands Pendennis Castle, built at the same time (1543) as its twin St Mawes (for both, *see p240*), a mile across the estuary. Just below, a road runs all around the point, taking in the docks on the way. In 1860, the foundation of Falmouth Docks created a focus for maritime industries, and an extensive ship repair and maintenance industry. Beneath the road that leads around the point, a number of narrow paths weave between the rocks, trees and remains of defensive batteries. The castle road then takes you to the town's three main sandy beaches, which have clear waters and views of the bay: Blue Flag-winning Gyllyngvase is the nearest to town, with Swanpool and Maenporth stretching out to the south (all have public facilities and cafés, and are ideal for families).

In season, consider doing away with parking headaches and use the Ponsharden Park & Float (01326 319417, 01872 861910, www.kingharrys cornwall.co.uk, closed Nov-Apr), which takes you down the Penryn River by boat, all the way to the quay in the centre of Falmouth.

The Carrick Roads is home to the last remaining oyster fishery in Europe that is still dredged under sail and oar, with traditional boats working between October and March. The beginning of the season is celebrated every October with the Falmouth Oyster Festival.

Around Falmouth

Effectively conjoined to Falmouth, but once a harbour town in its own right, Penryn has changed considerably since the foundation of the university

here. Where you might once have found odd charity shops in which to rummage, you are now more likely to stumble across an offbeat interiors boutique, a gallery or a deli along its narrow main street. Down on the water, new eco development Jubilee Wharf houses Miss Peapods bar-café (*see p237*). Before leaving Penryn, pick up some multi-award-winning smoked fish and cheese down by the river at the Cornish Smokehouse (Islington Wharf, 01326 376244, www.cornishcuisine.co.uk, open Wed-Fri).

Across the Penryn river from Falmouth are the attractive and affluent yacht-heavy villages of Flushing and Mylor, accessible by ferry from Falmouth. The Long Close Farm Shop (Tregew Road, 01326 373706, www.tregewfarm.co.uk) in Flushing is excellent for seasonal vegetables.

Pendower beach. See p241.

The serene waters and exotic gardens of the north bank of the Helford River – around five miles to the south of town – are also easily reached from Falmouth; see p259.

Where to eat & drink

There are bars, restaurants and cafés around every corner in Falmouth. As well as those reviewed in full below, we also recommend Jam (32 High Street, 01326 211722, www.jamrecords.co.uk, closed Sun & Mon Jan-June), a café in a record shop; Cinnamon Girl (4-6 Old Brewery Yard, 01326 211457), a friendly organic café with great food, and outdoor tables in a cobbled yard; and, also in Old Brewery Yard, the Tap Room (01326 319888, closed Sun), a small Berlin-esque cocktail bar with a vintage feel, good for late-night drinks and music.

Our pick of the fish and chip outlets is Harbour Lights (Arwenack Street, 01326 316934, www.harbourlights.co.uk), a restaurant and takeaway; it's cheery and clean, staff will grill fish on request – and children get their meals in 'beach buckets'.

Watering holes near the water include the Front (Custom House Quay, 01326 212168, www.thefrontfalmouth.co.uk), a small bar on the quay that has a thriving music programme (including Cornish folk nights), and a vast selection of rum and ale; Harvey's Wharf (01326 314351, www.harveys-wharf.co.uk), a smart bar and brasserie on Discovery Quay; and the Shed (Discovery Quay, 01326 318502), a colourful, kitschy bar and restaurant, and one of the few places in Falmouth to catch the evening sun.

As we went to press, fish restaurant Indaba on the Beach (www.indabafish.co.uk) was poised to open in the old Three Mackerel premises, perched above Swanpool Beach.

Cove Restaurant & Bar

Maenporth Beach, TR11 5HN (01326 251136, www.thecovemaenporth.co.uk). Open Summer 11am-11pm daily. Winter 11am-3pm, 6-11pm Tue-Fri; 11am-11pm Sat; noon-11.30pm Sun. Food served Summer noon-9.30pm daily. Winter noon-2.30pm, 6.30-9.30pm Tue-Fri, Sun; noon-5pm, 6.30-9.30pm Sat.

This friendly, stylish restaurant, a few paces from the shore at Maenporth, has a café and tapas menu for beach breaks, along with more substantial lunches and dinners. The short but creative menu changes every six to eight weeks to make the most of local ingredients, especially seafood (Falmouth Bay scallops, for instance, or Cornish sole steamed with coriander and lemongrass). There are some well thought out options for vegetarians too, such as red onion and pear tarte tatin with feta and endive salad. The large terrace has gorgeous views over the beach, and the decor is tasteful and minimalist. Off-season, there are regular culinary masterclasses (fish, game, chocolate), which cost from as little as £12.95 per person.

Eight Bar

8 Webber Street, Falmouth, TR11 3AU (07767 838846, www.eight-bar.co.uk). Open 8pm-3am Mon-Sat (last entry 1.30am). No credit cards.

CORNWALL

Touting itself as Falmouth's 'hidden late night cocktail bar', Eight Bar's low, curved ceiling, eclectic music, candlelit tables and steamy front windows create something of a speakeasy feel. The cocktail menu is a sophisticated affair, incorporating fresh herbs and spices, own-made syrups and infusions, plus local ingredients such as Cornish apple juice, elderflower and pears – in short, not Sex on the Beach territory. With musicians playing every Wednesday night, and DJ sets running from Thursday to Saturday, things can get lively later on – so arrive early if you'd prefer a quiet conversation over a mojito.

Gylly Beach Cafe ★

Gyllyngvase Beach, Cliff Road, TR11 4PA (01326 312884, www.gyllybeach.com). Open Summer 9am-midnight daily. Winter 9am-midnight Wed-Sun. Breakfast served Summer 9-11.45am daily. Winter 9-11.45am Wed-Sun. Lunch served Summer noon-5pm daily. Winter noon-5pm Wed-Sun. Dinner served Summer 6-9pm daily. Winter 6-9pm Wed-Sun.

Despite the slick look – lots of white, blond woods and trendy (though actually very comfortable) white plastic chairs – prices are perfectly reasonable at this bar-restaurant, right on Gyllyngvase Beach. Menu options include gourmet burgers (in Baker Tom's ciabatta) with chunky skin-on chips, and posh fish and chips. But the wide, wraparound beachside terrace at the front, giving far-reaching views of the estuary, is the real draw (fleece blankets are provided on nippy nights). Gylly attracts a mix of well-heeled tourists and locals of all ages, as well as students (particularly for 'curry and a pint for a fiver' night on Sunday), while the serving staff are bright young things who have perfected the art of speedy service.

Hunkydory

46 Arwenack Street, Falmouth, TR11 3JH (01326 212997, www.hunkydoryfalmouth.co.uk). Dinner served Summer 6-10pm daily. Winter 6-10pm Mon-Sat.

This airy blue-and-white restaurant on Falmouth's main drag is a longstanding favourite for its stellar array of local seafood. Crab, clams, mussels, prawns, squid and lobster are all present, and daily-changing specials might include line-caught sea bass, monkfish and john dory. The menu takes a predominantly Modern European stance, with occasional Asian accents (as well as a sushi tasting plate). The crowd-pleasing dessert menu takes its inspiration from closer to home, with crème brûlée, sticky toffee pudding and a platter of Cornish cheeses. Choose between the cosy wooden-beamed front room or the brighter, steamship-style back room with its big booths – book in summer.

Miss Peapod's Kitchen Café

Jubilee Wharf, Penryn, TR10 8FG (01326 374424, www.misspeapod.co.uk). Open 10am-4pm Tue-Thur, Sun; 10am-12.30am Fri, Sat. Breakfast served 10-11.30am Tue-Sun. Lunch served noon-2.30pm Tue-Sat; 12.30-4pm Sun. Dinner served 7-9pm Fri, Sat.

The eco chic haven of Miss Peapod's occupies an enviable position in Penryn's new wind- and sun-powered Jubilee Wharf development, located right by the water. The affordable, Med-inspired menu demonstrates considerably more than a passing interest in sustainable practice: eggs come from Penryn's own Boswin Farm, meat from the Lizard, coffee from Constantine and beer from a local boutique brewery. All of Miss Peapod's china and furniture

is recycled, and the floor once graced a London nightclub, so you can pull up a chair out on the decking (made of sustainably sourced timber, naturally), order a glass of organic wine and feel a warm, worthy glow. There's an eclectic programme of musical performances and DJs at weekends.

Oliver's

33 High Street, Falmouth, TR11 2AD (01326 218138). Food served Easter-Sept 8am-11pm daily.

Located in Falmouth's characterful Old High Street area, this tiny new restaurant already enjoys a sizeable reputation. There are only eight tables, so booking is a good idea. Offering 'a fresh twist on old favourites', the daily-changing menu takes classic British ingredients and dishes and subtly invigorates them: pot-roasted pheasant with roasted vegetables on a giant crouton, pesto-grilled monkfish with a creamy spring onion risotto or king prawns in a red Thai broth, say. The stripped down decor sports a relatively understated retro theme (except for the staff's Easyjet-style orange aertex shirts), but the desserts (knickerbocker glory, banana split, apple crumble) are straight-up nostalgia.

Pandora Inn

Restronguet Creek, Mylor, TR11 5ST (01326 372678, www.pandorainn.com). Open 11am-11pm daily. Lunch served noon-3pm, dinner served 6-9pm daily.

This thatched 13th-century inn is famous for its ridiculously poetic setting, with its own pontoon bobbing on the calm waters of Restronguet Creek. Inside is a warren of interconnected rooms, with low beams, dark wooden panels, benches and fireside tables; the restaurant upstairs serves the same likely-looking menu of seaside pub classics in a more formal setting. In summer, though, most people are here for a picnic table out over the water. For extra romance, you can take the Aqua Cab from the pier in Falmouth (07970 242258, www.aquacab.co.uk, closed Nov-Apr) right up to the pub.

Provedore ★

43 Trelawney Road, Falmouth, TR11 3LY (01326 314888, www.provedore.co.uk). Open 9am-4pm Mon, Tue; 9am-10.30pm Wed, Thur; 9am-4pm, 6-10.30pm Fri; 9am 3pm Sat. Breakfast served 9am-11.30am, lunch served noon-3pm Mon-Sat. Dinner served 6-10.30pm Wed, Thur, Fri.

This minute neighbourhood restaurant used to be a deli specialising in the finest French and Mediterranean imports, with delicious soups, paellas and stews to take away. But the cooking was so good, and the welcome so warm, that everyone wanted to eat in and it morphed into a tapas bar and café. Saturday morning breakfasts (local sausages, foraged wild mushrooms, great coffee) have reached near-cult status, while the Cornish octopus, authentic bouillabaisse and paddle crab bisque have to be tasted to be believed (the seafood is delivered alive early evening). Ox tails, spicy meatballs and fresh tortilla also feature, and the drinks list allows for a preprandial oloroso and fino sherry, and a Spanish brandy digestif.

Star & Garter

52 High Street, Falmouth, TR11 2AF (01326 318313). Open 11am-midnight daily. Lunch served noon-2.30pm, dinner served 6.30-9.30pm daily.

Gylly Beach Cafe. See p237.

The prettily fronted Star & Garter pub, with original tiling and blue-painted windows, has always had fantastic, 180-degree views across the harbour and over to Flushing. But in recent years, it has also garnered a reputation for great food (particularly its Thursday sushi night) and music (jazz on Mondays, folk on Thursdays and blues on Sunday).

Where to stay

Falmouth Townhouse

Grove Place, Falmouth, TR11 4AL (01326 312009, www.falmouthtownhouse.co.uk). Rates from £85 double incl breakfast.

Given its arty air, Falmouth was long overdue a hotel with design flair – and with the arrival of Falmouth Townhouse, crafted with care from a lofty, double-fronted Georgian house, it finally has one. The ten rooms at this retro-styled hotel are scattered with vintage modernist design classics, original art and bespoke furniture, amassed with care by the owners. They also offer king-size beds, spacious luxury bathrooms (with Korres toiletries) and an unbeatable location in the centre of town – right opposite the harbour and National Maritime Museum. The cool little bar, serving tapas, wine and cocktails, is a neat addition.

Greenbank Hotel

Harbourside, Falmouth, TR11 2SR (01326 312440, www.greenbank-hotel.co.uk). Rates £135-£185 double incl breakfast.

Dating from 1640, this is the oldest hotel in Falmouth, and has a distinguised history to prove it, boasting Florence Nightingale and Kenneth *Wind in the Willows* Grahame as former guests. History is evident all around you, in the shape of high ceilings, sweeping staircases and tasteful but traditional decor. Situated on the Falmouth harbour front with unrivalled views of Flushing – and its own 16th-century private quay to boot – the hotel is popular with the yachting crowd, but is also a great base for anyone wanting a touch of class within a stone's throw of the town centre. Modern British cuisine, with the emphasis on fish and seafood, and twinkling harbour views are the order of the day at the hotel's Harbourside restaurant.

St Michael's Hotel & Spa

Gyllyngvase Beach, TR11 4NB (01326 312707, www.stmichaels-hotel.co.uk). Rates £72-£198 double incl breakfast (min 2 night stay).

Less prominent than the imposing Falmouth Beach Hotel, St Michael's has the advantage of being situated right opposite Gyllyngvase Beach (and ten minutes' walk from

town). Set back from the main road behind subtropical gardens (which include a children's play area and an outdoor massage pagoda), it has a host of extra features to add to the business of bed and board – including an indoor pool, sauna, jacuzzi, steam rooms, gym and sundeck. The fresh, nautical-inspired interior is light and airy (where else would you find a boat for a reception desk and beach hut-style toilets?), the comfortable rooms are amply equipped, and there are a number of scenic lounges and outdoor terraces.

Sixteen
16 Western Terrace, Falmouth, TR11 4QW (01326 319920, www.sixteenfalmouth.co.uk). Rates £65-£80 double incl breakfast.
The stylish rooms at Sixteen set themselves apart from average seaside digs with French antiques, flatscreen TVs and handmade Cornish soaps – and the all-round whiff of quality. Both rooms are ensuite but shower only. It's a 15-minute walk into town, and about the same to the beach.

ROSELAND PENINSULA
Famously favoured by holidaying surrealist artists (Lee Miller, Roland Penrose, Max Ernst, Man Ray et al) in the 1930s, the glamorous yachting set in the

1950s and '60s, and a string of A-listers in recent years, the Roseland Peninsula could hardly be described as an insider secret. But even in the busy summer months, it somehow manages to feel like one. It's easy to escape the crowds, and the area offers a very peaceful brand of tourism: row your boat up a quiet creek, learn how to sail, or curl up with a book and a bucolic view.

A large part of the Roseland's charm lies in its deep seclusion. Attractive as its winding roads undoubtedly are, skirting open fields framed with leafy hedges and dipping down through wooded valleys, a couple of return trips by road to Truro or Falmouth are usually enough to make you swear to take the boat or the ferry next time. There are regular boat crossings from St Mawes to both Falmouth and Truro (Enterprise Boats, www.enterprise-boats.co.uk, 01326 313234, closed Nov-Apr), while the year-round King Harry Ferry (01872 862312, www.kingharryscornwall. co.uk) is the only vehicular crossing of the Fal, and one of only five remaining chain ferries in the country. The King Harry takes just five scenic minutes to cross this section of the Fal, flanked on either side by thick woods.

An upmarket holiday resort since Edwardian times, St Mawes is the largest settlement on the peninsula. Neat white cottages and smart townhouses cling to the hillside above the small, sheltered harbour, with the dramatic shapes of dark Monterey pine trees framing the skyline on the brow of the hill behind – and St Mawes Castle (*see p240*) keeping watch on the headland. Across the sheltered mouth of the Percuil river, the views of St Anthony lighthouse have graced the covers of many a glossy holiday magazine citing comparisons with the South of France. The retreat was given further polish in 1999, when celebrated interior designer Olga Polizzi renovated the Hotel Tresanton (*see p241*).

From St Mawes, take the little ferry ★ (www.king harryscornwall.co.uk/ferries/place_ferry, closed Nov-Easter) across to Place; it's a short but very scenic excursion, and gives access to some superb walks on St Anthony Head and to the lovely church of St Anthony (*see p294*). There are no food and drink purchasing opportunities once there, so it's worth stocking up at the tiny St Mawes bakery (01326 270292) on the quay beforehand – their pasties are excellent.

The Roseland is awash with exquisite views, charming villages and untouched coves with clear waters, so you could strike out in almost any direction and encounter scenes of rare beauty. One soothing route is to head north of St Mawes and up St Just Creek to St-Just-in-Roseland Church ★, set in steep subtropical gardens on the side of the creek, with its sandbar and moored yachts. It is a breathtaking spot – 'to many people the most beautiful churchyard on earth', according to John Betjeman.

Along the south coast, stop at the charming village of Portscatho, which has a tiny harbour, a scattering of shops and cafés – including well-stocked deli and village shop Ralph's (The Square,

Places to visit

National Maritime Museum Cornwall

FALMOUTH

National Maritime Museum Cornwall ★
Discovery Quay, Falmouth, TR11 3QY (01326 313388, www.nmmc.co.uk). Open 10am-5pm daily. Admission £8.75; £6-£7 reductions; £24 family.
Housed in an impressive wooden building, the five-year-old NMM features a huge collection of restored sailing craft and nautical objects, as well as hands-on interactive displays, audio-visuals, talks and special exhibitions, covering all aspects of maritime life, from boat design to fascinating tales of survival at sea (the exhibition on the history of diving is particularly good). One highlight for all ages is the Tidal Zone, where you can go underwater and look out into the harbour through two large windows; stand there for long enough and you'll see the tide rise and fall. Another is the 360 degree views over the harbour and towards Flushing from the top of the 95-foot Look Out. One ticket buys you annual unlimited access – and given the vast scope of the museum, it's worth considering a second visit. There is a stylish glass-fronted café on the first floor, looking out over the water.

Pendennis Castle
Pendennis Headland, Falmouth, TR11 4LP (01326 316594, www.english-heritage.org.uk/pendennis castle). Open July, Aug 10am-6pm daily. Apr-June, Sept 10am-5pm daily. Oct-Mar 10am-4pm daily. Admission £6; £3-£5.10 reductions; £15 family.
Sitting fatly on the rocky peninsula overlooking one of Falmouth's best beaches, Pendennis cannot be ignored. It was constructed between 1540 and 1545 to form the Cornish end of the chain of coastal castles built by Henry VIII to counter the threat from France and Spain. In the centuries that followed, the fortress was frequently adapted to face new enemies, right through until 1945. In 1646, prior to the Civil War, the fort played host to the future Charles II before he sailed to the Isles of Scilly, when it withstood five months of siege, before becoming the penultimate Royalist

garrison on the British mainland to surrender. Pendennis also saw significant action during World War II. The Guardhouse has been returned to its World War I appearance; underground, there's a network of magazines and tunnels, including the World War II Half Moon Battery, as well as the original 16th-century keep with its recreated Tudor gun.

In summer, battle re-enactments take place on the gun deck, and open-air concerts and plays are performed on the lawn; in July and August, there's the daily ceremonial firing of the Noonday Gun. Christmas shopping and Cornish yuletide events are also held here.

ROSELAND PENINSULA

St Mawes Castle
St Mawes, TR2 5DE (01326 270526, www.english-heritage.org.uk/stmawescastle). Open July, Aug 10am-6pm Mon-Fri, Sun. Apr-June, Sept 10am-5pm Mon-Fri, Sun. Oct 10am-4pm daily. Nov-Mar 10am-4pm Mon-Fri. Admission £4.20; £2.10-£3.60 reductions.
Like its larger sister across the water, Pendennis Castle, St Mawes Castle was built between 1539 and 1543 to defend against attacks from the French and Spanish that never came. When the castle was finally threatened with some serious action in the Civil War, its occupants quickly surrendered it to Parliamentarian forces, hence preserving its immaculate state (it is one of the finest, most complete examples of Henry VIII's south-coast forts).

St Mawes has the same clover-leaf design as Pendennis, but the three semicircular bastions that surround the four-storey central tower make it the more architecturally distinguished of the two. The castle also enjoys the benefits of its remote location; whereas Pendennis Point sees ice-cream vans, daytrippers and canoodling teenagers crowding the car park day and night, St Mawes enjoys nothing but exposed rocks and fresh, panoramic seascapes.

Tregothnan Estate

Tregothnan, TR2 4AJ (01872 520000, www.tregothnan.co.uk). Tours by arrangement only.
The beautiful old country estate of Tregothnan, not far from Truro, has been owned for 450 years by the Boscawan family. It is now best known for its line of premium tea, grown in its gardens – the first tea to be produced in the UK – and honey (including manuka honey). Private two-hour tours of the historic botanical garden, including a cream tea, cost £50.

TRURO

Royal Cornwall Museum

River Street, Truro, TR1 2SJ (01872 272205, www.royalcornwallmuseum.org.uk). Open 10am-4.45pm Mon-Sat. Admission free.
The county's best exhibition space is a must-visit for anyone interested in Cornwall's history and culture. There is a permanent display on the history of Cornwall, from the Stone Age to the present day, and the museum also has a selection of paintings by Newlyn School artists, a collection of rare mineral specimens, and old master drawings in the De Pass Gallery (John Constable, Van Dyck, Rubens). Attached to the museum is the Courtney Library, which specialises in local history resources, and there's an attractive café by the entrance.

Trelissick ★

Feock, TR3 6QL (01872 862090, www.national trust.org.uk/trelissick). Open Jan 11am-4pm daily. Feb-Oct 10.30am-5.30pm daily. Nov, Dec 11am-4pm Mon-Thur, Sat, Sun. Admission £7; £3.50 reductions; £17.50 family.
Gloriously sited on the river and surrounded by (free) walking trails (through the woods, along the water and criss-crossing the estate), Trelissick is a fine example of a grand Cornish garden. The 30 acres feature an apple orchard and an array of mature trees and plants, many of which are rare and exotic enough to excite the most jaded of gardeners. Only the grounds and gardens are open to the public, together with a café with pleasant courtyard seating, the inevitable NT gift shop, and a rather more charming gallery showing work by Cornish artists and craftspeople. Best of all, the gardens lead down to a couple of ferry landing stages, making the gardens easily accessible from the south coast (*see p246*).

Truro Cathedral

St Mary Street, Truro, TR1 2AF (01872 276782, www.trurocathedral.org.uk). Open 7.30am-6pm Mon-Sat; 9am-7pm Sun. Admission free.
Cornwall's only cathedral, a vast, late 19th-century Gothic Revival edifice, is so imposing it seems to dwarf the rest of this low-rise county capital (indeed, it is said the architect had to build a clearly discernible bend in the nave to fit it into the tight city-centre space). With three Bath stone spires, an ornate façade and some of the world's finest Victorian stained glass, it can't fail to impress. At the time of writing, there were major regeneration plans on the table to breathe new life into the gardens behind the cathedral and restore the central spire.

01872 580702), which sells pastries, bread, locally caught fish and local ale – and a tempting pint stop in the shape of the Plume of Feathers (*see below*). Its nearest beaches are just around the curve of Gerrans Bay: secluded Porthcurnick (limited parking), and Pendower and Carne, which join at low tide to form a long, sandy stretch.

A few miles on, follow the narrow lane down to the tiny fishing village of Portloe, whose whitewashed and pastel-painted cottages are tightly packed around a steep rocky inlet and harbour. Although fishermen still sell the day's catch on its small, pebbly beach, the four-wheel drives and Mercedes parked up the hill tell a different story about the village's full- and part-time inhabitants. The coastal path heading westwards from here gives yet more stunning coastal views back towards the Roseland and nearby Gul Rock.

Inland, the quaint village of Veryan is famous for its curious thatched and crucifix-topped roundhouses, built in the 19th century by a local minister for his five daughters. Constructed without any corners, these houses apparently ensured that the devil would have nowhere to hide.

Where to eat & drink

Outside of the hotels, the Roseland's sleepy villages are not the place for complicated food and fine wine. Nonetheless, they do have a pleasing selection of smart yet traditional pubs. The Plume of Feathers (The Square, 01872 580321) in Portscatho serves good, low-key food and Cornish ale; the King's Head (Ruan Lanihorne, 01872 501263, www.kings-head-roseland.co.uk, closed Mon, Sun eve Nov-Easter) is a popular gastropub in the hamlet of Ruan Lanihorne; and the Roseland Inn (01872 580254, www.roseland inn.co.uk) in Philleigh has its own microbrewery. In St Mawes, the Victory Inn (01326 270324, www.victory-inn.co.uk), formerly a fishermen's haunt, now sees more chinos and blazers than it does yellow fishing overalls.

Before catching the King Harry Ferry, take refreshment at the quirky Smugglers' Cottage (01872 580309, www.newmanscruises.co.uk, closed Nov-Easter), signposted right on the road to the ferry. Serving chunky slices of cake, cream teas and lunches, this 15th-century riverside cottage has the added interest of having served as the embarkation point for US troops for the D-Day landings. Along the road, you will even see a sign directing you into the thicket to examine the Americans' latrine.

The best restaurants for high dining are found in hotels. The dining room at the Tresanton (*see below*) is the standout choice, but the Lugger and the Nare (for both, *see p242*) are also accomplished.

Hotel Tresanton ★

27 Lower Castle Road, St Mawes, TR2 5DR (01326 270055, www.tresanton.com). Lunch served 12.30-2.30pm, tea served 3.30-5.30pm, dinner served 7-9.30pm daily.

Dinner at the Tresanton exudes effortless quality: everything from the cut-above waiting staff to the thick, starched napkins, smart decor and elevated prices is a statement of serious gastronomic intent. The food delivers too: choose from a daily-changing Modern European menu of fresh fish dishes, classic meat selections or imaginative vegetarian fare (pappardelle with wild mushrooms and truffle oil, for example), all executed with flair and precision. Summer brings cocktails and dinner on the terrace, with views over the St Anthony lighthouse and Fal Estuary. For food and service of this quality in the area, the Tresanton has few peers. If your budget won't stretch to dinner (£42 for three courses), instead call by for a light lunch or a cream tea on the terrace.

Where to stay

The most distinguished self-catering accommodation on the Roseland is located on the romantic private estate of Rosteague (01872 580346, www.rosteague.co.uk), where there are two gorgeous old properties for rent.

Driftwood Hotel

Rosevine, TR2 5EW (01872 580644, www.driftwood hotel.co.uk). Rates £195-£250 double incl breakfast.
This privately owned beach house stands amid seven acres of gardens, with a path leading down to a private beach. Catering to families (there's a small games room for children) as well as couples, the Driftwood is all about carefully considered comfort. Design is crisp but informal, with lots of natural fabrics and stone. The smart white restaurant is another enticement, as are after-dinner drinks watching the moon on the water from the decking area. A beautiful but isolated location makes this one for willing escape artists rather than those on a whistle-stop tour of Cornwall.

Hotel Tresanton

27 Lower Castle Road, St Mawes, TR2 5DR (01326 270055, www.tresanton.com). Rates £190-£360 double incl breakfast.
Renowned interior designer Olga Polizzi's Hotel Tresanton has become synonymous with waterside chic, having played host to a stellar cast of celebrities since it opened in 1999. Nevertheless, it still has an intimate and homely atmosphere that will make mere mortals feel welcome. Originally created in the 1940s as a yachtsmen's club, the hotel became a well-known haunt for yachties and tourists in the 1950s and '60s. Polizzi bought the place in 1997 and spent two years and a cool £2 million renovating and restoring it, adding personal touches to every room (guests are even provided with wellies).

Occupying a cluster of houses built into the hillside on different levels, 27 of the Tresanton's 29 rooms have views out to sea and the St Anthony lighthouse on the headland beyond. Nautical patterns influence the design of some rooms, while others blend natural cream and beige hues with dark wood and richly coloured fabrics. Original works of art adorn the hallways and lounge areas, with pieces by Terry Frost, Barbara Hepworth and acclaimed St Mawes sculptor Julian Dyson in the collection. Unlike many seaside retreats, Tresanton is a hotel for all seasons: spend a day aboard the *Pinuccia* (a 48ft classic racing yacht built to represent Italy in the 1938 World Cup), followed by dinner on the terrace in summer; in winter, make the most of the bridge and treatment weekend packages, DVD library and cosy lounge. The upmarket restaurant is superb (*see p241*).

Lugger Hotel

Portloe, TR2 5RD (01872 501322, www.luggerhotel.com). Rates £80-£150 double incl breakfast.
The interior at the Lugger is elegantly simple with contemporary touches, but its unassailable asset is a remarkable setting. The 17th-century inn (ask about the landlord who was hanged for smuggling in the 1890s) and fishermen's cottages that now collectively form the 21-room hotel are built right into the cliffs above the tiny cove and fishing village of Portloe, mere yards from the water. Public areas include a lounge with a well-stoked log fire in winter and a terrace in summer, as well as a swanky British-European restaurant with sea views.

Nare Hotel

Carne Beach, TR2 5PF (01872 501111, www.the nare.com). Rates £250-£466 double incl breakfast & afternoon tea.
Standing proud above Carne Beach on Gerrans Bay, the four-star Nare is an elegant, wholeheartedly traditional retreat. First opened in 1925, the extended 37-room hotel still retains much of its original character, with winding corridors, glowing log fires and rooms bursting with antiques. The bedrooms add to the sense of old-world charm, with carriage clocks, floral fabrics and high-backed armchairs. It's also worthy of note for its exceptional service, which is all about old-fashioned manners and attention to detail (hot-water bottles as standard in winter, fine leaf tea at breakfast, greetings by name). Facilities include indoor and outdoor pools, subtropical gardens leading down to the beach, sauna, hot tub, gym, beauty salon and billiards room, plus two restaurants with views.

Rosevine

Portscatho, TR2 5EW (01872 580206, www.rosevine.co.uk). Rates £950-£1,550 per week for 2 people; £1,300-£2,350 per week family room.
This luxury family-oriented apart-hotel has some of the best looking accommodation on the Roseland. Its 15 studios and mini apartments are equipped with compact kitchens and decorated in fresh pastels, New England stripes and rejuvenated antiques, and there is a well-stocked DVD library. Other facilities include a children's play area, large gardens, a heated indoor pool and a games room – and, most usefully, the unspoilt beach of Porthcurnick at the end of the road. The Dining Room, serving rustic British food, looks out across the exotic gardens to the sea. Cots and baby monitors are provided at no extra cost, and babysitters can be called in from a local agency.

St Mawes Hotel

Marine Parade, St Mawes, TR2 5DW (01326 270266, www.stmaweshotel.co.uk). Rates £70-£140 double incl breakfast.
This friendly waterfront establishment, in the centre of town, has nine simple but attractively decorated rooms for B&B (or dinner, bed and breakfast), along with four rooms in the newly converted fisherman's cottage out back. Prices are reasonable for this well-heeled town. The sea-view brasserie and bar downstairs are very popular, so be warned that this may not be the most serene of retreats in the summer months.

Falmouth Townhouse. See p238.

Truro Farmers' Market

CORNWALL

TRURO

Located at the head of the Carrick Roads estuary, the 'capital' of Cornwall has an air of cultural and financial self-sufficiency that sets it apart from the rest of the county, with rows of pastel-painted Georgian townhouses and a triple-spired Gothic Revival cathedral (see p240). As a comforting microcosm of urban life, with boutiques, cocktail bars and fancy delis, Truro tends to attract big-city refugees wishing to live out the country dream without wanting to get their feet muddy.

There is hardly a trace now of the working quays that once ran along the river, but the piazza, on the old Lemon Quay, is a busy outdoor space with café tables, markets and a plethora of outdoor events year-round. Truro Farmers' Market (01637 830958, www.truro farmersmarket.co.uk/truro php) takes place here every Wednesday and Saturday, as does the Cornwall Food & Drink Festival in September (www.cornwallfoodanddrinkfestival.com).

The well-heeled satellite villages of Truro – Kea, Feock, Point and Devoran – spread out south along the banks of the Carrick Roads. At Kea, farm-based butcher Ralph Michell (01872 271066, closed Sun) sells fantastic free-range meat; peacocks and bantams roam the farmyard, and in the next-door field, huge pigs roll in the mud.

Truro is linked to Falmouth by an attractive branch line, which takes 20 minutes, and a ferry that leaves from Town Quay, near Tesco, or from Malpas just downriver if the tide is low; see www.enterprise-boats.co.uk for details.

The tourist office (01872 274555, closed Sun Summer, Sat, Sun Winter) is next door to the City Hall – now the Hall for Cornwall (see p246) – on Boscawan Street.

Where to eat & drink

Café culture is thriving in Truro, with no shortage of lattes and posh paninis served in smart surrounds. Among the nicest spots are the Duke Street Sandwich Deli (10 Duke Street, 01872 320025, www.duke-street.com, closed Sun) for paninis, freshly made sandwiches and salad boxes; the Lemon Gallery café (01872 271733, closed Sun), within Lemon Street Market (see below); and veggie havens Archie Browns (105-106 Kenwyn Street, 01872 278622, www.archiebrowns.co.uk, closed Sun) and Lettuce & Lovage (15 Kenwyn Street, 01872 272546, www.lettuceandlovage. com, closed Sun).

For picnic provisions, stop at Lemon Street Market (www.lemonstreetmarket.co.uk). There's bread by the much-lauded Baker Tom ★ (08453 884389, www.bakertom.co.uk), including honey and lavender loaf, rock salt and rosemary foccacia, and 'beer bread' made with Betty Stogs Cornish ale, as well as quiches, cakes, made-to-order sandwiches and picnic hampers at the Larder deli (01872 275218, closed Sun). The Cheese Shop ★ (29 Ferris Town, 01872 270742, www.cheese-eshop.com, closed Sun) is also excellent, with

FIVE SCENIC BRANCH LINES

Back in the 1960s, the Beeching Axe saw the controversial closure of numerous branch lines (secondary railway lines that branch off a main route), as the government attempted to cut the cost of maintaining the railways. Since then, many have reopened, with several now existing purely as heritage railways. Others are part of 'rail ale' trails (www.railaletrail.com) – routes that encourage rail travellers to sample the local brews at pubs near the lines. For more information on the following routes, visit www.greatscenicrailways.com.

Atlantic Coast Line
This 20-mile community railway runs from the village of Par to Newquay. En route, it passes through the steep-sided, densely wooded Luxulyan Valley, designated a World Heritage Site thanks to its early 19th-century industrial remains.

Looe Valley Line
Just under nine miles long, the Looe Valley Line offers access to some of Cornwall's finest walking and cycling terrain – not to mention some excellent country pubs. The route runs from the market town of Liskeard to Looe, via Coombe, St Keyne, Causeland and Sandplace.

Maritime Line
Following the valley of the River Fal, the Maritime Line connects Truro and Falmouth, with stops at Perranwell, Penryn and Penmere. After Perranwell, the lines crosses a lofty viaduct, with views of the Carnon Valley – a former tin-mining area – below. Walking trails run from (and sometimes between) the various stations.

St Ives Bay Line
Taking just 12 minutes to make the journey from St Erth (where it connects with the mainline), along the birdlife-filled Hayle Estuary and Lelant Saltings, past the white sands of Carbis Bay and into the heart of St Ives, this has to be one of the most dazzlingly scenic branch lines in the country. There are also two or three direct services from Penzance, on the south coast, to St Ives, which takes around 20 minutes.

Tamar Valley Line
This glorious 14-mile stretch of track runs between Plymouth, on Devon's south-western edge, to Gunnislake, over the border in Cornwall. It follows the River Tamar and its estuary, before crossing the river on the mighty Calstock viaduct, completed in 1907.

CORNWALL

Things to do

FALMOUTH

Enterprise Boats
66 Trefusis Road, Flushing, TR11 5TY (01326 374241, www.enterprise-boats.co.uk). Open Mar-Oct; times vary, check website for details. Admission £12 return; £8 single.
Enterprise Boats links Falmouth, Truro and St Mawes, as well as Trelissick garden (*see p241*), with its small, charming ferries. The tranquil journey from Falmouth to Truro takes around an hour, and makes for a brilliant sightseeing trip. Boarding in Falmouth is from the Prince of Wales quay, and in Truro from Town Quay (tide-dependent). Check the website for timetables.

Orca Sea Safaris
Discovery Quay, Falmouth, TR11 3QY (01872 861910, www.kingharryscornwall.co.uk/ferries/orca). Trips by arrangement only. Admission £39.50; £28 reductions; £125 family.
Setting out from Falmouth, a 12-seater Rigid Inflatable Boat takes you out to sea to spot dolphins, seals and basking sharks (and even a whale, if you're lucky). The scheduled trips can be booked on the website year round.

Sea Fans Scuba School
(07916 931038, www.seafanscuba.co.uk). Open phone for details. Courses from £40.
Sea Fans is an affordable, family-friendly centre with taster dives for children over ten. After a briefing, you're off into the sea with a wetsuit and tank for anything up to an hour, swimming with fish, peering into caves and tumbling off underwater cliffs. For younger ones or those not too keen on the idea of all the equipment, Richard and his team will organise snorkelling safaris.

Sea Kayaking Cornwall
Swan Beach, Falmouth (07768 382010, www.sea kayakingcornwall.com). Open by arrangement only. Courses from £150.
Based in Falmouth, SKC runs one- to five-day kayaking (and surf-kayaking) courses for all levels and abilities. Budding adventurers will be tempted by the multi-day expeditions, which might involve wild camping and foraging; destinations include the Isles of Scilly.

Ships & Castles Leisure Centre
Pendennis Headland, Falmouth, TR11 4NG (01326 212129, www.shipsandcastles.co.uk). Open times vary, check website for details. Admission £5.40; £4.40 reductions; £13.50-£16.50 family.
On days when the real sea is out of the question, families might try the wave machine and little 'beach' at this pool. In addition to areas for lengths, the fun pool has a flume, a rapid river ride, a ridewave machine and jacuzzis (with bubble pools for toddlers). Located on the Pendennis Headland, it's an attractive place to paddle, with a large glass ceiling making it feel much sunnier than your average leisure centre.

ROSELAND PENINSULA

Fish & Trips of St Mawes
01326 279204, www.fishandtripstmawes.co.uk. Open Apr-Oct. Trips from £15 per person; charters from £7 per person. No credit cards.

Skipper James Brown offers fishing trips (mackerel, live bait and trolling for bass) out of St Mawes, as well as private charters and day trips.

St Mawes Sit-on Kayaks
The Quay, St Mawes, TR2 5DG (07971 846786, www.stmaweskayaks.co.uk). Open Apr-Oct 9am-6pm daily. Hire from £10. No credit cards.
Hire out easy-to-paddle, family-friendly kayaks from St Mawes harbour and venture up the creek, around to St Anthony Head or all the way to St Just.

TRURO

Bike Chain Bissoe
Old Conns Works, Bissoe, TR4 8QZ (01872 870341, www.cornwallcyclehire.com). Open Summer 9am-6pm daily. Winter 9am-5pm Mon, Thur-Sun. Hire from £12 per day.
This place has a bike for eveyone, from tandems and tricycles to hybrids and mountain bikes. There's free parking for customers, so you can leave the car behind and pedal off along the Coast to Coast Trail on your new set of wheels.

Hall for Cornwall
Back Quay, Truro, TR1 2LL (01872 262466, www.hallforcornwall.co.uk). Open Box office by phone 9am-6pm daily. In person 9.30am-7pm daily. Tickets £10-£35.
Having worked with Sam Wanamaker on the rebuilding of the Globe Theatre in London, entrepreneur Chris Warner campaigned vigorously during the 1990s for the establishment of a venue west of Plymouth in which to stage commercial productions of any size. There is little in City Hall's grand Italianate façade to hint at its modern interior, but inside you'll find a slick 950-seat auditorium, as well as a coffee shop, bars and a restaurant. Entertainment here ranges from Abba cover bands to opera, world-acclaimed dance companies and big-budget musicals. It also hosts various fleamarkets and craft markets in the daytime.

Loe Beach Watersports
Feock, TR3 6SH (01872 300800, www.loe beach.co.uk). Open times vary, check website for details.
A wide range of watersports are on offer at this friendly Watersports Centre, including sailing, kayaking, rowing, windsurfing and motor boating. There's a compact pebbled beach here, and a small café just next door (*see p249*).

Skinners
Riverside, Newham, TR1 2DP (01872 245689, www.skinnersbrewery.com). Open Shop 9.30am-5.30pm Mon-Sat. Tours Apr-Oct 12.30-2.30pm, 7.30-10.30pm Mon-Sat. Admission £6.50 afternoon tour; £10-£12.50 evening tour.
The names might be jocular – Betty Stogs, Ginger Tosser, Cornish Blond – but the Skinners are serious about ale. This family-run operation is one of Cornwall's leading brewhouses, and visitors are welcome for tastings and tours on the riverside Truro premises. We consider Skinner's Betty Stogs to be one of Cornwall's top five ales; see p210.

Place ferry leaving St Mawes harbour. See p239.

Portloe. See p241.

a full range of Cornish specialities as well as European imports, plus some deli items.

A fledgling cocktail culture is apparent in a number of new venues in the centre of town, including the Old Grammar School (*see below*), Vanilla Bar (1-2 Duke Street, 01872 242466, closed Sun), Vertigo (15 St Mary's Street, 01872 276555, www.vertigotruro.com) and the One Eyed Cat (116 Kenwyn Street, 01872 222122, www.oneeyedcat.co.uk). In Truro's move upmarket, only a handful of pubs seem to have escaped with their soul intact – the Old Ale House (7 Quay Street, 01872 271122, www.oahtruro.co.uk) is one, a spit and sawdust sort of place that serves a vast range of real ale. Worth leaving town for is the pretty, blue-windowed Heron Inn (Trenhaile Terrace, Malpas, 01872 272773, www.heroninn.co.uk), fronting the river.

Bustophers
62 Lemon Street, Truro, TR1 2PN (01872 279029, www.bustophersbarbistro.com). Open 11am-11pm daily. Lunch served noon-2.30pm, dinner served 5.30-9.30pm daily.
A bistro stalwart on Lemon Street, Bustophers has been trading on its lively atmosphere, crowd-pleasing food and classically stylish digs for decades. Now with a classically modern look and an open kitchen, Bustophers is perennially popular for Fowey river moules-frites, classic lasagne, risotto with rocket salad or just a warming lunch of house soup with Baker Tom bread.

Loe Beach Café
Feock, TR3 6SH (01872 864433, www.loebeach.co.uk). Open times vary, phone for details.
It's little more than a shed with some benches and spotty bunting, but the Looe Beach Café serves better food than you might expect. There were three fish specials on our last visit, including very good whitebait, plus an all-day menu of freshly cooked family-friendly comfort food (ham, eggs and chips, and burgers). The cheery young staff happily sell mugs of tea and Twix bars to young kayakers from the watersports centre next door, and this place is popular with both locals and trippers.

Old Grammar School
19 St Marys Street, Truro, TR1 2AF (01872 278559). Open 10am-midnight Mon-Sat. Lunch served noon-3pm, dinner served 6-9.30pm Mon-Sat.
Truro's hippest hangout is a neat, sleek space in the centre of town with the best cocktails around (from £6 each), each one attentively mixed with premium spirits, plus a DJ booth and a small repertoire of tapas. The posh glasses, prices and vibe tends to attract late twentysomethings and up, but this place still manages to be way too cool for school.

Old Quay Inn ★
32-33 St Johns Terrace, Devoran, TR3 6ND (01872 863142). Open 11.30am-11.30pm daily. Lunch served noon-3pm, dinner served 6-9pm daily.
An old, white-painted village pub that's been brought up-to-date without being spoilt. An unfussy, spick and span interior is given warmth by a handsome fire; there's a friendly atmosphere, with no background music to hinder conversation. Real ales include Sharps' Doom Bar and

Skinner's Betty Stogs and there's a guest ale at weekends. Fresh, local ingredients are transformed into hearty dishes such as slow roasted pork belly or beer-battered haddock and chips – excellent stuff, and much anticipated after a walk or cycle (Devoran is on the Mineral Tramways path). The setting, in a village on Restronguet Creek, is very pleasing, and a beer garden out back is a further plus. It also has three B&B rooms (£70-£90 double incl breakfast).

Saffron
5 Quay Street, Truro, TR1 2HB (01872 263771, www.saffronrestauranttruro.co.uk). Open Summer 10am-10pm Mon-Sat. Winter 10am-3pm Mon; 10am-10pm Tue-Sat. Lunch served noon-3pm Mon-Sat. Dinner served Summer 5-10pm Mon-Sat. Winter 5-10pm Tue-Sat.
On the surface of it, Saffron is an unassuming small-scale Truro restaurant with rustic decor. Inside, though, it delivers some of the most accomplished new Cornish cooking around – and a short, genuinely seasonally led menu that makes for inspiring reading. With everyone and their sous-chef banging on about the local provenance of their ingredients, it's sometimes hard to separate serious source-local policies from token flourishes. But at Saffron, the breadth of knowledge of Cornish ingredients is self-evident: not only does it feature all the foodie headliners (Bocaddon 'real' veal, Tregothnan Tea ice-cream, Helford crab, Rodda's clotted cream, Cornish Cuisine's smoked trout), but it also employs more unusual wild food accents (wild gorse sorbet, say, or wild garlic spätzle) and seasonal specialities (Kea plum eve's pudding, say, made with a uniquely Cornish variety of plum harvested around the River Fal in August).

Where to stay
Truro has a bizarre lack of desirable lodgings, possibly due to its inland location – it isn't especially popular with holidaymakers as a base, even though it is very centrally placed for outings. Historically, the Alverton Manor Hotel (Tregolls Road, 01872 276633, www.alvertonmanor.co.uk) is considered to be the city's most luxurious – but while the rooms are undoubtedly comfortable and the building is grand, the decor is looking dated.

Mannings
Lemon Street, Truro, TR1 2QB (01872 270345, www.manningshotels.co.uk). Rates £95-£109 double incl breakfast.
The most up-to-date property in Truro, and the one with the best city-centre location (right on the piazza), Mannings has chic, businesslike guestrooms, nine apart-rooms next to the hotel, and a smart bar-restaurant downstairs.

Tregye Farm House ★
Tregye Road, Come to Good, TR3 6JH (01872 863162, www.tregyefarmhouse.co.uk). Rates £95 double incl breakfast. No credit cards.
With high-end fittings and fabrics (flatscreen TV, Vi-Spring bed, Nespresso coffee machine) in its two guestrooms, flawlessly hospitable hosts and a quiet location near the tranquil waters of the estuary (but only a short drive to Truro), Tregye Farm House is one of Cornwall's top B&Bs. Book early.

CORNWALL

The Lizard Peninsula

In the rush for posh fish and chips in Padstow, surf shacks in Newquay and gallery-hopping in St Ives, visitors often overlook Cornwall's most remote corner. The Lizard Peninsula, the bulge of land south of the Helford River – south, in fact, of everywhere in mainland Britain – is on the way to nowhere. It is miles from anything you might class as a big town, barely served by public transport and almost completely surrounded by water. For all these reasons, it is one of the county's most rewarding areas.

For a relatively small expanse of land, the Lizard offers tremendous scenic diversity. The placid waters of the Helford River and the pulverising swell of Porthleven Sands are separated by just a few miles of countryside, and the colossal serpentine cliff-faces of the south coast are just a few snaking lanes away from creek-side beaches so small they look like scale models. Running down the centre of the peninsula are the eerily barren Goonhilly Downs, giving way at the edges to gently rolling countryside.

Keep an eye out for the chough, a jet-black bird with distinctive scarlet legs and bill. This rare member of the crow family, which takes pride of place on the Cornish coat of arms, disappeared from the Lizard in 1952 but returned to the area to breed in 2002, and now seems to be making a slow comeback.

HELSTON & AROUND

Helston
The only town of any size in the area is the pretty country town of Helston, famous for its annual Flora Day celebrations held on 8 May (unless it falls on a Sunday or Monday). During this ancient festival, the town is decorated with bluebells and gorse, and schoolchildren dress in white and wear garlands in their hair. Festivities include the play-like ritual known as the Hal-an-Tow, in which St Michael slays the devil and St George slays the dragon, and culminate with the processional 'Furry Dance', in which townsfolk dress up in their finery and dance in and out of the houses. Amid the springtime revelry, much Cornish ale is imbibed – in particular the potent Spingo from the Blue Anchor pub (see p252).

Helston lost its role as a river port in the 13th century, due to the silting up of the Cober estuary. However, it remained an important stannary (tin mining district) and market town. Today, it's a delightfully old-fashioned sort of place, boasting a number of attractive buildings, many of them on Coinagehall Street. The neo-Gothic monumental gateway at the end of the street was built in 1834 in memory of Humphry Millet Grylls, a Helston banker and solicitor who had helped to keep the local tin mine open, thus safeguarding 1,200 jobs.

There's a farmer's market in the Cattle Market by the boating lake on the first Saturday morning of every month. South-west of Helston, pretty woodland paths take you through the National Trust's Penrose Estate to Loe Pool. The largest freshwater lake in Cornwall, it is cut off from the sea by a sand and shingle bank known as Loe Bar.

Porthleven
The prevailing winds whip straight into south-west-facing Porthleven, restricting its development into anything larger than a fishing village. Massive sea defences are testament to the village's vulnerability to gale-driven winter waves – and entry into the harbour remains a perennially hazardous undertaking. But the odd storm lashing doesn't stop Porthleven being perfect for an amble. In contrast to Cornwall's more cutesy fishing villages, its atmosphere is that of a bustling, year-round community.

Along the front, there's a scattering of shops, including a few galleries, a good fishmonger (Quayside Fish, Fore Street, 01326 562008) and Kota restaurant (see p252). The recent arrival of the Corner Deli (see p252) and a Wednesday food market by the harbour reflects a burgeoning local food scene – as does the new annual Porthleven Food Festival, which takes place in April.

In bad weather, watching the breakers crash over the high sea wall is a stirring spectacle. If the wind happens to be blowing offshore, this is also a good place to watch advanced surfers in action – Porthleven offers some of England's best waves, surfed by a hardcore group of locals. Visiting surfers make pilgrimages here too, but this is a dangerous place for novices. Bathing off the long and attractive beach, especially near the Loe Bar, is also risky due to the strong currents and undertow.

Where to eat & drink

In the formal dining department, Helston is represented pretty much exclusively by the smart new restaurant at Nansloe Manor (*see p255*), on the outskirts of town. For picnicking purposes, stock up on pasties from the Horse & Jockey (41 Meneage Street, 01326 563534) or assemble a hamper of Cornish goodies from Olivers deli (65 Meneage Street, 01326 572420, www. oliverscornwall.com).

In Porthleven, the Ship Inn (Mount Pleasant Road, 01326 564204), above the entrance to the port, is an old smugglers' grotto and an excellent perch from which to survey the seascape.

Blue Anchor ★

50 Coinagehall Street, Helston, TR13 8EL
(01326 562821, www.spingoales.com). Open
10am-midnight daily.
With more than 600 years of beer-making behind it, the Blue Anchor is reputedly the country's oldest continuously operating brew-pub. More importantly, it's still one of Cornwall's finest boozers, with a thatched roof, time-smoothed wooden tables and flagstone floors. Settle into one of the many nooks with a pint of its famous Spingo ale; there are few other places in Cornwall where you can get your hands on this locally revered liquid gold (*see p210*). You might be permitted a peek at the brewhouse at the end of the passage if you ask nicely. No food is served, but you can bring in your own.

Corner Deli

12 Fore Street, Porthleven, TR13 9HJ (01326 565554).
Open/food served Summer Deli 9am-6pm daily; pizzeria
6-9pm Mon-Sat. Winter Deli 9am-6pm Mon-Sat;
pizzeria 6-9pm Wed-Sat.
This appealing deli is miniscule – one counter, a few shelves and two tables and chairs – but it packs a lot in: premium Cornish (and occasionally Italian) produce, including loaves by the esteemed Vicky's Bread, Camel Valley wine and Moomaid of Zennor ice-cream, as well as local duck eggs, organic carrots and muddied potatoes in baskets. It also serves superior sandwiches on organic flatbreads in the daytime, and pizzas from a wood-fired oven in the evenings. Seating is extremely limited, so you may find yourself eating outside on Porthleven harbour – no great hardship.

Kota ★

Harbour Head, Porthleven, TR13 9JA (01326 562407,
www.kotarestaurant.co.uk). Lunch served noon-2pm
Fri, Sat. Dinner served 5.30-9pm Tue-Sat.
Kota is Maori for shellfish and, taking full advantage of its fishing village location, chef Jude Kereama – half Maori, quarter Chinese, quarter Malaysian – oversees a menu of super-fresh Cornish seafood, crafted into Asian-accented cuisine. Monkfish green Thai curry is spicy and complex, and tempura Falmouth oyster appetisers with wasabi tartare (and a lettuce leaf for a spoon) are essential nibbling at £2 a pop. We'd be happy to declare this the best Asian food in Cornwall, but the distinct lack of competitors renders it a rather hollow statement; instead, we'll just say that Kota is quietly superb. This being an old mill, the decor is rustic and beamed, with big old wooden sideboards. Service is of rare efficiency, and prices where they should be for food of this quality.

CORNWALL

Kynance Cove. See p255.

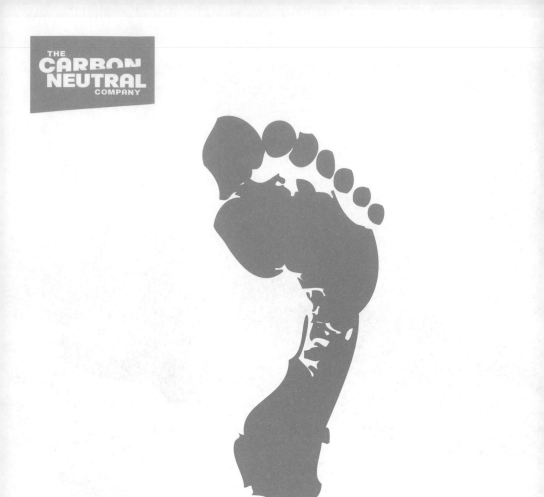

Whatever your carbon footprint, we can reduce it

For over a decade we've been leading the way in carbon offsetting and carbon management.

In that time we've purchased carbon credits from over 200 projects spread across 6 continents. We work with over 300 major commercial clients and thousands of small and medium sized businesses, which rely upon our market-leading quality assurance programme, our experience and absolute commitment to deliver the right solution for each client.

Why not give us a call?

T: London (020) 7833 6000

Where to stay

Two unfussy B&B rooms are available upstairs at Kota (*see p252*), one with harbour views.

Beacon Crag

Porthleven, TR13 9LA (01326 573690, www.beacon crag.com). Rates £65-£85 double incl breakfast. No credit cards.

It's not often that B&Bs bag the big views – but this handsome white house, on the edge of the cliff near Porthleven, is a notable exception. The setting really is in a league of its own, with far-reaching views along the coast in both directions; the remains of mine stacks can be seen on the cliffs. There are three chintz-free rooms to choose from, at mid-range prices.

Nansloe Manor

Meneage Road, Helston, TR13 0SB (01326 558400, www.nansloe-manor.co.uk). Rates £114-£240 double incl breakfast.

Accommodation in Helston is generally limited to a few basic B&Bs and the odd room above the pub, but if you're willing to venture just out of town – down a long, tree-lined driveway – you come to the ever-so-private and amazingly underpublicised Nansloe Manor. The 15 rooms in this Georgian manor are fresh and classically modern, all looking out of huge windows on to the suntrap lawn. The accomplished restaurant is an equally elegant affair, and the 'modern country' menu comes care of chef Neil Martin, who has the rare privilege of a decent-sized kitchen garden at his disposal.

THE LIZARD

South from Helston, the peninsula takes on an altogether more untamed character. The underlying serpentine rock, a greenish metamorphic stone, is covered by dour, dramatic sweeps of heathland (collectively named the Lizard National Nature Reserve), whose unusual geological make-up means it is home to some of Britain's rarest plants. The swathes of pink-flowering Cornish heath (erica vagans), at its prettiest in summer, are particularly glorious.

On the coast, there are towering cliffs and rousing seas, preposterously pretty fishing villages and tempting sandy coves. Most visitors gravitate inexorably to Lizard Point, in order to spend a few moments as the most southerly person in mainland Britain.

Mullion & around

Just inland, Mullion is the largest village on the peninsula, with a good deli, a traditional pub – the Old Inn – a gallery and the pretty 16th-century church of St Mellanus, with its richly carved pews and a large Celtic stone cross outside. The village also has the virtue of being within easy striking distance of three beaches: tiny but dramatic Mullion Cove, with its small harbour beach and cluster of buildings; secluded Polurrian, accessible only by footpath and devoid of facilities; and popular Poldhu Cove, a fine, sandy enclave with a little café and ice-cream shop. Poldhu's main claim to fame, however, is the Poldhu Wireless Station, from where

Guglielmo Marconi sent the first transatlantic wireless signal in 1901. The remains can still be seen on the rugged cliffs above the beach – and the Marconi Heritage Centre (*see p265*) tells the story in brief.

Just to the north of Poldhu, but involving a considerable detour inland if travelling by car, Church Cove is a peaceful, unspoilt family beach, with a precariously sited old church. Its idyllic sands belie its long history of smuggling and shipwreck. Nearby, the forbidding mass of the 200-foot Halzephron Cliff has claimed many ships. The bodies of sailors washed ashore along this unforgiving coastline were refused burial in hallowed ground, and until the early 18th century were unceremoniously dumped in a clifftop pit. Over the centuries, enduring tales of buried treasure have led numerous fortune-seekers to dive for the two tons of Spanish coins reputedly lying off this rocky coast.

Lizard Point & the coast

Like Land's End, Lizard Point – Britain's southernmost tip – is a tourist magnet. Other than stopping for one of Ann's legendary pasties (*see p257*), there's no cause to dally in Lizard village, whose charms are somewhat subsumed by dull cafés and tacky gift shops. But the blustery outcrop itself has escaped the worst of the tourist excesses, being marked only by the twin towers of the Lizard Lighthouse (recently opened to the public; *see p264*) and a few attendant cafés and shops selling carved and polished serpentine ornaments. All the same, it's the surrounding coastline that deserves attention: the jumble of cliffs, caves and coves oozes drama.

The coastal path leads north-east towards Cadgwith, passing the Devil's Frying Pan – a 200-foot-deep collapsed blowhole that makes for a memorable sight, especially when the 'pan' is spitting. The mood changes as you reach idyllic Cadgwith Cove, where fishing boats line up on the pebble beach and pretty thatched cottages cling to the steep terrain. There's a wonderful 300-year-old pub, the Cadgwith Cove Inn (*see p257*), a few small shops and a hatch selling crab and lobster sandwiches by the beach. Park at the top to avoid becoming entangled in the village's narrow lanes.

On the east side of the Lizard, Kennack Sands is easily accessible and offers good bathing and a little surf. It's one of the area's most generous stretches of sand, backed up by crag and rock pools. There's a car park, and a small café/shop.

Kynance Cove ★

It may not be the place to hire pedaloes, surfboards and deckchairs, and getting there involves something of a walk, but Kynance Cove is undoubtedly the jewel in the Lizard's crown. 'Kynans' means gorge in the Cornish language, and this particular gorge is backed by vast cliffs and scattered with striking green-blue stacks, pinnacles, arches, caves and rock pools, all set against turquoise waters. In the right light, the combination of brilliant seas, pinkish sands and rocks calls to mind Bermuda, *The Tempest* and

Things to do

HELSTON & AROUND

Cornish Camels
Rosuick Organic Farm, St Martin, Helston, TR12 6DZ (01326 231119, www.cornishcamels.com). Open July-Sept 9am-5pm daily. Oct-June 11am-2pm Sat. Admission free.
Over at Rosuick Farm, an organic farm near St Keverne, the owners have imported 14 rare Bactrian camels. In season, the friendly camels take visitors on short treks around the grounds, but on special request you may be able to arrange treks across the Cornish Heathland area of Goonhilly Downs (a surreal landscape, even before you add camels into the equation). There's also a farm trail, tractor trailer rides, peacocks, wallabies, an organic farm shop selling the farm's meat and a play area.

The Flambards Experience
Helston, TR13 0QA (01326 573404, www.flambards. co.uk). Open Feb-Dec times vary; check website for details (closed Jan). Admission £7.95; £4.50-£6.95 reductions.
Flambards was an aviation museum when it opened 30 years ago. Now it's a far more broad-based family day out. There are thrill rides (Thunderbolt, Hornet Coaster and Canyon River Log Flume are among the white-ish knuckle ones), an animal section and Hands On Science Experience, a Victorian village with cobbled streets, an exhibition on Britain in the Blitz, an indoor theatre and, hanging on in there, the exhibition of aircraft relics and models. The school holidays also bring weekly firework displays.

THE LIZARD

Coverack Windsurfing Centre
Cliff Cottage, Sunny Corner, Coverack, TR12 6SY (01326 280939, www.coverack.co.uk). Rates Windsurfing from £20; surf skis from £5. No credit cards.
Based in the secluded Coverack Bay and open from April to November, this centre offers tuition for all levels, as well as residential holidays and courses.

Mullion Golf Course
Cury, TR12 7BP (01326 240685, www.mulliongolfclub.net). Open all year.
England's most southerly golf club has 18 holes and magnificent clifftop views.

Porthkerris Divers
Porthkerris Cove, St Keverne, TR12 6QJ (01326 280620, www.porthkerris.com). Open all year.
This family-run dive centre offers great shore dives to the sunken shipwrecks off the notoriously treacherous Manacles.

Roskilly's ★
Roskilly's Ice Cream & Organic Farm, Tregellast Barton, St Keverne, TR12 6NX (01326 280479, www.roskillys.co.uk). Open Summer 9am-dusk daily. Winter 11am-3pm Mon-Fri; 11am-5pm Sat, Sun.
At this idyllic organic dairy farm you can feed the ducks, watch the cows being milked or just stroll around the meadows and ponds in the grounds. Entrance is free, but you won't be able to hold on to your money when you see the farm shop and the Bull Pen Gallery, selling sweet wooden toys, furniture and the work of local artists. There's also the cosy restaurant (Croust House; *see p257*), and, of course, 24 scrumptious flavours of Roskilly's ice-cream on sale.

THE HELFORD RIVER

Helford River Boats ★
Helford Passage, TR11 5LB (01326 250770, www.helford-river-boats.co.uk). Open Ferry Easter-Oct 9.30-5.30pm daily. Tickets £5; £1 reductions.
There is no better way to take in the quiet beauty of the Helford River than from the water. This boating company, which operates a kiosk at Helford Passage (on the north bank), hires out self-drive motor boats by the hour, day and week (from £35 for one hour, maximum six people), for which no experience is required. Kayaks are also available for £10 an hour. The same company runs the ferry service between the north bank and the south from April till the end of October.

Helford River Boats

any number of treasure islands. Its beauty has lured creatives down the ages, including, most famously, Tennyson and the artist William Holman Hunt. One of the original Pre-Raphaelites, the colour-obsessed Hunt was naturally taken with the cove, whose hues feature in his work of 1860, *Asparagus Island*.

At low tide, Kynance's azure waters and countless sandy nooks, caves, rock pools and crannies are the stuff of fantasy. On a calm day, having a splash or a body surf in these sparkling waters is a joy. If, however, there is mild to moderate swell, and the tide is high, swimmers – especially children – should take care, as it is easy to be lulled into a false sense of security by the peaceful scene. And be careful not to be cut off by the tide if you stroll over to nearby Asparagus Island, accessible on foot via the Bellows, a stretch of white sand that emerges at low tide. Wild asparagus, a spiky flowering plant that grows only in a handful of places, flourishes on this hump of rock.

It's a steepish climb down from the National Trust car park at the top of the cliffs to the seasonal café and shop on the edge of the sand.

St Keverne & around
The B3293 heads south-east through Goonhilly Downs to the village hub of St Keverne, a mile or so inland. Arranged attractively around a main square are its two pubs, shop and distinctively steepled church. Within easy striking distance are Porthallow Cove and Porthoustock, quiet fishing villages with uncompromising grey shingle beaches. Between them, Porthkerris has become something of a diving hotspot (*see left*) thanks to its proximity to the notorious Manacles – a jagged, mostly submerged two-mile offshore reef, upon which many ships and men have come to grief.

More conventionally appealing is the fishing village of Coverack, with its tidal beach. Once a centre of smuggling, it is now favoured for its quiet coastal setting, with traditional granite cottages and a few cafés and galleries lining up along an arc of sand and shingle. There's a working harbour at the southern end of the bay, a pub (incongruously named the Paris Hotel, after a French liner that was wrecked on the headland on which it stands), the old lifeboat station (now housing a restaurant and fish and chip shop) and glorious views out to sea.

Where to eat & drink
In addition to the Halzephron Inn (*see below*), we are partial to a pint in the cosy Cadgwith Cove Inn (01326 290513, www.cadgwithcoveinn.com), which comes alive every Friday night to the rousing strains of the Cadgwith Singers and their Cornish fishing shanties.

Croust House ★
Roskilly's Ice-Cream & Organic Farm, Tregellast Barton, St Keverne, TR12 6NX (01326 281924, www.roskillys.co.uk). Lunch served 11am-3pm Mon-Fri; 11am-5pm Sat, Sun.

The excellent restaurant at Roskilly's (*see p256*), converted from the old milking parlour, is all about homely, comforting fare (pasty and salad, jackets, baguettes, quiche and soup) at sensible prices. The atmosphere here is refreshingly low-key – you order from the counter, and are welcome to hang out on the farm for the rest of the day. With ample bench seating in the large courtyard, a dedicated kids' menu and farm activities on site, families are in their element.

Halzephron Inn
Gunwalloe, Helston, TR12 7QB (01326 240406, www.halzephron-inn.co.uk). Open 11am-2.30pm, 6.30-11pm daily. Food served 11am-2.30pm, 6.30-9pm daily.
Ruling the roost on top of a particularly formidable stretch of cliff ('halzephron' derives from the Cornish for 'cliffs of hell'), this famous old inn has a longstanding – and deserved – reputation for good pub food. Expect solid renditions of standards such as ploughman's, spaghetti bolognese, burgers, steak and chips and scampi, and more adventurous specials. With the pick of the Cornish ales on tap, including Doom, Betty Stoggs and the local Chough Brewery ale, this is one of the most popular stops along the south coast of the Lizard. Choose from the old-school bar, a smarter restaurant, the family room or the bracing front terrace – the same menu applies to all.

The Lizard Pasty Shop
Beacon Terrace, Helston, TR12 7PB (01326 290889). Open Jan-Mar 9.30am-2.30pm Tue-Sat. Apr-Dec 9.30am-2.30pm Mon-Sat.
Ann's pasty shop at the Lizard (you can't miss it, it's bright yellow) is justly famous for its first-rate rendering of the Cornish classic – and even more so now that a certain super-chef from Padstow has given it his stamp of approval. Indeed, despite the touristy setting, this is the real deal. Note that the shop closes early if the pasties have sold out.

Where to stay
This being probably as far as you can go off the tourist trail in Cornwall, there isn't a lot of accommodation on the Lizard – and what there is tends to predate the boutique hotel boom. Still, a number of the big hotels on the coast make up for what they lack in design nous with jaw-dropping clifftop settings and impressive old buildings. The Mullion Cove Hotel (01326 240328, www.mullion-cove.co.uk) and the Housel Bay Hotel (01326 290417, www.housel bay.com) are two such traditional hotels with panoramic vistas.

Roskilly's (*see p256*) farm has self-catering cottages for hire and, at Lizard village, the endearingly eccentric Henry's Campsite (01326 290596, www.henryscampsite.co.uk) is the most southerly campsite in Britain. Cider is served by the jug, most pitches have sea views, and pigs, ducks and guinea pigs roam at will.

In the tiny village of Kuggar, Namparra (01326 290040, www.namparracampsite.co.uk, closed Nov-Easter) is another delightful campsite, 20 minutes' walk from Kennack Sands. Campfires are allowed – or you can rent a freestanding clay chimenea.

The Bay

Coverack, TR12 6TF (01326 280464, www.thebay hotel.co.uk). Rates £67-£97 double incl breakfast & dinner.

A small, independently owned hotel on the waterfront at Coverack, the Bay is a good-value hideaway on the Lizard. The decor, while not in the business of chasing trends, is modern, attractive and soothingly toned – and rooms at the front have knockout sea views, as does the conservatory restaurant.

Chydane

Gunwalloe Cove, Helston, TR12 7QB (01326 241232, www.chydane.co.uk). Rates £110-£130 double incl breakfast. No credit cards.

Chydane's two polished B&B rooms – classily decorated with plenty of white, antiques and high-end fabrics – are spectacularly sited at the cliff edge above Gunwalloe. The long beach and growling sea are a few metres away, and it's a short walk to the Halzephron pub (*see p257*).

Coverack Youth Hostel

Parc Behan, School Hill, Coverack, TR12 6SA (0845 371 9014, www.yha.org.uk). Rates from £15.95 per person; £11.95 reductions.

This small, simple youth hostel, set in a Victorian house with spectacular views over the cliffs and coves of the eastern coast of the Lizard, is much loved by watersports enthusiasts and walkers. Of the nine bedrooms, six have double beds and five are en-suite. Breakfast, picnic lunches and evening meals are all available.

Lizard Point Youth Hostel

Lizard Point, TR12 7NT (0845 371 9550, www.yha.org.uk). Rates from £15.95 per person; £11.95 reductions.

From the driveway and manicured gardens, you'd think you were about to check into a luxury clifftop hotel. Instead, this smartly painted old Victorian hotel is now a first-rate YHA hostel, offering fresh, homely rooms (including some doubles and triples) – most of which have sea views.

Lovelane Caravans

Cartshed Cottage, Retallack Farm, Constantine, TR11 5PW (01326 340406, www.lovelanecaravans.com). Rates from £150 3 nights for 2 people. No credit cards.

Fans of retro will be in their element in Lovelane's period caravans, restored to their former glory and equipped with nostalgic touches such as thimble-like gold-rimmed cups from the Queen's Coronation, a Goblin Teasmaid or a hand-embroidered tablecloth. These touring vans might be relics, but they are still very much mobile – and can be towed to campsites, remote fields or a place of your choosing. Guests requiring the comfort of hot showers and flushing toilets should plump for a campsite, but the more adventurous can take advantage of the near self-sufficiency of the caravans, which are equipped with their own water tank, gas-run lights and an integrated (if tiny) kitchen; a surprisingly inoffensive 'earth' toilet is positioned nearby. We asked for 'remote' and couldn't have dreamed up a more secluded experience: we found our cute two-berth caravan parked deep in the Lizard countryside in a circular Iron Age Fort. A quirky treat.

The Polurrian

Mullion, TR12 7EN (01326 240421, www.polurrian hotel.com). Rates £122-£208 double incl breakfast & dinner.

Taken over by the owners of the elegant Budock Vean hotel (*see p260*) on the Helford River, this stately old Edwardian building has undergone a much-needed facelift. The style is still strait-laced, but the rooms are fresh and comfortable. More excitingly, the hotel is set in 12 acres of rugged coastal moorland – there are notices in the rooms reminding guests to shut the windows during gales, and in the sea view rooms you drift off to sleep to the sound of waves crashing outside. There are tennis courts, a family putting green, children's climbing frames, a football area, indoor and outdoor pools and a jacuzzi; the hotel's own sandy beach is a quick abseil below. Indoor facilities include a squash court, a toddlers' play area and a games room that includes PlayStations, a pool table, table football and table tennis.

THE HELFORD RIVER

In *Frenchman's Creek*, Daphne Du Maurier's tale of passion and piracy, she paints the Helford River as a 'symbol of escape', a place paused in time. And the effect on today's visitors is remarkably similar. The Helford, whose spidery creeks intersect the sheltered northern shores of the Lizard peninsula, is one of few places in Britain to which time has been so gentle – thanks to its profound geographical isolation, lack of fast roads and the commitment of various interested parties to preserving its peace and natural beauty.

Du Maurier fans will still find plenty to feed their imagination in and around the Helford's hidden waterways and in the dense woodland that grips its shores – some of the last pockets of wild woodland in the country. From the choppy waters of the open sea at the mouth of the 'river' (technically it's a ria, or drowned river valley) to the small port of Gweek at its head, the scale gradually diminishes: the creeks, coves and inlets become calmer and more hidden, and the tiny shingle beaches are perfect miniatures.

Plenty of footpaths (consult an OS map) weave through the thickets, leading walkers deep into the woodlands and down to the water's edge. Our favourite walks are the short circular trail from Helford village to Frenchman's Creek, via lovely Penarvon Cove, and a longer excursion through Trelowarren estate's tall, echoey woods down to National Trust-managed Tremayne Quay (open Feb-Sept; ask at the estate's reception for a leaflet with a map) – a tranquil spot, only accessible on foot or by water.

Heading inland, sinuous lanes lead to the heart-meltingly pretty villages and hamlets – Manaccan, St Anthony, Gweek and Mawgan on the south side, and Helford Passage, Port Navas, Mawnan Smith and Constantine on the northern banks – dotted with thatched white cottages, village shops, pubs and church steeples reminiscent of slower times.

The affluent north bank of the river, home to two stunning gardens (*see p265*), is most easily accessed by road from Falmouth. Alternatively, a

Lovelane Caravans

foot ferry makes the very short crossing from Helford village on the south side to the cluster of houses and the pub at Helford Passage to the north (£5; 9.30am-5.30pm Apr-Oct, until 9.30pm July, Aug).

Where to eat & drink

Also in the area are South Café (Manaccan, 01326 231331, www.south-cafe.co.uk), a casual but chic bistro with a modern British menu, and the low-key Down by the Riverside Café (Helford Chapel, 01326 231893, closed Nov-Easter), in the little old chapel at the top of Helford village, which serves a mean crab sandwich.

Ferryboat Inn

Helford Passage, TR11 5LB (01326 250625, www.wrightbros.eu.com). Open 11am-11pm daily. Lunch served noon-3pm daily. Dinner served 6-8.30pm Mon-Fri; 6-9pm Sat, Sun.
Overhauled in 2009 by the Wright Brothers of Borough Market, probably the country's most respected oyster wholesalers, this venerable old riverside pub – with dreamy views of the water from the terrace at the front – has been transformed into a thoroughly upmarket affair. The design, menu and prices now place the Ferryboat on a posher plane than your average gastropub, and there's even a seafood counter serving local oysters and champagne. It's an incongruously urbane set-up for such a remote locale, but there can be no doubting the quality of the produce: with the Wright Bros running the Duchy Oyster Farm at Port Navas, less than a mile away, these could well be the freshest oysters in the land.

Gear Farm & Bakehouse

St Martin, TR12 6DE (01326 221150). Open Summer 9.30am-4.30pm Mon-Sat. Winter 9.30am-4.30pm Wed-Sat.
Gear Farm, just outside the small village of St Martin, sells its superior own-baked bread and pasties out of a small farm shop, as well as a range of local – and usually organic – produce, including meat, milk, cheese and fish from the Helford River. The jolly little café attached to the shop (really just a handful of tables) is perfect for a pit-stop. The menu keeps things very simple indeed: pasty or pizza, both from the bakehouse. There's a small campsite overlooking the Helford River opposite.

New Inn

Manaccan, TR12 6HA (01326 231323). Open noon-3pm, 6-11pm Mon-Sat; noon-3pm, 7-10.30pm Sun. Lunch served noon-2.30pm Mon-Sat; noon-2pm Sun. Dinner served 6.30-9.30pm Mon-Sat; 7-9pm Sun.
There's nothing new about this picture-perfect, cream-and-thatch inn. In fact, it has barely changed for decades and, from the outside, probably centuries. A fine specimen of a country pub, it has just one room, with a log fire, real ale and the quiet, cosy feel of another era.

New Yard ★

Trelowarren, TR12 6AF (01326 221595, www. trelowarren.co.uk). Lunch served noon-2pm Tue-Sat; noon-2.30pm Sun. Dinner served 7-9pm Tue-Sat.
Such is the beauty of this riverside country estate, we'd settle for any excuse to visit Trelowarren – so the fact that its chic,

airy restaurant is also the best place to dine on the Lizard is a happy bonus. In the evening, prices dictate that New Yard, converted from the old carriage house, is somewhere for a Nice Meal Out rather than a casual bite, but thankfully it's not a tense, cutlery-scraping kind of place – the warm, friendly service and deep country setting keep things pleasantly relaxed. In line with the green credentials of the estate, new chef Oliver Jackson's menu is full of ingredients sourced from within a ten-mile radius of the restaurant: Helford fish, Falmouth Bay crab and Cornish cheeses (super-mature Menallack Farmhouse cheddar, ripe Cornish camembert) are all fortes. There are half a dozen outdoor tables in the pretty courtyard.

Shipwright Arms

Helford Village, TR12 6JX (01326 231235). Open/food served 11am-2.30pm, 6-10.30pm Tue-Sat. Winter opening hours vary.
The absurdly picturesque Shipwright Arms, right on the water in Helford Village, was a smugglers' hangout back in the days when these winding creeks provided a bounty of hiding places for smugglers, pirates and fugitives. These days, it's a pleasant spot in which to smuggle yourself away for a pint and a spot of lunch (crab sandwiches, a pint of prawns or a ploughman's) overlooking the creek, watching birds duck in and out of the water, and the sailing boats quietly come and go. There is no parking on these narrow streets – leave the car at the car park at the entrance of the village.

Where to stay

Budock Vean

Helford Passage, Mawnan Smith, TR11 5LG (01326 252100, www.budockvean.co.uk). Rates £152-£243 double incl breakfast & dinner.
Sitting proudly on the prosperous north bank of the Helford River, this lavish four-star resort presides over its own golf course, tennis courts, pool and spa, and vast, organically managed gardens. (The latter lead down to a private foreshore on the river, complete with private sun lounge.) The emphasis here is on the traditional values of service and comfort – and the decor is more old guard than avant-garde. As you might expect, afternoon tea is a hallowed institution – splash out on the Celebration Tea, which includes champagne. Gentlemen are required to don a suit and tie for the main restaurant and cocktail bar after 7pm (special dispensation available in hot weather). Ask for a room in the original hotel building, rather than the modern extension.

Trelowarren

Trelowarren, TR12 6AF (01326 221224,www. trelowarren.com). Rates from £450 per week for 4 people-£650 per week for 10 people.
Since its inception, the UK's first 'eco timeshare' – in the green and peaceful grounds of the Trelowarren estate – has been stacking up awards, thanks to its exacting environmental agenda and green technology (coppice-fired heat and power system, rainwater harvesting, low-energy appliances). Owner Sir Ferrers Vyvyan, who has ambitions for an entirely self-sufficient estate in his lifetime, considers the timeshare concept, despite its unfashionable ring, to be a potentially low-impact form of tourism, avoiding the

Vicky's Bread

A rising sensation in these parts, Helston-based Vicky's Bread – the brainchild of Vicky Harford – produces a small range of superb hand-made bread, and delivers daily to dozens of small independent shops and delis across west Cornwall. The process, and the results, could not be more different to mass-produced loaves. The ingredients are all organic, and no artificial preservatives or enhancers are added – the sourdough culture (inspired by the French *pain au levain*) used in the loaves naturally gives the bread a longer shelf life, as well as lending the finished product a beautifully springy, moist texture. The loaves are shaped by hand and then allowed to rise slowly – for maximum taste – in willow baskets, with the divinely crunchy, brittle crust created by steam baking.

Vicky's everyday range consists of five breads – the classic baguette, multigrain, sourdough, spelt sourdough and, our favourite, the rustic bordelais – with speciality loaves often available at weekends. Look out for the small baskets with a hand-written 'Vicky's Bread' sign sitting modestly on the counters of delis and grocer's throughout west Cornwall – great things lie within.

Vicky's Bread (www.vickysbread.co.uk).
See website for a list of stockists.

'empty second home' syndrome afflicting many Cornish towns and villages. When not booked by their part-owners, the high-spec houses – located next to whispering woodland, and a short walk from the Helford River – are available to everyone for rent. Tennis courts and a swimming pool occupy the old walled gardens.

PRAA SANDS & AROUND

Praa Sands

A mile-long stretch of golden sand, backed by dunes, Praa Sands (pronounced 'pray') may be one of West Cornwall's most popular beaches, but it suffers from something of an identity crisis. Geographically, some people consider it part of the Lizard, others part of the Penwith peninsula. Although it lacks the star quality of some of its Cornish brethren (Kynance Cove, say, or St Ives), being backed by some weathered beachfront shops and cafés and a bevy of old-fashioned bungalows,

it is an excellent family beach, with clean water, good swimming and plenty of space.

It's surfing that really put Praa Sands on the map, though. The summer boarding hordes may flock to Cornwall's north coast, but, on the right swell and especially in winter, this is the place to be. To lose the crowds, head to the eastern side. From here, there's great walking to be had around Rinsey Head, where a grand old mansion, often used as a filming location, stands in total isolation on the edge of the cliff.

Perranuthnoe

The tidal beach of Perranuthnoe, just a few miles along the coast towards Penzance, offers less crowded conditions than Praa and a more secluded setting. Like Praa, Perranuthnoe has beachbreak surf, working on big south-westerly swells held up by a north-easterly wind. It also boasts a reef break, known as the 'cabbage patch', at the eastern end of the bay. However, high tide is not the time to

Helford River. See p259.

CORNWALL

262 **Time Out** Devon & Cornwall

Places to visit

HELSTON & AROUND

Future World @ Goonhilly
Helston, TR12 6LQ (0800 679593, www.goonhilly. bt.com). Open July, Aug 10am-6pm daily. Apr-June, Sept, Oct 10am-5pm daily. Winter times vary; phone for details. Admission £7.95; £5.95-£7.25 reductions.
The Goonhilly Downs, at the heart of the peninsula, might be agriculturally barren, but they have managed to grow an impressive crop of hardware. At one point the largest satellite earth station in the world, Goonhilly's vast BT-owned satellite dishes are an arresting sight, silhouetted against the heathland of the Lizard National Nature Reserve. There's also an array of marketing-oriented attractions on site, including Future World, with its resident robot, a children's play area, the Xbox play zone, nature tours and film shows, including the first live intercontinental satellite images, which were received here from America in 1962.

Godolphin House ★
Godolphin Cross, TR13 9RE (01736 763194, www.nationaltrust.org.uk/godolphin). Open Garden Apr-Nov 10am-5pm Mon-Wed, Sat, Sun. Admission £2.70; £1.35 reductions.
The National Trust's most recent acquisition in Cornwall, this wildly romantic country house looks a bit like an Oxbridge college dropped deep in the west Cornish countryside. Hugely advanced for the 17th century, the architecture is impressive despite its state of disrepair, and the historically significant formal gardens are thought to be the oldest in the country. The Grade I-listed house, which staff hope to reopen to the public in early 2011, is a stunning evocation of the period, with mullioned windows, original Elizabethan stables and a glorious colonnade leading through the screen wall into a courtyard. The overgrown gardens – little changed in centuries – and work-in-progress feel won't be to everyone's tastes, but we couldn't help but fall for the untamed beauty of it all, and the tangible sense of history.

Helston Folk Museum
Market Place, Helston, TR13 8TH (01326 564027, www.cornwall.gov.uk).Open 10am-1pm Mon-Sat; extended opening times during school hols. Admission free.
Behind the Guildhall, in the old market building, the Helston Folk Museum displays an intriguing miscellany of local domestic, industrial and agricultural artefacts of the 19th and 20th centuries, plus Helston man Henry Trengrouse's original Rocket Apparatus and Bosun's Chair. Although his invention was ignored by successive British governments during his lifetime, it later evolved into the Breeches Buoy, a winch now used all over the world for sea rescues.

Poldark Mine
Wendron, TR13 0ES (01326 573173, www.poldark-mine.co.uk). Open Apr-June, Sept, Oct 10.30am-5.30pm Mon-Fri, Sun. July, Aug 10.30am-5.30pm daily. Admission free. Tours £8; £5-£7.50 reductions, £20 family.
North of Helston, Wheal Roots tin mine, as it was originally known, dates from 1725, making it probably the oldest complete mine workings open to the public in Europe. Subterranean guided tours (not for the claustrophobic) detail the life and work of the miners, while the surrounding buildings house pieces of old mining equipment and attendant amusements – very much of the old school – for younger visitors (candle-dipping, panning for gold, remote-controlled boats). And yes, scenes from the classic '70s BBC series *Poldark* were filmed here.

Trevarno
Crowntown, TR13 0RU (01326 574274, www.trevarno.co.uk). Open 10.30am-5pm daily. Admission £6.50; £2.25-£5.75 reductions.
A few miles outside Helston, Trevarno is a 750-acre estate, dating back to the 13th century. In the mid 1990s it was bought by two businessmen, who originally came looking for a country-house headquarters for their business. Distracted from the task at hand by the beauty of the grounds, and the desire to save them from being parcelled up and sold off in lots, they bought the entire estate, embarked on an ambitious restoration project, and opened the gardens to the public in 1998. This is now one of Cornwall's best-loved visitor attractions, receiving over 70,000 visitors every year. The extent of the grounds – and the mixture of formal gardens and wilder woodland – makes for a lovely hour or so's amble, past the Victorian boathouse and lake, bamboo wood and the walled kitchen gardens. Take tea in the conservatory afterwards and watch the peacocks parade on the front lawn, posing for pictures. The estate also houses the National Museum of Gardening, a café in the conservatory and a shop selling Trevarno's organic skincare range.

THE LIZARD

Lizard Lighthouse Heritage Centre
Lizard Point, TR12 7NT (01255 245011, www.lizardlighthouse.co.uk). Open Apr-June, Sept, times vary Mon-Wed, Sat, Sun. July 11am-6pm daily. Aug 11am-7pm daily. Oct-Dec times vary Mon-Wed, Sun. (Closed Jan-Mar). Admission £4; £2-£3.50 reductions; £10 family.
Warning ships off this perilous headland since the 18th century, Lizard Lighthouse, a striking white hexagonal structure, opened to the public in 2009, along with a

Trevarno

CORNWALL

Trebah

jungle-like setting – roped-off flowerbeds are pleasingly absent – will appeal to families, with the 19th-century laurel maze and Giant's Stride rope swing providing added entertainment. A covered outdoor café serves good, solid lunches and snacks.

National Seal Sanctuary

Gweek, TR12 6UG (01326 221361, www.seal sanctuary.co.uk). Open Summer 10am-5pm daily. Winter 10am-3pm daily. Admission £12.95; £10.95 reductions.
Opened in Gweek in 1975, this sanctuary for rescued seals is now a popular family attraction. The seals are brought here to convalesce, before being released back into the wild. There are nursery pools, a hospital, and a pool for the centre's permanent residents rescue seals that wouldn't survive in the wild. There's also a nature trail with other animals to see, and a children's play area.

Trebah ★

Mawnan Smith, TR11 5JZ (01326 252200, www.trebah-garden.co.uk). Open 10am-5pm daily, times may vary. Admission Mar-Oct £7.50; £2.50-£6.50 reductions. Nov-Feb £3; £1-£2.50 reductions.
Originally laid out by the outrageously creative Charles Fox – brother of Alfred, who owned Glendurgan next door – Trebah has 26 acres of lush, subtropical vegetation tumbling down a wooded ravine. Legend has it that Fox was a stickler for detail, even asking that the head gardener put up scaffolding towers to indicate the eventual height of each tree. The garden design cleverly saves the best till last: the view from the bottom leads the eye up past a pond, reflecting a pretty white bridge, beyond the vast bed of pastel-hued hydrangeas, the gunnera (or 'giant rhubarb') and flanks of mature trees, all the way up to the white house at the top. Children can whoop it up on the climbing frames, swings and paraglide (over-fives only) in the Tarzan's Camp play area; there's also a conservatory selling plants, a shop and the Planter's Café, with its appealing seasonal menu.

Trelowarren

Mawgan, TR12 6AF (01326 221224, www. trelowarren.com). Open varies; check website for details. Admission free.
Occupying 1,000 acres between the Helford River and Goonhilly Downs, the beautiful Trelowarren estate has been passed down through the Vyvyan family for some 600 years. Visitors are welcome, and it would be easy to fill the best part of a day exploring the exquisite parkland and on-site microbusinesses. The converted outbuildings now house the superb New Yard restaurant (*see p260*), a plant nursery and an excellent gallery run by the Cornwall Crafts Association (open Mar-Oct). You can even venture into a well-preserved Iron Age fogou (underground chamber), the purpose of which is lost in the mists of time. But the most magical part of any visit is a ramble along the woodland tracks leading down to the secluded riverbank (open to non-guests Feb-Sept; ask a member of staff for a map). Daphne Du Maurier described the estate as a 'a shock of surprise and delight, lying indeed like a jewel in the hollow of the hand', and it provided the inspiration for *Frenchman's Creek*.

smart new visitor centre. The lottery-funded exhibition is full of interesting snippets about lighthouse life through the ages – you can sound a foghorn, listen to lighthouse keepers' tales and tap out dots and dashes by morse code. But by far the most exciting part is the enthusiastically narrated lighthouse tour, during which you climb 62 feet up into the hothouse at the top. Here you gain sweeping sea panoramas, and an up-close encounter with the equipment that emits one powerful white flash every three seconds – visible for up to 26 nautical miles.

Marconi Heritage Centre

Poldhu, Mullion, TR12 7JB (01326 241656, www.gb2gm.org). Open July, Aug 7-9pm Tue, Fri; 1.30-4.30pm Wed, Thur, Sun. May, June, Sept 7-9pm Tue, Fri; 1.30-4.30pm Wed, Sun. Jan-Apr, Oct-Dec 7-9pm Tue, Fri; 1.30-4.30pm Sun. Admission free.
This tiny but informative multimedia exhibition is a tribute to Italian radio inventor Guglielmo Marconi. It marks the location on the headland above Poldhu Cove where Marconi built his wireless station in 1901, later using his vast antenna on the cliff to transmit a message – albeit a weak one – over 2,000 miles to Newfoundland (now Canada).

THE HELFORD RIVER

Glendurgan Garden

Mawnan Smith, TR11 5JZ (01326 250906, www.nationaltrust.org.uk/glendurgan). Open Aug 10.30am-5.30pm Mon-Sat. Mid Feb-late July, Sept, Oct 10.30am-5.30pm Tue-Sat. Admission £6.40; £3.20 reductions.
Planted by devout Quaker Alfred Fox in the 1820s, Glendurgan is one of Cornwall's most exotic gardens. Its theatrical subtropical planting includes tall, swaying palms and tree ferns with vast fronds, with greenery cascading all the way down the steep, wooded valley to a sandy beach on the Helford at the bottom. The

CORNWALL

New Yard. See p260.

new yard restaurant

come for a surf, a walk or anything else for that matter, as the beach all but disappears. The pretty village is home to the Cowhouse Gallery (www.cowhousegallery.org.uk, closed Jan, Feb), a pink-painted gastropub (the Victoria Inn; see below) and the beachside Cabin Café (see below).

A walk along the coast path to Prussia Cove – actually a group of isolated coves – is a must. The romance of the landscape is enhanced by its history: the cove was named after a notorious smuggler, John Carter – alias the King of Prussia. Carter got his nickname as a boy, when he played soldiers on the beach and pretended to be the Prussian monarch. As an adult, his rich pickings were stashed away in Piskies and Bessy's Coves. Between the two coves, an iron post and chains are relics of the HMS *Warspite*, which ran aground here in 1947 and was the largest wreck ever to occur on the Cornish coast. There are no ice-cream kiosks or cafés in these parts, and access is via footpaths; leave your car in the car park.

Where to eat & drink

Cabin Café
Perranuthnoe Beach, TR20 9NE (07907 691639, www.peppercornkitchen.co.uk). Open Apr-Sept 9am-5pm daily. Oct-Mar hours vary. No credit cards.
Improbable as it might seem on arrival, this modest outdoor café – essentially a shack and a handful of open-air tables

next to Perranuthnoe beach – serves praiseworthy food, prepared from scratch at the Peppercorn Kitchen, a catering business based right next door. Stop by for a slice of cake and a glass of own-made cordial, a hefty bacon butty, or one of the tempting daily specials. Vegan, vegetarian and gluten-free meals are also available.

Sandbar
Praa Sands, TR20 9TQ (01736 763516, www.sandbar praasands.co.uk). Open 11am-11pm Mon-Fri; 10am-11pm Sat, Sun. Food served 11am-9pm Mon-Fri; 10am-9pm Sat, Sun.
This beachside hangout – a 1970s disco reborn – has a nicely low-key, sand-worn feel and a large terrace overlooking the sand. Flip-flops and soggy hair are perfectly acceptable attire for a hot chocolate stop, post-surf pub food (locally sourced fillet steaks, Sunday carvery, fish pie) or a round of pool or table football.

Victoria Inn
Perranuthnoe, TR20 9NP (01736 710309, www.victoriainn-penzance.co.uk). Summer Lunch served noon-2pm daily. Dinner served 6.30-9pm Mon-Sat. Winter Lunch served noon-2pm Tue-Sun. Dinner served 6.30-9pm Tue-Sat.
Since husband and wife team Anna and Stewart Eddy took over in 2006, this lovely old thatched inn – furrowed away in sleepy Perranuthnoe – has been quietly making a name for itself. Previously of Hunstrete House in Bath, where he garnered a Michelin star, chef Stewart gives fresh local produce his undivided attention. This means that fish won't just be vaguely local but very local, the pork is from the

village of St Buryan, and you won't find asparagus on the menu until spring. The modern British menu features plenty of exciting flavours, presented without pretension (you're unlikely to find anything as fussy as a 'foam'). We loved the melt-in-the-mouth gooseberry pavlova with own-made elderflower and lemon ice-cream, and a dressed crab starter served with a fennel-laced salad. If you just want an old-fashioned pint and a toasting from the fire, that's fine too. There are a couple of basic guest rooms upstairs (doubles, £65 incl breakfast).

Where to stay

In keeping with its understated appeal, Praa Sands doesn't have a single hotel – just a few old-fashioned B&Bs.

Ednovean Farm

Perranuthnoe, TR20 9LZ (01736 711883, www.ednoveanfarm.co.uk). Rates £85-£105 double incl breakfast.

Technically we must call this a B&B, although its three exquisite rooms – Pink, Blue and Apricot – feel more like a luxurious country hotel, with the bonus of being within walking distance of the lovely Victoria Inn (*see p266*). The rooms are romantically furnished with sumptuous antiques and fabrics (toile de Jouy, vintage Liberty), as well as roll-top baths, fluffy towels, DVD players and private terraces. Best of all, you are free to roam the huge, impeccably landscaped gardens, which afford changing coastal panoramas and are dotted with hidden seats and benches. Note that check-in isn't until 4pm.

Prussia Cove

Prussia Cove, Rosudgeon, TR20 9BA (01736 762014, www.prussiacove.co.uk). Rates from £73-£662 per week for 4 people-£326-£1,565 per week for 12 people.

The family-owned Porth-en-Alls estate, comprising numerous cottages and houses for rent around Prussia Cove, offers get-away-from-it-all properties amid untamed scenery. A world away from beach bars, celebrity chefs and surf shops, this is Cornwall at its best: wild and untouched.

Praa Sands. See p261.

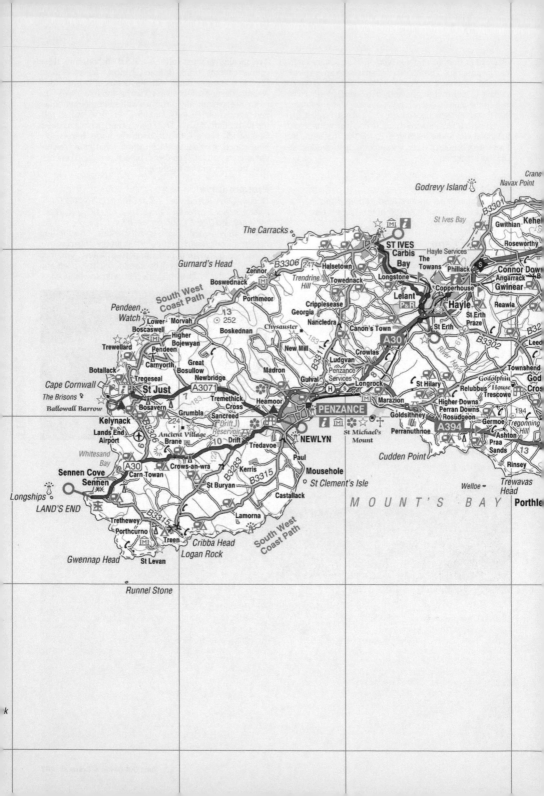

The Penwith Peninsula

There is something infinitely head-clearing about pushing on in the direction of the setting sun, all the way to the end of the line, the end of the 'motorway' (as the A30 is locally known), and eventually, of course, the end of the land. In this remote corner of the country, the cliffs drop dramatically into the relentless swell of the Atlantic and you can, should you feel so inclined, find a blustery perch, gaze out to sea and ponder the nothingness in front of you stretching all the way to North America.

Also known as Land's End Peninsula, the Penwith Peninsula could be another country: it's wild, distant and bounded by so much sea it's almost an island in itself. The primitive landscape – a granite wilderness of open moorland, sea-ravaged cliffs and prehistoric remains – and the area's famous clarity of light continue to exert a magnetic pull on artists, hundreds of whom call it home. If you think our prose excessive, consider instead the words of DH Lawrence, who, on arrival at the pretty village of Zennor in 1916, attempting to escape the hostilities of war, felt like 'a Columbus who can see a shadowy America before him... a new continent of the soul'. Or turn to the Cornish poet John Harris, for whom Land's End's 'granite arches mock the rage of Time'.

Inspirational landscapes aside, the peninsula also has dozens of unspoilt sandy beaches and coves, a quietly flourishing food scene and, of course, galleries galore.

ST IVES BAY & AROUND

St Ives

The approach to St Ives by train – a journey holidaymakers have been making since the line was built in the 1870s – is a veritable sight for sore eyes. The single-carriage train chugs along the curve of St Ives Bay, opening up glorious vistas of golden sands and treating you to a bird's-eye view of the UK's most perfect seaside town: a pretty old granite harbour scooped out of the Bay, filled with water the colour of lime cordial, and a tangle of cottages and lanes nudging each other for space.

Long a magnet for artists, on account of the extraordinary quality of light, St Ives still has a wonderfully exotic feel. The vivid colours rebel against the restrained English palette, and its island-like setting means there are soft, white sand beaches and glimpses of the sea at every turn. A scattering of Cornish palms – not to mention the more recent arrival of frothy cappuccinos, fancy restaurants and fluffy white towels – combine to make it all feel considerably more French Riviera than Cornish Riviera.

In the 1850s, St Ives was a thriving centre of the fishing industry, but by the 1900s pilchard stocks had declined and the town was attracting schools of artists instead. Abstract painters and sculptors such as Barbara Hepworth, Ben Nicholson and Naum Gabo put St Ives firmly on the creative map. This small seaside town still has a big reputation when it comes to art, cemented by the construction of the third branch of the Tate

(see p282) in 1993, right on the beach, and the reopening of the Leach Pottery (see p282) in 2008.

St Ives is best explored on foot; its narrow, winding streets are no place for a car, and parking can be problematic. Besides, one of its great pleasures is to take an aimless stroll through the twisting 'downalong' alleys and lanes behind the harbour, where the fishermen used to live. These endlessly picturesque streets, forming an 'old town' of sorts, are lined with pint-sized white and granite cottages, decorated with bursting windowboxes and pastel-coloured paintwork. The town's main shopping street, pedestrianised Fore Street – now as much home to bijou boutiques, delis and galleries as to old-fashioned fudge shops – is a good place to dive in, with the subtropical Trewyn Gardens close by.

Alongside the inevitable tourist tat of a seaside town, St Ives has some characteristically creative small enterprises, such as I Should Coco (39 Fore Street, 01736 798756, www.ishouldcoco.co.uk), for fresh, hand-crafted chocolates and truffles of Cornish inspiration (try the Cornish sea salted caramel); Beaten Green (St Andrews Street, 01736 796799, www.beatengreen.co.uk, closed Mon, Sun Nov-Mar) for quirky vintage furnishings and design; and Seasalt (4 Fore Street, 01736 799684, www.seasaltcornwall.co.uk), a Cornish mini chain specialising in organic clothing. On Fore Street, St Ives Bookseller (no.2, 01736 796676, www.stives-bookseller.co.uk) is a dapper little establishment, and a rewarding place for a browse.

At the entrance to Smeaton's Pier, you can stick your nose into the miniature stone-built

St Ives harbour. See p269.

Porthminster Café. See p275.

St Ives Bay. See p269.

St Leonard's Chapel, where fishermen prayed before they went to sea. On the opposite side of the harbour stands the Lifeboat Station, open to visitors in summer. Between the two is the atmospheric Sloop Inn (01736 796584, www. sloop-inn.co.uk), one of the oldest pubs in Cornwall, and with tables right on the harbour. Stretching out north of the harbour like a big toe is the area known as 'the Island', an outcrop whose grassy footpath takes you on a short walk around the headland to Porthmeor Beach, and the Tate, on the other side.

Town beaches

It is hard to imagine a town of these diminutive dimensions with more (or better) beaches: if you count the harbour, which also transforms into a soft, sandy beach at low tide, St Ives has four beaches, all with clear waters and bright, clean sand. There's little Porthgwidden, hidden away in a nick on the Island, which is great for kids; Atlantic-facing Porthmeor, St Ives' surf star and home to the Tate gallery; and palm-trimmed Porthminster ★, whose waters and sands have been awarded Blue Flag status. Barely a mile out of town (and an exquisite walk along the coastal footpath) is another fine, Blue Flag beach at Carbis Bay.

Hayle

Gently curving round the north-eastern reaches of St Ives Bay are Hayle's impressive (and much-touted) 'three miles of golden sand', reaching from the mouth of the Hayle estuary all the way around the bay to Godrevy Point, an epic spot guarded by the Godrevy Lighthouse (thought to have been the inspiration for Virginia Woolf's novel To the Lighthouse). A world away from the cuteness and crowds of St Ives across the bay, the beaches of Gwithian and Godrevy, joined at low tide, are altogether more elemental scenes, pounded by some of Cornwall's best surf and with big open skies and sunsets.

The surf peters out as you walk south and, in the bay's sheltered south-western elbow, at Hayle Towans, fishing boats putter along the glassy estuary. Behind the harbour, the long, thin town of Hayle is slowly shedding its dated skin. It has a smattering of boutiques, including a good surf shop (Down the Line, Market Square Arcade, 01736 757025, www.downthelinesurf.co.uk), Mr B's ice-cream parlour (24 Penpol Terrace, 01736 758580, www.mrbsicecream.co.uk, closed Mon, Tue & Sun winter), boho veggie café Johnny's (50-51 Penpol Terrace, 01736 755928, closed Sun winter) and a contemporary art gallery. Up on the dunes, however, Hayle Towans, with its holiday parks and chalets, still has an air of Butlins about it.

Zennor

In the opposite direction, the scenic B3306 road heads west towards St Just, taking in some heart-stopping moor-meets-sea scenery along the way – as well as the famously pretty village of Zennor. DH Lawrence and his German wife Frieda spent two years living here during World War I, first staying at the Tinner's Arms, then renting a cottage

for the sum of £5 per year, until their eventual expulsion from Cornwall amid allegations of spying; their story is evocatively told, and the scenery painted, in Helen Dunmore's 1994 novel Zennor in Darkness. Little has changed in this tiny hamlet, and there is a timeless quality to the old buildings, the surrounding remains of ancient field systems and the wilderness of the granite moors.

Stop for a pint in the delightful one-room Tinners Arms (see p276), and wander around the pretty St Senara church, which has a famous carving of the mermaid of Zennor that is thought to be over 600 years old. There's also the Wayside Folk Museum (01736 796945, closed Nov-Mar & Sat term-time), with its working waterwheels, tools and domestic relics of days gone by.

Stunning coastal walks stretch out to either side of Zennor, and it's well worth taking in the windy drama of the Gurnard's Head, which pushes out into the Atlantic a mile or so to the west, before eating at the superb inn of the same name (see p274).

Where to eat & drink

The best harbourside spot for an honest pint in St Ives is the 14th-century Sloop Inn (see above), with benches by the water. Good café stops include the simple but chic Tate café, looking out to sea; deli-café the Digey Food Room (6 The Digey, 01736 799600, closed Sun); and Ocean Grill (Wharf Road, 01736 799874), with a seagull's-eye view over the harbour. Or eat on the beach with a hand-made pasty from blue-and-white-striped St Ives Bakery (52 Fore Street, 01736 798888).

Over at Gwithian, the Sunset Surf Shop & Café (10 Gwithian Towans, 01736 752575, www.sunset surfshop.co.uk, closed Tue, Wed Nov-Feb) lives up to its name, with views out to sea and to Godrevy Lighthouse – ideal for when the sun melts into the sea. It's a busy, post-surf refill station (with surf school attached), its tables usually packed with groups wolfing down chunky burgers and spicy wedges. A few doors down, the Jam Pot is a cosy caff serving mugs of tea and monster breakfasts.

A short drive out of Hayle, near Conner Downs, is one of Cornwall's most successful farm shops, Trevaskis Farm (Gwinear, 01209 713931, www. trevaskisfarm.co.uk) – renowned for its sausages, but stocking a huge variety of local produce. Meanwhile, its rustic Farmhouse Kitchen Restaurant serves solid bistro fare in generous portions.

Alba

Old Lifeboat House, The Wharf, St Ives, TR26 1LF (01736 797222, www.thealbarestaurant.com). Lunch served noon-2.30pm, dinner served 5.30-9pm daily.
Not a million years ago (as few as six, in fact), the Alba was the only destination restaurant in St Ives: a sleek, chic haven serving top-class Modern European cuisine with a dash of the Far East. In the face of stiff competition, we're pleased to report that it is a still a major player in newly gastro-centric St Ives. The harbourside location, in the old Lifeboat Station, is an irresistible draw; more importantly, the food is immaculately prepared – fillet of grey mullet on noodles

Things to do

ST IVES BAY & AROUND

Gwithian Academy of Surfing
Godrevy House, Prosper Hill, Gwithian, TR27 5BW (01736 757579, www.surfacademy.co.uk). Open phone for details.
The British Surf Association-approved Gwithian Academy teaches surfers of all levels in the beautiful setting of St Ives Bay.

Paradise Park
Trelissick Road, Hayle, TR27 4HB (01736 751020, www.paradisepark.org.uk). Open Mar, Apr, Oct 10am-4pm daily. May-Sept 10am-5pm daily. Nov-Feb 10am-3pm daily. Admission £7.95; £5.50-£6.50 reductions; £27.25 family.
In the event of beach overload, you might consider seeking distraction in this family-oriented wildlife sanctuary. It contains parrots and tropical birds galore, many of them rare and endangered species (among them the rare Cornish chough, the symbol of Cornwall, now making a comeback on the Lizard). There are regular free-flying bird shows and the flamingos roam free in the gardens, making for irresistible photo ops. There's also an indoor playground, a mini railway and, of course, a shop stacked to the rafters with brightly coloured parrot toys and paraphernalia.

MOUNT'S BAY

Cornish Way Cycle Path
www.sustrans.org.uk
Following the sea all the way from Penzance to Marazion (with access to St Michael's Mount), this very manageable, flat section of the Cornish Way cycle track takes you around the sweep of Mount's Bay. It is traffic-free most of the way, apart from a short stint at Marazion, and the views are fantastic. Bikes can be rented from the Cycle Centre Penzance (1 New Street, 01736 351671, www.cornwallcycle centre.co.uk, closed Sun) for £10 per day. For a longer ride, set off from Mousehole, which is part of the same designated national cycle route.

Jubilee Pool ★
The Promenade, Penzance (www.jubileepool.co.uk). Open end May-early Sept 10.30am-6pm daily. Admission £4; £2.30-£3.40 reductions.
Penzance's stunning art deco lido, which points gracefully into the waters of Mount's Bay, was built to mark George V's silver jubilee in 1935. Saved from destruction a few years back, the triangular pool, which is fed by sea water with the flowing of the tide, is now a listed building. The curving white edges, lines of changing cubicles and Cubist pale blue tiers and steps,

Jubilee Pool

and a fragrant ginger- and coriander-infused Asian-style broth, say, or hake with a creamy leek and mussel sauce – and the service assured.

Blas Burgerworks ★
The Warren, St Ives, TR26 2EA (01736 797272, www.blasburgerworks.co.uk). Food served July, Aug noon-3pm, 5-10pm daily. Sept-June 6-10pm Tue-Sun. Closed mid Nov-mid Dec, mid Jan-mid Feb.
St Ives' very own gourmet burger company occupies a pint-sized space secreted down a pretty, narrow lane. Seating is on stools at communal tables and elbow room is scarce, but once you've sunk your teeth into one of Blas's chargrilled burgers, comfort seems a secondary consideration. In the absence of an available seat, grab a burger and walk a few yards to the seafront (keeping a watchful eye on the circling seagulls, renowned for their barefaced swoop-and-steal operations). Cornish meat is used in all the beefburgers, and Blas has a committed green agenda: all organic waste is composted, the furniture is made from reclaimed timber and

local produce is king. Service is exemplary. Note that opening times do vary – and that sometimes (spring half-terms, for example) lunch is served out of season.

Gurnard's Head ★
Treen, nr Zennor, TR26 3DE (01736 796928, www.gurnardshead.co.uk). Lunch served 12.30-2.30pm, dinner served 6.30-9pm daily.
With the desolate Penwith moorland on one side and the foaming sea on the other, this coastal inn – named after the rocky outcrop a few fields away, shaped like a gurnard's head – boasts a splendidly isolated setting. Although the gastronomically astute menu, confident service and rustic chic decor place the Gurnard's well out of the pub grub bracket, the atmosphere is buoyant and informal, the prices fair and the food fuss-free. This is hearty British comfort food of the highest order: pork belly with mash, cabbage, cider and thyme, rabbit and partridge terrine or gurnard with roasted fennel and zesty mash. Also the owners of the celebrated Felin Fach Griffin inn in Wales, the Inkins are

Minack Theatre

set against the background of the open sea, are a photographer's dream (several books of images are for sale around town). Its beauty is no protection against the often limb-numbing water temperatures, though, and savvy locals often wear a wetsuit. There are deckchairs for hire, and the lichen-coloured Poolside Indulgence café (www.poolside-indulgence.co.uk) is the perfect spot for a light lunch or a late afternoon tipple with views out to sea and across to Newlyn. Needless to say, the pool closes in winter.

300 Cornwall Explorer
0845 600 1420, www.firstgroup.com.
Tickets £6-£6.50.
Set aside any predjudice about bus tours – this open-top double decker does a good-value circuit of the Penwith peninsula for just £6.50 (hop-on, hop-off).

It's a round trip from Penzance, stopping at Newlyn, Porthcurno, Land's End, Sennen Cove, St Just, Geevor Tin Mine, St Ives and Marazion. There are four services a day from May to August, leaving Penzance at 10.55, 12.55, 2.55pm and 4.55pm.

LAND'S END & AROUND

Fat Hen ★
Gwenmenhir, Boscawen-noon Farm, St Buryan, TR19 6EH (01736 810156, www.fathen.org).
With the help of two specialist chefs, ecologist Caroline Davey runs gourmet Wild Food Weekends and foraging outings deep in the West Cornwall countryside.

Minack Theatre ★
Porthcurno, TR19 6JU (01736 810181, www.minack.com). Visitor Centre Open Summer 9.30am-5.30pm Mon, Tue, Thur, Sat, Sun; 9.30am-noon Wed, Fri. Winter 10am-4pm daily. Admission £3; £1.20-£2.20 reductions.
There can be few more memorable theatre trips for children (or adults, for that matter) than a performance at the open-air Minack Theatre, a Greek-inspired amphitheatre carved out of a granite cliff 200 feet above Porthcurno Beach, with the ocean as the backdrop. The theatre was founded by the quite extraordinary Rowena Cade, and its first production in 1932 was, aptly given the wild surrounds, *The Tempest*; the visitor centre tells the story. Performances take place from June to September: book early and bear in mind that performances go ahead in all but the most extreme weather conditions – bring jumpers, anoraks, a picnic and cushions (the Minack also hires them out, for a charge).

Sennen Surfing Centre
Churchtown House, Sennen, TR19 4AD (01736 871227, 01736 871561, www.sennensurfingcentre.com). Open Easter-Sept; call in advance to book. Lessons from £25.
There can be few greater settings for a surf lesson than Sennen in the far west, where long-haired, youthful instructors take group and private lessons.

firm believers in 'the simple things in life done well'. And so now are hundreds of hungry hikers, urban refugees and locals getting together for a family roast – so bookings are essential in high season. One of Cornwall's best eats.

Moomaid of Zennor ★
The Wharf, St Ives, TR26 1LG (01736 799285, www.moomaidofzennor.co.uk). Open Summer 9am-10.30pm daily. Winter 11am-5pm daily.
Made in the nearby village of Zennor, Moomaid is a cool new contender for the Cornish ice-cream crown – and the competition is fiercer than ever (*see p277*). Its new boutique ice-cream parlour on the front at St Ives beats the more mainstream offerings hands-down. Note: opening times are a guide, rather than gospel.

Porthgwidden Beach Café
Porthgwidden Beach, St Ives, TR26 1PL (01736 796791, www.porthgwiddencafe.co.uk). Food served Summer 8-11am, noon-3.30pm, 6-9pm daily.

Winter 8-11am, noon-3.30pm Tue, Wed, Sun; 8-11am, noon-3.30pm, 6-9pm Thur-Sat.
The Porthminster Café's (*see below*) more easy-going sister restaurant is a delightful spot for a full English, a light lunch or just a good Lavazza coffee overlooking St Ives' most secluded beach. The white-walled and wooden-floored interior is beachside breezy but in summer it's all about the terrace, with its blue gingham tablecloths and fabulous views out into the bay. Prices are very fair given the prime location (from £1.95 for buttered crumpets to £14.50 for Cornish rib-eye steak, and no wines over £20) – and it's open year-round.

Porthminster Café ★
Porthminster Beach, St Ives, TR26 2EB (01736 795352, www.porthminstercafe.co.uk). Food served Summer noon-4pm, 6-10pm daily. Winter noon-3pm Tue-Thur, Sun; noon-3pm, 6-9pm Fri, Sat.
The name rather understates its case: far from being your average beach-side caff, the Porthminster Café is a serious

restaurant in the body of a laid-back beach house – albeit a very classy one. Australian chef Michael Smith's sunkissed menu sets the perfect tone for holiday dining, with the emphasis on Mediterranean flavours and fresh seafood, as well as posh fish and chips (with white balsamic vinegar, naturally). Friendly, slick service, fresh decor and dreamy views over the white sands of Porthminster Beach make this the ideal perch from which to contemplate the light dancing in the bay with a glass of local bubbly (try the Polgoon Aval or Camel Valley brut). Porthminster is not only one of St Ives' best kitchens, but is quickly making inroads into the upper echelons of Cornwall's burgeoning restaurant scene. Booking recommended.

St Andrews Street Bistro

16 St Andrews Street, St Ives, TR26 1AH (01736 797074). Dinner served Feb-Oct 6-10.30pm daily.
A supremely quirky, low-lit counterpart to the light, bright eateries of modern-day St Ives, retro-styled St Andrews Street appeals to St Ives' boho set with oodles of atmosphere, compelling modern art on the walls (there's nary a quaint fishing village scene in sight) and an eclectic, globetrotting menu, which might include anything from goat curry to ostrich fillet, as well as more classic bistro fare (fish cakes, pasta, pâtés). Best of all, prices are accessible and it's BYO – though a limited range of wine and spirits is also served.

Tinners Arms

Zennor, TR26 3BY (01736 796927, www.tinners arms.com). Open 11.30am-11pm Mon-Sat; noon-10.30pm Sun. Lunch served noon-2.30pm, dinner served 6.30-9pm daily.
A peaceful little pub in Penwith's prettiest village, the Tinners feels like it probably hasn't changed a great deal since it was built in the 13th century. And we mean that in

a good way: flagstone floors, a log fire, good beer, no musak, no TV and no fruit machines. In short, just the sort of place you daydream about stumbling across after a windy walk on the moors. The White House next door (*see p278*) has simple but tasteful white rooms.

Where to stay

Blue Hayes Private Hotel

Trelyon Avenue, St Ives, TR26 2AD (01736 797129, www.bluehayes.co.uk). Rates £150-£210 double incl breakfast.
The 'private' tag is fitting: tucked discreetly away above Porthminster Beach (a mere ten minutes from the harbour), Blue Hayes has just five luxuriously appointed suites and a guests-only restaurant. Owner Malcolm Herring spent two years overhauling an old 1920s guesthouse, halving the number of rooms and creating a clean, classic interior design with the odd touch of glamour. The rooms have spacious terraces, dazzling sea views and immaculate bathrooms – but the icing on the cake is the balustraded white terrace. Here, you can take breakfast (or a cocktail at sunset) overlooking the harbour. More St Tropez than St Ives.

Boskerris

Boskerris Road, Carbis Bay, St Ives, TR26 2NQ (01736 795295, www.boskerrishotel.co.uk). Rates £105-£230 double incl breakfast.
Over the past six years, this 1930s hotel – on the southern edge of St Ives in Carbis Bay – has been transformed by the Bassett family into a haven of contemporary coastal chic. It's furnished with unerring good taste (Osborne & Little outsized floral wallpaper, perspex coffee tables, pristine white rugs) and run with admirable attention to detail

Zennor. See p273.

(perfectly placed mirrors to reflect the sea, fresh milk for tea). The panoramic terrace is in pole position to take in the sweep of the whole bay, with St Ives on one side and the white horses crashing into the Godrevy Lighthouse on the other, and nearly all rooms have ocean views. Breakfast is sure to satisfy the fussiest of foodies – a named-local-source menu includes ricotta hot cakes with berry compote and French toast with pan-fried bananas and maple syrup. The centre of St Ives can be accessed via a 20-minute walk along the coastal path, or a three-minute train journey on the charming branch line train.

Eleven Sea View Terrace

11 Sea View Terrace, St Ives, TR26 2DH (01736 798440, www.11stives.co.uk). Rates £90-£115 double incl breakfast.
Technically it's a B&B, but aesthetically this Edwardian townhouse is breaking well out of its bracket. The three rooms are stylish and understated, with white walls, navy blue accents and spotless modern bathrooms. In terms of views, the address says it all: located at the top of town, it has two rooms with views over the old town below; the other has a private south-facing terrace by way of compensation.

Gwithian Farm Campsite ★

1 Church Town Road, Gwithian, TR27 5BX (01736 753127, www.gwithianfarm.co.uk). Rates £12-£20.50 for 2 people.
Despite boasting the kind of coastal setting that leads many a campsite to nonchalance, Gwithian Farm shows an unwavering commitment to high standards, providing the sort of cut-above facilities that usually involve braving a large, expensive holiday park. Campsite luxuries include a state-of-the-art shower block, a plethora of child-friendly features, large pitches and an incredibly well-stocked campsite shop (miniature bottles of Felippo Berio olive oil, locally picked strawberries, a visiting fishmonger, OS maps, national newspapers). There is a solid village pub just across the road, and the beach is a 15-minute walk away. Advance booking is essential in high season.

Primrose Valley Hotel

Porthminster Beach, St Ives, TR26 2ED (01736 794939, www.primroseonline.co.uk). Rates £100-£165 double incl breakfast.
This lovingly run hotel is one of St Ives' best boutique options, with a quiet but central beachside location, contemporary styling and keen attention to guests' needs. Just metres from the soft sands of Porthminster Beach (ask for directions, as the location is decidedly discreet), white-fronted Primrose Valley has the feel of a seaside villa; request a front-facing room with sea views for the full effect. Despite hip hotel accents (kitschy floral wallpaper, retro lamps, pink and purple hues), this is an unpretentious place, where substance is as important as style. Expect a superb organic breakfast, personal service, a small bar that goes well beyond the call of duty (a 50-strong wine list and Riedel crystal glasses) and a commitment to reducing its ecological impact. There's even a stylish REN therapy room on site.

Treliska Guest House

3 Bedford Road, St Ives, TR26 1SP (01736 797678, www.treliska.com). Rates £64-£80 double incl breakfast. No credit cards.

FIVE CORNISH ICE-CREAMS

Jelberts Ices
A splendid scoop of ice-cream nostalgia, Jelberts (New Road, Newlyn, no phone) has been selling vanilla, and vanilla alone, out of these tiny Newlyn premises since time began… Or since the 1950s, at any rate. Measured against the wacky flavours doing battle across the county, its adherence to own-made vanilla might seem old-fashioned, but with clotted cream and a flake, it's ice-cream heaven. Small, fresh batches of unadulterated ice-cream are made daily, and the slightly grainy texture tastes wonderfully home-made. Closed out of season.

Kelly's of Cornwall
Available in supermarkets nationwide, and at almost every beach in Cornwall, Kelly's (www.kellysofcornwall.co.uk) is hardly an artisinal operation. Nonetheless, it does sterling service in producing just under ten million litres a year of very commendable (and affordable) clotted cream vanilla ice-cream. Its 'whip' cones are the smoothest around.

Moomaid of Zennor
The new kid on the ice block, Moomaid (www.moomaidofzennor.co.uk) has speedily made inroads into the very competitive Cornish ice-cream market with its fantastic range of 'creams and fruity sorbets, and some inspired flavours (peach bellini, anyone?). It has a cute parlour on the front at St Ives (*see p275*).

Roskillys
Producing high-grade artisan ice-cream on its dairy farm on the Lizard, Roskilly's (www.roskillys.co.uk) stands out by dint of its texture; there's no stinting on chunk size either. It's available all over west Cornwall, although true devotees head for the farm where it's made on the Lizard (*see p257*).

Treleavens
South-east Cornwall's finest parlour produces a tasty, all-natural product that can be found in the Treleavens shop in Looe (www.treleavens.co.uk) and various other outlets all over east Cornwall. Award-winning flavours include panna cotta with summer fruits and orange and mascarpone.

A few minutes' walk from the harbour and just off the high street (there's no dedicated parking area, though staff can arrange a private space nearby at extra cost), Treliska has some of St Ives' best-value rooms – modern, clean and tastefully decorated. Breakfast warrants a mention, with own-made breads and muesli, as well as a fine full English and American-style pancakes, and hosts Gill and Mike are supremely accommodating.

White House
Tinners Arms, Zennor, TR26 3BY (01736 796927, www.tinnersarms.com). Rates £90 double incl breakfast.
Attached to the lovely old Tinners Arms in Zennor, this tiny guesthouse is one of those rare places where you can find simple good taste and a beautiful setting and still get change from £100. The four rooms (two doubles, two singles) are decorated in fresh whites, with rustic wooden furniture and fresh flowers.

MOUNT'S BAY

Penzance
The best way to arrive in Penzance is by train – partly for the feeling of having escaped to the end of the line, but also because when the track emerges from the Cornish countryside on to the curve of Mount's Bay, it reveals a perfect view of the town on the hill above. The commercial centre for the western district of Penwith, Penzance was once a fashionable seaside resort – the trappings of which can still be seen in the fading but elegant architecture along Cornwall's only seaside promenade, notably the art deco Jubilee Pool (*see p274*).

These days, compared to Cornwall's more prettified seaside towns – Fowey, Padstow, St Ives – Penzance is rather frayed around the edges. But it is an atmospheric place, with plenty of bohemian charm, a smattering of seaside irreverence and a newly prospering art scene, consolidated by the opening of the Exchange, a major new modern art centre, in 2008. Leading commercial galleries include Stonemans (56 Chapel Street, 01736 361756, www.stoneman publications.co.uk), Cornwall Contemporary (1 Parade Street, Queens Square, 01736 874749, www.cornwallcontemporary.com) and the Rainyday Gallery (22 Market Jew Street, 01736 366077, www.rainydaygallery.co.uk), all of which are closed on Sundays. On Market Jew Street, Books Plus (no.23, 01736 365607, www.booksplusuk.com) stocks books on the local art scene amid its enjoyably eclectic stock.

The venerable Penzance Arts Club (01736 363761, www.penzanceartsclub.co.uk) occupies a splendid old listed building with a walled garden on Chapel Street, the town's original high street. As we went to press, it had changed hands and plans were afoot to update the tired premises and guest rooms, while keeping its bohemian spirit alive – watch the website for news.

Traditionally, Penzance is renowned for its mild climate and sun-trap feel. On a windy February weekend you may not be convinced, but subtropical plants genuinely thrive in havens such as Morrab Gardens and Penlee Park in the centre of town – and don't be surprised if you see banana trees and palms poking out of front gardens. Further evidence of clement climes comes in the shape of the recently cultivated Polgoon vineyard (Rosehill, 01736 333946, www.polgoon.co.uk) on the outskirts of town, which is open for tours. The first year's rosé garnered praise, and the Aval, a refined, French-style sparkling cider, is now served in Rick Stein outposts and the Porthminster Café (*see p275*), among others.

For many, Penzance is the jumping-off point for the Scilly Isles, 28 miles west – the *Scillonian III* leaves from the harbour and the heliport is on the outskirts of town. For the Isles of Scilly, *see p287*.

Marazion
Although it is now hard to believe, Marazion, not Penzance, was the major port and commercial centre in Mount's Bay until the 17th century, and it is one of Cornwall's oldest chartered towns. These days, its winding, narrow main street gets tourist-logged in summer, with visitors flocking to see the area's star attraction, St Michael's Mount (*see p283*). You can walk across to the island via a causeway that reveals itself at low tide, but ferries also run.

Even if you're not visiting the Mount, it's well worth walking or cycling the coastal trail (*see p274*) that hugs the bay from Penzance all the way to Marazion; in the right conditions, you'll see kite- and wind-surfers in action against the backdrop of the Mount. At the end, repair to the large terrace of the Godolphin Arms (West End, 01736 710202, www.godolphinarms.co.uk), a pint of ale in hand, to admire the bay twinkling in the foreground and Penzance in the distance.

Newlyn
Almost joined to Penzance to the south, Newlyn nevertheless retains a strong identity, with a history that is strongly linked to both art and fishing. Despite the decline in the fishing industry, this is still the country's biggest fishing port and the site of Newlyn Fish Festival, held over the August bank holiday. In contrast to Mousehole, a few miles round the coast, Newlyn has the look and feel of a working port, and anyone with an interest in fishing should take a closer look at the harbour – or at the very least, invest in some gleaming fish or fresh Newlyn crab from W Stevenson and Sons (01736 362982, closed Sun) on the main street; there's another branch in Penzance (Wharfside, 01736 331459, closed Sun).

Its importance as a centre of art in the late 19th and early 20th century, when the Newlyn School nurtured such names as Stanhope Forbes, Henry Scott Tuke and Walter Langley, is represented in the longstanding but recently revamped Newlyn Gallery (*see p283*), just off the promenade. There is little else to detain you, bar a couple of good commercial galleries along the main street and traditional ice-cream maker Jelberts (*see p277*), on New Road.

CORNWALL

Mousehole

On a sunny morning, before the summer crowds throng the harbour walls and car-owners make misguided attempts to navigate its minuscule streets, Mousehole (pronounced Mowzel) seems too perfect to be true. Its tiny harbour is fringed with soft, yellow sand, while the granite cottages huddling together behind are made all the more irresistible by carefully tended window boxes and the odd cat peeking out. But even if Mousehole has, by dint of its beauty, become a tourist magnet, with cramped fisherman's cottages attracting mind-boggling offers, the village has retained plenty of character, and has a strong sense of community year-round. The village's colourful Christmas lights, draped across the boats in the harbour and the quayside, are a sight to be seen. The best date for a visit is 23 December, when the village makes Starry Gazey pie in honour of Tom Bawcock's Eve; its namesake is said to have saved the village from starvation in the early 20th century, setting sail in stormy seas to land a bountiful catch of fish.

Where to eat & drink

Penzance has no shortage of pleasant cafés and small, laid-back eateries. Among the most appealing are Archie Brown's (Bread Street, 01736 362828, www.archiebrowns.co.uk, closed Sun), perennially popular for its healthy veggie food; the Deli (27 Market Place, 01736 350223, http://finefoodscornwall.co.uk, closed Sun), selling Cornish goodies and good coffee; the Honey Pot (5 Parade Street, 01736 368686, closed Sun), a cosy nook that has at least three types of chocolate cake on the go at any one time; and, in season, the alfresco Poolside Indulgence (Wharf Road, 0777 999 8590, www.poolside-indulgence.co.uk, closed winter), next to Jubilee Pool, has views out into the bay.

The best pasties in town can be found at Lavender's (6A Alverton Street, 01736 362800, closed Sun) or county-wide stalwart WC Rowe (73 Causewayhead, 01736 333193, closed Sun). After dark, head for recent arrival the Zero Lounge (Chapel Street, 01736 361220), an underground cocktail bar with outdoor seating.

On the way into Mousehole is the casually chic café-restaurant at the Old Coastguard Hotel (01736 731222, www.oldcoastguardhotel.co.uk), with palm-fronted sea views. If you'd prefer a boozer, we recommend the Ship Inn (South Cliff, 01736 731234, www.shipmousehole.co.uk), an archetypal Cornish pub that's right on the harbour.

The Bay

Penzance Hotel, Britons Hill, Penzance, TR18 3AE (01736 366890, www.bay-penzance.co.uk). Lunch served noon-2.30pm Mon-Fri, Sun. Dinner served 6-9pm daily. The restaurant at the Penzance Hotel has a superb view, out to St Michael's Mount and the harbour below, and a fine veranda with stylish rattan furniture from which to survey it. Dinner ventures into pricey terrain, but the lunch menu is good value, offering two courses for £12.50. The menu

Boutique Retreats. See p285.

Sennen Cove. See p285.

is a modern Cornish affair (smoked mackerel, goat's cheese and rocket, local catch of the day...), taking few risks – but the results, combined with the view, merit a stop.

Poets Café
Trereife House, Newlyn, TR20 8TJ (01736 362750, www.trereifepark.co.uk). Lunch served 10am-5pm daily.
On the outskirts of Penzance, Trereife is an impressive 18th-century manor house with a fine Queen Anne façade and beautiful 18th-century formal gardens (open to the public). For those in the know, though, the ridiculously pretty one-room café in the old stables is just as much of a draw. Tea, light lunches and hefty slices of cake are served; blue and white spotted tablecloths, wild flowers on the tables and Charles Trenet on the stereo complete the scene. There's an art gallery upstairs.

Turks Head
Chapel Street, Penzance, TR18 4AF (01736 363093, www.turksheadpenzance.co.uk). Open 11am-11pm Mon-Sat; 11am-10.30pm Sun. Lunch served noon-2.30pm, dinner served 6-9.30pm.
On historic Chapel Street, Penzance's oldest pub is a nicely worn nook dating back to the 13th century, which cries out for a cosy pint by the log fire. This place was originally a smugglers' hangout; ask about the underground tunnel

that once led from the harbour. With Doom and Betty Stoggs on tap, a quiet atmosphere and resolutely traditional furnishings, the Turk's is a fine antidote to Cornwall's new wave of blue and white bistros. There's a palm-shaded beer garden at the back. A few doors down, the Admiral Benbow (01736 363448), surreally decorated with objects retrieved from shipwrecked vessels, is another historic inn.

2 Fore Street
2 Fore Street, Mousehole, TR19 6QU (01736 731164, www.2forestreet.co.uk). Lunch served noon-3pm, dinner served 6-9.30pm daily. Closed Mon Nov-Mar.
A relative newcomer on the west Cornwall dining scene, this bright bistro on Mousehole harbour is as dinky and perfectly formed as the village itself. The kitchen isn't in the business of statement cooking, sticking instead to a short but sweet menu of favourites, prepared to a very high standard: shell-roasted Newlyn scallops with lemon butter, crab and chilli linguine or whole baked sea bream, and the likes of chocolate tart and lemon curd pannacotta for dessert. Own-made bread, cheerful service and locally sourced ingredients add to the appeal. There's not a huge amount of space – and you'll need to book early to get a window seat – but there's also a pretty, sheltered garden with a few tables at the back.

Places to visit

Barbara Hepworth Museum & Sculpture Garden

Leach Pottery

*Higher Stennack, St Ives, TR26 2HE (01736 799703,
www.leachpottery.com). Open Mar-Oct 10am-5pm
Mon-Sat; 11am-4pm Sun. Nov-Feb 10am-4pm
Tue-Sat. Admission £4.50; free-£3.50 reductions.*
Among the modernist heavyweights of the 1930s
St Ives art colony (which included the likes of Barbara
Hepworth, Ben Nicholson and Naum Gabo) was the
pioneering potter Bernard Leach, widely hailed as
the 'father of studio pottery'. After long years of
neglect, his internationally renowned Leach Pottery,
founded in 1920 with Japanese potter Shoji Hamada,
reopened in 2008 after a £1.7 million restoration
and redevelopment programme – furnishing St Ives
its third major artistic attraction, alongside the Tate
and the Barbara Hepworth Museum. Born in Hong
Kong, Leach spent his formative years mingling with the
artists of the Japanese Shirakaba folk craft movement;
when it opened, the Leach Pottery was the first in the
Western world to install a Japanese wood-burning kiln.
Now a scheduled monument, the kiln stands – as it did
the 1970s – in the most evocative part of the museum:
the old pottery, which has been left respectfully
unpolished. The Leach Tableware collection, produced
on site and sold in the shop, makes a classy souvenir.

Tate St Ives ★

*Porthmeor Beach, St Ives, TR26 1TG (01736 796226,
www.tate.org.uk/stives). Open Mar-Oct 10am-5pm
daily. Nov-Feb 10am-4pm Tue-Sun. Admission £5.65;
free-£3.20 reductions.*
The undisputed flagship of Cornwall's art scene, the
UK's smallest Tate occupies a striking, curving building
in an even more striking location: Porthmeor Beach.
At the heart of the building is an open-air rotunda
(representing the gas-holder that once occupied the
site at the old gasworks); the brightly coloured glass
display is the work of late Cornish artist Patrick Heron.
The museum's changing exhibitions (there is no
permanent collection) showcase the work of 20th-
century painters and sculptors, particularly those
associated with St Ives (the naive art of Alfred Wallis,
say, the geometrical paintings of Ben Nicholson or the
studio pottery of Bernard Leach), as well as exhibiting
contemporary artists as part of its artist-in-residence
programme. Take a breather in the top-floor café, which
has great views over the old town and out to sea.

ST IVES BAY & AROUND

Barbara Hepworth Museum & Sculpture Garden

*Barnoon Hill, St Ives, TR26 1AD (01736 796226,
www.tate.org.uk/stives/hepworth). Open Mar-Oct
10am-5pm daily. Nov-Feb 10am-4pm Tue-Sun.
Admission £4.65; free-£2.70 reductions.*
Owned and managed by the Tate, this small museum
is an engaging tribute to one of the 20th century's
most important artistic figures. Sculptor Barbara
Hepworth made this her home and studio from 1949
until her death in 1975. It offers a fascinating insight
into Hepworth's life, with her studio and garden
preserved as she left it. Her curving sculptures,
including *Fallen Images* (which was completed only
a few months before her death), are complemented
by biographical material, while the garden, which
she helped to design, displays her larger pieces in
a peaceful subtropical setting.

MOUNT'S BAY

Chysauster Ancient Village

*TR20 8XA (07831 757934, www.english-heritage.
org.uk). Open Apr-Sept 10am-5pm daily. Oct 10am-
4pm daily. Admission £3; £1.50-£2.60 reductions.*
This wild, exposed site dates from the first century
BC and features the best-preserved hut circles in the
UK – not to mention some awesome views over the
granite-strewn moors. More ancient village remains
and a fogou (an Iron Age underground structure) can
be seen at Carn Euny, near Sancreed, further west.

The Exchange

*Princes Street, Penzance, TR18 2NL (01736
363715, www.newlynartgallery.co.uk). Open Mar-Oct
10am-5pm Mon-Sat. Nov-Feb 10am-5pm Tue-Sat.
Admission free.*

The wave-like exterior of the old phone exchange building – after dark, pulsing with the sea blues and greens of Peter Freeman's light installation – announces your arrival at west Cornwall's major new contemporary art gallery, an offshoot of the Newlyn Art Gallery. The look is sleek and modern and the curating ambitious – you are more likely to find a boundary-pushing installation than a pretty seascape. There is no permanent collection, but four or so exhibitions a year spotlight local and national artists. The airy café/shop is good for a light lunch of smoked mackerel with salad, or soup and crusty bread.

Newlyn Art Gallery

New Road, Newlyn, TR18 5PZ (01736 363715, www.newlynartgallery.co.uk). Open Mar-Oct 10am-5pm Mon-Sat. Nov-Feb 10am-5pm Tue-Sat. Admission Free.

Once home to the Newlyn School of artists from the late 19th century, Newlyn continues to support a thriving art scene, with this long-standing gallery at its heart. It has occupied this site just back from the promenade for over 100 years, but underwent a much-needed redevelopment and expansion in 2007 (which included the addition of the affiliated Exchange gallery in the centre of Penzance, *see p282*),

St Michael's Mount

and holds exhibitions of national and international contemporary art. There is a small shop, but no café.

Penlee House Gallery & Museum

Morrab Road, Penzance, TR18 4HE (01736 363625, www.penleehouse.org.uk). Open Apr-Sept 10am-5pm Mon-Sat. Oct-Mar 10.30am-4.30pm Mon-Sat. Admission £3; free-£2 reductions; all admission free Sat.

A smart Italianate Victorian villa, Penlee House holds the largest collection of paintings by the Newlyn School. Look out for Norman Garstin's *The Rain it Raineth Every Day*, painted in 1889, and the earliest work in the collection – *Mount's Bay* (1794) by William Brooks, as well as key works by Stanhope Forbes and Walter Langley. Note that there is no permanent display and only a selection of paintings is hung at any one time. A small museum covers Cornish history in brief, with exhibits ranging from Stone Age tools to the mining safety lamp invented by Penzance's famous son Humphrey Davy (1778-1829). The Orangery café is an idyllic spot for an open-air lunch, amid exotic gardens.

St Michael's Mount ★

Marazion (01736 710507, www.stmichaelsmount. co.uk). Open Castle Apr-Oct 10.30am-5pm Mon-Fri, Sun. Tours Nov-Mar 11am, 2pm Tue, Fri (weather permitting; call to check). Gardens May, June 10.30am-5pm Mon-Fri. July-Oct 10.30am 5pm Thur, Fri. Admission £7 castle; £8.75 castle & gardens; £3.50-£4.40 reductions.

Just off the coast of Marazion, St Michael's Mount – bearing an uncanny resemblance to its namesake across the channel – is the stuff of fairytale; an iconic island castle holding court in the bay. Legend claims the mount was once the lair of the giant Cormoran, who tyrannised the local population but was defeated in true David and Goliath fashion by a little Cornish boy. Early records, however, show that the mount began life as a bustling port for the fishermen of Marazion. Its religious status was conferred when a church was added and, by the eighth century, a monastery had been founded. It was used as a store for Royalist arms during the Civil War, before becoming the residence of the St Aubyn family. St Michael's Mount was donated to the National Trust in 1954 by Lord St Levan, although his son, the fourth baron, still lives on the island.

For visitors, it's a rousing walk across the granite causeway at low tide (there's also a ferry), followed by a steep climb from the harbour up the Pilgrim's Steps to the castle entrance; pause to admire the giant's stone heart in the cobbles on the way. Inside, the castle is disarmingly cosy and compact, with paintings, weapons and military trophies dominating the displays.

Trengwainton Garden

Madron, TR20 8RZ (01736 363148, www.national trust.org.uk/trengwainton). Open Feb-Nov 10.30am-5pm Mon-Thur, Sun. Admission £5.80; £2.90 reductions.

The handsome pile at the end of the sweeping drive isn't open to visitors, but there is plenty to admire in the extensive gardens. At its best in springtime, the sheltered estate incorporates magnificent wooded walks through a stream-fed valley, gorgeous kitchen gardens with unusual sloped beds, and all manner of

Places to visit

▶ exotic plants. On a sunny day, the lawn terrace and summerhouses at the top, with views to Mount's Bay, invite a picnic break or even a siesta.

LAND'S END & AROUND

Geevor Tin Mine ★
Pendeen, TR19 7EW (01736 788662, www.geevor.com). Open Mar-Oct 9am-5pm Mon-Fri, Sun. Nov-Feb 9am-4pm Mon-Fri, Sun. Admission £8.50; £4.50-£7.50 reductions; £25 family.
Geevor was a working mine for over 80 years, employing some 400 at its peak, before its closure in 1990 after the crash in tin prices had rendered the huge clifftop operation economically unfeasible. Following a multi-million-pound preservation programme, which included the addition of the interactive Hard Rock Musuem in 2008, the mine has been brought back to life as a visitor attraction. The site has been sensitively adapted, leaving the workings of the mine wonderfully intact – everything from the hulking machines of the compressor house and the ore processing mill down to the helmets and paperwork of the employees remains in place. Visits culminate with an underground tour of the tunnels, conducted by ex-miners – an experience that is as emotive as it is claustrophobic.

Geevor offers a captivating insight into the scale of the mining operation in the area, and Cornwall's preeminence in the industrial world before it became better known for cream teas, beach holidays and surfing. With even a passing curiosity you could spend hours here, and with any sort of specialist interest you could be absorbed for days. One of Cornwall's great unsung sights – and serving a fine hand-made pasty in the café to boot.

Levant Mine & Beam Engine
Trwellard, TR19 7SX (01736 786156, www.national trust.org.uk/levantmineandbeamengine). Open July-Sept 11am-5pm Tue-Fri, Sun. June 11am-5pm Wed-Fri, Sun. Apr, Oct, May 11am-5pm Wed, Fri. Admission £5.80; £2.90 reductions; £14.50 family.

With a panoramic cliffside location, just around the coast from Geevor Tin Mine, Levant offers visitors the chance to see an original steam-powered Cornish beam engine in action. Originally used to winch men and materials up from the shaft, this one was restored after lying dormant for 60 years. Check the website for the times and days before setting out; underground tours are also conducted.

Merry Maidens
Off B3315, nr Lamorna.
One of the country's best-preserved stone circles, the Merry Maidens comprises 19 standing stones set in a tidy circle, next to the road from Newlyn to Land's End. There's no fanfare on arrival, just the occasional curious onlooker, but that makes the scene all the more bewitching. Legend has it that the stones are a group of women who were petrified for dancing on a Sunday.

Telegraph Museum
Porthcurno, TR19 6JX (01736 810966, www.porthcurno.org.uk). Open Apr-Oct 10am-5pm daily. Nov-Mar 10am-5pm Mon, Sun. Admission £5.50, £3.10-£4.90 reductions.
Now more talked about for its tropically coloured waters and white sands – and, of course, the Minack Theatre (*see p275*) – the remote cove of Porthcurno was also once a pioneering communications station, and the landing point for the first long-distance underwater telegraph cable connecting Britain with India. The Eastern Telegraph Company grew through the 19th century and into the early 20th (and eventually merged with Marconi's Wireless Telegraph Company, later to become Cable & Wireless), making Porthcurno a target during World War II. To this end, a bomb-proof underground tunnel, bored by local miners, was built: the bunker now houses part the museum. Overhauled and opened in 1998 as a visitor attraction, this is an absorbing museum, with interactive exhibits, an engaging talk (during which you get to hold sections of underwater cable) and clear explanations of what are – even for internet agers – tricky concepts.

Telegraph Museum

CORNWALL

Where to stay

Abbey Hotel
Abbey Street, Penzance, TR18 4AR (01736 366906, www.theabbeyonline.co.uk). Rates £105-£200 double incl breakfast.
The Abbey's restaurant may have lost the Michelin star it won under chef Ben Tunnicliffe (now heading up the kitchen at the new Scarlet hotel, *see p226*), but the hotel continues to offer some of west Cornwall's most sumptuous rooms. Owned by former '60s model Jean Shrimpton, and now managed by her son Thad and his wife, the Abbey casts a heady spell of away-from-it-all indulgence with heavy curtains, antiques and chandeliers. The eight spacious rooms are plush and flouncy, and the blue-painted, 17th-century manor house is a listed building, with a superb position overlooking the harbour. The old-world drawing room and private walled garden at the back are the stuff of minibreak fantasy.

Boutique Retreats ★
Mousehole (01326 231112, www.boutique-retreats. co.uk). Rates £270-£360 Fri-Sun.
This crossover concept falls somewhere between a swanky boutique hotel and a cute holiday cottage. You get all the perks of a high-end hotel – roll-top bath, king-size bed, goose-down duvet, freshly cut flowers, soft white towels, mini toiletries, Wi-Fi – all the while being in possession of your own key, and therefore total privacy. So no small talk with the receptionist, and no need to surface in time for the dregs of the breakfast buffet (you'll find your fridge stocked with an organic breakfast kit). Choose between two romantic boltholes in the pretty village of Mousehole, available for short breaks and week-long sojourns.

The Summer House
Cornwall Terrace, Penzance, TR18 4HL (01736 363744, www.summerhouse-cornwall.com). Rates £95-£125 double incl breakfast.
Squeezed into a little mews in Penzance, this blue-painted boutique B&B is just a few paces from the promenade. The rooms are invitingly fresh and stylish (and, with their baby blues, sunny yellows, pinstripes and lashings of white, 100% chintz-free). Breakfast can be consumed in the pretty patio garden, complete with Cornish palms, and guests can also take advantage of the Summer House's 12-table 'dinner club', serving superb Mediterranean cuisine care of Italian chef-owner Ciro. Book ahead as there are only five rooms, and they are much coveted.

LAND'S END & AROUND

Land's End
By all means go and get your photo taken at Land's End, the most westerly point on the mainland, with the sign pointing to New York, 3,147 miles away (for which you will be duly charged), but we recommend avoiding the Land's End Experience theme park. This sorry development, built in the late 1980s on the country's most remote headland, could only ever seem naff when compared to the unprocessed drama of the scenery, just metres away – and many locals continue to smart at the fact that planning permission was granted.

For the most atmospheric approach to Land's End, avoiding the theme park entrance, walk the short stretch of coastal footpath from Sennen, just over a mile away.

St Just
St Just in Penwith (not to be confused with St Just in Roseland), once the centre of the mining industry in the area, is the only significant town in the far west of Cornwall. It's a stark-looking, no-fuss sort of place, with granite terraces and old miners' cottages radiating out from a busy market square. It has a lively, arty community, a deli, several galleries, pasty shops, a few good traditional pubs and a grassy amphitheatre, the focal point during the town's Lafrowda Festival in July.

Stop for a pint of well-kept ale at the Star Inn (1 Fore Street, 01736 788767, www.thestarinn-stjust.co.uk), a 17th-century pub with a terrific 'no musak, no mobiles' policy – if your mobile rings you will have to pay a donation to the lifeboat fund. The pub doesn't serve food, but you can bring your own pasties.

For an unspoilt end-of-the-land experience, consider swapping Land's End for a walk at gusty Cape Cornwall, two miles west of the town. Topped by a 19th-century mine chimney, England's only 'cape' is but one degree east of Land's End proper – and was, before the arrival of cartographers, taken to be Britain's most westerly point.

North from St Just along the B3306 are the silent ruins of what was once hardcore mining territory. One of the most spectacularly sited mines is Botallack, right on the edge of the cliff, which can be seen from the coastal footpath. Around the coast at Pendeen, Geevor Tin Mine, the last operating mine in Penwith, is now a superb heritage centre and museum (*see p284*).

Sennen Cove
Shored up on the banks of Whitesand Bay, the stunningly scenic village of Sennen Cove perches on the very edge of mainland Britain, its weathered houses hatched into the hillside and a sweep of golden sand stretching into an arc below.

Britain's surfing cognoscenti have long flocked to Sennen, and there is a saying among locals: 'If there's no swell here, there's none anywhere.' They have a point. Even in summer, there is usually a wave to be had, as the beach takes the brunt of any swells driven by bands of low pressure in the Atlantic.

To walk the coast path the length of the bay and on to Land's End – just over a mile away – is to experience one of the most exquisite seascapes in the British Isles. On a clear summer's day, the Isles of Scilly can be seen, the sea looks wonderfully limpid, and Mediterranean gulls, shearwaters, puffins, kingfishers and Arctic skua are the local aviators.

There's a surf boutique and restaurant next to the beach (The Beach; *see p286*), the Old Success Inn (*see below*), a fish and chip shop, and an arts and crafts gallery in the Round House (01736 871859, www.round-house.co.uk).

Porthcurno & around

Porthcurno, three miles from Sennen Cove, regularly appears in 'top ten' beach lists. From the stone balustrades of the open-air Minack Theatre (*see p275*), carved into the cliffs above, you can gaze upon a scene that seems to have landed by some trickery from more exotic climes: creamy white sands and a shock of vivid turquoise sea. At low tide, an expanse of sand enables access to the secluded nudist beach of Pedn Vounder.

The sleeper

There is no getting around the fact that Cornwall is a long way away from London: six hours by car, nine hours by bus and only minimally served by plane. Even by 'express' train, a series of geographical obstacles – moors, hills and spindly creeks – add up to a five-hour jaunt. When a journey's that long, you might as well make an adventure of it.

The sleeper train from London to Penzance, a service locals fought successfully to save in 2005, is a vital connection for the Cornish, being the only way to reach the capital for a morning meeting. It's also one of only two remaining sleeper services in the country.

The Night Riviera, as it is romantically called, is also now a very comfortable way to travel, thanks to a £2 million renovation in 2008, care of Eurostar's interior designer Michael Rodber. Berths now feel almost like pod hotel rooms (albeit very small ones), with soft cotton sheets and towels, TV, a kit of mini toiletries, a sink with piping hot water, and breakfast (with filter coffee) brought in the morning half an hour before your destination.

Book yourself a solo berth, repair to the bar for a nightcap, and let the rocking motion lull you all the way to the end of the line. Top tip: sleeper berths count as first-class tickets, so you are granted access to the sleek first-class lounge at London Paddington, where you can help yourself to drinks and nibbles before boarding at around 11pm, or smarten yourself up on arrival. How thoroughly civilised…

From £69 return in advance (0845 678 6980, www.firstgreatwestern.co.uk).

Moving east around the coast, you'll come across a series of picturesque settlements: the sweet village of Treen, clinging to the clifftop; and the delightfully hidden-away fishing coves of Penberth and Lamorna. The latter was a muse for Newlyn School painters, with its steep, weather-sculpted granite stones creating striking geometric shapes, and is still popular with artists and craftmakers.

Where to eat & drink

As you might expect, this remote corner of the country is not about fine dining or wild nightlife, but that's not to say you can't get a good square meal and a nice pint of Cornish ale.

Cosy old pubs include the 17th-century Old Success Inn (01736 871232, www.oldsuccess. com) at Sennen, a characterful fisherman's inn by the beach; the Logan Rock Inn (01736 810495) in the idyllic coastal hamlet of Treen; and the sublimely old-fashioned Star Inn (*see p285*) in St Just. Less log fire and more white-hot is the über-chic Cove (*see below*) in Lamorna, whose restaurant-bar is pricey but first-rate, and open to non-guests; there's a smaller café on the front at Lamorna.

The Beach

Sennen Cove, TR19 7BT (01736 871191, www.the beachrestaurant.com). Open July-Oct noon-9.30pm daily. Nov-Feb noon-4.30pm Fri-Sun. Mid Feb-June noon-4.30pm Mon-Thur; noon-9.30pm Fri-Sun.
Just when the market for chic beachside restaurants with jaw-dropping views seemed thoroughly saturated, along came this aptly named hangout. Overhanging the sands at Sennen, it offers far-reaching views out into Whitesand Bay. It is family-run and friendly, with an easy-eating menu (falafel, steak, crab sandwiches, meatballs); in summer, you may have to queue for a table.

Where to stay

In 2009, the Sennen Surfing Centre (*see p275*) opened the neat new Brea Vean Surf Lodge (Brea Vean Farm, St Buryan, 01736 871748, www.cornishsurfhouse.com) just outside Sennen, with private doubles (with shared facilities) from £45 and sunset views.

The Cove

Lamorna, TR19 6XH (01736 731411, www.lamorna cove.com). Rates £123-£477 for 2-4 people.
One of west Cornwall's hottest hotels, the Cove – set into the steep hill above quiet Lamorna Cove, facing out to sea – brings a sprinkling of glitz to Britain's furthest reaches. Its 15 luxury self-catering apart-rooms have slick, glass-topped kitchens, and guests enjoy all the conveniences of an exclusive hotel, including a sauna, terraced gardens, a chic bar-restaurant and – best of all – a curvy outdoor pool. Decor is decidedly cosmopolitan: in fact, with its mirrored bedside tables, perspex chairs and turquoise accents, it feels a bit like staying in a supersized Tiffany jewellery box. The small bar-restaurant is excellent, with mojitos prepared to perfection, ultra-fresh fish and immaculate service.

Isles of Scilly

Small, quiet and extraordinarily beautiful, the Isles of Scilly are a low-lying archipelago strung out across the Atlantic, some 28 miles off Land's End – the last dots of land before North America. Basking in the warmth of the Gulf Stream, in summer the islands paint an exotic scene: softly curving, silver-sand beaches are splashed by clear, shallow waters, and a shock of weird and wonderful flowers and plants, many of which would struggle to survive in any other part of the country, run riot. Fiery red-hot pokers and purple-headed agapanthus, both natives of Africa, make themselves at home, and the waxy 'cactus roses' of aeoniums, originally from the Canaries, crawl over garden walls.

Only five of the islands are inhabited; St Mary's, which is the largest, and the 'off-islands' of St Martin's, St Agnes, Tresco and Bryher. Around them there are more than 100 unoccupied islets, rock formations, reefs, outcrops and ledges, which provide a sanctuary for grey seals, puffins, shearwaters, migratory birds and passing dolphins. Come winter, the islands show another face: when an Atlantic gale comes roaring in, the memory of more than 700 local shipwrecks is brought forcefully to mind.

INTRODUCING THE ISLANDS

Dotted with prehistoric burial chambers, standing stones and settlements, the Scillies have been occupied for at least 4,000 years, with even the Romans recognising them as 'Sun Isles' (the translation of their Latin name, Sillinae Insulae). In legend, this is the Lost Land of Lyonesse, to which King Arthur's men retreated after their leader's last fatal battle.

With a total population of around 3,000, these are small communities. Thanks to an almost complete absence of cars, the pace of life is slowed to an enjoyable stroll, and there's a pleasing pragmatism to even the most deluxe accommodation. Don't expect theme parks, nightlife or a cutting edge on anything except a fisherman's knife – just the unflashy excitement of stunning views and the chance to hide away. Happily stranded, visitors find themselves shifting swiftly down through the gears and entertaining themselves with nothing more complicated than shell collecting (the lovely cowrie shell is particularly prized), birdwatching, reading, walking or chatting over a pint of Ales of Scilly.

Tourism is carefully managed, which means there is a relatively small range of accommodation, especially on the off-islands and for short stays in peak season. As a result, occupancy levels and prices stay high, and advance booking is essential. B&Bs, self-catering accommodation and camping (there is a campsite on each of the islands, save Tresco) are the best ways to save money.

Thanks to the combination of a remote location and a cornered market, transport costs also stack up. The inter-island boats cost around £10 return per person, and the boat from Penzance starts at £80 return; the breathtakingly scenic helicopter ride, meanwhile, reaches well into triple figures. Still, at least when you make it back to the mainland

(via the Skybus, helicopter or the notoriously rough *Scillonian III* crossing), you're guaranteed to feel that you have come back from somewhere much further away, and a long way from England.

ST MARY'S

Although it measures just two and a half miles across at its widest point, St Mary's is the largest of the Isles of Scilly, as well as the most populous – it even has a recognisable road system. Its centre, Hugh Town, seems bustling if you've already spent time on the other islands, laid-back if you've come here first. Set on a narrow isthmus on the island's south-western side, the town is flanked to the south by pretty, sheltered Porthcressa Beach, and to the north by the less appealing Town Beach, where the Penzance ferry and inter-island passenger boats come and go.

Itineraries of tours and boats to the off-islands are chalked up on boards on the quay, and the Isles of Scilly Wildlife Trust (01720 422153, www.ios-wildlifetrust.org.uk) has an information centre in the harbour waiting room, with details of nature walks and tours. From May to September, the harbour also hosts the islands' famous pilot gig races. The gigs – 32 feet of brightly painted wooden rowing boat, some of them more than 100 years old – are raced on Wednesday and Friday evenings.

Above the harbour, west of Hugh Town, Garrison Hill offers brilliant views. It is dominated by the 16th-century, eight-pointed Star Castle, built as a defence against the Spanish Armada and now a hotel (*see p289*). In the other direction, Telegraph Road leads from Hugh Town towards the island's interior, and a pleasant trail around a dozen galleries, open studios and craft shops, making a comfortable circuit south to Old Town. En route

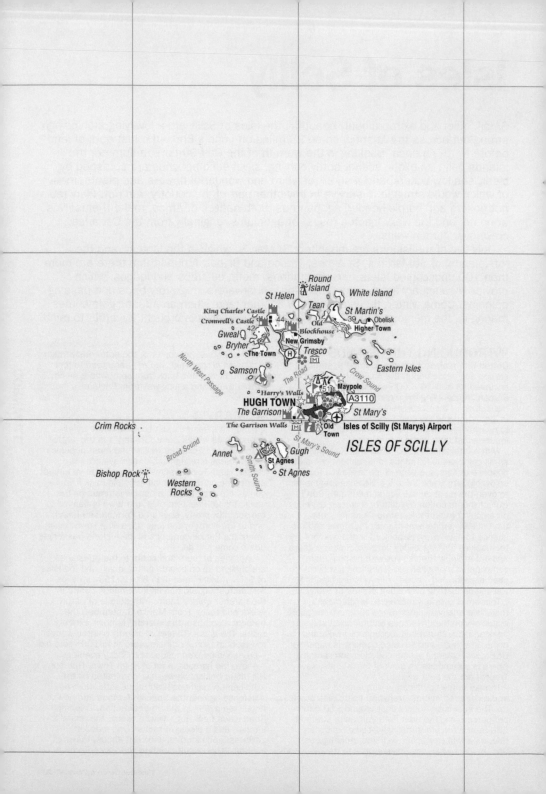

take a look at Carreg Dhu, pronounced 'Crake Dew' (01720 422404) – a small, volunteer-run community garden in a disused quarry.

Heading east from Porthcressa Beach, a path loops south around jagged Peninnis Head, passing some intriguing geological formations, such as the 'Kettle and Pans', near the lighthouse. Beyond is sheltered Old Town Bay, whose straggling settlement was, until the 17th century, the island's main port.

Near the airport, the small bay at Porth Hellick is overlooked by a monument to naval hero Sir Cloudesley Shovell, whose fleet ran into the rocks off the island during a storm in 1707, with the loss of 2,000 men. A mile north, Pelistry Bay is one of the most secluded and picturesque beaches on St Mary's, with the small Carn Vean Café (Pelistry, 01720 423458, closed Oct-Apr) providing sustenance. At low tide, a sand bar enables visitors to cross to the idyllic Toll's Island (don't attempt to swim across at high tide, as the sand bar causes vicious rip tides). Head north-west around the coast and you'll come to the most impressive prehistoric remains on the archipelago: Halangy Down has stone huts, a burial chamber and a standing stone that is thought to date from 2000 BC.

Where to eat & drink
Also worth trying – though check opening times before making a special trip – is Dibble & Grub (01720 423719), right on Porthcressa Beach. Brunch and light lunches are served from 10am.

Deli
Hugh Street, St Mary's, TR21 0LL (01720 422734). Open/food served 8.30am-8pm Mon-Sat.
A great place to put together a picnic, the Deli is housed in a delightfully converted butcher's shop – with some of the fixtures and fittings retained – and sells hams, cheeses and olives, and an array of Scillonian delicacies. There are half a dozen wooden tables for light lunches (quiches, pasties, salads) and drinks, with Wi-Fi available, or you could take out a mini tub of Troytown Farm ice-cream from St Agnes.

Juliet's Garden Restaurant
Seaways Flower Farm, St Mary's, TR21 0NF (01720 422228, www.julietsgardenrestaurant.co.uk). Food served Easter-Oct 10am-5pm daily; 6pm-late Mon, Wed-Sun.
A 20-minute amble along the coast from Hugh Town, Juliet's is a picturesque spot for lunch, with bird's-eye views of Hugh Town harbour and plenty of seating in the garden. Service is quick and upbeat, and the menu comprises simple café classics – cakes, sandwiches, quiche, soup, mackerel pâté with chunky granary bread – prepared with care. In the evening, with the lights dimmed and candles lit, there's a more formal menu.

Mermaid Inn
The Bank, St Mary's, TR21 0HY (01720 422701). Open/food served 10am-midnight Mon-Sat; noon-11.30pm Sun.
The Mermaid is a traditional local on the quay, greeting visitors as they come off the boat from the mainland. Hugh Town's social hub, it dispenses real ales downstairs

(including Scuppered, from the Ales of Scilly brewery), while the upstairs bar-restaurant is a more modern looking affair, serving light meals in the daytime and more substantial fare after 6pm.

Where to stay
Apart from the Star Castle Hotel, the only high-end accommodation on St Mary's is the St Mary's Hall Hotel (Church Street, 01720 422316, www.stmary shallhotel.co.uk, closed Nov-Mar), whose imposing old building, Italianate accents and wood-panelled hall combine to create a sense of occasion.

More affordable options on the island include the six B&B rooms at the handsome Belmont (Church Road, 01720 423154, www.the-belmont.co.uk, closed Nov-Easter), on the outskirts of Hugh Town, and the long-standing, friendly Mincarlo (Carn Thomas, 01720 422513, www.mincarlo.force9. co.uk, closed Nov-Mar). The latter has big windows and sea views; outside, steps descend to the beach.

Star Castle Hotel
St Mary's, TR21 0JA (01720 422317, www.star-castle.co.uk). Closed Jan. Rates £162-£362 double incl breakfast & dinner.
This star-shaped granite Elizabethan castle above Hugh Town is an atmospheric place to stay. Despite steady refurbishment, the prevailing style remains traditional; stay in one of the four rooms on the first floor to be in a point of the star, or the second floor for even better views through mullioned windows. Most of the accommodation is in the modern, more spacious 'garden' rooms out back, which are simply furnished, light and airy. The rooms on the western side look over the cliff path to the ocean, those to the east on to a lawn and green fields. There's a fantastically eccentric bar in the dungeon, and two restaurants, whose menus feature produce from the kitchen garden. One is a fairly formal affair, set in the castle's original, stone-walled officers' mess room; the other (summer only) occupies a bright conservatory, serving mostly seafood under the vines. There is an indoor pool and the grounds are lovely.

TRESCO & BRYHER

Tresco
For some, a visit to the Scillies' privately run and closely managed island estate (still leased from the Duchy of Cornwall by descendants of 19th-century reforming landlord Augustus Smith), Tresco, is altogether too cosseted. For others, it represents a life of delicious simplicity: one pub, one hotel, one café and no cars. The scene is set by the toy town jollity of the tractor ride between the heliport and your accommodation.

Two miles long and a mile wide, Tresco is the largest of the off-islands. The unassailable highlight – and the most impressive sight of the entire archipelago – is Abbey Garden (*see p292*). A walk around the island also takes in exquisite beaches, two peaceful lakes, tranquil woods and a solitary, heather-clad headland with two defensive fortifications – the 17th-century Cromwell's Castle and, above it, the earlier King Charles's Castle.

Tresco. See p289.

Hugh Town Harbour. See p287.

Most settlement on Tresco runs across the island between Old and New Grimsby. New Grimsby is home to Gallery Tresco (New Grimbsy Harbour, closed Nov-mid Feb), a single room of local art and souvenirs overlooking the sleepy little jetty, the New Inn and the newly built Flying Boat Club accommodation; Old Grimsby has the grander Island Hotel (for all, *see right*).

Bryher

Just opposite New Grimsby, separated by just a quarter of a mile of water, tiny Bryher feels like a place apart – even in Scilly. It takes its name from the Celtic for 'place of hills' and is a beautifully wild island, generally undeveloped and looking out on stunning rock fortresses such as Scilly Rock, Castle Bryher and Maiden Bower.

On the western shore, Hell Bay lives up to its name when a storm's up; the Hell Bay Hotel (*see right*), one of the most dramatically positioned hotels in England, is just to the south. Nearby, artist Richard Pearce (01720 423665, www.rpearce.net) has a similarly awesome outlook from a studio barely the size of a rowing boat (it is, in fact, a converted gig shed). The considerably more sheltered east shore has Green Bay, a fine sandy beach, along with boats and kayaks for hire from long-time islanders the Bennetts (07979 393206).

A circuit of Bryher takes little more than an hour on foot but is incredibly invigorating, with bees and birds around you as you walk and truly superb views. Gweal Hill offers the loveliest sunset in the Scillies, while Samson Hill opens up the whole archipelago.

Places to visit

ST MARY'S

Isles of Scilly Museum
Church Street, St Mary's, TR21 0JT (01720 422337, www.iosmuseum.org). Open Easter-Sept 10am-4.30pm Mon-Fri; 10am-noon Sat. Oct-Easter 10am-noon Mon-Sat. Admission £3.50; £1-£2.50 reductions. No credit cards.
There's no escaping the thread of disaster and loss, primarily from shipwrecks, at the endearingly low-tech Isles of Scilly Museum. Alongside the cases of flotsam and jetsam you'll find curiosities such as a Scilly shrew's nest in a discarded can, stuffed birds, shells, Iron Age axeheads and, fascinatingly, a Bronze Age sword found by a Bryher potato farmer in the 1990s. Downstairs are stuffed birds and fish, including 6lb 2oz of broad-nosed eel. Another exhibition is devoted to former prime minster Harold Wilson (including his famous Gannex mac), who is buried nearby at St Mary's Old Church.

TRESCO & BRYHER

Abbey Garden ★
Tresco, TR24 0PQ (01720 424105, www.tresco. co.uk/see/abbey-garden). Open 10am-4pm daily. Admission £10 Mar-Oct, £5 Nov-Feb; free reductions.
Even those not usually drawn to gardens find this exotic garden exciting, so confirmed garden geeks can safely expect to be catapulted into horticultural heaven. The Abbey Garden is without doubt Scilly's biggest attraction, but that rather understates their significance: for many, this is one of the most extraordinary gardens in the world, a singular experiment in horticulture – or, as author Walter Besant famously described it, 'Kew with the roof off'.

When Augustus Smith arrived in 1834 to take on the lease of the islands, Tresco was exposed to vicious winds and far from sympathetic to the kind of tropical vegetation now thriving here. A man of supreme vision and drive, Smith had tall windbreaks built around the remains of the 12th-century Benedictine priory to shelter sloping terraces, and the magnificent gardens now have over 20,000 plants from 80 countries, including succulents, palms, cacti and eucalyptus. It is a surreal sight to see such intense colour in Britain; red hot pokers, birds of paradise, pink proteas and

Abbey Garden

lobster claws all invite the attention of your zoom lens. These plants flourish thanks to the Scillies' mild climate, and many would not survive in mainland Cornwall. Thoughtful Italianate landscaping adds perspective and ensures that, even in high season, it's easy to forget your fellow visitors. Valhalla is the on-site collection of salvaged ships' figureheads, now colourfully restored. There's also a small shop, and the Garden Café for refreshments.

Where to eat & drink

The best upmarket dining on Tresco comes care of the Island Hotel (*see right*), which serves well-executed, traditional food in mannered surrounds. The Hell Bay restaurant is also open to non-guests.

Fraggle Rock Bar-Café

Bryher, TR23 0PR (01720 422222). Open 10.30am-4.30pm, 7-11pm daily. Lunch served noon-2pm, dinner served 7-8.30pm.

Based in a small granite house with a beer garden at the front, this relaxed spot serves lunches (double-decker crab sarnies, soup, burgers) and evening meals (pizza, risotto, and fish and chips on Friday), as well as pints of Doom Bar. The first floor has sea views, internet access (Wi-Fi, as well as access to the house laptop in exchange for a donation to the Wildlife Trust) and stripped pine decor – comfortable enough, but less cosy and pub-like than the downstairs.

New Inn

Tresco, TR24 0QE (01720 422844, www.tresco.co.uk). Open Apr-Oct 10am-11pm daily. Lunch served noon-2.15pm, dinner served 6.30-9pm. Nov-Mar 10am-2.30pm, 6-11pm daily. Lunch served noon-2pm, dinner served 7-9pm.

Tresco is at its liveliest in the New Inn's snug Driftwood Bar, lined with dark reclaimed wood. Sunny days seem to draw the entire population of the island to its shady outdoor terrace, where they are joined by cheekily well-fed sparrows and chaffinches. There's a fine selection of ales (including Ales of Scilly and Skinners) and wines (25 in total, about ten of which are available by the glass), as well as good pub food. Local produce is used as much as possible, on a simple but satisfying menu that might include bangers and mash and fish and chips with a choice of Cornish fish. An additional conservatory-style space serves Roskilly's ice-cream and calico. The adjoining hotel has 16 bright, comfortable rooms (£140-£210 double incl breakfast).

Where to stay

Tresco's only pub, the New Inn (*see above*), is a cheaper alternative to the Island Hotel for short-stay accommodation. Bryher has a pretty campsite (01720 422559, www.bryhercampsite.co.uk, closed Oct-Mar) with basic facilities.

Flying Boat Club

Tresco, TR24 0QQ (01720 422849, www.tresco.co.uk/stay/flying-boat-club). Rates from £1,375 per week for 6 people.

The Flying Boat Club, Scilly's newest digs, comprises a string of 12 luxurious, modern houses, built on the beachfront at New Grimsby. The curious name is a reference to the Royal Naval Air Station that stood on this site, which sent out seaplanes during World War I to counter German submarines. In line with the trend for self-catering/hotel crossovers, FBC's beach-chic houses combine the freedom of a holiday home (proper kitchen, breakfast when you want it, privacy) with the luxuries of a high-end hotel – flatscreen TVs, thick bathrobes and sleek bathrooms. Guests also get access to the Flying Boat Club across the road, with its restaurant and bar, tennis courts, spa and leisure club. As with everything on Tresco, and the Scillies in general, the prices sting. But tariffs do at least include entrance to the

Flying Boat Club

Abbey Garden – and where else in Britain can you climb down half a dozen steps from your holiday home, directly on to the soft sand of a deserted white-sand beach?

Hell Bay Hotel

Bryher, TR23 0PR (01720 422947, www.hellbay.co.uk). Rates £310-£600 double incl breakfast & dinner.

In an unbeatable position on the edge of the Atlantic, Hell Bay Hotel was a pioneer of contemporary – if not quite cutting-edge – style on the Scillies. Its relaxed, spacious suites sport a jaunty colour scheme of light greens and blues, and have portholes in the doors; most of the rooms open on to private balconies or patios, and all but two have sea views. Details are carefully attended to (fresh milk in the fridge, a personal cafetière) and there's some striking modern art in the expansive bar area, and sculptures dotted throughout – thanks to its art-collecting owners, the Dorrien-Smiths (who also own Tresco). Food can be served on the patio, as well as in the restaurant; expect the likes of seared Cornish scallops with cauliflower purée and pancetta, pan-roasted fillet of West Country beef, or burgers and superior sarnies from the bar menu. Facilities include a heated outdoor pool, a seven-hole golf course and a mini gym and spa.

Island Hotel

Tresco, TR24 0PU (01720 422883, www.tresco.co.uk/stay/island-hotel). Closed Oct-Feb. Rates £260-£720 double incl breakfast & dinner.

The front lawn of the Island Hotel sweeps down to the sheltered sands of Raven's Porth on one side, while the other side affords wonderful vistas of rocky islands and a line of surf breaking at the reef – though you'll need to fork out for the Menavaur suite to get the best view of it. This colonial-style hotel has a five-star location and a peculiar layout that provides most rooms with some kind of sea view. The old-school formal restaurant – with thick white tablecloths and punctilious service – offers local seafood and fine meat dishes; for more relaxed fare, try the bar's decked terrace. There's also a tennis court, croquet lawn and heated outdoor pool (May-Sept). The whole place is slated for a complete overhaul in time for the 2011 season, which will recreate the hotel as 25 self-catering units, available by the day or week.

ST MARTIN'S

Trimmed with sugary, silver-flecked beaches and translucent waters, St Martin's shores could, in the right light, pass for St Kitts – an illusion that tends to shatter the moment your toes touch the sea, which is rarely anything other than glacial. Entirely free from man-made construction (bar the grey hotel built on the westerly beach) and deserted by default, St Martin's sands are a special sight – even by the Scillies' high standards.

Flower-growing is the main industry, which accounts for the colourful fields, but St Martin's has attracted a number of sensitive entrepreneurial operations, from the organic smallholding and café at Little Arthur Farm to the St Martin's Bakery. Higher Town, the main hub, has few other attractions, so head instead for the stunning beaches and views – in particular from St Martin's Head on the north-east coast. Sparsely inhabited and virtually pollution-free, St Martin's is also fantastic for diving (*see p297*).

The main quay is on the magnificent Par Beach, a pure white curve of sand; the St Martin's Vineyard & Winery (01720 423418, www.stmartinsvineyard. co.uk, closed winter) is close by. On the southern coast, Lawrence's Bay is long, sandy and perfect for shell-collecting. To the west, Lower Town has views across to the uninhabited islands of Teän and St Helen's, and on the north-east coast, Great Bay ★ and Little Bay offer sweeping, isolated stretches of sand; the former is a strong contender for Britain's best beach. At low tide, climb across the boulders from Little Bay to wild White Island (pronounced 'Wit') to explore Underland Girt, a huge sea cave.

Where to eat & drink

Tiny St Martin's has a surprising number of eating options. The pretty Polreath Tearoom (Higher Town, 01720 422046, www.polreath.com, closed Sat & Nov-Easter) serves tea and light lunches in the café and courtyard or, best of all, under the vines in the greenhouse; it also has a curry night on Mondays.

Little Arthur Farm

Higher Town, St Martin's, TR25 0QL (01720 422457, www.littlearthur.co.uk). Lunch served Apr-Sept 10.30am-4pm daily. Dinner served 6.30-8.30pm Mon-Fri. No credit cards.
Looking down the slope to Par Beach, this wholefood café offers excellent salads and rolls filled with own-grown organic ingredients, soups, shellfish salad, ploughman's lunches and own-baked cakes and scones, served in a small conservatory. Adam's Fish & Chips (01720 423637) takes over on Tuesdays and Thursdays (6-8.30pm) for what has to be one of Britain's finest renditions of the dish, made with Adam's line-caught fish and homegrown, hand-cut potatoes.

TEN CORNISH CHURCHES

St Anthony, Roseland

Architectural historian Nikolaus Pevsner described this as the 'best example in the county of what a parish church was like in the 12th and 13th centuries.' But it's also worth a visit for its roof, loor tiles and stained glass, added during a 19th-century restoration. *See p239.*

St Enodoc, Trebetherick

The church of St Enodoc, part of which dates from the 12th century, is the final resting place of Sir John Betjeman, who was particularly fond of the building, penning a verse to it: 'Sunday Afternoon Service at St Enodoc'. His grave is near the south side of the church. *See p208.*

St Germans

The site of the church at St Germans, in eastern Cornwall, served as the county's cathedral from 926, and is mentioned in the Domesday Book; it's still the largest parish in Cornwall. Much altered over the centuries, the church is a mix of styles; don't miss the magnificent Norman door on its west side. *See p191.*

St Ildierna, Lansallos

Dominating the tiny parish of Lansallos (*see p187*) in south-eastern Cornwall, this 14th-century granite church was damaged by fire in 2005, finally re-opening in 2009 after massive fundraising efforts. Happily, the church's medieval pews, carved from English oak, survived the blaze.

St Just-in-Roseland, Roseland

The beautiful 13th-century church of St Just-in-Roseland, north of St Mawes (*see p239*) stands by the water's edge, on the site of a fifth-century chapel. Its beautiful riverside gardens are filled with semi-tropical plants, while the path to the church is lined with granite blocks carved with biblical verses.

St Martin's Campsite

St Martin's Bakery

*St Martin's, TR25 0QL (01720 423444, www.stmartins
bakery.co.uk). Open Mar-Oct 9am-6pm Mon-Sat; 9am-
2pm Sun. Nov-Feb bakery courses only. No credit cards.*
As well as organic bread, baker Toby Tobin-Dougan makes
homity pie, pasties with Scilly beef, quiches and pizza slices.
Sip own-made lemonade and tuck in at the outdoor trestle
tables, leaving a few crumbs for the chicken pecking about
your ankles. The bakery uses local ingredients, including
eggs produced on its farm, and own-smoked ham and fish,
and provides gluten free options. There's takeaway pizza in
the evenings, and baking holidays take place off-season.

Seven Stones

*Lower Town, St Martin's, TR25 0QW (01720 423560,
www.sevenstonesinn.co.uk). Open Mar-Oct 10.30-4pm,
6-11.30pm daily. Lunch served noon-2.30pm, dinner
served 7-9pm daily. Nov-Feb 6-11.30pm Fri; noon-
2.30pm Sun.*
It may look more like someone's front room than a pub, but
the Seven Stones is nonetheless a welcoming hideout, serving
Ales of Scilly and sturdy pub food, as well as seafood hotpot
with catch of the day. The views from the beer terrace are
sublime – and in wet weather you'll find the toasty interior
busy with de-anoraked campers from the nearby campsite.

Where to stay

Polreath Guesthouse & Tearoom (Higher Town,
01720 422046, www.polreath.com, closed Nov-
Easter) has three sea-view rooms, and Little Arthur
Farm (*see left*) also has a cute eco-cabin for rent.

St Martin's Campsite

*Oaklands Farm, Middletown, St Martin's, TR25 0QN
(01720 422888, www.stmartinscampsite.co.uk). Open
mid Mar-Oct. Pitch £16-£20 per night for 2 people.*

St Mary Magdalene, Launceston

One of Cornwall's most picturesque
towns (*see p165*) is also home to one
of its most imposing churches. St Mary
Magdalene's tower dates back to the
14th-century, but the rest of the structure
was erected in the late 16th century.
The church is best known for its ornately-
carved granite exterior – a tour de force
of the highly-skilled Cornish stonemasons.

St Morwenna & St John the Baptist, Morwenstow

Set near the cliffs on Cornwall's west
coast, Morwenstow's church is a 13th-
century Norman structure. A figurehead
from a ship wrecked nearby lies in the
graveyard, but the church is best known
for its eccentric vicar, Reverend Hawker:
he pioneered the notion of Harvest
Festival as we know it, dressed in long
sea boots and a pink hat, and wrote
poetry in a driftwood hut on the cliffs
(*see p211*), now run by the National Trust.

St Nonna, Altarnun

Known locally as the 'Cathedral in
the Moor' (it's made from unquarried
moorland granite), Altarnun's 15th-century
church (*see p166*) is topped by one of the
highest towers in Cornwall. Inside, carved
16th-century bench ends depict jesters,
musicians and religious figures; at the
entrance to the churchyard, a weathered,
weighty Celtic cross is thought to date
from the 6th century.

St Senara, Zennor

Extensively restored in the 19th century,
this lovely 12th-century church is known
for its carving of the Mermaid of Zennor.
In the past, villagers came here to give
thanks for the safe return of local
fishermen, and a good day's catch.
See p273.

St Winwaloe, The Lizard

A stone's throw from the sea at Church
Cove, St Winwaloe is said to be one of
the oldest churches in Cornwall. Its
precarious position (it was once known
as the 'church of the storms') has meant
is has been reinforced several times since
the main structure was built in the 15th
century. The detached belltower dates
from the 13th century. *See p255.*

CORNWALL

Things to do

The Scillies may not have much in the way of organised attractions, but those interested in simpler pleasures will be in their element. Rockpooling, birdwatching, butterfly spotting, shell collecting and walking are all pastimes that demand neither guide nor equipment. For others – boating, sailing, fishing, snorkelling, kayaking, diving, golf – the islands are well equipped.

ST MARY'S

Island Sea Safaris
Old Town, St Mary's, TR21 0NH (01720 422732, www.scillyonline.co.uk/seasafaris.html). Open Easter-Oct daily (weather permitting). No credit cards.
Take to the water on sightseeing boat trips (1hr £20 per person; 2hrs £30 per person) in RIBs (rigid inflatable boats), or embark on a snorkelling safari (£35/3hrs).

Island Wildlife Tours
01720 422212, www.islandwildlifetours.co.uk. Open Apr-Oct. Tours £10 per day.
Wildlife expert Will Wagstaff leads these walking tours of the islands. Tours tend to leave at 9.45am from St Mary's quay on weekday mornings, but times and itineraries vary. Call for further details, or check the board on St Mary's quay.

Isles of Scilly golf course
St Mary's, TR21 0NF (01720 422692, http://iosgolfclub.tripod.com/gcindex.html). Open 8am-dusk Mon-Wed, Fri-Sun. Green fee from £22. No credit cards.
Opened in 1904, after much bracken-clearing, this gently-sloping nine-hole course has great views.

Sailing Centre
Porthmellon Beach, St Mary's, TR21 0NE (01720 422060, www.sailingscilly.com).
A variety of watersports taster sessions, courses and equipment hire is offered here, including windsurfing, snorkelling, dinghies and kayaks. All ages and abilities are catered for.

St Mary's Boatmen's Association
Rose Cottage, The Strand, St Mary's, TR21 0PT (01720 423999, www.scillyboating.co.uk). Tickets £7.60-£11 return; £3.80-£5.50 reductions. No credit cards.
Information about the day's boat excursions can be found written up on the quay, outside the Atlantic Hotel and Tourist Information Centre in Hugh Town. The Association has a fleet of large boats and runs direct journeys daily to the off-islands, but also arranges wildlife spotting jaunts, fishing trips (colin, (mackerel or pollock for beginners, shark fishing for the more advanced) and birdwatching forays on Annet.

St Mary's Cycle Hire
The Strand, St Mary's, TR21 0PT (01720 422289, 07796 638506 off-season). Cycle hire from £7 per day; £40 per week.
Tandems and child seats are available too.

Scilly Walks
www.scillywalks.co.uk.
Katharine Sawyer offers guided walks with a historical angle on St Mary's and the off-islands.

TRESCO & BRYHER

Bennett Boatyard
Bryher, TR23 0PR (07979 393206, www.bennett boatyard.com). Open Apr-Sept 9am-6pm daily. Boat hire from £10-£90 per day. No credit cards.
The boatyard hires out kayaks, small dinghies, rigged sailing boats and even a glass-bottomed rowing boat – all available by the hour, half-day, day or week. You can also hire a fishing line to tow along behind.

Bryher Boat Services
Bryher, TR23 0PR (01720 422886, www.bryher boats.co.uk). Tickets from £7.60 return; £3.80 reductions. No credit cards.
The company runs scheduled boats from Bryher and Tresco to the other islands, plus private charter jet boats to Penzance, when the *Scillonian* sailing is fogged off.

Island Wildlife Tours

There can be few more effective ways of switching off than pitching your tent on a tiny off-island of the Isles of Scilly. One of the more sheltered campsites in these parts – protected, to a degree, by the dunes and the high hedges that divide the site into cosy strips – St Martin's also has the best facilities. The toilet and shower block is modern, and the showers are reliably hot. No electric hook-ups means minimal light and noise pollution, and the lack of cars, caravans or motorhomes is a rare treat.

St Martin's on the Isle
St Martin's, TR25 0QW (01720 422090, www.stmartins hotel.co.uk). Rates £250-£510 double incl breakfast.
The only hotel on St Martin's is a somewhat angular affair, built in stern grey stone, but its setting is beautiful: the hotel overlooks gardens dotted with incongruous Caribbean rush parasols and, beyond them, the quay and a beautiful white-sand beach. Many of the 30 rooms have enviable sea views, but are otherwise rather lacking in character – though this could change with the refit that's due to start in late 2010. Teän, the acclaimed main restaurant, is on the first floor and has several prized tables perched right in the angled window, looking over the channel to its namesake island. The menu draws on a wealth of local ingredients, particularly seafood – something of a necessity, one might imagine, when running Britain's most remote fine dining restaurant. A swimming pool is tucked away indoors.

ST AGNES
Craggy St Agnes, set apart from the cluster of islands, is the most south-westerly community in the British Isles – with a wild, windswept setting to match. What the island might lack in sandy beaches, it more than makes up for with edge-of-the-world scenery and weirdly weathered granite rock formations. The only inhabited island without a hotel, St Agnes has more of a community feel than the others – and the simple, outdoor life is fully embraced here.

Boats land at and leave from Porth Conger, under the watchful eyes of the Turk's Head pub. There you'll also find St Agnes's most attractive beach, Covean. When the tide is right you can walk across the sand bar to the tiny island of Gugh (pronounced 'Goo'), where there are rocky outcrops, a Bronze Age burial chamber and a standing stone – or rather a crazily leaning stone – called the Old Man of Gugh. In Higher Town, stop by the Bulb Shop (Higher Town Farm, closed Sat) for locally made soaps and crafts, postcards, plant cuttings and bulbs – as well as Fay Page's exquisite silver and gold jewellery, cast from shells found on the islands' shores.

Inland, St Agnes is dominated by the squat, white form of the Old Lighthouse, which dates from 1680, making it one of the oldest in England. Near to Periglis Cove, on the western side of the island, is Troy Town Maze – laid out in large pebbles in 1729 by, it is said, the lighthouse keeper's bored son.

The wild heathland of the wonderfully named Wingletang Down takes up much of the south of St Agnes, edged on its western side by impressive coastal scenery and on its eastern side by Beady Pool. This inlet takes its name from a haul of beads from a wrecked 17th-century Venetian trader that

Scilly Walks

Tresco Cycle Hire
Tresco Estate, Tresco, TR24 0QQ (01720 422849). Cycle hire from £6 per half-day.
Cycling is not only the best way to get around Tresco, it is also pretty much the only way. Hire mountain bikes from next to the Tresco Stores by the half-day, day or week.

ST MARTIN'S

St Martin's Diving Services
Higher Town, St Martin's, TR25 0QL (01720 422848, www.scillydiving.com). Open Apr-Oct. Diving/snorkelling from £38, min 2 people. No credit cards.
Thanks in part to the islands' ocean-edge location, the waters around Scilly are some of the most biodiverse in the country, populated by exotic species, ornate corals and colourful sponges. This, combined with the clarity of the waters and the numerous shipwrecks, makes it one of the best places to dive in the UK. The dive school offers diving courses, scuba outings and safaris snorkelling with seals.

ST AGNES

St Agnes Boating
The Barn, St Agnes, TR22 0PL (01720 422704, www.st-agnes-boating.co.uk). Tickets £7.40 return. No credit cards.
As well as daily passenger trips to St Mary's and the off-islands year-round, St Agnes Boating offers private charters (charged by the hour), two-hour fishing trips (gear hired at £15 a rod) and trips out to the Western Rocks and Bishop Rock Lighthouse.

Turk's Head

was washed up on the shores. Above the cove, two enormous boulders indented with a three-foot-deep basin form the Giant's Punchbowl, the most impressive rock formation on Scilly.

Where to eat & drink

Coastguards Café/High Tide
St Agnes, TR22 0PL (Coastguards Café 01720 422197, High Tide 01720 423869, http://hightide-seafood.com). Food served Apr-Oct 10.30am-4.30pm, 6.30pm-late Mon-Sat.

It's effectively just a tiny – and we really do mean tiny – stone outhouse, but there's something special about this place. Perhaps it's the wild views out to the Bishop Rock Lighthouse, the smart decor or the contemporary art (pop art takes on the cairns and crags of Scilly) on the walls. In true multi-tasking islander fashion, this place pulls off a great double act: by day, it's the Coastguards Café, serving toasties, rolls (including an inspired pastrami and rock samphire combination), cakes and St Agnes ice-cream. Come the evening, Emma and Mark Eberlein take over as High Tide, a licensed, globally inspired seafood restaurant that concentrates, quite rightly, on a short menu prepared with local produce (St Martin's microgreens are a highlight).

Turk's Head ★
St Agnes, TR22 0PL (01720 422434). Open Apr-Oct 10.30am-11.30pm daily. Lunch served noon-2.30pm, dinner served 6-9.30pm.

Our favourite Scilly pub has a superb location, looking out over the lucent waters of the island's mini harbour. It's perfect for tucking into one of the legendary pasties (get your order in quick) while taking in the view – or keeping an eye out for your boat home. Inside, it's all model boats, maps and flagstone floors. Sup on a pint of the pub's own Turk's Head ale, or a comforting hot chocolate braced with a nip of something stronger.

Where to stay

There is no hotel on St Agnes, just a handful of B&Bs and the dramatically sited Troytown Campsite (01720 422360, www.troytown.co.uk, closed Oct-Mar), occupying a spectacular if exposed position facing the Atlantic. At the sweet Covean Cottage guesthouse and café (St Agnes, 01720 422620, http://st-agnes-scilly.org/covean.htm), all rooms have sea views; picnic lunches are also available.

UNINHABITED ISLANDS & BISHOP ROCK LIGHTHOUSE

Samson, the largest uninhabited island, was populated until the 1850s, when poverty and the threat of eviction by Augustus Smith forced the islanders to resettle. A beautiful beach lies at the foot of North Hill, while significant prehistoric remains dot the slopes above. At low tide look out for the Samson Flats, the remains of ancient field systems that show up in the sands between Samson and Tresco.

Just off St Martin's, Teän has large, crescent-shaped sandy beaches; on St Helen's, just behind it, stands an interesting ruined church. On the other side of St Martin's, the milder Eastern Isles have fantastic beaches on Great Arthur and Great Ganilly, also home to puffins and grey seals. However, the best place to spot these captivating creatures is the storm-harried Western Rocks beyond St Agnes, the site of numerous shipwrecks.

Several miles further out west is the remarkable Bishop Rock Lighthouse, a miracle of Victorian construction that perches on a rock base little wider than its own circumference; it has been automatically operated since 1991.

For visits to Scilly's uninhabited islands, ask at your hotel or at the quay for details of boat trips.

Bishop Rock Lighthouse

Further reference

USEFUL ADDRESSES
www.cornwallclassiccarhire.co.uk
www.english-heritage.org.uk
www.enjoyengland.com
www.heritageopendays.org.uk
www.metoffice.gov.uk
www.nationalrail.co.uk
www.nationaltrust.org.uk
www.ordnancesurvey.co.uk
www.sustrans.org.uk
www.thegoodpubguide.co.uk
www.thetrainline.com
www.visitbritain.com
www.ukworldheritage.org.uk

COAST & COUNTRYSIDE
www.babo.org.uk British
Association of Balloon Operators.
www.bbc.co.uk/coast BBC Coast.
www.bcusurf.org.uk BCU Surf.
www.british-trees.com The
Woodland Trust.
www.britsurf.co.uk British
Surfing Association.
http://camping.uk-directory.com
UK Camping and Caravanning
Directory.
www.classic-sailing.co.uk
Classic Sailing.
www.countrysideaccess.gov.uk
Countryside Access.
www.cpre.org.uk Campaign for
the Protection of Rural England.
www.goodbeachguide.co.uk
Good Beach Guide.
www.lidos.org.uk Lidos in the UK.
www.nationalparks.gov.uk
National Parks.
www.nationaltrail.co.uk
National Trails.
www.naturalengland.org.uk
Natural England.
www.ngs.org.uk National
Gardens Scheme.
www.paddleandsail.com
Cornwall Sailing School.
www.river-swimming.co.uk River
& Lake Swimming Association.
www.ramblers.org.uk Ramblers
Association.
www.rya.org.uk Royal Yachting
Association.
www.sas.org.uk Surfers
Against Sewage.
www.surfingwaves.com/travel/
england.htm Surfing England.
www.surf-wax.co.uk Beach-based
sports in Devon and Cornwall.
www.ukclimbing.com UK Climbing.
www.uk-golfguide.com UK Golf.
www.walkingbritain.co.uk
Walking Britain.

www.walking-routes.co.uk
Walking Routes.
www.wildaboutbritain.co.uk
Wild About Britain.
www.wildswimming.com
Wild Swimming.

HOLIDAY HOME COMPANIES
The Big Domain 01326 240028,
www.thebigdomain.com.
Boutique Boltholes 0845 094
9864, www.boutiqueboltholes.co.uk.
Cottages4you 0845 268 0763,
www.cottages4you.co.uk.
**Duchy of Cornwall Holiday
Cottages** 01579 346473,
www.duchyofcornwallholiday
cottages.co.uk.
Landmark Trust 01628 825925,
www.landmarktrust.org.uk.
The Little Domain 01326 240028,
www.thelittledomain.com.
North Devon Holiday Homes
01271 376322,
www.northdevonholidays.co.uk.
Superior Cottages
www.superiorcottages.co.uk.
Toad Hall Cottages 01548
853089, www.toadhall
cottages.co.uk.
Unique Home Stays
01637 881942,
www.uniquehomestays.com.

DEVON

TOURIST INFORMATION CENTRES
More details can be found
at www.visitdevon.co.uk. The
main tourist offices are listed
below.

Barnstaple 01271 375000.
Exeter 01392 665700.
Newton Abbott 01626 215667.
Plymouth 01752 306330.
Tavistock 01822 612938.
Torbay 01803 211211.

USEFUL ADDRESSES
www.bbc.co.uk/devon Local
news, weather and events.
www.dartmoormagazine.co.uk
A quarterly magazine with features
on Dartmoor's heritage, news
and current events.
www.dartmoor-npa.gov.uk
Dartmoor National Park Authority.

www.devon.gov.uk Devon
County Council.
www.devon.gov.uk/buses
Devon bus services.
http://devon.greatbritishlife.co.uk
A monthly magazine with useful
listings of events throughout the
county.
www.devonguide.com/beaches
Information on Devon's beaches.
www.theexmoormagazine.co.uk
A quarterly magazine with lifestyle
articles and features on Exmoor's
heritage.
www.eyeball-surfcheck.co.uk Web-
cams and weather reports covering
North Devon's main beaches.
www.greenevents.co.uk A free,
bi-monthly publication detailing
green events in South Devon.
www.originalsurfboards.co.uk Retro
wooden surfboards and bespoke
bodyboards, crafted locally.
www.reconnectonline.co.uk
A bi-monthly alternative lifestyle
magazine, available free from
green shops.
www.visitdevon.co.uk Official
tourist information site.
www.westernmorningnews.co.uk
Main regional newspaper covering
Devon and Cornwall.

FICTION
Patricia Beer *Moon's Ottery*
Romance and intrigue in an East
Devon village, at the time of the
Spanish Armada.
RD Blackmore *Lorna Doone*
Victorian romanticism on the
wilds of Exmoor.
Agatha Christie *Evil Under the Sun;
The Mysterious Affair at Styles; And
Then There Were None* Local settings
abound in the Torquay-born crime
writer's novels.
Sir Arthur Conan Doyle *The Hound
of the Baskervilles; Silver Blaze*
Dastardly goings-on on Dartmoor.
Charles Kingsley *Westward Ho!*
The village near Bideford was
named after this rip-roaring tale
of adventure.
Rudyard Kipling *Stalkey & Co*
Kipling's experiences of public
school in North Devon come to
life in nine tales.
John Masefield *Jim Davis* A
smuggling tale set in 19th-century
Devon.
Henry Williamson *Tarka the Otter*
The naturalist and writer based his

St Ives Bay. See p269.

most famous story around the Taw and Torridge rivers, taking an otter as his hero.

NON-FICTION
William Crossing Guide to Dartmoor Written a century ago, Crossing's guides to Dartmoor and the surrounding areas are still in print and used to this day.
Nikolaus Pevsner Devon A classic exploration of Devon's architecture.

POETRY
Ted Hughes Moortown Diary; Collected Poems Yorkshire-born poet laureate Ted Hughes moved to North Devon in 1961, where he lived until his death in 1998. The natural world and rural life inspired many of his poems .
Samuel Taylor Coleridge Selected Poems Some of the Devon-born poet's most enduring works (including 'Kubla Khan', 'Rime of the Ancient Mariner' and 'Frost at Midnight') were written in and inspired by the Quantock Hills and Exmoor.

FILM
The Belstone Fox (James Hill, 1973) A sort of foxy Black Beauty set on Dartmoor, starring Bill Travers and a young Dennis Waterman.
The Hound of the Baskervilles (Sidney Lanfield, 1939) Basil Rathbone super-sleuths his way around Dartmoor in this classic Holmes mystery.
International Velvet (Bryan Forbes, 1978) Scenes from this feelgood equestrian tale were filmed on the Flete Estate, in Mothecombe.
The Remains of the Day (James Ivory, 1993) Shot at Powderham Castle in Devon, this film stars Anthony Hopkins as a repressed butler, struggling to deal with his master's Nazi sympathies and his own emotions.
Sense and Sensibility (Ang Lee, 1995) A number of Devon locations appear in this Austen adaptation, including Saltram House, the village church in Berry Pomeroy, Compton Castle, and Plymouth.
That Summer! (Harley Cokliss, 1979) Follow-up to the film Scum, the underrated That Summer also stars Ray Winstone, charting his character's trip to Torquay on leaving prison.
The War Zone (Tim Roth, 1999) Harrowing film based on Alexander Stuart's novel about incest and family breakdown in rural Devon.

TV
Fawlty Towers John Cleese's classic BBC sitcom was inspired by a real hotel in Torquay, visited by the Monty Python team.

MUSIC
Seth Lakeman Kitty Jay (2004) The songs on this Mercury Music Prize-shortlisted album were inspired by stories and legends from Dartmoor, where Lakeman was brought up and lives.
Joss Stone The soul and R&B singer grew up in Ashill, near Tiverton, and still calls Devon home, citing the county as a source of inspiration for her work.

ART
Beryl Cook Cook moved to Plymouth in the 1960s, and found considerable success depicting local people and places.
Joshua Reynolds The famous 18th-century portrait painter and founder of the Royal Academy was born in Plympton St Maurice. Plymouth waterfront features in the background of several of his works.

WALKS & CYCLE TRAILS
The website covering the South Devon Area of Outstanding Natural Beauty (01803 861384, www.southdevonaonb.org.uk) includes details of more than 30 walks and trails for walkers, cyclists and horseriders. Here are a few ideas:
Dart Valley Trail A 16-mile ramble, following the riverbank. The four-and-a-half-mile section between Kingswear and Greenway is particularly attractive, as it meanders through ancient woodlands.
Greenway Walk You'll be walking through Agatha Christie country on this trail, which links Greenway (see p135) with Galmpton (where the writer was a governor of the local school), Broadsands (one of her favourite beaches) and Churston (where she worshipped at the church of St Mary the Virgin).
South West Coast Path www.southwestcoastpath.com See p185.
The Tarka Trail www.devon.gov.uk/tarkatrail This 180-mile trail forms a rough figure of eight, with its pivot at Barnstaple. The southern loop extends through rural Devon and to the edge of Dartmoor, while the northern loop climbs to Exmoor and the coast, returning along the Taw-Torridge Estuary. A 31-mile stretch between

Braunton and Meeth is open to cyclists.
John Musgrave Heritage Trail Starting at the coast just north of Torquay, this 35-mile route then loops inland and ends on the coast at Brixham. It's split into four sections, marked by signs featuring a brown arrow with a yellow boot-print.

CORNWALL

TOURIST INFORMATION CENTRES
More details can be found at www.visitcornwall.com. The main tourist offices are listed below.

Bodmin 01208 76616, www.bodminlive.com
Falmouth 01326 312300, www.discoverfalmouth.co.uk
Fowey 01726 833616, www.fowey.co.uk
Isles of Scilly 01720 424031, www.simplyscilly.co.uk
Newquay 01637 854020, www.visitnewquay.org
St Ives 01736 796297, www.visit-westcornwall.com

USEFUL ADDRESSES
www.bbc.co.uk/cornwall Local news, weather and events.
www.cornishfish.co.uk Get freshly caught Newlyn fish delivered to your door.
www.cornwall-beaches.co.uk Cornwall Beach Guide.
www.cornwall-calling.co.uk/ surfing Surfing Beaches in Cornwall.
www.cornwall.gov.uk Cornwall County Council.
www.cornwall.gov.uk/buses Cornwall Public Transport
http://cornwall.greatbritishlife. co.uk A monthly magazine devoted to Cornish life, with comprehensive listings for events throughout the county.
www.stranger-mag.com A stylish, creative site, with Cornwall-focused reviews, features and news.
www.visitcornwall.com Official tourist information site.
www.westernmorningnews.co.uk Main regional newspaper covering Devon and Cornwall.

FICTION
Nicola Barker Five Miles from Outer Hope Quirky, appealing novel about a 16-year-old

misfit growing up in the
Burgh Island Hotel.
WJ Burley *The Wycliffe Novels*
This series of Cornwall-based
detective novels were later made
into an enormously popular
television series.
Sir Arthur Conan Doyle *The
Adventure of the Devil's Foot*
Holmes and Watson's holiday,
in a cottage near Poldhu Bay,
is interrupted by a grisly mystery
that only the great detective can
unravel.
Daphne du Maurier *The Loving
Spirit; Jamaica Inn; The Birds;
Rebecca; The King's General; The
House on the Strand* Du Maurier
made superb use of the Cornish
landscape's drama in many of
her novels.
Patrick Gale *Notes from an
Exhibition, Rough Music* Two
excellent, Cornish-set novels by
the acclaimed contempary novelist,
who lives near Land's End.
Winston Graham *The Poldark Novels*
A series of 12 historical novels, set
around Perranporth and St Agnes
and later made into a television
series.
Thomas Hardy *A Pair of Blue Eyes*
A tragic tale of love and class
conflict, partly based on Hardy's
Cornish courtship of his first wife.
Rosamund Pilcher *The Shell Seekers*
This hugely popular novel tells the
story of three generations of the
Keeling family, with much of the
action set in Cornwall.
Arthur Quiller-Couch *The Delectable
Duchy* Short stories set in Fowey
(loosely disguised as Troy Town),
at the end of the 19th century.
JK Rowling *Harry Potter and the
Deathly Hallows* Two chapters of
the boy wizard's adventures take
place in Cornwall, just outside the
fictional village of Tinworth.
Mary Wesley *The Camomile Lawn*
Set on the Roseland peninsula,
Wesley's novel charts the lives and
romantic intrigues of Richard and
Helena Cuthbertson's five nieces
and nephews.
Virginia Woolf *To The Lighthouse*
Despite being set on the Isle of
Skye, Woolf's masterpiece was
inspired by Godrevy Lighthouse.
St Ives, meanwhile, helped inspire
Jacob's Room and *The Waves*.

NON-FICTION

John Betjeman *Betjeman's Cornwall*
Prose and poetic musings on the life,
landscape and architecture of the
poet laureate's favourite county.
Tom Cross *Catching the Wave: Art
& Artists in Contemporary Cornwall*

A fine introduction to
the Cornish art scene.
Daphne Du Maurier *Vanishing
Cornwall* An eloquent evocation
of Cornish life and culture.
Henry Jenner *Handbook of the
Cornish Language* Jenner is seen
as the man who led the revival
of the Cornish language.
AL Rowse *A Cornish Childhood*
This autobiographical work describes
the eminent historian's childhood
in Cornwall in the early 1900s.

POETRY

Robert Laurence Binyon *For the
Fallen* Binyon penned his famous
poem, honouring the dead of
World War I, while sitting on the
cliffs between Pentire Point and
the Rumps in North Cornwall;
in 2001, a plaque was erected
there.
Charles Causley *Collected Poems*
Born in Launceston in 1917,
Causley is one of the county's
most beloved poets – best known,
perhaps, for his children's poems.
Thomas Hardy *Poems 1912-1913*
An ageing Hardy reflects on youth
and love in Cornwall.
John Harris *A Story of Carn Brea
1863* Harris's most important
work describes this mining area
of Cornwall.
RS Hawker *Song of the Western
Men, A Cornish Folk Song, the
Cornish Emigrants 1803-1875*
The eccentric Reverend Hawker
was a gifted poet as well as a
Cornish clergyman; indeed, his
Song of the Western Men is now
the Cornish national anthem.

FILM

Blue Juice (Carl Prechezer, 1995)
Sean Pertwee, Catherine Zeta
Jones and Ewan McGregor live
the surfing life in North Cornwall.
Ladies in Lavender (Charles Dance,
2004) Dames Judi Dench and
Maggie Smith star in this period
tale, set in a Cornish fishing village
in the 1930s.
The Manxman (Alfred Hitchcock,
1929) Although Hitchcock's last
silent film was set on the Isle of
Man, much of it was shot in North
Cornwall and Polperro.
Rebecca (Alfred Hitchcock, 1940)
Daphne du Maurier's classic tale
became a masterly Hitchcock
movie, starring Laurence Olivier
and Joan Fontaine.
Saving Grace (Nigel Cole, 2000)
Gently humourous film set in
Cornwall, about a widow who
tries to clear her debts by
growing marijuana.

Straw Dogs (Sam Peckinpah,
1971) Recently re-released, this
controversial film tells the story
of a mild American university
researcher who erupts into
violence in a Cornish village.
Swept from the Sea (Beeban Kidron,
1997) Based on a Joseph Conrad
short story, the film tells the tale
of a Russian vessel shipwrecked
near an isolated Cornish village
in the 19th century.

TV

Doc Martin *ITV, 2006-present* Set
in a fictional Cornish hamlet, this
mild-mannered comedy drama is
actually filmed in the fishing village
of Port Isaac.
Frenchman's Creek *BBC 1998*
This television dramatisation of
the Daphne du Maurier novel was
set and filmed around Charlestown.
Poldark *BBC, 1975-1977* A 1970s
classic, *Poldark* closely followed
the novels of the same name by
Winston Graham.
Wycliffe *ITV, 1993-1998* This long-
running detective series, based on
the novels by WJ Burley, was set
and shot in various locations
around Cornwall.

MUSIC

Eric Ball *The Fowey River Suite*
(1964) Ball wrote a number of
brass band compositions inspired
by the West Country; this one was
dedicated to the Cornwall Youth
Brass Band.
Dalla *Rooz* Singing in both Cornish
and English, this Cornish group
are known for producing music
for traditional Cornish *Noze Looan*
('happy night') dances.
Richard D James *Surfing on Sine
Waves* (1993) Also known as
Aphex Twin, James grew up in
Cornwall. The cover of *Surfing on
Sine Waves* which he released
under the pseudonym Polygon
Window, was shot on Porthtowan
Beach.
Brenda Wooton *The Voice of
Cornwall* (1996). The late Cornish
folk singer, who performed both in
English and Cornish, was seen as
an ambassador for Cornish culture.

ART
See p204.

WALKS & CYCLE TRAILS
For more, see www.cornwall.gov.uk.
South West Coast Path
www.southwestcoastpath.com
see p185.
**Camel Trail, Clay Trails,
Mineral Tramways** see p183.

Devon Thematic Index

Saunton Sands. See p49.

Devon A-Z Index

Where to eat & drink in Devon

INDEX

INDEX

Where to stay in Devon

INDEX

INDEX

Cornwall Thematic Index

INDEX

Helford river. See p259.

Cornwall A-Z Index

INDEX

Where to eat & drink in Cornwall

Gylly Beach Cafe. See p237.

INDEX

Where to stay in Cornwall

Advertisers' Index